The Rise and Fall of
North American Indians

The Rise and Fall of North American Indians

From Prehistory through Geronimo

WILLIAM BRANDON

A Roberts Rinehart Book

TAYLOR TRADE PUBLISHING

Lanham • New York • Toronto • Oxford

Taylor Trade
A Roberts Rinehart Book
A wholly owned subsidary of The Rowman & Littlefield Publishing Group, Inc.
4501 Forbes Boulevard, Suite 200
Lanham, MD 20706

Distributed by National Book Network

Library of Congress Cataloging-in-Publication Data

Brandon, William, 1914–2002.
    The rise and fall of North American Indians : from prehistory through
    Geronimo / William Brandon.
        p. cm.
    A Roberts Rinehart Book.
    Includes bibliographical references and index.
    ISBN 1-58979-036-7 (hardcover : alk. paper)
    1. Indians—History. 2. Indians—Government relations. 3. Indians—
Social life and customs. I. Title.
    E58.B83 2003
    970.004'97—dc21   2003011951

⊗™ The paper used in this publication meets the minimum requirements of American National Standard for Information Sciences—Permanence of Paper for Printed Library Materials, ANSI/NISO Z39.48-1992.

Manufactured in the United States of America.

Contents

PART TWO   Heritage of the New World

Maps

Acknowledgments

Most of the work on this book was done in European libraries and collections. I want to thank particularly the institutions and staffs of the Archivo General de Indias de Sevilla in Spain, the Archives Nationales of France and the Bibliothéque Nationale in Paris, the British Library in London, the Public Record Office now in Kew, and, above all, the Cambridge University Library. Other institutions almost literally of infinite number have been of endless help, without which, of course, no work of this kind would be possible at all. I thank them all collectively and most sincerely.

And I must add a special word of gratitude to the many friends and advisers over the many years and many miles of this work, a few of these being Terence and Iris Armstrong, Robert Arnold, Paul Bernal, Ray Billington, Sherburne Friend Cook, Nicola di Cosmo, Rupert Costo, Frank Darnell, Philip Durham, Bertha Dutton, Edgar Faure, Ping Ferry, Eric and Jane Force, Jerry Gambill, LeRoy and Ann Hafen, Helene Harris, Jeanette Henry, Wilbur Jacobs, Harry C. James, Richard Ketchum, Oliver La Farge, Claude Lévi-Strauss, Ronnie Lupe, William G. McLoughlin, D'Arcy McNickle, Russell Mortensen, Jean-Claude Narden, Abraham Nasatir, Joseph Needham, Allan Nevins, Tom Nixon, Essie Parish, Rodman Paul, Jane Penn, Harry Porter, Everett Rhoades, Morris Rubin, Alexander Saxton, Anne M. Smith, Annie Dodge Wauneka, Wilcomb Washburn, Oscar Winther, Hannah Marie Wormington, Robert Young; and most devout thanks to my wife Victoria, who not only endured with angelic patience and brilliant suggestions and helpfulness this long chore but also drew the maps and is even talking of the martyrdom of the index.

PART ONE

The Ancient Americas

CHAPTER 1

The Dawntime

The one thing we know about the origin of mankind is that it took a long time. Present thinking wobbles over how many million years ago (4 million? 14 million?) manlike creatures, hominids, and apelike creatures, pongids, definitely branched off in different directions in the briar patch of evolution.

When the hominids grew into actual human creatures, walking upright with hands free to use tools, and—the great miracle—beginning to speak intelligible language, also remains an open question: two million years ago? Or more? A million years ago? Or less?

The how and why of this development raises still more debate. Says a leading paleoanthropologist, there are "almost as many scenarios of human evolution" as there are paleoanthropologists.

On one point, however, there is general agreement—this long human evolution took place in Africa, Asia, Europe, but not in America. Throughout all those millions of years the Americas remained an untouched Eden; the earliest American human presence, in the opinion of most experts, was that of man in his present modern form, *Homo sapiens sapiens*. Identifiable fossils of anthropoid apes or of archaic human forms have not turned up in the New World—no beastlike *Australopithecus*, no manlike *Homo habilis*, not even any all-but-modern Neanderthals, now also classified as *Homo sapiens* but with only one sapiens as against the two now given the thoroughly developed model, ourselves. All ancient human bones thus far brought to light in the American hemisphere have been placed in *H. sapiens sapiens*, whose first appearance anywhere in the world was, in the time scale we have been considering, quite recent. It is usually estimated to date back no more than some 50,000 years ago, twice that at most.

At some unknown time, then, after (according to current belief) the emergence of man in modern form, the first forebears of the American Indians entered the New World.

The time and place of that entrance has excited a good deal of guesswork. In a more innocent age, when Archbishop Ussher's date for the creation of the earth (4004 B.C. at nine o'clock of a Friday morning) was still printed as a learned footnote in Bible margins, the American Indians were suspected of being Egyptians, Phoenicians, Greeks, Romans, Chinese, Japanese, Welsh, Irish, or descendants of the Lost Ten Tribes of Israel, or of having made their way to the Americas via a lost continent of Atlantis or a lost continent of Mu, or both.

It is now known that American Indians are far more ancient than any of these candidates. Finds have been made proving the presence of man in America at the time of such Ice Age big game as camels, mammoths, giant ground sloths, and primitive horses—in other words during the last of the Pleistocene glaciations, the last great Ice Age, which (in North America) approached its decline some 12,000 years or so ago. Even that remote date is being pushed back still farther into the past.

Such dates can be given with a fair amount of assurance, long ago though they are, due to scientific tests worked out in recent years that can sometimes provide almost calendar accuracy in archeological dating. Most of these techniques measure various substances in bone, wood, charcoal, and the like that decay or alter at a regular rate following the death of the host, thus pinpointing the age of the material tested with a precision only limited by the exactness of the measurement. The best known, and one of the first of such methods, radiocarbon dating, has now been joined by a whole panoply of other elaborate procedures, all wildly sci-fi but nevertheless (at least some of the time) workable.

Enough of these dates have accumulated, in conjunction with additional archeological and geological evidence, to place man in America well before the final finish of the last glacial period, 10,000 years ago.

Further indications support probabilities of 20,000 years ago and possibilities of 30,000 years ago or even more. These indications include distinct differences in blood-group patterns between American Indians and the Asiatic Mongoloids who were, presumably, their most ancient neighbors, patterns so strikingly unrelated they led long ago to speculation that the ancestors of American Indians may have left the Old World "before the primordial blood streams of man became mingled."

Consideration of such primary biological differences has led to the modern reclassification of American Indians from a Mongoloid group to a separate geographical race. Given a genealogy stretching back through the relatively closed history of the New World to those early people of 10,000 and 20,000 years ago, it would seem to be by far the oldest such identifiable race in existence.

Time is the tonic chord in the American Indian story.

With this sort of antiquity, it seems clear the first peopling of America must have taken place long before there were boats anywhere capable of ocean crossings. The only place of entry more or less accessible by dry land was Alaska at Bering Strait, separated from northeastern Asia by less than sixty miles. Two steppingstone islands, the Diomedes, break the water distance into still shorter stages, the longest only twenty-five miles. At times furthermore the Strait is frozen solid and can be crossed on the ice.

Much more important for ancient history, at times in the geologic past the Strait has been dry land, an isthmus up to a 1,000 kilometers' strike.

Obvious Mongoloid characteristics of some native Americans, implying later origins in later Asia, appear to corroborate the proposition of a long-used Bering Strait entry. This is so universally agreed upon by archeologists in the United States that it is now scarcely regarded as theory but as established fact—although a frequent theory among archeologists working on the other side of the Strait, in Siberia and Russia, pictures migration via the Kamchatka peninsula and the Aleutian Islands.

But entrance into the North, before 10,000 or 12,000 years or so ago, collides with those Pleistocene glaciations which sheathed the shoulders of North America in ice and may thereby have barred any migrations. Either the first people came between glaciations or a way must be found for them through the ice. Both are feasible.

There were four major Pleistocene glaciations, each enduring for many thousands of years, separated by interglacial periods that lasted even longer, when the climate probably was much as it is today—we are presumably living in one such interglacial period now. The last great glaciation, known in America as the Wisconsin stage, is believed to have lasted more than 100,000 years before its final retreat into the Holocene, the Present, some 8,000 to 10,000 years ago.

This particular Ice Age, the Wisconsin, is in turn divided into several substages of heavy glaciation separated by "interstadial" periods of glacial ebb and warmer times, each of these divisions extending through thousands of years.

The times of glaciation may have been distinguished by unimaginable rains and snow and winds rather than unimaginable cold. The seas were lowered many feet by the volume of water turned into snow and ice, and the weight of the ice buckled the crust of the land. Beaches and islands existed that are now ocean floor. It is indeed easy to imagine Bering Strait becoming a vast grass-grown plain during such periods. Geology dates a dryland Bering isthmus between about 22,000 and about 11,000 years ago, interrupted by a couple of periods of about a thousand years each when the isthmus was flooded. During those 11,000 years or so there were apparently several thaws and renewals in the glacial mass covering Canada.

These tremendous changes gradually—over vast stretches of time—urged animals and plants from one part of the world to another, and where there were people they must have been driven also, even though so slowly they knew not that they moved, the centuries if not millennia of each great change spanning multitudes of generations.

Perhaps the first human beings to drift from Siberia into Alaska were nudged along by great complexes of change into Alaska's sweeping valleys that were imperceptibly filling up with game nudged along with them. The ice sheets in North America did not spread from the North Pole but radiated in all directions from centers in the latitude of Hudson Bay. Most of Alaska was left ice-free, as was apparently much of northeastern Siberia. Or perhaps the first people drifted over during an iceless interglacial period, following only the ineluctable gradient of time. Time, enough time, can herd people along unaided; it doesn't need an assist from discernible motives of man.

Movement southward from Alaska during stages of heavy glaciation would have been limited, Canada generally being covered with plateaus of ice as much as 10,000 feet high. But there may still have remained a few passable routes.

The most detailed and authoritative timetable for the last life of the Wisconsin gives an ice-free corridor in Yukon Territory, northeastern British Columbia, and northern Alberta between about 35,000 and 25,000 years ago. This corridor was probably closed between about 20,000 and 14,000 years ago. But even in dubious times some travel might have taken place along the ocean coasts.

Nor were the areas of glaciation always necessarily lifeless. A modern population, the Greenland Eskimos, has cohabited with a heavily glaciated land for a thousand years historically, and probably for some ages before that.

The passages described would appear to suffice in getting people down into the continent from about 35,000 years ago at most. If archeologists date sites substantially earlier than that limit, it will raise the possibility of the first Americans appearing in the long ice-free interval known as the Sangamon interglacial that preceded the Wisconsin more than 100,000 years ago—a date that would also precede the supposed first appearance anywhere of *H. sapiens sapiens*.

Routes later open as the last of the Wisconsin died away after 11,000 to 8,000 years ago could have been and probably were used by later peoples. The gradual populating of the Americas went on for a very long time and involved numerous different groups of varying physical types, differing language structures, and differing social tendencies. Mankind's discursive march from Bering Strait to Tierra del Fuego may easily have taken, according to a geographer's calculation, something like 25,000 years; other geographical guesses have run as low as 8,000 or 9,000.

Probably the view back through time to the childhood of man can only be seen in distortion. The world becomes a still picture when it was alive with motion, or it moves when it was as still as eternity.

The ice sheets of the glacial "movements" did not come and go as far as people living among them were concerned. They had always been there, the white lands beyond and beyond, and the tumbling cliffs of rotting ice along the edges, snarled with sodden vegetation; they were as permanent as mountains, and the countless lakes as permanent as the Great Lakes of today. The mammoths had not "migrated" from Asia with their mastodon ancestors—they had always been there, filling the riverside groves with giant trumpeting; the horses and camels were not "migrating" anyplace but had always been there, racing in herds over the rainswept plain, and a man's mother's mother could tell how they had always been there in her day.

"When speaking of the migration of entire faunas," says a paleozoologist, "one must realize it is not the fauna that is moving." The whole ecosystem is moving; the fauna is only staying put in its place. When forests move over thousands of years the resident squirrels play on within it; when plains move over thousands of years the resident horse herds only keep on grazing.

Surely this could also apply to people of glacial times; it would seem highly unlikely they were consciously undertaking great migrations; they were only living. No doubt this place or that had always been home until eventually some families found themselves spending more time across the ridge, and for their children and their children's children that valley became in turn forever home.

"Anything seems possible that is not immediately necessary," wrote the philosopher J. H. Klaren; given enough time anything can come to pass, lands can be remade, beasts can become men, gods and ancestors can be forgotten.

The drift of the first populations may have followed the flanks of the Rockies and the Andes as principal north-south axes down into the two continents. From the Rockies they may have trended westward to the Great Basin and the pluvial lakes then watering the Southwest, eastward along the rivers leading to the Mississippi. In South America the shoulders of the Andes were also sheathed in ice, and the hypothetical first populations would have needed to thread new glacial passages to centers, perhaps in Venezuela and Bolivia, for subsequent penetration eastward and southward to the forests and savannas of Brazil and Argentina.

A French authority, Paul Rivet, thought many years ago (1925) that he detected various relationships, even linguistic, between certain South American Indians and some of the aboriginal people of Australia, and wondered about prehistoric travel from or to Australia via the Antarctic. According to ideas of continental drift then considered rather on the wild side, these regions had once been connected. Rivet guessed that connection at 6,000 years ago. Various features of the continental drift ideas, now known as plate tectonic theory, are widely accepted these days by geologists, but Rivet's 6,000 years would now be reckoned at several million, adding a few complications to his speculations.

The coming of the people and the sagas of their ancient wanderings are only matters for speculation after all. A figure stirs behind the mists across the river of time, nothing more. "The fogs of creation," goes a Zuñi legend, "the mists potent with growth."

But the story left in stone and bone is something more. Wherever she came from, however she got there, a young woman died some 12,000 to 20,000 years ago, by radiocarbon dating, in what is now west Texas near the New Mexico line at the site known as Midland; wind scoured the sand away from her scattered bones and a partial skull (assumed young and female from its delicacy) was found by an amateur archeologist in 1953. And men lived in a cave near the southern tip of South America (Fell's Cave) at a Carbon-14 (C^{14}) dated time of 11,000 years ago, as men lived in a cave at about the same time 4,000 miles away in Nevada (Gypsum Cave), in both cases seemingly butchering twenty-foot-long ground sloths that may sometimes have been kept penned up like cattle, and in both cases leaving behind stone tools and spearheads that were found in the bottom layers of successions of floor levels indicating thousands of years of occupancy. Stone and bone tools and points made by men of the same approximate time have been found at numbers of archeological sites elsewhere on both continents.

Years ago, in 1870, deep-ditching work in the region of Tequixquiac, near Mexico City, uncovered at a depth of forty feet a llama or related camelid bone, from an extinct species, carved to represent the face of a wild pig or coyote. Other artifacts and Pleistocene fossils have been found since in the same area, in two distinct geological formations, the younger dated at more than 11,000 years ago, the older far back in the middle of the Wisconsin glaciation.

Some 11,000 years ago or more, camel hunters cooked their meals beside Nevada lakes (Tule Springs), and people hunting mammoths on the shores of other Ice Age lakes near Clovis, New Mexico, left ivory spearheads as well as points of stone among the bones. Chopping tools of stone were found near hearths (Lewisville, Texas), hearths that gave radiocarbon dates of some 38,000 years ago.

In South America (Pikimachay, Peru) artifacts were found in a layer dated at 13,000 to 21,000 B.P. (Before Present), and at Taima Taima, on the Gulf Coast of Venezuela, with an age of more than 14,000 years. Monte Verde, Chile, has one well-documented site at 13,000 and further dates reaching beyond 33,000 years (as we shall see, further news will come from discussion of this site). The area known to archeologists as Sao Raimundo, Nonato (state of Piaui, northeastern Brazil), containing nearly 200 painted caves and shelters, has been the scene of recent exploration at the multisyllabic Boqueirao do Sitio da Pedra Furada giving a continuous chronology of occupation from 32,000 to 6,000 years B.P. Some of the painting has been dated to 17,000 years ago, making it the oldest cave art in America and one of the oldest examples of such in the world.

In Mexico at the famous site of Valsequillo Reservoir, near the city of Puebla, four sites have been explored since evidence of early man was first found there in 1959 (a broken mammoth bone bearing incised drawings of animals), with radiocarbon dates ranging to 21,000 B.P., and geologic dating of artifact-bearing levels appearing to reach the "essentially impossible" region of 250,000 years ago. Less than 100 miles away toward Mexico City, at Tlapacoya, a log over an obsidian blade has been there, according to C^{14} dating, some 22,000 to 24,000 years.

At Meadowcroft Rockshelter in western Pennsylvania a series of radiocarbon dates ran from 11,000 to 17,000 years B.P. In southern Idaho (Wilson Butte Cave) and Fort Rock Cave, southern Oregon, evidence of early people has given C^{14} dates of 13,000 to 14,000 years. Old Crow Flats, at the border of Canada's Northwest Territories and Alaska, has provided dates ranging from 33,000 to 25,000 years ago. The basin of Old Crow River has been the scene of intensive archeological search for some years, studying various indications that point to human presence in very ancient times; on the other hand several key Old Crow dates have been successfully challenged, and the interpretation of some worn Ice Age bones as crude tools has always been questioned.

Many other such early sites have been chanced upon and explored, from end to end of the Americas.

What were they like, the early people? They had fire; they roasted meat. Not even the dog had yet been domesticated. They used paint from a red iron oxide, and some of them at least made beads. They worked stone, bone, horn, and ivory (of mammoth tusks). They probably wore skins; tailbones are missing from skeletons of the great-horned bison, killed 10,000 years ago, implying the robes were used.

They were watching when Niagara Falls began, and when Crater Lake in Oregon exploded into being. "Come and see the world the Creator made," so sings a Piman prayer.

The world was filled with marvels, sunlight and night time, rain and fire and wind, health and sickness, birth and growth and death, fear and anger, joy and dread, wonder pondered for a hundred generations, the marvel of the myriad creatures sharing the magic of life. They sang to protect their children entering life and their old people departing, to celebrate food as well as to honor all invisible spirits everywhere, to fulfill unnamable desires and to guard against unknown perils. In such endless pondering they may have employed their unimaginable reaches of time.

And so the people came. They came before the arrival of the bow and arrow; the earliest, so some specialists have speculated, possibly before the use of any stone-tipped projectiles, they drew pictures that are filled with exuberant action, and they were there. Scattered bands of newmade people watching through the interminable dawn of a newmade world

Inference may be a more hazardous game than pure speculation, but it might be inferred that at least some of the people practiced at least some of those rites thought to be nearly as old as humanity, rites involving fire and thunder and lightning; or ceremonies involving physical demonstrations—dancing—by the entire family or band to show its wish to protect the individual member imperiled by such mysteries as birth, sickness, the rhythmic flow of woman's blood, injury, death. It might also be supposed they lived with the world rather than in it, as much a part of the setting fashioned by nature around them as fingers are part of a hand, and it would follow as a matter of course that the beasts, trees, winds, stars of that setting pondered and talked, aspired, feared, and desired as did anyone else. In fact what was life but a conversation between all such beings, of which man was only one? Pan had an ancient childhood.

The unimaginable thing about this world is time. The people can be imagined, and their thoughts and ways, everything but those limitless reaches of time, time so much longer than all the centuries of written history, when men leaned on their spears and dreamed and nothing really changed at all.

Such divisions of that time as exist are marked off for us principally by the changing forms of spear points and dart points and, later, arrowheads. These, and other weapons and utensils, are most often in stone. Time has consumed, usually, relics in other materials. A number of pieces remain in horn and bone, a few in worked wood, not much else as far as the earlier horizons are concerned. There are some scraps of basketry; fragments of fine twined work were found in Fort Rock Cave, together with dozens of pairs of partly burned sandals, made—and well made—of shredded sagebrush bark. They produce a radiocarbon age of about 9,000 years.

The meager number of human bones from these times has a special explanation all its own: most of the experts, before the 1930s, were not looking for them. They were looking instead for an American ape-man, evidence that a separate branch of humanity might have originated in the New World. It used to be generally agreed, under the forceful leadership of Dr. Ales Hrdlicka, physical anthropologist at the Smithsonian Museum, that modern man, in the form of the American Indians, could only have arrived in the Americas a very few thousand years ago at the earliest (2,000 to 5,000 then the favorite guess), and therefore the relative age of their bones was not important. The only important discovery could be an American ape-man. Skulls and human skeletal remains of supposed antiquity were examined, argued over, and judged on the basis of possible simian or other pre-human characteristics, and since no such characteristics were clearly established they were all discarded.

Nowadays some of them are being dusted off for another look—and for dating by the new techniques—and the sites of their discovery re-explored. They range all the way from large finds of many burials to single bones, and geographically from South America through Mexico to Canada, touching Washington and California and points east en route. Unfortunately the lapse of time since their discovery, and the possibility of contamination since from other articles in the jumble of museum basements, now handicaps their credibility.

Part of a skull found in Laguna, California, was knocking around among the experts for years until in 1968 it turned up a radiocarbon age of 17,000 years, which, if correct, makes it one of the oldest New World human bones so far found. "Minnesota Man" (also believed to be young and female) and Mexico's Tepexpan Man, both subjects of angry controversy, are among several that claim dates in excess of 10,000 years—a study of some thirty-odd years ago listed nineteen skeletal finds of "reasonably certain antiquity." Spirit Cave Man, partly mummified remains found in 1940, rested for decades in the Nevada State Museum at a supposed age of about 2,000 years until spectrometry tests in 1996 announced an age of more than 9,400 years, an antiquity also applying, evidently, to his well-woven tule-mat shroud and his moccasins. A skeleton found in 1972 near what was once the shoreline of a lake in what is now the Yuha desert along the California-Mexico border produced dates running from 20,000 to 60,000 years. Texas's presumably female "Midland Man," mentioned earlier, is regarded by many specialists as offering fairly sure proof of the cited age of 12,000 years, with 20,000 "possible."

The people who hunted mammoths on the shores of bygone lakes near Clovis, New Mexico, some 10,000 to 12,000 years ago, left stone spearheads that were grooved or "fluted" part way up the face. Similar fluted or "Clovis" points have been found at several places over the Southwest, together with bones of musk ox, mammoth, and the rest of the usual Pleistocene cast of characters. Occasional points of fluted type have been reported from the Texas Panhandle to the Atlantic coast, from Florida to Nova Scotia, and from Mexico to the Alberta-Saskatchewan plains of Canada.

Another fluted point, the famous Folsom point, seemingly came into use somewhat later, perhaps roundabout 10,000 years ago or a bit less. It is famous for having presented the first proof of the existence of American Ice Age Man, with the discovery in 1927, near Folsom, New Mexico, of one such point embedded between the ribs of an Ice Age buffalo. Folsoms have since been found over the general high plains region. It is smaller than the Clovis (one might assume meant for darts, the Clovis for spears), quite often beautifully made, distinguished by a long groove or fluting running up each face. This fluting might be distinctively American—such points have not yet been found in the Old World.

The mammoth had disappeared by Folsom times, at any rate from the Southwest; the giant ground sloth, an emigrant from South America, had spread from coast to coast, but the commonest big game kill for Folsom man appears to have been the colossal antique bison.

Assortments of implements in stone and worked bone have been found with all these various points, as well as occasional beads and pendants. At a Folsom site in northeastern Colorado (Lindenmeier) some mysterious bone disks decorated with tiny incised lines were discovered; there is a theory they might have been markers for a lunar count, or maybe even for a game of some kind. They look a little like poker chips.

With the Folsom people the last glacial period underwent its final decline and became the geological Present, which embraces the past 8,000 or 9,000 years.

By that time people had been in the New World for perhaps 20,000 years, in view of all the current notions of earliest dates hereinbefore noted—and possibly more people than one might think from the foregoing list of scattered finds. A generation ago an archeologist made a survey of some 25,000 artifacts claimed to date from Wisconsin Ice Age times, most of them in private collections, and commented on how many thousands of camp sites and artifacts must still lie buried for chance to have exposed such ancient remains in anything like such considerable numbers.

However, a rather serious controversy has erupted among American archeologists over these early dates; in fact it begins to look like an incipient civil war. A date of 12,000 years before the present has been adopted by one faction as the earliest date acceptable for the presence of man in the Americas, and all earlier dates—as we have seen, there are a great many—have been stringently attacked and left either dead on the field of battle or driven to cover under a hail of doubts.

Earlier radiocarbon dates? Erroneous. One of the leaders in the 12,000-year goal line stand, C.V. Haynes, a geologist who has also worked in a laboratory involved with radiocarbon dating, says, "If I have learned one thing . . . it is that radiocarbon dates can be wrong." Artifacts in geologically certified strata, such as the Calico site in California, which is in an alluvial fan with a minimum age of 8,000 years? Not artifacts at all but "flukes of nature," bits of rock that look like artifacts. Valsequillo's dates of plus-20,000? But the date is on shell, an "often unreliable" material. Tlapacoya's obsidian blade under a log dated plus-20,000? But the "blade could be intrusive."

The date of plus-20,000 attached to the Midland skull? But snail shells below give only 13,000. Meadowcroft's seemingly secure dates to 19,000? But the site is in a coal mining district, with contamination possible. Pikimachay in Peru, excavated by a most eminent American archeologist, Richard MacNeish, with dates to 22,000? But artifacts not really artifacts, and C^{14} dates for the layer above at 14,000 but the layer above that only 9,000. Could the two layers really be separated by 5,000 years? The dating "may be unreliable."

The seemingly insurmountable difficulty of moving early man all the way down to the tip of South America by 11,000 years ago, as the secure dates at Fell's Cave would seem to demand, with early man only permitted into North America from Beringia at 12,000 years ago, is answered by some rather unlikely demography. Simple arithmetic can show how one single hunting band of (let us say) twenty-five people could, by doubling each generation, multiply into 10 million in only 500 years or so, thus populating the entire hemisphere from top to bottom (leaving the many divisions among Indian peoples, some groups fat some groups lean, some tall some squat, some dark some light, some slant-eyed and growing the Mongolian spot, some of one blood-type some of another, leaving all these divisions to happen later), but anyway thus fitting the necessary dates with room to spare.

An archeologist specializing in settlement patterns speaks of a "remarkable growth rate" for a pre-industrial group in the climax of the great city Teotihuacan's population explosion with its population doubling every two centuries, one sixth of the growth suggested here for the New World's first primitive arrivals.

But in addition, this theory neatly explains the disappearance of the large Ice Age mammals, mammoths and such, at about the same time, rendered rapidly extinct by the sudden upsurge of those millions of hungry hunters.

That these large mammals also became extinct at the same time over all the rest of the world would seem to create a parallel problem. Mammoths had been so plentiful in Siberia that mammoth ivory, from the skeletal remains of animals long extinct, was exported to China and Europe for centuries, in medieval times and after. Research there tends to explain the extinction not by an instant upsurge of hungry hunters—billions?—but by the prosaic customary theory that the huge glacial melt brought drastic changes to vegetation, turning the landscapes into quagmires of sphagnum bogs and eradicating forage for many large herbivorous mammals.

The earth's zoological history contains many, a great many, extinctions—it will contain our own some day.

But the 12,000-year line and those 25,000 artifacts of alleged glacial age? Meaningless, since we don't know their provenance; the same thing applies to Pleistocene claims for the many skeletal finds from North and South America that "have been removed from their find-spots by non-professionals."

There is abundant evidence in the Old World of Ice Age man but American evidence is "very imperfect," wrote Ales Hrdlicka in 1912, and similarities between the present turmoil in American archeology and the iron rule of Dr. Hrdlicka have not gone unnoticed. In the words of a prominent Mexican archeologist, the "emotional campaign" of long ago "persists in some ways even to this day," particularly noticeable in the matter of steadfastly disqualifying "findings prior to a certain date."

One might even ask whether "Australia itself was as yet peopled," remarked Hrdlicka in demolishing Rivet's 6,000 years. A spokesman for the 12,000-year faction speaks of an "open-minded" view in looking beyond the 12,000-year line as "naive." A veteran of the opposition pronounces himself saddened to see the world of study "split into warring camps with anger and contempt boiling in the scholarly journals."

The opposition (arguing for a human presence much more ancient than 12,000 years ago) is supported by various heavyweight authorities, such as the ranking expert on the Bering Land Bridge, the U.S. Geological Survey's man in Beringia, David Hopkins, who published in 1982 his opinion that convincing evidence shows man "widely distributed" in Beringia 35,000 ago and "also present south of the ice sheets" as much as 10,000 years before the 12,000 year line. Recent genetic research analyzing mitochondrial DNA variations in American Indian populations has led to theorizing from that unexpected quarter proposing Indian residence in the New World for at least some 20,000 to 40,000 years if their mtDNA bill is to be filled.

All argument notwithstanding, neutral foreign observers have noticed that very few archeologists have changed sides during the past twenty years, and the thought has been ventured that "although archaeology likes to masquerade as science, its objectives are not fundamentally scientific," and that the conflict "is as much psychological as archaeological." Some impatience is making itself felt in American archeological circles. Says one recent protest (1989), "just as there is no compelling evidence to accept pre-Clovis occupation, there is no compelling reason to deny one either."

Very recently, however (February 1997), word has been announced of agreement between archeologists from both sides on pre-12,000 year dates for human occupation of the Chilean site, Monte Verde, occupation dating back to 12,500 years ago, thus setting back the earliest entrance from Asia some thousands of years earlier still. This single victory may not end the war, but does seem to reveal a touch of light at the end of the tunnel.

One parallel development of value may have come from all this, a focus of attention on the great deglaciation during the several millennia leading up to the 12,000-year line. Presumably the rising seas and lakes and rivers would have swept away at that time much preceding evidence, as the Old Crow material in northwest Canada—redeposited by flooded river action— seems to bear out.

Changes all but unimaginable took place during this wild period. In Alaska and adjacent Canada lakes filled and emptied over the centuries and refilled and emptied again and again. At various times before 16,000 years ago and again between 15,000 and 14,000 years ago giant Lake Bonneville dumped floods that brought rivers in present Oregon 200 to 300 feet above normal levels, carrying flows three times the average discharge of the Amazon, tumbling along huge boulders, even bedrock. The vast prehistoric Lake Missoula, covering some 3,000 square miles, exploded in "glacier bursts" time after time between 15,000 and 13,000 years ago, producing a raging flow of water greater than that of all the present rivers in the world combined.

But intensive search in the remains of this chaotic time, such as that in precisely the Old Crow basin, does seem to be revealing new information of real worth.

Quite a few other "point industries" have been identified for the several thousand years as the geological present took over from the deglaciating past. Nearly all these are considered more or less later than the fluted Clovis and Folsom although noteworthy exceptions are recorded, such as the mammoth hunters of Iztapan and Tehuacan in Mexico who used a point known as Lerma, that did not bear the fluted trademark.

Scottsbluff, Eden, and Cody are among the many site-names that have been bestowed on later points. There is a growing fashion of lumping together groups of point-styles under generic names derived from manufacturing techniques, for example "Parallel-flaked" points to cover all the above site-names, or from general locale, such as the term "Plano" to cover a very large variety of points associated with the Great Plains.

Some of the earlier New World "industries" are broadly comparable to Old World techniques that appear to have been roughly contemporary, but specific relationships are few and none too solid; the American tools seem to remain persistently American.

In far earlier times one of the first steps toward human behavior may have been meat-eating, in contrast to the largely vegetarian apes, as hominid and pongid turned to the parting of the ways those millions of years ago, and "man the hunter" emerged from the wings to take the prehistory stage.

Meat-eating, involved with the appearance of sharpened tools, flaked stones, necessary to cut through the tougher hides, sums up evolutionary complexities occupying all but infinite seas of time, as does almost any reference to such early matters, from bipedalism to larger brain size—this last limited by the size of the human pelvis.

(Will some future adoption of a standard surgical delivery, possibly developed from present Caesarian section, open the way, perhaps 10,000 years hence, to a quantum leap in the size of the human brain?)

But even the picture of man the hunter, apparently so simple and logical, brings with it problems covering no doubt many millennia, while man the hunter emerged, mayhap, from man the scavenger.

And as feminist critics have pointed out and specialists have agreed, the finished product, man the hunter, was really the hunter-gatherer; for even in the happiest hunting grounds there are all too many days when the hunter's luck goes wrong and supper has to be made from what the women and children have gathered. Only in the Arctic do populations appear to have lived largely on the kill of the chase; ethnologists studying modern groups of hunter-gatherers have found that hunting is rarely the primary source of food, regularly furnishing less than half the diet except in the far North.

Nobody knows how many different groups of people inhabited the Americas in earliest times. Probably a great many. Oldest legends indicate a world in movement. We came from the sunset or the sunrise, from the sky or from beneath the ground, from the roots of the holy mountain. In the beginning there was only the sea, said the Haida of the Northwest Coast, and the Maya, a continent distant from them. In the beginning there came white men with black beards, said peoples separated by thousands of miles and many centuries.

Some of these beliefs, notions, and customs may date back to the veriest beginnings of human society, and may be found in one form or another more or less worldwide. For example the effort to protect women, or perhaps protect everyone in the band, from women's periodic bleeding, obviously a link with the dangerous unknown. But some were not quite so universal, as the belief that once women ruled because they had the veritable magic, until men, stronger although not as bright, stole the magic away—in this might possibly remain some reference to women as the earliest factual scientists, who learned how to leach the poison from acorns or manioc, how to find and use scores of wild plants.

From end to end of the two Americas lived many differing groups of many diverse kinds of people, strangers to each other, unknown to one another except at each little ripple of contact. The ripples transmitted ways of life and thought, sometimes with amazing fidelity and sometimes monstrously garbled, to the farthest end of the inhabited land, and then rebounded with as much force as before. They started from nowhere and they never ended. They crossed and recrossed each other at all angles, and their patterns changed at each new voice.

A man might live out his life and never leave his valley, a family might never have seen foreigners as long as could be remembered, and the cycle of the years might never have been disturbed in their land that they knew bush by bush and that never changed, and yet life was in constant motion. New people crossed the sill of the world in the distant north and still another ripple was added, and another and another and another, at every fear or joy or thought or hope encountered in its passage. Seen against a scale of centuries, the knots of people moved, merged, split, multiplied, died, appeared, or disappeared at every compass point.

We climbed up to the light, we climbed down from the sky, say the legends. At first there was only the god Coyote or Raven, Serpent or Jaguar, or the twins of creation, echo of cosmic duality.

In ancient times a beautiful girl had a lover who came each night but would not let her see who he was, so she painted her hands, or rubbed them in soot, and that night embraced her lover again, and the next day she saw the marks of her hands on the back of her brother. She ran from him in horror and he ran after her, so she turned herself into the sun and he turned himself into the moon, and he still appears at night looking for her but she has always gone away; and the marks of her hands are still on his back.

Or, men lost their repose so the Creator gave them tobacco, but after a time they despaired and lost their repose again, so the Creator gave them women. This order was reversed in some myths that told of the tobacco plant's first appearance at the spot where a man and woman had lain to make love; the word for smoking tobacco among some New World peoples was a word also used for sexual union.

All about them the world comprehended simply by being and so did they. Of course there was meaning in the spring stars hanging in the gilded branches of the spring forest, and the autumn stars hanging in the antlers of a tall silent beast, or the terror of a storm bursting round your ears, or the dread illness of hunger in black winter days.

With such comprehension the American Indians came into existence, rather uniform genetically, infinitely diverse in look and manner, a people of infinite differences and remarkable sameness. Some feared the world and placated its ferocity, some worshiped with praise its goodness. Some apologized to animals they killed, and others insulted them. Some feared the dead—not so much death as the dead, with their unnatural sightless eyes and their ghosts that sprang up in the dark—and fled from the dead in panic, even while weeping with grief, to abandon them where they died; others hung up the dead in a place of honor in the lodging and kept them there.

One insistent tone is present in all these varying examples, an awareness of the harmony of things that can be struck out of balance at any moment, even by one's own actions. By a knife or a stone I can bring the abnormality of death; by careful and right behavior can I keep my normal world free of such abnormalities as death and sickness?

Varieties of thought underlying this belief are multitudinous, but regardless of separateness, of disparities, a pulse of contact ran endlessly through the huge body of time. If time is the tonic note in the story of the Indians, this theme of the world's precarious harmony is the dominant. This notion, the interdependence of all life (which has become of special interest to modern science), underlies one of the few traits that might be applied sweepingly to what we can know of the past of most American Indians, belief in a personal relation to the world at large. The widespread concept of ownership of land in common by an associated group of people might be another such trait.

These attitudes appear to have been overwhelmed in emerging societies elsewhere in the world by other sets of notions drawn from other primitive world views, but they gained the ascendancy in the Americas. Operated upon by untroubled time, they became distinctively Indian.

CHAPTER 2

In the Footsteps of the Ancients

In the dawn of the geological Present, or the Recent as preferred style has it, the giant beasts of the Pleistocene were gone—or nearly. By 8,000 years ago or so the usual big game had become pretty much modern from the caribou in the far North to buffalo over much of what is now Canada and the United States to guanaco in the Andes. Weapons for hunting and fighting were spear and spear-thrower (a rod acting as a sling in throwing the dart farther and harder), slings for stones, clubs, and bolas (cords weighted at each end with stones, thrown to whip around the animal's legs and trip him up, known chiefly in South America). It was still long before the bow.

Archeology headlines tools and weapon points, which provide a sequence of sorts in something like concrete evidence. Besides the stone points and tools of varying styles, burials have offered some information, the body cremated or in a basket or the bones painted red and oriented east and west.

In their life the people collected seeds and roots that made food, nuts and berries and wild fruit, set snares and built pitfalls and fish weirs—one existed 4,000 years ago in what is now Boylston Street, Boston, in which many thousands of stakes were used to build a fish-fence and traps in the tidal flats; elaborate weirs were spoken of in the earliest English accounts of Indian life along the Atlantic coast. ("No more dams I'll make for fish," sings Caliban, extolling freedom in Shakespeare's *The Tempest*.)

An early date of much interest comes from the Great Lakes area in and about Wisconsin, where the people of the Old Copper culture made lance points (some of them socketed) and a profusion of other articles from the copper native to the region. Carbon-14 tests and other data have traced the beginning of this culture to something beyond 5,000 years ago, a very early time for use of metal anywhere in the world, with its complex of tools and ornaments most common one and two millennia later, and continuing up to the arrival of Europeans.

Another interesting early date comes from the region of a great bygone lake, given the posthumous name of Lake Cochise, in the now blazing desert country where Arizona, New Mexico, and Mexico meet. Here are signs of continuous habitation for many thousands of years by a people as ancient as the Folsom hunters, and yet apparently quite different from them in their way of life. The chief items in all phases of this continuity are stones and pestles described as "milling stones," obviously used for grinding or pounding some sort of food in the form of wild grains or seeds. Here again is an extremely early appearance anywhere in the world, of such milling stones, for the oldest phase of this culture is dated at 9,000 years ago or more.

In the Cochise desert country plant food was "abundant," certain grass seeds (foxtail, for example) to be ground into flour or meal, mesquite beans, cactus fruit, sotol, and agave to be baked, mescal and honey for pudding, and a variety of additional plants, such as sumpweed, sunflower, and pickleweed that came and went with regional evolution.

Another early grain date comes from the same region, maize found in a cave, Bat Cave, in western New Mexico. It is primitive maize, "pod corn," each kernel enclosed in a husk of its own, but a hybridized form and thus undoubtedly cultivated by man. Domesticated squash was grown along with it. It is some 5,000 years old by radiocarbon dating.

It is generally supposed that agriculture began far to the south, in the land that later produced high civilizations; squash and tiny ears of pod corn have been found in central Mexico that were harvested more than 7,000 years ago. Along the coast of Peru in South America the first indication of those later high civilizations began appearing more than 5,000 years ago, with public buildings of stone, astonishing community achievement in pre-agricultural times. These dates are truly venerable, with real establishment of agriculture still to come, and villages of outright farmers far in the future.

Evidently most of these ancients also did a lot of moving; even though a people stayed in a general area for thousands of years the usual life must have been one of frequent movement, following the seasons from the hills to the valleys, from the valleys to the hills.

But exceptionally there may have been communities that stayed so close within favorite food-gathering precincts as to become wholly sedentary, although possibly this is an unnecessarily refined point, turning on a view of sedentariness rather too artificially limited. Some populations of Archaic peoples undoubtedly spent lives entailing less movement than the lives of sedentary urban commuters today. But signs of pre-agricultural permanent villages have also been found—for example, considering only North America, in southern Illinois (Koster Site) with evidence of post and daub houses solidly built more than 7,000 years ago, or houses in Virginia (Thunderbird Site) possibly as old or even older, or traces of earth lodges in northeastern California (Surprise Valley) a mere 1,500 years or so younger. And of course nonagricultural villages persisted into historical (or even present) times in regions such as the Northwest Coast, their people living, and living well, on seafood and wild fruits and vegetables.

The association of certain peoples with certain places over absolutely incredible lengths of time in the Archaic—the Archaic is generally reckoned at about 7,000 years duration—seems fairly well established. Seasonal fire-hunts, as one rather far-out example, are believed by some students (although not at all by all) to have continued so long so regularly that they created the great plains of the American West. Archaic-age people of the southeastern part of what is now the United States, including the "gracefully slender" peoples some archeologists believe were distant ancestors of such Siouan-speaking modern groups as the Tutelo and Catawba, are thought to have fired the southern woods for so long that the Southern longleaf pine became dependent on this seasonal burning to reproduce—without its hot flashfire the tiny seeds could not burst their shells and without the annual singeing off of the matted duff the rootlets could not reach the earth.

Still fainter shadows can be projected by speculation on the social intangibles of that seemingly endless and marvelously stable Archaic world. A number of experts caution against a notion of particularly "primitive" life in the Archaic or of necessarily sparse populations. On the contrary, the skillful use of all resources, of an optimum "forest efficiency" that did not disturb or destroy the "plant-animal-man-with-culture ecosystem" may have developed, in passing through these enormous chasms of time, a way of life teeming with riches and fulfillments by now long and utterly forgotten.

There have even been hints that these people of the Archaic waited so long for new ideas (such as pottery and agriculture) and the resultant elaboration of their basic culture simply because they were content in their timeless nirvana and not at all eager to change. Heretical reflections threaten to follow, that change—we call it progress—might not always be a result of "forward" social movement but possibly of something going wrong in the social animal.

The thought has been suggested that the Biblical "fall" of man from the Garden of Eden might picture metaphorically nothing more than the introduction of agriculture, with its life of toil.

There are some indications that those long Archaic times inclined to be peaceful, and a gradual change in this regard might identify at least one of the complex and subtle forces that might have stimulated (or sickened?) the strong and stable world of the Archaic until it was ready at last for progress.

Most current expert opinion sees the Archaic ringing down its curtain someplace in the time between 5,000 and 3,000 years ago, although the curtain took its own slow time in falling. In some regions the Archaic remained fairly well in business into historical times.

Its close is customarily marked by the appearance of pottery. Otherwise no great change is immediately visible in the Archaic complex—later Indian cultures generally appear to be built quite squarely upon it.

Earliest pottery on the east coast of North America is dated at 4,000 to 4,500 years ago, in Mexico at 4,400 to 5,000 years ago, in Colombia and Ecuador at 5,000 or even 5,200, in Peru at 4,100, Patagonia at 3,000. Points of origin have been suggested in Europe, Asia, and at various American sites as independent inventions, including inland tropical sites in South America.

The greatest revolution in all the history of mankind—before our own truly earth-threatening invention of nuclear weapons—must have been the development of agriculture.

Someplace, a people who doubtless had gathered wild seeds as part of their food since time immemorial found among the plants they came back to each year several that were favorites among them, and probably some that had been especially famous for many generations. The transformation of such wild plants into domesticated crops is a story riddled with marvels.

Plants (such as maize) that were eventually to produce fields of waving grain for the delectation of humankind had no interest whatever in that objective. On the contrary, it was their nature to scatter their seed as widely as possible over as long a period of time as possible, rather than keeping it clustered in one neat fat head for human consumption. Thus in the wild the seeds of a plant did not mature all at once, and fell over a lengthy period of time—but the people who found their wild seeds tasty naturally picked the biggest, fullest heads available, containing seeds that tended to mature all together. Weeding out these best heads would seem to have encouraged survival and dominance of precisely the variety people did not want, the plants with the shattered heads and scattered seed. Paleobotanists theorize that seeds of the variety picked by people accumulated in the scraps and refuse of the people's living places until, in time (centuries? millennia?), the desired plant made itself noticeable as a camp follower and all but insisted on being tended, ergo gardened.

There is much speculation among specialists as to the first American cultivated plants: perhaps not only for food but rather for fiber, raw material for baskets, mats, houses, boats, as the *totora* of the Andes (the tule of California), used to construct whole islands in Lake Titicaca, used as well for food and fuel, was also used for a noteworthy Andean specialty in being made into fans to fan fires, "a necessity at that altitude because of the rarefied air."

Or as a stimulant, or for coloring matter, or for use in ritual. The bottle gourd, useful not only as a bottle but as a rattle for accompaniment in ritual, in South America and Mexico from a very early date, 9,000 years ago or more, was apparently not even native to America but had seemingly come from Africa at some time in the past, floating across the ocean, it is believed, under nothing more than its own volition. Coconuts, a tropic delicacy in both Oceania and America, very probably did likewise.

Manioc, staff of life in the tropical forests of South America, came in two varieties, sweet and bitter, the bitter poisonous and requiring a complicated operation to leach out its poison. The theory was proposed many years ago that the bitter variety had been cultivated first, for the use of its poison to stun fish or poison war arrows, the food value of its residue only realized later.

North of Mexico, in what is now the eastern United States, some of the earliest plants gardened appear to have been sunflower, knotweed, lamb's quarters, pumpkin, and the previously mentioned sumpweed. Pumpkins may have been at first cultivated for their seeds, like sunflowers, although the sunflower also provided pigments. Both were keeping company with human admirers from very early dates, 4,000 to (in west central Illinois) 7,000 years ago. Sumpweed, *Iva annua*, also possibly a subject of horticulture 4,000 years ago or earlier, may have been displaced by corn and beans when real agriculture came along. There seems to be no trace of it as a cultivar in historic times. A couple of chenopods, probably wild, were much gathered from foraging times onward and by Woodland times (the close of the Archaic) may have been cultivated.

In Mesoamerica pumpkins (*Cucurbita pepo*) and various grass seeds of the colorful amaranth, red pigweed, may have received some special attention and tending in the most ancient of days, a like attention also certainly given to the wild teosinte (or a mysterious relative now missing), that over some thousands of years turned into the plant botanists now call *Zea mays* and corn belt farmers call corn. Archeological dates for these beginnings reach back 7,000 to 9,000 years in Mexico. Some peoples may also have tamed tobacco in pre-agricultural times. There are indications that beans and maybe chili peppers and somewhat later peanuts and sweet potatoes could have come from points of origin in South America to join the Mexican staples of maize and squash, chocolate, tomatoes, and avocadoes.

The view has sometimes been proposed that the ultimate point of origin for New World agriculture is to be found in the tropical forests of South America, among hunting-gathering and part-time gardening communities that remained in the Archaic while passing their discovery of agriculture on to the people of the western mountains, the Andes, who built civilizations upon it.

In South America sweet potatoes, white potatoes, lima beans, go back to very early times, up to 8,000 B.P. in Peru. The sweet potato, a prehistoric domesticate on both sides of the Pacific Ocean—principal item of diet for the Maori of New Zealand—raises a fairly convincing argument for transpacific contact by very early people, even if only by one accidental storm-tossed voyage. It is difficult to imagine this plant making the trip on its own. Botanists think northwestern South America a likely spot for its origin. Maize did not reach South America until long after its establishment in Mexico, found archeologically in Peru and Ecuador dating only to 4,500 years ago.

An agricultural frontier of sorts between North and South America—seed plants such as maize for North America, tubers such as potatoes and manioc in South America—has been noticed by searchers of the past, for what light it may throw on agricultural origins and dispersals: especially on the question of reseeding as against propagation by cuttings as first steps.

Certain plants, potatoes the commonest, flourished in the mountains, and certain specialized crops were grown at even higher altitudes (to 13,000 feet) in the Andes, a chenopod, called quinua, probably used as a cereal, is perhaps the best example. Quinua is still very much present in the altiplano scene, often grown mixed with dwarf maize and a lupine locally called *chochos*, that has to be leached free of poison before using but that is very rich in oil and protein, and "meat is a luxury to the Indians of Ecuador." Quinua is nowadays broadcast by hand in sowing, which may also have been the prehistoric practice, unusual if so for the New World, where as a rule seeds—maize for example—were planted individually. In this, as in several other agricultural matters, the New World and the Old World differed strikingly, sown seed the customary Old World way.

The greatest difference in New World and Old World agriculture, and a difference entailing enormous consequences, was pastoralism, fundamental to the Old World way of life, entirely absent in the New World except for some herding of llamas and related small camelids in the high Andes.

This—pastoralism—may have been a major factor, maybe the major factor, in the establishment of private property at the mudsill underpinning of Old World social structure, already basic law in 1800 B.C. when its legal specifics were carved on the stone tablet bearing the Code of Hammurabi. It does seem reasonable that private property may have come into being with the keeping of flocks, as the profit and loss problems between Jacob and Laban in Genesis 30: 30–43 as to just who were to own which of the straked and unstraked cattle might seem to bear witness.

New World agriculture, however, developed for the most part upon a chassis of group ownership, and as such produced civilizations of a high order—but with built-in disaster waiting, as we shall see, when the Old World arrived in collision.

CHAPTER 3

Art and Numbers

Pottery, agriculture, and permanent villages did not all come into being at the same time, as has been seen, but all were in business (3,700 to 2,800 years ago) in the young life of such new-forming villages as El Arbolillo, Tlatilco, and Zacatenco in the lofty central plateau known as the Valley of Mexico.

The people (faceless no more) march into view in the form of little clay figurines, usually naked except for string hats or turbans and ornaments and tattoos. Some are women with big hips, some, coming from villages to the south in present Puebla and Morelos, are young and graceful, their elaborate hair sometimes streaked red and white, as the thatched houses of the time were painted; they were popular in the valley for years.

A curious parallel came into being at about this time, in northern Peru and in southern Mexico, a religious cult worshiping, so it seemed, a cat god, a jaguar. (The name comes from a word, *jaguara*, in the language of the Amazonian Tupi, meaning "kills in one leap.")

This began happening some 3,000 years ago or so, and for the next 500 to 1,000 years the parallel new styles, or the new peoples, remained in mastery of the loops and whorls of evolving little worlds in the Andes and in Mexico.

They were evidently not the same people, in these regions so distant from each other, and there is no indication the new religion came to both areas at the same time. They may easily have been some centuries apart in their South American and Mexican arrival.

The birthplace of these two styles is not yet pinned down (the search has been turning now and then in recent years to Central America); until it is, the early story of these little new worlds is rather like the story of early Greece (a contemporary) without its forerunner Crete.

In Mexico, the most noticeable of these newborn works seems to be associated with the country later occupied by a people known as the Olmeca, the Olmecs; consequently these early residents are usually called Olmec too although they may well have been an entirely different people from the later Olmeca. Whoever they were, they made essentially the same sort of ornaments, pottery, and figurines that were customarily produced in the Valley villages, but they did it a great deal better and they added their own particular designs. Their snarling jaguar's head or a cat-faced human head or a peculiar "baby face" (maybe celebrating, some have suggested, a custom of infant sacrifice) and a truly modern preoccupation with whatever was monstrous, deformed, disharmonic, appeared on all they touched.

And these people themselves come into view in their turn, fat little men with ornamentally deformed heads and ornamentally deformed teeth. They made some of the most charming of the seductive little figurines spoken of previously, some of them with two heads.

Through the years, through the centuries, they developed important centers in southern Vera Cruz, the rubber producing country of Mexico. Archeologists have worked out a succession of three important Olmec centers in this region, the best known being the middle one in age, the island town of La Venta, dating from about 1,000 B.C. At La Venta (believed to be not actually a town but only a ceremonial center for the inhabitants of the countryside roundabout) multi-ton blocks of stone were carved into columns and monuments and especially gigantic heads (up to fourteen feet high) glorifying the typical "Olmec" features—the largest is carved from a block of stone weighing an estimated fifty tons that must have been transported, perhaps rafted, at least sixty miles from its nearest source through the surrounding mangrove swamps. Studies have considered the supposed element of magnetism in some sculpture, the shape of some structural groupings (in the form of birds?) and the "compass" orientation of their apparent direction. Turning from the monumental to the miniature, La Venta sculptors worked jade with wizard skill into jewel-like representations of their half-human jaguars, deformed people, bearded men, and other monstrosities.

Jade beads and jewels have been found occasionally in Mexican burials dating from early times onward, but nothing comparable to the exquisite jade work of the Olmec preceded their appearance—and nothing comparable has been done since. There is evidence that jade pieces executed by these consummate artists were treasured for generations by neighboring peoples, as we preserve today the works of Rembrandt or Michelangelo. The ancient Olmeca were more or less contemporary with the Chou dynasty in China, which also saw the highest point of jade working in Asia; naturally there has been speculation that there may have been some connection. The Olmec jade was jadeite, in general considered rather superior to the ancient Chinese jade, which was usually nephrite. Jade deposits have not yet been located in Mexico, but have been found in recent years in Guatemala.

In the region next door to the southeast, during about the same time as the flowering of the Olmec style, other maize-farming people were outgrowing the Olmec cat-face cults to create a distinctive world of their own. In it they spring as resplendently to life as any people ever have in the temples, the spectacular ruins of their architecture, the art they left behind them. But they created more than a style; they created a civilization, one of the great civilizations of antiquity. These were the Maya.

It was once believed that the Olmeca preceded the Maya by some centuries, but recent archeological work in Belize, on the southeastern edge of the later Maya world, has revealed undoubted Maya communities as early as, or maybe earlier than, the Olmec centers. At the Belize site called Cuello some fifteen centuries of development can be studied underlying the spectacular artistic and intellectual achievements of the following Classic Maya.

The basis around which these intellectual achievements were organized was the extraordinary Maya calendar. Whether this was an invention of the Olmec (who, for that matter, may themselves have been a group of proto-Maya) or of the Maya or of an earlier unknown people is still uncertain but it received by far its most notable use among the Maya, whose Classic age is marked for us by the introduction in monumental art of the calendric formula known archeologically as the Long Count.

The Maya calendar was in its totality a family of related calendars locked together in a gearbox of considerable complexity. The simplest was the *tzolkin*, or book of the days, a ceremonial round of 260 days, eventually in use all over ancient Mesoamerica; it may have originated in the annual coming and going of Venus, or it may have been founded originally on the period from autumn through spring, since the other 105 days of the year were devoted to the planting and growing season.

The 260 days of the tzolkin involved a series of twenty different day names revolving through an endlessly repeated number series of one to thirteen. This series meshed with the *haab*, a solar calendar using nineteen named months (eighteen of twenty days each and one of five days); the two calendars repeated their original conjunction after revolving through 18,980 days, or fifty-two years. This marked a century, so to speak, and was celebrated with special ceremonies.

Further systems, a lunar calendar brought into a fixed relation with the day count (with an error of less than five minutes a year; the "sophistication of their system of time-keeping," says a modern astronomer, "was quite staggering"), and a Venus calendar meshing five Venus years of a mean 584 days each with eight solar years of 365 days each, were all graced with complicated relationships. They created whole galaxies of cycles, wheels within wheels, all turning like the perpetual works of an infinite clock, the emphasis always on that marvelous repetition of time, a clock striking the hours of eternity.

These endless cycles were corrected by startlingly accurate observations of the sun, moon, and *noh ek*, the Great Star—Venus. They were noted down in a numbers system based on twenty (counting fingers and toes instead of only fingers, as in our system of tens) and using positional numbers and zero, two concepts unknown in Europe for another thousand years.

The Long Count was based on the *kin* (1 day), the *uinal* (20 days), the *tun* (360 days), the *katun* (7,200 days), and the *baktun* (144,000 days), all except the tun successive multiples of twenty. Long count dates were counted from a fixed point in the past, apparently in the neighborhood of 3,000 B.C. This beginning point may have historical meaning like our B.C. or it may not, like Bishop Ussher's 4004.

How long it took the stargazing priests, Maya or Olmec or whoever they were, to work out all their intricate machinery is anybody's guess. The fundamental calendar was fully established long before Classic Maya times. In fact the earliest date so far found in the "Maya" Long Count system was not found in Maya country at all but in the last of the three important Olmec centers, the site known as Tres Zapotes, where the date, carved on a stone monument, or stela, equates, in the most widely accepted correlation, with 31 B.C. However, no other definite proof has yet been found of the Long Count calendar's existence in other Olmec centers, so it is still an open question whether the Olmec or the Maya had it first.

The earliest undoubted Maya Long Count date so far known, carved on the famous Stela 29, was found at the great jungle center of Tikal, fifty miles north of Lake Peten in Guatemala, center of the Classic Maya world. The date, in the usual correlation, is A.D. 292. The monumental use of this date, as mentioned, is regarded as the opening of the 600 years of the Maya Classic age, although of course such early centers as Tikal had been in operation for centuries before this time.

Students of the Maya realized from the start that all these inscribed dates, buttressed with such obvious exactitude, would be of crucial value in learning the history of these remarkable Maya ruins—if they could be correlated with the Christian calendar, and many a valiant effort was made to accomplish this. The problem, however, revealed so many layers upon layers of difficulties that it began to seem thoroughly insoluble. There then appeared one of the more unlikely heroes in all the unlikely lists of nineteenth-century science.

Joseph Goodman as a young man in his twenties had been the owner and editor of a frontier newspaper in the mining town of Virginia City, Nevada, at that time (1860s) the silver-bonanza capital of the world. He hired a young out-of-work drifter named Sam Clemens, who developed, under Joe Goodman's enthusiastic encouragement, a useful knack for writing news stories that couldn't have happened, and adopted the fictitious name of Mark Twain for signing them. Together they had a fine time and, it may be, an effect of sorts on the Territory of Nevada. Goodman defended his paper's opinions with a Navy Colt, in keeping with publishing practice of the region, and one of his fire-and-brimstone editorials exploded, so it was said, the whole Territorial Supreme Court off its bench.

Mark Twain moved on to other spheres, and Goodman, when he decided on a quieter life, invested his mining-stock profits in a vineyard in California. A neighbor there, Dr. Gustav Eisen, was obsessed with the mystery of the Maya picture-writing and infected Goodman, but Goodman was less interested in the meaning of the picture-symbols, the glyphs, than in their age. At the time it was popularly supposed the stupendous Maya ruins had been the work of a long-vanished super race.

Eisen furnished drawings of the glyphs and of the temples and stelae, recognized Goodman's talent for calculation in regard to dates, and drove him on when Goodman "grew faint hearted and ready to give up the apparently hopeless task," until, after twelve years' labor, a satisfactory scheme was at last worked out that seemed to align all the necessary dates and conjunctions to provide a correlation with the Christian calendar.

The number totals reached were in error and soon revised, but a correct angle of jointure for the two calendrical systems, European and Maya, had indeed been pinpointed; the British Mayanist Alfred P. Maudslay agreed and published the Goodman correlation in 1897—and all other authorities in the field overwhelmingly rejected it.

It took thirty years for the Goodman correlation to win general acceptance, and then only after new archeological finds gave support, and two ranking professionals, Mexican and British, attached their names to it, after minor adjustments, as seals of approval, making it the Goodman-Martinez-Thompson (or GMT) correlation, which it remains today. A rival system, using the same key but connecting with the Maya calendar in a different century, was offered by the American anthropologist Herbert Spinden in the 1920s and gained a good many converts, but the GMT continued to hold first place, its general run of dating now regarded as all but official, although the problem is far from complete solution.

Many questions—and still more following each archeological or epigraphic discovery—are not yet answered and many may never be. The Long Count ceased with the end of the Classic Maya monuments, five to six centuries before Columbus, but the basic calendar was still in use (not necessarily, of course, keeping correct Maya time) when the Spaniards arrived, to create special difficulties in matching native dates with colonial records. Much work at present is directed toward astronomical evidence or toward the study of events involving not just separate Maya cities but the whole of the Maya world.

One such event of importance in Goodman's mind was the mysterious hiatus that apparently closed down the ceremonies in a number of the leading Maya centers for sixty years, just before the greatest Classic centuries. This lasted, in the Maya calendar, from 9.5.0.0.0 to 9.8.0.0.0; in the Goodman-Martinez-Thompson correlation, from A.D. 534 to 593.

What marvelous calendrical conjunction could have brought about such a massive sixty-year abstinence?

Joe Goodman, in 1895: "Now, in Maya chronology, the 9th cycle of the 54th great cycle embraced an event, an occasion, an anniversary, a conjuncture— I cannot find a word to express exactly what I mean—more significant and momentous than anything we can conceive of as possible to happen in our national annals or in the history of the world. It was a point at which all the multitudinous periods of their different styles of reckoning, except the cycle and the great cycle, came to an end and began anew."

But sixty years does seem a long pause.

As the biggest lies have been told in silence, possibly some revealing truths may be told in silence also.

CHAPTER 4

Under the Wheel of Time

The Maya world endured, reckoning from the earliest traces of impressive architecture so far discovered, through the long centuries of the Preclassic development period, through the six spectacular centuries of the Classic, and through the five to seven chaotic centuries of the Postclassic.

It was in cultural contact with a multitude of neighboring gods near and far. The cat-faced Olmec deities (jaguar skins marked the seats of authority for Maya leaders) were followed by little potbellied stone gentlemen (idols? victims? sages?) carved in staggering numbers roundabout southern Guatemala, particularly in the vicinity of the early Maya center, Kaminaljuyu; these were followed by the tortured and ornate Zapotec iconography from the great Oaxacan center of Monte Alban—a candidate for the place of origin of the Maya system of writing. The huge city of Teotihuacan in central Mexico (its site within suburban distance of modern Mexico City) had a noticeable effect on Maya activities in early Classic times, and some hundreds of years later Toltec invasion from the same central region brought warrior societies and chronic warfare to newly established Postclassic centers in northern Yucatan.

Throughout all these vicissitudes over this immense stretch of time the Maya remained substantially Maya.

Their country covered an area larger than Italy, crossing the borders of what are today Honduras, El Salvador, Guatemala, Belize, and the Mexican states of Yucatan, Campeche, Tabasco, Chiapas, and Quintana Roo. Their Classic age alone lasted longer than the entire life of the Roman Empire from Julius Caesar to Romulus Augustulus, with which it apparently overlapped in dates.

They practiced a form of agriculture known to primitive peoples all over the world since agriculture began, hacking down and burning trees and brush,

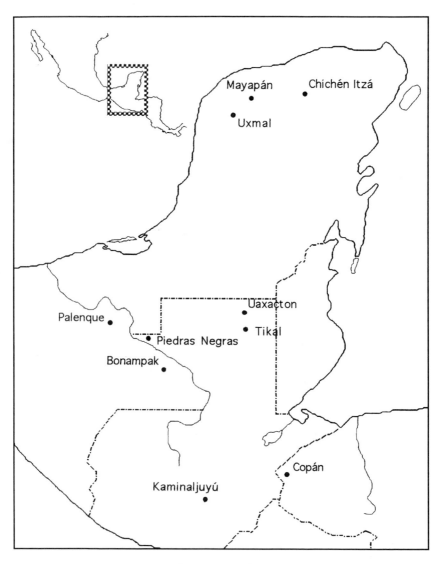

Some Maya Sites

planting a cornfield in the rough clearing, and slashing out a new such clearing a few seasons later. (Anthropologists call such a cornfield a *milpa*, a name taken from Nahuatl, the language of the Aztec.) In all the days of their greatness this technology was never improved. There is some indication here and there of more intensive gardening on mounds or raised beds (*chinampas*), but the milpa remained the standard.

Slash and burn farming, by its nature, operates against the growth of cities—the clearings are scattered, in contrast to the closely populated communities fostered by such group undertakings as irrigation. Very few of the Maya ceremonial centers appear to have been truly urban. House mounds studied by archeologists are typically dispersed, with no clear pattern of urban density; thus the Maya, in the days of their greatness, rarely built real cities, at least not in our sense of the word.

But their resplendent cathedral centers, civic centers—call them what we will—were unbelievably numerous; well over 100 have been excavated, and those who know the forest and the bush in Maya country say there are many more waiting to be found. The total population may therefore have been very large—aerial surveys of regions unscreened by jungle report evidence of "virtually continuous" habitation.

Burials, common and princely, and the voluminous mass of pictorial relics reveal social classes and priests conducting a complex religion, but there seems to have been no centralized government. The Maya never had an "empire" or anything approximating one, so far as has yet been determined.

They developed no metalworking, no metal tools. In common with the rest of the New World they developed no practical use of the wheel, even though they used rollers on the *sacbeob* (artificial roads), raised causeways that were built here and there to connect various of the temple clusters. It was not easy to get from place to place in the central Maya country; it still is not easy today. Although their world stretched from mountains to open savannas it reached its zenith in the swampy, difficult lowland rainforest.

In all these respects they differ from other early high civilizations in both the New World and the Old. They are the foremost exception to the apparent rules attending the birth of civilization.

They tattooed their bodies and sometimes painted themselves certain colors to go with certain professions or acts: blue was associated with sacrifice, warriors might be black and red, prisoners (captives) of later times striped black and white. They distended their earlobes with outsize earplugs, and a few pierced the septum of the nose to insert carved "jewels." Cross-eyes seem to have been highly regarded, and in the later stages of their greatest age the men wore artificial noses, evidently in keeping with an ideal of beak-nosed handsomeness. They flattened their foreheads and decorated themselves with feathers, breeding birds in aviaries for the most gorgeous plumes, and men wore brilliant little obsidian mirrors hanging in their hair.

But most obviously, they were obsessed with intellectual dimensions and with art. Temple pyramids in central Mexico reach a size twenty times larger than those of Maya construction, but the Maya architecture and sculpture and painting are by general consensus incomparably more distinguished. The "grandeur and the beauty," wrote Bishop Diego de Landa more than 400 years ago, "fill one with astonishment," opening the litany of awe—no other word will do—that has been repeated by artists and students ever since, summed up by a recent art historian: "The Maya created one of the great art traditions of the world."

Besides the temple-topped pyramids, various of the centers contained "palaces," monumental stairways, reviewing stands, vapor baths, bridges, aqueducts, ceremonial plazas for public spectacles, and astronomical observatories. Some of the larger "cities" were made up of building clusters around separate plazas, covering many acres or even extending for miles.

It is assumed the proportion of skilled artisans and artists in the labor force producing these public works was exceptionally large. There is no reason farmers may not have practiced some of these genteel skills. It fits ill with our treasured Old World image of a truly low class peasantry, but these farmers did not keep stock, as did Old World peasants, requiring steady work all year long, and the farm work, as has been shown, occupied only 105 days of the year. The possibility must therefore be considered that some farmers may have been also practicing artists, masons, and so on, and some artists may have been farmers. That farmers in their off time were used only for properly low-class manual labor (dragging heavy stone about, for example, under the whips of overseers) can scarcely be made to fit the population proportions.

The population contained, obviously, many highly trained groups, those savants learned in mathematics, astronomy, and literature, and the large number of artists and craftsmen constructing and decorating buildings, illustrating books, painting and decorating vases and other ceramics, carving jades, plaques, ear spools, gorgets, toys, and manufacturing the wealth of featherwork and textiles.

The books, except for a few remnants and tatters, are gone, destroyed by time and missionary zeal. The literature included history, science, the lives of great men, astronomy, astrology, prophecy, theology, ritual, legends, and fables, "cures of diseases, and antiquities, and how to read and write with letters and characters with which they wrote," as Bishop Landa was told in the 1560s, and seemingly "certain songs in meter," and "farces . . . and comedies for the pleasure of the public."

Three hieroglyphic books remain (Codices Dresden, Madrid, and Paris, named for the cities where they are now held), long accordion-folded sheets of pounded-bark paper sized with lime, bearing glyphs and illustrations painted on both sides. The British Mayanist J. Eric S. Thompson noted the constant repetition in these books of prophecies "of death, strife, war, evil, fierce burning suns, destructive storms, drought, woe to the maize, woe to mankind, woe to rulers upon their seats of authority . . . and the fewer tidings of joy and plenty." The repetitions themselves, involved in the endless analysis of all the interrelationships within the tzolkin, the sacred 260-day calendar (incidentally including numerous mathematical errors), appear to illustrate one cornerstone of Maya philosophy—the importance of the exact repetition of ritual down through time, complex and difficult though such exactness may be.

The intense Maya religion pervaded the obsessed art, and pervaded the astoundingly productive Maya life—astoundingly productive in ritual celebration. But in addition to ritual, the pantheon of gods enmeshed in their calendars required constant attention in the form of sacrifice and penance. The commonest act of penance was undoubtedly the drawing of blood from one's own tongue, ear, arm, or genitals, as it was the commonest act of penance for Aztec priests hundreds of years after Maya times. It is pictured in Maya art as a public ceremony, the blood dripped on sheets of bark paper or gathered in dishes and offered to the gods. The sting of a stingray was the preferred instrument for drawing blood; Thompson tells us such stings or artificial replicas thereof were buried with priests as insignia of office, and that in the large site of Tikal they have been found in burials by the hundreds.

Some human sacrifice took place in many Classic centers, evidently more frequently in later times, when bloodier invaders from central Mexico gained control of more and more Maya country—a ceremonial use of decapitated skulls, for example, is found in the Toltec-dominated late Classic and Postclassic Chichen Itza.

However, sacrificial offerings of all sorts of animals and vegetables are much more plentiful in the evidence: seeds, rubber, resin, copan, maize, honey, "pure" or "virgin" water, parrots, owls, fish, turtles, dogs, turkeys, even insects. The added offerings of continence, fasting, and often confession from the celebrants were necessary in celebrating all ceremonies, great and small. Later accounts relate that participants left their wives and lived in special quarters near the temples for sixty, eighty, or 100 days before scheduled rites, blackening their faces, praying, drawing blood, neither bathing nor combing their hair, fasting to the limit of their endurance, piously refraining from even raising their eyes to their wives or the women who brought their daily bread (some sources say one tortilla per day was the ration).

The special quarters near the temples where the ritual leaders stayed for their purification and preparation may have been in Classic times the misnamed "palaces," which could hardly have been meant for actual residence—cooking would not have been possible in the windowless rooms, and kitchen middens have not been found at their doorsteps.

Where the very important persons of Classic times really did live could pose interesting questions. Maybe sometimes in smaller stone houses, or maybe sometimes in tiny houses of poles and thatch, like the houses of ordinary people, maybe in compounds of such huts? It is reasonably certain the illustrious leaders wore their marvelous costuming only for ceremonial appearances; the fantastic and labyrinthian regalia of the stelae can scarcely be imagined at breakfast or upon taking a nap or when going to the toilet. Nor can the chieftain's (or victim's) litter, sometimes pictured, be imagined elsewhere than on the plaza or the sacbeob. It would be a careening wild ride traversing the jungle.

Rites inside the temple were all but secret. This can be regarded as certain, since the diminutive rooms of the Classic temples could not hold more than a very few people. But at the ceremonies in the plazas the people could all have marked the time together, in communion with the brilliantly arrayed priests and the revered *halach uinic* (chief celebrant), in ecstasy, perhaps, from the drumming and the dancing and the pageantry, the colors and the beauty and the meaning of the ritual that marked another passing point on the holy calendar.

It may be that the passing of time marked the triumph of life. To continue forever, as long as correctly celebrated: life-giving time. While the maize grew and the priests read and wrote and gazed over their crossed sticks at the stars, and the nobles nobled all day and raided each other on great occasions, and the people ate corn mush (*maadz*) in their houses and the women ground more corn and dangled bits of pitch between the baby's eyes to make him cross-eyed, and everybody, wearing fancy mantles and Sunday sandals, trooped in to the centers for the life-giving communion that kept the calendars turning.

We know a great deal about the Maya. Specialists can follow every step in the techniques that produced their buildings, sculpture, painting, unravel all the intricacies (well, nearly all) of their calendric calculation, tell us how they lived, loved, worked, slept, worshipped, died, what they ate and how they cooked it, how they dressed and how they wore their hair. And the people are still there, 5 million (even though Maya people by the thousand have been bombed, burned, and shot in recent times by a series of Guatemalan military dictatorships; a total of 120,000 Indian "war orphans" in Guatemala was reported in 1984) or so who speak the various related Maya languages, and in many cases are so similar in appearance to the muscular, delicately posed little men in the ancient art that they could be the frescoes come to life.

We know nearly everything about them, really, except that we really don't know the ancient Maya at all. They present the most profound enigma in American history.

Very early formative Maya communities, with a possible very early history covering 1,500 years, have been excavated in Belize, as has been mentioned. One of the earliest important ceremonial centers, in highland Guatemala (Kaminaljuyu, its ruins now pretty much swallowed up by Guatemala City), dates from more than twelve centuries before the Christian era. Maya agriculture may have first come into being some place nearby, much earlier, there on the flanks of the Central American Cordillera, a region of great beauty. Specialists in linguistics, studying structure and pattern in language families, have worked out shadowy forms of parent languages that reach back to still earlier times: thus a "Proto-Maya" spoken in 2500 B.C. is believed to have used words for "maize" and for "cotton cloth."

The highland Maya of the Guatemalan mountains were somewhat backward in Classic times in comparison with the lowland Maya, the typical Classic Maya, who expanded their way of art and life from the vicinity of Lake Peten in Guatemala to dominate all the rainforest country of central and southern Guatemala and adjacent areas of the Yucatan peninsula as well as, eventually, the dry brush country of northernmost Yucatan.

Throughout all these centuries of development, and the following six centuries of the Classic age, none of these many "cities," the communities exemplified by the numerous ceremonial centers, all remarkably alike, seemed to win hegemony over the others; all seemed to retain separate individuality.

In the Old World the civilization of the Sumerians in lower Mesopotamia came into being more or less simultaneously with the establishment of cities and war-won empire, one of its basic dates c. 2650 B.C. for the completion of the great wall of Uruk. The high civilization—and cities and empire—of ancient Egypt emerged at almost the same time. In ancient China the Epoch of the Warring States led within two centuries to the conquests of the First Emperor, who completed, with convict labor, the Great Wall c. 214 B.C., coeval with Maya Preclassic development. In ancient Greece the several city-states (to which the Maya communities have sometimes been compared) exhausted themselves in efforts to conquer each other, and, within three centuries after Solon, became subject states in the empire of Alexander the Great and two centuries later subjects of the Roman Empire.

This pattern, civilization = cities = conquest and empire, has been posited by many social scientists as law, but the Classic (and for that matter also the Preclassic) Maya don't seem to have obeyed it, thus presenting the first mask of the Maya enigma.

The previously mentioned Stela 29 at the ceremonial center of Tikal, fifty miles north of Lake Peten, the earliest stela so far found dated in the Long Count, was taken for many years as the starting point for the Classic Period. The GMT correlation gives its date as A.D. 292. The contending Spinden correlation reads these Classic dates about 260 years earlier; some radiocarbon tests appear to support the Spinden system for this period, but more seem to support the GMT—to the great relief of most Mayanists and their publishers, since most modern references are based on the GMT system. Although, as has been mentioned, the complex correlation question is still far from entirely settled.

The Classic Period came to a close some six centuries after A.D. 292, when the lowland Peten Maya, the people in the heart of the Maya country, departed from their shining temple clusters and drifted away and out of their rainforest homeland. They left no indications of invasion, war, or general unrest. They left, therefore, their chief enigma.

This was not at all the end of the Maya but it was the end of their central societies, their greatest age. Gradual exodus from the Classic centers began in the ninth century A.D. (GMT). A century or so later the towering pyramids, the monuments, and the buildings with their prodigious decoration (some buildings were left half-finished and some glyphs were left blank on interrupted inscriptions) were all but deserted. No one knows why. Apparently the few residents who stayed on for several generations after the halt of the sacred machinery tried, here and there, to keep alive the cult of the monumental stelae, reverently resetting broken fragments—but sometimes, in their helpless ignorance, placing the ancient inscriptions upside down.

Thus the second mask of the Maya enigma.

Perhaps both these baffling problems, the overall form of Classic government and the abandonment of the temple centers that composed their most important city-states, perhaps both these impenetrable masks are only different views of the same face, of the total enigma that is the central Maya Classic age, primitive, wise, industrious, poetic, artistic, credulous, seemingly the unique example in the history of the world of a people absorbed in watching the clock.

Both these masks could be removed in an instant by the discovery of new information, and in the 1960s new information was announced that for a time appeared to be on the point of providing such revelation. Tatiana

Proskouriakoff, a leading specialist in Maya monumental art, noticed that certain glyphs in a series of stelae at the ceremonial center of Piedras Negras followed patterns of dates within certain limits that could be reasonable lifetimes or lengths of reigns for rulers. Were the inscriptions therefore historical, rather than simply calendrical? Further work by epigraphers and art historians showed conclusively that many inscriptions were indeed historical, moving the Maya out of nonliterate prehistory into a background of, or at least a beginning of, written historical records, a truly momentous alteration.

However, attempts to follow the lead of this discovery to a more extensive Maya explanation have not been very satisfactory. Some ascriptions of individual names have been rather widely accepted, and the dubbing of local leaders as kings, and even a few tentative "dynasties." But a history of war and empire has not resulted, in spite of strenuous efforts to dig it out.

Stelae commemorating a calendar event such as the ending of a *lahuntun* (a period of 3,600 days) or a *katun* (7,200 days) often included a sculptured portrait of the local ruler or celebrant, accompanied by other figures and sometimes by a prisoner or two. It has usually been assumed the prisoners would figure in the ceremony (perhaps as sacrificial victims) and may have been captured for that purpose in raids on borderlands or on neighboring city-states.

Evidence of formal warfare among the Classic Maya has always been deemed conspicuous by its absence. (The first North American to study Maya ruins, in 1840, said of an unidentifiable object in a sculpture, "It may be a weapon of war, and, if so, it is the only thing of the kind found represented at Copan"). But if a glyph in the adjoining inscription seemed to refer to a neighboring city, the thought was now suggested that the stela commemorated a full-scale war between the two communities, perhaps concluding with the capture of the neighboring ruler. This new interpretation, however, without corroboration from art or archeology, seemed to need more work.

A corroborative Classic picture of genuine war was suggested, the newly discovered Bonampak murals. In 1946 the photographer and filmmaker Giles Healey was led by Lacandon Maya people to seventeen ancient Maya sites until then unexplored, the largest a ruin since become famous under the name Bonampak (the name invented by the Mayanist Sylvanus Griswold Morley), in Chiapas, Mexico. There, rare and wonderfully well-done murals pictured a series of events including a battle and the torture of captives, amongst whom lies a severed head. This, almost the only genuine war scene in central Classic temple art (dated c. A.D. 775), has been cited as proof that the Classic Maya were truly warlike, and together with the new interpretation of prisoners on lahuntun stelae proof that the Central Maya were in fact, as one enthusiast puts it, in a state of "constant warfare."

But it has been pointed out by other specialists that the enemy in the Bonampak battle scene appears to be unarmed. Further, in the later scene of torture, the severed head lying amidst the captives is oddly larger than life, and is actually more a face than a head—if cut from a real body it would have necessitated some neat skilsaw dividing of the skull. It very much resembles in fact the face of the young maize god seen so frequently on temple walls. One thinks of classic Athens and the sacrilegious defacement of images of Hermes understandably (if wrongly) associated in the public mind with Alcibiades and his playboy pals. Could something such as this be the background here? The torture of the captives consists in drawing blood from their hands, possibly by tearing off the fingernails, reminiscent of the penance so often seen exacted on the part of the body that had sinned: tongue, ears, hands, genitals. More work does seem needed, to turn such an ambiguous scene into evidence of chronic warfare down the centuries.

One thing though is clear: for the same data to bring opposite conclusions to different students has to mean that, in the previously quoted words of a sacred text, we are not seeing things as they are, we are seeing things as we are.

A great deal of discussion has been pursued in many other areas, of course, devoted to the search, in the light of the new information, for Classic Maya conquest and resultant empire, or at least some resultant central authority. Exceptionally large centers, such as Tikal, the biggest in Classic times, or Copan, the intellectual capital, clearly exerted some regional influence on smaller neighbors, or, in the case of Copan's astronomical leadership, on the whole lowland Classic world.

Tikal has been the scene of immense multidisciplinary investigation (finally financed by the government of Guatemala with tourism in view) which has shown Tikal to be more urban than the usual Maya norm, and with a more intensive agriculture, in the surrounding swampy lowlands, than the usual slash and burn technique would appear to provide.

But conquest, empire—even a single central authority—have not appeared. A meeting of archeologists, art historians, and epigraphers in 1986 considering the revisionist evidence and interpretations found that no important change had resulted in our picture of Maya society. Assumptions and speculations remained still basic to our definitions; proposed "dynasties" were without clear lines of descent; four out of five "kings" or local rulers were of unnamed parentage; some such rulers were clearly not direct descendants of predecessors; there were numbers of important rulers whose accessions were somehow irregular. The argument for constant warfare found Classic evidence that ten people of aristocratic (*ahau*) status could be definitely shown as captives—but a tiny total such as this in six centuries of war?

The findings concluded with warnings against undue significance for fragmentary decipherment of inscriptions. Most importantly, the romantic (Old World) view of masterful military power and kingly might as the only begetters of statehood still remains seriously questioned in the case of the obsessively religious Maya. In particular the Old World tradition of dynasty based on direct descent would seem incompatible with Maya astrological obsession—an obsession with the correct date of birth rather than the line of parentage.

One major issue put forward by the new interpretation continues very much in business: conjecture that the principal purpose of the monumental art was not celebration of calendric events but the personal aggrandizement of the local leader.

In this the great hiatus that so intrigued Joe Goodman, when for sixty years—in the midst of Classic times—all stela dedication in a number of the leading Peten centers ceased, may serve as a crucial issue. Personal aggrandizement would certainly seem to give way, for two long generations, to the purely calendrical pause. On the other hand if one of the centers affected, for example Tikal, or perhaps more plausibly Copan, could be shown to take the lead in this and, in effect, impose its will on the others, it might offer a hint of one central authority, at any rate for that lengthy occasion. The matter of this heavy silence might well be worth still more heavy consideration.

The longevity of Maya religion may have some bearing on its weight. Maya religion dated of course from long before Classic times; the Classic "markers" for archeology are (or rather, used to be) the Long Count, vaulted architecture, and a polychrome pottery, but construction of religious edifices had been going on for perhaps a thousand years before the Classic Period. The peak of construction at huge Tikal came before the Classic Period began, and the Preclassic site of El Mirador, "in sheer bulk larger than Tikal," contained platforms and pyramids even older. And the scriptures were still being recited a thousand years after the Classic collapse—"Then there sprang up the bouquet of the priest, the bouquet of the ruler, the bouquet of the captain; this was what the flower-king bore when he descended and nothing else, so they say. It was not bread that he bore."

The calendrical observances of the Maya clearly expressed an idea common to many American Indian religions, from those of the highest civilizations to the simplest desert groups of hunter-gatherers: a rite of renewal. The intricate Maya mind, counting so many wheels within wheels, all in motion, all bringing the past and the future bodily into the present, may have embellished this with a panoply of further abstractions, but the germ of renewal must have been present in the foundation.

Renewal has to imply a preceding ending. It is easy to believe that many ancient American peoples lived only to celebrate death. Hopewellian tombs of the Ohio Valley are remarkably rich with funerary offerings. In South America such cemeteries as the Paracas Necropolis are still richer, infinitely richer; some of the bundles of woven material found there, perhaps the finest weaving in all the world's history, would appear to be the product of entire lifetimes of virtuoso work.

Certainly the most dramatic fact of life is death. What a transformation so quickly wrought—and its absolute finality and utter universality! Death as theme of ritual is immediately understandable—as is its corollary, rebirth and renewal.

Says a remembered Maya prayer: "Let it dawn, let the day come, may the people have peace, may they be happy, give us good life."

The day, the year, the century renewed, what will it bring? Divination as a chief service of religion, the most commented aspect of Maya (and of many another) religion, is also easily understandable. How ancient can ideas be? Is it necessary to erect public monuments before man can be anxious about his destiny? Are irrigation systems necessary before men can wonder what the heavens are designing?

Death, renewal, divination, being key factors in Maya religion, may also have been factors in the ending of the Maya Classic age. A story was told centuries later of Maya resistance to Spanish invasion in a particular region, that the resistance ended because calendric divination said that at this point it would. Could one factor in the departure of the Classic Maya from their shining cities have been that divination told them to go?

CHAPTER 5

Turmoil and Temples
in Central Mexico

I spent the first three years of my life mostly in Maya country, on the borders of the Yucatan peninsula, where my father, a civil engineer, was working. In the remote village where we lived there was a whipping post soaked through with blood; my father had it cut down and made into a high chair for me.

Despite a whipping post's evidence of the brutal subjection of the people there, Maya people were good humored, outgoing—genial or merry would not be an overstatement, as I often heard my mother say in later years. And yet the War of Chan Santa Cruz, a desultory but widespread and violent rebellion, had been going on for generations by that time, its epicenter no more than 100 miles or so to the east of us.

My mother, the daughter of a devout Methodist family, thought these Yucateca people intensely religious, both in regard to the remnants of their ancient religion and to the forms of Spanish Catholicism under which they had lived for more than 300 years. And yet to her the most striking thing about them was their coarse and shocking frankness, even among the women—in fact especially among the women—in speaking of sexual matters. This became their principal trait in her memory, a trait that seems to be borne out in the theological literature of the region.

There may be a hint of it from Classic times in what was apparently a stock comic character in anecdotal ceramics, a boozy girl-chasing dirty old man—sometimes played by a young man in an old man's mask. At the least it seems to touch on a far from solemn view of sex among the solemn stelae.

"They are *so* contradictory," my mother would say, reminiscing, and would usually add, "but interesting people so often are."

The character of the ancient Maya is much discussed at present, as has been noted. Supporters of the current "revolution" in Maya thinking pronounce them warlike, tyrannical, sadistic, savage. "S&M history," an archeologist suggested, punning on the names of the best selling authors, Schele and Miller.

But regardless of current controversy, the ancient Maya certainly continue to hold star billing as interesting people. It is not easy to keep in mind that their Classic world preceded the Aztec and Inca worlds by 1,000 years. The questions left by the Classic Maya outlived all their New World successors; it is possible they will outlive us.

It is also necessary to keep in mind that the ancient Maya were only one among many peoples in America to build pyramids and surround them with courts and avenues and buildings dedicated to religion. Their art, as mentioned, is considered by general consent to include the finest in the New World and some of the finest anywhere, but they may not have been the first among their neighbors to develop it. The corbelled vault distinctive to their architecture, some aspects of their written language, and possibly their use of zero, seem to have been exclusively their own; but they may not have been the first to use the principles of their famous calendar mathematics. They were far from being alone in the growing world of their time, and ideas are no respecters of state lines. All the middle zone of the Americas, from Mexico south to Bolivia and Peru, was spawning varicolored towns and cities. Agriculture, especially corn farming, and the revolution in living that went with it—new gods, new wealth, new ways, new worries—had spread far beyond this highly cultured heartland.

Some 700 miles to the west of Classic Maya country were the brilliant mountaintop cities of the Zapotec—where various fundamentals of Mesoamerican civilization may have been invented. Three hundred miles farther west another people had built the great city of the epoch, huge Teotihuacan. Two thousand miles or so farther north (by land), in the Ohio valley in North America, a people who may possibly have included descendants of long-ago émigrés from someplace in that Mesoamerican heartland were establishing villages, making pottery, and building enormous burial mounds, hundreds of years before the beginning of the Maya Classic period.

Centuries before the first dated Mayan monuments, corn was under cultivation among the already ancient Cochise people in the adjoining southerly regions of what is now Arizona and New Mexico, and not long afterward was

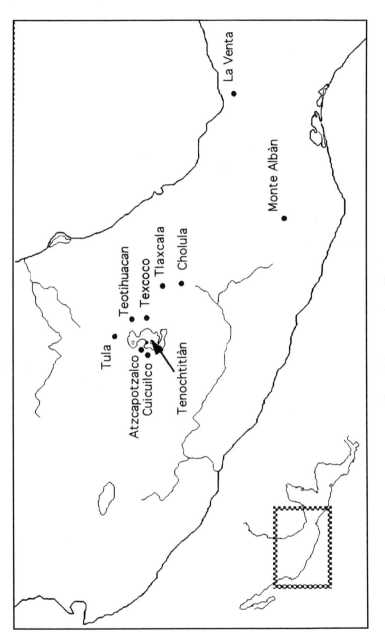

Some Mesoamerican Sites

La Venta

Monte Albàn

Teotihuacan

Texcoco

Tlaxcala

Cholula

Tula

Atzcapotzalco

Cuicuilco

Tenochtitlàn

being grown by incipient villagers of the Southwest who were ancestors of the modern Pueblo Indians.

And everywhere beyond the belts of little slashed-out planted fields, everywhere throughout the boundless areas surrounding these few frontiers, the wandering tribes, untouched, lived as they always had. "People of the wood," the Maya poets called them in the Popol Vuh. "There are generations in the world, there are country people, whose faces we do not see, who have no homes, who only wander."

While the Maya were building their earliest temples some of these people then living in the Grand Canyon of Arizona were making tiny symbolic figurines, figurines of little deer fashioned from twigs, with twig spears run through them: if this unnatural phenomenon is modeled and inserted in the world, might not the world produce it in response? (Archeologists first discovered these for sale at a roadside curio stand in Arizona; they are more than 3,000 years old.)

Trading in more than ideas went on between the towns and cities— trading in everything from slaves to kitchenware. Articles of commerce found their way from town to town and covered, sometimes, astonishing distances, crossing countries of high culture as well as lands inhabited only by peoples of the wood. It can be assumed that commercial and cultural interchange seeped, slowly but inexorably, everywhere that topography permitted.

Interesting information from the Pueblo country of the American Southwest indicates that prehistoric trade, meaning direct contact, normally covered an area with a radius of about thirty days' foot travel, or (very roughly) a radius of 500 miles or so in average distance. However, direct contact could reach much farther under exceptional conditions, as Maya influence on the Huasteca, a splinter group of Maya people in the region of Vera Cruz, easily traversed distances of 700 miles or more, and mighty Teotihuacan made itself felt very noticeably in Classic Maya centers 1,000 miles away.

A look at the neighbors of the Classic Maya, in what is now Mexico: west along the Gulf Coast from the Yucatan Peninsula was the old and faded Olmec center of La Venta. A possibly related people, known to us as Totonac, may have built Tajin, a town coming into importance farther west along the coast, a town of a famous pyramid, ball courts, and many temples.

Inland, within several hundred miles to the south and west, a profusion of towns and cities were inhabited by a profusion of peoples not yet altogether clear in the archeological record, from the Zapotec in their mountaintop showplaces of the Oaxaca area on westward 250 miles or so to the great religious center of Cholula, for generations evidently the capital, cultural capital at least, of the Mixtec people.

The Zapotec city of Monte Alban grew into being on a very ancient site, and apparently experienced a variety of histories in its long life. Hundreds of puzzling bas-relief stone figures were produced there in early days, the so-called *danzantes*, perhaps picturing the agonies of torture. They are dated centuries before the opening of the Maya Classic period. In Classic times the city was the home of a funeral cult whose high style urns were traded far and wide. Some archeological studies have reported that the Classic Monte Alban was a center of learning; one study finds that it was under the rule of a birthright oligarchy. The Zapotec country may have been the birthplace of the god Xipe, central Mexico's god of springtime, in whose honor the priest danced in the skin of a flayed sacrificial victim.

At Cholula an immense sacred pyramid was augmented by successive enlargements until it eventually exceeded in volume Egypt's Pyramid of Cheops. A mural of butterfly gods decorated one of its inner rooms, together with a painting of Quetzalcoatl, who, as the Plumed Serpent, God of the Morning, Morning Star, the Bearded Man, Lord of Life, Lord of the Wind, Bringer of Civilization, and in countless other guises, was known to many of these differing peoples of central Mexico from the earliest times.

As far as present comprehension comprehends, these urban glories reached their apex in the Valley of Mexico, a high landlocked basin wrinkled with networks of lakes and vales and ringed by smoking volcanoes, set in the southeastern end of the vast plateau that is mid-Mexico. Here in this "valley" at an altitude of nearly a mile and a half were numerous towns and villages and cities, most of them congregated around the great salt lake, Lake Texcoco, and its freshwater feeder lagoons, sizable lakes in themselves.

The Classic period in this Valley of Mexico was in some respects uncultivated and immature compared to the Classic period in the Maya jungles, but its works made up in dimension what they lacked in elegance and subtlety. Teotihuacan, the great city of the Valley in Classic times, was a solid procession of majestic public buildings and religious barracks from the Pyramid of the Moon to the Temple of Quetzalcoatl, dominated in the center by the tremendous Pyramid of the Sun. A paved area more than three miles long and nearly two miles wide was occupied by these structures, decorated with the serpents, beasts, and feathered men of heaven. The public buildings were surrounded by their plazas, parks, and avenues—and by what were evidently closely packed houses, leading to the supposition that Teotihuacan was no uninhabited ceremonial center but a genuine city in the modern urban sense.

The emergence of this city appears to have been marvelously rapid, as well as the planning and building of much of its public architecture, constructed in the final centuries B.C. The raising of the Pyramid of the Sun, with a volume of about 1,000,000 cubic meters, was completed within two centuries, "the largest single-phase structure ever erected in the pre-Columbian New World," according to the archeologist William Sanders. Such intense effort would seem to bespeak powerful rulers and a people driven under the whip, but there is no evidence of a coercive society. Sanders tells us there is "no other situation in the historical or archeological record" that is comparable.

The crippling of a rival city, Cuicuilco, by a volcanic eruption at the beginning of this activity, may have played some part, calling attention, possibly, to the watchful presence of the gods.

The population had been doubling every two centuries, noted as a "remarkable growth rate" for a pre-industrial group; the city eventually numbered more than 125,000 people, possibly at times reaching 200,000. (The zenith population of Athens, c. 400 B.C., may have numbered 100,000, of which only a small fraction lived in the city proper.) The Teotihuacan urbanites were at first overwhelmingly agrarian, living in town and going into the country to work their fields. This was a pattern very different from that of the Peten Maya, who as has been mentioned lived in their scattered rural communities roundabout the temple centers. Population density in the largest Classic Maya city, Tikal, was at the most only in the hundreds per square kilometer—in Teotihuacan it totaled in the thousands. But Tikal's area was 60 square kilometers (or 120, counting fringes), Teotihuacan's 25.

As time passed—Teotihuacan's dominance in Mexico lasted for 500 years—more and more of the people there turned to some sort of specialized work, up to one-third of the population finally, with the largest bloc of this, some 10 percent of the city's households, engaged in the obsidian "industry" (mining long-dead lava flows).

Such a vast community certainly became a place famed throughout the land, to which the faithful must have thronged on holy occasions, joining the black robed priests in celebrating the mysteries that kept the world in balance: rain and fire, planting and harvesting, and the endless mystical renewal of the calendar.

Varying forms of the typical Mesoamerican calendar systems—including most of the Maya calendrics except for the Maya long count—were in use among all the cities of Mexico, the calendar that swallowed itself, like the two-headed serpent, every 260 days and every fifty-two years, spinning out the revelation that everything comes to an end and yet is reborn, everything changes and yet remains the same, only the circle, revolving forever, remains unchanged.

The sacrifice of flowers, birds, dogs, human beings—the sacrifice, in short, of life—was an act meant to recognize and sustain this process of the gods.

Teotihuacan's gods were in the rain and the sunlight that brought growth—the American gods were hungry, hungry for the death that brought new life. Was not death the final objective of life, and therefore its food? In common with many other peoples before and since, the Teotihuacanos ate the god, in ritual cannibalistic feasts, to achieve communion.

Obsidian may have been the core of Teotihuacan's extensive trade, a trade that marked even the distant Maya country with very recognizable Teotihuacano traits. Ancient Kaminaljuyu, in the southern Maya highlands, is believed by some specialists to have become an outright Teotihuacan conquest. Two notable rulers of Tikal itself, in early Classic times, were seemingly apostles of, or even natives of, Teotihuacan.

The touch of magnificent Teotihuacan—in architecture, pottery, in its gods—can be traced for century after century over all central and southern Mexico until about A.D. 600, when began the generations of disruption or invasion or revolution that continued until the great city was destroyed or abandoned.

Before that final ending Teotihuacan was twice rebuilt, lower rooms filled in and buildings covered with cut stone and adobe to provide platforms for new and larger buildings. Temples were often enlarged or rebuilt at the close of each fifty-two-year century, but these reconstructions apparently indicated something more, possibly clean sweep changes of political administration. Religion and politics were evidently so entwined as to be one and the same thing; when the party of the old gods was overthrown the party of the new gods raised new temples as well as a new society, and perhaps fed the new gods with any priests of the defeated opposition who could be chased down and caught. Such changes may or may not have meant invasion of new people, perhaps only a shift in alignment of powerful families or clans. Or they may sometimes have reflected a climax of discontent among the more numerous poor relations—a revolt of the masses.

The old gods, in many cases, changed their masks but never really disappeared. Tlaloc, the rain god who was defeated at Teotihuacan, had the teeth of the long ago Olmec jaguar, and with new added attributes later reappeared in the front rank of the pantheon. Quetzalcoatl, whose ornately sculptured temple was completely covered over and turned into the foundation for new construction, remained nevertheless a star actor in the march of the following centuries. The old gods melted into the new, the new gods became new disguises for the old; the gods of good and the gods of evil, locked in their eternal confrontation, were all, conceivably, only opposing manifestations of the same beings—even, one might venture, of the same single being.

In the generations after A.D. 600 turmoil ran wild among the city-states of central and southern Mexico, and the Classic Age was pulled to pieces.

During this time, Cholula of the great pyramid took a leading place as a holy city, caught the fallen metropolitan mantle of Teotihuacan, so to speak, or so some present readings of the archeological records appear to indicate. Although it also seems that the Mixtec people, while still clinging to their center at Cholula, were pivoted still farther down country to come in conflict with the Zapotecan people of Oaxaca.

It may have been due to some such pressure that the Zapotec people abandoned their mountaintop city of Monte Alban—many generations later Mixteca were using the ghost town of Monte Alban as a cemetery, and some of the richest treasures of ancient Mexico have been found there in their tombs.

It appears that people along the Vera Cruz coast, any remaining Olmec descendants and related Totonac people (if they were indeed relatives), raged inland into the mountains of Oaxaca and Puebla, adding to the disturbances among the Mixtecan and Zapotecan peoples there.

A number of towns and cities throughout the civilized regions of central Mexico were abandoned, as the Maya were abandoning their lowland jungle centers at about the same time.

If the GMT correlation of the Maya calendar is followed, the wave of collapse appeared first in central Mexico and later, a couple of centuries or so later, among the Maya; the Spinden correlation brings the decline in both areas closer together in date. It seems easier to find reason for the breakup outside the Maya borders, but still the war-making migrations that seem to have been one immediate cause must have been in turn set afoot by something, some prodigious set of motives—famine, disease, signs and portents in the troubled skies. The dislocations they set in motion went on for centuries, whatever the cause.

CHAPTER 6

From the Toltecs to the Incas

People (if there are any) a thousand years from now may well see our twentieth century as a tremendous explosion of titanic wars, violent revolutions, demonic famines, and demoniac massacres, all attending the opening of eternity's smash hit, nuclear weaponry. Students will wonder how, in the midst of this chaos, Einstein and Fermi found any time to think. But we can bear witness that ordinary dinnertimes, ordinary bedtimes, ordinary lifetimes continue to exist even in an epoch of furious change.

The epoch of furious change that struck Teotihuacan in the seventh century A.D. seemed to bring disruption rather than sudden destruction. The view formerly held of barbaric invaders from the north destroying and burning the city is not supported by recent research. Instead there was apparently a gradual decline over several generations of ordinary lifetimes. The decline may have been caused by civic unrest, breakdown of trade or in agriculture (from unusual frosts or drought, for example), some raids or invasions from troublesome neighbors or northern barbarians, and possibly from other causes still outside the experts' guesswork, all combining to disrupt repeatedly the basic stability that had prevailed for centuries.

The people of the woods who crowded down from the north to harass the Valley of Mexico during this age of chaos may have been driven by the fever of unrest endemic in the time or may have been a germ of its beginning.

Long afterward, a thousand years afterward, the grandson of the last "king" in the Valley of Mexico compiled a set of annals from records then still existing in books of picture writing. Fable, myth, and legend mingle in them, evoking all the more movingly the distant shadows. Listen to the saga of the Tolteca, a nation of barbarians who have dwelt for ages in "the country towards what is now called California, in the Southern Sea" (which is to say,

Mexico's Pacific coast), who have learned the calendar (strayed into the magnetic field of civilization and absorbed its beginnings), and who now have been split by civil war—a bitter but natural process among the wild tribes of splitting and dividing whenever they grew so large as to be unwieldy units for their way of life.

The expelled faction (driven forth in grief and anger) sojourned for eight years here, three years there, left families to populate this land or that, traveled on to new sojourns of seven years or eight years, until after 122 years and a series of thirteen temporary homelands, "they marched on . . . and founded the city of Tula, which they were six years building."

The site of Toltec Tula is believed to be on a ridge (on a defensive height, reflecting the temper of the times) above the present community of Tula de Allende, a couple of hours from Mexico City by car, just outside the northwestern edge of the Valley of Mexico. Evidence has been uncovered there of houses by the thousand, a small (but elegant) ceremonial center, and heavy occupation some 900 or 1,000 years ago in the countryside roundabout. The city's rise was rapid, its florescence brief, and its decline headlong. Its total life as the great capital of its time lasted only a half dozen generations or so, from about 950 to 1150. But its fame was immense and has lived on ever since.

By the time of the city's fall the Toltec conquests extended as far as the heart of the ancient Maya country, in Guatemala and northern Yucatan. The Maya abandonment of their lowland jungle centers at the close of Classic times had been followed by appearance of new or enlarged centers to the north of the Peten jungle, in the Puuc hills, in the region of the Rio Bec, all the way through the peninsula of Yucatan to the Yucatan coast beyond. Some of these Yucatan centers, most notably the famous Chichen Itza, reflected Toltec domination throughout a long Postclassic Indian-summer renaissance. Such Toltec conquests may have been achieved by Toltec displaced persons following the fall of Tula, as, several centuries before, displaced Teotihuacanos had emigrated to the ends of the known earth.

It would please our taste for sequence, maybe, to think of the Tolteca as uncultured conquerors with the esthetic sensibilities of rich drug dealers, but this doesn't seem to have been the case. Mexican tradition has remembered the Toltecs as the master architects, the brilliant innovators, and the ideal expression of ancient Mexico. For centuries after the Toltec empire had vanished, ruling families from Yucatan to Texcoco insisted on claiming Toltec descent. This is puzzling in view of the brevity of Toltec dominance, compared to the great antiquity of contemporary and powerful Cholula, the previous lengthy preeminence of Teotihuacan, the antiquity and influence of the people of Oaxaca and Tlaxcala. Simply a result of Toltec military successes? Possibly—but the thought that the Toltec, as near predecessors of the Aztec, enjoyed therefore great Aztec renown, a renown subsequently passed on to the Aztec successors, us, is perhaps more reasonable.

The scholars and the diggers have revealed much of the New World's tangled past, the least known and therefore the most intriguing of ancient histories, but there are so many things not yet understood and that may never be. The pattern changes with each shifting wind that stirs the ashes. But here and there a coal is glowing yet, alive with a memory still warm to the touch. These bring a pulse of reality even though the cleverest of the specialists may be unsure—precisely the cleverest are the least sure—as to their exact place in the pattern.

Such are the Maya and such are the people we call the Toltecs—the Maya alight with meditation, the Tolteca with energy.

Tradition says the Toltec as conquerors brought to Mexico the black god Tezcatlipoca, Lord of the Night, to war with white Quetzalcoatl, Lord of the Morning, and that as invaders they introduced human sacrifice to the Maya. Tradition says they introduced the sacred ball game, at which whole populations bet, won, and lost everything from lip jewels to lives. And in the time of the Toltec ruler Iztacaltzin, says tradition, a lady of blessed memory named Xochitl (commonest girl's name in the Nahua language, meaning flower) invented *octli*, booze concocted from the maguey plant, today called pulque and still the national drink.

But human sacrifice, as we have seen, had been known long before, although apparently practiced with less frequency, among the Maya as elsewhere in Middle America. No one can guess how long ago the practice began of sending dead souls to help the sun in his war against the stars, and feeding the rain with blood. What more could devotion offer, and who wouldn't be glad to go? "Quickly slay me, trample me with thy feet! May my body come to rest!" in the words of an ancient Mexican prayer.

And Tezcatlipoca, whose symbol was a jaguar skin (and the jaguar of the Olmec had arrived 2,000 years before), had been fighting the sun on temple walls for hundreds of years before Toltec times.

And surely most of the ball courts in various cities were many centuries pre-Toltec. The origin of the Mexican ball game, in which players, without using their hands, tried to knock a solid rubber ball through the goal of a vertical ring set in the wall of a ball court, is believed to be very ancient indeed—it figures prominently in at least one creation story. The game was surrounded by ceremonies that were evidently of a sacred character. Ballgame terminology (as in the verse from a Nahua hymn: "He plays the ball game the servant of marvelous skill he plays at ball/ Youths make yourselves equal in the ball court to your forebears") could express the most solemn religious feeling.

And if the alcoholic Maya *balche*, so much used in ritual, had not wafted its idea northward to Mexico proper in times long before it would be surprising.

Tradition says the most glorious Toltec leader, Topiltzin, being born on the day called in the calendar *Ce Acatl* (One Reed) was given its name, after their custom, and since he was educated as a priest of Quetzalcoatl he therefore was given the god's name too, as was the custom, so that he was called in full Ce Acatl Topiltzin Quetzalcoatl. He ruled with unparalleled goodness and wisdom.

But now tradition dissolves the priest into the divinity and says the vengeful god Tezcatlipoca appeared on earth and drove Ce Acatl Topiltzin Quetzalcoatl from Tula to Cholula and then to Yucatan, and that as Topiltzin Quetzalcoatl passed through all these places he "taught them by his words and by his works the road of virtue. . . . After having taught . . . he departed by the way he had come, that is to say, to the East, and . . . told them that in time to come, in the year of Ce Acatl, he would return." So says Ixtlilxochitl, the previously mentioned (Spanish-educated) grandson of the last "king" of the Valley of Mexico.

Quetzalcoatl says, in the translation of the Nahuatl manuscript known as the Florentine Codex, "I am called hence. The sun hath called me."

Quetzalcoatl taught and left behind him, they say, all the arts of peace, from metalworking to featherworking, from writing to weaving. He tried to abolish human sacrifice in Tula, and limit worship there to the burning of *copal* (resin) as incense and the sacrifice of flowers and butterflies; but as Kukulcan he demanded human sacrifice at Chichen Itza—where, says legend, he came to live, as he came to live in Mayapan.

Possibly much of this contradictory clamor of tradition is based on bits of truth. The Toltecs seem to have brought a burst of energy, new ideas or a restructuring of old ideas, new learning or an altered application of old learning, in short a blazing rekindling of the old cultural fires all but snuffed out in the collapse of the Classic Age. Every flying spark could have set off a different conflagration, blown this way and that by different many-sided gusts, leaving different memories in different places.

The greatest Toltec figure may very well have been Topiltzin. His time is variously ascribed to the ninth or tenth centuries. Metalworking was rather clearly introduced to Mexico during this period, in the neighborhood of A.D. 900 (at last the sun could be made tangible in the splendor of gold, "excrement of the gods"), and trade was greatly expanded. Cargoes of everything from macaw feathers and jaguar skins to drinking tubes and chewing gum traveled the trails in the tumpline packs (back packs held by a band passed around the forehead) of merchants and their slaves.

Certain areas exported products—salt, rubber, dogs fattened for the table, cacao for the delicious foaming chocolate so much in demand that cacao beans were used for currency. Other regions worked up manufacturing specialties—yarn, embroidered cotton cloth for mantles, loincloths, skirts, hair ribbons; war clubs with inset sword blade edges of obsidian; rope, carved jade and turquoise, flutes and tobacco pipes of clay; pottery, paints, and dyes.

Some trade went by sea—the Maya imported at this time the famed Orange pottery from the region of Vera Cruz, that had to be freighted more than 600 miles by seagoing canoe. Dugouts of the coastal Maya, crewed by as many as twenty-five paddlers, carried for trade such building materials as lime, clay, and the metal-hard sapodilla wood, as well as corn and vanilla, wax and honey, stone cutlery from razors to hatchets, and chiefly (so wrote an early European explorer) "draperies and different articles of spun cotton in brilliant colors."

The machinery of trade, the markets, that developed in the New World may have been built upon formations difficult for us to comprehend: apparently they were not profit-oriented. They appear instead to have been simply mechanisms for exchange, systems of a redistributive economy, as the specialists put it, in which populations in regions of environmental diversity could swap excess goods and thereby obtain different necessities required.

In accordance with this picture, ancient Mesoamerican trade dealt principally with goods of use in everyday living. Religious articles were sometimes present, such as cat-faced carvings or green-feathered birds, but there seem to have been few items aimed at an elite personal taste.

Old World contrasts with this profitlessness are of interest here: the typical market of classic Greece "a set place in the middle of the city, where men come together to cheat each other and forswear themselves."

By circa A.D. 1000 the growing of corn and the companion crops that followed (or sometimes preceded) it, such as squash and beans, and its accompanying art, the making of pottery, had spread over nearly all North America where climate permitted, except the far west coast.

The descendants of the Cochise people built ball courts for the sacred game in the Arizona deserts, where their irrigation ditches had already by this time been carrying water for perhaps 200 years. And in the cottonwood canyons of the rainbow country where New Mexico, Arizona, Utah, and Colorado join, the golden age of the Pueblos was dawning, with the phenomenal burst of construction in and near Chaco Canyon in northwestern New Mexico where towns, roads, structures containing hundreds of rooms and spacious ceremonial chambers (*kivas*) came into being.

A basic controversy has come into being with study of this locality: was the complex settlement here a result of independent processes or a reflection of distant Mexico? Contact with distant Mexico seems fairly definite—live parrots were brought here in trade, carried perhaps from markets in central Mexico (or perhaps from the Chiricahua mountains in southern Arizona, depending on secure identification of species).

A corridor of maize-farming peoples extended from this Arizona–New Mexico outpost country down the eastern slope of the Sierra Madre Occidental to the northwestern frontier of the Mexican civilization to the south, this frontier falling in the western borders of the land of the Zacatecans, nearly as far above the Valley of Mexico as the Maya country was below it.

It seems that another corridor, a sea-lane, may have reached across the Gulf of Mexico to the Mississippi, and a long list of trade items, some markedly Mayanesque in style, went from hand to hand through what may have been a grand network of prosperous little nations in and about the Mississippi valley. Many of these people built earthwork walls and mounds as burial monuments, ceremonial designs, or embryonic temple platforms.

Ripples of contact carried ideas, customs, fragments of holy ceremony, to the most distant people of the woods as well as to these settled farmers, and brought back new ideas in return.

The bow was working its way down from the far north, whizzing along at the rate of some 2,000 miles in 1,000 years, and in the northern forests moccasins were replacing bark sandals. A sporty small-caliber weapon, the blowgun, shooting little clay bullets to knock down birds and small game, had appeared in Classic Teotihuacan. But the universal Mexican arms in A.D. 1000 were still the mace, knife, spear, and spear-thrower.

Worked gold came to the Maya toward the end of Classic times, about A.D. 700–900, from Panama and Costa Rica, presumably drifting up from Colombia and Ecuador and Peru, where metallurgy had developed long before this time. The Maya never became metalworkers but the Mexican city-states above them, receiving worked gold at about the same period, eventually produced goldsmiths and silversmiths whose achievements, in a specialist's accolade, rank with "the greatest works of art of all time."

The use of metals in prehistoric America is believed to have been discovered independently in several different centers. Fragments of gold foil, hammered out possibly from bits of gold in river beds, have been found in the very early Peruvian village site of Waywaka, dating to before 1500 B.C. Tiny sheets of hammered copper at another Peruvian aite, Mina Perdida, date possibly to 1000 B.C. Only a few centuries later, in the area of 600 B.C., gold and silver objects bearing religious motifs from Chavin de Huantar were appearing. Copper in South America roundabout Lake Titicaca, high in the Andes between Bolivia and Peru, and the presence of tin in the same area led in time to the making of bronze, which has been found in fairly early prehistoric graves in Peru.

In North America, as has been mentioned, native copper was used in early times in the vicinity of Lake Superior, at the present international boundary between Canada and the United States.

The art of casting in molds and the copper-gold alloy called tumbaga may have been developed in Colombia. Goldsmiths in the region of Ecuador and Colombia eventually became expert in repoussé, die stamping, chasing, hammering, plating, gilding, inlaying; in the use of blowpipes (but, oddly enough, no bellows), furnaces and crucibles, anvils and hammers, and molds in the lost-wax process; and in northernmost Ecuador practiced a technique for working platinum (of which more later). The growth of this work to such advanced and sophisticated levels over many generations is fairly clear.

When metallurgy reached central Mexico, metal smiths there worked out the use of an investment compound of clay and powdered charcoal that could be carved for cores, in casting gold and silver, superior to modern compounds that become too brittle for carving. Modern cores have to be mold made, a technique relegated by the ancient Mexicans to cheap mass production.

Virtually all this extraordinary work in metals in the high-culture Indian Americas was for ornamental or religious use. Some copper atlatl-hooks, mace heads, lance points, even digging-stick blades have been turned up, but for the most part metal tools and weapons were emphatically absent—even though alloys of useful hardness (tumbaga and bronze) were known. Here again a comparison with the direction of Old World progress is of interest.

Mention has been made of parallels between the widely separated— widely separated both in time and in space—early centers of high culture in Mexico and in Peru. Each shared in early stages some all-but-identical pottery styles and some, though not all, of the same basic crops. Each built ceremonial centers and then towns and cities, temple mounds and step-pyramids; and most strikingly each worshiped (so it seems) a cat-god, a god that lived on for stupendous ages of time.

It is worth repeating that these levels of culture were not synchronized as to dates.

The Peruvian coast is a narrow strip of blazing desert cut by numerous small rivers and wintertime streams. The distance from the coast over the sky-high Andes to the tropical forest on their east can be 120 miles or less, crossing twenty of the earth's thirty-four life zones en route—a setting unique in world geography. Communities of people appeared in these three major areas, coast, highlands, forest, in very early times and with some interaction and to some degree interdependence among them.

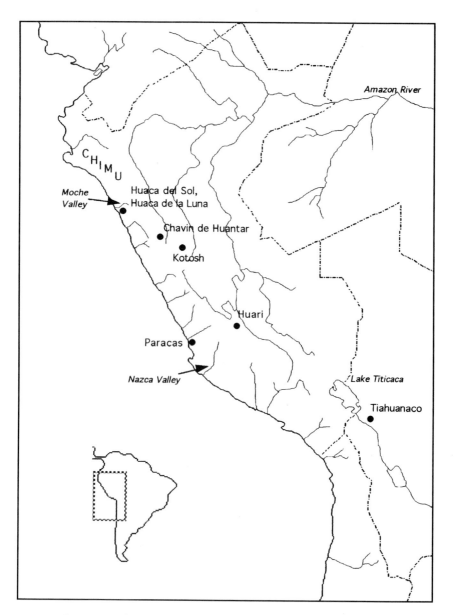

Some Sites from the First 4,000 Years of Andean Civilizations

The oldest cultivated plants in the New World were found in a sheltering cave on the Peruvian coast, leftovers from a repast of 10,000 years ago. They included chili peppers and beans, foreign to the area, clearly migrants from someplace to the eastward. A young man buried in a very early seaside village was accompanied by his pet monkey, from the tropic jungle on the other side of the great mountains.

Eventually monumental religious architecture (one of the generally accepted symptoms of "civilization") began appearing in communities of this region—a dozen or so such sites have been excavated along the coast, ten or eleven more in the highlands, with much public architecture that has been dated to an amazingly early period, 3000 B.C. This was before these communities had an organized agriculture, and an incredible 1,000 years before such symptoms appeared in Mexico.

And likewise long before any evidence of hierarchy and a "coercive" state apparatus, supposed by many social scientists of our present culture to be necessary for the construction of public buildings. Presumably the group effort required here was produced only from religious impulse (although some archeological opinion does claim to detect the rise of hierarchy "upon which [it insists], civilization rests.")

After many centuries this dawning civilization seemed to find a central focus around the site of Chavin de Huantar, located inland from the coast in the steep mountain valley of a little river, the Marañon, deceptively modest commencement of the Amazon. The cultural dominance of Chavin and its feline god reached a peak in the last millennium B.C., its influence visible over an immense period of time and a sizable area in the central Andes and along the central and northern coast.

Parallels between these Peruvian centers and Olmec Mexico are prominent only in the overlapping earlier periods of each. A common source in the beginning is argued against by the great variance in earliest dates and by certain differences in basic crops, such as the retarded spread of maize in Peru after many generations of maize cultivation in Mesoamerica. This apparent "frontier" between the two agricultural areas has been cited previously. Any ready communication in following times is belied by metallurgy only reaching Mesoamerica after 1,000 years or more in South and Central America. The wonderful Mexican calendar never reached the Andes at all.

The style of building, public building, of the Chavin region, temple platforms and religious complexes of massive construction faced with dressed stone, remained essentially unchanged during all pre-Columbian Andean civilizations. Farming by digging-stick and hoe was established, never to change—the plow was unknown in the New World. Fundamental ceramic techniques were fixed—the potter's wheel never came into general New World use. Mummification of the dead, practiced by the very early Chincheros people on the Peruvian coast long before its appearance in Egypt, continued into Inca times.

Finally, after its long stardom during the last millennium or so B.C., the dominance of Chavin faded and a half dozen "regional" styles of life labored into view, to shine forth here and there during the succeeding centuries. This period, lasting until along in the sixth to the eighth century A.D., was the flowering of the Andean Classic age, designated as such because art and technology were at their highest point.

That the time of this Classic age appears to be pretty much in step with the time of the Classic periods in Mesoamerica (Maya to Teotihuacan) has attracted very little comment. A general consensus on detailed chronology is perhaps a bit less prominent in South America; investigation there has been hampered by the enormous size of the country, the enormous looting of archeological sites (begun by the first conquistadors and still going on), and by the stubborn persistence of various dating debates, leaving some scattered clouds of uncertainty.

Beyond this, the remains of these centuries, intricate mountainside terracing, systems of irrigation canals running for miles, flood-fields patterned with ridges for high-yield cultivating, wide roads, monumental fortresses and ceremonial centers, terraced houses of stone and adobe and underground stone paneled galleries, skilled work in precious metals—above all, the weaving and the pottery—have been buried under so many superlatives that their creators have for the most part lost real-life identity, like the artists of Renaissance Italy.

Real-life identity, though, certainly comes through in the work of the Mochica people, from the Moche, Viru, and neighboring valleys of the north coast. Their pottery (for the most part meant to be placed in tombs as religious offerings) reproduced with portrait-and-caricature realism their lives, from birth (women delivered on their knees) to war and death, from the ritual of religion to sexual extravaganzas, much of this anti-erotic, heavy on suffering, cruelty, punishment, sermonizing. Or captives are sacrificed by being hurled from cliffs, helmeted warriors swing trophy heads, surgeons cut off a convict's, or perhaps a priest's, lips. But savagery is only part of the program; many scenes picture familiar everyday subjects as recognizable to us as TV comedy—comedy, incidentally, was given high billing, although without television's primmer restrictions.

The uncanny plastic skill and a certain taste for the maimed and the monstrous are oddly enough reminiscent of the ancient Olmec mind, dead for many lifetimes before the Mochica appeared, and also oddly enough a feline returns to their pantheon, after an absence of centuries, in the cat fangs and whiskers of their monster-god, Aia Paec (the Creator). Quite a few ceramic representations show a man with lips and nose amputated; Rafael Larco Hoyle, the great collector of Mochica pottery, saw this as punishment for some offense. Cat-faced gods or priests, however, are common in Mesoamerican sculpture, from Olmec beginnings on, over many centuries and many regions, as well as in earlier South American styles, and it could be by the amputation of nose and upper lip that a cat-faced human visage might be made. It seems not unreasonable that this ancient iconography might have reappeared among feline-worshipping Andean people of Classic times. It has also been suggested that disease could have caused the pictured deformation of nose and lip, and a representation of such a disease affecting a woman has been cited, but nearly all the Mochica examples do appear clearly surgical.

Mochica textiles of delicate pastel colors arc also strangely eloquent, but textiles made by the Paracas and Nazca people of the Peruvian south coast represent in the opinion of experts, as has been remarked, some of the finest textile art ever produced anywhere. They were woven from cotton and the wool of llamas, alpacas, guanacos, and vicuñas, into every sort of cloth from gauze and lace to brocade and tapestry, in every sort of color—archeologists have classified as many as 190 hues in seven color ranges. Apparently the most remarkable were woven as clothing for the dead, who were wrapped in luxuriant mummy bundles of dazzling damask and richly embroidered brocades.

The deserts of the Nazca valley and northerly environs also contain most unusual relics dating from the South American Classic age: giant geometric and pictorial figures etched on the earth, figures so huge some have only been noticed since the advent of air travel. They were made over many years, evidently, by the simple process of picking up stones to leave bare ground along the lines desired. The earliest are believed to represent animals (birds, fish, spiders) and monsters shown on early textiles; later trapezoids, spirals, zigzags, would seem to be abstractions organized around meanings so far indiscernible—although some are believed to indicate the sun at summer and winter solstices. A single line may run straight (and allegedly blueprint-straight) for several miles, a considerable achievement without instruments. Guesses as to the significance of these "geoglyphs" have ranged from world-view equations to individual memorials to landing strips for extraterrestrials.

An extraordinary medical practice, trephination, cutting baseball-sized holes in the skulls of people suffering, presumably, various mental or cranial disorders, appeared in the area of southern Peru before Classic times and remained a fashionable practice during Classic centuries. A similar sort of surgery occurred also here and there in the prehistoric Old World, more often a cauterization that sometimes burned through the skull, and was continued in medieval times in Europe as a treatment for epilepsy and dementia (cauterization in the form of a cross, in Christian times), and was still being taught at the Charity Hospital, Berlin, in the 1840s. New World surgeons managed a healthy ratio of survivors, judging by later bone growth in some trepanned skulls.

Andean surgery, in addition to trephination, was skilled at amputation, which appears to have had at times a religious connection—possibly the loss of an arm or leg may have been in some wise an act of sanctity, perhaps commemorated by a golden arm or hand in an attitude of prayer or devotion.

(According to Japanese legend, Zen Buddhism was created by the great teacher Daruma and the monk Eka—who proved to Daruma his earnestness as a student by cutting off his own arm.)

And while wandering odd byways mention should be made of a supposititious system of writing among the Classic Mochica, ideographs indented in lima beans, in which some have seen similarities to Maya glyphs.

Agriculture was successful, with a great variety of plants to complement the nutritive limitations of basic crops (such as potatoes), and successful also in distribution to the growing populations. The organization involved was impressive: *pampa isla* ridged fields in Ecuador, Bolivia, and Colombia required causeways that in some vast agricultural networks could total more than 1,000 miles, or cover as much as 50,000 acres. Ducks and guinea pigs had been domesticated, and in the high mountains llamas and alpacas. Coca had come into use, mixed—in the worldwide way of masticatories—with a pinch of lime or ashes to release the narcotic. A beer, *chicha* (very tasty, say some modern reports), was fermented from corn or fruit.

The suggestion has been noted that agriculture in South America may have first begun in rainforest villages far from the later Andean centers of civilization. Possibly a memory of jungle origins may account for the appearance in some classic costuming of the penis sheath, so common among the jungle tribes. This detail (embarrassing for us) may have represented some sort of official or religious insignia in cities of Classic times or later.

The permanent central Andean clothing had evolved by the Classic age: loincloths, waistbands, knee-length shirts, a variety of hats, headbands, or turbans. Mochica aristocrats wore splendorous headdresses, agleam with gold.

Balsa boats, large and small, traveled the oceans and lakes. The bladed club and spear-thrower (*estolica* in Mochica) were still the standard weapons. Feather masks and musical instruments from tambourines to coiled trumpets were used in the ceremonial dances.

Everything, in fact, had been created that the Andean world was to have, except really widespread conquest and empire.

Something like this came along in due course during Classic times—perhaps not conquest, but a fairly widespread uniformity of sorts. The capital and center may have been the city of Huari, although this period of first "empire" has been more customarily associated with Tiahuanaco, the holy place in Bolivia near Lake Titicaca. Under whatever name, its influence (heavy and fearful feline gods, weeping gods, condor gods) became evident in many of the little nations from the Nazca valley in the south to the Moche valley in the north, unifying to some degree the people of the central Andes for the first time since the decline of Chavin and the ancient cat cult many centuries before.

Lake Titicaca (just visible from Tiahuanaco) was the focal point of cultural history for an immense area over a rather impressive length of prehistoric time. Thus a Tiahuanacan influence, whether or not channeled through the secular arm of Huari, seems nevertheless to have been essentially religious, in keeping with this long tradition.

Whatever it was, straggly "empire" or spiritual radiation, the Classic age came to an end after some few centuries, and the sprawling city of Huari was abandoned, as was also the temple center of Tiahuanaco, at some time near the end of the eighth century A.D.; this was within a century or two of the abandonment of the Mochican capital city, Huaca del Sol and Huaca de la Luna, in the Andean north. That this suggested date roundabout A.D. 800 is also the date of the abandonment of the Maya cities and within a couple of centuries of the collapse of great Teotihuacan seems to have attracted very little comment.

It could perhaps be hypothesized that a Classic period, a peak of art and technology, may have been reached at the same time by developing societies far removed from each other, but that collapse and abandonment would then follow also simultaneously seems a bit too much for any reasonable theorizing as to simple coincidence.

The Andean region and its seacoast are given to natural disasters. Earthquakes, tidal waves, tremendous year-long dust storms, tremendous year-long cataclysmic rains and flooding can reach literally world-shaking dimensions—some earth scientists claim their magnitude can slow the earth's rotation, altering the day-length and the seasonal food chain on land and sea. The commonest culprits are tectonic forces busy with mountain-making (the Andes are "new" mountains) and a warm and wayward Pacific ocean current, known as El Niño, that appears periodically, sabotaging the usual Humboldt current, killing the phytoplankton on which the usually rich marine life feeds and thereby driving the marine life away. It also brings rains and droughts that destroy plant cover on the land, and winds that remove resultant dust and floods that remove resultant mud. (North America received a rare visit from El Niño in 1993, blamed for the Mississippi River floods of that year—and is receiving another at this writing, 1997.)

It might be supposed that a climax of such events could provide major factors in triggering the movement of peoples. One difficulty is that preceding centuries of stability must have survived somewhat similar events; there is evidence that El Niño made three Peruvian appearances in the sixth century, plus a thirty-year drought, and five visits in the seventh century. But it does appear that El Niño could cause effects that at their most rampageous may have destroyed not only cities but also civilizations.

In any case, if the earth's rotation was indeed slowed in South America by El Niño at its most cataclysmic, it was likewise slowed in Mesoamerica, possibly with somewhat similar results.

Still other more or less parallel internal factors might be imagined, for example something such as growing problems of sewage and garbage as the cities grew older and older and larger and larger. Or maybe, as has been mentioned in regard to the Maya, there was something in the divinatory air.

The collapse at the end of the Andean Classic period was followed by renewed activity in separate centers, building of large cities and larger agricultural systems, and an increase in the neighborly making of war.

The Mochica reappeared as hub of the Chimu state, star of this time, whose cities along the northern Peruvian coast reached a high state that has led some archeologists to dub the epoch Chimu or City Builders. More goods of all kinds were made during this period, and very skillfully, but the masterworks of old, of the Mochica ware, of the Nazca and Paracas weaving, of the profusion of arts which poured forth in Classic times, were not again equaled—exception noted for metalwork, much more gold and silver being worked (in Ecuador even some fish hooks were of gold) and Chimu gold and silver artistry reaching spectacular heights. The making of bronze was further developed, restricted to the high mountain country of Bolivian tin (a mighty feat of leapfrogging if introduced by sea from some other land).

Social classes were sharply divided into ruling classes and commoners, according to early Spanish chroniclers. One such chronicler learned that Chimu nobility and commoners were thought to be products of separate creations (although perhaps it should be noted that the same chronicler's pages may set a record for the number of miracles surrounding the work of his missionary order). Multiple creations are of course common in creation myths worldwide; some readers see in the Bible two creations (if not three), Genesis 1:27 and 2:18–22.

In the mountain valley of Cuzco, between Tiahuanaco and Huari, a backwoods tribe of Quechua-speaking people who called themselves the people of the Inca composed one of the many little nations trying to survive in the war-making atmosphere of those post-Classic fragmented times. They had done well enough in the past: Cuzco, a town laid out in old-fashioned pre-Classic style, separated by farm fields from its surrounding villages, was said to be one of the few never to have been absorbed into the Tiahuanaco sphere.

Hearsay dynastic history, processed through the ears of early Spanish chroniclers, can give the Inca story palace intrigue, noble machinations, royal dudgeon, valorous battles enough to satisfy the three musketeers or even match those romances of chivalry that drove Don Quixote mad. With European trimmings somewhat subdued, we learn that Viracocha Inca was eighth in a line of local chiefs, that the neighboring city-state of Chanca sent invading warriors, and that Viracocha fled with the heir apparent, Inca Urcon, to a mountain fort, abandoning his city.

In the high Andes, everything is larger than life. You could drop an ordinary mountain in any chasm, said Alexander von Humboldt, and lose it there. The country cried out for Wagnerian music and gods in the guise of heroes. At this moment it got one. Yupanqui, a son of Viracocha, refused to run and at a critical moment the stones of the battlefield became warriors, so they say, and fought on the side of the people of Cuzco. The Chanca were defeated and the city was saved. Viracocha returned and at his death was given the priest-ruler's customary deification (his women and servants danced ceremonially until they were drunk on the ceremonial wine, when they surrendered themselves to the strangler so they might accompany their lord), but Inca Urcon was then either put aside or died, and Yupanqui took for himself the strip of braid that was the Inca crown. He also adopted a new name, Pachacuti (Cataclysm).

This was said to be in the year 1438 (or thereabouts); during the next fifty-five years Pachacuti Inca Yupanqui and his son, Topa Inca, by a process of propaganda, diplomatic maneuvering, power politics, and the persuasive matter of eight major military campaigns, built and organized the Inca empire, extending over 2,000 miles from north to south—on the map of Europe, as if from Sweden to Egypt. Population estimates have run from 3.5 million to 32 million (currently 12 million is favored). The population of England at about the same time was some 4 million. The Andes were named from Spanish *andenes*, terraces for channeling runoff and rain in the enormous agricultural system—satellite photos show that more land was then involved than is under cultivation today.

The things the people made in this great empire (which seems really to have been an empire) were stamped with a very identifiable Inca style but were essentially the same things made in preceding ages. The subjects of Tawantinsuyu (Quechua name for the empire, meaning "The Four Quarters") built, and built marvelously, in their cities, fortresses, terraces, temples, basically what had been done before, but a great deal more of it. In general, Inca art in ornamentation, woven fabrics, ceramics, did not approach in quality the best work of earlier times, although in quantity it was truly inspired. It has been sometimes supposed that the Inca produced a great deal of work in gold as religious symbolism of the Sun, but the great Inca treasures in gold and silver appear to have been adapted so clearly from predecessors, most notably from the Chimu, that the possibility arises of Inca goldwork being in fact Chimu, seized after the conquest of Chimu or made by Chimu goldsmiths under Inca supervision.

One genuine Inca development may have been something approaching true war and true military conquest, conquest in which conquered lands were to some degree permanently occupied and conquered peoples to some degree organized into the world of their new masters. Views on all this have fluctuated through the years, but the Inca do seem to have been pretty much alone in the New World in achieving real military organization, constructed on actual soldiering, not warrior societies playing games. Inca slingers were professionals; they wore to their graves their slings wound round their heads, as badge of office. Or so it seems.

The Inca world appears to have been built on the social group called the *ayllu*, a community of families living together who may have been related, usually working land that was owned in common and periodically redistributed in family lots. Certain fields (coca fields among them) were cultivated for support of the political and religious apparatus, and taxes were paid by such labor; there was no money.

There were a number of royal ayllus, about a dozen at the beginning of Spanish records, or perhaps in this case they should be called lineages—the word in Quechua was *panaca*; the fashion among some archeologists today is to call them royal corporations. *Inca* meant a kin-group that ruled as a noble caste; the word also seemed to be applied to the emperor, who was chosen from among the males of these special lineages. There were probably some 500 of such eligible individuals at the time of the Spanish invasion.

The Inca himself, once maneuvered into his top job, was an absolute ruler but on the other hand was obligated to care for his people's needs. This was carried out by an immense bureaucracy, from imperial, territorial, and provincial officials down to local ward heelers. Territorial governors and the heads of the four great quarters into which the empire was divided formed a council advisory to the Inca. But the Inca's decision was law, as was, apparently, each subordinate's word all the way down the line.

A Spanish conquistador who settled in Peru stated in his will ("to relieve his conscience") that in the country when he had first entered it all was peace and order, there were no beggars, no thieves, no prostitutes, no poverty, no hunger. Juan de Sarmiento, president of the Council of the Indies, visited Peru in 1550 and was even more panegyric about what he could learn of the Inca government—the best for the people, he concluded, of any government imaginable. Modern comment has tended to emphasize the totalitarian aspects of the Inca state and the regimentation of all aspects of life for the conquering Inca people as well as for their conquered subject peoples.

However, some recent opinion has questioned this picture of a monolithic Tawantinsuyu, finding the empire far from a uniform state, rather a mosaic of diversity, a diversity deliberately maintained, even unto a "Frank Lloyd Wrightian" integration of differing villages into the dramatic Andean landscape. The indirect system of government was evidently supported more by organized feasting and ceremonies than by any police authority, although the enthralling play of ceremony was probably meant to legitimize Inca rule—in short, a system of government "almost impossible to conceive of in terms designed for European nation states."

Religion structured the complex ceremonialism and, as elsewhere in the ancient New World, played a major role in architecture and city-planning, but in Tawantinsuyu celebrated chiefly the deity of the Sun and the divinity of the Inca as a son of the Sun, as well as majestic manifestations of nature such as the Thunder, the creator Viracocha (who had made the world, taught all goodness and virtue, and then walked away on the water across the Pacific), and rigorously observed the sacredness of the *huacas*—holy things, holy places, such as the tombs and the mummified bodies of ancestors, the extremely sacred bodies of dead emperors, the miraculous stones of Pachacuti's first battlefield.

The endless rites were administered by innumerable priests and priestesses housed in innumerable temples and convents. Every act of life was adorned with religious meaning; each day at sunrise priests cried out to the Sun to remember that we are thy children, and in the lavish public ceremonies before the gold-sheeted Temple of the Sun each step of the glittering dance, each drumbeat and each note of a flute, was exactly prescribed. Human sacrifice occasionally took place, especially of children, and sacrifice of llamas, as of Old Testament lambs, was frequent, but the most reverent moment came with the simple offering of a chalice of wine to the Sun by the Inca, and by far the commonest sacrifice was that of beautiful cloth: garments apparently possessed a magic or particularly religious quality. Shirts, robes, beautiful weaving, were paid as taxes, or were made by women of the special category known as *aklla*, "the weaving women"; some of this was used for ceremonial costuming but much of it went for sacrifice, 100 pieces a day sacrificed in the usual rites at such a ceremonial center as Cuzco.

The Four Directions, or Five or Six if counting Up and Down, have been the cornerstone of cosmography for many American Indians, the symmetry of a universe in tune. But while the practical Inca policymakers administered their state in four political and traditional quarters, they recognized in their religion only east and west, the rising and setting of the sun.

The Inca world, of busy city streets and the greatest collection of art in gold and silver ever known, with everything meticulously but simply organized, from the education of the flawless girls chosen to be priestesses, sacrificial victims, or imperial concubines, to the orderly rows of farmers digging their fields in unison, brought nothing really new to Andean civilization except the subtle direction of its organization. (Aristocracy by family relationships it may have taken from the preceding Chimu.)

So far as present study has shown, the Inca world touched only erratically the many peoples beyond its boundaries.

Southward the Calchaqui, of northwestern Argentina, part of the larger language group called the Diaguita, were farmers and town dwellers similar in many ways to the Pueblo people of the southwestern United States, with stone houses, pottery, textiles, and Inca-style (Chimu?) metalwork. Eastern neighbors of the Diaguita included the Guiacuruan hunters of the Chaco; some of these, notably the Abipon, developed striking parallels to the hunting tribes of the North American plains.

Farther south still, in central Chile, the Araucanians, farmers and llama herdsmen extraordinarily fond of freedom, lived in family villages, worked gold, grew the same crops (they may have been the first to domesticate the potato) but were otherwise thoroughly unlike the class-conscious, temple-building central Andeans and gave Tawantinsuyu as little shrift as possible.

Below them only people of the wood roamed the stormswept bush of Patagonia, some of them living in the same caves that had been the homes of hunter-gatherers 8,000 or 10,000 years before. Some of them, incidentally—the towering Tehuelche of eastern Patagonia—were the tallest of all Indians and among the tallest people in the world.

Except in a few somewhat isolated instances, Andean ways, and the imperial Inca state, seem not to have penetrated very deeply into the continent east of the Andes—although, as has been noted, some theorists suspect the high civilizations west of the Andes had their beginnings in the eastern lowlands, finding evidence in early agriculture and in the early Andean motifs of jaguar, serpent, monkey, and other jungle memories.

The New World epicenter for the ceremonial use of narcotics was (and still is) in Andean country and in the Amazon rainforest; the Andean use of coca was, judging by anecdotal pottery, as casual a matter as the modern use of tobacco—coca leaves chewed into a ball, unslaked lime in the lime-box ground to powder, the rod ready in the box and a bit of lime brought on the rod with great care to the mouth and thrust into the cud of leaves. The great care involved was not ceremonial but because the slightest touch of the lime to lips or gums was wildly painful.

On the other hand, the Jibaro people of the riverine forests in the easterly reaches of modern Ecuador and Peru drank with great formality a datura, *maikoa*, in rituals attending boys' puberty rites and before going on a raid to capture their famous trophy heads. In the course of the ceremonies associated with the "shrinking" of the trophy head, or *tsantsa*, a narcotic called *natema* (*Banisteria coapi*) was drunk, to bring visions believed to be divinatory. Among the Zapora, traditional Jibaro enemies, along the interior borders of present Colombia and southern Venezuela, a powerful infusion of tobacco was ritually drunk as well as various other drugs, above all *ayahuasca* (a Quechua word meaning vine of death or vine of dreams), a violent narcotic strictly reserved for men (so they say).

The vast lands of Amazon drainage, roughly the size of the continental United States, contained peoples and histories in undoubted abundance that are now lost without a trace, the terrain being generally unfavorable for archeological preservation. Some widespread traits included use of the poisonous bitter manioc for flour, tobacco rolled into cigars, drugging of fish, signal drums, skirts of shredded bark, and God made manifest in masks.

The incredible profusion of plants and animals in the American tropics— the tiny country of Costa Rica contains more species of birds and trees than all of North America—naturally led to an incredible knowledge of their use. The present-day Secoya people in the northwestern Amazon rainforests, perhaps now a twentieth of their pre-Columbian population, identify 2,000 species of plants used for food, medicine, hygiene, clothing, adornment, furnishings, dwellings, transportation, and rituals and 224 species in daily use.

In the Amazonian rainforests lived, in what early accounts described as uproariously stinking villages, possibly the jolliest cannibals on earth; some of the many bands of Tupian people were said to have bred their women to captives of war (who would presumably be gone before they could follow the riverine rule of a father taking to his hammock to rest for a certain number of days after childbirth or the baby would sicken and die) and raised the resultant children like veal calves for butchering. In such accounts it is well to note the phrase "were said to"—of which more anon.

To the north of Tawantinsuyu, in what is now Colombia, Ecuador, Venezuela, and the southeasterly states of Central America, were a number of barbaric kingdoms and petty priest-ruled states, the best known being the extensive domain of the Chibcha, centering in Colombia. Some of these peoples had histories of more or less high culture as old as many of those in the Andes or Mexico, and with more archeological work in the future may assume a larger share of the record than they are given at present; that troubling origin-point of New World metallurgy may even be found here. Alien touches appeared in the border regions but most of the people were clearly South American (Chibchan the commonest language) all the way to the southern Maya frontier in the region of the Ulua River in Honduras.

Arawak is still one of the largest language families in lowland South America, and it was Arawak-speaking village people, mainly, who had populated the islands of the Caribbean—gentle and kindly and ridiculously inept at war, although some had learned the high style ceremonial ball game of Mexico. During Inca times or thereabouts raids and invasions began among the islands from a people of northern South America, the Caribs, whose name was given to the sea as well as to the word "cannibal" in the English language; the raids continued for generations, fine sport for the Caribs (so said Arawak tradition).

Erratically, some Andean ways migrated during the centuries across the Gulf of Mexico to the melting pot at the mouth of the Mississippi, and even the farming people far to the north who were later called the Sioux, and who might have been descendants of the people who built temple mound communities in the Mississippi valley hundreds of years before the Inca rise to power, used the word *wakan* (identical in sound to the Quechua word *huaca*) for something holy, sacred, supernaturally inspired.

CHAPTER 7

Empires of the Sun

Sources for the history of the great New World civilizations are mainly post-Conquest "chronicles," which might or might not be reasonably correct. For want of anything better, we'll pretend here that they are more or less trustworthy. We learn from them that in Mexico drought, famine, and wars of the gods, which is to say heretical revolutions and invasions by heathen neighbors, caved in the Toltec empire roundabout (perhaps) the twelfth century. Tula ("a very large city, and truly a marvel . . . many powerful and wise men lived there") died in the year corresponding to our calendar's 1168, some say, and the same year is one of the traditional dates for the beginning of new invasions from the north by various barbarian tribes, tough, brutal, and hungry. The northern barbarians were sometimes contemptuously referred to collectively as Chichimecs (Dog People), but these Chichimeca were inferior to no one—they were armed with deadly new weapons, bows and arrows.

They pushed their way into the Valley of Mexico, probably over a period of many years, seized, sacked, and destroyed everything in sight, and emerged toward the end of the thirteenth century as rulers (usually claiming Toltec lineage) of some of the various city-states rebuilt, bigger and richer with gods than ever, about the great salt lake, Lake Texcoco.

They were a fiercely pious people and brought a tremendous increase in the pattern of human sacrifice and of wars instigated at least partly for the purpose of capturing prisoners as sacrificial victims. They were also a supple people, and within a very few generations had become as aggressively cultured as they once had been savage—grand patrons of the arts, swooning esthetically over tastefully arranged bouquets and manipulating feather fans with a fine aristocratic grace. If they were not already Nahua-speaking they became so, and forgot the tongue of their uncouth grandfathers.

However, they did not lose their muscles. Besides the wars customary to ducal states jostling for gain, power, dominance, there were the hungry gods and that constant need for prisoners to be fed to them: warriors and priests remained the elite castes. For several centuries, ever since the rise of the Tolteca, warriors had vied with the priests—previously the unrivaled culture heroes—for space on the wall and column-carvings, with the warriors slowly but surely gaining, an obvious reflection on the way the world was trending. "Then the man dexterous in arms . . . such honor he won that no one anywhere might be adorned like him," says the *Florentine Codex*. While the ascetic priests, praying in the mountains, sawed skewers and cords through their own tongues, lips, ears, hands, genitals, to pour out their own blood in a thousand midnight fountains for the gods, penance from the part of the body that had sinned.

Curiously, bows and arrows, after their apparently successful introduction, largely gave way (except for the use of fire-arrows in sieges) to the old standard arms of spear and spear-thrower and battle-axe, and of these it is the obsidian-bladed club that is most often pictured in the codices. It would be hard to take prisoners with long-distance bows and arrows, of course, which may have been one reason.

Wars were battles royal, hand-to-hand; you either disarmed your opponent and made him surrender or beat him unconscious and then dragged him away. Battles were gorgeously costumed affairs, men in headdresses and shirts of yellow parrot feathers, sprays of costly quetzal feathers set off with gold, whole squadrons uniformed in jaguar skins or golden hoods with feather horns, carrying shields decorated with golden disks, butterflies, serpents, wearing embroidered sandals with thongs of orange leather. And they raised a gorgeous din as well, with the two-toned drums, conch-shell trumpets, shrill clay whistles, screams full voiced (so heaven could hear), and slyly designed besides to shock and terrify the enemy, calling on God for help and witness. The priests led the way to combat, carrying the gods, and then chanted sacred magic and blew encouragement with piercing trumpet blasts while they waited with ready obsidian knives for the first prisoners to be dragged out from the battle for sacrifice on the spot, to be yanked spread-eagled on their backs, their chests slashed open, their hearts torn out and triumphantly raised "there toward where the sun came forth." Decision gained, the victorious warriors charged into the defeated town, burning the temple, butchering and capturing the noncombatants, until finally they deigned to listen to the losing leaders' applications for peace and promises of tribute.

These combats were not, to be sure, the constant pleasures of all. While every able-bodied man was supposedly ready to take up arms if need be, the most practiced of the warriors tended to become an exclusively military class. Others—artisans, farmers, and artists—worked at their work as they always had. But even the everyday world was colored with spectacle, excitement, terror, and joy, so why resent a famous warrior's glory? He didn't get there without sweat either; and for that matter anyone, with a lucky birthday and the help of the gods, could become a bedecked warrior or an awesomely learned priest. And anyway, tortillas were yellow as sunlight or white as snow, green chocolate was tender, delicious, and foaming, and the girls, with their beautiful teeth and their blue-dyed hair, as pretty as spring rain.

The accounts of battles and "wars" have a pronounced air of ritual; at the least it is obvious that war in the New World reveals certain basic differences from war over the rest of the world. Most notably there appears never to have been any organization, with possible Inca exception, for prolonged campaigning of a sizable military unit. Mention is made of large armies, nowadays ascertained by estimating numbers of men of military age in an estimated general population, but the stomach on which these armies travel remains decently out of sight among the unmentionables.

Military studies of the campaigns of Genghis Khan in the early thirteenth century have emphasized the organization, discipline, and "clock-like coordination" of tactical movement, terms that could not fit any New World evidence (even Inca). The armies of the Liao empire (A.D. 907–1125) developed this organization 200 years before the Mongols, and it was still a ruling principle in the Manchu armies of the seventeenth century: the journal of a low-ranking officer, c. A.D. 1680, relates years on the march, a personal organization of servants, goods, horses, an incessant attention to supply ("I sold a woman to buy extra horses").

Still more telling, analysis of German organization for war in the sixteenth and seventeenth centuries reveals every little movement with a meaning all its own aiming at the bottom line of profit—even in the fiercest religious wars of Europe's history.

War as the chief element in the Old World ancient history has been mentioned; some past and present pundits have promoted it to the rank of the great civilizer, or as the only plausible explanation of the origin of states.

These suppositions do not seem to hold for the New World, as we have seen in the case of the Classic Maya. Instead, recent Mesoamerican archeology appears to find more substance concerning social development in the role of the land than in transient human conflict. Some specialist thinking finds conflict over land and its produce leading to an institutionalized elite and resultant social change; others find regional trade—in salt, chert, obsidian, cotton textiles, any surplus furnished by the land—as prime mover in society's evolution. The environment could at least, in dealing with similar peoples, express itself in terms of time: the region of Tlaxcala-Puebla next door to the southeast of the Valley of Mexico was several hundred years "ahead" in development, due primarily to differences in natural surroundings—shorter frost season, heavier rainfall.

Population in the Valley of Mexico as a whole declined after the fall of Teotihuacan. Tula, during the time of its greatness, grew a cluster of suburban communities along the northwestern borders of the valley, ten provincial centers, nineteen large villages, 120 small villages, 555 hamlets, fairly comparable to the total population of Teotihuacan's greater shopping area but with much more of the total dispersed in the hundreds of rural hamlets—nearly four times as many as Teotihuacan had possessed.

Population in the Valley proper shifted from north to south following the decline of the powerful northern neighbor, Tula. Intensified agriculture in *chinampas*, prodigiously fertile raised beds in flooded fields (Mesoamerican version of South American *pampas islas*), became widespread at this time. And now cities emerged around the valley's great central lake, Lake Texcoco, although most of the population remained largely rural, centered in the south end of the Valley, around the flooded shores of the freshwater Lakes Chalco and Xochimilco.

The question of the division of labor has been touched on, in regard to the Maya. How many people were engaged in the production of the Mesoamerican art objects that today furnish the immense worldwide trade—to museums and collectors—in such items? How long did it take neolithic sculptors to chisel and grind, without metal tools, the great stone warriors of Tula? (Tula's metropolitan population was about equal to that of a present-day Midwestern small town, 30,000 to 40,000.)

We have noticed that some of the Paracas textiles in South America are believed to have been the work of lifetimes, and some jades (Olmec and others) are believed to have required generations to complete. Ceremonial centers (Maya and others) were periodically rebuilt, a huge labor of urban renewal carried out repeatedly in Classic times in scores if not hundreds of communities, very few (before the Aztecs) more populous than Kokomo, Indiana.

Where did they all come from, the stonemasons, sculptors, feather workers, potters, painters, weavers, and, outside the Maya country, the consummate artists in gold and silver? The art in stone and clay and metal can still speak to us with passion, enthusiasm, and dedication. Good work is hard work, usually, in art. They produced some wonderfully good work, and in an abundance difficult to explain.

Azcapotzalco, on the west of Lake Texcoco, was the city of the Tepanecs; on the east of the lake laid the city of the Acolhuas, called Texcoco; on the south Culhuacan of the Culhuas. All were rivals, all growing in power. The city of the Acolhuas had seventy towns paying it tribute.

The Culhuas employed as mercenaries a landless tribe of spearmen, the Mexica, who had a heavy date with the future. They took a first step toward it when, wishing on a certain occasion to flatter the Culhua chief of council with the highest honor they could think of, they sacrificed his daughter and invited the ruler to watch the solemn climax of a priest dancing in the girl's skin. To their amazement the chief was enraged, caused the individuals responsible to be sacrificed or enslaved, and drove the rest of the Mexica people into exile. The dismayed fugitives founded a town on a miserable little group of islands in the lake, partway between Culhuacan and Azcapotzalco; they called their shantytown Tenochtitlan, which may have meant Place of the Cactus in the Rock or maybe Place of the Hard-as-Rock Cactus, or maybe was named after Tenoch, a revered elder (as their name Mexica may have been taken in honor of a former leader named Mecitli). The founding of Tenochtitlan took place, according to the traditional date, in 1325; other dates have been suggested ranging from 1280 to 1362.

Such is one of the stories given by the chroniclers relating the establishment of the Mexica city. Another version has it that the Mexica were being held in slavery in Culhuacan, and escaped to their island hideout. On one point though most of the chronicles are in agreement—only yesterday the Mexica were the rankest of nobodies: "nowhere were they welcomed . . . they were told, 'Who are these uncouth people?' . . . They could settle nowhere."

Installed on their mud-caked islands the beggarly Mexica split into two rival factions, one of which founded a neighboring island town called Tlatelolco and became, some say, auxiliaries of the Tepanecs at Azcapotzalco—at any rate, Tezozomoc, *tlatoque* (supreme chief of council) of Azcapotzalco is said to have given them one of his own sons as governor. The rival faction at Tenochtitlan received as governor a grandson of the tlatoque of Culhuacan, presumably indicating an alliance with their quondam masters, the Culhuas. But when, some time later, Culhuacan was destroyed by the voracious conqueror Tezozomoc, the victory was followed by signal favors granted to the people of Tenochtitlan, possibly hinting that their alliance with Culhuacan may have contained a dash of perfidy and possibly helping to explain why, although the twin cities of Tlatelolco and Tenochtitlan continued to live together and grow, Tenochtitlan grew faster. Tezozomoc even condescended to give his daughter in marriage to Huitzilhuitl II, its chief (who being the son of the Culhua governor was of course better born than the low-brow Mexica);

and Tenochtitlan thereupon assumed identity as a full-fledged city state and flourished to become Tezozomoc's stoutest and most worthy vassal, and the Mexica people there began calling themselves Tenochcas, after the name of their proud new city.

With the constant help of the Tenochcas, Tezozomoc extended his conquests for many miles beyond the valley. Each new expansion of power tightened his rivalry with the only remaining other great valley power, Texcoco, across the lake.

At last, in the year 1416, when Tezozomoc was in his nineties and had to be wrapped in down and cotton and carried in a basket, he raised the curtain on the big war and sent his warriors of Azcapotzalco against Texcoco. Huitzilhuitl and his Tenochca Mexicas gave good service among the troops of subject warriors; Tezozomoc conducted the campaign with relentless craft; Texcoco was besieged, invaded, and finally taken. Its tlatoque, Ixtlilxochitl, tried to escape from the conquered city with his son Nezahualcoyotl (Hungry Coyote). The father was caught and died under the spears and battle-axes of Tezozomoc's warriors. But the son escaped, to become Mexico's most resplendent legend.

He hid in the forests and the mountains, or in disguise in friendly cities; he wrote poetry, studied philosophy, discovered a personal religious faith in an Unknown God to whom sacrifice should not be made but only prayers; he was absolutely valorous, completely skilled in arms; he never did wrong, he always did right.

The followers who flocked to his secret standard (under the green oak greenwood tree) were loyal unto death; when he was once captured and put in a wooden cage to await execution a guard released him and died in his place. The incredibly aged Tezozomoc—he was now past 100 years old—could conquer the world but was powerless against the destiny of Nezahualcoyotl. A dozen times, according to the stories, Hungry Coyote miraculously eluded capture and certain death when Tezozomoc all but had him in his grasp.

"The goods of this life, its glories and its riches, are but lent to us. . . . Yet the remembrance of the just shall not pass away." So sang, more or less, the poet Nezahualcoyotl—while the armed men of Tezozomoc went from house to house in vanquished Texcoco slaying out of hand all children who mistakenly answered "Nezahualcoyotl" when asked who was their tlatoque.

And Tenochtitlan become strong and formidable and putting on airs, perhaps began to seem less a vassal than a rival to great Azcapotzalco, for it appears that two opposing factions now came to grips in the Azcapotzalco ruling council, one no longer trusting the Mexica, one—headed by ancient Tezozomoc—still warmly trustful. When Huitzilhuitl II of Tenochtitlan died, the Tenochca elders and chief priests and warriors elected his son Chimalpopoca (Tezozomoc's favorite grandson) their new leader. But the anti-Tenochca party at Azcapotzalco decreed that Chimalpopoca must die and Tenochtitlan be fully subjugated and incorporated into the Tepanec state. It is said that his despair over this decision finally killed old Tezozomoc, at the age of 106, finding himself at the end quite powerless in his all-powerful capital of Azcapotzalco.

Chimalpopoca was duly murdered (by stranglers in the night, some stories say), and Tezozomoc's successor as tlatoque among the Tepanecs, Maxtla, as implacably hostile toward the Mexica as Demosthenes against the Macedonians—and evidently for the same reason, fear of a growing power—insisted on either total surrender or total war. The Mexica, urged on by a young (twenty-nine-year-old) councilor named Tlacaelel, reluctantly, and, one gathers, fearfully, chose war.

But they elected a new leader, the famous Itzcoatl, and formed an alliance with the exiled Nezahualcoyotl. Armies of the faithful sprang up from Texcoco to follow Hungry Coyote. A third member joined the alliance, the strategically situated town of Tlacopan, which provided a beachhead for fleets of canoes sent across the lake from Texcoco. Maxtla was defeated and his city of Azcapotzalco taken by storm, although seven years—until 1434—were needed for the gradual conquest of all the Tepanec towns, as far afield as Cuernavaca.

Nezahualcoyotl returned in triumph as the rightful tlatoque of Texcoco, married 100 wives, built a matchless palace at his summer place of Texcotzingo, and lived a long life of matchless wisdom and probity. So they say.

And Tenochtitlan, the island shantytown of a century before, suddenly found itself (with Texcoco) one of the two chief cities of the entire country.

As the Mexica people of Tenochtitlan had risen in power and eminence they had given themselves a suitable family history, and taken as their own a suitable god, Huitzilopochtli, "omen of evil . . . creator of war." (Teoyaotlatohuehuitzilopochtli, "Divine Lord of War, Great Huitzilopochtli," to give him his formal epithet.)

They had originally come from some place in the northwest of Mexico, a place they called in their legends Aztlan, and so they called themselves the People of Aztlan, or Aztecs.

Their god had told them to wander until they came to a cactus growing from a rock on which an eagle would be perched, holding in his beak a serpent—the symbol of water and abundance. The promised land had been found, cactus, eagle, snake and all, exactly as predicted, at the site of Tenochtitlan. (The first Inca people had been given a golden staff by the Sun and told they would find their promised land where the staff should enter the ground—which had been at the site of Cuzco.)

Huitzilopochtli (or perhaps the councilor Tlacaelel, who may have been gifted at divine interpretation) had also told the Aztecs they were his chosen people and would rule the world. Together with Texcoco, and with Tlacopan for a junior partner in a continuing triple alliance, they proceeded to do so, as far as their known world of Mexico was concerned. Their conquests multiplied, extending far to the north and south. Tribute and captives poured into the city, and Tenochtitlan exploded in size.

Tenochtitlan's sister city of Tlatelolco became a commercial center, famed for its market, and in an interborough war in the 1470s was at last taken over by the Tenochcas and absorbed into Tenochtitlan. This may have represented a final victory for Tlacaelel, who according to some accounts had by then served as the principal administrator of the Tenochca state for more than forty years, during the rule of three "kings," or chiefs-of-council, and the initial great expansion of Aztec influence. (Among his other achievements, it is said that Tlacaelel led a purely scientific expedition to the north searching piously but in vain for Aztlan, the place of Azteca origin.)

Now the island foundations of the city were enlarged, for the use of houses and buildings and for the enormously productive chinampa agriculture, its Mexica variety still practiced today among the "floating gardens" of Xochimilco. Swampland was reclaimed, blocks of new temples were raised, a three-mile-long aqueduct (double-barreled so its channels could be closed alternately for cleaning) was built to bring fresh water from the mainland, and a second built soon afterward. A thousand people, so they say, were employed each day in washing down the streets. There were in the city, so some contemporary records seem to suggest, an estimated 300,000 white-mantled people. Recent study of settlement patterns supports some such ultimate population figure—perhaps 1,000,000 for the entire valley, with nearly half that in the core area of the huge city and for fifteen miles or so roundabout. At any rate, it was by far the largest concentration of settlement in prehistoric Mesoamerica. (The population of London at the same epoch was 120,000.)

How did this large population get food? Mainly by everyone farming, so says one early report—the government urging each person to follow his trade and be a farmer as well.

An interesting point: house size in Teotihuacan was large enough for sixty to 100 people; in Tula for thirty to sixty; in Tenochtitlan for ten to fifteen people.

Texcoco became the artistic and intellectual capital of the Valley, but Tenochtitlan became the center of power and wealth for all Mexico, gradually assuming leadership over Texcoco. Tlacopan was gradually forgotten as any kind of partner at all. After the death of Nezahualcoyotl in 1472—he left a reported sixty songs—Aztec ascendancy grew still more pronounced.

Sometime in the 1470s, in Peru, another renowned leader died—
Pachacuti. His son Topa Inca had been in command of military
matters for some years while Pachacuti concerned himself with organizing
administration; now Topa Inca campaigned to the south, whereas he and his
father had previously driven toward the north. He marched his mace-men
and peltists down into Chile, across the Atacama desert, where rain has never
been recorded, into the frontier zone of the country of the Araucanians, and
set up, for all time, the southern boundary-markers of the empire on the
banks of the River Maule, at what is now the town of Constitución. He spent
his later years perfecting the Inca machinery of rule over this giant country,
something more than eighty-five provinces (probably more than 100), far and
away the largest political state yet known in the New World, and in the last
year of his reign could see this creation trouble-free, perfectly functioning,
magnificently complete.

This was in the year 1492.

The Aztecs conquered from sea to sea, from the Gulf Coast to the
Pacific. They ran into setbacks with the Tarascans to the west,
murderous bowmen who walloped them with a resounding defeat, and they
were never able to crush the Tlaxcalans to the east, who used squadrons of
Otomi archers as auxiliaries, although the Aztecs surrounded Tlaxcala with
satellite Aztec states that left its independence isolated and precarious, and
its people deprived of the luxuries of commerce. Or Tlaxcala had been deliberately left unconquered, say some of the chroniclers, to serve as a nearby
training (and captive-catching) ground for Tenochca warriors: a policy attributed to Tlacaelel.

Nearly all the rest of Mexico below Tampico and Guadalajara paid Aztec
tribute—more or less, with frequent defections requiring frequent reconquests.

The Aztecs established no real empire in the Inca or Roman sense; they
never thought of fighting wars for keeps in the modern sense. War remained
at least partly a captive-catching game, its most notable feature the delayed-
action battlefield casualties, the captured victims who played out their death
roles later in ostentatious temple ceremonies rather than in the anonymous
immediacy of battle. Occasionally some portion of conquered lands was
placed under direct Aztec dominion, but in general defeated states were looted
and then, in effect, left alone—as long as they continued to furnish the often-
heavy tribute assigned, and recognize Aztec political hegemony.

Some peoples, theoretically subjugated, were in such a constant state of
revolt that their names became almost synonymous among the Aztecs with
the terms for captives, slaves, sacrificial victims—such were the Huastecs (a

splinter group of Maya cousins) and the Totonacs (relatives, possibly, of the long ago Olmecs), both in the Vera Cruz region along the Gulf Coast.

Even so, there were still not enough wars to furnish enough prisoners to feed the gods with sacrifice, and so artificial wars—Wars of the Flowers they were called—were instituted between neighboring states for the sole purpose of capturing victims from each other. These battles were formally arranged, each side fought until enough prisoners had been taken to satisfy the gods, and all parted friends, with no hard feelings. So they say.

It will bear repeating that the Aztecs did not introduce human sacrifice into Mexico. It had existed, at least to some degree, from the earliest times. They simply did the same things that had always been done but, according to all accounts, much bigger and better.

Anyone or any group, a war captain or a trade guild or a warrior society or the merchants' association or someone ill with a galloping infection, needing the intercession of a god, bought a slave and on the god's feast day had him (or her—goddesses, naturally, were fed with women and girls) ceremonially bathed and slain. The priests at the many temples needed slaves, or captives (all captives of war were slaves, although all slaves were not captives; one might sell himself or a family might sell its children into bondage and possible sacrifice, and many did when times were hard), as victims for the established, official temple rites. Military organizations needed victims for their established religious observances. In the case of the Aztecs, the state needed victims constantly for the state god, Huitzilopochtli, who fought each day against the darkness of the night; without blood and human hearts the very order of the world might fail.

Each of the eighteen twenty-day months of the year had its ceremonies and sacrifices. Hearts were torn out for Huitzilopochtli, and then, at Tenochtitlan, the heads of the victims were impaled on the towering skull-rack in the central plaza. Captive warriors were given mock weapons and led by their celebrated keeper Old Wolf ("he in whose care lay the captives, as if they had become his sons") to be tied to the gladiator's stone and killed in a pretense of combat by warriors armed with real weapons, and then the priests danced with the heads of the captives ("And Old Wolf wept at this; he wept for his sons who had died"). Priests danced wrapped in the skins of victims, "stained, dripping, gleaming" with blood, "so that they terrified those whom they followed," in honor of Xipe Totec. Victims were lashed up as targets and shot full of arrows and darts so their dripping blood would fertilize the earth; children were sacrificed to the rain god, Tlaloc; victims were burned alive to celebrate the August heat of harvest. Crowds danced and sang hilariously around the slave girl dressed as the Earth Mother, laughing and joking to conceal from her fate, and the young war captive chosen to represent Tezcatlipoca lived a full year as the god, amidst every comfort, pleasure, and delight, and at the end of the year climbed the temple pyramid, breaking at each step a flute symbolic of his joyous incarnation, to meet his death on the sacrificial stone at the summit.

The deep-voiced drum, the huehuetl, throbbed like an enormous pulse, and the people celebrated, "jostling, howling, roaring. They made the dust rise; they caused the ground to smoke. Like people possessed, they stamped upon the earth."

The Aztecs were full of contradictions: arrogant and yet prizing humility, implacable and yet emotionally tender and affectionate, and like the ancient Greeks devoted equally to law, order, and loot. A boisterous, ebullient, but intensely earnest people, with an absolute certainty of the superiority of their way of life, they were well structured, technically and psychologically, for the mastery of the less zealous world around them.

Tizoc, supreme chief of council of Tenochtitlan from 1479 to 1486, was poisoned by the clan councils (it is said) because he was weak in war, for all that he performed the devout service (the chief of council was also one of the two supreme chief priests) of having a gigantic block of stone dragged to the city where it was carved into a monstrous bowl for burning human hearts.

Ahuitzotl, his brother and successor, left a more satisfactory trail of terror up and down the land, conquering forty-five provinces. Together with Nezahualpilli, son of Nezahualcoyotl and tlatoque of Texcoco, he campaigned for two years in Oaxaca to gather a fitting mass of captives for dedication of the new temple to Huitzilopochtli. Twenty thousand people were sacrificed on this occasion—or so some say; others say 80,000 (but more about this later).

Ahuitzotl gave his niece, daughter of Axayacatl, to Nezahualpilli for "wife"—she was only one among several "noble" maidens sent as concubines, or possible wives, but was too young for consideration. While she was quartered in the palace to age properly she not only took lovers from the court of Texcoco with royal abandon, but had statues made of them and worshiped them as her gods (the story may have picked up here a few post-Conquest frills that may hint at memories of pre-Conquest politics). Nezahualpilli, in the role of a true son of the just and austere Nezahualcoyotl, had her publicly judged, condemned, and executed, along with several hundred wicked domestics and other "accomplices" (so they say) in 1498.

Her brother Moctezuma II (the familiar Montezuma of history, his name being Motecuhzoma in Nahuatl, usually rendered Moctezuma in modern Spanish, "Angry Lord" in English translation), who became the ruler of Tenochtitlan five years later, never forgave him, and after several years of strained relations took cold revenge by allowing the Texcocan force to be wiped out when the ostensible allies were attacking (unsuccessfully, again) the Tlaxcalans. When Nezahualpilli died in 1516, Moctezuma named his successor, as if Texcoco were a subject state instead of an equal ally; an opposing candidate raised a party of revolt, and the alliance was, at last, totally broken.

But by this time there were other even graver matters weighing on Moctezuma's mind. A temple burst into flame without cause and burned to the ground. In a school for musicians, a ceiling beam sang a prophecy of national doom. A comet fell in broad daylight, in sunlight. In the year 1511 a column of fire appeared by night in the east, piercing the heavens; the people watched in terror, striking their mouths with their hands, "all were frightened; all waited in dread." Cihuacoatl, Serpent Woman, the Earth Goddess who wailed in the night streets to tell mothers when their children were to die, was heard weeping at night, crying out, "My beloved sons, whither shall I take you?" A marvelous bird was brought to Moctezuma, a crane with a mirror in its head, and in the mirror could be seen people "coming massed, coming as conquerors, coming in war panoply. Deer bore them upon their backs." Moctezuma summoned his soothsayers and wise men, but the bird vanished before their eyes.

The New Fire ceremonies were held in 1507—the critical rites celebrating the end of a fifty-two year cycle in the sacred calendar. Temples were enlarged or rebuilt; old debts were paid, injuries forgiven, enmities reconciled. Sins were confessed (at any rate by those too old to sin any more) to the goddess Tlazoteotl, goddess of carnal knowledge.

On the night of the New Fire all old fires were put out, and until midnight demons were free and the world hung in delicate balance—pregnant women were locked in windowless rooms so they could not be changed into animals, and children were kept forcibly awake so the demons could not eat them in their beds.

The priests knew the world had been destroyed four times before, and would be destroyed again—this time by fire—in a divine rhythm that was inescapable, although it might be delayed by correct action. It would happen on such a night as this, when the New Fire would refuse to respond to the priests' control.

But at midnight the fire priests succeeded in kindling the New Fire on the Hill of the Star and raced with it along the miles of causeway to the city, and rejoicing burst forth over all the land. The sun would rise again, the world would continue; all would go on as before.

CHAPTER 8

When Worlds Collide

For Europe, on the authority of sundry sages, the discovery of the New World was the most important event in the history of mankind. Trade, land, and wealth were expanded exponentially. To a people obsessively interested in trade, land, wealth, this was of miraculous importance.

To the people of the New World, obsessed with living the mysteries of religion, it was, in the beginning at least, a simple miracle absolute.

Cristoforo Colombo (Italian), Cristobal Colon (Spanish), Christopher Columbus (Anglicized Latin), Christ-bearing Dove (as we would literally translate the name if it were Indian) wrote while on his way home from his voyage of 1492, "The lands . . . are all most beautiful . . . full of trees of a thousand kinds, so lofty that they seem to reach the sky. And some of them were in flower, some in fruit, some in another stage according to their kind. And the nightingale was singing, and other birds of a thousand sorts, in the month of November. . . . The people of this island, and of all the others that I have found and seen . . . all go naked, men and women . . . they are artless and generous with what they have, to such a degree as no one would believe but he who had seen it. Of anything they have, if it be asked for, they never say no, but do rather invite the person to accept it, and show as much lovingness as though they would give their hearts . . . they believed very firmly that I, with these ships and crew, came from the sky; and in such opinion they received me at every place where I landed, after they had lost their terror. And this comes not because they are ignorant; on the contrary, they are men of very subtle wit, who navigate all those seas, and who give a marvelously good account of everything. . . . And as soon as I arrived in the Indies, in the first island that I found, I took some of them by force, to the intent that they should learn and give me information of what there was in

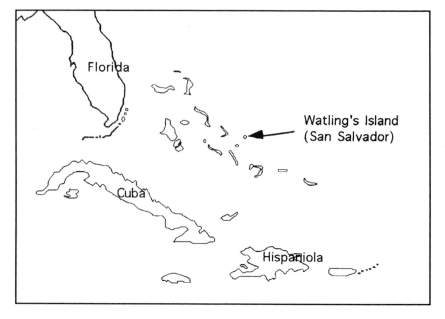

The Bahamas and Watling's Island

those parts. And so it was, that very soon they understood and we them, what by speech or what by signs. . . . To this day I carry them who are still of the opinion that I came from heaven, from much conversation which they have had with me. And they were the first to proclaim it wherever I arrived; and the others went running from house to house and to the neighboring villages, with loud cries of 'Come! Come to see the people from heaven!'"

Twelve islands in the Bahamas (or their respective tourist hotels) vie for the honor (and profit) of being the scene of Columbus's first landing, October 12; Watling's Island is the most likely; Columbus named this island San Salvador. Then, doubtless with the help of Arawak-speaking guides, he went to Cuba and then to Santo Domingo, which he named Española, a "densely settled place," that appeared to be "more populous than England," where all the land was "fully cultivated." Here the *Santa Maria* was wrecked, and here he left a few dozen of his men to establish and hold a little fort, La Navidad. He sailed away to return to Europe on January 4, 1493, taking with him his six Indian interpreters, and returned to the Caribbean the following autumn with seventeen ships and 1,500 more people from heaven, most of them coming as colonists. He also brought horses, twenty stallions and mares surviving from thirty-four at the start of the voyage.

Other islands in the Antilles were explored; a town was founded on Española and later moved to the south coast of the island (and called Santo Domingo) when gold was discovered there.

Christ-bearing Dove attacked the cannibal Caribs (the interpreters said they were cannibals, which made them fair game for enslavement) wherever they were found. Six hundred were shipped to Spain to be sold as slaves in 1498—but he did his best (as long as he could) to enforce just treatment of the guileless and defenseless Tainos, as the Arawakian island people called themselves. Two days after first encountering them on that October day in 1492 he had noted in his journal that "These people are very unskilled in arms . . . with fifty men they could all be subjected and made to do all that one wished." But he had also written, "I knew that they were a people who could better be freed and converted to our Holy Faith by love than by force . . . they remained so much our friends that it was a marvel."

But the Spanish settlers needed laborers for their plantations and mines, and the Indians were uninterested in work; the priests also protested that the Indians couldn't be taught and converted unless they were gathered into congregations. More settlers came—200 more in 1498, 2,500 in 1502, and 1,000 to 2,000 a year thereafter. It became necessary, of course, to congregate the Indians in villages under Spanish jurisdiction and see that they stayed congregated, and lived and worked decently.

Some of the Tainos tried to rebel, more fled to the hills and other islands and the mainland, more still died in the epidemics of the strange new diseases that came with the people from heaven.

And the invaders, hunting cannibals and other native peoples classified as hostile who could properly be made slaves, as well as following the incessant rumors of gold, were cruising the other islands of the Caribbean, the coasts of Florida, Panama, and South America.

The first Indian children fathered by the people from heaven grew to adulthood. The survivors, if there were any, of the first naked islanders who had ventured down to the beach to approach the hairy, shining strangers became old men, and their stories had long ago lost all their wonderful savor. Christ-bearing Dove sailed away for the last time, aged and certain of nothing. Some of the surviving Tainos may have heard that he died a year or two later.

But they may have been too much occupied with their own dying. By that time there were seventeen chartered towns in Española, and an estimated 14,000 Tainos left out of an estimated original several million on the island.

A colony was founded on the Panama isthmus in 1509, and reinforced in 1514 by 1,500 Spanish settlers. Spanish shipyards came into being, and horse and cattle ranches to supply the settlers with livestock.

Throughout these years the Spanish never heard, except in dream-sequence Indian tales describing golden cities in a gilded cloudland, of the Aztec and Inca empires.

But in the year 1511 a Spanish ship, bound from Darien in Panama to Santo Domingo, struck a reef and sank in the Caribbean. Survivors reached the east coast of Yucatan, where, ragged and starving, they were found by coastal Indians. Some were killed and (it was said) ceremonially eaten, others died in slavery; eventually only two were left, two men named Aguilar and Guerrero, enslaved to Maya chieftains.

At about the same time, far up the Nahua coast of Mexico, a little girl named Malinal was stolen and sold into slavery. That this could happen is implied by the stringent Aztec laws against such kidnapers; but some say the little girl's father, chief and governor of the town of Paynala, had died, and her mother, remarried, had Malinal secretly sold to make secure the position of her new children. In any case, Malinal was owned by some people in Xicalingo, who in turn sold her to someone in Tabasco, on the frontier of the Maya country of southeastern Mexico.

Among the Maya the ancient life of grandly marking time, the ancient cycles of solemn observance, had ended long ago. If it is to be assumed Toltec invaders had taught them (or some of them) the arts of pride and war, the Maya had learned exceedingly well. The cowering Maya warriors of the eleventh-century sculptures had become, by the sixteenth century, some of the toughest fighters in the New World.

A number of Postclassic Maya centers on or near the Yucatan coast had been for centuries communities of opulence and importance, such as the huge Tiho, at the site of present Merida, or nearby Dzibilchaltun, both in a region crowded with Maya settlements throughout a very long time.

The 8,000 or more structures at Dzibilchaltun formed a number of separate clusters around the principal ceremonial center, a fairly frequent Maya arrangement. Research using colonial records of some remnant groups in this area that survived into Spanish times has turned up a theory suggesting that political power and offices at Yucatecan sites may have rotated among several kinship groups. If so, it is thought these clusters may have been centers for such separate lineages, and some such rotational pattern may have been an ancient form of Maya social and political organization in northern Yucatan. It is a common pattern in Indian Mexico still today.

The most subtle of specialists pondering the perplexing question of Maya "rule," finding that it will not fit the coercion or riches familiar to the Old World, wonder if it could have been founded on nothing more than a sense of propriety, on ancient custom—that can seem as immutable as the stars.

Whatever it was, it was clearly altered (perhaps by warlike Toltec intrusion) at the two most famous Postclassic Yucatan centers, Chichen Itza and Mayapan. There, two truculent lineages, the Itzas and the Cocoms, came into dictatorial power. A third such family, the Xiu, ruled at a neighboring capital, Uxmal.

After centuries of feud and intrigue the Itzas (who claimed Toltec descent) were driven with their followers back into the jungles of the Peten, where the Classic Maya world had flourished a thousand years before. Mayapan was devastated by the Xiu in the middle 1400s, and all the Cocoms murdered except one son, absent on a trading trip to Honduras at the time. The little Mayapan confederacy broke up into many quarreling city-states and the surviving Cocom, with what was left of his people, established a new city and carried on a smoldering cold war against the Xiu family.

The Xiu also claimed Toltec descent (and had their name, a Nahuatl word meaning "fire," to prove it; on the other hand the name may be Mexicanization of the Maya word *ciu*, meaning "lord"). After all but annihilating the Cocoms, the Xiu leaders and their supporters abandoned Uxmal and built a new city at Mani ("It is passed"). Truly so, and the gods knew it: in 1464 a hurricane smashed Yucatan, in 1480 a pestilence decimated the people, and in the 1490s furious war became so general that the dead in the towns outnumbered the living.

In 1516 a terrible new pestilence swept over Yucatan, a disease never known before, with "great pustules that rotted the body," and the people died so quickly from it that the Maya named it "the easy death." It was apparently smallpox, passed along on ripples of contact from Panama, perhaps, where a wildfire epidemic had followed the arrival of the colonists in 1514. It came like the first trumpet call announcing the people from heaven, for the next year a Spanish slave-hunting ship from Cuba touched on the Yucatan coast, not far from where the slave-girl Malinal was living.

The Maya people there were unimpressed by the first white men they had ever seen and drove the Spaniards away in a hot fight, in spite of gunfire. But the Spanish leader heard of cities and saw gold; he died of his arrow wounds not long after getting back to Cuba, but the next year four more Spanish ships came to tack along the Yucatecan coast. Again they were driven away, but again, a few months later, the Spanish returned, this time with eleven ships and 500 men. They also brought sixteen horses. Warriors gathered from Maya towns along the coast and fought "face to face, most valiantly," and continued fighting off and on for three days, until the Spanish were able to disembark their horses and field a little troop of barely over a dozen mounted lancers. The Indians, who had never seen horses before, fled in panic, and this time the Spanish stayed.

The new Spanish captain, a young man named Fernando Cortés, had heard of bearded men in the Maya towns and gotten a message through to Aguilar and ransomed him from his seven years of slavery. The other surviving Spaniard had become a Maya and would not leave. ("Brother Aguilar, I am married and have three children and the Indians look upon me as a Cacique and captain in wartime—You go and God be with you, but I have my face tattooed and my ears pierced, what would the Spaniards say should they see me in this guise?" so said Guerrero, the other Spaniard living among the Maya, as recorded by Bernal Díaz del Castillo, a twenty-seven-year-old soldier with Cortés.) And among other gifts of tribute, the now subdued people of the Maya coast gave to Cortés their choicest girls, and among these the slave-girl Malinal.

Malinal had grown up to be not only pretty but also bright ("good looking and intelligent and without embarrassment," said Bernal Díaz). She spoke Nahuatl as a birthright tongue, and in Tabasco she had learned the Maya language spoken there, Chontal, and also, possibly from merchants visiting the household where she lived, Yucatecan. She could talk to Aguilar in Yucatecan Maya, and Aguilar could then translate into Castilian for Cortés.

The Spanish called her, after she was baptized, Marina. She proved herself such a brilliant and valuable girl Friday that some historians are almost tempted to think of her as the real conqueror of Mexico.

"[A]nd thus God," wrote Bishop Landa some forty years later, "provided Cortés with good and faithful interpreters, by means of whom he came to have intimate knowledge of the affairs of Mexico, of which Marina knew much." Landa's modern editor adds, "God also provided Cortés with a mistress . . . she lived with Cortés and bore him a son." (Cortés at first allotted her to one of his lieutenants, but before long took her for himself.)

It was in March 1519 that the people of Tabasco gave the Lady Marina (as Bernal Díaz always speaks of her) to the strangers, and this was in the shadowland country at the far frontier of the Aztec realm. That realm (including much of present central and southern Mexico, composed of numerous provinces surrounding the Valley of Mexico and the capital city of the Aztecs) was a land larger in extent than all Spain, filled with towns and cities that astonished the Spaniards, who in a generation in the New World had not yet seen anything more than villages of thatched huts. Estimates of the population—over this vast territory—have run from 3 to 30 million, with the best recent guesses, based on Aztec tribute-rolls, hovering close to 10 million, although other plausible guesses can run somewhat higher. (Spain at the time had a population of 4.5 million.) And these were no timorous Tainos or unorganized Caribs; city after city could produce armies of thousands, war-loving fighters whose courage and tenacity were never belittled by anyone who had fought them—they went to church to death daily. Even on the remote Tabasco coast the great city of Tenochtitlan, sometimes called Mexico after the Aztecs' other name, the Mexica, was famous, the center of the world, and the omnipotent Moctezuma, who ruled there, was obeyed to the ends of the earth.

But by the end of the year the Spanish expedition, by then only some 400 men, held Moctezuma prisoner in the center of the city of Mexico, and through him commanded all the country.

The Spanish had superior weapons—but not that much superior. The quilted cotton armor of the Mexicans was superior, in fact, to the Spanish steel breastplates—and the Spaniards were quick to change. No more sudden decisions were won by the sight and sound of horses or cannon.

The important point is that throughout the first march on Mexico, after they were joined by Malinal, the Spanish were forced to fight in only one instance—where only their immensely superior tactics saved their lives. Otherwise, the road of their first penetration into the country—the perilous interval while they were still without important allies and could have been wiped out a dozen times over—was paved by a string of diplomatic victories as remarkable as so many straight passes at dice.

On the Vera Cruz coast, where the little Spanish army sailed from Tabasco, Cortés played a double game, first with the fat Totonacs, who lived

there, encouraging them to rebel against their Aztec oppressors, and then with
the Aztec ambassadors from Moctezuma, convincing them that he was on
their side against the treacherous Totonacs. The Totonacs provided workmen,
food, and warriors; Moctezuma sent as gifts a solid gold disk as large as a cart
wheel, designed to represent the sun, a larger silver disk designed to represent
the moon, a helmet full of grains of gold, 100 bearers loaded with other gifts
of richly embroidered mantles, gold ornaments, crests of feathers, and decla-
rations of friendship—and a polite refusal to permit the mysterious strangers
to visit the city of Mexico.

But the refusal was evasive and half-hearted; for who, indeed, were the
bearded white men?

Quetzalcoatl, the bearded white god (born as the Toltec Topiltzin, it will
be remembered, in a year of Ce Acatl), had said, so the legends recorded, that
in another year of Ce Acatl he would return from the sunrise to reclaim his
kingdom, and by a coincidence out of grand opera the year 1519 was another
year of Ce Acatl in the Aztec calendar. Was it possible?

It is reasonable that Malinal, fully aware of this stage setting of prophecy,
would have intimated that truly it was very possible, when she talked for
Cortés to the chief men of cities and to the chief priests of temples—the longhaired ones, the Nahuatl annals call them, their ears shredded from acts of
penance and their waist-long hair matted with the blood of sacrifices.

Everywhere the troubled people flocked to the temples; at each town the
strangers entered they found sacrificed bodies on the altars, hearts before the
idols, and the temple walls desperately splashed with blood. (One of the most
memorable things about the temples, not surprisingly, was their overpower-
ing stockyard smell.)

Deftly juggling friendly Totonac allies and uncertain Aztec ambassadors,
and with flowery expressions of the sincerest respect sent ahead to the great
prince Moctezuma, the Spaniards marched inland for Mexico City.

The one instance of fighting was found in the independent city-state of
Tlaxcala, where stubborn armies threw themselves against the strangers in a
running engagement that went on for days. Javelins fell as thick as straw on a
threshing floor (said the Spaniards), and the Tlaxcalans and their Otomi
archers, far from panicking at the explosion of gunpowder, drowned its noise
with their shrill whistles and threw dust in the air while they rushed the dead
and wounded away, so no one could see what damage the little cannons might
have done. They killed a mare, a good and handy mare belonging to Pedro de
Moron, and almost captured her rider. Three times, by day and by night, the
Spaniards only survived by the hottest of sword work while holding their
ranks exactly intact. Repeatedly Cortés requested peaceful passage through

their country, and repeatedly the Tlaxcalans responded with attacks of redoubled fury and, if we are to believe the communiqués, in enormous numbers. The gifts Cortés sent, including "a fluffy red Flemish hat, such as was then worn," were sacrificed on the Tlaxcalan altars, and the Tlaxcalan war leader, Xicotencatl, insolently presented the head of Pedro de Moron's mare "on the point of his lance" to the Tlaxcalan Senate.

Bernal Díaz credits Doña Marina with wringing victory out of this equivocal and exceedingly dangerous situation—several of the Spaniards had been killed, a faction was for retreating to the coast, and "all of us were wounded and sick"—by discovering so readily the plans of enemy war-councils that the Tlaxcalans might have been pardoned for deciding the strangers were genuine wizards; and then by delivering with unfailing valor ("although she had heard every day how the Indians were going to kill us and eat our flesh with chili") arguments of a most telling mixture of threat and persuasion to the Tlaxcalan envoys. The problem for the Tlaxcalans seems to have been to decide if the strangers were pro- or anti-Aztec; Cortés ingratiatingly presented himself as anti-, but he was traveling with Indian allies from the coast who were Aztec subjects, and the Tlaxcalans had learned through a century of bitter conflict to trust nothing that smacked even faintly of Aztec brewing; obviously the sort of problem Marina's fluent explanations might well have helped solve.

Once decided on friendship the Tlaxcalans remained the firmest of allies, and the march was continued with an added ball to keep in the air—a large Tlaxcalan detachment trailing along, implacable enemies of the Aztecs and all their subject states.

At the ancient metropolis Cholula, of the great pyramid, and very much an Aztec subject state, Cortés tastefully encamped the Tlaxcalans outside the city, again juggled exchanges of friendship with the Aztec ambassadors, discovered a plot against him in the city, and arranged instead for the Tlaxcalans to rush into the town at a prearranged signal and join the Spaniards in a massacre to punish the Cholulans' planned treachery. The surprise massacre—and accompanying looting—went off elegantly, except that Cortés had a hard time getting the Tlaxcalans to stop, once he thought the punishment had gone far enough. Cortés reported 3,000 of the city's inhabitants killed; others say 6,000 or more.

Evidently there really was a plot against the strangers on the part of a faction in the city—"for it is a large city and they have parties and factions among themselves"—conspiring with agents sent from Moctezuma. All of these were doubtless profoundly disconcerted by the strangers' ability to read their most secret thoughts, which is to say by the alertness of the Spaniards' intelligence service, which is to say the Lady Marina.

Cortés, through Malinal, blandly forgave everyone concerned, assured the Aztec ambassadors that he knew Moctezuma could have had no hand in such an ungentlemanly plot, even succeeded in representing himself to the Cholulans as their protector against the Tlaxcalans—henceforward to be friends with one another—and marched on to the capital, the city of Mexico, Tenochtitlan.

There is no way of telling, of course, whether the extraordinarily effective cunning and guile displayed all the way along this march was chiefly due to the devious genius of Cortés or to that of the Lady Marina. Cortés, as he proved often enough in other situations, was one of the great nonlosers of all time. Regardless of the odds or setbacks he seemingly could not lose, and until he tangled with lawyers he never did. Perhaps one reason was that he knew how to make true use of such loyal confederates as the Lady Marina. A modern historian writes, "Had it not been for her devotion to Cortés and his various and sundry captains, she could well have caused the destruction of the small Spanish army.... Most great captains in history found their defeat in the arms of a tender morsel—not so Cortés, he conquered Malinche and thus the New World." The Nahua people called her Malinche, or so it sounded to Spanish ears (her supposed Nahuatl name of Malinal may have been only the Nahuatl pronunciation of Marina—where Cristo became Quilisto—and Malinche could have been made by a suffix of some form of *cihuatl*, "lady"). Cortés was known to the Nahua people as Malinche's Captain or, for short, also as Malinche. Marina is given much importance in the Spanish chronicles, and it is even more striking that, in such Indian chronicles as the *Lienzo* (picture history) of Tlaxcala, Marina not only appears in every important scene but is customarily drawn larger than any of the other actors, including Cortés.

All the wonders the Spaniards had seen had not prepared them for the numerous cities around Lake Texcoco, the towers and temples rising out of the waters of the lake, the long straight causeways eight paces wide jammed with welcoming crowds, the dignitaries tall with the dazzling plumes of the scarlet spoonbill, hung with jewels of gold and jade and pearls, sent to greet them, and finally the capital, the city of Mexico; the soldiers asked each other if they were dreaming, "for it is," Cortés wrote, "the most beautiful city in the world."

No doubt the strangers were of equal interest to the Aztec public, with their curious weapons and dress, the one black man among them, a slave owned by Juan Sedeño, the richest soldier in the company, the tired and scarred but caparisoned horses (there were thirteen or fourteen left and one six-months-old foal, it being Juan Sedeño's mare, naturally, that had foaled), the two greyhounds, the loads of mysterious baggage borne by Indian servants from all the allies they had so far made—Totonacs, Tlaxcalans (who had given Malinal alone 300 handmaidens, so some say), Cholulans, as well as a half dozen foreign Indian servants brought from Cuba.

Moctezuma himself was carried out in his litter to meet them; all the people bowed their heads so as not to affront the chief-of-men by looking into his face; and Moctezuma quartered the strangers and all their people in an immense house, with courtyards and many rooms and with walls of sculptured stone, the palace, so they gathered, of his father Axayacatl, the conqueror of Tenochtitlan's twin city of Tlatelolco fifty years before.

After a week or so of polite visits back and forth, during which Moctezuma showed the strangers his city, his temples, the Tlatelolco marketplace greater than Rome's, so said the soldiers who had served in Italy, Cortés came calling one day with a handful of men and the Lady Marina, and took Moctezuma prisoner. This was accomplished with no more than a flimsy pretext and "smooth speeches"; it took Malinal an hour or two of smooth speeches—coupled with the most courteous of threats—to convince Moctezuma it would be best for him to come along quietly. He went with the Spaniards to their quarters and remained from then on in their custody, although treated with the greatest respect, accompanied by his household, and free to carry on each day the business of state.

The pretext for this action involved news of an attack, purportedly at Moctezuma's orders, on soldiers of a garrison Cortés had left at Vera Cruz; the immediate reason, however, was that the Spaniards were beginning to feel seriously uneasy, so few as they were in this great and warlike city, and a hostage of such quality was their best and boldest security; the basic reason, of course, was that they had come on conquest and it was high time to set about it.

Moctezuma swore fealty (said Cortés) to the strangers' Don Carlos, King of Spain—in fact, according to Cortés, he explicitly abdicated, presumably in favor of the strangers as emissaries of Quetzalcoatl. (If so, subsequent events would illustrate how wrongly the Spaniards interpreted his "kingly" power.)

At the suggestion of Cortés, Moctezuma got together a princely present for the lord across the sea—his family's heirlooms, and what he could raise from his empire; gold, Cortés wrote, such as no monarch in Europe possessed. The Aztecs regarded gold as of small value except when transformed by the goldsmith's art; jade was the precious stone. The Spanish preferred gold, and they liked it in the raw; they had the worked pieces melted down. Scholars disagree on the total value—Prescott made it some 6 million nineteenth-century dollars, exclusive of silver, carved ornaments, and some of the delicately worked gold figures left unbroken.

Only the royal fifth was set aside for the lord across the sea. The rest was divided, with many angry rows, among the company of the people from heaven. The Spanish captains had their shares made into heavy chains of gold, and wore them wound around their doubleted shoulders.

The war was still to come, but the conquest was accomplished. From the moment of the magic touch of so much gold so tamely taken the strangers were masters and could never believe otherwise. These sumptuous people in their glorious cities were only naked natives after all.

This whole unbelievable interlude, 400 Spaniards coolly taking over a capital that could (and eventually did) raise an army of many thousands of fanatically determined warriors, has troubled historians ever since. Moctezuma had but to lift a finger, in the good old prose of Prescott, and the little band of strangers would be stormed under and destroyed.

Maybe the smooth speeches of young Malinal really were enchantment. Maybe Moctezuma did believe the strangers were gods; maybe he reasoned that only gods would have their audacity. He seems to have been hopelessly uncertain, anxious to get the strangers to go away, but equally anxious not to anger them. It is possible that he did not quite realize a conquest was going on. Who knows the proper protocol for visitors from outer space?

And so months passed, and in the spring of 1520 a new Spanish army—a much bigger one—landed at Vera Cruz. This was a force of 1,400 men under the command of red-bearded bully boy Panfilo de Narvaez, come not to help but to hijack; Narvaez had emerged from high-level political maneuvering back in Cuba, whose high-level politicians would have liked a share of the Aztec treasure, with authority to make Cortés his captive, dead or alive, and assume command of Cortés's forces.

Cortés sent emissaries loaded with gold to talk to various of Narvaez's captains, arranged for a couple of thousand mountain Chinantecs to meet him at the coast as allies (he had his own men armed and trained with long Chinantec lances, as an improvement over Spanish arms for fighting horsemen from the ground), and then, with 250 or so of his men—266 including the drummer and fifer, says Bernal Díaz—went to deal with these interloping people from heaven.

He left Pedro de Alvarado in charge in the city, where a highly touchy situation had developed: the Aztec priests were beginning to urge death or expulsion for the strangers. Moctezuma's scientists were reporting, in effect, that the visitors from outer space were radioactive and would melt the country's marrow.

Alvarado was blonde and handsome (the Aztecs called him Tonatiuh, "Sun God"), chatty, edgy, covetous, and vicious. Apparently with some shaky idea of terrorizing the Aztecs by a repetition of the Cholula massacre, and maybe with some idea of a repetition of the Cholula looting, he ordered an insane attack on the people dancing at the feast of Huitzilopochtli, and the city, shocked and enraged, burst into violence.

Cortés returned, having whipped Narvaez handily, and bribed or persuaded most of his fine big army into changing sides—Narvaez lost an eye in the battle—and found a full-scale war in preparation in the city of Mexico. He forced Moctezuma to try to calm his subjects (and the great Moctezuma said with grief, "What more does Malinche want from me?"), and Moctezuma was killed in the attempt, some say by the infuriated Aztecs, some say by the desperate Spaniards.

The strangers had to fight their way out of the city and make for the safety of Tlaxcala. Cortés escaped, with Marina, but of his handsome new army—the thousand or so additional recruits from Narvaez's forces and his own 400 veterans—more than 800 were killed in the fighting, drowned in the canals by the weight of gold they were trying to carry, or captured and sacrificed. The gods ate well on this midsummer Noche Triste, Cortés's Night of Sorrow.

It took a year to gather armies of Indian allies and return to attack Tenochtitlan again. The real war was fought during this year, a war for empire between the Aztecs and the invaders, a war of intrigue, deals, and ruthless force where needed, carried out in a land torn from end to end not only by dissension but by disease: the first smallpox epidemic of record swept over Mexico in 1520, set off, says Bernal Díaz, by "a black man whom Narvaez brought covered with smallpox." This, though, was evidently the still-running wave of the great epidemic reported from Panama in 1514, from Yucatan in 1516, from Española in 1518–1519, and no doubt found many more entrances than only one into Mexico in 1520. The Indians had no immunity whatsoever to this first hot breath of civilization and, worse, their custom of frequent bathing in groups (the unwashed Spaniards knew that had to be unhealthy) helped fan the spread of the disease.

In the marshaling of power, Tlaxcala and the Totonac towns and the anti-Aztec factions in many subject-states, including Texcoco (Moctezuma's vengeance for his sister turned out to be costly), threw in enthusiastically with the Spanish. States loyal to the Aztecs were put to fire and sword by Cortés and his insurgent allies, and their populations were branded on the face and sold as slaves. Captured Spaniards were sacrificed in the temples; sometimes their faces were skinned (with the beards) for trophies to give to the gods. The heads of horses as well appeared on the skull rack in Tenochtitlan. Cortés's policy with prisoners of war was to free them, if there was any chance of making peace with their people; if not, he had their hands cut off and sent them home.

It was a long and bitter war, but the strangers pulled away more and more of the confederacy, and the Aztecs could never trap and destroy them—there was always Tlaxcala for refuge; and eventually it became clear that the invaders had won and the Aztecs had lost. When at length the strangers came back in massive strength to besiege the capital the issue could not be in doubt.

The attack on the city was mounted from Texcoco, where the anti-Aztec leader, Ixtlilxochitl II, helped work out the same sort of operation that his grandfather Nezahualcoyotl had used with the Aztecs against the then capital of Azcapotzalco—heavy attacks by water and encirclement by land. The pincers closed and the island city was held under siege until fresh water and food became more precious than jade. Many thousands of allied warriors, a great number, Cortés wrote, were supporting the Spanish.

But seemingly inexhaustible squadrons of Aztec spearmen fought like demons, from house to house, from temple to temple, along the canals that were the city's streets—the streets were (except for a few principal avenues) all of two lanes, one of hard earth like pavement, the other of water, "so that they can go out along the land or by water": so said the Anonymous Conqueror, one of Cortés's soldiers as yet unidentified, in an account that deals almost entirely with a description of the city of Mexico and its people.

Cuauhtemoc, a nephew of Moctezuma and the new Aztec leader, had told his people they would either be victorious or die fighting. They did, almost to a man—in the usual hyperbolic sense of the term. Losses of Aztecs and their allies in the city were put by Cortés at 117,000; survivors, excluding women and children, at 30,000. Losses of the Texcoco troops were estimated at 30,000.

"It was useless to tell them," Cortés reported, "that we would not raise the siege, and that the launches would not cease to fight them on the water, nor that we had already destroyed the people of Matalcingo and Malinalco, and that there was no one left in the land to bring them succor, and that there was nowhere whence they could procure maize, meat, fruit, water, or other necessaries, for the more we repeated this to them the less faintheartedness they showed. On the contrary, both in fighting and in stratagems we found them more undaunted than ever."

The battle lasted eighty-five days (more or less; accounts differ) and ended on (or about) August 13, 1521, when Cuauhtemoc, trying to escape by boat, was captured, and the last few defenders in the northeast corner of the city were cut down.

"All through the Colonial era, and even up to now," writes a modern archeologist, "the northern district of Mexico [City] has found favor neither as a residential quarter nor as a business center. Today there are railroad yards and slums where the Aztec civilization bled to death. The ghosts of its heroic defenders still haunt the place."

Nothing in all that has been written about the Aztecs tells as much about them as one of their songs, a hymn, that runs:

> We only came to sleep
> We only came to dream
> It is not true, no, it is not true
> That we came to live on the earth
> We are changed into the grass of springtime
> Our hearts will grow green again
> And they will open their petals
> But our body is like a rose tree:
> It puts forth flowers and then withers.

The last thing the Spanish learned about the most sacred idol of the Aztecs, that of Huitzilopochtli, "was that it was hidden in an unknown cave near Tula, where it may still remain today." Perhaps it will so remain.

In Peru at about the same time, sometime in the early 1520s, barbarians crossed the Andes from the east and raided the border provinces of the Inca Empire. They came from the wild brush country called the Chaco, a Quechua word meaning hunting ground. They were Guarani people, bowmen (and, of course, said to be cannibals). This was not their first plundering appearance on the Inca frontiers nor their last—Huayna Capac, the Inca, son of Topa Inca, built three fortresses to guard against them. But on this occasion they were accompanied by a few white men, shipwrecked castaways from an exploring fleet commanded by Juan de Solis, chief pilot of Spain. In 1515 and 1516 Solis had sailed down the east coast of South America as far south as the Rio de la Plata, where the expedition had come to grief. The European survivors with the Guarani must have spent the intervening five or ten years wandering the length and breadth of interior South America, from the region of the present Buenos Aires to Peru, some of it country still only sketchily explored today.

One of these Europeans, and the only name we have from among them, was Alejo Garcia, a Portuguese. Along with what may have been one of the most imposing lists of firsts in all exploration, he was the first European of record to see the wealth and civilization of the Incas. His name might be more than a footnote to history except that his Guarani friends killed him on the way back east.

Tawantinsuyu, the Realm of the Incas

The importance of this invasion to the Incas is in the sudden pestilence that followed it. (Maybe there was no connection or maybe the Guarani and their guests had been carrying it wherever they went, or maybe this too was a rolling wave of the great smallpox plague sent forth from Panama in 1514, taking a dozen years to roll its way to the highlands of the Andes.) For during the epidemic Huayna Capac died, so quickly and unexpectedly that he did not have time to make the usual formal announcement of his successor. He meant his son Huascar to succeed him, and Huascar was invested with the office at Cuzco by the high priest. But Huayna Capac happened to die at Quito in the north, where he had a separate wife and a son by her named Atahuallpa. Atahuallpa assumed the governorship of Quito and the northernmost regions of Tawantinsuyu (the northerly regions of modern Ecuador) and command of the army that had been with Huayna Capac when he died.

The two leaders of that army, Quisquis and Challcuchima, gave Atahuallpa their complete loyalty. They were the empire's foremost generals, and their seasoned troops by far the empire's best. In the civil war that followed, and lasted for five years, Quisquis and Challcuchima won a solid string of victories, ending in a decisive triumph north of Cuzco. Huascar was taken prisoner, his forces scattered, his lieutenants executed.

Huayna Capac died in 1527. In the same year word came of strange beings (perhaps Viracocha returning?) at the far northern outposts of the empire. The Viracochas went away, but five years later they returned. Atahuallpa was at the town of Cajamarca in the north central highlands when he received the great news of the final victory over Huascar and, at the same time, a visit from the Viracochas. The Viracochas (164 Spaniards, 62 horses) were led by the hard-eyed old soldier Francisco Pizarro, who sent his brother Hernando and a young captain named Hernando de Soto to invite Atahuallpa to visit the Viracochas's quarters. The next day, November 16, 1532, Atahuallpa came in his litter accompanied by several thousand warriors. The Viracochas (who had been planning this expedition in search of the fabled Biru for years, and meanwhile listening attentively to tales of the way Cortés did things in Mexico) met him with a prepared ambush, blew his soldiers to pieces with cannon, rode down the remnants with cavalry, and took Atahuallpa prisoner.

The story of the conquest of Peru contains no psychological mysteries, no gifted and beautiful heroines, no heroics, and above all no heroes. It is a simple tale of unrelieved double dealing and violent crime. Francisco Pizarro, illiterate, sixty-one years old, with a lifetime of blood on his hands, was a plain man with uncomplicated notions: blunt treachery, suspicious self-interest, and a sword-thrust for persuasion.

With the sacred person of the Inca as hostage the Spanish were immune from attack, and Atahuallpa was now ordered to produce a ransom. Among the Inca people there was some feeling that the Viracochas may have appeared and seized Atahuallpa in answer to the prayers of Huascar, who was still the prisoner of Atahuallpa's generals and still claiming to be the true Inca. When the captive Huascar managed to get into communication with Pizarro, the captive Atahuallpa smuggled out orders to put him to death. Tradition says Huascar was drowned by his jailors. A few months later, in August 1533, the gigantic ransom having been collected, melted down, and distributed among the enraptured Viracochas, Pizarro had Atahuallpa publicly strangled.

And again a conquest was completed, although the war was still to come. In this case it was a savage, stubborn war that lasted forty years in Tawantinsuyu itself, and 300 years longer in the border country to the south. In the wild Chaco and Montaña to the east (where the first of the Viracochas appeared and disappeared, and where tribes still exist who have scarcely seen white men) it hasn't been completed yet.

Atahuallpa's huge ransom, cooked into bullion, amounted to a treasure more than twice as large as Moctezuma's—Baron Humboldt made it 20 million nineteenth-century dollars. It included the gold sheeting torn from the Temple of the Sun at Cuzco and such masterpieces of the goldsmith's art as a golden ear of corn sheathed in silver leaves with a tassel of silver threads.

Of all the marvelously worked gold and silver art objects gathered in the first decades of the Conquest over all the New World, not one piece, says a modern expert, survives. Those currently exhibited in the Museo de America, Madrid, came as gifts from Latin America on the 400th anniversary of the Discovery, and inventories from 1596 to 1878 at Vienna indicate that not even the exhibits there were among the first pieces received. All these first pieces were subsequently "plundered" or their gold decoration replaced with gilded bronze.

CHAPTER 9

Through the Lookinglass I

The great civilizations of the New World were as ancient in many respects as the ancient civilizations of the Old World. We have seen that monumental architecture in the coastal valleys of Peru dates from 3000 B.C., the date also of the first dynasties of Egypt and of Ur that have long stood alone as the veriest beginnings of civilized society.

Archeological opinion sees the site of Sechin Alto in Peru's Casma Valley, with its plazas and ceremonial platforms stretching for nearly a mile and its pyramid as high as a nine-story building, as one of the world's most impressive architectural creations at its peak time, the thirteenth century B.C. But sites of massive public building that date to more than 1,000 years earlier have been located in the same region, a dozen along the coast (it is supposed still others may have been drowned by changes in the sea level), eleven in the nearby highlands. No less than thirty small sites of similar sort, dating from the last two millennia B.C., were disclosed along a limited section of the Jequetepeque valley by a hasty survey carried out in 1978–1981 before a new dam flooded the area.

These early expressions of organized humanity in both worlds, Old and New, had certain similarities: fearsome gods, worshipful heavens, and triumphant warriors.

The New World populations eventually grew to staggering totals, as has been recounted. The sculpture, ceramics, masonry, architecture, unsurpassable textiles, ultimately the treasures in gold and silver works of art, at least equaled the artistic production of the Old World.

In war, in tools and weapons, in technology in general, the two worlds were separated by a gulf so huge as to seem astronomical.

Where could this New World have sprung from, with its myriad samenesses to the Old World, its dreamlike divergences?

The samenesses prompted presumptions that the New World civilizations were merely offshoots in some manner of the civilizations of Asia and Europe. The origin of the Inca people, wrote William Hickling Prescott in his *Conquest of Peru*, "may afford a tempting theme for inquiry to the speculative antiquarian," and for centuries there has been no lack of speculative antiquarians offering evidence to prove that the civilizations of Peru or Mexico sprang readymade from some Old World point of origin.

Some demonstrated an Egyptian parentage, others the far-reaching empire of Alexander the Great. Some found the Inca civilization a creation of the "Grand Khan Kublai." A learned French traveler saw in 1746 in Canada, "900 leagues to the west of Montreal, a tablet of stone fixed in a sculptured pillar" on which was (so someone translated) a Tartar inscription—the Chevalier de Beauharnais, governor of New France, had it presented (so someone said) to the minister, M. de Maurepas, in Paris; who could question such respectable names?

The Spanish historians Oviedo and Gómara, among others, decided on the authority of no less than Aristotle that the Indians of the New World were Carthaginians, Aristotle having related that some Carthaginians were storm-driven to an unknown island. Another Spanish scholar, Vanegas, supporting their theory, showed that both the Carthaginians and the Americans "practiced picture-writing, both venerated fire and water, wore skins of animals, pierced the ears, ate dog, drank to excess, telegraphed by means of fires on hills, wore all their finery on going to war, poisoned their arrows, beat drums and shouted in battle." However, the Spanish historian Acosta, after seventeen years in Peru, was rather more convincing in proving that America was really the Ophir of Solomon. The early-nineteenth century British scholar, Edward King, Viscount Kingsborough, spent his life, his fortune, and his sacred honor (he died in debtors' prison) proving that the Hebrews built the Mexican civilization. (He made it to debtors' prison by giving to the world, among other costly gifts, a truly magnificent printing in seven sumptuous volumes of the Codex Mendoza, a picture-manuscript painted by Aztec artists in 1541 at the behest of Viceroy Antonio de Mendoza.) Lord Kingsborough was withal only one of many who filled great volumes with the numerous Aztec-Holy Land parallels (circumcision, for example) that had a most persuasive ring to Bible-conscious Victorian ears.

All unanswered questions, and the endless parallels real and apparent, spur on such speculation. Anthropologists noticed long ago fairly lengthy lists of correspondences between New World and Old World culture traits, ranging from similarities in certain folktales to similarities in such occasional items as various games or widespread addiction to gambling, ritual giveaways of food and property, specific fire-making techniques, blowguns, scattered use of wooden pillows, stilts, plaited fans, litters for leaders, and on through dozens of examples. Some of these may have been part of the universal baggage of Paleolithic man, some may well have been incidental imports (or exports), and some may have been independent convergences or coincidences. Most, regarded as elements of culture growth, appear to be trivial.

It would seem in a general sense that the development of the New World civilizations over such great stretches of time offers few nooks and crannies for sudden mysteries. As has been seen in these pages, the outlines of this development show slow growth and accretion during many thousands of years.

The developing civilization of the Andes had witnessed Chimu warriors, coeval with iron-gauntleted Crusaders in the Old World, trotting past relics of Tiahuanacan idols that were already as ancient to them as Saxon England is now to us, and past stone felines of Chavin as ancient to them as Cleopatra is to us. It had seen cat-cult priests of the pre-Chavin period, coeval with the Druid priest-rulers of England, invoking magic over farm fields already more ancient to them than the Crusaders are now to us. Roughly similar gradations mark the Mesoamerican time scale.

Evidently there is no scoring here for the unexpected trombones of mysterious culture-bringers.

Nevertheless Old World claimants have continued to appear, sometimes in veritable armies ready for either siege or assault.

Pottery offered some possibilities. It was apparently first introduced among North American Woodland peoples in late Archaic times via Siberia, Bering Strait, Alaska and points southeastward, although some early occurrences are suspected of being independent designs born from previous stone bowls. Later ponderings of earliest North American pottery came up with transatlantic introduction as more acceptable than trans-Siberian, alleging striking resemblances to Neolithic ware in north Russia and Scandinavia. No one proposed such hypothetical contacts with primitive north Europe as transmission points for a ready-mixed high culture, but very early pottery at the very early site of Valdivia in Ecuador provided a glorious and well foughten field in the 1960s and later for those who saw this pottery as Japanese and those who did not.

Even wider and wilder hostilities were touched off by the publication in 1947 of botanical evidence that prehistoric New World cotton may have been a cross between Asiatic cotton and American wild cotton. The sensational prospect arose of Asiatic immigrants (from the brand new Indus Valley culture, the only embryonic civilization in those parts old enough to fit) landing some time before 3000 B.C. on the bleak north Peruvian coast, at some such pre-ceramic site as Huaca Prieta, associated with early cultivation of this cotton.

Here, then, might be the civilization-bringers so long sought by the more persistently Old Worldian speculative antiquarians.

Later studies have brought increasingly skeptical reaction in regard to the Japanese pottery, and have found the American cotton genetically all-American after all.

But the idea of transpacific contact at such an unlikely early period engendered considerable excitement, and by the time of these verdicts enthusiastic theorists had ransacked Asia searching for still further connections or parallels between its ancient civilizations and the ancient civilizations of the New World.

They have found many, almost as many as had previously been found proving a connection with the Hebrews, although none seem to be very weighty additions to the lists of parallels already familiar to anthropologists.

Some archeologists are inclined to give serious consideration also to arguments that New World metallurgical techniques derived from outside stimulus. Work in alloys, including diffusion-bonding, fusion-gilding by flowing the alloy over the pre-heated metal object, surface enrichment by acid, casting by the lost-wax method, and a very long list of further complex procedures previously noted were carried out, and magnificently carried out, by New World metal-smiths—could these things really have been invented twice?

But could they have been brought to the New World without bringing along one of metalworking's simplest and most basic and most essential tools, the bellows? Present in the Old World in great antiquity, the hand bellows was followed by the foot bellows, found in general use in the seventeenth century B.C., pictured in an Egyptian wall painting of c. 1450 B.C. The Americas were apparently unique among civilized worlds in not possessing the bellows. It seems quite inconceivable any Old World teacher could have taught any aspect of metalworking without introducing the bellows. It could be fashioned in minutes from its merest description—and without it all metallurgy was more difficult and whole areas of metalworking were impossible, including the largest and grandest. Entirely apart from its incalculable value in metalworking it would have been truly a blessing everywhere in the high Andes, where the thin air required wearisome and only erratically effective fanning even to light a fire.

The earliest definite presence of metallurgy in the New World, as has been mentioned, is in Peru during the last millennium B.C. The exquisite work that appeared so early does pose a sore mystery—but for that matter so does the exquisite early work in Sumeria in the third millennium B.C., "amazing" technically, "breath-taking" artistically, and the marvelous early work in Egypt even more so.

Far more wonderful is the fact that platinum was worked in pre-Columbian Ecuador and Colombia (centuries before it was known in Europe) by a process usually thought to be a strictly modern method of working high-melting-point metals, and is the first known application anywhere of this basic principle, called nowadays powder metallurgy.

Maybe metalworking was introduced via contacts with Mount Olympus. (But no, Hephaestus had twenty bellows there, which worked spontaneously at his order; surely he could have spared one for the New World.)

The absolute origins of the various early New World pottery complexes and the root origin of New World metallurgy are still open questions and are likely to remain so for at least some time to come. But the early primitive pottery, wherever its origins, scarcely determined the shape the great New World civilizations would assume. Metallurgy could have had even less effect on the Maya world, where it never appeared at all, or on Mexico in general, where it appeared only toward the end of Classic times, when the form and structure of the Mesoamerican world had been firmly fixed for many centuries.

The majority of the proposed Asian influences have been art motifs, some of which may have merit as possible actual resemblances, but much more than this would be needed to give even slight support to Old World participation in the creation of New World civilization. One leading proponent offers much more indeed—a speculative theory arguing in some detail how various Asian societies may have transported these civilizations across the Pacific piece by piece in a fairly regular traffic of transpacific sailings continuing for more than 2,000 years and barely ending, circa A.D. 1200, in time to make way for Columbus.

An extraordinarily thorough survey of pan-Pacific resemblances has been made, including the use of Chinese points of reference from the work of Chinese specialists little known in the West, by the historians of science in China, Needham and Lu. Subjects dealt with include gods and calendars, art and music, mathematics and magnetism, technology from irrigation to suspension bridges to royal Tyrian purple dye to distillation to metallurgy. Many of these matters, discussed in some detail, are of great interest, but the conclusions reached express agreement with the well-known statement of Glyn Daniel that any contacts were slight and infrequent "and had little effect on the native development of pre-Columbian American culture."

Some of the advocates of the Old World as father of the New express a zeal that is of interest in itself. The center of this faith has remained pretty much in the Old World, particularly in Europe, for many generations. One factor in this may have been the principle of universality—in effect the unity—of world history which became popular in Germany early in the nineteenth century and still carries a certain authority in European academic circles. This concept of world history can of course not survive if the pre-Columbian New World maintains its position as a major isolate, which may have something to do (along with a sensible conviction that naked savages can't build civilizations) with the determined, if not at times fervent, efforts to achieve what the European theorists frankly designate the desired "breakthrough."

But the civilizations of the Old World were based on sown cereals, the plow, the cow and the ass (or the goat or the pig), and the wheel. Is it possible the technicians sent to America could have left all those behind to bring only countless cargoes of art motifs instead? And obviously none of them, on the return voyages, carried back the New World products that after Columbus took the Old by storm: potatoes, tomatoes, corn, rubber, chocolate, all the list of more than 100 agricultural items that now make up three-fifths of the world's crops. Of all these products, only a half dozen or less seem to have occurred in both the Old and New Worlds in pre-Columbian times: coconuts, calabashes, sweet potatoes (rather clearly carried from the New World to Oceania), and maybe peanuts are the most likely candidates for this rare honor.

More significantly still, apparently none of the supposed Old World culture-bearers brought the new diseases that, as we have seen, within only a few years after Columbus were well begun on their death-dealing work of wreaking the greatest demographic catastrophe in recorded history.

These diseases are now believed to have had their Old World origin, for the most part, in the herds kept by Old World people at the distant beginnings of Old World societies. The multiple effects on these societies of their pastoral foundations will be discussed later. It will suffice at present to note that the societies so formed differed in important fundamental dimensions from the New World societies, which, except for the minor enclave of llama herding in the Andes, had no past of flocks and herds.

The important point is that the American high cultures differ basically from those of the Old World, as they differ also from each other.

Clearly pre-Columbian contacts with Old World civilizations can have been of no great significance in the direction taken by the development of the American civilizations, or those basic differences would not have remained basic.

Undoubtedly there were occasional contacts, transoceanic, even transpacific. There were some 10,000 years for them to be made in, and any craft, no matter how primitive, once launched on the bosomy deep can conceivably be carried to very strange and faraway places indeed. Perhaps some of the earliest contacts by sea came by way of the Aleutian Islands. Appearances of Norsemen on the eastern coast of North America unquestionably took place. Chance trips (involuntary) between Africa and South America would have been fairly probable.

With the beginning of settlement on the nearer Polynesian islands, beginning about the tenth century A.D., some trips back and forth (with a bow to *Kon-Tiki*) certainly must have occurred. There were indubitable later contacts between Asia and the Northwest Coast; some of the results re-echoed to Hawaii and thence the far western Pacific, back to the doorstep of Asia, to create scholarly confusion today. There are a number of recorded instances of Chinese junks and Japanese fishing vessels driven ashore on the Northwest Coast; there must have been many more during the previous unrecorded centuries. But except for the Northwest Coast, landfall for the Kurushio current in the north Pacific, chances would have been better for accidental crossings from South or Middle America to Asia rather than the other way around. The sixteenth-century Spanish, champions of their day when it came to voyaging, tried for thirty-seven disastrous years before they found the Kurushio current and were able to make their way eastward across the Pacific to the northern California coast and eventually Mexico. Chance trips to and from Africa would have been more probable still.

Phoenicians, Egyptians, Greeks, Chinese, Vietnamese, Britons, Irish—how many wandering boatloads of lunatic marooners stumbled ashore on this land as strange as the moon in time unimaginably long ago? If the greatest epics were unsung, here they are.

And there is plenty of matter (other than metallurgy) for mystery in the marvelous fabric of New World cultures and peoples. There are the Negroid characteristics some see, or imagine, in the Olmec of long ago, or the bands of so-called white Indians, such as the highland Chachapoya of the Inca empire, famous fighters. There is the sometimes white, sometimes bearded, sometimes bald Quetzalcoatl, much too ancient, alas, to be a Viking, as the old favorite theory had it. There are the black-boned, black-fleshed Araucanian chickens that lay blue eggs that might be pre-Columbian, and might be related to the Silkies, a breed of Africa and Asia. There are the resemblances some see, or imagine, between certain written ideographs from the pre-Inca Andes and the so-called "rongo-rongo" Easter Island script, from 2,000 miles out in the Pacific and 1,000 years later in time.

Some culture elements must have been exchanged to be sure, and it is interesting to guess what they may have been. None could have been fundamentally important in the formation of New World civilizations, for the reasons previously noted. The culture exchange business is notoriously deceptive;

some alleged resemblances turn out on closer examination to be quite doubtful; some root back to the primitive Ice Age soil out of which both the Old World and the New World grew.

But the Old World civilizations turned one direction and the New World another. Besides the basic differences already noted—the plow, the wheel, the herd, sown grains (to which could be added an all but endless list of other highly practical possessions, from iron and the keel and the chimney and the bellows to stringed musical instruments)—prevailing patterns of Old World civilizations were tailored around a core of kingship and inherited personal wealth, private property particularly in landed estates, individual competition for acquisition of wealth, this leading to an individual spiritual and intellectual freedom and commercial and technological progress, but also leading to true war and the ultimate business of genuine military conquest.

New World civilizations exhibit these various aspects, so fundamental to the Old World, as exceptions rather than the rule. Communities were usually under the rule of councils, a veritable kingship pattern being exceptional. Much property, and particularly land, was usually held by groups. Individual competition for individual acquisition of wealth at the expense of one's neighbors was uncommon. As a consequence individual spiritual and intellectual freedom was not customary; spiritual and intellectual activity was pursued, rather, in group participation. Belonging, as is said elsewhere in this volume, was more important than belongings. One believed, felt, strived, rather as a member of a group than as a solitary individual, in comparison to a typical subject of Old World societies.

The basic unit of social construction in the New World was kinship—family relationship. The basic unit of social construction in the Old World was property relationship.

The great reigning motive of life in the New World civilizations was always religious—from the earliest archeological reconstructions to the arrival of the Europeans religion appears to have been the principal and almost the only key to the organization of society, religious behavior the chief force everywhere, from the wildest people of the woods to the most dazzling Maya cities.

The great reigning motive of life in the Old World was acquisition of wealth, property, business, the commerce of individual gain and individual ambition, leading to (as noted) the ultimate business triumph of veritable military conquest, and in this worldly welter religion was only one of many forces. Business assumed so large a role so early that Pindar, in seeking to illustrate how much he loved his homeland, said, "I will put your interests even before business."

A society must be the product of its total time, not merely of this or that hypothetical instant of culture-contact. Every impulse that enters or goes out from it, crosses over it or clashes with it, develops within it or is rejected by it, the thoughts that are not thought as well as the thoughts that become ideas, all must contribute to any society's complex pattern, a pattern infinitely too intricate for glib dismemberment into similarities of art motifs or furniture styles. In the New World patterns were formed that were elaborately distinctive from those formed in the Old World, and distinctively American Indian.

CHAPTER 10

March of the Metal Men

To Europeans with an eye on income, the New World was a disappointment from the first; Columbus's two sons, pages to the queen, were bedeviled in the summer of 1500 by a crowd of malcontents returned from Columbus's Indies who (wrote the younger son, Ferdinand, in later years) would shout after the boys, "There go the sons of the Admiral of the Mosquitoes, of him who has found lands of vanity and delusion, the grave and ruin of Castilian gentlemen."

In the same year, 1500, Columbus and his brother (appointed governor of Española) were sent home to Spain under arrest to await the settlement of open civil war in Española over who got what part of the colonial profit, such as it was. In those days, before Mexico and Peru, ready colonial cash came mainly from Indian slaves or brazilwood, or, for officials, from the crown as salaries, frequently in arrears—so far, for the crown, expenses were outrunning returns.

To Europeans with an eye on a broader vision of genuine wealth rather than quick loot, Columbus's great discovery announced truly a new world, where nothing would ever be the same again. Columbus's first letter from the New World, written on shipboard in February 1493, was published in some thirty editions in Spanish, Latin, Italian, and other languages during the next five years. On his way back to Spain as a prisoner in 1500, Columbus wrote in another letter, less often quoted: "I should be judged as a captain who went from Spain to the Indies to conquer a people numerous and warlike, whose manners and religion are very different from ours . . . and where by divine will I have placed under the sovereignty of the King and Queen our lords, an Other World, whereby Spain, which was reckoned poor, is become the richest of countries."

For the people of this New World, meeting strangers whose manners and religion and military might were very different indeed, their world was not merely changed, it was shattered, to be dismembered piecemeal in succeeding generations.

Christian Spain, at the time of Columbus's discovery, was in the first flower of a militant nationhood, newly united under Isabella of Castile and Ferdinand of Aragon. At the same period came the final end of the long reconquest of the last of Spanish land from the Moors; the fall of Granada, marking the close of that age of troubled enchantment in which war had seemed the natural order of life, came in 1492. The first objective of Ferdinand and Isabella was to unify their raw, jangling, quarrelsome domains under the strict rule of an absolute monarchy. They made efforts to expel the Moors and the Jews, and among the many councils they established for various special tasks was the Council of the Inquisition. They extended royal sway over towns and castles with the help of their secret police and seized for the crown the grand commanderships of the powerful orders of knights.

They followed what were then, in the hour of Europe's birth of nations, the newest and most modern ideas: one nation, one speech, one God, one king, adaptations raptorial as well as defensive, particularly well suited to the consumption of prey; adaptations creating a rigid dictatorship in which the king's word cut through any law and the king's hand covered every thread of the national existence.

With the establishment of colonies in the New World a foreign trade office was set up in Seville and later placed under the supervision of a royal Council of the Indies. Through this council the crown controlled—and closely—all colonial matters; until her death in 1504 the "crown" meant Isabella alone, for she alone had title to the Indies operation. Multitudes of laws were placed on the books dealing with overseas trade, exploration, mining, church, colonists, and Indians. (One of the earliest, instigated by a well-meaning Isabella years before any smallpox epidemics, was a law to prohibit Indians from taking so many baths, as bound to be injurious to their health.)

Columbus, governor general in the Indies, distributed lands to the colonists and tribute payments to be met by the Indians. Endeavoring to appease rebellious colonists in 1499, he gave to each settler not only a grant of cultivated land but also the Indians living on it, to be exploited as the new owner wished for the new owner's profit. This was the beginning of the *encomienda* system, formally decreed a few years later (1503): villages of Indians were "commended" to the care and protection of an *encomendero*, who could exact their labor, but as free men (technically) and for pay (technically). This resulted, in most cases, in total slavery. Encomenderos commonly spoke of owning their Indians; Cortés raised money by mortgaging his encomienda of Indians in Cuba when, being a young man long on promise but short on cash, he was appointed to lead the expedition to Mexico.

Expedition after expedition received the royal commission and sailed forth, first from Española, then from Cuba. One after another hurled itself against Panama, in search of its storied gold and pearls and Southern Sea, only to be beaten back by tropical fevers and by the poisoned arrows of the people of the little chiefdoms there, who were usually friendly at first but customarily alienated in short order by slaving, murder, torture, and extortion.

A number of questionable notions are widely held of the early Spanish conquests, one being that the Spaniards merely walked in and took possession, frightening the simple Americans into fits of submission by their horses and godly cannon. As has been seen in the case of Mexico and Peru, it seldom worked that way.

It was true that the Indian inferiority in offensive weapons and especially in tactics was immense; in many cases the Spaniards (well-armored) were up against nothing more serious than rock-throwing mobs. The infinitely superior organization and supply of the Europeans were certain to prevail in the long run—if a long run could be managed. It was also true that the strangers often gained a foothold with the help of a peaceful or even hospitable welcome, and with the help of Indian allies. But with all this, the opening of hostilities could still bring man-sized fighting in which the Spaniards could lose as well as win.

The Spanish soldier was considered (after the Swiss) the best of his time, as the Spanish horse, sprung from the breedy Barbs and Arabs of the Moors, was the toast of Europe. Ingrown chivalry reached its most rococo luxuriance among the Spanish knights but so far it had only made them unbelievably vain and valiant: lean, fanatical El Grecos not yet distorted into Don Quixotes. They habitually tackled matters that required more guts than sense, and more greed than either—they raised their war cry "Santiago!" (Saint James!) in the face of any odds, if the smell of gold was in the offing. Above all, they were bounteously equipped with grand gestures—Cortés literally burned his boats behind him on the beach at Vera Cruz when he started inland to the Aztec capital city, and hanged a couple of his men and cut off the feet of another who conspired to return to Cuba.

The driving forces of hot new nationalism, zealous religious solidarity, and capable armed strength under direct central authority eventually gorged Spain on fat New World pickings, but it was far from easy. The *Conquistadores* earned their name.

(The chief expansionist power in Europe at the time, the Ottoman Turks, conquered and held more territory in Europe—fighting Europeans—during the first century after the discovery of America than the Spanish, with all their early conquests, were able to take in the same period from the Indians of the New World.)

But with all their boldness and ultimate superiority of arms and organization, it is (to repeat) noteworthy that those Conquistadores who won usually did so with some Indian help. As a rule those who lost, such as the leaders of the first two formal expeditions to Panama, who met utter disaster and left hundreds of Spaniards dead in the jungles and sand dunes, had none.

And so Vasco Núñez de Balboa, a destitute ex-colonist from Española, too poor to outfit himself as a proper conquistador (it was an expensive line of work), stowed away in a barrel on a ship bound for Panama, there successfully romanced the daughter of Careta, cacique of Coiba, made friends with Panciaco, son of Comogre, cacique of Comogra, and with God's grace and such allies became a leader of men and fought his way to the Pacific.

And now expeditions went forth from Panama as a base, from Mexico, and later from Peru, and from every little conquest in between, like hungry wolves plunging into a giant carcass in search of the richest mouthfuls. The royal permission to explore continued to provide the explorers with a percentage of profits and governor-generalships of new lands found—powerful incentives for rapidly expanding exploration. But the geography of territory assigned was necessarily vague, leading to contest, intrigue, and conflict between rival would-be conquerors. And so when expeditions bumped against each other they fought or sued or preferred charges before the king. Superior courts, the *Audiencias*, were set up in the New World to unsnarl such imbroglios.

Expeditions sent north from Panama by the governor there met and fought with expeditions sent south from Mexico by Cortés, and prospective conquistadors from Española who had wangled new royal permissions met and fought with both. One of the faithful comrades in Balboa's wild surmise was Francisco Pizarro; when five years later a new governor of Panama had Balboa arrested and beheaded as a too-dangerous rival, faithful old Pizarro made the arrest.

The first to enter the country of a chief named Nicaragua brought back more than 30,000 recorded baptisms, and gold trinkets and pearls in the amount of more than $100,000. In the next five years at least four more expeditions plundered up and down the Costa Rica-Nicaragua-Honduras region, often accompanied by hordes of Indian allies happy to help the mighty strangers destroy their traditional enemies beyond the mountains.

Survivors of the destroyed people were branded and sold as slaves. A missionary usually thought of as biased in favor of the Spanish conquerors wrote in the 1540s that in Mexico the Indians "were treated inhumanly, and regarded as being lower than beasts . . . great flocks of them, like sheep . . . were branded so often that, in addition to the principal royal brand, their whole face was marked up, being rebranded each time the slave was bought and sold."

The usual ultimate fate of the allies was to be granted in encomiendas, although important men among them might be rewarded with fiefs of their own, to help hold their people in line. Although there was a risk that persons of means could sooner or later find themselves in the hands of the torture squad, the Spanish military professionals operated on the European model, knowing no other. In Europe the velveteened burghers of a submitted town who hadn't paid enough to buy their safety were as a matter of course given a touch of torture to make them cough up the last of their silver spoons. You got at the real marrow of truth by cracking joints. Were these people of the Indies any different? Didn't they too have joints to pull apart?

Bartolomé de Las Casas, the first priest ordained in the New World and son of a veteran of Columbus's first voyage, thundered against the encomienda practice, but it persisted. The encomenderos enjoyed being feudal lords and enjoyed their profits; the Council of the Indies continued to hope abuses could be corrected; all agreed it was certainly vicious and absolutely destructive of Indians; but it was certainly convenient for the encomenderos and above all it was certainly worth money.

Las Casas received his baptism of fire when Cuba was "reduced" by blood and terror. He tried in vain to stop the carnage, and at last was impelled to call down on reducer Panfilo de Narvaez a wrathful, wholesouled, and formal curse. (One of Columbus's gentle Tainos, being burned at the stake, refused baptism for fear that in heaven he would find more Christians there.) From this time on Las Casas raged through the New World, and back and forth to Spain, swinging a propaganda sword of truly archangelical proportions on behalf of oppressed Indians.

Racing each other for the fattest mouthfuls, the people from heaven coursed the seas and the shores, the mountains and the plains. Another Mexico, another Peru, might be just beyond—the pagans always said so. Mines of gold or silver might be anywhere, or spices or pearls; and there were sure to be slaves for the taking, and souls to be saved for Christ.

The Huasteca, on the old northeastern frontier of the Aztec country, threw back a Spanish attack from the sea, were swamped by an invasion of 40,000 (so they said) allied warriors under the leadership of Cortés, rose again against the strangers when Cortés turned to fight and defeat a new rival Spanish intrusion. An officer under the orders of Cortés subdued them in a manner recalling Aztec days—he rounded up 400 of the principal men and sacrificed them to the new gods by hanging.

Tangaxoan, a chief among the heretofore never-conquered Tarascans to the west, was one of the many local caciques from all over Mexico who visited Cortés, made submission, was appointed a Spanish satrap, and gave the strangers a center in his territory. But many other Tarascans refused satellite status, and their country long remained a fighting frontier. A leader of the Otomi to the north was commissioned a captain-general of Spain by Charles V, made a Knight of the Order of Santiago, given the Christian name of Nicolas de San Luis, and with the help of another Otomi satrap, Fernando de Tapia, held the northern frontier for Spain for thirty years.

The Maya gave up hard, with wars and repeated invasions that went on for years. At one time five different Spanish adventurers were stalking each other in the highland Maya country—Cortés, as usual, came out the winner. Pedro de Alvarado, the febrile young Sun God, marched to Guatemala with 400 Spaniards and 20,000 Mexican allies, and then spent an equal amount of time in Spain politicking to keep the profit from the rather meager winnings he had seized. He gained an extraordinarily villainous reputation, deserved or not, even among his Indian confederates. He went through the country, wrote Las Casas, "killing, ravaging, burning, robbing, destroying."

Las Casas won that round—the battleground of frontier Tuzulutlan (Land of War) was given to the Dominicans in 1540, who renamed it Verapaz (True Peace) and kept it pretty much as such for three centuries.

Cortés, when he marched to Honduras himself to settle matters, became involved in one of the great epics of Central American exploration just getting there through the jungle. He took along Cuauhtemoc, his captive Aztec king; crushed though the Aztecs were he seems to have been wary of Cuauhtemoc, and watched him as if he were a time bomb. On this Maya campaign Cortés's nerve broke and he had Cuauhtemoc executed, charging rumors of a conspiracy. Bernal Díaz was skeptical, and wrote that the killing "was thought wrong by all of us who were along on that journey." Recently discovered documents, though, lend some support to a possibility that Cortés acted in the genuine belief of a real threat.

On this trip, Cortés married off the Lady Marina to one of his captains, Don Juan Xaramillo, and presumably she lived happily ever after. Cuauhtemoc's widow, the fair Tecuichpo, his cousin and a daughter of Moctezuma, later became the wife of a prominent Spaniard, Don Thoan Cano, and mothered an illustrious Spanish family.

Among the Maya, the Xiu family frequently made alliance with the Spaniards, giving aid that is regarded as crucial to the eventual establishment of Spanish authority. Most of the other Maya chiefdoms kept up an incessant guerrilla warfare that by 1536, after more than ten years of fighting against two major invasions, succeeded in driving—for a time—all the Spanish out of Yucatan.

During the following interval of comparative peace, the Xiu people and the Cocom people continued their long feud, ornamented with murder, treachery, and massacre, until the repeated Spanish invasions at last prevailed.

The ancient and powerful Itza family, however, remained a problem for another century and more. Finally, in December 1695, having just refused again a Spanish embassy (led by a member of the Cano family), they sent word that they would be ready to accept conversion after one more year, which they did, in 1697. Some scholars have wondered if this may have been an instance of Maya intervention in history to make events conform to prophecy: for more than 1,000 years the Itza had been defeated and driven from their homes every Katun 8 Ahau (recurring roughly every 256 years). A Katun 8 Ahau fell in the 1690s (there is uncertainty as to the exact year, either 1695 or 1697)—could the date of ultimate defeat for the Maya gods have been chosen to match the ancient pattern?

The last shreds of the Maya civilization went with their books "as they contained nothing but superstition and lies of the devil, we burned them all, which the Indians regretted to an amazing degree and which caused them great anguish." Thus wrote Bishop Landa from Yucatan. ("With rivers of tears we mourned our sacred writings among the delicate flowers of sorrows," wrote the unknown poet of the Book of Chilam Balam of Tizimin.)

Bishop Landa's zeal in torturing idolaters brought scandal, investigation, churchly rows, and left a persistent touch of sullenness in the air. The subjugation of some Maya groups went on for generations longer. The Lacandon Maya of the Chiapas forests have held out into our own day. But the grandeur was gone, and the Maya renown. They sank into the anonymity of "indigenes."

With the conquest of Mexico and Peru the carcass of the hemisphere had lost its liver and lights. But the magnitude of early Spanish penetration is more evident in its extent of contact than of conquest. Early conquest was limited and insecure, but by the middle 1530s, when men who had sailed with Columbus were still living, the Spanish had already built solid contact with by far the largest population blocs in the New World.

Estimates of the total hemispherical population before Old World invasion scatter all the way from 10 million to more than 100 million. Middle-of-the-road guesses thirty and forty years ago assigned 7 million or so for Mexico and something near the same for Andean South America, but these numbers have by now been revised (again) dramatically upward.

Projections calculated from detailed analysis of Aztec and Spanish tribute rolls reached some 25 million for the pre-Spanish population of the area of the present country of Mexico (modern Mexico did not get to that figure until after 1940). Later estimates have now gone as high as 30 to 37 million (modern Mexico did not get there until after 1960). This teeming population, whatever its precise level, was reduced by disease and other Conquest-related disasters to an eventual seventeenth-century nadir of 1 to 2 million.

Most of the total hemispherical population was of course concentrated in the Mexican and Andean areas, chief targets of early Spanish activity, usually presumed to have been roughly equal in numbers.

In the vast fringe area that was North America north of Mexico, population estimates allow a far smaller total than that concentrated in the high-culture areas below the present Mexican border, and yet here too recent guesses have brought drastic revision. Five to 6 million souls for the present contiguous United States, Canada, and Alaska seems acceptable to many specialists, with possibilities of twice that or even rather more under consideration. The U.S. nadir was 250,000 in 1890.

But though Spanish penetration had reached the heaviest populations, the total body of the New World's nations had only been scratched. The number of separate tribes, or distinctive groups, then inhabiting the Americas is all but immeasurable; estimates here really run wild.

Conservative guesses put the number of mutually unintelligible languages in North America at 500 or so, with twice that easily possible. South America, the world's greatest land of Babel for variety of language, would have contained perhaps 1500, to make a grand total for the hemisphere of something between 2000 and 2500. Linguistics people prune these language thickets into families of several hundred or several score or still fewer (sometimes far fewer), tracing and arguably (sometimes very arguably) connecting various relationships.

But linguistic diversity is one of the worst of scales for measuring separate groups of people. Neighboring populations may be very closely related in everything except language—as are the speakers of some provincial languages in modern France; while many independent societies widely differing culturally and racially may speak the same languages—as in the varieties of English-speaking people over the world at present.

The evolution and descent of language lie in perhaps the most mysterious corner of all humanity's history.

What shall I do (says a song from Texcoco), you who hear me?

CHAPTER 11

The Plumed Serpent

The Valley of Mexico, with the heaviest populations and richest economy of sixteenth-century Mesoamerica, was centered on Tenochtitlan and such provincial hubs as Chalco, Azcapotzalco, Culhuacan, and the like. This region suffered the most spectacular damage from the generations of disaster that followed the Spanish conquest.

Twenty-eight huge epidemics ravaged the country between 1520 and 1597, multiple epidemics in 1545–1548 and 1576–1581. The estimated population of the entire valley in 1519 was cut by more than half in fifty years, by more than half again in the next fifteen years, finally to a residue of some 100,000 by the middle 1600s.

Survivors were relocated into *congregaciones* or encomiendas; agricultural terraces fell into disuse and became grazing lands in the vast holdings of new Spanish owners.

A new city was laid out on the site of Tenochtitlan and crushed Aztec gods were used in the foundation of the Cathedral of Saint Francis. Cuauhtemoc, the last Aztec leader, having been captured alive, was put to the torture to make him reveal the rest of the Aztec treasure, but there wasn't any left. (Cortés had to answer for this indignity to a royal person later in a formal trial before the royal Council.)

The people of Tlaxcala, as a reward for their faithful services, were specifically exempted from being distributed in encomiendas. Cortés wrote the king that he had wished to avoid the system altogether in New Spain, but the Spanish settlers could not exist without it (so they said). The Council of the Indies, less and less encomienda-minded, decided they would have to exist without it and revoked the encomiendas, but the colonists, as was usual with unacceptable commands, found ways to get around the Council's ruling.

In theory, land grants to Spaniards were given an appearance of legality, either by being made from lands not under Indian use, or by being obtained in one manner or another from Indian "lords." Some of these "lords" and "kings" were maintained in their supposed hereditary authority by Spanish support, and several, such as Ixtlilxochitl of Texcoco, were officially ennobled and became grandees of Spain.

The rightness or wrongness of this Spanish supposition became a lively issue in later studies, the crux lying in the presumption of private property and a landed hereditary aristocracy.

The Azteca, to use them as a paradigm of the various Mexican peoples, founded their social and political organization on a group (possibly a kin-group) known as the *calpulli*, the basic structural unit of society, from which all larger organizations, towns, cities, city-states, were built. Although, says a leading authority, "We are still a long way from understanding either the composition or the structure of this basic unit."

Most *calpultin* appeared to be well-defined groups that could include farmers and craftsmen, administrators and commoners and nobility, to the number of several hundred or even several thousand people, but that were not necessarily geographical units. Thus the calpultin did not make up the standard territorial divisions used in administration—these were distinctive neighborhoods, called *tlaxilacalli*, eighty or more making up the city of Tenochtitlan. Recent research indicates the calpultin in the city may have numbered sixty; twenty used to be the usual guess.

Local officials of bewildering identity—the Spaniards found themselves calling the same person "captain of the guard" and "abbot"—served in each calpulli, as well as a *tlatoani*, or "speaker," who was also a member of the city's ruling council. This council in turn chose four executives for the four quarters of the city. A supreme ruler was selected by the ruling council from among these four principal executives.

This top job was for life, and was filled from the same family or patriclan, which could explain why the Spaniards referred to such officials as kings. Primogeniture was not followed, and the election appears to have been really an election ("they cast votes for . . . brave warriors . . . who knew not wine . . . the prudent, able, wise . . . who spoke well and were obedient, benevolent, discreet, and intelligent") but otherwise the *tlacatecuhtli* (chief-of-men), *hueytlatoani* (revered speaker), or *tlatoque* (usual title for chief of council in the Nahua cities), or by any other name, was a right royal figure, even godlike.

The residence of the revered speaker, in an administrative center called in Nahuatl *tecpan* but called by the Spanish a "palace," contained halls and patios where top officials did their daily work, judicial, diplomatic, military, conferring with subordinates or with local groups summoned to discuss or perform this or that task. Another large "palace" occupied by the official known as the Cihuacoatl was filled with functionaries busy with the mundane operation of the city-state—water, sanitation, hygiene, streets, and canals.

The nub of the problem of Spanish interpretation was not in calling the elected tlacatecuhtli a king—after all, their own Charles I, grandson of Ferdinand and Isabella, had just become Emperor Charles V of the Holy Roman Empire by election—but in assuming the tlacatecuhtli enjoyed absolute one-man rule as a real king should; in calling the councilors "nobles" and assuming they possessed individually all the hereditary rights and privileges, particularly in property, that the title implied to the title-worshiping and property-worshiping Spanish mind; and in assuming as a matter of course the private ownership of property, especially land.

As we have seen in the case of the great Tezozomoc, powerless in the midst of all his mighty power, or Moctezuma, stoned to death by his people when he tried to urge them to a questionable course of action, the apparent ruler, godlike figure though he might be, was far from being any absolute monarch.

It appears that as long as his gestures were perfectly proper the illusion of absolute rule might prevail. But clearly a major policy conflict could reveal him for what he evidently was, a symbol only symbolizing authority, possessing none of his own beyond that of any elder with the right to speak in council.

The propriety of his acts seems to have been determined by their religious correctness. As a specialist has put it, religion "intervened" in areas we would regard as remote from its bailiwick: religion controlled commerce, politics, and war; religion expressed the purpose of the state, the purpose of education and right action, the purpose of life. Everything, even conquest with all its pleasures, was subordinated to religion.

This situation we have noticed before and will see again in these pages. The Inca world seems to have come close to breaking out of the crystal shell of religion, providing thereby one measure of the profound differences between the Inca and Mexican worlds. And yet across its gulf of difference, Inca organization, with its ayllu corresponding to the calpulli, its council of state presided over by the regents of the four quarters of Tawantinsuyu, strikes note after note of sameness with the Mexican city-state, as well as with many other examples of American Indian political organization.

The Aztec tlacatecuhtli, the "emperor" as the Spaniards called him, fulfilled important priestly functions; it may be rather as representative or even as the personification of Quetzalcoatl. The second in rank in the Aztec state, mentioned above, represented the earth goddess, Cihuacoatl, Serpent Woman.

The great minister Tlacaelel held this post during much of his public life; after his death the minister in this job was called the Cihuacoatl, possibly as a result of Tlacaelel's history-propaganda program designed to give the Aztecs a proper prestige.

Together these two leaders, the Quetzalcoatl and the Cihuacoatl, embodied the concept of dualism that appears again and again as one of the basic ideas in American Indian thought. They were the dualism of state and religion, the dualism of the things of the spirit (Quetzalcoatl) and the things of the earth (Cihuacoatl). They were, in the view of some students, representative of the dual government, the government outside the walls and the government inside the walls, so commonly met with in American Indian political structure. For the world outside the walls, the tlacatecuhtli seemed to personify the totality of the city-state; for the world inside the walls the Cihuacoatl was the very model of real workaday authority.

In actual authority both were without doubt principally dependent on the consent of the council, and all that entailed of clan and family intrigue, ward politics, factional logrolling, and, most markedly, of theological dexterity.

Somebody (possibly Tlacaelel?) popularized the idea that the revered speaker, the Quetzalcoatl, was actually the direct descendant of the real god, Quetzalcoatl. Somebody (possibly Tlacaelel?) popularized a story that the last of the famous Aztec predecessors, the last of the Toltecs, and thus (of course) genuinely a descendant of Topiltzin Quetzalcoatl, had impregnated twenty maidens from the leading Nahua lineages so their descendants would all be genuine descendants of Quetzalcoatl, thus creating, for the enchanted Spanish chroniclers, the hereditary nobility. (A few minutes with *Nobiliario Español* or *Burke's Peerage* or an old *Almanach de Gotha* might leave a suspicion that twenty maidens and one progenitor could in 100 years create only wild confusion in the blueblood business, even—maybe especially—with the help of precise written records.)

The problem of ownership has always provided great difficulty in our understanding of the Indian world. This is particularly true with the Aztecs, one of the most highly stratified and in our sense of the word one of the wealthiest Indian groups in North America. But with few if any exceptions land was in group ownership, used by the calpultin, religious groups, warrior societies, administrative groups, or any or all such groups in combinations that were doubtless clear and reasonable to Mexica understanding but in the sources available to us are contradictory and puzzling.

On occasion, lands seem to have been bestowed by the Aztec leadership on noteworthy persons for noteworthy services—Tlacaelel was said to have bestowed such grants. These may have been special tracts set off for the purpose of raising tribute from areas of recent conquest, the crops to be gathered by slaves for the grantee or perhaps for his associated group or groups. One of the most thoughtful of specialists on this subject suggests the possibility of some heads of patrimonial estates exercising "such tight and enduring control" that one could speak of private estates. Much present opinion, however, sees such "private" estates of minimal importance and probably linked to the role of their "owners" in the administration of the state.

Such rare examples might point up the basic generality that the ownership of land, or as the social scientists like to put it, the accessibility to specific lands and produce, seems to have been inextricably involved with the function of the agency in ownership—never as something to be individually bought and sold. The same fundamental situation existed in Inca Tawantinsuyu, as has been seen, and—with a few exceptions, such as on the Northwest Coast of North America—was as universal throughout the New World as the concept of private property in the Old.

It is probable that certain groups, certain lineages, held a preferred position in regard to certain offices or sorts of activity, or to certain perquisites. It is possible that among the Aztecs and their predecessors, and among the Inca and their predecessors, the use of various sumptuary items—jade, turquoise, gold and shell, featherwork, sandals with ocelot ears—was supposed to be limited to certain groups. It is possible that the "emperor" held custody of various treasures, predominantly works of religious art, in his position as the living embodiment of the godhead, similar in some wise perhaps to religious treasures held by a European cathedral or religious chapter. But there is no indication they were owned as personal property in the European sense—treasured up as wealth, to be spent for the owner's personal pleasure, invested at interest, sold at the owner's personal whim.

A special conception of ownership—that we cannot own things, no matter how desirable they may be—is visible at the very foundation of ancient Mexican thought. It is the constant theme, as has previously been mentioned, of the finest poetry: we can own only our own soul, the quality of our own behavior, "the remembrance of a good act."

The description by Nahua priests of one of the principal Aztec religious observances, the sacrifice of the matchless (captive) youth who had spent a year as the personification of the god Tezcatlipoca and who climbed alone the pyramid to his death, casting aside at each step the gorgeous and valuable possessions he has (temporarily) owned during the year of his godly role—the description concludes with the words:

For whoever rejoices in possessions and
prosperity
sweet things and riches
ends in nothing and in misery.

The point is ownership precisely, and its unreality, its ephemeral quality. It is a strain not unknown in the West: Book Two of Boethius's *De Philosophiae Consolatione* makes much of the fact that "we cannot lose external goods because we never really had them. . . . The beauty of fields or gems is theirs, not ours." And the theme of carpe diem delighted dangerous Rome ("put out the wine and the dice," says Virgil, or at any rate a poet some claim is Virgil, "and perish who thinks of tomorrow"), but a minor strain, a philosopher's game.

But in ancient Mexico, the basic idea.

The youth chosen to impersonate Tezcatlipoca was dressed and adorned in the greatest magnificence (Moctezuma himself arrayed the young man, arrayed him as the god), taught to converse with the greatest grace; he went where he pleased attended by his servants and his beautiful women, and everywhere he was honored, before him the people bowed and kissed with reverence the earth. Someone who didn't know might have mistaken him for the "emperor" himself; wherein, probably, lay the whole idea: the daily statement, before the eyes of all, of a philosophy incarnate.

The significant fact will be discussed later in this book that the theme of sudden riches so common in Old World literature—Ali Baba, Aladdin, Jack and the Beanstalk, and their countless relatives—is (with a few exceptions such as in Northwest Coast cultures) absent in the songs, poems, and tales of the New World peoples. Great Rabbit of the North American woodland stole magic to impress the people. Coyote of the North American West stole the heart of God to invent death. The Aztec children were decked in rich finery when they were taken to be sacrificed for the magic of rain.

Magic yes, riches no.

Even among those Northwest Coast people obsessed with wealth, the attitude was strangely distorted: witness a Haida Air,

A rich woman
cedar bark and slaves within reach
sitting above a dish of steamed halibut
eating with a spoon

someone too powerful to look upon
came in and stood there
the house shaking

and cut her through and buried her bones
and wore her skin
and became
a rich woman
cedar bark and slaves within reach
sitting above a dish of steamed halibut
eating with a spoon.

The ownership of things in common had been remarked upon from the first by Europeans. Columbus wrote, "Nor have I been able to learn whether they held personal property, for it seemed to me that whatever one had, they all took shares of." Even the simmering pepper pot, Columbus noted, seemed to be free to any neighbor who wanted to fill a gourd, even—to his amazement—in starving times.

But it struck too deep a root of difference to be grasped. Europeans simply could not comprehend. Likewise, the people of the New World had nothing in their experience comparable to the European spirit of competition for personal gain.

Much more was at issue here than a difference of abstract ideologies. Ramifications ran through every tissue of life. These two worldviews, each never dreaming of the other's existence, had really created two totally different worlds.

On the one hand, the communal outlook produced attitudes tending toward cooperation and group identity that were reflected to some degree in every gesture of Indian existence, from practical jokery to religion. On the other hand, the ingrained custom of personal acquisition at the expense of one's neighbors, of striving in constant competition against each other, colored every aspect of Old World life and thought.

In ancient Mexico, "freedom of thought, individual liberty, personal fortunes, were non-existent," wrote one of the most penetrating of modern archeologists, but "an Aztec would have been horrified at the naked isolation of an individual's life in our Western world."

The major point I am making here is the closeness of an interrelation (symbiosis is the favored word at present) that Europeans could never have felt, but that could exist in all levels of a New World community.

But a symbiosis quite beyond conquistadorial perception; and since the only thing to be done with the incomprehensible is to pretend it does not exist, the Spaniards blithely designated council members "nobles" and owners of "estates," dealt with them as landed aristocrats, called on them to furnish feudal tribute and service from their peasants, and married their daughters, thereby founding some of the leading families of a later Spain as well as of a later Mexico.

The Spanish gave deeper thought to what they could see of Aztec religion, especially after the missionaries settled in and the whipping and burning of the so often "sullen" and persistently idolatrous natives became a common topic of official correspondence.

The famous Aztec sacrifices have fascinated one and all to the exclusion, nearly, of the rest of Aztec history. The offering up of human lives in the belief that this gravest of transactions would keep the shaky world upright and maintain their cherished way of life is again something inconceivable to our civilization, even though we fight wars today for rather the same reason, offering up everybody's life. Or the Mexican sacrifices might be compared to the Old World's public executions—800 hangings for crime in a normal sixteenth-century English year, crime that could be theft of more than a shilling or 199 other capital offenses, and the more edifying beheadings of political losers or the spectacle of the best and the brightest (Joan of Arc, Giordano Bruno, and their ilk) burnt alive, or those of incorrect religious views put to death in an endless variety of excitingly painful styles.

Or for more detail, the county clerk of Middlesex County, the country about the city of London excluding the city itself, kept statistics on crime and punishment for ten years beginning with 1609: 736 people hanged or pressed to death, thirty-two of these by the *peine forte et dure*, three of these women. In the pressing to death of peine forte et dure, the accused was fastened to the dungeon floor on his or her back and weights piled on the chest until death; the purpose of this was to extract either a confession or a plea of not guilty, for without one or the other the accused could not be sentenced to death and the forfeiture of chattel property. Thus the accused could save his or her property for the family by refusing to plead, and dying in "unutterable agony instead of by hanging." The author sums up however by stating that the "most brutalizing punishments of the time were the public whippings" of both women and men.

All these were in a very obvious sense sacrifices to gods of property and propriety.

A widespread general impression that Mesoamerican sacrifices were relished by their savage and bloodthirsty public is clearly in error. The most authentic descriptions, such as those in the Florentine Codex, dwell more on tears than on blood—the chief at dread Culhuacan wept that the god Tezcatzoncatl had to be fed with death. He wept that it might not be; he wept. He wept that the god Axalaco had to be fed. He wept that it might not be; he wept. And Old Wolf, in charge of captive warriors held for sacrifice, wept for them at their death, as if for his sons Old Wolf wept.

The annual death of Tezcatlipoca, object of reverence by all during his year's life on earth, was a tragic business but absolutely essential, if the gods were to permit the people to maintain their cherished way of life. Sad necessities have always been a part of life, and very likely the general Aztec public thought no more often of these necessary deaths than we think of traffic accidents.

In fact, the automobile and its enormous toll in traffic deaths and injuries may offer a fairly apt comparison in the world of today: anyone seriously suggesting that we should abolish this custom of human sacrifice by abolishing the divinity, the motor vehicle, would surely be regarded as out of his mind, and all our highest priests—economists and political scientists—could easily explain that the motor industry, spewing out an ever-increasing stream of roaring idols, is a principal support of our cherished way of life.

Even a modest request to reduce our traffic sacrifices by reducing the top speed of all vehicles to, say, fifteen or twenty miles an hour would surely be greeted by universal refusal if not universal derision. Power may well be enthroned at the head of the modern pantheon, the weaker we become as individual animals the more we idolize the god of power, and communion with this dearest of gods is at our instant command simply by stepping on the gas.

And while we are shocked if someone we know is chosen for one of these random sacrifices, we nevertheless when driving past cannot resist slowing down, stacking up traffic behind us for miles, to ogle the smashed bodies, our eyes as avid as any Aztec's.

Concrete facts and figures concerning the Aztec sacrifices are suspect, having been composed or interpreted after the Conquest by converts who may have been eager to please their new holy men. For example, the recorded 20,000 victims at the previously mentioned dedication of Huitzilopochtli's temple: several post-Conquest chroniclers give the number of victims all the way from 20,000 to 80,000. All agree that the victims stood in long lines, extending far out on the causeways, that the two sponsoring kings themselves tore out the hearts of the first two victims, and that two teams of priests then took over, relieved by other teams when they tired. Some say the work took one day, others that it required up to four days, from sunrise to sunset.

Now the feast of Huitzilopochtli occurred in May, when the days between sunrise and sunset are about twelve hours. So we picture the four sacrificial assistants seizing a victim, throwing him on his back and holding him down on the convex altar stone, while the fifth man of the team gouges into his chest at the fork of the rib cage with an obsidian knife, finds the heart, saws and tears it loose, offers it to the sun, and deposits it in the Stone of Tizoc. The body is then dragged away and hurled down the temple steps, and the next victim is seized.

Even allowing for the most practiced efficiency on all hands, it is hard to imagine this being accomplished in less time than, say, one minute per victim. At that rate two teams could theoretically finish off 120 victims an hour, or 1,440 in a twelve-hour day, or 5,760 for the outside limit of four days.

Sherburne Friend Cook, a professor of physiology as well as one of the finest American historians of our time, allotted three minutes per sacrifice rather than the one minute my ignorance of physiology is willing to imagine. Applying his three-minute time to my foregoing calculations yields a grand total of 1,920, rather closer to 2,000 than 20,000—a reasonable error in reading the commemoration stone?

CHAPTER 12

Cornfield and Kiva

The impracticability of trying to express American Indian history and society in European terms may be one of the most important revelations conveyed (unwittingly) by the work of early missionary chroniclers. This has been recognized for quite a while by a number of scholars who have turned instead to analyses that might shed light on Indian thought as a frame for New World history.

This approach has been useful not only in the study of literate groups—Yucatec Maya for example, with possibly a very ancient literature indeed, accompanied by an unusually abundant ethnography—but also for the history of nonliterate societies, where ethnography and archeology can sometimes work together in presenting a picture of the past. (Although, as an archeologist has confessed, ethnologists and archeologists don't talk much to each other.)

Ethnographic information can reveal New World communities concerned more with ritual, belief, group gratification, than with profit and production. Says an apologist for this information, "This is not to argue against a materialist approach as one way of looking at archaeological data; it is to refute the suggestion that it is the only way."

The deepest unbroken past thus found among New World societies may be in the Southwest of what is now the United States. Here, in timbered mountains and semiarid river valleys and sunburnt deserts dwelt (and still dwell) peoples descended from inhabitants of this same country, living in basically the same way, never catastrophically disturbed, for at least 9,000 years. Such seems archeologically probable, judging from what appear to be related sequences of artifacts stretching across this giant reach of time. While every conquering Ozymandias in all history rose and fell and was forgotten, these people, peaceful people, grinders of meal and singers of songs, lived on, as natural as sunlight.

They appear to have sprung from the primitive culture given the name Cochise by archeologists, their relics consisting more of grinding stones (for wild seeds) than projectile points, thus embryonic farmers thousands of years before farming came into being. They lived along the banks of lakes and streams that then existed in their country, left over from the Ice Age, then just ended. The women gathered seeds among cottonwoods and hickory trees and the men hunted among such roaming beasts as mammoths and dire wolves (which may have lingered on a little longer here than elsewhere). Some 7,000 years later, the lakes and Ice Age animals long since vanished, the nearest hickories hundreds of miles away, their land a yellow desert of salt bush, mesquite, scarce water and rare rivers, and tall dust devils rising each noon to dance, they emerge as gardening if not quite farming peoples given by archeologists the names Anasazi, Mogollon, Hohokam. These groups are regarded by most students as clearly ancestral to the Pueblo people of New Mexico and neighboring regions, and to the Piman-speaking people of southern Arizona and neighboring regions in Sonora.

Our imaginations are so constructed that we cannot envision time: time is invisible unless we see it in relation to something in motion—a river standing still while life comes and goes on its banks. There are not many other places on earth, perhaps none, where time in this sense, uninterrupted time, has gone on so long as among these Southwestern communities, still living today where their remote ancestors had lived so long ago, still farming as had their recent ancestors of only 2,000 years or so ago.

The Hohokam of the deserts and rivers of southern Arizona had many things familiar to the belt of farming villages that ran all the way south to the Valley of Mexico and beyond, all the way to Central America—little clay figurines (sometimes turbaned, and with earrings, and often, of course, ripe, and female), a snake and bird as the commonest religious motif, mirrors made of flakes of iron pyrite set like mosaic work in stone plaques, ball courts (after about A.D. 500) and the rubber balls to go with them, and the jingling copper dance bells that were traded so widely from Central America and Mexico. While the Maya flourished and declined, while the Toltecs came and went and the Aztecs took their place, these people planted their corn and pumpkins, hunted the little desert deer, and squeezed some sort of benefit out of nearly everything that grew on their sundazzled horizon. Around A.D. 1000 someone among them seems to have developed a process of etching, using weak acid possibly made from fermented cactus juice (from the fruit of the saguaro, source of their ceremonial wine) to etch designs on seashells that had come

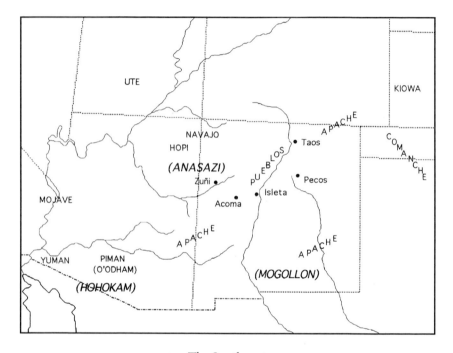

The Southwest

by trade from the Pacific. After a century or two the practice ceased; it may have been a single family's magic secret. It is the first known use of etching in the world.

The Hohokam who lived in the river valleys, their center in the region where the Gila meets the Salt, in the vicinity of present-day Phoenix, developed some of the most heat-tolerant and drought-resistant plants in existence, and built miles of irrigation canals, tremendous undertakings comparable to the city-building in the Valley of Mexico not only in their construction but in their constant maintenance. Scholars and modern farmers (and modern politicians) argue about how many thousand acres were under irrigation, but single ditches, some as large as twenty-five feet wide and fifteen feet deep, have been surveyed that ran as far as sixteen miles, and one network alone along the Salt River totaled 150 miles. The irrigation systems were well under way by A.D. 700 and reached their maximum size 600 or 700 years later. The first Europeans to see them naturally but wrongly supposed they had watered large cities; a Spanish priest wrote more than 200 years ago of "a very large canal still open for the distance of some two leagues [six miles] . . . it appears to have supplied a city with water, and irrigated many leagues of the rich country of those beautiful plains."

One reflection of the great civilizations far to the south is the occasional occurrence of rather rudimentary (at the most about ten feet high) mounds, evidently meant as platforms for temples; one recently excavated near Gila Bend, Arizona, offers a hint of its purpose in the presence nearby of a large cremation area, containing burned human bones and offerings of dance bells and the points of darts or arrows. But some things the Hohokam had not at all in common with the mighty world of far-off Mexico—among such things they possessed, especially, a resolute democracy and peaceableness, an almost aggressive nonaggressiveness.

There was no division into classes, in spite of the organized labor the canals must have demanded, involving close cooperation among numbers of villages. There are few indications of war and fewer of aggressiveness in the archeological record, and while there is a sharp decline in their material culture after about A.D. 1400, maybe with the entrance of Diné raiders from the north, forebears of the Apache, the later Hohokam descendants seem to have retained much of the same spirit, a spirit of quietness and peace.

For a long while in modern times these people were called the Pima, a misnomer applied by missionaries due to a misunderstanding, and still remaining as the name of their language stock, Piman. (To the missionaries' questions they answered, "Pima," a word meaning "No, I don't know," but taken by the missionaries to be their name.) They are now known by their own real name, O'odham, meaning, as tribal names often mean, The People, usually elaborated into River People (Akimel O'odham). Their cousins, living south of present Tucson, were long known as the Papago (from Papa O'odham, Bean People), but have now also adopted their own more common name, Tohono O'odham, Desert People. This tribal name was often spelled in the last century Aw-aw-tam, giving an indication of traditional pronunciation. Obviously "Hohokam" is a cognate.

Each family among the Hohokam as among the historic O'odham lived in the same sort of earth-and-pole house built over a dropped living room floor, and even the house of the most respected elder, the house of the most holy priest who lived with august dream beings and gods, the "house, enveloped in white winds and white clouds, into which we went to perform our ceremonies" (in a later Piman description), was only somewhat larger than the others, if different at all. The manner of government might have survived in the Tohono (Papago) council of four from whom was chosen one, the best and wisest, to be the principal leader—we seem to have heard of this before. But the spirit that made this government work is best revealed in a line from a Piman children's tale, a line expressing, in fact, a spirit typical of aboriginal America, from the disciplined Aztecs to the befuddled Amazonian ayahuasca-heads: "I . . . went to consult a man of authority, to whom a boy should not have had the temerity to go."

When, eventually, habitual war did come to Pimeria and the people discovered a knack for it and fought well and hard, like beasts of prey, like raptorial birds, so say their songs, a successful warrior returning (bringing the four hairs from his enemy's head that customarily served them as scalp or trophy) had to undergo the sixteen-day cure for insanity. Many Indian societies required purification ceremonies for warriors who had killed, but not usually quite this purifying. Ceremonial war speeches of the O'odham collected in 1900 by Frank Russell all close with the ritual phrase: "You may think this over, my relatives. The taking of life brings serious thoughts of the waste; the celebration of victory may become unpleasantly riotous."

Studious individuals with their gaze fixed on the past sooner or later go a little nutty; every now and then someone springs up shouting he has found the secret of it all. Today, when historians and archeologists work with biologists, geophysicists, agronomists, chemists, the whole palette of the solemn sciences, and when the comparative advantages of solid carbon or gas sample methods in radiocarbon dating, or the beautifully esoteric mechanics of submarine geology, have become as meet for discussion as pottery sequences or Etruscan inscriptions, the secret of it all seems much nearer. The intricate wizardry in the darkened laboratories, the awe-inspiring formulae in the physicists' notebooks, can only reveal Truth, can't they? But it is really very difficult to fit scientific theories of human behavior around ancient fears that the celebration of victory may become unpleasantly riotous.

For the real stumbling block is that these attitudes of peace and quiet may be rooted very deeply indeed, as deeply as any attitudes of savagery. There has been a tendency for a long while to associate the deepest instincts with the most savage, the underlying idea being that all men are ferocious by nature but that some (like us) have been steadily moving upward from their savage beginnings when they brained each other daily. There is, in addition, a current fashion of extracting structures of natural (and therefore unavoidable) fascist human behavior from the behavior of animals from apes to ants, positing thereby an instinct for mayhem, especially in connection with some notion of "territoriality" as the deepest bias of all life.

But the history of Indian America is riddled with instances of inexplicable (to us) pacifism, and with instances of the willing surrender of territory or seemingly anything else—even lives—merely when asked. We have seen this with the peaceful Tainos who died by the millions after welcoming Columbus with such open hearts to Española. The people, wrote Columbus, are "wonderfully timorous . . . timid beyond cure." Their general lack of serious resistance to outrage—any outrage no matter how outrageous—leaves our best experts lost at sea: "*Although* peaceful and lethargic, they possessed considerable intelligence and were quite emotional," says one of the best, with my italics.

The peaceful Taino and the savage Carib raiders who preyed upon them, both of a reasonably equal "primitiveness" in their material culture, might be supposed to represent survivals of equally primitive attitudes. For an extreme example of instinctive pacifism and meek surrender of territory—even to the ultimate territory of life itself—the Arawakan Chané of the eastern slope of the Andes were seemingly dominated, enslaved, eventually destroyed as a separate entity by bands of Guarani, all without any evidence of fighting back; an early Spanish explorer reported 400 Guarani "owning" 4,000 Chané, regularly rounding up a few (said the early explorers) to butcher and eat.

The peaceful people of the Southwest (although far from being this peaceful, nor particularly "primitive") could trace their pedigree of nonaggressiveness back to a very early root, surely one of the deepest roots of their being. Maybe the sons of Abel have always been with us too.

In this connection a further word might be ventured about the famous Hohokam irrigation canals. Theories sometimes put forward by present-day scientists of society insist that large community undertakings such as irrigation systems require a class-ordered community culminating in despotic masters and submissive commoners driven under the whip. But, as has been remarked, the considerable work of constructing the Hohokam irrigation ditches and the continuing work of maintaining them did not, evidently, trouble the resolute egalitarianism of the Hohokam people.

We have seen a similar mystery among the very early stone buildings on the coast of Peru, leading a few heretical observers to suspect there may be more than one road to civilization (or, even more heretical, more than one sort of civilization).

East of the Hohokam country, in what is now southwestern New Mexico, was the land of the Mogollon culture, possibly ancestral, it is believed, to some of the present Pueblo Indian groups a bit to their northward, such as, perhaps, the Zuñi.

Their homeland centered in the Mogollon Mountains for the thousands of years from Cochise times to their gradual disappearance from this region in the fourteenth or fifteenth century A.D. They achieved what is probably the all time highest point in the art of Southwestern painted pottery, with the marvelously clean and beautifully executed Mimbres style, dating from about A.D. 1000 to about 1400, when, coeval with the change in Hohokam ways, they vanished, possibly, as mentioned, to merge into Puebloan beginnings in country on their north.

The Anasazi ("Ancient Ones," the name bestowed by modern Navajo in speaking of the ruins of long-ago towns) heartland was in the high, broken country where the four corners of New Mexico, Colorado, Utah, and Arizona come together: red-rock canyons and sagebrush flats, grasslands in the rolling foothills, juniper ridges and pine-clothed mountains.

The multi-thousand-year past of the Cochise culture is sometimes given by archeologists a special designation of San José for the Anasazi area, where ties with this past are particularly obvious. The earliest Anasazi are called the Basketmakers, from the many examples of their extraordinary basketwork that have been found—some of them watertight for cooking vessels (hot rocks were tossed in until the mush boiled). The Basketmakers appeared during the final millennium B.C. in or about their Four Corners heartland; they too lived in houses built over a dug-down floor until, about the seventh or eighth century A.D., they began building their houses entirely above ground, of logs and adobe mortar and then of stone. At about the same time they acquired the cultivation of cotton and beans to add to their crops of corn and squash, and slowly changed their way of life in becoming genuine farmers.

Clans—a mother and her married daughters and their families—joined their houses together in a single structure of a number of rooms, and finally a whole village dwelt in the same many-roomed, multistoried building.

The pit houses remained as religious centers for the men—subterranean chambers, usually circular, entered from the roof, with paintings of gods around the walls and the mystical hole in the floor, the *sigapu*, to remind the devout of the birth of their first ancestors from the belly of the earth. These chapels are known today as kivas, from their Hopi name.

It was for a long time believed that the Basketmakers and the modern Pueblo Indians were separate peoples, representing two distinct "migrations," since the earlier Anasazi, the Basketmakers, seemed to be a long-headed people, and the later Anasazi, the Pueblos, a relatively roundheaded people. It has since been found that in Europe as well as America most people's heads have been getting rounder down through the centuries, for reasons still not altogether clear. It was also discovered that the later Anasazi had picked up the fashion of skull deformation, flattening the backs of their heads by strapping infants to cradle boards, which made their skulls look rounder than they were naturally. It is now generally agreed that the Basketmakers were direct ancestors of the Pueblo, although there have been other intermixtures.

Seen in close focus, a given Anasazi "pueblo" (Spanish for "town") was a right little, tight little, closed little world, and years passed, sometimes a great many, while the people sang up the corn, called the rain with puffs of pipe smoke and clouds of eagle down, danced together with their mother, the Earth, worked together, laughed together, gradually became grandparents and died and watched with their mountain-mahogany faces through the unchanging masks of the dancing gods while their grandchildren gradually became grandparents—and nothing interrupted, nothing penetrated, nothing interfered.

House timbers from a single site in the Canyon de Chelly, now part of the Navajo country in Arizona, give tree-ring dates from A.D. 348 to A.D. 1284. Dates from the Mesa Verde complex of cliff and cave pueblos, and pueblos built in the open, cover 1,000 years, A.D. 300 to A.D. 1273. The mesa-top pueblo of Acoma, New Mexico, has been continuously occupied for more than 600 years to date. The Hopi are believed to have lived on or about their same three mesas in Arizona for 1,500 years or more, and their modern villages of Old Oraibi, Shungopovi, and possibly Walpi have been continuously inhabited for at least some 800 years.

But seen from a long view, the Anasazis moved, merged, split, built, and abandoned towns, appeared and disappeared from every compass point. Strangers entered, and sometimes learned Anasazi ways and themselves became Anasazi—and sometimes did not. In an early Anasazi burial there is a foreigner wearing moccasins, centuries before moccasins replaced the Anasazi sandals, and his body had been cut in two and then sewed together again; did the Basketmakers wonder what he was made of? But the Anasazi world seems to have offered a happier way of life than most of its neighbors knew and so it expanded willy-nilly, naturalizing many varied groups of people.

Nonaggressive though this expansion generally appeared to be, there must have been contentions, with each other as well as with wandering people of the wood such as the Utes of the Colorado Rockies; the communal buildings were sometimes made as defendable as fortresses. But the more usual motive that put people in motion seems to have been the death of old fields through drought or erosion—or other natural disasters such as a volcano eruption (it left a scar now called Sunset Crater near Flagstaff, Arizona) c. A.D. 1066 that sent a pre-Pueblo people fleeing from their surrounding homes; when they came back years later to fields now fertile with volcanic ash, Puebloan and Hohokam people came with them.

The square-shouldered figures in Basketmaker petroglyphs range over a wide area. The clearest religious symbol—if it was a religious symbol—of later Pueblo times, a humpbacked ithyphallic love god usually shown in petroglyphs playing a seductive flute, may perhaps be another indication of a religion not exactly marked by austerity.

By the time of the Classic Age of the Great Pueblos (1100–1300) the way of life of the Pueblo world had grown offshoots and tendrils that reached from Nevada to Texas. These people spoke different tongues in different villages and were in no sense a single "tribe." They were related only in that they all followed a remarkably similar way of living.

The art and architecture of this way of living came to its finest hour in the Great Pueblo Age. In the canyon of the Chaco River (northwestern New Mexico) are the ruins of a number of giant community houses. The best known of these, Pueblo Bonito, rose four and five terraced stories over three and a half acres, contained 700 to 800 rooms that may have housed up to 1,200 people, and great circus-ring ceremonial chambers, kivas, never equaled in later construction; and, like a medieval cathedral, was a 150 years building, from the year 919 to 1067 (by tree-ring dates).

Eight towns were built in the canyon, four others on nearby mesas. Some seventy other sites in the general region have been identified, such as the recently located Salmon Ruins, near Farmington, New Mexico, with 300 rooms, built in six years at the end of the eleventh century.

Networks of roads from the canyon to outlying communities ran as far as forty-five to sixty miles, with widths up to thirty feet, reminiscent of the Maya sacbeob. Ceremonial avenues for religious processions? In addition to flood-plain gardening some irrigation systems were worked out in Great Pueblo times, one in Colorado using a mother ditch more than three miles in length. The course of streams may have been sometimes altered—for agricultural purposes only, or for ritual purposes, as suspected in certain instances in Peru? (In Peru's Cajamarca valley two sites dating to the second millennium B.C., Layzón and Agua Tapada, may have been joined into a single ceremonial system by the famous Cumbemayo Canal, nine kilometers long. The first 850 meters are carved in bedrock in an elaborate series of zigzags, presumably with some cultural meaning.)

Judging from the many kivas and dance courts, religion must have been a constant occupation, an indication that the congregations regarded it as the best part of life as well as sacred duty. Constant duty tends to become onerous; hence the usual necessity of high-powered high priests to keep up its enforcement. But among the Great Pueblo people, as among the Hohokam, there were no distinguishable high priests—distinguishable, that is, by any upper-class attributes. The highest-ranking theocrats were evidently only simple farmers like everybody else.

The people made feather cloth and colored cotton cloth (high style sashes, masterfully designed, have been found in burial caves where they had kept like new in the dry air of the Southwest), beautifully decorated pottery and elegant jewelry, particularly of turquoise, some necklaces containing thousands of worked stones.

Other impressive ruins of this period have been found in the northern reaches of San Juan River, and along McElmo Creek and other San Juan tributaries within the previously mentioned Mesa Verde complex, and in the Kayenta region on the Arizona–Utah state line.

Roundabout the end of the thirteenth century this Great Pueblo world began to shrink in upon itself. The people drifted away from the principal northern centers until many were left abandoned.

Tree rings tell of a long and murderous drought, a period of twenty-three almost utterly rainless years (1276–1299). This would seem to have been enough in itself to have filled the land with the dispossessed.

It is also possible that wolf packs of the immigrant Athapaskan-speaking Diné began to push their way in from the north at about that time, a little earlier than reaching the Hohokam, twanging their new and improved weapon, the sinew-backed bow (as against the flimsier oak or skunkwood bow of the Pueblos) with a new and improved arrow-release (arrow held between first and middle fingers, pull on string with fingers) that pulled three times the power of the less sophisticated release (arrow held between thumb and first finger, pull on the arrow) then apparently in general use in the Southwest.

For whatever reasons, times were hard and troubled here and there in the Pueblo country, and burned villages here and there and butchered unburied bodies were left to prove it.

Or, the desertion of many of the great communal dwellings has also led to theories from some archeologists that perhaps they simply grew too large for the local-option Pueblo democracy, and the people chose to stick with neighborhood rule and small towns. And yet even larger towns appeared in the following centuries—Zuñi in western New Mexico, and, the biggest of all, Pecos at the farthest eastern frontier of New Mexico.

An odd and perhaps profound episode from these times: a Puebloan population in the Tonto Basin of Arizona pulled up stakes and moved gradually southward until eventually, during the thirteenth century, they began moving in with the Hohokam along the Salt and Gila rivers. There was no invasion, no fighting, no conquest physical or spiritual on either side, so far as any evidence attests. The two peoples lived mingled together for several generations, probably about a century, and each people followed its own customs— the Pueblos made tobacco pipes (the Hohokam smoked ceremonial cigarettes); the Hohokam got drunk once a year on their cactus juice, welcoming the green sun of summer (the Pueblos didn't drink); the Pueblos buried their dead (the Hohokam practiced cremation). Kitchenware and houses remained pretty much in their separate styles, which were considerably separate, with the single exception that in both cases house entrances faced the east, as did the house entrances of many other right-thinking Americans everywhere. Otherwise the houses of these Puebloans—the Casa Grande ruin in Arizona is an example, described in 1764 as "of four stories which are still standing; its ceiling is of the beams of cedar . . . the walls of a material very solid, which appears to be the best of mortar"—were a far cry from the humble Hohokam dwellings.

About the year 1400 these Puebloan people by then resident so long among the Hohokam began moving on again, maybe south into what is now Mexico, maybe northeast to the Zuñi towns of western New Mexico, ending an instance of tolerance between strangers that has left archeologists bedazzled, not to say bemused. The Hohokam people stayed where they were, eventually to become the Piman-speaking O'odham of today.

For the Pueblo world in general the center of things shifted a little southward, from the present New Mexico-Colorado line to the pueblos in the country of the upper Rio Grande in New Mexico and scattered villages in the same latitude westward among the deserts and mesas into Arizona and eastward to the headwaters of the Pecos.

In the reeds along the rivers, in the willows on the creeks, in the dust-veiled red-streaked canyons, the still wind of time never died. In their heaped-up earth-colored towns the Pueblos prospered, diverse and yet identical. Some said one thing and some another, "Posoge," "Tséna," "Pajo," "Paslápaane," for the Big River, the Rio Grande, or "mowa," "piki," "hewe," for the paper-thin cornbread everybody made; everybody also made the sweetened dumplings— blue cornmeal mixed with ashes, sweetened by mouthfuls of chewed stale bread—that the old men traditionally filched from the pot, spearing them with splinters as quickly as they cooked.

Among some, the people were divided into two birthright groups, the Summer People and the Winter People, each group taking turns at running the town for half a year. Among others, the head of a certain society automatically became the town leader. Among most, men grew the corn and women ground it, and among some the husband owned the house but among more the wife owned the house and everything in it, including the corn as soon as it was brought in from the field, and a man belonged more to his mother's house than to his wife's, and was more the preceptor of his sister's children than his own. Among some, membership in the various societies whose important activities filled the days was inherited; among others, one could choose what religious, war-making, hunting, medical, or social clubs he might wish to join. Some wore cotton clothes and some, living too high in snow country to raise cotton, wore buckskins.

But the Milky Way was to all, with different words, the Backbone of the World, and all knew, under whatever names, the Corn Maidens, and the powerful gods, the kachinas, who had granted men the right to wear masks and represent them in dances of prayer. Most also knew the koshare, gods of sunshine and laughter and instruments of discipline by public ridicule, who had granted the same privilege of remembering them in masks when they had gone away long ago to their homes in the east. To most, in common with many other people all over the Americas, the first gods on earth had been two brothers, and men of authority were still called elder brother (the Aztec term for, so to speak, an army colonel).

All knew the fragility of the world's harmony and the danger of throwing it out of key by wickedness, ignorance, or accident. Evil magicians did so on purpose, and when one was caught (you could sometimes tell them by their harsh and aggressive nature; they also gave themselves away by such acts as peering in through a window at night), he might be hung by the thumbs until his shoulders were crippled for life, or until he died.

There were beasts, trees, snakes, birds, mountains, stars, of supernatural power, and a right way of living in concert with them, from presenting a newborn baby to the sun to the wealth of pageantry surrounding the growing of the varicolored corn. Some of these rituals were complex and the formal property of specified organizations of priests, but some were not, such as cleaning up the pueblo for the arrival of the harvest (so "the corn will be glad we bring it in"). Anyone could pray anywhere, as long as it was done the heedful way, with a good heart, and votive offerings were also optional (a feathered prayer stick from a man, generally, a sprinkle of cornmeal from a woman).

The first rule of this living, above all, was everything in moderation, nothing too much. None of the ecstatic religious visions of the Mexican eaters of the narcotic peyote or the narcotic mushroom, the *teonancatl*, although a powerful narcotic, *datura* (Jimson weed), grew at hand. This was sometimes used as an anesthetic at Zuñi for putting a patient to sleep while the director of a curing society set a broken leg or, with an agate scalpel, cut out a tumor, but even then it was usually given only to women or children; men did not need such nonsense. The Pueblo people knew and used at least seventy medicinal plants, some restricted by secret power-invoking, evil-averting ritual, some free to all—in moderation, and if used with a good heart. Plants too were living beings; one talked to them, and if the words were genuine the plants talked back.

There was none of the furtive, self-conscious fear of sex so important to many other peoples, Indian and otherwise—he's a likeable fellow; he's always in trouble over women; so ran a common, casual phrase in some pueblos. Puberty, menstruation, even childbirth, were not ringed around with supernatural terrors. There was little dread of the dead, or the dramatic, hysterical grief so common among many other people, Indian and otherwise. Grief was kept deep but decently within, and the most beautiful of pottery was broken in the grave. There was none of the ascetic self-torture, the gashes, the blood, the wild saintly suffering so important to many other deeply religious peoples. The body was purified for certain rituals by induced vomiting, as among many Indians, but a yucca-suds shampoo was more usual. There was little of the dour, haughty exterior associated with such warrior people as the Aztec; most of the Pueblos liked a man who, as the saying still has it, talked easy and talked lots.

No excesses; industry, sobriety. But the women were expected to make a social bee of the never-ending community work of grinding corn, and the right way of doing things could also include a man at the door of the grinding room, playing the grinding song on a flute.

Each gesture of living was an obeisance to living the right way, in unison with each other and with the past and with the rest of the living world, an acceptance of living, a reverence for living—in moderation. The Pueblo people made a divinity of living, in moderation.

Nothing too much, said the classic Greeks, and these words were placed on the wall of the temple of Apollo at Delphi, their most venerated shrine. Nothing too much, moderation in all things, one of the foundation stones of the ancient Greek world.

These sentiments would have been equally at home in the land of the Pueblos.

On a day in May in the year 1539, foreigners appeared at Hawikuh, the westernmost of the Zuñi towns; they were Indians from the south, some 300 in number, most of them furnished by the governor of New Galicia (Francisco Vásquez de Coronado), but they were led by a man who was a new thing to Pueblo eyes, a man who was black. He was Estevanico (Stevie), a Negro from the west coast of Morocco, a Spanish slave, and (for the European history books) the discoverer of New Mexico. He was a veteran at meeting strange Indians, but whatever it was he did at Hawikuh, it must have been wrong.

Some say, with a TV ring, that the medicine rattle he carried was recognized by the Zuñis as having been made by a people who were their "traditional enemies." Some, leaning more to the adult Western, say the Aristotelian epistemologists of the Zuñi council were affronted by the black man's doubly fantastic claim that a white man was coming along three days behind him. Some say Estevanico made piratical demands for girls and turquoise. Perhaps some of Estevanico's Indian bearers happened to reveal that he represented a people who would come bringing war.

Whatever it was, the Zuñis, after a long deliberation, took up their bows and killed him. Panicked fugitives from among Estevanico's Mexican Indians fled with the news to the party of the white man three days down the back trail, a Franciscan friar, who sprinted back for Mexico "with his gown gathered up to his waist." But in midsummer of the next year, when the corn was just beginning to ear, a terrifying army appeared from the south that contained not only white men, along with more Indians from Mexico, but hundreds of weird and gigantic beasts that were horses and mules.

The Zuñis collected at Hawikuh the warriors from all their six or seven towns, sent the women, children, and old people of Hawikuh to hideouts, probably high on the top of Corn Mountain, their sacred mesa, and telegraphed each movement of the approaching strangers with smoke signals from town to town. When the strangers arrived at Hawikuh, the Zuñis were inflexibly defiant. The Spaniards begged them repeatedly to submit without fighting, while the Zuñis came up to the very heels of their horses to shoot arrows at them and try to drive them away, until at last the "Santiago!" was raised and the town was stormed.

The Spanish leader, Francisco Vásquez de Coronado, was battered with so many rocks hurled down on his gilded helmet that he was knocked unconscious and carried from the field "as one dead," but the taking of the town was only the work of an hour.

An even larger army, the main force of the Vásquez Coronado expedition, came up from the south in September, with more horses and mules and even odder animals—pigs, sheep, goats, cattle, and with white women and children. The whole horde moved on to the pueblos of the Rio Grande for the winter.

The reports of the expedition list seventy to eighty pueblos, with a total (at a broad guess, probably low) of some 20,000 to 30,000 inhabitants, stretching from the Hopi towns in the west, almost as far west as the Grand Canyon country, to metropolitan Pecos (with its five plazas and sixteen kivas) on the edge of the great plains to the east; and from Taos in the north to the Piro towns in the south, in the region of the present Socorro, New Mexico. The Zuñis spoke their own language, the Hopis a Shoshonean tongue, and the other towns a variety of languages now gathered into two general groups, Keresan and Kiowa-Tanoan (this last including Tewa, Tiwa, Towa—spoken in great Pecos—and Piro), which does not mean that all the speakers of each group could converse with each other, any more than an Englishman can talk Dutch.

But they were all the same people by their way of life, as the Spaniards immediately realized, and what one of Coronado's private soldiers (Pedro de Castañeda) wrote of Zuñi he meant for all: "They do not have chiefs as in New Spain, but are ruled by a council of the oldest men. They have priests, who preach to them, whom they call *papas*. [This was the Zuñi word for 'elder brothers.'] These are the elders. . . . They tell them how they are to live, and I believe that they give certain commandments for them to keep, for there is no drunkenness among them nor sodomy nor sacrifices, neither do they eat human flesh nor steal, but they are usually at work."

During the winter of 1540–1541 they were usually at work for the Spaniards, who took their food, blankets, women, and houses, and when the people resisted took their lives by sword, fire, and rope—although with real regret. It comes through rather clearly that in spite of their disappointment at not finding riches, the Spaniards genuinely liked these brave and modest little people and were impressed by them. Vásquez de Coronado earnestly did his utmost to avoid violence. But why wouldn't they submit? Unfortunately the Pueblos didn't have any history of submission. They didn't know how. Even the quiet Hopis insisted on a fight.

The Hopis' name, by the way, is their own word for themselves, from Hopitu, "peaceful ones"—most names Indian people use for themselves simply mean people, or people of such and such a place, as Englishmen means men of England, but the names by which we have come to know them are seldom their own. The Zuñi name for themselves, for example, is Ashiwi, "the flesh," while Zuñi is a garble of the name the Keresan-speakers called them: Sunyitsi, meaning unknown. The Zuñi called the Keres people "drinkers of the dew," one of the few examples of poetic names. The Tewa Pueblo people got their name from a Keres word meaning "moccasins," which might provide a hint as to the order of their coming to the Southwest (or as to their taking up first a new style?).

In the summer of 1541 Francisco Vásquez Coronado led his army eastward onto the great plains looking for cities of gold and found only Indians living in grass houses; he returned discouraged for another winter, and in the spring of 1542 all the strangers trailed away and went back to Mexico except for a couple of small missionary parties that stayed, one at Pecos (consisting of "a very saintly lay brother," a young slave, and a flock of sheep) and one that returned to the people far out on the plains, in the country the Spaniards called Quivira, this a sizable operation under the command of an ordained priest, with two Indian "donados" (lay brothers) from Zapotlán, a Portuguese soldier-gardener, a black freedman with wife and children, and sheep, mules, and a horse. This, doubtless the first Christian mission regularly established in what is now the United States, came to grief in short order with the death of the priest at the hands of unknown natives. The Portuguese gardener, Andrés do Campo, accompanied by the two donados, made it to Mexico after an epic journey of several years; he arrived "longhaired and his beard hanging in braids." The report naturally got about that the lay brother and his servant left at Pecos had also been martyred, but nothing definite of them was ever learned.

It was forty years before any Spaniards returned (1581), and then only a tiny party of Franciscan friars and a few soldiers from the mining frontier in what is now Chihuahua; two of the friars stayed among the Rio Grande pueblos with a few Mexican Indian assistants, expecting martyrdom, which they received, probably as soon as they tried to interfere with the dances of prayer. A pious merchant came up with a small group the following year to find how they were faring and learned they had been slain, but also found several Christian Indians who had come up from Mexico with Francisco Vásquez Coronado forty years before and had lived among the Pueblos ever since, and who told great tales of great riches they had heard about—among other trifles a lake of gold. So in the following years a few more small bands of the white strangers appeared, mining-camp toughs for the most part, hanging Indians right and left along their way in approved mining-camp style; Spanish soldiers sometimes came along in pursuit and took them away.

But in 1598 a whole population suddenly arrived, 400 men, women, and children, 7,000 head of stock, more than eighty ox-carts, *carretas* (that is, more than eighty started; sixty-one got through). The land of the Pueblos was being colonized.

Only the desert pueblo of Acoma, seemingly impregnable on the summit of its steep-walled mesa, made any serious resistance; when some of the strangers tried to take blankets and food they were shot down with arrows. Other Spaniards came and fought their way up to the town, impregnable or not, killed the warriors in their kivas, and took 500 women and children back to the Rio Grande for trial. The few men over twenty-five years of age who had been captured were sentenced to the loss of one foot and "personal service" for twenty years; women, and children above the age of twelve, were given only the twenty years slavery; children under twelve were put in the care of the priests. Two Hopi men who happened to be visiting Acoma at the time were sent home with their right hands cut off, as a warning. The Spanish governor, Don Juan de Oñate, was later (fifteen years later) fined and stripped of his honors and titles by a Spanish court for these forbidden acts of violence, among other charges.

Oñate, son of one of the richest of the fabulously rich Zacatecas mine-owners, and with a wife who was descended from both Moctezuma and Cortés, colonized the new province at his own expense, in the usual way of such affairs, and lost his shirt. The country was too poor. There was no gold or silver, and not even enough corn and cotton to feed and clothe the colonists—regular supply caravans had to be sent from New Spain (Mexico), at the public charge. The tribute from the pueblos—a yard of cloth or leather and a bushel of corn a year from each house seems to have been standard, although firewood was a common substitute—helped the colonists survive but was far from enough to turn a profit. The whole project would have been called off after a few years, except that the priests had by then (so they said) baptized thousands of Pueblo people, and insisted that these new converts could not be abandoned.

This was a reflection of religious politics; testimony at Oñate's trial gave the total of a few score baptisms only, of women and children in the Spanish service ("the reason why no more had been baptized was that the friars were not interested as they believed the land was poor and that it would not be maintained permanently"). But there was sudden news of thousands of fresh baptisms, indicating either a sign from on high or a basic shift in policy here below, resulting in a new royal order retaining New Mexico in the Spanish Empire after all. Conflict between churchly orders or individuals played a role of occasional weight in empire matters.

Succeeding governors, who bought the office and had to get their money back somehow, made desperate attempts to squeeze more return out of the Pueblos. The priests, angered by the stubbornness of the Pueblos in clinging to their "devil-worshiping" dances, took increasingly stringent measures against them. The Pueblos, angered by the public whippings (occasionally fatal) of their most respected elder brothers, now and then martyred a few more priests.

After fifty years of enduring, the Pueblos joined with their ancient enemies the Apaches (who were, of course, subject to a continual open season of outright slave raids, being unsettled infidels) and tried to raise a fight against the Spaniards. It was beaten down before it got started. Twenty years later disasters struck in clusters—there was a year of death-dealing famine, and the next year a sweeping plague, and the next year a furious onslaught of the Apaches, who "totally sacked" the entire province; and two years later officials in Mexico stopped sending the supply caravans. The year after that a new governor, determined to put an end to the complaints of the priests, hauled forty-seven Pueblo "medicine-men" into custody, hanged three, and kept the others imprisoned in Santa Fe.

One of these was an elder brother named Popé, from the Tewa pueblo called by the Spaniards San Juan. He was released after several years, filled with bitterness over the punishments he had received, and went into hiding in Taos, where in the summer of 1680 he organized a real rebellion. Concerted action was very hard to achieve, due to the fairly strict Pueblo adherence to the unanimity rule—if the council of a given pueblo did not agree unanimously on the point at issue, no action was taken. ("We are in one nest," runs a Tiwa saying.) But this time all the towns except those farthest down the Rio Grande—Isleta and the Piro villages—joined in, and this one worked.

Families were massacred in outlying haciendas, priests were murdered in their mission churches, Santa Fe was held under siege for days, until the Spaniards there broke out and fled to the south.

The Pueblos attacked "with shamelessness and daring" reported the governor, and of the total Spanish population of 2,500 or so in the province, nearly a fifth were wiped out. The rest, leaving their possessions and their homes of almost a century, made their way south along the blast-furnace desert trail the muleteers called Dead Man's Road, and didn't stop until they reached El Paso del Norte, the present El Paso, Texas. The governor summed up, with infinite sadness, the Pueblo situation: "Today they are very happy without religious or Spaniards."

And the celebration of victory became unpleasantly riotous. Not only churches, church furniture, and Spanish houses were burned but pigs, sheep, anything living or dead that had been brought by the Metal People (Tewa for Spaniards). Popé, the Spaniards learned, "saw to it that they [the Indians] at once erected and rebuilt their houses of idolatry which they call *estufas* [kivas] and made very ugly masks in imitation of the devil in order to dance the dance of the cacina." The Indians said, so the Spaniards were told, that "God, the father of the Spaniards, and Santa Maria, their mother, were dead." Popé ordered that everything Spanish should be destroyed, including the plants they had introduced—watermelons, onions, peaches, wheat—but here he went too far for people who saw god in every flower and knew plants by their first names (generic words for tree, plant, bush, are often lacking in Pueblo languages); the Pueblos "obeyed in everything except with regard to the seeds."

Popé was carried away by his success, and became, or tried to become, a dictator, demanding obedience from all, seizing whatever caught his eye, and ordering instant execution of any opponents. War broke out between the towns, Taos and Pecos and the Keres pueblos remaining loyal to Popé, the other river pueblos insurgent against him. He was deposed, later restored to power, eight years after the rebellion, shortly before his death—but long before that, reaction had set in.

The excesses, the civil wars, the bewildering despotism of a leader preaching freedom, were followed by repeated Spanish attempts at reconquest, four in eight years, and for a final nightmare touch the plague returned. Many went away to the wild mountain canyons of the north, in the vicinity of the present Colorado line, and hid out for years with Ute and Apache people, while thinking serious thoughts of the waste. Others went west to the country of other "traditional enemies," the Navajo. A couple of Rio Grande villages moved all the way west to settle among the Hopi—one (Hano, settled c. 1700) is there yet. The Hopi moved their villages to the tops of their mesas, and the Zuñi people moved up to their sacred fortress-mesa, the gorgeously colored Corn Mountain that stands like a red and white banner in the desert, and stayed there for some ten years.

Twelve years after the revolt, in 1692, the Spaniards at last returned in sufficient force for a reconquest. It took four years of sporadic but sometimes heavy and brutal fighting. Some of the Hopi were now mounted "on good horses" and offered a show of force, "giving fearful yells," when the Spaniards approached their mesas, but were pacified when the Spanish commander, Don Diego de Vargas Zapata Luján Ponce de Léon, told them "I did not come to do them any injury nor ask them for anything." Eight years later, though, in 1700, a mission was re-established in the Hopi town of Awatobi; it was destroyed almost immediately, and the town around it for good measure, by the people of the other Hopi towns, after which the stubborn Hopis were left alone.

And when at last the people of the Rio Grande pueblos rebuilt their towns—most of them in new sites—they locked the years of war away and never, as a people, returned to them.

But neither, even yet, did they submit. The dances and the old ways continued, in secret in the kivas if necessary. But Spanish rule was never again as muscular as before the revolt. For Spain by then was a different Spain.

Some modern historians place the downfall of Spain, the finish of Spain as a first class power in Europe, at the Peace of Westphalia (1648), some at the Treaty of the Pyrenees (1659). Both were a very long way from New Mexico, but the echo eventually made the trip.

CHAPTER 13

Blood, Gold, and Souls

Old World history begins with empire (Egyptian, Akkadian) and continues on the same theme in our own time (American, recently-fallen Soviet).

Spain, a nation on the move toward empire, met Zuñi, a nation that wasn't going anywhere, and conquered it with an almost casual "Santiago!" in a few minutes of a hot July desert afternoon.

Zuñi wasn't going anywhere because Zuñi, in Zuñi's opinion, was already there. But Spain was on its way to building the greatest empire, as we say, that the world had ever known. It was built of Indians—without the Indians there would be no Indies, said the Conquistadores, who were bristling believers in totally immoderate power—and in this monstrous, sprawling edifice, burnished with blood and crowned with a cross of solid gold, the trifling conquest of Zuñi was surely one of the most insignificant of architectural details.

At the time of Zuñi's fall to Francisco Vásquez Coronado (1540), the Chibcha people of the Andean plateau at the topmost shoulder of South America (present Colombia) had met the conquistador Quesada and been vanquished after two years of war in a grade A conquest to rank with the invasion of Mexico or Peru. The confederacies of what is now Venezuela had experienced colonization and exploitation by agents of the Augsburg banking house of the Welsers—Charles V had given the Welsers, to whom he was in debt at the time, hunting rights in that area, the only major deviation from the early Spanish policy of Spaniards only. The Welser adventure is highly confused, everyone from priests to freebooters seems to have bought a piece of the show, but it was clear enough as far as the Venezuelans were concerned, since it scored in the aggregate one of the finest achievements in the history of New World conquest for heartless and wholesale enslavement,

147

mass murder, torture, and general rapine. The Welser concession was revoked after some twenty years.

Peru was the scene of large-scale fighting for a generation. Collaborationist Quechua troops served with the Spanish (there may have been some class-war feeling involved, subjected populations perhaps tending to swing to the Spaniards as bringers of liberty from Inca rule) against the neo-Inca Manco, a youthful brother of the murdered Huascar, who almost turned the trick of equaling his great-grandfather Pachacuti—but not quite. He held the Spaniards under extended siege in Cuzco, his peltists fired the city with white-hot projectiles, but the gods were gone. This time the stones of the battlefield remained merely stones. The new Viracochas ultimately prevailed.

In 1538 the honest old soldier Francisco Pizarro and one of his original (supposedly equal) partners, Diego de Almagro, turned to fighting each other over the spoils of Peru, Almagro being defeated and executed. Almagristas assassinated Pizarro a couple of years later and set up Almagro's son as leader, who was defeated and executed by a royal governor sent out from Spain.

In the north, at Quito, lieutenants of the murdered Atahuallpa had led a war against one of Pizarro's lieutenants, known as Belalcázar, who had bought out Almagro for the privilege of looting in the north; Almagro had previously bought out the golden boy Pedro de Alvarado, who had come down from Guatemala with 500 followers to horn in. Above them in Colombia the famous Welser advance man Nikolaus Federmann collided with Quesada, and while they argued jurisdiction Belalcázar fought his way up from Peru and joined in—all three went back to Spain to clamor before the king.

In all these turmoils Indian auxiliaries furnished the main bodies of sol-diery, Indian cities and towns the battlefields, and Indian possessions or Indians themselves the objectives—one of the bitterest issues of the civil wars and rebellions was the right of holding encomiendas and exacting forced per-sonal service, which the conquistadors indignantly refused to give up even if it meant defying king and council.

Above all, Indians remained the symbols: the son of Inca Manco, Sayri Tupac, was given a little court, possession of the rich encomienda of Yucay, and a pension as long as he appeared safely tamed; his daughter Beatriz married into a wealthy and illustrious Spanish (Basque) family, her husband the nephew of Saint Ignatius Loyola. But after Sayri Tupac's death his younger brother, Tupac Amaru, stirred the fears or ambitions of Viceroy Francisco de Toledo and in 1571 the last of the Incas was publicly beheaded in the plaza of Cuzco. Philip II was "alleged" to have given a reprimand to Toledo for this act, which appears to have been part of the viceroy's energetic campaign to vilify the memory of the Inca Empire and make the Spanish rule look good in comparison.

In keeping with this campaign, relics of Inca ceremony were stamped out with vigilance—if they could be caught in time. A notorious incident occurred in Cuzco when "the Indians participated enthusiastically in a procession in honor of St. Ignatius of Loyola; they seized the opportunity to revive one of their ancient Inca dances without the Spaniards being aware until it was done."

A lasting effect of Viceroy Toledo's presentation of Inca times as total tyranny was to cast Andean peoples in a role of immemorial serfdom, Aristotle's natural-born slaves to the life. As a result gross enslavement prospered, the encomienda had a long career, the *mit'a* continued in force throughout all the colonial period. Two centuries later the reformist Bourbon administration in Spain sent two young naval officers to Peru as members of a French scientific expedition (La Condamine's) with the assignment of preparing a confidential report on the state of colonial administration, which their report (1749) found corrupt, wasteful, vicious, "no greater cruelties are conceivable to the human mind . . . than the tyrannical activities" of the colonial officials—religious officials, alas, included. And in the words of an authority writing in the 1960s, "Even today in Andean countries many people believe the Indians to be 'subhuman' and in their treatment of Indians conduct themselves accordingly."

Elsewhere in South America in the early years of conquest, one of Francisco Pizarro's brothers, Gonzalo, led a disastrous expedition across the Andes to the upper Amazon, looking for a reported Land of Cinnamon. The countless river tribes of the lower Amazon were treated to a glimpse of the people from heaven when one of Gonzalo's lieutenants, Francisco Orellana, succeeded in a wildly surrealistic journey through the Amazon rain forests all the way to the Atlantic (1541). Eight years later another Spanish explorer, Benavente, spent some time among the Jibaro people (Shudra, in their own name) of the upper Amazon forests and may have been the first European to examine the shrunken heads they kept as instruments of sacred power. More than a trophy, the famous Jibaro "shrunken head"—actually the skin of a head (human or animal, sloth or jaguar preferred), contracted by heat to about the size and hardness of a baseball—was and is fetish, status symbol, and a most powerful religious relic. The magical ceremonies surrounding its preparation and purification required weeks; the quest for it came close to providing a respectable man's reason for being in Jibaro society. Eight years after Benavente's exploration the Jibaro country was granted in encomiendas, but the landlords who came so innocently to take possession didn't stay long; most of those lucky enough to escape were gone by 1600.

From Peru the conquistador Pedro de Valdivia made his way south across apparently limitless deserts to the pleasant farmlands of the Araucanians, in present Chile. He had the gold from his plunder—there wasn't much—made into stirrups and scabbards so horsemen could transport it to Peru. A half dozen of his men started (in 1541) with this richest equipage such cavaliers had ever boasted but were cut off by Araucanians on the way, who took the golden trappings back and left only two of the cavaliers alive to tell the tale. The Araucanians killed Valdivia himself a dozen years later and made his skull into a cup.

The New World's lure of riches came to mean silver as much as gold after 1545, when two Peruvian Indians (legend gives their names as Gualca and Guanca) made the first silver strike on the tall sugarloaf mountain, lost in the remote heights of the Andes, known as Potosí. The immense yield of the Potos's mines brought the king's fifth alone to 3,000 pesos daily in the early years—and those in the know said that in spite of official watchfulness not two-thirds of the silver taken out was registered. The beehive-shaped native smelting-oven, *huayra* (the word meant "air" in Quechua), sprang up by the hundreds on the surrounding hillsides. As has been mentioned, the New World did not possess the bellows; to achieve a fire hot enough to smelt ore it was necessary to build an enclosed fireplace on a windy hillside, with a bottom opening to catch the wind and funnel it in a draught to the fire above.

In the mines, files of Indian laborers toiled up the long rawhide ladders in the shafts, each with a fifty-pound pack of ore on his shoulders, the leader with a candle tied to his thumb; there was a resting place every 140 feet. The Indians worked under varying degrees of servitude, commonest being the *mitayos* working out the *mit'a*, or tribal labor tax, a neat custom carried over intact from Inca times.

Commonly, however, teams of Indians contracted with the *mineros* to produce a certain amount of ore, keeping the surplus for their own use, and for the earlier years the huayra was the only workable means of transforming any of the ore into silver. Some groups of Indians thus became rich. Since they were prohibited by law from wearing Spanish dress, the Indian section of the boomtown of Potosí produced native Andean costumes as elaborate as any the Incas had ever known. All could buy the coca that was "indispensable for the Indians working in the mines," and some could even pay the wildly inflated prices for luxuries that found their way from all over the world to Potosí during its boomtown years (1572–1650), when the "Imperial City" was the New World's greatest, with a population exceeding 100,000. And the universal beggar's cry all over the Spanish New World became "No tengo Potosí!" ("I have no Potosí!")

In northern Mexico the infamous Nuño de Guzman, bent on conquest toward the north, in Sinaloa, led 10,000 (so they say) Indian allies in a two-year career (1529–1531) of unmitigated atrocities, for which he was later imprisoned. Another result of this campaign was the so-called Mixton war of 1541, in which Guzman's ex-victims (or more accurately survivors therefrom) rose against the Spanish, killed priests, prospectors, and encomenderos, and destroyed crops and cattle. They dug in near present Guadalajara and fought off the ubiquitous Alvarado, who happened to arrive from Guatemala in time to participate and lose his life in this war. The revolt was finally put down by the viceroy, with 450 Spanish troops and a reported 30,000 Indian allies.

In 1548 the Zacatecas silver mines of northern Mexico were opened; they made their four proprietors (the father of Don Juan de Oñate among them) the richest men in America of their day. More mines were found, rushes of prospectors overran new country so that the frontier strode northward in seven-league boots and ranchos and towns came into being seemingly overnight—by the 1560s the area around Querétaro, 120 miles north of Mexico City, was sending thousands of head of cattle south to market on yearly trail drives, and by 1586 one of the Zacatecas bonanza kings branded 33,000 head on his ranch in what is now Durango, some 600 miles northwest of Mexico City, and even so was not the biggest operator of his region.

Indians were sold to slavery in the mines or held in serfdom on the vast estates of the conquerors, and in the incessant search beyond the frontier for fresh supplies of slaves still new country was explored, still new mines discovered, the process exploding its way along as naturally as the wind and the rain.

But the progress of such a storm front was of course furiously turbulent. Desperate fighting ran before and followed after; supply trains and cattle drives now and then included armored wagons elaborated into rolling fortresses. Indian states were laid waste in "a crusade of fire and steel, of death and enslavement" and whole populations were smashed into scattered bands of fugitive guerrillas. As one consequence history for years thought of northwestern Mexico as containing originally only "nomadic tribes," although today archeology gives us indications of high civilization all the way to the modern states of Zacatecas and Durango, with tombs and ruins still offering up pre-Columbian art objects of the highest order.

The Indian world was violently remade by these convulsions of growth in the brand-new Spanish empire, and the changes, once triggered into being by genes of greed and piety, continued in something very like spontaneous reaction, as blind as pulsing blood. Had the Zacatecas frontier leaped north to the Pueblo country, as it might well have done if the reports of Francisco Vásquez Coronado had been favorable rather than otherwise, the Pueblos too might have been obliterated as independent and identifiable societies. And it was precisely during the following decades of interlude that the Spanish government, urged on by growing criticism at home and abroad, took the most extreme measures in New World history to try to safeguard newly subjected Indians from enslavement and wanton destruction. Reforms were terribly slow, enforcement being so difficult, but efforts were pressed with dogged persistence and by the end of the century, when Oñate brought colonists to the Pueblo country, survival chances for Indian groups enmeshed in the frontier were really somewhat better.

But blind reaction also played its part in the reconquest of New Mexico, twelve years after the Pueblo revolt of 1680, a blind reaction prompted more by the story of the Sierra Azul than by any political (either churchly or stately) strategizing, the Sierra Azul being a quicksilver mine someplace in the Hopi country (so they said), a deposit so rich that little pools of liquid mercury just stood here and there over the ground, waiting for somebody to use it.

The mines of Spanish America were always in need of quicksilver, for use in the amalgamation of silver ores. One important such mercury discovery was made in Peru in 1563, at Huancavelica, and came to be regarded as Peru's "greatest mineral contribution to the empire," beyond all mountains of bullion. Only two other sources in the world supplied mercury in the needed amounts, Almadén in Spain and Idrija in Slovenia—in the seventeenth century there was a severe shortage, for various reasons, from all three. The legend of the Sierra Azul remained for a long time one of the brightest of the Spanish frontier's many golden dreams.

But who could say dreams when the reality of riches lay everywhere in this New World, for all to see? Peru was producing two-thirds of the whole world's precious metals by 1600, and the New World has produced by far the largest share of the world's silver ever since. Peru itself was for years nothing but one of those golden dreams, the fabled Birú, until the swords of Almagro and Pizarro cut it open to the light of (Old World) day. Who wouldn't dare the barbarous nations to find another Peru, another Mexico, another Potosí? To find the Land of Bimini, the Land of Cibola or Cali or Quivira or El Dorado or the marvelous realm of the White King, or the Golden Temple of Dabaiba?

And even if these were only mirages forever retreating behind the ranges, there were the lesser treasures men actually found from day to day, so common they weren't worth reporting (the king would never miss his fifth); even in ordinary graves, as in the Colombian Andes, country of the Treasure of Quimbaya and the long, long tradition of working gold, where all hands were put to work disinterring the dead, opening the graves, graves so rich they yielded thousands of pesos each.

In 1528 a certain Captain Francisco César, with Sebastian Cabot at the Rio de la Plata in South America, came back from a scouting trip of some weeks up the Paraná River to report tales of a land of great wealth to the west—he may have gotten near enough the Andes to have heard of the Incas. In 1540 the flagship of an ill-starred expedition sent down to the foot of South America to colonize Patagonia capsized in the strait—probably many of the 150 men aboard reached the nearby shore. Indian stories began to drift up to Peru of a land some place down in the mysterious south populated by white people, and these stories mingled with the old report of Captain Francisco César, which had lost everything but his magic name.

And the land of the Caesars came into being: "a city, commonly called the city of the Caesars." Rich, of course. Could there be a mysterious land in the New World that wasn't rich? "beautiful church buildings . . . Indians for their service . . . many mines of gold and silver . . . ranches of many cattle . . . farms, where they gather an abundant harvest of grains and vegetables . . . cedars, poplars, orange trees . . . delicious fruit . . . climate the best of all the Indies, so healthful and cool that people die of sheer old age. Unknown here are the diseases of other places; all that is lacking is Spaniards to settle and exploit the great wealth."

Who wouldn't go searching for it? And expeditions did go, at least a half dozen from 1540 to 1600; the city of Córdoba in present Argentina was founded (1573) as a base for, among other urgent needs, Caesar-searchers. In 1604 the governor of Buenos Aires led the largest expedition in Spain's colonial history—800 men—hunting the City of the Caesars. Some fifteen years later his son-in-law (and grandson of another noted Césarista) inherited the quest, and led still another expedition "inland from Chile, toward the Strait . . . a nation called the Caesars."

With such rich dreams and the grace of God, and in one tremendous generation of widespread war-making—always remembering the massive support of native American auxiliaries—the Spanish turned their first contacts into conquests over immense areas in South and Central America, Mexico, and the Caribbean. The probing contacts northward into the great unknown continent above Mexico and Cuba were, unless they should turn up a new Mexico, a new Peru, minor elements in that grand design. By the time of the fall of disappointingly minor Zuñi, other probes, far to the east, were reaching up into the northward mainland, into the country the Spanish knew as the Floridas.

The first Spanish slavers there met on the coast of what was to become the Carolinas a "gentle, kindly, hospitable" people they called the Chicoreans— the first two shipmasters to meet them traded for the few gold trinkets they had, then invited as many on board as their ships would hold, then invited them to inspect the interiors of the vessels below-decks, then closed the hatches on them and sailed away. One ship foundered but the other made it to Santo Domingo and sold the cargo to work in the mines. One of these kidnap victims turned up later, somehow, in Europe, and gave Peter Martyr information on the Indians of "Florida"—surely some of the earliest authentic East Coast ethnography.

A hidalgo adventuring in Santo Domingo, Lucas Vázquez de Ayllón, owner of several ships engaged in the standard pursuits, including slaving, was given a commission as *adelantado* (explorer, colonizer, and potential governor) of the Floridas, and in 1526 took a would-be colony to the Carolina coast to look into the source of the gold trinkets. (The source was probably storm-wrecked Spanish treasure ships cast up on the beaches.) The Chicoreans were hospitable as ever, and according to one account invited a number of Vázquez de Ayllón's people to one of their principal villages and there gently slew them all. The rest of the colony, after a struggling year or two, collapsed.

Later in the 1520s a commission to conquer the Floridas was wangled by Panfilo de Narvaez, now a one-eyed bullyboy, who landed near Tampa Bay with some 400 men and 42 horses. Slavers had also visited Gulf Coast villages before then but Narvaez finally coaxed a chief and his family into the Spanish camp. He then had the chief's nose cut off and his mother torn apart by dogs.

Exploring along the coast, the expedition then ran into the Apalachee, famous at the time as fighters. The expedition took to homemade boats, all rapidly wrecked on what is now the Texas coast.

Four miserable survivors then spent more than six years getting to the frontier of New Spain in Sinaloa.

One was Alvar Núñez Cabeza de Vaca, treasurer of the expedition, middle-aged, evidently guileless and honest to such an unusual degree he is still being puzzled over by poets.

Another of the four was the "bearded Negro" Estevanico, discoverer of New Mexico who died at Zuñi, a slave belonging to one of the other two Spaniards in the group.

All four were enslaved by wandering people of the Texas coast and shared, season after season, a poverty-stricken life of moving from the land of the pecan groves to the land of the prickly pears and back again and starving in between. During the starving times the famished people scrabbled for anything they could get, bark, bugs, bones, or whatever could be bitten into, including on occasion each other. Wild was the rejoicing when by good fortune a deer was surrounded, driven into the ocean, and clubbed to death.

Núñez Cabeza de Vaca and his companions, after sundry adventures, became practicing physicians, at which Núñez particularly became famous. He says simply, and with unquestionable sincerity, that he prayed over sick people and they got well—even a man thought dead being brought back to life.

In the end Núñez Cabeza de Vaca and his three fellow travelers were passed from band to band in a blaze of glory and reached the Mexican frontier accompanied by hundreds of faithful followers, whom Núñez then had to save, at considerable effort, from enslavement by the welcoming Spaniards.

The stories the four men had heard of the wonderfully wealthy Pueblos (no doubt they seemed wealthy, by report, to the underprivileged Muruam people of the Texas coast) and especially of the wonderfully rich Zuñi towns (the Seven Cities of Cibola) were responsible not only for the Vásquez Coronado expedition to New Mexico but also for another entry via the Floridas—a well-equipped army led by Hernando de Soto, Pizarro's dashing young captain of horse in Peru, and financed by Soto's cut of the ransom of the Inca. From 1539 to 1542 this invasion force, led on by constant reports of riches just beyond, pushed and struggled and fought its way from Tampa Bay to the mountains of North Carolina and westward across the Mississippi as far as present Oklahoma. Not surprisingly Soto (who died on the Mississippi in the course of the expedition) found more war than peace in Narvaez's legacy, and the venture was as much a total financial loss as the Vásquez Coronado expedition.

But in spite of blind alleys, setbacks, internecine feuds, and hollow dreams, the Spanish empire laboriously persisted in trying to construct a strictly profit making enterprise from the world of American Indians.

The people thus constructed were seldom grateful for their destiny. Their gods and homes were shattered, and from an enjoyment of living they were turned to working for it. They lost their subtle mystic pride and forgot their very names, and they called themselves by the mocking Spanish names of Big Ears or Short Hairs. They died by millions from measles, smallpox, malaria, influenza, yellow fever, cholera, tuberculosis, from starvation, from preposterous overwork, from desperation, from sheer horror at inhumanities they could not believe even while they were happening. They died drunk, they died insane, they died suicides; they died, they said, because their souls were stolen. They vanished in such numbers that African blacks could not be shipped in fast enough to take their places. Women finding themselves pregnant "took drugs to lose their babies" or killed newborn children "with their own hands." Or children were born dead, from syphilis; or the women, rotted with syphilis, became unable to bear children at all.

And so they went mad and rebelled and fought, fought and rebelled, escaped and fought, murdered and burned, and the Indios bravos, the wild Indians, filled with dread, became only wilder still.

Wrote the French essayist Montaigne, in the 1570s: "So many goodly cities ransacked and razed; so many nations destroyed or made desolate; so infinite millions of harmless people of all sexes, status, and ages, massacred, ravaged, and put to the sword; and the richest, the fairest, the best part of the world topsy-turvy, ruined, and defaced for the traffic of pearls and peppers! Oh, mechanical victories, oh, base conquests!"

There were outraged Spanish consciences, quite a few of them among the conquistadors themselves. Mention has been made of contemporary comment by European witnesses that there were no beggars, no prostitutes, no persons "vicious or lazy," no poverty, resources "were all so administered that everyone had enough," in the Indian societies that had been conquered and destroyed.

But those who really got something done about saving at least some of the Indian population from total destruction were such as the friar Bartolomé de Las Casas, or Julian Garcés, bishop of Tlaxcala. There were many of these voices; they were as much the Spain of the time as the Pizarros and Guzmans. They could not hope to win outright, cash profit was not on their side, but their share in the spirit of the Spanish Indies was—and still is—its salvation.

One of these was Fray Bernadino de Minaya, who was with Pizarro in Peru (although as unauthorized personnel) when some Indians were sent to Panama to be sold as slaves: "I notified Pizarro of Your Majesty's law against enslaving Indians even when they were the aggressors. He proclaimed the law but at the same time stopped giving me and my companions maintenance."

The whole matter of Indian slavery in all its aspects was a lively issue at the time in the Council of the Indies, and Cardinal Loaysa of that Council, being informed that some Indians had thought the Ave Maria was something to eat, decided they were not capable of learning the Holy Faith ("no more than parrots") and so could be enslaved at will. Brother Bernadino begged his way to Spain, saw the puissant cardinal but could not change his mind, upon which Brother Bernadino set his jaw and begged his way to Rome to see the pope "although merely a poor friar, I should not fear to oppose a cardinal on this matter."

He saw the pope (Paul III) and the bull *Sublimis deus* of 1537 resulted, accompanied by various papal briefs outlawing Indian slavery in any form. Unfortunately Brother Bernadino sent the glorious news direct to the Indies instead of through channels (the Royal Council), and a major international incident ensued; Charles V, feeling his sovereignty impugned, forced the pope to call back the briefs, and had Brother Bernadino Minaya tossed into prison to reflect on diplomatic procedures while the affair was being settled—it took a couple of years. But *Sublimis deus* still stood.

Las Casas's monument, the *New Laws* for the Indies, was unveiled to the New World in 1544. They provided for the gradual abolition of encomiendas, at which the Spanish pioneers in Peru staged a full-scale revolt, under Gonzalo Pizarro, who defeated and killed the viceroy and among other rampages raided the royal treasury at the silver mines of Potos'—one of his lieutenants took 1,500 llama loads of silver bars in a single raid. But the king's long arm bore him down, and after four wild years Gonzalo was captured and executed.

The abolition of encomiendas simply could not be enforced and was delayed another half century, and Las Casas kept on battling until he died. He "has twenty-seven or thirty-seven Indian carriers with him—I do not remember the exact number—and the greatest part of what they were carrying was accusations and writings against the Spaniards, and other rubbish," wrote his angry opponent, the friar Motolinía, in 1555, when Las Casas was eighty-one years old.

In 1550, the year in which Spain reached her "zenith of glory," the king and the Council of the Indies ordered that all further conquests and explorations be halted while the justice of warring against and enslaving Indians was debated. This debate took place in Valladolid, before a panel of jurists and theologians, between Las Casas and the great champion of the propriety of Christian conquest, Juan Ginés de Sepúlveda. The specific point of debate: "How can conquests, discoveries, and settlements be made to accord with justice and reason?" was subordinated to argument over the best way to spread the faith (by force or otherwise) and over the Aristotelian point that some are born to be slaves, Sepúlveda arguing that this last applied to the rude and infidel Indians.

This great debate is in effect still going on, but the basic point established by Las Casas that "mankind is one, and all men are alike in that which concerns their creation and all natural things, and no one is born enlightened" and that "the law of nations and natural law apply to Christian and gentile alike, and to all people of any sect, law, condition, or color without any distinction whatever" and that, in short, "all the people of the world are men" became the basis of modern international law, holding that treaties must be honored even between peoples of opposing faith, race, and customs.

Slowly but inexorably reform won the day in the lawbooks. Indian slaves in Mexican mines—160,000 of them—were to some degree actually, not only technically, freed from forced labor in 1551, and a special court for protection of Indian rights was established in Mexico the following year. Juan de Zumárraga, bishop of Mexico and lifelong friend of Las Casas, had already started schools for Indian boys and girls and produced books written specifically for Indian students, incidentally bringing the first printing press to America.

Encomiendas, revoked, restored, reverted, regranted, the subject of furious lobbying, were in the end not made perpetual (a final victory for Las Casas). Encomiendas, being built of Indians, died when the Indians died, and many had become empty title to the ownership of corpses, but there were always new-found Indians to parcel out in new encomiendas.

Now the mission (often accompanied by a presidio with troops, just in case) began to take the place of encomiendas in frontier organization.

In what is now Paraguay along the present border with Brazil and in the neighboring Misiones Territory of Argentina, the Jesuits built, among Guarani people they characterized as peaceful and altogether unwarlike, a network of missions that for more than 150 years was a veritable model of a successful and prosperous theocratic state. Even the Indian converts increased in population, directly counter to all the apparent laws on such matters, until their notorious Arcadia was ended with the expulsion of the Jesuits (1767).

The conquistadors had been obliged by law (technically) to read a rather lengthy legal document to any Indians before making war on them—it explained the growth of humanity since Adam and Eve, the supremacy of the pope, who had given the New World to the king of Spain, and concluded by requiring the Indians to submit to said king. In the middle 1500s this was changed to a friendly, downright genial proclamation of greeting, rather as from one monarch to another, from the king of Spain to the "kings and republics of the mid-way and western lands." The *New Laws* of 1573, reflecting much of Las Casas's position in the great debate of 1550, stated that even the word "conquest" was no longer to be used; the word from now on was to be "pacification," in order not to furnish any possible color or cause for aggravation to the Indians.

There were still 4,000 encomenderos left in the Americas in 1574, out of some 32,000 Spaniards then settled with their families in the New World. There were about 1.5 million male Indian taxpayers recorded in the Spanish colonies, representing a population of perhaps 5 million left from the original populations of eighty years before. These original populations in the centers of Mexico and Andean South America are now estimated, as previously noted, to have totaled 50 to 70 million. Of Peru's people, originally 9 million or more, less than 1 million were left by 1620, and the decline here continued until after the final great epidemic of 1719 (Andean native population in general has made a remarkable recovery since—at present there are 10 million or so speakers of Quechua and Aymara, principal languages of the Inca empire). Colombia's population dropped by 75 percent in the first thirty years; Hispañola's so often cited hundreds of thousands or "many millions" were only a few hundred by 1570.

While some part of this stupendous population drop, this "tremendous demographic fact," this "phenomenon without parallel," may be attributed to flight out of the white man's reach—an occasional complaint of the authorities—most of it clearly came from disease, raging epidemics of small-pox and measles and other such Old World favors visited upon the totally non-immune New World peoples. These epidemics swept the Andean regions as well as Mexico and Central America; a modern investigator summed up the Andean death toll as "in all likelihood the most severe single loss of abo-riginal population that ever occurred."

War and conquest, pillage and enslavement, with attendant malnutrition, exposure, overwork, and psychological devastation, played at least some role in addition to disease, even allowing for what is now seen as gross exaggera-tion in the "black legend" of Spanish mistreatment of the Americans; and it would be very wrong to assume this role was entirely terminated with the enlightened new laws of 1573. There was a touch of truth in the old Spanish saying, "Obedesco, pero no cumplo" ("I obey, but I do not comply"), and in the words of an ironic professor at the University of Mexico in the sixteenth century, that although there were now 400 defenders for every Indian, Indians continued to be enslaved, bought, sold, and forced to labor.

Trials of conquistadors accused rightly or wrongly of atrocities against Indians became almost standard procedure, as increasingly rigorous laws pro-hibited any punishment of Indians, even for refusing to become Christians—leaving a single loophole for punishment of those who "hindered the teaching" of Christianity, a clause much used by missionaries in commend-ing troublesome elder brothers to the lash or the gallows.

Indian wars and outbreaks continued, and many of them. For more than 200 years there was a major uprising about every ten years in the mine-and-mission frontier of northern Mexico, from Sinaloa and Sonora to the Pima country.

Nor were such disorders confined to the frontiers. Profitable silk culture, introduced into Mexico by Cortés, was killed not only by the rapid decline in the labor force but by the demand of officials for higher and higher quotas from their villages of Indians until, in the 1580s, Indian workmen destroyed their mulberry trees, wrecking the whole costly silkworm industry that had taken years to build up.

In the capital itself the *tumultos* that were to give Mexico City such a riot-spangled history frequently had their origin among the most downtrodden, the most undernourished, the most oppressed of all the miserable urban poor, the Indios. In a fairly real sense, Latin America has been in a constant state of revolution from its beginning.

But an uneasy balance was at length achieved that made possible the comparatively stable colonial centuries, and that ultimately left traces of a Spanish stamp on the great majority (90 percent, at a moderate guess) of all surviving Indians of the entire hemisphere.

From the beginning, as has been seen, outbreaks of Indian rebellion had been put down with the help, often substantial, of Indian allies. But by the end of the sixteenth century the Spanish were finding an even more urgent use for Indian alliances—as buffers against other European encroachment in the New World. This consideration was to become an increasingly important part of Indian policy as time went on, not only for the Spanish but for the other European encroachers as well.

Portugal, formally if reluctantly given a bite of the Indies by treaty with Spain, had ceased to be a threat for the time being, with the union of the two kingdoms in 1581. But France and England, Spain's blood enemies, and Holland, just breaking free of Spanish subjection, were interloping with growing insolence.

Francis of France, noted for his wit as well as his women, had mentioned that he would like to see the will by which Adam had divided the world between Spain and Portugal—this while admiring part of Moctezuma's treasure, intercepted by a French privateer on its way to Spain from Cortés.

Thereafter, France had taken a piquant interest in the Americas from Canada to Rio de Janeiro. French Huguenots in the 1560s were building Fort Caroline in the Carolinas to overlook the passing Spanish plate fleets, and finding, so they claimed, the natives kind to them because of hostility toward the Spaniards.

Spain had at that time just failed in yet another attempt to colonize Florida, even though the colonists had been instructed to set a good example, with good works and presents. But now a do-or-die Spanish effort founded St. Augustine, massacred the French colony at Fort Caroline, and installed there a Spanish garrison. A private French vengeance party returned to Fort Caroline a couple of years later and with Indian help massacred the Spanish garrison, hanging those who surrendered, but by then, at last, the Spaniards were firmly settled in St. Augustine.

The Spanish governor, Menéndez de Avilés, a renowned naval officer, negotiated an alliance with Florida's most powerful nation, the Calusa, by marrying the sister of their chief, Carlos, equally renowned in his world. Missions and presidios were planted up the Atlantic coast as far as South Carolina, and inland to western Georgia.

Sometime about 1560 an Indian youth had been taken to Mexico from the Atlantic coast region the Spanish called Axacan. He was given the Christian name of Luis de Velasco (the name of Mexico's great viceroy of the time) and was sent to Spain for a European education. In 1570 a party of Spanish Jesuits returned with him to Axacan to establish a mission. Luis de Velasco went home to his village of Chiskiac, where he was the nephew of one of the leading men and should have been able to get friendly support for the missionaries; but it didn't work out that way. Perhaps the Chiskiac people were scandalized at Don Luis's European ways. Anyway they got him into proper clothes forthwith, and were thenceforth suspicious and resentful of the priests, who were finally martyred, putting a stop to the mission before it really got started.

The Chiskiacs became part of the strong and influential Powhatan Confederacy; some thirty-five years later the English were established among them and named the country roundabout Virginia, the First Families of which might now have somewhat different names if it hadn't been for young Don Luis's hose and doublet.

The Chiskiac country was along the York River in present York County, Virginia, and marked the point farthest north in the Spanish effort to create an Indian bulwark against other Europeans on the Atlantic coast.

As already intimated, a gaze fixed on the past becomes more and more untrustworthy (eventually even reporting that there is no past at all, only a boundless present), but one thing it does sometimes seem to see is that the seeds of greatness, as we call it, are also the seeds of self-destruction. The forces of hot new nationalism under total central authority, crusading religious passion, and the lure of gain, profit, quick riches, that hewed out Spain's huge empire became the forces of its ruin.

The hot new nationalism, kept sealed in a vacuum bottle for Spaniards only, cooled to stagnation. Central authority grew rigid and inflexible, and changed from a whip to a bar—nothing could be done without royal permission; every detail had to be reported, at officious length, through endless official channels. Oñate was kept marking time for several years, his army of colonists already assembled, while royal authority decided whether or not to let him colonize New Mexico. Alvar Núñez Cabeza de Vaca, made governor of Buenos Aires and Asunción in present Argentina-Paraguay, tried to protect the Indians and thus earned the hostility of the local slavers; it was the royal pleasure to throw both Núñez and his principal opponents in prison, not being certain which side had the right of it.

Ecclesiastical zeal, solidly ensconced and grown unrecognizably fat, devoted itself to a chronic war with the miners and ranchers (and between rival religious orders) over Indian jurisdiction. It became customary for each faction to blame the other for every Indian upheaval, sometimes with justice, and the spectacle of priests inciting Indians to murder settlers and settlers inciting Indians to murder priests was not unknown. Each courted the Indians with one eye and winked at subterfuge slavery with the other.

The king poured the wealth of the Indies into European adventures, and crusading religious passion put Spain in the forefront of the war against the Reformation. The gold and silver brought by the shipload from across the sea (from the opening of Potosí in 1545 to the end of the sixteenth century, silver flooded into Europe at six times the amount of the previous half-century) brought wild inflation with it—5 percent a year in Andalusia all through the sixteenth century, blighting small business and sinking the Spanish masses into a poverty that endured until modern times.

Those in Spain with access to the empire's riches were the church and the wealthy, who between them became landlords of more than 95 percent of Castilian land. The church grew until one-third of the country's 8 million people were in some manner of religious employment, and the nation sustained 9,000 monasteries. The rich—the royal family and the 120 great nobles—grew richer, with estates more and more enormous, ostentatious entertainments more and more costly, carriages, jewels, luxuries of fairytale magnificence (the duke of Alva had some 16,000 pieces in his silver dinner service). The overswollen court and grandees are regarded by historians as principal factors in Spain's downfall ("a vast court, a monstrous tumour swelling larger and larger, and relentlessly consuming the life of the nation"); the unbelievable poverty of the people in general followed close behind as another. There were in the 1600s, so some calculate, 20,000 beggars on the streets of Madrid.

Public finances were in chronic short supply—no ministers of state were powerful enough to square the deficit by taxing the powerful grandees. Spain repudiated its debts three times during the sixteenth century, the last time, in 1596, abrogating a debt of 14.5 million ducats owed to European moneylenders and leaving the state with ruined credit. In 1608 the state income was not quite 6.5 million ducats (2.25 million from the Indies), as against expenses of more than 7 million. The war in Flanders dwindled from lack of money; Spain managed in 1609 to wangle a truce with the Dutch for twelve years, whereupon northern goods flooded the Spanish-world markets and Dutch ships sailed away with the Spanish silver. Eventually most of the empire's business found its way into the account books of the businesslike Antwerpers.

Empire oriented to dreamland profit flipped magically to bankruptcy. Bankrupt empire passed its dead hand upon all the works of its once-vigorous people, from agriculture to commerce. The Spanish knights were no longer chivalric, eagle-eyed Grecos but Velazquez dwarfs, with tragic, noble faces and helpless, stunted arms.

In 1559 the new Spanish king, Philip II, severely pious, attended in person, along with an audience of some 200,000, an auto-da-fé at Valladolid, at which ten heretics were strangled and two burned alive. But the new king was also so severe in his repression of the slave trade that he opened up bright new fields for the enterprising English, one of whom, John Hawkins, numbered Queen Elizabeth herself among his backers on his illicit slave-run in 1564–1565 from Africa to the West Indies—she provided one of his ships (the Jesus). He successfully brought and sold 400 blacks for a fine profit on the operation.

And throughout the generations, from one century to the next, still more Spanish expeditions toiled hither and thither through the howling winds of Patagonia and along lost pampas streams "haunted by flamingoes and Magellanic swans," inquiring of the towering Tehuelche the way to the City of the Caesars.

Nothing in this high point of Old World civilization, the Spanish Empire, would seem to fit with the American Indian societies we have seen in all these preceding pages. In the most basic respects the two worlds seem to have been markedly different.

Perhaps the absence of beggars in the American world, compared to the thousands (even if merely hundreds) on the streets of Madrid, provided a key point of difference. Perhaps the superior military organization of the invaders was a critical difference (in the words of a modern paleontologist, with the growth of "materially-based societies, warfare has increased steadily in both ferocity and duration"), perhaps the technological superiority in general of the invaders, perhaps their immunity to those wild epidemics, perhaps their simple madness for acquisition that would stop at nothing and could be stopped by nothing short of death.

Perhaps a signal difference can be seen in the very early monumental Peruvian public architecture, rivaling Egypt and Sumeria in antiquity but apparently without the oriental despotism theoretically essential in the Old World and, millennia later, the Hohokam irrigation systems without evidence of the Old World keystone of high culture, a whipswinging ruling class.

Possibly a great difference was in food, New World crops, led by manioc and white potatoes and maize, providing abundant food for huge populations even with only simple farming methods: no plow, no draft animals. Possibly the nonprofit markets remarked upon by archeologists in Mesoamerican studies, and the absence of folktales dealing with sudden riches, may illustrate significant differences.

A profound difference might be discernible in art: signed works by celebrated individual artists seem to be lacking in all New World history before modern times. In the Old World the Greek music drama was being revived in the birth of European opera at the end of the sixteenth century, although the Old World tradition of the star performer (the Roman emperor Nero's greatest ambition was to be a superstar singer) had never died, even in medieval Europe, being continued in the churches. Some Maya anecdotal sculpture may hint at star performers but dramatic representations (religious and secular) in the New World seem never to have celebrated the author.

Differences in religion were especially profound. A missionary in Brazil in 1500 wrote that the Indians had not a single "vestige" of religion, but later most missionaries described Indian religious activities in great detail. New World people offered sacrifices and prayers to panoplies of gods; in time new gods could be accepted, throughout time old gods could remain. The invading Old World religion (Christian) compelled all to submit to the one God and none other.

New World liberty, universal bosslessness already attracting much comment, would entrain many enduring consequences.

Differences could extend through sexual attitudes to parental behavior or emotional structures of every variety, in other words through all of life from birth to death, all of human organization from family to nation, or empire.

Clearly, differences between the New World and the Old, between American civilizations and societies and Old World civilizations and societies, differences in aim and direction, in basic fundamental ideas, were bedrock-deep, truly worlds apart.

But if the New World really was, as an anthropologist has put it, a second earth, this may have something crucial to tell us not only of our past but also of our present and, in its implication of a free and unconfined horizon, of our future.

PART TWO

Heritage of the New World

CHAPTER 14

Through the Lookinglass II

History is a record of relationships. Sometimes, like children of unwise fathers, such relationships may not be recognized until well after the event.

The presence of the Indians in the history of western America, wrote James Bryce in 1887, has "done no more than give a touch of romance or a spice of danger to the exploration of some regions . . . while over the rest of the country the unhappy aborigines have slunk silently away, scarcely even complaining of the robbery of lands and the violation of plighted faith."

In the early 1920s, as he approached the close of his teaching career, Frederick Jackson Turner summed up the presence of the Indians in the history of eastern America: "Between the beginning of the seventeenth century, when the West lay along the Atlantic coast, and 1850, when it had crossed the Mississippi . . . the Indians had step by step, in successive wars, been defeated and removed. . . . Indians had influenced white development by this retardation of advance, compelling society to organize and consolidate in order to hold the frontier; training it in military discipline; determining the rate of advance, particularly at the point where the mountain barriers broke down."

Indians are traditionally viewed as natural features of the land, rather like mountains or rivers or buffalo or troublesome, if colorful, wild varmints, affecting American history only by at times impeding the civilizing progress of advancing settlers.

This attitude remains dominant even though in recent years a veritable flood of important work has appeared in local and regional Indian history. Expert testimony of historians and anthropologists in connection with hun-

dreds of legal cases before the special commission for Indian land claims that
has been in operation since 1947 has furnished further raw material by the
bale for tribal histories.

However, only relatively few works have made any serious attempt to analyze Indian history as an effective force in American history in general—for
example, its role in the origin of the Civil War. The study of main currents in
American history continues to regard Indian history as a distinctly separate
and distinctly unimportant eddy.

Pressure groups have obliged history textbooks to give a certain amount
of space to various minorities, including American Indians, but a serious historical relationship between American Indians and the history of the birth
and growth of the United States has not yet been found acceptable.

Still apropos today is Bernard DeVoto's statement of fifty years ago that
most of our history has been treated as if it were "a function solely of white
culture—in spite of the fact that till well into the nineteenth century the
Indians were one of the principal determinants of historical events."
Disregarding Parkman's "great example," said DeVoto, American historians
have made "disastrously little effort" to understand how the Indian world
affected white history.

Parkman's example, though, is all too frequently the kind of befriending
that leaves no need of enemies. His Indians are truly wild, they skulk, screech,
slay with the mindless gluttony of weasels, and otherwise behave as barbari-
cally as possible and hardly ever (if not never) permit themselves to be seen
acting like reasonable beings. A lone camper in the forest is no doubt an
Indian, lurking in concealment, "watching to kill some passing enemy." Or the
ferocious Iroquois are on conquest bent: "Yet it was not alone their homici-
dal fury that now impelled them to another war. Strange as it may seem, this
was in no small measure one of commercial advantage."

Parkman summed up his period's judgment of Indians (in the introduction to *The Jesuits in North America*): "It is obvious that the Indian mind has
never seriously occupied itself with any of the higher themes of thought."

Parkman's persistent picture of the Indian as "man, wolf, and devil, all in
one," was undoubtedly of some consequence in rendering its subject historically ineffective. Painted savages who capered about in indecent clothes, ate
nasty foods, and howled unintelligibly whenever they came in sight obviously
could not have been of much more importance in the course of American history than so many grizzly bears.

But today we are not quite so confident of the self-evident superiority
and manifest "progress" of our civilization. We are not even altogether confident as to who is savage and who is civilized. As long ago as the beginning of

the present century anthropologists of rank concerned themselves with the question of what is primitive and found it a difficult question to answer.

A. L. Kroeber took stock of the aboriginal Australians, at the time assumed to be the most primitive people available, and noted that from the point of view of a spiritual rather than a financial balance their culture was one of the most highly integrated in the world; he concluded that this marvelous integration may have been achieved rather in proportion to their voluntary renunciation of material possessions, "say somewhat on the principle of those who have riches hardly entering into the kingdom of God. But this leads us off from the question of primitiveness into something quite else." Franz Boas came to the conclusion that some of the more primitive people on earth, in the fullest sense of the word, might actually be found among aimless, valueless groups in our own modern civilized society: "Greater lack of cultural values than that found in the inner life of some strata of our modern population is hardly found anywhere."

Claude Lévi-Strauss summed up the matter by suggesting a standard of relativism to "utilize all societies in revealing principles" of social structure.

Principles of surprising ramification stand ready for revelation in the study of ancient New World societies—for example, the general absence of a pastoral background in the New World appears to have been of effect in accounting for not only the general absence of private property, the general absence of both riches and poverty and for that matter the general absence of beggars, but also the generally low level of technical progress especially in warfare, and even the absence of immunity in the New World to Old World diseases.

Whatever present-day social scientists decide to think of them, it can be supposed that most citizens of American Indian societies thought of themselves as properly civilized, in that they made a conscious effort to try to live in the right way, toward what their society regarded as right and proper objectives. It would follow that in general their behavior was a product of the nature of that society, a deliberate behavior motivated by a conscious, deliberate point of view.

There were numerous avenues by which the peculiarly Indian behavior of American Indians clearly affected, directly and indirectly, the development of the United States and the history of the rest of the post-Columbian world. The introduction into the Old World of Indian medicines, such as ipecac, curare, coca, cascara, quinine (although as to quinine "the Indians were ignorant of it, having no use for it until we diffused malaria to them"), and farm products, such as maize, potatoes, tomatoes, manioc, beans, chilies, avocados, vanilla, chocolate, rubber, tobacco—in total well over half of all modern agricultural products—has been assessed time and again and need only be mentioned. The same is true of the minor contributions of such items or complexes of items as bark canoes, snowshoes, signaling systems, and the like.

But there were other indirect effects of the Indian world that are extraordinarily interesting and have not been given the attention they surely merit. One was the weight of the New World on the development of social ideas in Europe during the centuries after Columbus, most clearly seen in the New World influence on European notions of liberty.

From the beginning of European exploration in the Americas, Indians were reported to spend their time in "Idlenes and playe" and to be beautifully free to do so—"ever too used to live at libertie," all these the words of the New World's earliest historian, Peter Martyr of Anghiera, 1511. No king, no lord, no wealthy, no one to obey, such sentiments were echoed by many travelers in the heart of the Americas, the Indian world real before their eyes, year after year, generation after generation.

Such sentiments were still being stated after nearly 200 years of acquaintance—"they live, all, at liberty; they drink and eat when they are hungry or thirsty, they work and rest when they please; they have no care," from the Caribbean islands in the 1650s.

Or one could instance, for the area of what was to be the United States, the missionary Lafitau whose incomparable work of ethnography first published in 1724 described the "entire liberty" and yet beautiful dignity and "good sense" of the Iroquois, or the Jesuit historian Father Charlevoix from the same time and region, on the Huron "Simplicity and Freedom of the first Age of the World." One might also include such unexpected frontier encomiums as that of Major Robert Rogers, writing of the Illinois and Missouri Indians of the 1750s: "These people of any upon earth seem blessed in this world; here is health and joy, peace and plenty; care and anxiety, ambition and the love of gold, and every uneasy passion, seem banished from this happy region."

Leading minds of Europe picked up the refrain, the poet Ronsard ("Leave these people alone in their freedom and tranquility"), the great essayist Montaigne ("to live still under the sweet liberty of the first laws of nature, I assure you that I would very willingly paint myself all over and go naked"), the philosopher Leibniz ("pursuit of a better and happier life"). Wrote Geoffroy Atkinson, a student of this body of literature in France, "Many travelers and missionaries had mentioned, even in the sixteenth century, the lack of private property among primitive peoples. Early writers had called attention to the generally happy condition of a primitive society founded upon equality and liberty. The cumulative force of such expressions in accounts of voyages published before 1700 would be a fascinating study."

An aspect of the Indian image that was to develop a galaxy of repercussions was observed by Montaigne, who had talked to three Indians touring Europe and learned something of the common Indian custom of dividing a community into halves, or moieties, for ritualistic or administrative purposes. The three Indians told him they had noticed that in Europe there seemed to be two moieties consisting of the rich, "full gorged" with wealth, and the poor, starving "and bare with need and povertie." The Indian tourists not only marveled at this division, but marveled that the poor endured "such an injustice, and that they took not the others by the throte, or set fire on their house." (Some 300 years later an American anthropologist brought these particular New World notions to the attention of Karl Marx and Friedrich Engels, as will be recounted elsewhere in this text.)

Rousseau is of course the eighteenth-century climax, congealing the Idea of the New World as liberty, equality, and revolution against tyranny. His early friend and adviser, Diderot, repeated Rousseau's "savage" litany, c. 1770: "I am convinced there cannot be nor one cannot have true happiness for the human species except in a social state in which there is neither king nor magistrate nor priest nor laws nor thine nor mine nor property moveable or real, nor vices nor virtue."

How much Rousseau's thinking had to do with the overthrow of Europe's thrones or how much the image of the American Indian really had to do with Rousseau's thinking are both eminently debatable, but the debate can only be concerned with the matter of degree. Both are undeniably present.

All this vaunted Indian freedom may have been indeed only a persistent illusion, and certainly the testimony as to the alleged nobility of the unspoiled savage can be matched by testimony showing the unspoiled savage as brutish, depraved, insensate, unclean, ill mannered, impious, unregenerate in his addiction to his nasty foods and indecent clothes, and in every respect far from respectable. (Recall Mark Twain's reflection on the Gosiutes of the Utah deserts: "the wretchedest type of mankind I have ever seen. . . . I refer to the Goshoot Indians . . . indolent . . . prideless beggars . . . savages who, when asked if they have the common Indian belief in a Great Spirit show a something which almost amounts to emotion, thinking whisky is referred to.")

But whether the freedom was illusory or not, the point is that the Indian *seemed* free, to European eyes, gloriously free, to the European soul shaped by millennia of toil and tyranny, and this impression operated profoundly on the process of history and on the development of America.

The essential difference between the Indian and European worlds may well have been in the attitude toward property. The European way of life (with some notable exceptions) was basically one of individual competition for the acquisition of property, to the point that it would be more correct to describe white frontier expansionists as property-hungry rather than land-hungry, to encompass the powerful forces of land and mineral speculation as well as the humble settlers content with small land-holdings.

The basic Indian attitude (also with some notable exceptions) leaned more toward cooperation in the use of property in common, rather than competition to acquire private property. This would have helped create an appearance of classless freedom in Indian life, along with an apparent lack of striving and an emphasis on the nonmaterial satisfactions that would result from a prevailing interest in matters other than work for profit. It might be said, in sum, that the Indian world was devoted to living while the European world was devoted to getting.

This essence, an incalculable force in American history, was at the same time the structural weakness that made inevitable the defeat of the Indian world when it came into general confrontation with an aggressively materialist civilization.

This essential difference has also been a principal obstacle throughout the centuries in keeping the white and Indian worlds from genuine and direct communication, from genuine and direct understanding of each other.

The effects of Indian participation in American history may appear wherever Indians have appeared, directly or indirectly.

A most striking direct participation was the assistance given by various Indian groups to embryonic colonies of Europeans. Massasoit and his Wampanoags were the salvation of the struggling colony of Plymouth, along with Tisquantum, who was called by Governor Bradford a "spetiall instrument sent of God for their good beyond their expectation" and by Sir Ferdinando Gorges one of "the meanes under God of putting on foote, and giving life to all our Plantations." The Wappinger people of Manhattan "preserved" the first Dutch traders "like the apple of their eye" and gave them "their Turkish beans and Turkish wheat" when the foreign invaders "sometimes had no victuals." At Jamestown Captain John Smith said of the neighboring Indians, with whom Captain Smith and his colonists had already fought, that "it pleased God (in our extremity) to move the Indians to bring us Corne, ere it was half ripe, to refresh us, when we rather expected . . . they would destroy us." Such was the weakness of the colony, said tough Captain Smith, "that had not the Indians fed us, we directly had starved. Indians taught the Jamestown people how to plant corn, and, after the strategic marriage of John Rolfe to Pocahontas, Indians taught the Englishmen how to raise tobacco. This gave the colony a cash crop and its first profit, and the appearance of the eagerly awaited profit entrained enduring consequences for all English North America.

Commonly, in the earliest days of exploration and colonization, first arrivals were greeted with friendliness rather than hostility: "being of simple faith, the natives evinced for Collomba tenderness and friendship," reported a foreign agent at the Spanish court, in sending out the first news of Columbus's discovery. Jacques Cartier landed on an island in the St. Lawrence in 1535 and "met with five men, that were hunting of wild beasts, who as freely and familiarly came to our boats without any fear, as if we had ever been brought up together . . . one of them took our captain in his arms, and carried him on shore." Alvar Núñez Cabeza de Vaca, traveling alone as a seashell peddler among Texas coast Indians who had probably never before seen a white man, this being circa 1529, wrote: "With my merchandise and trade I went into the interior as far as I pleased. . . . Wherever I went I received fair treatment."

Accounts of early explorers furnish almost at random such passages as, "Food was placed before them, and, as the Illinois code of courtesy enjoined, their entertainers conveyed the morsels with their own hands to the lips of these unenviable victims of their hospitality while others rubbed their feet with bear's grease . . ." or of the Arkansas, "I cannot tell you the civility and kindness we received from these barbarians." Or among the people of the Hasinai Confederacy, "a tribe then powerful but long since extinct. Nothing could surpass the friendliness of their welcome" or among the Sioux, where old men welcomed a stranger with caresses and tears. Alvar Núñez Cabeza de Vaca also spoke of weeping in welcome (as did many other accounts from both North and South America), "They have a custom when they meet, or from time to time when they visit, of remaining half an hour before they speak, weeping."

Wrote Pedro de Castañeda of the buffalo-hunting people of the plains he saw in 1541 who centuries later were to become the fearsome Apache, "They are a gentle people, not cruel, faithful in their friendship." Said Raleigh's envoy Captain Barlow in 1584 of the Atlantic coast people among whom ill-fated Roanoke was established a few years later, "most gentle, loving, faithful, void of all guile and treason, such as live after the manner of the golden age."

The policy of the various Indian peoples, in these first meetings between two strange worlds, was obviously a vital factor in the success of colonies and exploration. When in these early relations the Indians became opposed to the foreigners, colonies or trading posts or missions could not as a rule survive.

The varying policy in this regard of the various Indian peoples could scarcely derive from any imposed outside control. Manipulation of the simple Indians by guileful Europeans has sometimes been stressed and may have been of moment now and then, but it seems unlikely that it could have been very often very weighty in the earlier centuries when the balance of power and consequent occasion for initiative were extravagantly on the side of the Indians. The weightiness of this factor is sometimes questionable even in later times, as in the interesting case of Pierre Vial, a champion frontiersman sent north from Santa Fe in 1805 in the employ of Spain to stir up the Plains Indians against Lewis and Clark. Vial couldn't get his own expedition out his own front door, so to speak, being stopped by hostile Indians (identity mysteriously unknown) at the Arkansas River. He tried again, in vain again, while the inexperienced Lewis and Clark were successfully passing through dozens of Indian nations all the way to the Pacific.

Other factors in early Indian behavior may have been, at one time or another, desire for trade or for knowledge of new things or fear of new things, domestic political conditions or relations with rival communities, the season of the year, the state of the corn crop, heavenly signs and portents, religious laws, any of the multifarious motives that bear on human conduct, especially on group conduct in social and political actions. These factors and these Indian political decisions were of import in our history and deserve thoroughgoing study, but the point is not simply this. The point is also that they all refer to the underlying attitudes and ways of life of the societies making up the Indian world, the attitudes and ideas that shaped the nature of those societies and the character of their people.

If there was a tendency for Indians to welcome foreign invaders with more benevolence than otherwise, this is important. At most it might indicate that the Europeans were invading what was in a sense a higher civilization. At least it is an indication of New World character that appears to deviate considerably from the more customary and familiar Old World character. The question of how much this peculiar Indian behavior had to do with the health and growth of the nursling colonies and the later careers of colonial conquest takes on still more significance.

When the Indian world was moved to resist, it could become a world most difficult to penetrate and conquer, in spite of the great technological military advantage possessed by the invaders. Scattered bands of Apaches and their even more scattered allies declined to permit secure occupation of their country by foreigners for more than two centuries, enduring volumes of epic warfare and several earnest attempts at total extermination by Europeans allied with other Indian nations. The Jibaro of Ecuador and Peru drove out Spanish colonists in the sixteenth century and have not accepted colonization of their country yet. In the closing years of the seventeenth century French armies and allied Indians mounted repeated invasions that should have utterly smashed, but did not, the Five Nations Iroquois. In the middle years of the eighteenth century the French staged repeated full-scale campaigns against the Chickasaw and were repeatedly defeated. These two French failures played their part in the ultimate defeat of France in the New World. Some Indian conquests thought of as facile were, in actuality, not. The conquest of the Aztec state in Mexico required, even after the capture and death of Moctezuma, a year of desperate campaigning and Machiavellian diplomacy and the final bitterly fought months-long battle for the Aztec capital city, Tenochtitlan, besieged by the Spaniards and their "untold number" of Indian allies. The conquest of Peru required, even after the capture and death of the Inca, a long generation of tangled wars to end organized military resistance. The Spanish were lavishly assisted in these wars by many Indian allies, but even so they came within an ace of total defeat in Manco Inca's great war raised against them in 1536.

Clearly, an intact Indian nation could be a formidable opponent to overthrow by force alone, superior European tactics, and arms notwithstanding, even with the help of Indian allies. Without Indian allies, invasions by blunt force were often, if not usually, disastrous. Such were the first large-scale invasions of Panama, which, as has been related, cost hundreds of Spanish lives and ended in utter defeat, until Vasco Núñez de Balboa paved the way to victory with powerful Indian friends. In short, strictly military conquest was seldom easy, and seemed to have need of Indian help to succeed at all.

If American conquest was this difficult, and since nevertheless it was accomplished, even against heavy numerical and logistical odds, the existence of factors other than the strictly military would certainly seem to be implied.

Presumptive among such factors, again, would be attitudes and ideas, fears and desires, foolishness and philosophies, founded upon the peculiar character of the Indian peoples.

The customary pattern of American conquest was for an initial penetration to be made by guile, diplomacy, or in response to open Indian invitation, as has been mentioned. Once pierced or broken, an Indian society, like any other, was naturally more susceptible to conquest. In most such conquests, as noted, Indians also played a part, sometimes a major part, as allies leagued with the conquerors.

Indian activity as auxiliaries of various European powers in the Europeans' wars against each other was likewise of considerable magnitude in the multitude of North American conflicts, great and small, through the War of 1812. Indian activity as trade allies of various colonial powers was sometimes of decisive importance in the course of colonial affairs. It is unlikely that the position of organized Indian communities in these activities was always or even usually one of vassals under the control of their white associates. Too many events testify to the independence of Indian action.

The French were as a rule extraordinarily canny and persuasive in Indian dealings ("practice therein," urged Edmond Atkin in proposing to the British Lords of Trade his Indian policy of 1755, "the same little ingratiating Arts as the French do") but the catastrophic war waged against the French in 1729 by the Natchez, who had previously been sound friends, damaged the French severely in Louisiana. At the same epoch, in the Great Lakes country, the French were seriously hurt by the Fox wars, brought on by missionary mismanagement, says recent research, among other more obvious factors. The stubborn neutrality, and sometimes hostility, of the Five Nations Iroquois was a baffling problem to the French in Canada for more than a century. French inability to solve this problem or to wipe the Iroquois out of the way had its effect, as previously mentioned, on the final fate of France in North America.

Spanish traders, missionaries, colonial officials, and soldiers had more experience with Indians than all other Europeans combined and much more permanent success than other Europeans in altering Indian manners and ways. And yet the Spanish world was rejected not only by the aforementioned Apaches but also by (among many others) the highly cultured Pawnees. The destruction of the Villasur expedition in 1720 by Pawnees was a blow to Spanish dominion of the Plains country east of the Rockies. The Yuman-speaking Quechan (then known as the Yumas) had been sound Spanish friends, but in 1781 (the year of the founding of Los Angeles) they destroyed Spanish farms and missions and outposts that had been established at the "Yuma towns" on the Colorado River and closed the overland trail to California, thereby rendering more remote and precarious—and therefore a riper plum for eventual U.S. conquest—the struggling new California missions and settlements. Another overland route was not established for commercial caravans until 1830. The Apalachee people of Florida were famous fighters in the sixteenth-century days of the earliest Spanish explorers, but accepted, in fact are said to have requested, Spanish missionaries in the seventeenth century. After some fifteen years the Apalachees rebelled against mission rule, defeated a Spanish force sent to subdue them, and then reversed themselves "apparently through a counterrevolution in the tribe itself" and returned to the Spanish fold.

The Creeks generally refused Spanish overtures, although there were at times strong pro-Spanish factions in some of the Lower Creek towns. Together with allied Indians and, eventually, English slavers and traders from Carolina, the Creeks fought sporadically with the missionized Apalachee, and in a great raiding party of 1704, composed of fifty English volunteers and 1,000 Creeks, destroyed the flourishing Apalachee missions, permanently impairing Spanish strength in the Southeast.

Creeks welcomed English colonists in Georgia and gave them every assistance. Creeks, Cherokees, Chickasaws, and some of the Choctaw towns gave alliance to the English on many occasions, of value to the English and of pronounced effect on the history of the region. Iroquois partiality for the English at critical moments had its effect on the history of the Northeast. But Pontiac's partiality for the defeated French threw the West into a turmoil that was ultimately of heavy cost to the British and of some effect on the history of the American Revolution: William Christie MacLeod wrote many years ago, in *The American Indian Frontier*, that the "Indian policy of the Crown did more than anything else to alienate the borderers from loyalty to the Crown, and led the frontiersmen to throw their weight on the side of sedition in the forthcoming struggle between constituted government and rebellion. . . . Turbulence on the border was continual from 1765 to 1775 when the torch of rebellion was lifted."

Delawares who had been victimized by fraudulent shenanigans from Pennsylvanians and the Iroquois and assorted land speculators became the hard core of the "French" Indians at Fort Duquesne who helped ruin Braddock in 1755. But other Delawares in Pennsylvania insisted on the risky peacemaking policy of the Delaware leader Shingas and the Moravian missionary Christian Post, in 1758, whose success with the quondam French Indians on the Ohio was such that Fort Duquesne then fell to the English without a fight. Pennsylvania's inability to carry out the terms of Indian agreements made at this time no doubt contributed a glowing coal or so to Pontiac's war, as the British government's efforts to live up to agreements forced by Pontiac's war provided some sparks for sedition.

"American" Creeks and allied Yuchis and Cherokees bore a fair share of the fighting and the casualties against anti-American "Red Stick" Creeks in the Battle of Horseshoe Bend—the victory that first brought Andrew Jackson national recognition. The determined friendliness of the Northern Shoshoni and the Nez Perce for Americans from the time of Lewis and Clark to Chief Joseph's gentlemanly war seventy years later was of moment in the settlement of the Northwest; the results of this friendliness are easier to analyze than its origins.

Examples could be added ad infinitum. Many of these Indian actions simply will not fit any interpretation of Europeans dominating the policies and decisions of the Indians with whom they associated. Nor will the infinite variety of circumstances bear out easy notions of simple primitive diplomacy—of whites controlling Indian actions at one remove merely by overawing them with shows of force or winning their favor with trinkets and trade.

European tutelage in both warfare and trade is obvious in post-Columbian Indian history, but white efforts to influence Indian policies and decisions cannot be reckoned the dominant factors in most such decisions any more than France or Germany can be shown to have controlled historically the policies of each other or even of such lightweight colleagues as the Swiss Confederation.

We are accustomed to thinking of the Spanish and "their" Indians, the French and "their" Indians, and so on, but Indian nations doubtless thought of "their" European colonies and "their" European business connections and military allies in much the same way, and connived and intrigued to get the support of this or that European community for their own sovereign projects—projects certainly sovereign in their own plans and intentions, at least. Sir William Johnson, England's enormously successful superintendent of Indian affairs in the northern colonies, remarked that "many mistakes arise here from erroneous accounts formerly made of Indians; that they have been represented as calling themselves subjects, although the very word would have startled them had it ever been pronounced by an interpreter. They desire to be considered as allies and friends, and such we may make them at a reasonable expense and thereby occupy our outposts and carry on trade in safety until, in a few years, we shall become so formidable throughout the country as to be able to protect ourselves and abate of that charge." Edmond Atkin, England's superintendent for Indian affairs in the southern colonies, wrote at about the same time, in the 1750s: "No people in the world understand and pursue their true National Interest, better than the Indians. . . . in their public Treaties no People on earth are more open, explicit, and Direct. Nor are they excelled by any in the observance of them." Atkin recommended "above all, to begin with building Forts in their hearts . . . after which we may build Forts wherever we please."

The shape of the Indians' own sovereign thoughts, to repeat, was drawn from the underlying attitudes and ways of life of the Indian world. These attitudes pervade Indian history. Indian attitudes toward war, for instance, naturally had a direct bearing on the outcome of various Indian wars. Most Indian societies appeared to look to matters other than war as the principal objectives of their organization, and in the midst of war could give fighting a back seat to religious ceremonies, or, like the classic Greeks, could be swayed in their battle strategy by omens; white communities were usually organized much more effectively for sustained war.

War in the Old World definition, as has been noted, seems on the best evidence to have been an almost unknown concept in the untouched Indian world, with the possible exception of the Inca state. It has been remarked that even among the militaristic polities of Mexico martial victory is pictured in the codices by the burning of the enemy temple, religion being by far the dominant motif in both war and peace.

Religion permeated hierarchy and, in the form of divination, much political action, perhaps most such action among especially pious people such as the Maya. The visage of the enemy appears to have been seen in the enemy gods; an incredible effort was sometimes expended, as in certain instances among the ancient Olmec, in stabbing or otherwise disabling the stone bodies of conquered gods.

There is little indication of whole countries being overrun by war in prewhite times. The raids that were usually called wars customarily involved only a fraction of the available fighting men and these only briefly. Utterly defeated nations were assimilated rather than annihilated. Even among the Aztecs no armed troops met Cortés, no "guard" came to Moctezuma's rescue; it would seem that a permanent standing army did not exist.

Military forces based on Indian attitudes toward war could not usually maintain strength in the field over a prolonged period; thus against Europeans a clear-cut Indian victory could usually come only from a clear-cut knockout—a decision on points would mean a negotiated truce after which the Indian troops would melt away home, leaving the Europeans (with their organized military establishments) to interpret and enforce the truce terms as they saw fit. This was fairly often the upshot in Indian wars with Europeans.

The control of specific territories by communities or social groups was a familiar concept to many Indian societies, but private ownership or private buying and selling of land was, as must frequently be repeated in these pages, outside most Indians' experience. Above all, the common European ambition to own a landed personal estate as the ultimate symbol of success was to most Indian people as incomprehensible as would have been an ambition to own the sky.

The free and easy Indian land policies that were for centuries a central issue of Indian "troubles" are related to such basic attitudes. The U.S. Court of Claims, in an opinion of 1893 later upheld by the Supreme Court, stating, "Apart from the Indian tribes, communal property is with us a thing unknown," held that each member of the Indian community has an "absolute and complete" right of actual ownership. "Chiefs and headmen" have no authority to dispose of these rights, and even a majority of the tribe or community has no authority to sell the communal property, which would seem to constitute (said the Court), "taking away the property of the minority and disposing of it without their consent." The Court specifically remarked, of this matter so difficult for the Old World mind to grasp, "It is, indeed, not improbable that many of our troubles with the Indian tribes have sprung from the fact that our treaty-making commissioners and agents were ignorant of its nature, and of the fact that all Indian lands were communal property."

Indian influence on the movement of frontiers is another important example of direct Indian participation in American historical processes. Very few if any frontiers, especially before 1800, were opened without the prior consent, if not the invitation, of at least some of the Indian peoples concerned. The Ohio River country of eastern Tennessee and parts of present West Virginia and Kentucky was largely uninhabited at the time of European appearance and regarded by neighboring Indians as an open domain, not under the dominion of any Indian nation. When shattered remnants of Delawares, Shawnees, Hurons, Kickapoos, and others drifted into the region during the eighteenth century this country became a political football for these Indian refugee groups and for powerful nations in the background such as the Six Nations Iroquois and the Cherokee. Indian political maneuvers carried out for Indian purposes were vital in opening this no man's land to white settlement—the earliest trans-Appalachian English settlements.

Once established, the white frontier became very much a force in itself, but even so continued for some time to depend rather more than less on Indian actions and decisions. The Kentucky Shawnees who were goaded into Lord Dunmore's War in 1774 were first abandoned to this fate by the Cherokee and by most of the Iroquois, an abandonment that permitted Lord Dunmore's high-handed course of action. The devious reasons behind these Indian decisions are perhaps as important to our history as Governor Dunmore's devious motives, but have received considerably less attention. The objection is customarily brought that materials are lacking for studying these or other Indian decisions, although, as mentioned earlier, new materials are appearing in ever-increasing amounts. But the need at this moment seems to be less for new materials than for a more serious approach to already extant materials. Existing materials of course include the mountainous literatures of archeology and ethnology; historians who would consider Indian participation in American history as the participation of reasonable and politic peoples worthy of serious attention would presumably wish to become fluent in anthropology just as scholars of ancient history study ancient languages. At present the anthropologists seem to be doing most of the rapproching, with a growing interest in historical relevance, an interest at times reaching a degree that would have been regarded as downright frivolous not many years ago.

Direct white contact was not always the agency responsible for the shattering or transformation of Indian nations in the path of the white frontiers. A major aspect of the movement of frontiers was the purely Indian shock wave running ahead of the actual white frontiers, sometimes many years and many hundreds of miles ahead—such as the disease frontier, which sometimes disrupted patterns of population before invading Europeans had even been heard of, let alone seen.

Indian groups in actual contact with Europeans, stimulated by revolutionizing ideas and tools and weapons, hurled themselves into conflict or into revolutionizing trade with other Indian groups who might not yet have seen white men. The resultant disruptions affected the subsequent movement of white frontiers. The earliest frontiers did not move in response to European settlement but as a result of the military or commercial actions of Indian nations who, in effect, had the bomb first—which is to say, who were in touch with Europeans. There were, in other words, two networks of frontiers, one strictly Indian, the other, often profoundly influenced by the kinetics of the first, European. The far-reaching conquests of the Iroquois and the farther-reaching consequences therefrom are a familiar example of this Indian-versus-Indian frontier in operation.

Further, the Indian-versus-Indian frontier is amenable to still more delicate divisions, such as the horse frontier and the gun frontier, both traveling without benefit of white companionship. The horse frontier rolled across the American West from New Mexico far in advance of most white traders and sometimes as much as a century and a half in advance of tangible white frontiers, reaching the Northern Shoshoni in the 1690s or even earlier. Shoshoni horsemen were terrorizing their earthbound Blackfoot enemies by the 1730s. The gun frontier, moving from the east, reached the Great Plains at about the same time. The convulsions of these several Indian-versus-Indian frontiers sent reverberations rolling in all directions, changing in many ways the Indian world, and thus affecting in many ways the setting and the course of American history—in areas where white men had not yet set foot. Obviously these frontiers moved only because Indians moved them, only Indians being present.

All the whys and wherefores of the Indian actions create patterns teeming with complexities. There were marked differences between the attitudes and behavior of intact Indian nations and the attitudes and behavior of scattered bands of broken nations. Often it was the latter who represented the faceless "Indian tribes" in our frontier stereotypes—as in the conglomeration of refugees, migrants, and malcontents who made up the enemy Indians in Lord Dunmore's War, or the motley armies of displaced persons commanded by Pontiac. There were great differences also between the various Indian nations or groups, and great differences between the people of the same nation or group in different epochs. Differences in religious outlook influenced attitudes and personalities as readily as does TV today.

A principal difficulty in treating Indian history in depth is its fragmentation. The task of examining each group and each time-phase of each group from the point of view of teleology and all-pervasive religious ethic and of conducting this investigation at least partly in such other languages as that of anthropology is, to put it mildly, forbidding. The Indian reality was of an astonishing diversity, a diversity that presents a constant problem in any wide-angle view. Some Indian peoples tended to be quarrelsome and quick to violence, some were more gentle and peaceable than Quakers, some were taciturn, some were jolly and voluble, some were wildly emotional, some were as reserved as well brought up Englishmen. The general impression that among Indians farming was woman's work is to some degree correct for the eastern woodlands of North America, but not among the Pueblos or in the great agricultural states in Mexico and beyond to the south, where men did most of the farm work. Even minor touches present tangles: for example the widespread early report that Indians did not punish their children seems to have been generally true for many groups, but Creeks and Aztecs, for two, were resounding exceptions. Tattooing, so common among New World people as to seem nearly universal, was not practiced by the Hopi or by the Aztecs or, to go as far afield as possible, by the Yahgans at the tip of South America.

Such are only a few of the many significant differences among the various peoples of the Indian past, countless differences variously reflected in the varieties of Indian decisions and actions. Indian history is far from easy.

Fluctuations in the white point of view down through the centuries are also important. For a highly consequential example, Indians who had been for generations town-dwelling farmers, as were the majority of Indians in the present United States area at the time of European contact, came to be characterized as raggle-taggle nomads, interested only in keeping their lands as "hunting grounds," which of course made it easier to justify seizure of those lands. People living along the coast of California altered their actual appearance, if one is to believe sixteenth-century reports of the early Spanish explorers and Sir Francis Drake, who found them tall, handsome, and "merry"—and the comments of irritable immigrants a couple of centuries or so later who found them squat, squalid, sulky and contemptible. Indians who had been thought of as first class soldiers during the seventeenth and eighteenth centuries came to be pictured at certain later times as childlike primitives supposedly unable, for instance, even under circumstances that solved for a time the usual Indian problem of sustained organization and supply, to conduct a military siege of more than a few days—

even though Pontiac's siege of Fort Pitt and Red Cloud's investiture of the Powder River road are among the longer sieges in all American history.

Criteria of barbarism have rung through many changes; barbaric to the Puritan as well as the Victorian mind was the previously mentioned spared rod, resulting in the "unbridled and unruly children" that Parkman listed along with fleas and no privacy as among the chief annoyances of "savage" life. The nineteenth-century historian Henry M. Brackenridge, after a visit to the Missouri River Indians in 1811, wrote, "One thing I remarked as constituting the great difference between the savage and the civilized state, *their youth undergo no discipline*" (his italics). A missionary found the Opatas of the 1760s retained in the slough of barbaric heathenism by, among other things, a skepticism that made them say only, "Perhaps thou speakest truth," to any asserted fact they hadn't seen with their own eyes. "Until the ministering Father is able to banish this phrase from his neophytes they cannot have the faith required by the infallible authority of God and Church."

There are innumerable further areas of possible Indian historical effect, some rather likely, some rather tenuous. The federation of the United Colonies of New England in 1643, for one, was the first union of English settlements in America, and came not only as a result of the Pequot war but possibly in some imitation of the many Indian confederacies, which appear to have been the typical supra-tribal states in aboriginal North America.

The first formal intercolonial conference outside New England was held in 1684 at Albany, at the urging of the Iroquois and to meet with Iroquois spokesmen.

The six most important colonies met in 1754 with the object of working out a plan of colonial union; these delegates met at the urging of the Mohawk leader Hendrick and also in Albany, where for so many years by that time delegates from the several colonies had been gathering to meet with the Iroquois.

The prevalent Indian institution of government by council (most Indian chiefs were inventions of Europeans) may have been one of the various factors contributing to the form of modern American republics.

Or the amalgam of tribal identity and corporate structure now appearing in some hypermodern Indian societies (Navajo and Crow, for example) may foreshadow future forms of mainstream American society.

Or, at the opposite end of the spectrum, effects of the subtlest sort may be ascertainable—scars on the American soul, perhaps—from acts of more or less open conspiracy and persecution, as in extremist (but profitable) anti-Indian policies carried out in Mississippi, Alabama, Georgia, and Texas. Or effects may exist of such subtlety they have not yet been recognized: said the governor of Isleta Pueblo in 1940, "History tells us that conquerors frequently are conquered by the culture of their victims. If this is so the white man eventually will learn from the Indian—but he'll have to be brighter than he has so far shown himself to be."

Or hitherto unexpected links may be discovered between Indian images and modern views of art, philosophy, or morals.

Or studies of Indian attitudes based on a prevailing interest in matters other than work-for-profit may have something to offer in visions of a future anticipating an immense technological unemployment. A modern economist writes, in speculating on this future: "What takes the place of wages in a workless society? . . . Does profit remain a useful standard of accounting in a propertyless society? . . . The wampum hoard that confers prestige in one culture becomes the potlatch of another."

New World liberty, of much influence in Old World colonies and in Europe itself, may shape the future in ways we cannot begin to foretell.

Or Indian studies may bear on the future in a different direction in the view of the late Benjamin Lee Whorf, whose analysis of Hopi language led him to wonder if those American Indian languages which represent the world "not in the form of separate object-things (sky, hill, swamp, etc.)" but as a unity might not open "the way to possible new types of logical thought and new methods of perceiving the universe."

The important point is that the Indian world may really have been a genuine, influential civilization worth taking seriously in American history.

It may really have been a civilization so firmly committed to its strange attitudes that it nourished its own conquerors and abetted its own conquest.

It may really have been a civilization so incomprehensibly foreign to Europeans that Europeans could not recognize its existence even while in mortal embrace with it, somewhat as in the case of the "dark planets" imagined by Alfred North Whitehead that move on a scale of space and time so radically different from our own as to be undetectable to our senses and instruments.

And finally it may have been a civilization affecting not only our past but still to affect our future.

Within this still-unexplored civilization, said Pierre Teilhard de Chardin, "some general and fundamental laws in human development are certainly hiding."

From the collision of this New World civilization with the Old, the modern world and particularly modern America was born. Without the Indian side of that story its history is not yet written.

CHAPTER 15

Serpent Mound to Tattooed Serpent

Poverty in Spain was, in a favored phrase of Sancho Panza's, older than the itch. The peasantry, with a long history as feudal pawns, knew hard times well. With the flood of New World riches into the country, they became even better acquainted; the multi-thousand-piece silver services of wealthy nobles were matched in a grotesque ratio by the growing population of beggars clustered about church doors. Inflation brought ruin to the common people, destroyed the middle class, and left the country bankrupt.

But the wealth of the Indies also excited, naturally, the cupidity of Spain's European competitors. Hungry rivals shouldered their way into the New World, and Spain, gorged and corrupt with glorious empire, could not hold them off.

In what is now the eastern United States the Spanish were centered in Florida, the English above them on the Atlantic coast, English and French pirates and later colonies below them on heretofore-unoccupied West Indian islands. By the beginning of the eighteenth century the French had driven a wedge down from Canada to the mouth of the Mississippi, between Spanish Florida and Spanish Mexico.

The American nations caught in the middle of these European confrontations took sides, often with gusto, for most of these people of the Southeast were lovers of fighting.

Some of them were also people with a long and notable history. Current archeology dates various Midwestern people at 8,000 years ago or so. Ceremonial burials (painted with red ocher) among Atlantic Coast peoples have been dated to 5,000 years ago. Old Copper artifacts from the Great Lakes region are as old or older. Pottery (origin unknown) occurred in the Southeast as early as 2000 B.C. The ceremonial burials, preferably placed as high as possible on east-facing hills, went on for thousands of years, the tombs containing ornaments, tools, weapons, some articles "killed" by being broken. Cremation became common in the latter ages, during the last millennium B.C., and continued for many centuries. Mounds were built to take the place of hills.

There may have been some gardening along with the principal business of hunting and gathering wild foods but the elaborate culminating burial-mound societies that came into being, more than 2,000 years ago, from these beginnings, appear to have developed without the support of agriculture. Two distinctly different leading cultures have been identified as appearing within this general frame of time and manner. One, somewhat earlier (emerging by about 700 B.C.), is called Adena after the name of one of its sites in southern Ohio, and the other, appearing three or four centuries later and overlapping Adena in both time and place, is known as Hopewell, also after a site in southern Ohio.

There are indications climatic changes may have accompanied these arrivals, and there is some belief that the Adena people may have differed physically from their neighborhood predecessors and from the Hopewell people, and may have been culture-bearers from somewhere else. They did bring, evidently, an increased interest in stylish funerals and a new sophistication in art.

The Hopewell world reached its maximum development from about 300 B.C. to about A.D. 300 or 400, perhaps involving a confederacy of different peoples, and eventually spreading far beyond its Ohio valley heartland, down the Mississippi and through extensive regions reaching from the Gulf of Mexico to Wisconsin, from New York to Kansas.

Complex differences existed in these various outposts; it seems likely the widely separated communities grew from a movement of influences rather than from an expansion of a specific people. The people in and about the Ohio center built great burial mounds and extensive earthwork systems of a religious nature, sometimes enclosing as much as 100 acres in their riverside towns or ceremonial centers. In later Hopewell times and for long centuries afterward a distinctive Effigy Mound culture in various areas fashioned religious mounds in the form of great totem figures—birds, pumas, and the like.

Most Hopewellians everywhere apparently traded for raw materials (pipestone, seashells, mica, obsidian, copper beads, and such) from the Rockies to the Atlantic, and made art objects of a high order to leave for posterity in their rich and splendid burials.

Maize has been found at only a few Hopewell sites, one in Illinois dating to the first century B.C., and some other plants (sunflowers, for example) were cultivated, but agriculture in the East was still in its infancy. There may have been further climatic changes, this time favorable to agriculture, in post-Hopewell times, when a new order of things then developed, centering along the Mississippi south from present Cairo, Illinois.

This new order definitely entailed a farming way of life, around stockaded towns and villages built beside streams and bayous, featuring ceremonial centers of flat-topped temple pyramids made of earth, sometimes quite large—seventy or eighty or even 100 feet high, and covering considerable space. "The sides so upright," as a traveler wrote of one in 1790, "that the cattle cannot get upon it to feed." This Temple Mound tradition, usually called Mississippian nowadays by the archeologists, flourished for many centuries, reaching a peak of operation from about A.D. 1300 to A.D. 1500, and was still in business to some extent, although perhaps only on a remnant basis, when the first Europeans appeared in the Southeast.

The great center of Cahokia, one of the largest of these sites, just across the Mississippi from modern St. Louis, may have ruled its stretch of the river for nearly 1,000 years.

The pyramids resemble the pyramids of Mesoamerica and were topped by wooden temples in the manner of the early Maya, and were built in successive layers, probably at periodic renewal ceremonies, as in Mesoamerica. An eternal fire was kept burning in the temple, as in Mexico, and was regularly renewed at a new-fire ceremony, although once a year, at least in the later times we know about, rather than every fifty-two years, as in the Mexican calendar ordained. The thatched houses resembled some Mexican village (nonurban) houses. Sacrifice of war captives was evidently an enthusiastic community activity. Occasionally the victim was tied spread-eagled in a wooden frame, as in the ancient Mexican fertility rite, and pierced with arrows to bring the symbolic rain of blood. There are so many points in common, even to some specific pottery styles, with the Maya and other early civilizations of Mexico and Central America and even of South America that archeologists assume there must have been contacts, the only real question being the routes of transmission.

Recent speculation favors routes for such transmission north from Mexico heading eastward well inland, since it does not seem likely that scattered gangs of emaciated indigents feeding among the cactus flats of Texas, such as those described by their sometime slave and physician Alvar Núñez Cabeza de Vaca, would have handed on the torch of learning by way of the Gulf Coast. Or connections may have been by sea, across the Gulf, possibly from the Yucatan peninsula, possibly from points (maybe Huastecan points) along the Mexican east coast, a theory that has had some adherents since the 1920s.

This Temple Mound society, believed by many specialists the most vigorous of aboriginal societies in the area of the eastern United States, thus exhibited influences that were clearly Mesoamerican operating upon prototypes that were clearly local, some extending back to Hopewell times. A particularly rich climax, sometimes dubbed the Southern Cult, an emotional religion, captivated much of the area of the Southeast: skulls and bones, weeping eyes, feathered serpents, cat-man gods, and cryptic mystic symbols of an eye in the palm of a hand, a swastika in a star. Weeping in greeting was a common custom in much of the New World, over large areas of time as well as of space, and may have been a factor in this religious outburst.

Here in the Southeast as elsewhere populations had entered and vanished, merged and divided—only more so. Probably more than any other region north of Mexico, the lower Mississippi and environs had been a maelstrom of those currents and ripples of contact. The loose Burial Mound confederacy, and the even looser Temple Mound confederacy or confederacies—if confederacies they were—were apparently composed of tangled multiplicities of peoples, of varying customs and cultures, speaking different languages. The buzzard symbol of the Southern Cult spread its wings over a medley of nations from the numerous Caddo people west of the Mississippi, on the shores of the Great Plains, to the villagers of Georgia (probable ancestors of some of the later Creeks) who built the mound town of Etowah and crammed its graves with spectacular Southern Cult ornaments.

In a general sense, all were hoe farmers growing the same crops, fishermen using the same tackle, hunters coursing the same piney woods, cypress swamps, canebrakes, and gaudy hardwood ridges where bears started up and ran like rolling drums. Buffalo as well as deer were hunted on the Mississippi bluffs, and along the rivers a fearsome game was the "crocodile . . . it squashes people with its murdering tooth," as an erudite traveler reported (the line is a quote, more or less, from Ariosto). All rode the winding rivers in similar models of dugout canoes or poled the swamps with similar cane rafts. All boiled corn soup and hominy from the same recipes, and took the same extras and delicacies from the larder of wild nut trees and berry bushes. The village systems were more or less alike: a large town of perhaps 200 or 300 cabins, sometimes palisaded and moated for defense, serving as the hub for a number of smaller outlying communities.

But the deepest underlying unity seems to have been one of a passionate and mystic endeavor. Living was on a high note. Death was the great crescendo.

This traced back to an antiquity so remote it was in another world (the world of the first elder and younger brother, or the first mother—made pregnant by a snake—who gave birth to the first life and the first death). A story told by the Alabama people deals with a familiar Indian theme, people descending from heaven, in this case "in a canoe singing and laughing," and a man on earth who catches and marries a girl from among them. But later she and their children sail back up to heaven, "singing and laughing, continually singing."

In the Alabama ending to the story the husband tries to follow, in another canoe: "He went on for a while, singing, but looked down to the ground. Then he fell back and was killed."

The Alabama and the Mobile, two nations of considerable size at that time, joined forces under Mobile's famous war chief Tuscaloosa to resist Hernando de Soto's army—at "Fort Alibamo" according to one Spanish record—on October 18, 1540. If the Spanish records are correct this must have been one of the largest Indian battles ever fought in the area of the present United States; after heavy losses for the Spanish and enormous losses on the Indian side, the Spanish prevailed. Estimates of population in later centuries are far too low to fit the Spanish accounts, perhaps another indication of population losses to epidemics of new diseases long before Europeans were permanently installed in the region.

Mobile people of these later centuries gradually moved in with the Choctaw—they spoke the same language. Some Alabama people moved westward with the French after 1763 and a number of families stayed on in east Texas, but the principal groups joined the loose confederacy dominated by several nations of Muskogee people—the Alabama spoke a variant of the same language.

There is a feeling, perhaps, that in later times the meaning of this music of passion and aspiration had been forgotten, and that it was only followed because it had always been followed. Or, rather, that the theme was in a stage of change, modulating to a new key, as it must have done many times down the years.

But the order of living remained: the great midsummer renewal festival, requiring purification from the celebrated "black drink" (usually made from the leaves of the holly, *Ilex cassine*)—the purifying emetic of the Southeast, taken, says an early account, "until the blood comes"—and from physics that sometimes left the purified crippled from violent convulsions.

Midsummer also featured the mass ball game in which arms and legs and sometimes necks were fractured. The engrossing game of sliding sticks and stones called *chenco* (English traders called it chunkey), on which wild bets were made, was played any time, weather permitting.

The order of living included, in headlines, the taboos heaped on sex, which was charged with endless perils. The heart-springing excitement of battle and raid was limited to the young men who participated, but there was the dramatic torture-sacrifice of captured enemy people, as gripping as a play, open to all. It is hard to escape an impression that simply the entertainment involved had become a major force behind the ritual torture of captives of war; with certain exceptions, religious significance is either absent or disguised out of recognition by the time European observers arrive. There seems also to be a reasonable likelihood that such events did not by any means appeal to all the populace.

In essence, however, this was no world of contentment but a world in search of rapture and excitement; this was no land for people of moderation.

When, in the seventeenth century, the Spanish, French, and English established the battlefronts of empire in the Southeast, the largest and most powerful Indian group was a tenuous confederation of some fifty towns (perhaps 30,000 people all told) in the area of present Georgia and Alabama dominated by a nucleus of associated tribes known as the Muskogee.

Early English traders from South Carolina first met people of this confederacy living along a river the English called Ocheese Creek (now Ocmulgee River) and spoke of them as the Indians of the Creek, the Creek Indians, by which name members of the confederacy have been known ever since to speakers of English.

Composed of a number of different peoples and fragments of several earlier groups, most of them related but some utter aliens (a half dozen languages were spoken within it) the Creek confederacy was divided into two principal parts—the Upper Towns, and, in theory below them on the rivers, the Lower Towns, a division reflecting the frequent Indian arrangement of double government.

The Summer and Winter people of the Pueblos became in the Southeast (and quite a few places elsewhere) the Peace and War people. Among the Creeks the Upper towns (again only in theory, since in practice these matters got mixed up) were primarily the Peace Towns, the White Towns, controlling important civil ceremonies such as the *puskita* (the *bosquito*, the *busk*) the festival of the first corn that could run on as long as eight days. During this time new fire was made, grudges were forgiven, plazas were swept and sprinkled with new sand, all life was scrubbed, shined, and started afresh on another year.

The principal chief of the confederacy was supposed to be chosen from a White Clan. The Lower Towns were the Red Towns, consecrated to ceremonies of war, and the elders of the council, the Beloved Men, were supposed to choose the confederacy's battle chief, the Great Warrior, from a Red Clan.

West of the Creeks were the people whose road to their landing place on the Father of Waters, the road known later as the Old Chickasaw Trail, first led English traders to the Mississippi. The traditional Chickasaw river port, more than 150 miles west of their central villages, was on the site of modern Memphis.

Below the Chickasaw toward the coast of the Gulf the most important nation was that of the Choctaw, who gave their name to a lingua franca used thereabouts in trade, the Choctaw Jargon—also called, depending on where one was trading at the moment, the Chickasaw Jargon or the Mobile Jargon, these languages all being somewhat similar. The Choctaw, Chickasaw, most of the Creeks, in fact most of the people over all this deep south country from the Mississippi River eastward to the Atlantic, spoke languages related to various divisions of the Muskogee language family.

Related languages, as has been said before and I'm afraid may be said again (and again), did not have to imply related, or even friendly, people. The Choctaw and Chickasaw, for example, with very similar languages, were considerably less similar physically and in their natures: the Chickasaw far-ranging, quarrelsome, aggressive; the Choctaw close-mouthed farmers inclined to stay home and tend their gardens, which in the rich bottom lands of southern Mississippi and Alabama were some of the best in North America. The two were "traditionally," of course, bitter enemies.

In this Southeastern sea of Muskogean tongues there were islands of Siouan speech (notably the Biloxi) and Algonquian (notably bands of Shawnee). Up the Atlantic coast in North Carolina were the Iroquoian Tuscarora people, and north of the Creeks were the Cherokee, most populous single tribe in all the area (at a wild guess some 20,000 souls in sixty villages) speaking variant (the most variant known) Iroquoian dialects.

As noted, linguistic relationships are often purely technical morphological connections charted by linguistic anthropologists—they were or were not recognized as relationships by the Indians involved—depending on the circumstances. Speakers of English today might or might not feel a kinship to speakers of German, a closely related language, as has been mentioned—the two have probably not been separate languages as long as Cherokee has been separate from Iroquois—but it is doubtful that English speakers would feel any sense of linguistic relationship with, say, peoples who speak Hindustani or Kurdish, which are nevertheless in a technical sense distantly related to English, somewhat as a Muskogean tongue of one division might be related to a language of another Muskogean division.

The main Siouan frontier of the seventeenth century, zigzagging northward up the west bank of the Mississippi, might be said to begin in the south with the Quapaw (the name means "downstream people"). Their territory lay generally westward of the Chickasaw country, most of it across the Mississippi, centering on the mouth of the Arkansas. Below the western range of the Quapaw, over an immense region with its heart in present east Texas, were the principal Caddo confederacies.

The lower Mississippi, from the Yazoo to the delta, was controlled by a series of little riverine states, small in area compared to their surrounding neighbors, but not necessarily always weaker in population or influence, the best known of these being the famous Natchez.

The Natchez occupied nine or more villages, most of these on the east side of the present city of Natchez, and at the close of the seventeenth century may have numbered approximately 4,000 in total population, including two villages of refugee foreigners they had taken under their wing (the Grigra and the Tiou; the Tiou, at least, were refugees from Chickasaw aggression). This, as single "tribes" north of Mexico go, is a considerable size: twice as numerous as the Quapaw, almost equal to the Chickasaw, a fourth as large as the Choctaw, who almost equaled the great Cherokee in number.

It should be mentioned again that these estimates of early population figures are only guesses, somewhat as if we might guess the population of various foreign places after a summer in Europe, and estimates especially untrustworthy as any indication of the pre-Columbian state of things.

Even the earliest reports of European explorers and colonists are not at all likely to reflect normal pre-Columbian conditions, since disruptions and epidemics had in this area undoubtedly preceded the first appearance of any people from heaven, sometimes, perhaps, by many years. Three great outbreaks of pestilence ravaged the villages collected around the Spanish missions in Florida during the seventeenth century (1613, 1649, and 1672), and there was certainly no reason for any contagion to confine itself to Christian Indians.

Thus the population of 420 estimated for the Biloxi in 1699 may easily be far less than earlier numbers, and the 214 given by a report of 1715 for the Apalachicola, a leading people among the Lower Creeks, one of the original organizers of the Creek Confederacy, known among the Muskogee as the ancients of the country, must surely be, as it might seem from this impressive history, nothing more than a shadow of former strength.

The Natchez told of a great sickness in which "multitudes of people" died, lasting four years, and reducing them from a great nation of fifty towns, stretching fifteen days' journey in one direction and twelve days' journey in the other, an unheard-of calamity caused, so some said, by an unfaithful temple guardian who had let the sacred fire go out.

In any event, the celebrity of the Natchez is out of proportion to their size, but comes from their position as a preeminent, if perhaps not typical, example of a Temple Mound state surviving into modern times.

They were ruled by a king, a descendant of the sun and called the Great Sun. Every deference was shown him, and his power over his individual subjects, their lives, labor, and property, was absolute and despotic; although in political decisions involving the nation as a whole the Great Sun in turn was controlled by the council of respected old men.

His residence, in the principal village, was a large cabin (45 x 25 feet) built on a long, flat-topped mound some 8 to 10 feet high. Nearby on a similar mound was another large cabin, decorated with two carved birds perched at each end of the roof. This was the temple, in which two guardians watched the eternal fire, and in which were the sacred bones of previous Great Suns.

No one but the Great Sun, who was high priest as well as king, and the few appointed temple officials, was permitted to enter the temple. Whether its forbidding sanctity came primarily from the fire within it or from the bones interred there or simply from its religious symbolism is uncertain; experts disagree. Remains of larger pyramids dating from earlier times, such as Emerald Mound in Mississippi, 35 feet high and covering seven acres, could be seen not far from the Natchez towns; archeologists find a fairly orderly background for the Natchezan culture reaching into burial mound times 1,000 years before, long enough certainly for mystic structures to take shape.

The relatives of the Great Sun (with the exception of his children and his father) were Little Suns. His mother or sister was the principal woman Sun and chose the successor, from among her own sons or brothers, when the Great Sun died. This descent through the mother was common throughout the Southeast and familiar in agricultural social arrangements all over the world.

The Great Sun appointed the two war chiefs of the nation, the two masters of ceremony for the public rites in the plaza before the temple, and other important functionaries, from among the Little Suns, relatives (to repeat) of his mother or sister, excluding his own children.

Below the Suns in importance was a class of Nobles, and below the Nobles a class called Honored Men (to which anyone could aspire by distinction in piety or war), and lowest of all were the commoners, the masses, treated like dirt by the aristocrats, say the early accounts, and referred to as Stinkers (*Miche-Miche-Quipy* in the Natchez tongue, rendered in French as "Puant"), although the term was not used in the presence of the Stinkers themselves, as it offended them.

Suns could not intermarry—all Suns, great and little, male and female, had to take their husbands or wives from among the Stinkers, and children of all male aristocrats always fell one degree in the social scale: children of male Suns were born only Nobles, children of male Nobles were reduced to Honored Men or Women, and children of Honored Men were Stinkers. But children of female Suns were Suns, children of female Nobles were Nobles, children of Honored Women were Honored People. Children of two Stinker parents were of course absolute Stinkers.

This Gulliveresque system appears to be unique. As a possible worn down relic of ancient Mesoamerican rule by dominant lineage it may have much to reveal.

Female Suns, naturally, must have held a decisive power, as well as living the life of a maiden's dream—at any rate the dream of a maiden of the gallant court of Louis XV, whose Louisiana subjects recorded most of this.

There would be a temptation to suspect the reporters' powdered wigs were getting in their eyes except that five reasonably plausible contemporary accounts all agree in essential facts. Even so, one wonders. We are told the Stinker husband of a woman Sun had to stand in her presence like a servant, shout his praise of her every remark, was not allowed to eat with her, and if he displeased her, particularly by any infidelity, she could "have his head cut off in an instant." Privilege of rank permitted her, of course, as many lovers as she pleased. She could also, if the whim struck her (so they say), have her base-born husband thrown out at a snap of her fingers, and pick another Stinker in his place.

And yet this was a warrior society and the situation in the usual Natchez home (so they say) was that the husband "alone commands." Old men were held in such respect "they are regarded as judges. Their counsels are judgments."

The Natchez may have been the people spoken of in a chronicle of the Hernando de Soto expedition as worshipers of the sun, to whom Soto sent word that he was the sun's younger brother. They replied that if he would dry up the Mississippi they would accept his credentials. Possibly they joined other Mississippians in merrily chasing the Spaniards down the river. It was not until a century and a half later that their old life was definitively interrupted by Europeans who came to stay, when the French founded the colony of Louisiana, first established at Biloxi (1699) and then on Mobile Bay (1702).

The Natchez had seen Frenchmen occasionally for several years previously, leathern strangers who came floating down the river in canoes beautifully fashioned of bark, marvelously swift—the first of these (of record) had been a band led by a fretful trader named Robert Cavalier, Sieur de La Salle, an overnight guest with the Natchez in March 1682.

Now, in the 1700s, French missionaries began appearing and newcomers not only from Canada but direct from France, seamen in great boots, soldiers in steel breastplates, clerks from counting houses, farmers from Gascony—and three Carolina Englishmen came by way of the Chickasaws, already stout English allies, to visit the Natchez villages of White Apple, the Hickories, Grigra, and Tiou. The French would enslave the Natchez in their own country, the English traders said, and furthermore French guns and hatchets and knives were not as good as the English, and furthermore the English would trade for a lower price in pelts.

The Englishmen fled back to the Chickasaws when a French trading post was opened at the Great Village of the Natchez in 1713. But some of the Natchez (from the villages of White Apple, the Hickories, and Grigra) murdered several Frenchmen and brief hostilities followed—armed parleys rather than a war—resulting in the execution of six village war chiefs, and delivery by the Natchez of the heads of three others; their heads not their scalps, the French governor specified, "in order to recognize them by their tattoo marks."

Another result was a garrisoned French stockade, Fort Rosalie, established in the Natchez country.

These first French colonies had been a business venture on the part of a rich French businessman who had obtained sole exploitation rights for all North America from the Illinois to the Gulf, from the Carolinas to New Mexico, but could not make his investment pay.

In 1717 the revolutionary financier John Law took over his grant on speculation, formed a company that was given total power over this land and anyone in it, and propagandized for colonists and trade so successfully a huge financial boom was generated that still dwells in history under the name, alas, of the Mississippi Bubble.

Agents of this company obtained large tracts among the Natchez towns for plantations, the region became the most flourishing section of the Louisiana colony, and seemingly every Frenchman there who knew how to write recorded his observations on the remarkable Natchez—who are given more space in the literature of the period than all the other fourteen Indian states of the lower Mississippi put together.

Natchez warriors are seen again and again, heads flattened to a mitred point, hair cut in whatever bizarre fashion the wearer likes—shaved on one side, left long on the other, or trimmed to a single scalp lock, or tonsured like a priest's. They stroll the plaza, tattooed (tattoos were, so to speak, war medals) from face to ankle, negligently waving fans, or recline on their mats while the women work the fields.

All Natchez girls, however, seemed to live the life of a Louis XV maiden's dream in certain respects, such as the social approval seemingly given to sexual promiscuity before marriage and (female Suns apparently excepted) their virtuous fidelity afterward, fairly precise reverse of French fashion at the time.

Homosexuals appear, male concubines as one French observer calls them, men who wear their hair woman-style, long and braided, wear skirts instead of loincloths, and work with the women. Many Indian societies gave transvestites some recognition, ranging from an embarrassed tolerance to a sort of priestly distinction—although Maya tradition was reported as saying they had never heard of homosexuality before the Toltecs came, and the Aztecs and Incas punished it by law; Inca soldiers, about to make war on a notoriously homosexual nation, joked about the danger of rape. Sodomy was one of the common charges brought by early Spanish priests to justify punishment of various stubborn peoples. Las Casas claimed the reports were exaggerated, as the stories of Central American caciques who kept "hundreds" of effeminate men in "harems" might seem to indicate.

In a sense the whole Indian attitude toward what Europeans regarded as obscenity seemed shameless and arrantly sinful to European eyes and ears, and still does—even today scholarly translators of Indian literature make occasional use of Latin to veil the (to them) dirty passages. On the other hand many Indians found (and a few still find) some European attitudes, for example such as not isolating women during menstruation, not only obscene but arrantly wicked.

The sensational torture scenes were painted by all. Captured enemy warriors were the finest of prizes, brought back to dance and sing before the temple and then scalped and lashed up naked in a wooden frame to be tortured and burned. Etiquette demanded that the victim sing his death song so long as life remained, and some, says Le Page du Pratz, the best of the Natchez reporters, "have been seen to suffer and sing continually during three days and three nights."

Captive women and children had their hair cut short, badge of slavery, and were put to work pounding corn. As among most Indian groups, it was also possible for captives to be adopted into the nation, and even attain later eminence.

But it was the marvelously revolving caste system that made the Natchez remarkable to their French neighbors, who saw in this complicated hereditary aristocracy the surest proof that civilization's gentle step had once trod these woodlands rude, sometime or other.

When it came to the Great Sun, his Louis Quinze admirers were downright charmed. There were dissenters. The first French governor wrote of the Great Sun of his day (1700): "He appeared to me the most absolute savage I had seen, as beggarly . . . as his subjects." But other witnesses sing panegyrics on the reverent abasement of his subjects, his absolute authority, and his kingly demeanor.

"When he gives the leavings (of his dinner) to his brothers or any of his relatives, he pushes the dishes to them with his feet." "The submissiveness of the savages to their chief, who commands them with the most despotic power, is extreme . . . if he demands the life of any one of them he comes himself to present his head."

Wearing his crown of swan feathers tasseled in scarlet, the Great Sun was carried in a litter to the festival of the new corn; his platform bed of state was furnished with a goose-feather bolster and heaped with the richest buffalo robes and bearskins, and he was wakened in the mornings by the most distinguished old men, who saluted him with respectful cries and bows that he didn't deign to notice (a *lever du roi* to the life).

And "these people blindly obey the least wish of their great chief . . . for whatever labors he commands them to execute, they are forbidden to exact any wages. The French, who are often in need of hunters or of rowers for their long voyages, never apply to anyone but the great chief."

This last hints at a practical charm in addition to the regal romance of it all. One suspects the Natchez warriors did not spend too much time reclining on their mats after the French appeared.

This may have been one reason, along with constant English-Chickasaw agitation, for the fairly clear emergence of two political parties among the Natchez: pro-French and anti-French. There may have been some tendency for certain classes to cleave to one party or the other. The Great Sun and his brother, war chief of the nation, whose name was Tattooed Serpent, and their mother, the principal woman Sun, whose name was Tattooed Arm, were all strongly pro-French. The majority of the higher aristocracy seems to have followed them in pro-French leanings.

The clearest division was among the villages (of which only six seemed to exist after 1713): the Great Village and the Flour Village were pro-French centers, while the Hickories, White Apple, and the immigrant districts of the Grigra and Tiou seem to have been hotbeds of anti-French feeling. Although here again some of the chiefs of these seditious villages, Suns all, appear to have maintained a sturdy pro-French loyalty as long as possible.

In the autumn of 1722 a young sergeant of the Fort Rosalie garrison had an argument with an aged Natchez warrior over a debt and "threatened to give the old man a cudgeling," at which the old man, riled, said they might see who was the stronger. "At this defiance, the soldier, crying 'murder,' summoned the guard to his assistance." The old man, walking toward his village "at an ordinary gait," was shot in the back. He died the next day of the wound. The commandant of Fort Rosalie reprimanded the young sergeant.

Some White Apple men a few nights later (drunk, the Tattooed Serpent said) shot and wounded one of the directors of the plantation (called the concession of St. Catherine, giving the name it still bears to the creek running through the Natchez towns) neighboring their village, and killed and scalped a French soldier. A detachment of troops was immediately sent up the river from the recently founded capital of New Orleans. Tattooed Serpent managed to make peace, and forced the villages of White Apple, the Hickories, and the Grigra to pay an indemnity to the French troops.

Not long afterward resentful individuals from these villages killed some cattle on the concession of St. Catherine and this time a larger army, with Choctaw and Tunica allies, came up from New Orleans, the French after vengeance for the murdered cows, the Choctaw and Tunica along for incidental plunder.

Again, Tattooed Serpent made every effort for peace, but the French commander, this time the governor himself, was bent on blood, although he at length agreed to spare the Great Village and the Flour Village.

The expedition marched by stealth against White Apple, but on the way they came in sight of three Natchez women pounding hominy in front of a lone cabin, and since the governor had inspired his troops, among whom were many New Orleans volunteers, by promising that they could keep as slaves any females they could catch, the whole army stormed the three women and the cabin with such an uproar and fusillade that the White Apple people were alerted and abandoned their village.

Thereafter the army found only empty villages to burn. Although by chance an old woman was encountered, "who was perhaps more than 100 years old, since her hair was entirely white, a very rare thing among these savages. . . . The general . . . after having questioned her . . . abandoned her on the spot, as a useless encumbrance, to the discretion of a little slave he had, who took her scalp and killed her."

The Choctaws and Tunicas managed to scare up four women and one man during several tiresome days of marching, and the governor, who wanted "blood worthy of being shed," summoned Tattooed Serpent and told him they were going to destroy the Great Village and the Flour Village after all, since they couldn't find anyone at home elsewhere.

Tattooed Serpent, "who was really a friend of the French, made no other reply than to ask for peace." The governor finally granted it, on condition that the head of the chief of White Apple be delivered to him. This was a Sun of great distinction named Old Hair, particularly respected by the entire nation, and, very probably, the bulwark of the hard-pressed pro-French party in White Apple. Being a Sun, he was supposed to be exempt from capital punishment for any reason whatever. But Tattooed Serpent submitted, and after two days for the necessary ceremonies and leave-takings brought the head of Old Hair.

The governor, rather as an afterthought, also demanded and got the head of a free black man who had come to live with the Natchez—"It was justly feared that he would teach them the manner of attack and defense, and for that reason it was of the utmost importance . . . to get rid of him."

Sometime later a malefactor from Tiou cut the tail off a planter's mare (a trophy as good as a scalp). Tattooed Serpent bought peace this time with a tribute of corn from the entire nation, "more than sufficient to pay an entire regiment of cavalry."

Tattooed Serpent died in 1725. The whole nation (and quite a few of his friends among the French) wept, for he was much beloved. His two wives, his chancellor, doctor, principal servant, pipe bearer, and various other followers went joyously to the funeral rites, at which they were drugged and then, with their heads concealed in skin bags, strangled. Several other volunteers insisted on being strangled to go along, one of them a Noble woman, a great beauty, a particular friend of Tattooed Serpent, and "intimate only with distinguished Frenchmen." The French called her La Glorieuse. A Stinker couple sacrificed their child and threw its body under the feet of the pall-bearers (a means of being raised to Honored rank), and the Great Sun himself, wildly grieving, had to be restrained from suicide.

One cashiered warrior marked for sacrifice didn't want to go, and Tattooed Serpent's favorite wife sent him away: "it is not good that you come with us and that your heart remain behind you on the earth." To French friends who begged her not to die, she said "with a smiling air": "Do not grieve. We will be friends for a much longer time in the country of the spirits than in this, because one does not die there again. . . . Men do not make war there any more, because they make only one nation. I am going and leave my children without any father and mother. When you see them, Frenchmen, remember that you have loved the father and that you ought not to repulse the children of the one who has always been the true friend of the French."

She was, it will be remembered, from the class of Stinkers.

The Great Sun died three years later, in 1728. The succeeding Great Sun was young and less effective. The old queen mother, Tattooed Arm, was left alone as the mainstay of French support. The White Apple chief who had taken the place of Old Hair was hotly anti-French, and of growing influence. Pro-English Chickasaws, according to an English account, won the Natchez for their side in the year of the Great Sun's death. "But as the Indians are slow in their councils on things of great importance, though equally close and intent, it was the following year before they could put their grand scheme in execution."

For a final argument there came now as commandant at Natchez an unbelievably villainous ass (all accounts agree) named Chépart (also given as d'Etcheparre and Echepare), who tyrannized over everyone in sight, French as well as Indian. The best plantation land being taken up, he commandeered the Great Village itself for his plantation, and ordered the youthful Great Sun to move his people away instantly. He granted a delay until harvest time (the first corn having just sprouted), on consideration of a sufficient rental paid in fowls, bear's oil, corn, and pelts—but at first frost (the year was 1729) the people would be gone or he'd haul the Great Sun down to New Orleans in irons.

The old men met in secret councils. There could be no other decision than war. Messages were sent to some of the Choctaw, who agreed to join in and attack New Orleans. Tattooed Arm, in desperation, tried to warn the Sieur Chépart—he paid no attention to her messengers except to have them jailed.

At the first frost of 1729 the Natchez attacked the French everywhere in their country, killed more than 200 and made prisoners of several hundred women, children, and blacks. Natchez warriors refused to touch the Sieur Chépart with their weapons, but had a Stinker beat him to death with a stick.

The Choctaw faction supposedly allied with the Natchez played a double game and sided with the French, so this was, of course, the end. Even so it was a long time coming, and required two full-scale comic opera invasions from New Orleans, some genuine hard fighting here and there, and a grand display of power politics up and down the river as each side tried to line up support.

In town after town the red-painted war posts were set up and hung with red feathers, red arrows, and red tomahawks, and, after furious vomiting, warriors danced and struck the post with their red-painted war clubs, with all their might, to signify enlistment. The Yazoo Indians murdered the French among them, and one of them dressed himself in the clothes of their slain missionary to go to the Natchez and announce allegiance. The French secured the home front by sending black slaves to exterminate thirty inoffensive Chaouachas, the nearest Indians to New Orleans.

But the Choctaw defection had been decisive, even though only the western villages of the colossal Choctaw nation were involved—the Choctaw also were divided into two parties, pro-English in the east, pro-French in the west. These internal politics undoubtedly played a part in the devious course of Choctaw policy.

Eventually, after more than a year of maneuvering, the French managed to persuade a few dozen Natchez warriors and several hundred women and children to surrender. These included most of the leaders of the aristocratic pro-French party.

Tattooed Arm refused to come along, but it is reasonable to suppose the children of Tattooed Serpent were among them. The French commander selected a few men and women for public burning; the rest, including the Great Sun and his wife and children, were sold as slaves to the French colony in the Caribbean, on Saint-Domingue.

For a long while afterward bands of implacable Natchez harassed French voyageurs along the river, but the largest groups went into exile and established towns among the Chickasaw, Creeks, and Cherokee, where they acquired some reputation as mystics, possibly because of their antique traditions.

The Natchez had not had enough time; several thousand years were perhaps needed, to learn to be properly humble peasantry European style. A possible clue in this to the centuries of Indian wars to come, along with the bold determination of the three Christian nations, Spain, France, and England, when in collision to fight to the last Indian.

CHAPTER 16

People of the Forest

From the time men first began using the native copper along the shores of Lake Superior until the time of pottery along the upper Mississippi is believed to be some 3,000 years. From the time of the appearance of pottery until the flourishing midpoint of the extensive confederacy (as it seemed to be) of the Hopewell peoples was another 1,000 years or somewhat more. From the Hopewell high point until the general invasion of Europeans along the Atlantic coast was another 1,500 years or a bit more.

Beside the lakes and rivers, in the hills and fields and in the long reaches of forest of the Northeast, people lived, multi-tongued, of great diversities and many samenesses, who at the European arrival still traveled the worn paths of all these accumulated ages.

They hunted with the skill of neolithics, and the Deer, Bear, Wolf, and Turtle were their brothers. They used wild plants with the magic incantations and racial memories of women who had made meals of seeds, leaves, roots, nuts, berries, in this country for millennia before any knowledge of farming was in use.

Trade networks moved precious goods, probably band to band, across the entire country, obsidian from the Rockies to Ohio, tobacco from Virginia to the St. Lawrence, copper from the present Canadian border to the Carolinas and Georgia, flint and salt and pipestone everywhere.

The common political structure was the confederacy, a nucleus of associated bands in hegemony over other bands and fragments of bands, related or not, ex-enemies or ex-allies, ancient or recent acquaintances; immigration into the tribe was probably, as a rule, open to all.

They sought guidance in the supernatural dreams of the solitary hunter, and in the united prayers of a community of farmers. They raided each other for loot, glory, revenge, trophy heads or the skins thereof, or for captives to sacrifice or adopt to take the place of lost relatives.

It will bear repeating that Indian "war" north of Mexico in pre-white times was most often a private activity triggered by the death of a relative at the hands of foreigners. Evidence from later ages indicates that group conflict customarily splintered into scattered ripples of small engagements, continuing through long periods of time. The concept of national war was apparently all but unknown.

In later ages captive killing was embroidered with tattered vestiges of sacrificial ceremony, including occasional ritual cannibalism, and often with frenzied excesses of public torture that suggested an emotional religious background.

Here and there over the spruce and fir of northern woods appeared Quetzalcoatl, disguised as the Morning Star.

Various gods have survived to the present, from the solemn Master of Breath, the supreme being, to the deity straight out of a cartoon pantheon, the Great Rabbit, who went skipping about setting a chaotic world to rights (right by his wild lights), playing jokes (the funniest the dirtiest by European standards), and getting himself into (and always out of) terrible trouble. Great Rabbit's home was from the Great Lakes in the north to the canebrakes of the south, but he reappears again and again anywhere in the continent, sometimes wearing other identities (Coyote, Old Man, Raven, Raccoon, and many more); he is, in fact, the Trickster God known round the world, one of the universal inventions of the human mind.

Most of these forest dwelling people were, in the millennia following the appearance of agriculture, farmers and townsmen. Slash and burn cornfields were cultivated as far north as the climate permitted, although some groups spent much time moving from place to place and only touched base at a more or less permanent village during certain seasons. Their dwellings were of many varieties, from skin or brush shelters to long barracks-like multifamily houses to huts of pole and wattle "much like the wild Irish," as a New Englander of the 1620s observed.

Some organized society into clans that claimed descent from the spirit of an animal, Bear, perhaps, or Beaver, some into special societies formed for specific purpose such as war, ceremonial observances, healing. Some reckoned descent from the mother, some from the father. Some, notably the Huron, north and east of Lake Ontario, practiced elaborate mass-burial ceremonies, when the collected bones from the accumulated deaths of ten or twelve years were formally interred together with mountains of rich funeral gifts, from furs to beautifully worked tools and arms.

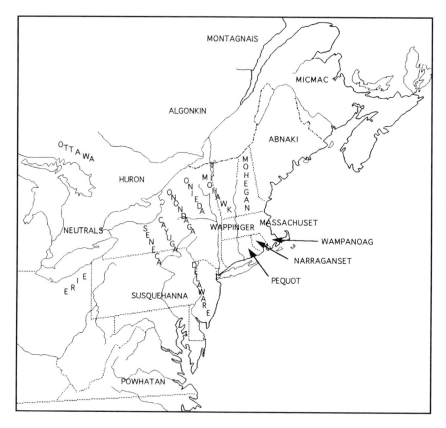

The Northeast

The southern ball game, with racquets, was played. French traders called the racquet, and the game as well, *la crosse*. An East Coast innovation introduced in the centuries following the decline of the Hopewell world was in wide use: seashells strung on strings or beaded into belts, used almost like money, and exchanged between nations at diplomatic councils as guarantees of earnest intentions. English traders called it wampum, after an Algonquian word, *wampompeag*.

These Northeastern people enter our history to the cries of woodland battle. "The place where they fought was of great advantage to the savages, by means of the thick trees, behind which the savages through their nimbleness, defended themselves, and so offended our men with their arrows, that our men being some of them hurt, retired fighting to the water side where their boat lay, with which they fled towards Hatorask," says an account from the year 1586, of a little engagement near the short-lived colony of Roanoke, in Virginia.

Or, in a description of Indians fighting Indians published in 1634 by the trustworthy William Wood, a Plymouth settler, the Mohawks come "running, and fiercely crying out, *Hadree Hadree succomee succomee* (we come we come to sucke your blood), not fearing the feathered shafts of the strong-armed bow-men, but like unruly headstrong stallions beate them down with their right hand Tamahaukes, and left hand Javelins . . . Tamahaukes be staves of two foote and a halfe long, and a knob at one end as round and bigge as a football . . . one blow or thrust with these strange weapons, will not neede a second to hasten death, from a Mohackes arme."

The Indian story gives an impression of being writ larger in war whoops in the neighborhood of the English colonies along the Atlantic coast than elsewhere in the invaded hemisphere.

It is important to realize that this is a distorted impression. The Indians of the Northeast were, most of them, warlike enough, but no more so than many others Europeans had met, and less so than some. Their wars were of critical importance for the persons concerned but they were fewer and smaller than the wars in a number of other areas of European colonization. Not only is a background of war a distorted view as regards the nature of the considerable Indian participation in American colonial history, but also in regard to Indian life in the region before European contact.

The subtler turmoils of peace were of equal or greater importance, and there were more of them. Will Wood's foregoing picture of charging Mohawks has been often quoted; another line in his 1634 survey has received less attention: "But to leave their warres, and to speak of their games in which they are more delighted and better experienced." Speaking of a New England tribe he remarked, "Take these *Indians* in their own trimme and natural disposition, and they be reported to be wise, lofty-spirited, constant in friendship to one another."

Thomas Morton, the merry trader of Merry Mount, Massachusetts, who probably knew the Indians of New England as intimately as any Englishman of his time, wrote of their festivals in the 1620s when "they exercise themselves in gaminge, and playing of juglinge trickes, and all manner of Revelles, which they are delighted in, that it is admirable to behould, what pastime they use, of several kinds, every one striving to surpasse the other, after this manner they spend their time."

In the untouched Indian world, even among peoples of dreaded warlike reputation, there was a great deal more peace than war. It will bear repeating (yet again) that war in the Old World definition was virtually unknown, only approached by such highly organized states as those of the Aztecs or, more particularly, the Incas.

Prehistoric burials reveal now and then plenty of violence, far less to be sure than is in our own daily news but larded enough with varied mayhem, women with broken arm bones (shielding themselves from husbandly blows?), sometimes murder. But there is little indication of whole countries being overrun by war. A meeting between strangers, as seen in early contact records, was more likely to be peaceful, even open and hospitable, than hostile. The raids that were called wars usually involved only a fraction of available fighting men and those only briefly. Defeated nations were sometimes assimilated, not annihilated.

All this was to change somewhat under European tutelage but the point is that the life lived by these woodland people in their stockaded bark-built towns, while it had its sudden storms and dangerous events, was by no means one of constant strife.

Their life was obviously built upon a certain sense of security, perhaps only born of the endless continuity of their world through the countless past generations. It was certainly a life filled with discomfort, and with institutionalized uneasiness anent ghosts and goblins. But above all it may have been pervaded by the feeling of rightness surrounding people who have lived a very long time in a very old garden.

The nations inhabiting the Northeast at about the time of the first European landings were for the most part divided among three language stocks: Algonquian, Iroquoian, and Siouan.

What had been so long ago the Old Copper country, from Lake Michigan to Lake Superior and environs, was now the Wild Rice country, where on the countless lakes and northern marshes, under a sky alive with waterfowl, people thrust their canoes and rafts, harvesting the rice. Judging from the reports of early European explorers this region was teeming with a surprisingly heavy population, the most important groups being the Siouan Winnebago, in the vicinity of Lake Winnebago and Green Bay; the Kickapoo, Sauk, Menominee, and Foxes west and north of them; the Ojibwa west and north beyond, on the shores of Lake Superior, these people speaking Algonquian languages; and various towns of the Siouan Dakota in the Wisconsin woods stretching westward to the Mississippi.

The Ojibwa made up one of the largest nations north of Mexico, with a wild-guess population of 25,000 or more—very probably more. The last syllable of Ojibwa is pronounced "way"; the name refers to the peculiar puckered seam of their moccasins; Europeans garbled it into Chippeway and stuck to it so persistently that many Ojibwa people today are officially called Chippeway (some today prefer another more ancient name for themselves, Anishinabeg or Anishinaubag).

North of the Ojibwa an almost identical people known as the Cree controlled the enormous spruce-fir country that ran all the way up to Hudson Bay. At the eastern end of Lake Superior, at the present Sault Ste. Marie, the Ojibwa joined with the Ottawa and Potawatomi in a loose confederacy known to white traders as the Three Fires. In the traditions of all three of these tribes they were originally one, and that not too many centuries ago (some ethnologists still list them all as Ojibwa).

The Miami confederacy of Indiana and environs (one of their villages was called Chicago, said to mean "skunk place") and the perhaps somewhat more populous Illinois confederacy to their west were not large in numbers, at any rate in historic times. These people too were of Algonquian speech. The Erie to their east, below Lake Erie, spoke an Iroquoian tongue.

Strongholds of Shawnee towns were south (the name means "Southerners") of the Miami and extended to the hills of the Chickasaws and the Great Smoky Mountains of the Cherokees, with the traditional Shawnee center in the Cumberland valley in present Tennessee. But the Shawnee appear to have been nearly everywhere throughout the Middle West and Middle South at various times. They were closely related, in language, style, and way of life, to the Sauk and Fox people, the Kickapoo, and to some other Algonquian peoples on the Atlantic coast.

The Ohio Valley, that had been the heart of the Hopewell burial-mound commonwealth some hundreds of years before, had apparently become surprisingly sparse in population since that time. A large area embracing parts of present Kentucky, southern Ohio, and West Virginia was so thinly settled that portions of it were regarded as practically uninhabited, a sort of no man's land, a hunting ground and battlefield open to all.

At least southern Ohio and contiguous Kentucky seem to have been empty at the time of the first European look. Since this was for so long the very epicenter of the ancient, thriving, town-dotted Hopewell world some small riddle seems to be afoot, beyond those mists of time that hang like fogs of a frosty Indian Summer over the beautiful Ohio.

Tidewater Virginia and adjacent beaches and backwoods, scene of some of the earliest European exploration and settlement along the Atlantic coast, were the home of a union of Algonquian-speaking nations called the Powhatan (accent on last syllable) Confederacy. The name means Falls of the River and was specifically applied to the falls of the James River (present Richmond).

The "king" whose home village was located there was called by the English colonists after the name of his town, and is in our folklore as King Powhatan. His real name was Wahunsonacock. In accordance with a widespread Indian usage his real name was as much his own discreet private property as is a film star's real name today; the evil-intentioned, by pronouncing one's real name, could gain a handhold on one's soul; thus one was more customarily addressed by a title, Brother, Uncle, Warrior—as we might say Senator or General—or by a nickname.

The giant Powhatan Confederacy numbered some 200 villages and included quite a few separate tribes or little states, each ruled (so it seemed to the English) by a minor "king," known as a *werowance*—said to mean "rich man."

"The great king Powhatan hath devided his countrey into many provinces and shiers (as yet were), and over every one placed a severall absolute weroance or comaunder . . . and his petty weroances, in all, may be in number about three or fower and thirty, all which have theire precincts and bowndes," wrote William Strachey, Gent., first secretary of the Colony of Virginia. Captain John Smith gave the number as twenty-eight, with a total population of perhaps 8,500. (Modern students like a higher number.) The English sometimes referred to the ruling chief as "The Powhatan," reinforcing the idea that the name was a title.

It appears that the patriarchal Powhatan (at least sixty years old when the English first met him) had constructed this confederacy almost from scratch during his own lifetime. Early reports of several other confederacies indicate they were in the process of being created by conquest and diplomacy—or dying from dissension—at the moment of European invasion.

Since archeological evidence hints at previous confederacies throughout much of the long past, it might be suspected that the centuries had seen a slow but incessant rise and fall, alignment and realignment, of such unions large and small, and that the confederacy was the normal American pattern.

Some, at least, of the confederated provinces of Virginia paid tribute to Powhatan, but quite a bit of autonomy was apparently enjoyed by the several werowances or the councils of oligarchs that the English also mention as ruling the destinies of various groups.

This or that village could and did separately make war on the English settlers while the confederacy was nominally at peace—Strachey, speaking of a "weroancqua, or queene," of one of the confederacy's towns, says, "Howbeyt, her towne we burnt, and killed some of her people, herself miscarieng with small shot in pursuit in the woods in winter 1610, for a treacherous massacre which she practiced upon fourteen of our men." Similar incidents are far from uncommon in the early history of the Virginia colony.

Howbeit, peaceful coexistence was the general rule during the ghastly early years of the Virginia colony, when the settlers died in batches in the miasmic Jamestown swamps (of the first 900 colonists landed during the first three years, 1607 to 1610, only 150 were still alive in 1610). Old Powhatan could have stamped it out or left it to starve with the greatest of ease—as easily as, it may be from only a slightly different turn of Indian politics, Roanoke had been weeded out only twenty years before, only 100 and some miles down this same coast. In fact, the 150 miserable Jamestown survivors were in the process of abandoning the colony, and were aboard ship to depart when a vessel arrived with reinforcements and supplies.

There was frequent and furious dissension among the colonists; rivalry amounting to gang warfare among different factions seemed to be particularly frequent in the early days of colonies particularly short on immediate profit. Such warfare had sent Columbus to Spain in chains from Hispaniola, and similarly sent Captain John Smith back to England a temporarily lambasted loser, after a serious burn from the accidental explosion of an ammunition-bag of gunpowder had left him for a time unable to cope with his foes.

There was distrust and blundering on each side, European and Indian, in this meeting of worlds so disparate, quarrels between Indians and the German, Irish, French, Polish, and English artisans and would-be gentry who made up the colonists. There was deliberate trouble stirred up by the Spaniards to the south—Spanish embassies to the Powhatans in 1609 are blamed for Indian attacks on Jamestown in 1610, and might have been responsible for the treacherous massacre practiced by the above-mentioned weroancqua. Other such Spanish embassies followed.

But peace, even though ill-policed, persisted. There were two immediate reasons for this: the directors of the joint stock company in London that owned and operated the Virginia colony voted, as the most profitable and least expensive course, to conciliate Powhatan as an independent sovereign rather than make war upon him as a savage, and sent him a copper crown to wear; and Powhatan himself earnestly desired peace. Some historians, who see Powhatan as striving to drive away the English by guile, dispute this but it does seem the benefits of English trade may have outweighed the various frictions.

Said Powhatan to Captain John Smith, so Captain Smith reported: "Why should you take by force from us that which you can obtain by love? Why should you destroy us who have provided you with food? . . . I am not so simple as not to know that it is better to eat good meat, be well, and sleep quietly with my women and children, to laugh and be merry with the English, and being their friend, to have copper hatchets and whatever else I want."

No king, but a kingly figure ("such majesty as he expresseth," marveled Strachey), Powhatan kept the peace.

The first settlers sometimes obtained Indian help by force or cajolery, but also, wrote Captain John Smith: "it pleased God (in our extremity) to move the Indians to bring us Corne, ere it was halfe ripe, to refresh us, when we rather expected they would destroy us . . . [and later] . . . the Indians brought us great store both of Corne and bread ready made."

But still later, when the shoe was on the other foot and the colonists had corn to sell to some starving Indian villages near Jamestown, the English governor traded 400 bushels for "a mortgage on their whole countries."

It was impossible, naturally, for Europeans (born businessmen) not to feel contempt for such people, and once again a conquest was completed, in effect, although the war was still to come.

Peace was badly strained during the troubles of 1609–1610. A little army of colonists seized and held for a while Powhatan's own village at the falls of the James and its 300 acres of cornfields and gardens, as being simpler than building a new town and clearing fields of their own, and wished to tax the Powhatans for the privilege.

But quarrels among the colonists brought the most urgent difficulties at the time, until tranquility was hammered out by the acting governor Sir Thomas Dale (1611–1616), who saved the colony by sparing not the lash, hanging captured runaways, and holding as hostage Powhatan's beloved daughter Pocahontas.

Pocahontas (a nickname meaning something like "Frisky")—her real name was Matowaka, the nickname was a "baby name" (attached in childhood)—is the most famous woman in early American history, and justly so, judging by subsequent events.

"Blessed Pocahontas, the great King's daughter of Virginia, oft saved my life," wrote Captain John Smith, never a man to mince sonorities; and apparently she oft saved the colony as well, being "much at our fort," and a great friend of the English, supplying their wants and filling their jars with corn. "She, under God, was the instrument to preserve this colony from death, famine, and utter confusion," testified Captain Smith.

At the time of her kidnapping she was seventeen years old and married to a warrior named Kocoum, of whom nothing more is heard, for she married within a couple of years one of the leading men of the colony, John Rolfe, a widower with one child. Rolfe wrote to Sir Thomas Dale that she was "an unbelieving creature to whom my heartie and best thoughts . . . have for a long time bin soe intangled and inthralled in soe intricate a Labarinth that I was ever aweried to unwind myself thereat." He wrote that he had feared his love was wicked, but he had decided it was pure, in spite of the allegations of vulgar persons that it was merely to gorge base carnal desire, and he wished to marry her for "our country's good, the benefit of this Plantation, and for the converting an irregenerate to regeneration."

Pocahontas was "a well-featured but wanton young girl," as Secretary Strachey had described her, and evidently had been much in English reveries since the early days when, half grown, she would "get the boyes forth with her into the market place, and make them wheele, falling on their hands, turning their heels upwards, whom she would followe, and wheele so herself, naked as she was, all the fort over."

The marriage was a smashing success for all concerned. The bride, "O princess whose brown lap was virgin May" (as says the best of her hundreds of poets), was crowned with English immortality; and even the father of the bride was eminently pleased, and real peace resulted.

More significantly, John Rolfe learned, presumably with Indian advice and assistance, the cultivation and curing of tobacco. He "experimented" for a year or two with a plot that may have been at "Varina" (the name perhaps not unrelated to the name of the best Spanish tobacco, Barinas) in Henrico, where he and Pocahontas lived after their marriage. He became so successful that he sent a shipment to England in March, 1614—and married Pocahontas the following month. He became the colony's first tobacco exporter, and the colony had what it needed, a fortune-founding cash crop. When his consignment sold at a good price in London, "the permanence of English colonization in America was assured."

A couple of years later he took his bride (along with her brother and several Indian maidens) to London at the invitation of the company, which paid her the truly princely sum of £4 a week—a farm laborer earned at the time £5 or so a year ("plus meate and drink") —as a publicity venture. She was something of a sensation and tradition still remembers her as the first lady of quality to enter a pub; the many pubs still named the Indian Queen supposedly honor this wanton breakthrough. She met everyone from the English queen to a drunken Ben Jonson (who had a character remark in a play several years later that the "great King's daughter of Virginia, hath/ been in womb of tavern"). She died of smallpox in the spring of 1617, at the age of twenty-one or twenty-two, on shipboard just at the start of her return trip to America, leaving an infant son from whom a whole hall full of illustrious Virginians have claimed extraction.

But it was tobacco that fathered all Virginia and had its effect in turn on the broader future of the English elsewhere in America. It had an even profounder effect on the future of Powhatan's people.

It was not a king, nor Christianity, nor knighthood gone adventuring that muscled the conquest of the Atlantic seaboard north of Florida. It was the joint stock company. The joint stock company was organized and operated simply for profit and nothing but profit, and recognized no other purpose higher, lower, or in between. It emerged in Elizabethan England in the mid-1500s in trade with Russia, triumphed in British business by the early 1600s, and provided the foundation of colonial Indian policy in much of non-Spanish North America.

Bows were made in the direction of patriotism and piety, but for the most part they were frankly cynical. Said an early promoter (Sir George Peckham, High Sheriff of Buckinghamshire, whose promotions left him broke in 1595): "First and chiefly [are those benefits to the Indians] in respect to the most gladsome and happy tidings of the most glorious gospel of our Saviour Jesus Christ, whereby they may be brought from falsehood to trueth. . . . And if in respect of all the commodities they can yeelde us (were they many more) that they should receive this onely benefit of Christianity, they were more than fully recompenced."

Or said Sir Ferdinando Gorges, arch-genius of early English colonization efforts: "what can be more pleasing to a generous nature than to be exercised in doing publique good . . . and what more pious than advancing of Christian Religion amongst People, who have not known the excellency thereof, but seeing works of Piety and publique good, are in this age rather commended by all, then acted by any; let us come a little near to that which all harken unto and that forsooth is profit."

French investors picked up with alacrity on the joint stock money machine, even though the usual French policy of royal monopoly gave it no official welcome whatever. An Act of Association drawn up in France in 1651 used several pages to describe the pious intent of the Society and Company before getting to the cost and the necessary hope of some fortune and thus stating, "We have judged apropos to our principal design, the Preaching of the

Evangel, to add as an instrument of aid and administration trade in *Negroes and Commerce* which could be made in those places which would be conquered and occupied by us."

(America was described—drawing on fanciful reports already ancient—in this prospectus, "frankly, without adding or altering anything, and without hyperbole," as enjoying all year long "a perpetual Spring or an Autumn, or better said, both together, so that the trees are seen covered with leaves, with flowers and with fruits: The country is sprinkled with diverse springs which render it as fertile as agreeable, the water is very healthy, and the air so temperate that sickness, rarely seen, is cured by the climate's quality, no one suffers the assaults of fever, and the natives of the country live to 150 years and more.")

The earliest ventures into Virginia, from Raleigh onward, envisioned profits from gold mines, peltries, a passage to India, or such commodities as sassafras, believed at the time to be a specific for syphilis. William Strachey, Gent., proposed that the Virginia Company corner all sassafras, hold it until the price skyrocketed, and then sell to all Europe "thereof at good rates."

Tobacco offered the first genuine indications of a profit, a real profit (sixteen pounds of tobacco could sell for the price of a good horse), indeed a stunning potential for instant riches, to the new Virginians and their stockholders. Tobacco, introduced to Europe via Spain and Portugal (and the French ambassador to Portugal, Jean Nicot, whence nicotine) in the 1500s, had become the rage of fashion to Englishmen of 1600. No devout Indian offering tobacco to the gods of the four directions could have equaled English eulogies bestowed on "this pretious herbe, TABACCO most divine," and "[t]he sweet and sole delight of mortall men," to quote some laudatory verses of 1602. It was believed at first to possess more or less miraculous powers for healing and well-being (an early name in Europe was *herbe panacea*) and was also believed to bring "the pleasure of drunkenness" because with it the Indians "unsettle all the fibres of their brain, and intoxicate themselves as if they had been drinking wine to excess."

With this kind of promotion it had become a desired item everywhere, in spite of the occasional opposition of authorities, which included stringent penalties sometimes even unto capital punishment or even excommunication. ("A custom," said King James in 1604, "loathesome to the eye, hateful to the nose, harmful to the brain, dangerous to the lungs, and, in the black stinking fume thereof, nearest resembling the horrible Stygian smoke of the pit that is bottomless.")

Not surprisingly tobacco turned into the Virginia colony's only export, and Sir Thomas Dale had to force the colonists to give some of their time and land to the planting of grain, since they couldn't eat money.

Not only did potential profit demand constantly expanding acreage, but tobacco used up the soil, and new fields had to be found every two or three years. It was usually easier to take fields from the Indians than to clear new land; early in the life of the colony Captain John Smith succeeded, by Herculean efforts, in having forty acres of land cleared, but not long afterward the village of Kecoughtan at the mouth of the James River was taken over and its inhabitants driven away, its cornfields (according to Secretary Strachey) encompassing 2,000 to 3,000 acres. Even allowing for a tenfold exaggeration on the part of the Honorable Secretary, it wouldn't take a canny eye long to see in this the birth of a pattern. The Americans loved their homes but they loved their peace and quiet (to say nothing of their lives) more. They wept but they moved.

It was easy to believe, each time, that the Coat-wearing People (the commonest Algonquian term for Englishmen) would now have all the land they could possibly want, but if the Indian mind grasped only dimly the European notion of land title it grasped not at all the European notion of great personal estates.

A strong feudal flavor lingered in these early joint stock companies. Some were given the right to grant titles of nobility; all had the right to grant landed estates. The principal officers of the Virginia Company were to be put in possession of personal estates of no less than 1,500 acres each—more if they owned extra "great shares," which brought the estates of some officers to 5,000 acres. Junior executives were granted 500-acre estates. The company created a 12,000-acre estate for itself. Other promoters who guaranteed certain numbers of settlers were given large tracts of land.

Land encroachment was not the only cause for conflict on this first Virginia frontier. Livestock introduced by the settlers damaged the unfenced Indian gardens, hogs being the worst offenders. But if you damaged the hog, the hog's owner would damage you, and if your friends then damaged the hog's owner, the English would then burn an Indian town and put a dozen people to the sword (the second most common Algonquian name for Englishmen was "cutthroats") and another little war would be afire that would take all old Powhatan's influence to smother.

Trading, theft, rowdyism, liquor, women, and attempts at taxation brought contentions, and as the English grew more numerous and bolder, and the inevitable felons, toughs, and whores were swept over from London streets to fill colonist quotas, contentions grew more common, regrettable outrages more outrageous, and exactions of the English always more exacting.

Nothing personal was involved, and it is a mistake to think of settlers and Indians as making two hard and fast opposing camps. The "old settlers" of the colony often had closer ties with the neighboring Pamunkeys or Appomatocs or others of the Powhatan league (or even more so among such as the anti-Powhatan pro-English Chickahominy) than among the Johnny-come-lately new settlers.

What was involved was the inexorable trending of the colony's basic official policy. Founded purely on economic considerations, this policy conciliated the Powhatan people while they were of use, and pressed them remorselessly, facelessly, mechanically, as innocent of conscious ill will as a turning wheel, when they became of less value than their acreage.

Old Powhatan died in 1618, the year after Pocahontas's death in England. Some time passed, during which the council members of the Powhatan Confederacy may have fought out a behind-the-scenes battle between pro- and anti-English parties. The aged Opechancanough, a half-brother of Powhatan's and an implacable English-hater ever since the days of 1607–1608 when he and Captain John Smith had taken turns capturing each other, came out the winner. (Opechancanough might share with Pocahontas in family trees of the later South—he was claimed as an ancestor by President Jefferson Davis of the Confederacy. An entertaining Virginia legend also makes Opechancanough the youthful Spanish-educated coastal Indian known as Don Luis who returned to his home village with the ill-fated Spanish Jesuit mission of 1570. A hint as to the pronunciation of his name may be found in Captain John Smith's map of 1612, where Susquehannock is Sasquesahanogh.)

In the spring of 1622 Opechancanough's Powhatans exploded under the unrelenting English pressure in a savage flash that left nearly 350 colonists dead (John Rolfe was said to be among them) and a number of settlements destroyed in the space of a few hours.

The English population just before Powhatan's death had been put at this same figure, 350, scattered in a half dozen villages. But in the five years since, the number of colonists had quadrupled, while the Indians had suffered disastrously from pestilence. Opechancanough was four short winters late.

The surviving English swore to scourge the Powhatans from the face of the earth, and did succeed in practically exterminating those along the lower James and York rivers. Three punitive campaigns a year were carried out, year after year, giving the Powhatans no chance to plant or harvest corn or rebuild destroyed towns. Men, women, and children were slain without quarter; the English captains were under oath to make no peace on any terms whatsoever.

The heaviest Indian losses were achieved when numbers of them were slyly persuaded to return to their villages, under promises of peace, and were then trapped and massacred. The greatest single victory came in 1625, with the defeat of 1,000 Pamunkeys and the burning of their town.

The war continued for fourteen years, and ended with a peace of mutual exhaustion. During this time, King James had secured an annulment of the Virginia Company's charter in the courts (for reasons having to do with European politics), and Virginia had become a Crown colony.

But the Indian policy established by the original joint stock company remained substantially unchanged. After a few years of peace, land-grab pressures again rose past the danger point; the outbreak of the English civil war in the year 1642 was also apparently a factor in Opechancanough's plans, as were wars and rumors of wars in other new colonies up the coast, and freer availability of firearms from various European traders.

On April 18, 1644, the aged chieftain, now in his nineties and so frail he had to be carried in a litter, struck once more. Again, hundreds of English lives were lost in a single flaming day, in a carefully coordinated sneak attack that took the colonists completely by surprise. There is a tradition that after this first attack the Powhatan war parties slacked away without pursuing their advantage, possibly frightened by an omen.

Opechancanough was eventually captured, shot (against orders) by a guard, and the war came to an end; this time the Powhatan Confederacy came to an end with it.

The English broke up the league, made peace separately with the member tribes and assigned them to reservations which were subsequently whittled down at the colony's pleasure, and—within less than forty years after Jamestown's founding—the once mighty Powhatans turned their faces toward the oblivion of beggary.

At the time of the American Revolution there may have been perhaps 1,000 people left of all the "three or fower and thirty" provinces, most of these survivors moved by then to the more thinly settled Eastern Shore of Chesapeake Bay, with only a few tribal societies, notably Pamunkey, Chickahominy, and Mattapony, still functioning.

A traveler wrote of late colonial Virginia (1759): "Indians and Negroes . . . they scarcely consider as of the human species; so that it is almost impossible, in cases of violence, or even murder, committed on those unhappy people by any of the planters, to have the delinquents brought to justice."

With local variations this is the story of most of the nations of the Atlantic seaboard from the Carolinas to New England during the period of early European colonization.

Unlike the Spanish structure, there was little official English interest in the Indians as a labor force or as souls to be saved.

Here, where plantation exports rather than mines or Indian trade became the infant colony's main road to profits, and where other European rivalry was not imminent enough to be a commanding factor, dealings with the American Indians followed a fairly simple and generally uniform course: initial friendship and cooperation, followed by dismissal of the Indians, so to speak, when their help was no longer needed.

The dismissal usually took the dramatic form of growing hostility, outbreaks of violence, war, and eviction. But in essence it was, as previously described, merely a matter of business.

It was not complicated by any of the soul-searching that beset the Spanish conscience; there was exceedingly little self-criticism of the Las Casas genre. There was no body of law designed to protect the Indians from exploitation or deliberate extermination. The governor and council (corresponding to chief executive officer and board of directors) of the parent joint stock company were answerable to no one for any action against Indians, up to and including enslavement or annihilation. There was, in the beginning, little control by central authority, and an almost total lack of home-government concern with Indian welfare; in sum, "There was no body of imperial law to protect the Indians."

Some of this was to undergo considerable modification after the colonies were taken over by the crown, but Indian policy was to remain for generations a major problem in colonial politics. And at bottom it was to remain what the hardheaded company directors in their paneled council-rooms in Europe's capitals had first made it, a matter of business, basically a problem in economic expediency.

CHAPTER 17

Puritans and Indians

The pattern of European colonization north of Mexico was remarkably constant in what was usually its major early concern, displacement of the Indian nations. A local variation in the Powhatan story was the meager use of Indian allies by the Virginia colonists when war came.

More commonly, Indian auxiliaries made up the bulk of the little European armies, as was the early tradition in Spanish America. Says a specialist in the history of North American colonial warfare, "The success of English arms was in direct proportion to the willingness of the English to use large numbers of Indian auxiliaries." Next door south of Virginia, in North Carolina, the Iroquoian people who composed a confederacy known as the Tuscarora were effectively dismissed, when the time came, by two English-led invasion forces, the first made up of thirty-three Europeans and 498 Indians from eighteen nations, the second numbering again some thirty white men and more than 900 Indian auxiliaries. These figures are those of the formal organization of the two expeditions, and thus were subject to fluctuation as the campaigns progressed. In the informal warfare of the time, many campaigners—white or red—headed jubilantly for home as soon as they had taken slaves or loot, while new recruits joined up along the way.

North of the Powhatans, along the Maryland shore, were a people known as the Nanticoke (an anglicized version of their own name, Nantego, said to mean "tidewater people"), nucleus of a confederacy that had existed, so they said, for thirteen generations before the arrival of Europeans. They were near relatives of Shawnees, Powhatans, and especially of a neighboring division of the people who came to be known as the Delaware. The Nanticoke were reported to be of unusual skill in hunting, fishing, and witchcraft.

A local variation in their story is the brevity of the initial interlude of peace after the beginning of colonization. The first English settlement in Maryland (1634, on cleared Indian fields) was followed by the beginning of annual war parties against the Indians in 1639; formal warfare lessened by 1644 but continued in some wise until 1678. By the end of the seventeenth century the remnants of the Nanticoke were placed on reservations, where a few hung on, but most, during the next generation or two, forsook their homeland and entered other countries as immigrants or suppliants.

The Delaware, so called later by the English, after the English name for the river along which many of their towns were located, were reputed a leading people of all the eastern Algonquian speakers, known to relatives, friends, and even to some of their occasional enemies as the Grandfathers. They occupied a very large territory centering in present New Jersey, eastern Pennsylvania, lower New York, and Delaware. Their precolonial population has been estimated at 8,000 to 12,000, scattered in some forty villages. Legends tell of their migration, long before, from the northwest to this "east land, large and long, rich and good." The migration was long ago indeed according to archeological studies that see these sequences growing pretty much where they were over at least some 3,000 years.

Speakers of Unami, one of their two principal dialects, used as a name for themselves the word Lenape, meaning, as usual, something like "real people," a name that gained wide currency as the native name for the Delawares. Speakers of the other principal dialect, Munsee, were often referred to by the name of their language, stamped on later maps from Muncy, Pennsylvania, to Muncie, Indiana, to Munceytown, Ontario, and in many a moccasined footprint more.

Hollanders of Dutch joint stock companies and Swedish colonists sent out by the New Sweden Company were the first Europeans to establish themselves in the country of the Lenape, in 1623 and 1640, respectively. Both Dutch and Swedish colonists bought Indian land, perhaps to legalize their occupancy in the eyes of other Europeans. The prevailing English usage (with some exceptions) at the time of early colonization was simply to seize, when they could, what was wanted, claiming English ownership of all North America by right of prior "discovery"—even the Indians, in this view, could only clear title to their lands by grant of the English king.

In 1749 Old Nils Gustafson, then ninety-one years of age and son of one of the original Swedish settlers, related, "when the Swedes arrived, they bought land at a very inconsiderable price. For a piece of baize, or a pot full of brandy, or the like, they could get a piece of ground, which at present would be worth more than £400, Pennsylvania currency."

Old Nils also recalled walking with an Indian and meeting a red-spotted snake in the road; Nils got a stick to kill it, but the Indian begged him to let it live "because he adored it." On hearing that it was to the Indian a deity, Old Nils killed it "in the presence of the Indian, saying: because thou believest in it, I think myself obliged to kill it."

The Swedish company made a vigorous effort to provide colonists, but failed—the grand total for ten years was less than 200. Dutch colonizing companies were reduced to one, the West India Company, interested at first mainly in the fur trade; one of the main early colonies was planted well inland, at Fort Orange, near the site of modern Albany, many miles beyond Lenape country. But in 1626 these colonists were brought together with others to found Fort Amsterdam on Manhattan Island, a woodland island that is now the center of New York City, which had been bought from the Indians that spring. The often-quoted price of $24 may be based on a questionable exchange rate: a modern economist has estimated the sixty gulden worth of trinkets would have been closer in contemporary value to several thousand dollars.

The Indians who made the sale were Delawares. In the beginning their relations with the *swannekins* (Algonquian for Dutchmen) were cordial, as in the usual pattern. Manhattan Island, at the mouth of the Hudson River, was something of a trading center, especially for furs brought down the rivers from the interior, and had been the site of a Dutch trading post for some time before the settlement of New Amsterdam. The Manhates ("Island People") were obviously pleased that the swannekins were gathering together in a settlement there. With their odd ideas of land tenure the natives may have believed they were only inviting the strangers to come and share the land with them or, at most, only selling the use of an area for a season or so.

Such land sales were numerous, often simply to individuals, to be regularized by the company later, as with the purchase by several persons of Breukelen (we call it Brooklyn) from the Delaware subtribe called the Canarsee.

But afterward cordiality cooled as the Indians, no longer of any use, became a nuisance, hanging around the settlements, and the usual sort of unpleasant incidents began occurring.

A new Dutch director-general (governor) arrived, who went about the business of subduing troublesome Indians in a businesslike way. When several hundred Delaware people, refugees from Indian-versus-Indian battles up the Hudson, retreated for protection to Manhattan Island and to Pavonia (now Jersey City), the governor, according to some accounts not only exasperated but also inebriated, ordered their massacre, as exemplary punishment for past troubles.

The relation of an eyewitness (who did not love the governor), and an anonymous contemporary pamphleteer, tells us this was carried out in the still of the night and eighty heads of men, women, and children were brought back from Pavonia to Manhattan, to Fort Amsterdam, where (say the atrocity stories in these sources) a colonial dowager played kickball with them in the street. A captive Lenape from a subtribe called the Hackensack was (says a perhaps less unlikely story) tortured to death, while the "poor, naked, simple creature," flayed from fingers to knees, castrated, dragged through the streets, persisted to the end in the quaint custom of singing his death song.

The Dutch were dismayed that "eleven tribes"—evidently most of the Lenape "river people"—joined in the war that followed. It lasted for two years (1643–1645), Indian losses were heavy, and Dutch colonists addressed a memorial to the company in 1644 saying the "fields lie fallow and waste, our dwellings and other buildings are burnt," crops could not be harvested, and the survivors were ready to abandon the colony. All their misery was blamed on the governor. The company directors shared their displeasure at the "bloody exploit" of the massacre that had opened the war, but were more seriously disturbed, the company being bankrupt at the time, by all the expense, with, as they said of such warfare in general, "so little appearance of profit."

A board wall built across lower Manhattan in the course of this war gave its name to Wall Street.

The company provided a new governor (no improvement, said the colonial critics), but the colony got back on its feet and prospered. Occasional trouble continued with the Indians, who remained indolent, insolent, and as thievish as monkeys. When a farmer caught and killed one of their females who was stealing peaches, her relatives or friends wantonly slew the farmer, and their tribe refused to turn these murderers over to the New Amsterdam authorities. A much more serious Indian attack was peaceably resolved. Conciliation went so far as the repurchase of some lands that had been bought once before, largely to soothe Indian ignorance regarding real estate.

New Netherlands took over the rival Swedish colony in 1655, with the help of a Dutch fleet, and just in time, as New Sweden was finally, with the active assistance of the Swedish crown, beginning to expand. The much more populous English neighbors to the east, with the help of an English fleet, then took over the healthily expanding Dutch province in 1664; with the Treaty of Breda four years later the Dutch gave up the last of their New Netherland claims in return for a free hand in Surinam.

Sweden during these times was beset by chronic political troubles natural to its role as a temporary great power. Holland, just breaking free of Spanish sovereignty, war on every side, was naturally zooming to one of the highest points in modern European history, its commerce all over the world making Amsterdam the financial center of the period, creating a flood of Dutch art— among others, from both the southern and northern provinces, Rubens, Hals, Van Dyck, Ruysdael, Vermeer, Rembrandt—unequaled since the Renaissance. But England, torn by Puritan factionalism that would lead to civil war, produced by the thousand, as shall be seen, the settlers for a New World, the one factor that ipso facto turned the others out.

These changes were of less moment to the Lenape people than the routine events on the Indian side of the frontier: murderous epidemics and incessant moving from here to there to avoid the wildfire beaver wars of the interior.

But Lenape were on hand in full force for the famous treaty meetings with William Penn in 1683. The best known Delaware leader at these meetings (in brand new Germantown, situated on the site of a traditional Lenape capital, on the edge of brand new Philadelphia) was the councilor Tamanend; of him a missionary wrote more than a century later, repeating Delaware yarns: "he was an ancient Delaware chief, who never had his equal. He was in the highest degree endowed with wisdom, virtue, prudence, charity, affability, meekness, hospitality, in short with every good and noble qualification." The English spelled his name Tammany; the political society of New York that adopted his name was not celebrated in its later days for practicing his virtues.

The most densely populated section of eastern North America in aboriginal times may have been the coastal area, roughly from New York to Boston, that was the birthplace of New England. East of the Wappinger country, in Connecticut, were the Mohegan, a separate, eastern branch of the Hudson River Mahican (the same name, of course, through different ears; it meant "wolves"); beyond the Mohegan, in the region of present Rhode Island, the Narraganset made up the principal nation; beyond the Narraganset the Wampanoag (a word cognate with Wappinger, both meaning "Easterners"); and beyond the Wampanoag the Massachuset. All these were Algonquian speakers, and in many ways similar peoples.

European deep-sea fishing vessels had been working the New England coast since the early 1500s, Dutch and English traders had been appearing along the Hudson River or on the coast since at least the early 1600s. English shipmasters had been pausing to pick up slaves or guides, either by kidnapping or smooth speeches, since at least 1605, when five New England Indians were brought into Plymouth in England; one of them named Tasquantum, was "seized upon" by Sir Ferdinando Gorges, then governor of Plymouth. The Plymouth (joint-stock) Company was actively interested in the New England coast a few years later when they employed the redoubtable Captain John

Smith to explore it for them; Captain Smith, exploring his way along in 1614, renamed a Wampanoag village in honor of his employers—the Wampanoag name was Patuxet, the new name bestowed by Captain Smith was Plymouth.

In the following year (1615) an English slaver, one Captain Thomas Hunt, kidnapped a Patuxet citizen reportedly named Tisquantum, and sold him into slavery in Malaga, whence he escaped to England. In 1616, the year after Captain Hunt's visit, an epidemic, very possibly measles or smallpox, broke out among the people of the New England coast "with such a mortall stroake," wrote an English trader, "that they died on heapes . . . and the living . . . would runne away, & let them dy, and let there Carkases ly above the ground without buriall."

It raged for three years. The Wampanoag and their nearest neighbors, the Massachuset, who lived north of them in the region of modern Boston, seemed to be in the center of this long storm of sudden death. The Massachuset were so nearly destroyed that, in some estimates, their population fell from 10,000 to 1,000 people.

A congregation of English Separatists then living in Holland as religious refugees organized themselves into an unchartered company, financed by a group of "merchant-adventurers" (merchants willing to venture some money). In 1620 they sailed as colonists, aiming for the northern reaches of the territory assigned to the Virginia Company—their choice of destination influenced by the Virginia colony's new tobacco prosperity; Guiana in South America, the scene of Sir Walter Raleigh's final golden dreams, had also been considered. Apparently the master of the Separatists' ship, the *Mayflower*, had no definite instructions as to a specific destination. Gossip later current in England had it that the shipmaster had "been bribed by the Hollanders to carry them and land farther to the northward," beyond the Virginia colony's northern boundary, which fell within the sphere of Dutch trade.

These colonists were the Pilgrim Fathers of the schoolbooks, searching for a place where they could be free from religious persecution; a bitter and tormented people, grimly industrious, as mercenary as purses.

In the region where they were landed they were squatters, without legal rights of settlement until a revised charter should be granted, which caused the colonists to draw up an agreement as to how they would run the colony. This agreement, known as the Mayflower Compact, was the first appearance in an English colony of a social contract based on the will of the colonists rather than the will of the sovereign—or of the controlling joint-stock company.

They found the forest clearings of their new country bespangled by the scattered bones of plague victims. The village of Captain John Smith's Plymouth, née Patuxet, was a ghost town, the people dead in the houses or fled from the plague in horror and despair. The colonists made the village and its fields their own, fields so handsomely cleared, said a delighted colonist later, there was "scarce a bush or bramble, or any cumbersome underwood to be seene in the more champion ground."

There was many a tale extant relating perfidies and murders between the local Indians of this coast and previous sea-borne English traders and slavers, but after a certain period of remaining "aloof" the Pilgrims made the acquaintance of a local sachem, or chief, named Samoset, who had picked up some English from such previous traders. He brought the noble Massassoit, grand sachem of the Wampanoag people (Massassoit, again, was only a title of address, as we would say Senator; the great sachem's real name was Wasamegin, meaning "Yellow Feather"), to pay a state visit to the colony, and Massassoit brought in his train a survivor of Patuxet's people who could speak marvelously in English.

This was, says orthodox history, the ex-slave Tisquantum kidnapped by Captain Hunt in 1615. But Sir Ferdinando Gorges said that his Tasquantum, brought to Plymouth, England, in 1605, "must be acknowledged the meanes under God of putting on foote, and giving life to all our Plantations."

Whoever he was, to the Pilgrims he became "a speciall instrument sent of God for their good beyond their expectation," so wrote the historian of the colony. "He directed them how to set their corne, wher to take fish, and to procure other commodities, and also their pilott to bring them to unknowne places for their profit." His name to the colonists was Squanto, and until he died of an "Indian feavor" in 1622 he was of inestimable use to the struggling colony.

A special study of some years ago devoted to the origins of New England concluded that seventeenth-century colonies "could not survive for long without obtaining some of their supplies from the natives." In Plymouth's first winter deaths from scurvy were terribly common (indicating that the colonists were still living on the stores brought by sea), leaving in the spring only a handful of persons able to work.

For survival, all labor and produce were then held in common. This endured for two years, but was discarded as soon as possible, the first and principal objection being that "the young men, that were most able and fit for labour and service, did repine that they should spend their time and strength to work for other men's wives and children without any recompense. The strong, or man of parts, had no more in division of victuals and clothes than he that was weak and not able to do a quarter the other could, this was thought injustice."

Plymouth kept peace generally with the Wampanoag and cultivated profitable Indian trade, principally in furs, so assiduously that after seven years a combine of the colony's eight leading men bought out the stock of their troublesome financial backers and formed a joint-stock company of their own; the remaining debt from this purchase was paid off in six more years from the profits of trade.

In the meantime other English colonies were sprouting along the coast and rivers, among them the Puritan colony of Massachusetts Bay, at Salem, which from the first quarreled piously with Plymouth. Thomas Morton, agent for Sir Ferdinando Gorges, founded with several dozen followers his colony of Merry Mount (near present Quincy), called Episcopalian and regarded as utterly godless by both Plymouth and Massachusetts Bay, who at last sent a force against him that seized his goods, burnt his buildings, and sent him a prisoner to England. Morton blamed their hostility on interest in profit, saying he had harmed "the benefit of their beaver trade," which "action bred a kinde of hart burning in the Plimouth Planters."

Between 1630 and 1642 more than 16,000 settlers, many of them entire congregations with their ministers fleeing increasingly rigorous attacks on nonconformists in England, joined the "Great Migration" to Massachusetts Bay. They were urged on by such promotional literature as the Rev. William Morrell's verse description of New England, published in 1625:

> The fruitfull and well watered earth doth glad all hearts . . . and
> yeelds an hundred fold for one . . .
> O happie Planter if you knew the height
> Of planters honours where ther's such delight

The godly colonists exulted, with reverence, over the frightful epidemic of 1616–1619 that had cleared so many heathen from the path of the Chosen People.

"The Wonderful Preparation the Lord Christ by His Providence Wrought for His People's Abode in this Western World," wrote a Puritan chronicler, pointing out with particular satisfaction that the plague had swept away "chiefly young men and children, the very seeds of increase." Even Thomas Morton of Merry Mount, who had more affection for the Indians than for the Puritans, observed that in "this, the wondrous wisedome and love of God, is shewne, by sending to the place his Minister, to sweepe away . . . the Salvages."

But there were still enough seeds of increase left to be troublesome, as happie planters multiplied, trade moved inland, and the Indian nations near the coast became of no benefit whatever.

In 1636 the Massachusetts Bay Puritans found themselves seriously at odds with a group of Mohegan people known as the Pequot ("destroyers"), an Indian nation reckoned as one of the strongest in New England.

Propaganda at the time (and since) pictured the Pequot as latecomers to the area, brutal invaders barely preceding the English, basing this on the similarity of the name Mohegan to that of the Mahican on the faraway upper Hudson River. Modern archeology, however, can only find evidence showing that the Pequot and Mohegan, like other southern New England peoples, had developed in place over many centuries.

The great sachem of the Pequot, Sassacus, was said in the middle 1630s to claim dominion over eastern Long Island and much of Connecticut, and to rule over more than two dozen subchiefs. Being on the border between the Dutch and the English, Sassacus played shifty politics with both, although Will Wood said of the Pequot, two years before war was opened against them, that "they were just and equall in their dealings; not treacherous either to their Country-men, or *English*."

The Dutch and the several English colonies for their part played shifty politics with the Pequot and the other Indian groups, notably the powerful Narraganset; for example, Plymouth disputed Pequot rights to lands on which the city of Hartford now stands in order to strike by this means at the Dutch, who had just bought land in this region from Pequot salesmen—Plymouth claimed the land still belonged to Indian groups who had held it prior to alleged Pequot conquest. The Pequot war came into being behind such devious maneuvers.

A real issue seems to have been, as the colonies grew larger, a possible alliance between the powerful Pequot and their customary enemies the powerful Narraganset (heretofore English allies) to oppose the colony of Massachusetts Bay. The Pequot endeavored to persuade the Narraganset by arguing that the English were beginning to "overspread" the country and in time would dispossess the Pequot and if the Narraganset assisted in this "they did but make way for their own overthrow," for the English would then sooner or later turn against the Narraganset and "take occasion to subjugate them."

These "very pernicious arguments" (says the contemporary record thus quoted) had the Narraganset "wavering" in spite of their usual hostility to the Pequot, until the timely intercession of Roger Williams won them back to the English side. Roger Williams had been banished the year before from Massachusetts for advocating the eccentric heresies of religious tolerance and Indian land rights; he had been given shelter in what is now Rhode Island by the noble Canonicus, the leader (with his nephew Miantonomo) of the Narraganset people.

Ostensible issues were related to the murder two years earlier of a lawless Virginia trader at the hands of unknown Indians, supposedly Pequot. Some of the Puritans were inclined to think he had received his just deserts, but for most (says a modern specialist in the matter), "it was enough that he was an Englishman; retribution was necessary."

In addition, the recent murder of another trader, evidently by Indians allied if not subject to the Narraganset, was blamed on the Pequot by reason of Narraganset testimony that some of the guilty parties were now living with the Pequot. (Nearly all the guilty parties had been killed by a passing group of Englishmen—two who surrendered were bound and thrown into the sea, but a few were believed to have escaped.)

The colony of Massachusetts Bay now sent a force to kill all the men of the band involved in the recent murder and bring the women and children back as slaves, and then to demand from the Pequots the return of the fugitives still with them plus heavy damages plus some of their children to be surrendered as hostages.

This punitive force failed in all its objectives, although an Indian guide (Cutshamekin, a Massachuset) did manage to kill one Pequot, which served at least as a declaration of war.

The English settlements in Connecticut and Plymouth were dragged into this state of war by the precipitate action of the Massachusetts Bay Puritans. A splinter party of Sassacus's own Pequot people had broken away, under a malevolent leader named Uncas, and had become the Pequots' bitterest enemies; this small group retained the name of Mohegan. They entered the hostilities on the English side with pleasure.

Skirmishes and isolated violent acts took place, accompanied by appropriate savageries—Pequot warriors captured an English soldier and cut off his hands and then, to hasten dilatory death, his feet; Puritan soldiers captured a Pequot and bound one of his legs to a post and tied a rope around the other leg and tore him apart.

The decisive action came on a night in late May 1637 when the English army (ninety colonists, mostly from Connecticut; an uncertain larger number of Narragansets; sixty Mohegans) made a stealthy approach on a stockaded Pequot town near the Mystic River in Connecticut. They reached the town "before day" and in a surprise attack burned the town and slaughtered nearly all the inhabitants, several hundred people. English losses were two killed, one apparently by accident, and perhaps twenty wounded; perhaps forty Indian allies were mistakenly wounded.

Wrote the governor of Plymouth, relating the news at second hand: "It was a fearful sight to see them frying in the fire and the streams of blood quenching the same, and horrible was the stink and scent thereof; but the victory seemed a sweet sacrifice, and they gave the praise thereof to God."

This massacre, which took little more than a half hour, seemed in some magical way to shatter the Pequot nation. Possibly Indian unfamiliarity with the European habit of total war may have been involved. (The incredible sack of the city of Magdeburg, X-rated climax of Europe's Thirty Years' War, had taken place only six years before, almost to the day.) An illustration of the Pequot massacre prepared by the victors showed unarmed Indians being shot down by the English; it was agreed that no more than seven people had escaped, from the entire population of the town.

The only other engagement of the war, aside from mopping-up operations, brought the surrender of a number of families trapped in a swamp (near modern New Haven). Adult males were killed, boys sold to the West Indies, women and girls parceled out as slaves.

Refugees fled in all directions. Some Pequot survivors were placed under the sovereignty of their old enemy, Uncas, and so sweet was the savor of his revenge thereof that the colonies mercifully took them away from him a few years later. The great Pequot sachem Sassacus, with a few followers, escaped to the Mohawks and requested sanctuary; the Mohawks put them to death—bribed by the Narraganset, said gossip.

The year following this war the New England colonies, pursuing the idea of united action that had worked, sort of, against the Pequot (Plymouth had not participated, and the Bay colony only piecemeal), began negotiations that led to the federation in 1643 of the United Colonies of New England, the first union of English settlements in America (Roger Williams and his heretical Providence firmly excluded).

The destruction of the Pequot left the Narraganset the strongest nation in New England. Uncas, commanding only a small number of warriors in comparison with the Narraganset military potential, was nevertheless able to maintain an Indian balance of power by the threat of his influence with the English. He boiled with ambitious plots, and ceaselessly stirred up English suspicion against the Narraganset and Wampanoag. The usual hostile incidents accumulated, and there were endless rumors of general Indian "conspiracies." Most modern historians are skeptical of these frequent alarms—although the hundreds of deaths in Virginia at that time were of course much in the New England mind.

One "hostile" incident was the murder of a sachem of the Narraganset, the well-known Miantonomo, a murder in which the Commissioners of the United Colonies and Uncas appeared to conspire.

For a time, even so, an uneasy peace was sustained.

It should be pointed out again that many individual settlers and Indians were not only peaceful neighbors but friends. It was from these Algonquian peoples of the Atlantic seaboard that most of the common Indian words in the English language were borrowed: squaw, papoose, moccasin, wigwam, succotash, hominy, and many more. The settlers adopted New England Indian cookery from clambakes—a clambake on the beach was a "squantum," from the name of an Indian seaside village on the site of present Quincy—to baked beans. The Indians adopted not only European arms and tools but European design in beadwork, as well as European rum and brandy. A colonial dancing-match, or play party, was called a "cantico," from a word of Algonquian root, and many a time Indians and colonists cut a cantico together, as the phrase had it—although really proper Puritans, of course, frowned on such frivolity.

The period's friendliest view of Indians comes from trader Thomas Morton, of the Maypole at Merry Mount so scandalous to the Puritans. Said Morton, "it was my chance to be landed in the parts of New England, where I found two sorts of people, the one Christians, the other Infidels, these I found most full of humanity, and more friendly than the other." He summed up, in typical Merry Mount terms: "their life is so voyd of care, and they are so loving also that they make use of those things they enjoy (the wife only excepted) as common goods, and are therein, so compassionate that rather than one should starve through want, they would starve all, thus doe they passe away their time merrily, not regarding our pompe (which they see dayly before their faces) but are better content with their owne, which some men esteeme so meanely of. . . . They may be rather accompted to live richly, wanting nothing that is needefull; and to be commended for leading the contented life."

There were indeed, and always had been, some Englishmen who esteemed but meanly of the Indians and their way of life. One youthful veteran of the Pequot war, with a couple of juvenile delinquent pals, stabbed and robbed a Narraganset man they met in the forest (the young leader "said he had killed many of them") but the Indian lived long enough to identify his murderers, who were hanged by a Plymouth court in September 1638. Some of "the rude and ignorant sort" protested against any Englishman being put to death because of an Indian, but the Government pressed that justice must be done "or else the country must rise and . . . raise a war."

And there were many, among these godly people, who worked selflessly for the heathens' salvation. John Eliot studied the Algonquian languages with a captive from the Pequot war, and after thirty years of labor published the Bible "translated into the Indian language." He founded at Natick on the Charles River the first of his villages of "praying Indians," and by 1674 had four congregations totaling 2,000, mostly, alas, from the weaker Indian towns located between the proud and pagan Narraganset, Wampanoag, and Mohegan. The missionizing Mayhew family worked among subjects of the

Wampanoag confederacy on Martha's Vineyard; four generations of this family remained in business as missionaries there for a consecutive 116 years. At Providence (where church and state continued impiously separate) Roger Williams continued to agitate for Indian land rights (at least on paper) so successfully that purchase of Indian lands, on the Dutch model, gradually became the accepted practice up and down the coast in the English colonies.

But the New England settlements grew in strength and property. The weighty, propertied men at the direction of affairs waxed inexorably weightier. The wheel of basic policy inexorably turned, to complete its inevitable full circle.

Plus, in this instance, a few extra added weights attached to the inexorable wheel: the Restoration in England (1660) with its high handed social reaction against puritanism naturally caused concern in the New England colonies. Pro-French and possibly pro-Catholic Charles II and his brother James (James became openly Catholic in 1668) naturally caused religious concern. Restoration of the royal prerogative, this time possibly on a stricter French model, naturally caused political concern, especially in the Commonwealth of Massachusetts, that had been rather more at ease with the Commonwealth of Cromwell. Colonial merchants found the Restoration Acts of Trade damaging to their business; in Massachusetts "the commercial spirit was steadily growing, and with it went a decline in religious fervor," in the words of the most thorough study of these colonies. Good old inflexible puritanism as a ruling force was rather relegated to the smaller communities of the interior. The presence within the colonies of Indian nations still strong and independent was no added comfort in this uncertain climate. Prescient political minds could see on the horizon a possible Indian alliance with New France, French "Canada and its Indians" just then becoming all too visible to the north of the Massachusetts provinces of New Hampshire and Maine.

The noble Narraganset Canonicus, whose help had been of value to Massachusetts in the Pequot war, died in 1647, full of years. The noble Wampanoag Massassoit, who had succored Plymouth colony in its first years, died in 1662. He had remained all his life a friend of the English, notwithstanding English "usurpations," as a nineteenth-century authority put it, upon Wampanoag lands and liberties.

The weighty men at the direction of affairs in Plymouth then began a campaign to place the Wampanoag people under outright subjugation. The Wampanoag were willing enough to profess themselves subjects of the English king, but Plymouth demanded that they also admit themselves subjects of Plymouth. Massachusetts supported the Wampanoag view of equality with Plymouth, an indication that business and politics might be intruding, as previously suggested, on religious solidarity—the Wampanoag were notably stubborn in refusing conversion.

The Wampanoag leader Wamsutta, known to the English as Alexander, eldest son of Massassoit, died suddenly on his way home from a more or less forced conference at Plymouth; his young wife Wetamoo believed he had been poisoned.

Plymouth now threatened Wamsutta's young brother (twenty-three years old) Metacom, known to the English as Philip, "King" Philip, with war if he refused to acknowledge Plymouth sovereignty.

Philip at last bowed to the yoke, committing his nation to pay £100 a year tribute to Plymouth. He may have submitted only to gain time to prepare for an apparently decided war, but English pressure increased, regardless. The drum-blows of hostile incidents came at a steadily accelerated tempo.

Today's leading expert on colonial military matters sees the situation in 1670 as an essentially colony-versus-colony rivalry in which "Massachusetts, Rhode Island, and Plymouth were contesting for hegemony in the area where their boundaries came to a point." Fictional or at least imaginary fears of an "Indian conspiracy" were "buttressed by the special interest each colony had in obtaining control over the lands of the Wampanoags and Narragansetts, portions of which were included in the Rhode Island boundaries that each of the other colonies, in its way, sought to violate. Still another factor was the colony of New York, which, under its governor, Edmund Andros, sought to assert its claim to all the territory formerly claimed by the Dutch, which claim included half the territory of Connecticut."

Obviously the colony that took Wampanoag and Narraganset lands by outright conquest would settle the issue.

But if covert competition between Plymouth and Massachusetts Bay had been a factor it was dropped as the reality of general war developed. The colonies joined together and both Philip and the United Colonies maneuvered for allies. Philip showed an unexpected gift for statecraft in these preliminaries.

The neutrality of the dreaded Mohawks (far to the west in upper New York but nevertheless a significant power element even unto the Plymouth coast) was secured by both sides. And when war burst out, in 1675, the Narraganset threw in with Philip (or were pushed in, some say, by the jittery English), as did most of the lesser tribes nearby. Uncas, well pleased at the prospective ruin of his last American rivals, brought 500 Mohegan gunmen and bowmen in on the English side. The Praying Indians remained loyal to their missionaries—although they had to be moved to Boston for protection from the enflamed populace, after the war got rolling.

For it was the most devastating war New England has ever experienced, before or since, ancient or modern.

Young Metacom had indeed been underrated. The Indians had not yet learned proper battle tactics but they were better armed with muskets than had been expected, and they had made some progress in learning how to do their own gunsmithing. Not enough, for inability to repair their arms remained a handicap, but enough so that Indian forges in the forests became prime military objectives for the English. (And some Indian war chiefs were resplendent in English armor.)

Metacom also revealed a possible talent in the direction of war psychology: the Wampanoags and Narragansets seemed seriously to believe they could win, perhaps in reflection of an attitude instilled by their leader. Their persistent courage mentioned many times in contemporary accounts appeared to be founded, at least in part, on such optimism.

The use of Mohegans and Praying Indians and other English allies as scouts and spies is instanced by some later historians as a valuable if not decisive factor in the ultimate English victory. But perhaps they romanticize. There were now more than 50,000 European colonists in New England. The total population of the Indian states combined against them could not have exceeded 20,000 and was probably much less, possibly less than half that figure.

English superiority in basic military ability was unquestioned. The European organization for war—as in stable sources of supply—was infinitely superior. There may have been more Indian casualties from exposure and malnutrition and the illnesses incident thereto than from military action.

Metacom's "genius" notwithstanding, the final issue could not be in doubt. That is easy to say now, of course, totting up the statistics out of books, but those on the scene at the time, both red and white, may have been a little too busy wiping the sweat (and fear) out of their eyes to see how simple and clear it was all going to look in books, later on. In the first few months of the war the outcome appears to have been felt in real doubt.

As before, the Puritans distinguished themselves by wholesale massacres of noncombatants that could scarcely be credited if not for the fact that it is the Puritans themselves who record them, often with relish—although not always; the shrieks of several hundred victims, mostly women and children, dying in the burning of a large Narraganset village in the winter of 1675 "greatly moved some of our soldiers. *They were much in doubt* and afterward inquired whether burning their enemies alive could be consistent with humanity and the benevolent principles of the gospel." (Italics in original.)

Some modern scholars, suckled on Freud, have made much of the dark side of Puritan psychology, which exhibited a holy ferocity toward "heretics" as well as toward defiant Indians—four Quakers, including the renowned Mary Dyer, had been hanged on Boston Common in 1660. But in their day Puritan psychologists were stricken with horror at the triple Tyrant's bloody Piemontese, that rolled Mother with infant down the rocks (John Milton, 1655, "On the Late Massacre in Piedmont"). Real war, with its massive ferocities and outrages, was the Old World's birthright. Europe's Thirty Years' War has been mentioned as an example of the seventeenth century in action, but of course any century in history (in Old World history) up to and most emphatically including our own can provide plenty of such examples.

The New World, with a past outside written history, may have been lacking in such a fine perennial crop of big and bloody true warfare. This possibility has been previously mentioned.

In any case the colonists needed no blood-warming this time, with fifty-two of New England's ninety towns attacked, a dozen utterly destroyed and others heavily damaged, and 600 men—"the flower and strength of the country"—killed, and unknown numbers of unrecorded noncombatant losses. But it was warmed again anyway by the divines of the New England theocracies, who repeatedly proved by Biblical interpretation that it was the sacred duty of the Christian English to root out the godless Canaanites.

Root them out they did. Canonchet, a Narraganset sachem, great-nephew of the noble Canonicus and Philip's most famous field commander, was trapped by the English, taken into Stonington and there executed, technically by Indian allies of the English although the obsequies performed upon his body, drawing and quartering, hath an English smack.

The month following this loss Philip's forces suffered a crucial defeat in a battle near the falls of the Connecticut River (Indian dead 100 to 200, including many women and children). This was, by now, the summer of 1676, and the war had been going on for more than a year. Anawon, an old man, one of the noble councilors from the time of the noble Massassoit, surrendered to the English on promises of quarter and was executed, over the bitter protests of Captain Benjamin Church, who had taken him prisoner.

The same Captain Church captured, early in August, Philip's wife and nine-year-old son, at which Philip is reported to have cried out, "My heart breaks; now I am ready to die," while the Reverend Increase Mather said with gusto, "It must be bitter as death for him to lose his wife and only son, for the Indians are marvellously fond and affectionate toward their children."

Later in August, in what proved to be the last battle of the war, Metacom himself was killed (by an Indian ally of the English). The confederacy was finished. Survivors, as usual, fled or were hunted down. Refugees turned up a half dozen years later far to the west, in the Mississippi valley, working as hunters for La Salle.

Hundreds were sold as slaves, 500 being shipped from Plymouth alone. Proceeds from these sales were divided among the colonies (Uncas was dismayed at not being cut in, but there was no more need of him now) to help defray in some small part the expenses of the war, usually called the most costly Indian war in U.S. history. Outright military expenses alone have been estimated at £100,000 (Philip's tribute for 1,000 years?), plus the immense damage. Said the orator Edward Everett a century and a half later, "No period of the revolutionary war was to the interior of any part of the United States so disastrous." And for nearly 100 years after the war, no farm or village in the Connecticut valley was safe from, in Mr. Everett's rolling tones, the incursions of the savage foe.

Recent analysis of this war has given increasing attention to arguments that the English were the aggressors, shed the first blood, attacked Narragansets and Pennacooks and Connecticut Valley Indians without justification, and had military successes only when they used more Indian allies than English troops.

Philip's crippled hand (injured by the explosion of a pistol in former years) was given to "Alerman, the Indian who shot him, to show to such gentlemen as would bestow gratuities upon him; and accordingly he got many a penny for it." (Said Alerman to the dead Philip, according to veterans' reminiscences later current, "You may have been a great man, but I'll chop your ass for you.") Philip's head was exposed on a pole in Plymouth (along with others of the slain enemy, men and women, in a New England version of the Aztec skull rack). Cotton Mather, writing more than twenty years after the war: "It was not long before the hand that now writes, upon a certain occasion, took off the jaw from the exposed skull of that *blasphemous leviathan.*"

Philip's wife and son, held prisoners in Plymouth, became the subject of high deliberation as the clergy decided their fate. The Reverend John Cotton of Plymouth and the Reverend Samuel Arnold of Marshfield quoted Deuteronomy 24:16 as authority for sparing the boy's life but the "scripture instances of Saul, Achan, Haman, the children of whom were cut off, by the sword of Justice for the transgressions of their parents" as deciding their vote for death to the child of him who had dared to attack the "whole nation, yea the whole Israel of God."

The Reverend Increase Mather of Boston also voted for death, quoting the instance of "Hadad, who was a little child when his father (the chief sachem of the Edomites) was killed by Joab; and, had not the others fled away with him, I am apt to think that David would have taken a course, that Hadad should never have proved a scourge to the next generation."

The Reverend James Keith of Bridgewater urged milder treatment, writing, "I know there is some difficulty in that Psalm, 137:8, 9," but "That law, Deut. 24:16, compared with the commended example of Anasias, 2 Chron. 25:4, doth sway with me."

Mildness prevailed, and Philip's wife and the grandson of the noble Massassoit were sold as slaves to the West Indies.

They and other Indians sold by the English and French to "the Isles" could join there the 80,000 Irish captives shipped as chattel slaves by Cromwell, and the survivors—if there were any—of the Highland Scots sold there after the battle of Worcester in 1651.

CHAPTER 18

European Cannon Meet Longhouse Diplomacy

Northward from New England through the unbroken woods there lived other Algonquian peoples, and still others dwelt farther north, north as far as corn could grow and farther still, all the way to the freezing black spruce forests and the treeless subarctic plains encircling Hudson Bay.

From the Abnaki of Maine through the Micmac of Nova Scotia and the Montagnais and Naskapi of Quebec and Labrador, hunger was increasingly a part of life and legend, in direct proportion as farming dwindled and hunting became the principal gainful occupation. Even in a country teeming, as the saying goes, with game, the chase is at times a shaky provider, there being nothing constant about a supply of wild meat.

But through fat times and lean, snows and spring, meat had to be brought in. Inevitably there were strings of empty-handed days, with nothing at all for dinner beyond barely edible wintry bits collected by the women and children. Then starving times, always waiting, the veritable wendigo, the mythical monster of the north woods, moved in to creep among the lodges. Especially at the end of the long winters there were weeks when the woods seemed to grow magically still, all game vanished, and the world sank into the semblance of death that preceded the first stirrings of spring. Famished people ate broth made of smoke, bark, snow, and buckskin, and the rash of pellagra appeared like tattooed flowers on their emaciated bodies—the roses of starvation, in a French physician's description; and those who starved died covered with roses.

Naskapi and Montagnais are umbrella-names for a considerable number of related groups that roamed over their immense northern territory. A distinguished ethnologist working among these people in the early decades of the 1900s published several papers dealing with their family-owned hunting territories, paternally inherited, dating (he gathered) from aboriginal times, within which conservation of game and fur animals was practiced. This discovery created much interest, the idea of a "natural" recognition of private property and a market economy being quite an important potato to unearth in those bolsheviki haunted days.

It became even more important as time passed and cold war thinking became so institutionalized that American anthropologists were hesitant about using the time-honored term "primitive communism," but substituted instead the more comfortable "corporate." At this point (1954) a later distinguished ethnologist discovered, upon "meticulous" examination, that these family territories had originated with the coming of the trading post. Earlier Montagnais-Naskapi lodge groups had not been centered on any such family plot, and until the European-introduced fur-trade economy "never had the band been a landowning unit." This return to the nineteenth-century consensus that the primitive ages "of egalitarian sharing" had molded our beginnings is bringing a veritable counter-revolution that threatens the entire thought-control pattern bequeathed by our cold war century.

The Micmac, remote in the Nova Scotia land's end country that sticks out like a sore thumb into the Atlantic, spoke an Algonquian dialect only remotely related to the Algonquian languages of their neighbors, and provided further exemplars of the trading-post-related family hunting territory. Some geographers have speculated that the Micmac may have been descendants of very early arrivals in the Americas, gradually pushed to the outermost fringes of the continent. Although not quite the last outermost fringe—the little-known Beothuk, a timid, retiring people who painted their unusually white skins red with ocher, were still beyond, on the island of Newfoundland.

The Abnaki (another variation of the word for "easterner") of Maine were rather close kin, in language, with the Algonquian peoples hundreds of miles to the west, around the Great Lakes.

But between the Algonquian-speaking nations of the Atlantic coast and those of the Great Lakes there stretched another world, the world of the Iroquois.

Archeological evidence appears to support the presence of Iroquoian people in the region of the lower Great Lakes from a period at least as ancient as 1,000 years or so before the time of Columbus. Their original ancestors may have been in the area much longer, but earlier (and later) discernible strains intrude from the Ohio Hopewell and from the Southeast, possibly only an influx of ideas, possibly of peoples.

At some unknown date during that long expanse of time, an unknown number of centuries ago, five Iroquois nations in and about what is now upstate New York, from the Genesee River valley to Lake Champlain, organized a confederacy. They were, reading from west to east, the Seneca, Cayuga, Onondaga, Oneida, and Mohawk.

In the customary frame of reference, these five nations are regarded as the Iroquois proper. Other Iroquois nations and confederacies north, west, and south of them are usually given the qualificative Iroquoian.

The confederacy formed by these five New York nations became the farfamed League of the Iroquois.

North of the Five Nations were the Hurons, a populous confederacy made up of four aristocratic tribes, richest in tradition and ceremony of all the Iroquoian people, and a number of dependent tribal groups, one of these an Algonquian community.

West of the Five Nations was the Iroquoian state that came to be known as the Tobacco nation, and the Iroquoian confederacy that came to be known as the Neutrals.

Southwest of the Five nations were the Erie ("long tail") people, also known as the Cat nation, from the meaning of their full name in Iroquois: "People of the Panther."

South of the Five Nations, along the Susquehanna River in eastern Pennsylvania and adjacent New York and Maryland, were the Iroquoian Susquehannock, Susquehanna for short, praised by Europeans from earliest meetings as not only admirable but exceptionally strong, able, and handsome. Said Captain John Smith in speaking of them: "Such great and well proportioned men are seldom seen."

But all the Iroquoian peoples were subjects of superlatives, from the earliest days of contact with Europeans. Will Wood wrote that the Mohawks "be people of a tall stature, of long grimme visages, slender wasted, and exceeding great armes and thighs." Jacques Cartier's men in 1535 were as much impressed by the fearlessness as by the strength of the five Iroquoian hunters (probably Huron) they met on an island in the St. Lawrence, one of them carrying Cartier ashore as "lightly and easily as if he had been a child of five years old; so strong and sturdy was this fellow."

Numerous French writers remarked on the exceptionally fine minds of the Hurons. Other reports speak of the impressive farms of Iroquoian people (of which the Five Nations farms were the poorest, by some accounts), the miles of fields of corn and beans and squash, and of their well-built multifamily longhouses and their log forts (their "castles" as the English called them). And still other reports emphasize the dirt, the dogs, and the eternal racket of laughter, horseplay, and constant multifamily chatter.

The Five Nations Iroquois were traditionally hostile toward most of the surrounding Iroquoian peoples, according to early reports. According to most reports, they were also traditionally hostile to surrounding Algonquian peoples. According to legend, the Five Nations were traditionally hostile even to each other before the founding of their League.

Legend says the League was organized by the saintly statesman Dekanawida (son of a virgin mother), assisted by the great councilor Hiawatha, a Mohawk, for the purpose of putting an end to the constant broils and battles among the Five Nations, and establishing a universal peace based on harmony, justice, and a government of law.

For the Five Nations the choicest superlatives in many early accounts are reserved for their ferocity, and of the Five Nations the Mohawk in this repute led all the rest.

The name Mohawk stemming from an Algonquian word meaning "man-eater," some historical summaries have taken rather seriously a notion that the Iroquois did indeed practice cannibalism, perhaps as a normal item of diet, bringing in support scary stories later white pioneers told each other.

Authoritative evidence finds it only in religion, in rare instances of ritual, a ritual of warriors eating the heart of a brave man, for example, to partake of his bravery.

The Old World's interest in cannibalism is of long standing: an apparently straight-faced work relates of the super-civilized Southern Sung dynasty in China that survivors of twelfth-century wars and famines in the north had opened in Hangchow restaurants offering human meat; dishes "made from the flesh of women, old men, young girls and children each had a special name, and were served in the same way as mutton."

This ancient interest evidently became in nineteenth-century Europe something of an obsession—as said a work of 1851, cannibalism was "presque universelle chez les nations entièrement sauvages." From W.S. Gilbert's *Bab Ballads* to Sir James George Frazer's *Golden Bough* (Frazer after years of pondering remained indignant "that certain depraved wretches should gratify their hereditary craving after human flesh in this disgusting manner") the literature of the time shuddered and shivered and gamely quipped. At present, however, anthropologists are debating whether cannibalism, as a habitual diet, ever existed at all.

One real reason the Mohawks led all the rest in ferocious repute was their geographical location: the most easterly of the Five Nations, they were the nearest to the frontiers of the first European colonies, and so better known to the first European reporters. Some early records refer to all the Five Nations Iroquois indiscriminately as Mohawk, thus giving the Mohawks credit for all the rip-roaring deeds of the whole confederacy.

The Iroquois were an "evil people, who go all armed even to their fingers ends," Cartier was told by some of their neighbors in 1535; a century later Will Wood, quoting other neighbors, referred to the Mohawks as being "more desperate in warres than the other Indians . . . a cruell bloody people." This reputation flourished for 150 years and among European settlers reached perhaps its highest pitch during the American Revolution.

Iroquois cruelty in torturing captives was notorious. There is a description of a woman burned as sacrifice to Arekwaskwa, god of war, but, in general, tales of Iroquois cruelty were told simply to raise the listener's hair, and any underlying religious significance, if present, was not mentioned.

As among the people of the southeast, a captive was supposed to perform a ritual dance after entering the town of his captors—while gold-star mothers showered him with blows, paying the accompanying soldiers a little tobacco for the privilege. Then, lashed to an elevated platform, he was supposed to continue singing his defiant death song while the jubilant, screaming women and children burned him with torches, gouged out bits of his flesh with pieces of seashell, or while a warrior tore off his scalp and poured red hot coals over his bleeding skull, all this cunningly managed to delay as long as possible the moment when the last glint of life, like a melting snowflake, died from the body.

This high estate of torture may have sometimes made a reputation for public sadism a political advantage, as with one Aharihon who (allegedly collecting vengeance for a brother killed in the Erie wars) developed down through the years refinements of psychological torture that would have done credit to a modern police state, and by 1663 boasted that he had tortured a total of eighty people to death with his own hand—and attained a responsible and eminent position as an Iroquois leader.

The best early ethnography (published 1724) on the Iroquois, though, presents some reservations: "When one burns a Slave [captive] among the Iroquois, there are few who do not show pity, and who do not say that it is worthy of compassion. Many, especially the women (if one excepts some furies, as are everywhere more savage than the men), have not the courage to be present at such an execution. Among those men and women who are present, some do nothing; those who torment the victim, often do so . . . because they feel obliged to; some, passing above this respect of custom, solace the victim when he asks for something. . . . At last, after a certain time, someone authorized by age and position gives the victim the coup de grace, and saves him from tortures he might still suffer."

Maybe Iroquois torture was a trifle too notorious, considering that most of their neighbors indulged in similar delights. Also considering that the Iroquois were particularly noted for adopting captives into their nations, to the point that at various periods naturalized Iroquois may have outnumbered the native born; it seems obvious that such wholesale adoptions must have cut into the torture supply. And also considering that Iroquois torture, like the black legend of Spanish cruelty used by the English and Dutch to excuse their own more conscienceless behavior, served various propaganda purposes for some of those who passed along the tale and let it lose nothing in the telling.

In later accounts, and subsequent history, superlatives have been lavished on another aspect of the Five Nations Iroquois—their political sophistication. This aspect too may have been sometimes overdone, in the comments picturing the League of the Iroquois as the best organized, in certain political respects, of any of the many confederacies north of Mexico.

It was operated by a council of fifty, made up of the ruling councilors of each of the Five Nations. These sachems were chosen from specific families by the mothers of their clans (groups of related women and their families), and were appointed for life—although the matriarchs of his clan could have a sachem deposed if he turned out to be a bad choice.

Dekanawida, the organizer of the great League, had been only a naturalized citizen (born a Huron, according to tradition), and so ineligible for a place among the council of fifty, but had become a chief on his merit, and had forbidden the appointment of a successor to his office. This may have given rise to the second class of sachems to which anyone (man or woman) could aspire by merit, rather than birth; the "solitary pine trees," they came to be called. These Pine Tree chiefs had the right to speak in council and made up a house of representatives, so to speak, as against the senate of the hereditary councilors. The most frequent road to Pine Tree honor was, as might be expected, via fame in war.

Each of the Five Nations was left alone in its own domestic affairs, but theoretically they were to act together in matters international. They seldom did. Individual nations, or even factions within the individual nations, went their own jolly way again and again in making peace or war—except when it came to fighting each other. The League, or the Great Peace as its founders called it, did keep the peace among its member nations.

No doubt it was also of value as a shadowy bugaboo for use in power diplomacy. My tongue speaks for all the Iroquois, said the Mohawk ambassadors, when they didn't even have authorization to speak with finality for their own nation.

One other value that perhaps should not be omitted was the spiritual sense of union. However often the League may have proved a fiction in actual political practice, it was a reality in the minds of the honored old men who composed the council, and doubtless in the mind of the general nonpolitical public.

The great council of the League held each summer at the principal Onondaga town (the Onondaga also furnished fourteen of the fifty councilors, and the council's presiding officer) was an impressive show that could not have helped but instill this sort of feeling, as it continued year after year, generation after generation.

A pooling of the religious power of the Five Nations—unity in prayer as well as in war—had been one of the main objectives of the League's founders. This objective was not achieved, either. But to some degree the magic of friendship was established, the emotional (even if not quite sound) conviction that come what may one's country did not stand alone, that all the way from the Seneca to the Mohawk the west wind streamed over a forest of brothers.

The unimpressive performance record of the Great League notwithstanding, the Five Nations Iroquois wrote a crucial chapter in the story of colonial North America. This came about in the following way.

North of Maine the first European colonies were French, and their reason for being was fur, primarily beaver. By 1608 when the first permanent colony, Quebec, was founded, French fur traders had already been active along the lower St. Lawrence for seventy years or so, and Grand Banks fishing crews from the French port of St. Malo had been pulling ashore for casual trading for a generation before that. Fur, primarily beaver, remained the grand preoccupation of the French in Canada.

Furs were obtained by trade with the Indians. French fur traders courted the Indians with whom they did business. They were partners. The Indian nations were essential to the enterprise. The Indians wanted the wonderful kettles and hatchets of the foreigners, but the French wanted even more the help and good will of the Indians, their woodland skills, their knowledge of winter snowshoe traveling, their birchbark canoes (up to 40 feet in length) and the paddlers to man them, their familiarity with the river-and-lake waterways leading to still more treasures of fur; and above all the French wanted to maintain in working condition the tribal channels of trade.

Whereas the English colonists usually destroyed, as soon as convenient, the Indian cocoon around them, the French more often supported and sustained the Indian world in which they found themselves, for out of that world came fur. Thus Indian communities here were in some cases strengthened and enriched by European contact.

Early fur-trading partners of the French were the Hurons and the Algonquian people of the lower St. Lawrence, principally the Montagnais and the numerous bands along the river who were known collectively as the Algonquian proper—one of these bands, on the Ottawa River, the Algonkin, being the original bearers of the name later applied by anthropologists to an enormous network of related languages.

Samuel de Champlain, lieutenant of the owner of the French fur trade monopoly, looked over Boston Bay and Plymouth harbor fifteen years before the landing of the Pilgrims (his Plymouth chart shows Patuxet filled with thriving fields of the people who were to be all but wiped out in the epidemic of 1617), but founded his colony at Quebec. At the end of February skeletal starving Montagnais people appeared, so famished they roasted and ate a dead cat and dog and pig the French had put out as fox bait, while the French immediately dug out for them a share of their winter's stores. In the spring (1609) Champlain and some of his men went with a war party of Montagnais, Algonkin, and Huron warriors on a long canoe journey to the lake now known as Lake Champlain.

There he won a battle for them, single-handed, against a little army of their hated enemies, who had never before met firearms. The foe were bold in arrow-proof body-armor made of plaited sticks, but Champlain killed two of their three war-captains and wounded the third, and the bold foe broke and ran.

So goes the usual story, which usually adds that the bold foe had been Mohawk, and that this was the origin of the basic animosity of the Five Nations Iroquois toward the French.

But questions arise from some details in the story, first and very much foremost Champlain's own detailed account, that he loaded his arquebus with four bullets, fired, and with one shot killed two of the enemy's three war chiefs and mortally wounded the third.

To declare this flatly impossible might be a little too rude, but to express a touch of doubt can surely be forgiven. Such a version may well have seemed to the author more believable than to have recounted three separate shots, the cumbersome business of reloading, applying the match, and firing an arquebus being familiar to too many readers of the time.

The identification of the enemy as Mohawk also could raise some uncertainty. The place of the fight—later site of Fort Ticonderoga—was at that time, according to most authorities, in Mahican country. The Mohawk did not succeed in pushing the Mahican on eastward until many years later, in 1664.

In any case, this engagement seems quite lightweight as a possible founding factor in the generally brilliant Iroquois maneuvering between the French and the English during the following two centuries.

The Dutch fur-trading post up the Hudson, near the present location of Albany, was first established only five years later. The Dutch were also primarily in the beaver business, eager to uphold and sustain the forest nations who might act as district jobbers for them. Within twenty years or so, Iroquois fur salesmen were procuring guns from Dutch, English, and French traders.

Trade in firearms to Indians at this early period was usually illegal, but the Five Nations Iroquois were favored in it by their location, remote enough from principal Dutch and English settlements to seem harmless, and in any case remote enough from any European settlements to make trade-supervision impossible.

It was standard colonial practice, naturally, to be more watchful about keeping guns from nearby Indian neighbors than from remoter nations, safely distant in their far-off woods, who had a legitimate use for guns anyway in coaxing more furs out of the gunless people still beyond them, and for use in attacking (one might hope) rival European trading posts. The Swedes of the Delaware country were chary of handing guns to the nearby Delawares but freely armed the Susquehannock of the distant interior, even supplying their forts with cannon and professional military instructors.

An area of conflict came into being, as networks of trade were extended, between French, English, Dutch, and Swedes; and an area of conflict also emerged between Indian nations, those farther from trade and those nearer the trade centers.

As has been previously discussed, the earliest frontiers did not move with westering European settlement but with the businesslike expansion of Indian nations who were in contact and trade with Europeans—there were thus, in effect, two frontiers: one strictly Indian, the other, following years behind, European. Out of the hurricane belt of these Indian-versus-Indian frontiers came winds that affected and sometimes determined the course of early American history.

The Five Nations Iroquois became the determining force of this Indian-versus-Indian frontier in the Northeast. Favored by their strategic location, they were no colony's creature. They were from the start their own masters. They traded, when all the magnificent oratory of the councils was done, with whoever offered the best deal, all things considered. All the things considered made for a bewildering tangle of loyalties, emotions, and motives, as does any group action. But no European business partner could be confident of calling the tune, either for any of the separate Five Nations who so often went their separate ways, or for the broad policy of the confederacy as a whole.

During the first half of the seventeenth century the Five Nations were sometimes at peace and sometimes at war, as single states or as a group, with the French and the "French Indians," the Indians to the north, Hurons, Algonquians, and the river traders to the west known as the Ottawa, all these much involved in fur trade with the French. This was especially true of the Hurons, who brought to the French many canoe-loads of pelts from the north and west of the Lakes.

There were several Iroquois attempts in this period to form a coalition with the populous Huron nation. Failure of these efforts may not have been due only to Mohawk and Seneca resistance among the Iroquois, and French machinations among the Hurons to keep them at odds with the Five Nations, but these things at least played a part.

The Hurons funneled through to New France, as mentioned, whole canoe-flotilla-loads of pelts taken in trade from the country north and west of the Lakes, a limitless country sparkling with streams and beautiful with beaver. The French felt they had the Hurons, and this trade, in their pocket, and naturally feared losing them to the more independent Five Nations.

Missionaries had been accepted by the Huron people and from the time of Champlain had acted as French agents in stirring up anti-Iroquois sentiment when needed. The Huron themselves being an Iroquoian people, the missionary priests distinguished between them and the Five Nations by calling Hurons the "good Iroquois." Letters from missionaries published in France were loaded with extravagant praise of Hurons (for all that the name Hurons, bestowed by the French, was an old French word with a meaning similar to "slobs"), and a continuous propaganda barrage against the Five Nations Iroquois.

In the summer of 1639 Hurons captured and burned a total of 113 Five Nations Iroquois people, some from roaming war parties or hunters, some casual travelers. Nevertheless, Hurons remained to the French the good Iroquois, while the Longhouse People, the Five Nations, were those demons, those tigers, and those wolves. "Did I not hope that you Frenchmen will wreak vengeance for such cruelties, I would be unable to speak," a French Jesuit quoted a weeping Algonquian woman, ex-captive of the bad Iroquois, as saying, while she related atrocities.

When in the 1630s repeated epidemics swept through the Huron people, reducing their population from an estimated 30,000 to an estimated 15,000, French administrators, writing home for more money, sometimes forgetfully attributed these plague losses to battle deaths at the hands of the bad Iroquois.

Some twenty years after this, a French governor mentioned, "It was politic to exaggerate more than ever the cruelties of the Iroquois," revealing more by the qualifying phrase than by the statement.

Spheres of power swelled. Guns became more common everywhere. Cardinal Richelieu's joint-stock company, which had taken over (and kept until 1645) the French fur-trade monopoly, permitted trade in guns to Christian Indians and there were thousands of baptized Hurons who could have qualified, but the French monopoly policy, with its attendant high prices, may have made them too dear a luxury.

The usual view has it that the Hurons were not as well armed as the Iroquois, who are made the possessors of some 400 muskets in 1643. But the tensions rising on the Iroquois-Huron frontier seem to have come from equally aggressive pressures on each side.

In 1648 Mohawk and Seneca war parties deliberately broke a truce with the Hurons that had been made in the name of the League. Their reasons for doing so are unfathomable, but intra-League politics presumably played a part. Economic motives involving the fur trade are often emphasized by American historians, sometimes to the exclusion of any other factors at all, but while it seems likely hostilities were heightened, or perhaps even genuine war first introduced, by the glittering presence of European trade, it also seems likely that other factors—religious, emotional, fraternal, national—continued to exist.

At the Mohawk-Seneca action a statesmanlike Onondaga councilor, Scandawati, who had pledged his word to the truce, invoked the ultimate diplomatic protest of killing himself. To no purpose. In the dead of the following winter, in March 1649, an overwhelming army of no less than 1,000 Mohawk and Seneca warriors suddenly invaded the heart of the Huron country in the area of Lake Simcoe and Georgian Bay, north of modern Toronto. Most of these troops are said to have wintered in Huron country, living off the snow-drifted land, without the Hurons suspecting their presence, while the massive strike was being prepared.

In two days of fighting they took and burned two Huron towns, were repulsed from a third, and vanished with many captives and much loot.

The Huron losses could not have been ruinous; their casualties were possibly 300 warriors killed as against 200 of the enemy. But panic followed. With no thought of provisions or shelter, the Huron people fled from their towns. Before the long northern winter ended many had died from starvation and exposure. Survivors kept on fleeing, literally, for years. In those two days of invasion the mighty Huron confederacy had been utterly smashed. The ancient desultory war that had gone on so long between the Hurons and the Five Nations, those evil people all armed even to their fingers' ends, was over.

The question of what caused this collapse of a confederacy that had experienced battle losses many times before, down through generations if not through centuries, does not seem to be answerable with the information we have. Possible clues may be suggested—similarity to the Pequot collapse, for example, and many others still to come. It could simply be argued that something new had arrived: Old World war. But while that may well be part of the picture it seems too simple for the whole explanation.

Some Huron refugees went to join their conquerors, in keeping with established New World tradition, occupying a town to themselves among the Seneca, and identifiable Huron neighborhoods in Mohawk and Onondaga towns. Others emigrated to the Iroquoian nations of the Tobacco-growing people, the Neutral people, or the Erie. Many fled to nowhere and turned up in later years everywhere, calling themselves Wendat, their own name. It became Wyandot in white literature.

The sense of utter defeat when there had been no utter defeat, the inexplicable demoralization that so suddenly destroyed the Huron state, left a magic roll of thunder in the air. For from now on the Iroquois frontier was alive with lightning.

Neighbors of the Hurons were thrown into panic, and the People of the Longhouse interpreted their panic as hostility and anti-Five Nations agitation, as no doubt it sometimes was.

The Tobacco people living at the western door of the Huron country were blasted by the Iroquois thunderbolt in December of 1649. These people appear to have been Hurons in everything but the name, and were famous for cultivating, besides tobacco, immense fields of corn and large quantities of hemp, used for making fishnets. They seem to have been a larger nation, in population, than all the Five Nations put together. Each of the opponents the Iroquois demolished, one after the other, seems to have outnumbered the Five Nations, whose combined population at this time may not have exceeded 12,000.

The next great Iroquoian confederacy to the southwest of the Huron country, called by the French the Neutral confederacy because of its neutrality in Five Nations-Huron troubles, was shattered by the Iroquois in 1651, with mopping up continuing for several years more.

The next Iroquoian people to the south, the People of the Panther, the Erie, apparently a Goliath in size compared to the Five Nations, struck first at the Longhouse People in 1653. An Iroquois counter-offensive the following summer, led by Onondaga soldiers, won a desperate battle in taking by storm an important Erie town located near the present Erie, Pennsylvania.

Here 3,000 to 4,000 Erie warriors were defeated by an army of 1,800 Iroquois (whose guns probably made the difference) in a victory that should have won the war on the spot, but this time the enemy reformed and fought back again and again, and two more years of fighting were required before the Eries, too, were finally vanquished.

One of the temporary Iroquois-French friendship pacts was in effect during the Erie war; a couple of the Iroquois war chiefs even wore French uniforms, and a French Jesuit mission was given a brief try among the Five Nations. This peace ended in outright war, and in 1666 the French made a full-scale, organized military invasion of the Iroquois country, burning towns and cutting a swath of devastation that should have been enough to destroy any nation. The Iroquois, furthermore, were in a disastrously weakened condition. There had been too much war. The Five Nations were bled white by war. It was at this time, in the expert opinion of the Jesuits, that the native-born Iroquois were reduced to a minority in their own towns, outnumbered by the immigrants they had adopted. They were still further reduced by a death-dealing epidemic in the 1660s.

But they made their enforced peace with the French, and somehow the Great League still stayed on its feet.

It faced continual wolf-pack attacks from remnants of the shattered nations to the north and west, and now a new major threat appeared from a new direction: from the south. The Susquehannock, armed with the best of guns and tall from easy pretension of conquest over their unarmed eastern neighbors, the Delaware, gave a humiliating beating to Seneca and Cayuga war parties and were evidently prepared to sweep the Five Nations from the face of the earth.

It has been observed that Europeans had furnished guns to the Susquehannock who in return had formed a firm alliance with the colony of Maryland, an alliance of mutual defense against the Iroquois. Maryland occasionally sent detachments of militia to aid the Susquehannock, the Swedes gave them cannon and military engineers, and on one occasion Maryland even conscripted every tenth man in the colony to raise a company of 410 men for Susquehannock assistance. This had been going on since the 1650s. Now, lording it over the grandfatherly Delawares become their humble vassals, and with such powerful allies at their back (and with the Dutch friends of the Iroquois out of business in New York since 1664), the Susquehannock might reasonably have expected a resounding victory over the Seneca, their special foe, with the rest of the enfeebled League too feeble to object.

Something intervened—perhaps fate, perhaps Tahiawagi, Holder of the Heavens, the Iroquois national deity. The Susquehannock lost staggering numbers of their people in waves of epidemics. By 1674 they were reduced to only one village of a few hundred people in Maryland and not many hundred more in Pennsylvania. White opportunists along the borders of the Maryland and Virginia settlements attacked (in 1676) these helpless remnants—in direct contravention of the official policy of their colonial governors, who had so long valued the Susquehannock as a frontier buffer. But Maryland had already discreetly forgotten its mutual-defense treaty with the Susquehannock and come to terms with the Iroquois, acknowledging them masters of Susquehannock territory without even the necessity of a major battle.

With this the Indian-versus-Indian wars of the Iroquois, their "beaver wars," as some historians call them, came pretty much to an end.

From their worn-down low point of the 1660s they bounced back with astonishing rapidity, strong with adopted immigrants, rulers of a vast woodland "land of Souls, where all was laid waste by war and terror, where on the fields was only blood, in the cabins only corpses," in the words of an orator from one of the nations they had destroyed.

Ghost-filled it may have been, but in this paramount area of conflict between rival European invaders the Great League now stood alone, king of the hill, the sovereign power, holding the key to the entire interior of the continent. More than beaver wars, more even than wars for land (which the Iroquois could now sell at a price higher than anything paid for peltries), their conquests had given them custody, as far as colonizing Europeans were concerned, of a continent.

Their decisions, in effect, would determine the nature of the country to be built thereon, so maintain some other American historians, possibly with some justice.

During the 1680s and 1690s the French, with Indian allies, smashed again and again at this Iroquois barrier, sending invasions that again and again should have broken forever the confederacy of the Five Nations, but did not. Iroquois crops and towns were destroyed and crowds of Iroquois souls went to join the wandering dead of their recent victims but the Iroquois state remained, frequently still capable of delivering heavy reprisals. ("Men make a state," wrote Alcaeus, "not walls nor empty ships.")

The Tree of Peace (as the Five Nations orators also liked to call their Great League) still stood.

Old World war, maker and destroyer of states since Sumerian times, could only roar in vain against certain communities of naked savages—why? The question will come up again.

It was from this point on that the League really began to function as a more or less unified force. At no time in the thirty years of great wars had the Five Nations all worked together—the Seneca at the western "door" and the Mohawk at the eastern had followed the devious paths of their own intricate interests, sometimes frankly opposed to each other, sometimes making common cause against the Onondaga in the center, who had sometimes conspired against other League members with the Hurons or the Susquehannock or even with the French.

But now, it seems, all the Five Nations began to realize the strength of their position and made the most of it. Swedes and Dutch were gone, as official entrants among the European invaders; English and French remained. The Iroquois learned to play them off one against the other with a certain amount of artistry.

Governor Edmund Andros of New York, who held an Indian signature of no more account "than a scratch with a Bear's paw," was nevertheless sufficiently agitated by New England's King Philip's War to organize in 1677, with an Onondaga councilor, a (very) loose alliance known as the Covenant Chain, linking the English colonies, New York at their head, with a number of Indian nations, the Iroquois at their head.

One of its ultimate results was the British disaster, two generations later, of Braddock's defeat. As domestic aggrandizement it didn't do much for its English participants either—New York would have to wait 200 years to assume actual ascendancy over New England. (And in only a dozen years Sir Edmund Andros was in jail in Boston at the end of the first American Revolution.)

But it worked quite well for the Five Nations, formally advertising the Iroquois as the Indian superpower.

They could never be true friends of the French: "between us and them there is no more good faith than between the most ferocious animals," said, with a Tartarinesque touch of exaggeration, a French administrator. At bottom, Iroquois sympathies were with the English, as they had been previously with the Dutch. This was especially true of the Mohawks, with what influence (frequently plenty) they could bring to bear on the rest of the League, for English trade, as had the Dutch, came first to their eastern door.

But the Mohawk as well as the League in toto fashioned a broad policy of independent neutrality that kept the balance of power in their hands for nearly a century.

"We are born free," a French governor was told in 1684 by Haaskouan, known to the French as La Grande Gueule (both names meaning Big Mouth), renowned Onondaga spokesman. And he spelled out exactly what he meant: the Iroquois would go where they wished, allow passage through their country only to "those who seem to us good," buy and sell with whom they pleased, English as well as French, or anyone else. They wore no muzzle, neither French nor English. "Listen, French Governor, my voice is that of the five Iroquois houses." And in this case it really was.

The French governor retired to his tent to rage and curse (so a witness reported), and a long line of French and English empire-builders raged and cursed, threatened, wheedled, devised, lied, and schemed. The Iroquois, those "subtle, adroit, and arrant knaves" (in the accolade of a French Jesuit), remained blandly independent and in command.

Their country lay athwart the one good water-level route to the interior and dominated the St. Lawrence and Ottawa River trade routes, the lower Great Lakes, the Ohio country, and the wilderness thresholds of New York, Pennsylvania, Maryland, and Virginia. In every plot and plan of French or English expansion, in every real-estate project to penetrate the interior or beguile the interior tribes, in every move of complicated fur-trade politics, the position the Iroquois would take had to be considered, often as the problem of foremost importance. There was no help for it. Neither side could afford to let the other take possession of the Iroquois and their country, highroad to the center of the continent. Neither side could afford to let the other become the Iroquois' one and only good true friend.

And so the latest decisions from the council of the Great League of the Iroquois became matters of moment to the busy strategists of St. James and Versailles. A French frontiersman was elevated to the peerage for his valuable work as interpreter to the Iroquois. Thirty-six (or some say thirteen or some say twenty-one) Iroquois councilors, seized during a parley and sent in chains to the galleys of Marseilles as a means of cutting their arrogance down to size, were apologetically freed, dusted off, dressed in "gorgeous French" robes, and returned in state to the dignity of their senatorial mats. ("A dirty troupe squatting on their behinds like monkeys, knees at ears, or sprawling back belly in air, everyone his pipe in his mouth, treating the affairs of State with as much coolness and gravity as the Junta of Spain or the Council of Doges at Venice.")

In even more state, four Iroquois councilors were escorted to London to visit the Queen—Queen Anne, this was, in 1710, and they were showered with gracious attentions and official favors, for, it was said, they were about to sign an important treaty with their friends, the English. The governor of New York, at about this same time, spoke glowingly of the Iroquois as the "bulwark between us and the French." The New York Indian commissioners at Albany reported that the Iroquois held "the balance of the continent of North America," and a French missionary in Canada recorded the same thing in almost the same words. The secretary of the Pennsylvania colony wrote to William Penn, "If we lose the Iroquois we are gone."

The Iroquois were even an influence in the temporary reversal of French colonial policy in 1696 when all traders (except Henri de Tonty, La Salle's old lieutenant, and his partner) were recalled from the forests and all expansionist activity ceased, although the mainspring of this extraordinary interlude was the brief rise to power in France of the Abbé Fénelon and his League of the Public Good with its revolutionary ideas ("I love my family better than myself, my country better than my family, the human race better than my country").

Colonial delegates from Massachusetts, New York, Pennsylvania, Maryland, Virginia, and the Carolinas traveled to the Iroquois eastern door at Albany to meet with the representatives of the Great League. The Iroquois themselves are said to have urged the colonies' concerted participation in these assemblies, expressing wonder that the colonies did not meet together over common interests, as did the Five Nations. Such irregular meetings had gone on for seventy years when, in 1754, the first great intercolonial conference (outside New England) was held (at Mohawk request—of which more later) to work out a design of colonial union; it took place, as a matter of course, at Albany.

The Tuscarora, driven from North Carolina in the years following 1712, were an Iroquoian people: "they were of us and went from us long ago, and now are returned," said the Five Nations, who gave them land for a new home, and made a place for them in the council of the Great League. Thereafter, the Five Nations were the Six Nations. The event caused concern among the colonies, for fear that it would embroil the Iroquois in southern Indian troubles. To prevent this, the governors of Virginia and Pennsylvania together with Indian ambassadors from the South went to Albany in 1722 and persuaded the Six Nations to agree to a dividing line between North and South. The line was laid down from the high ridge of the Alleghenies to the Potomac—forty-five years before the portentous Mason and Dixon survey to establish a Pennsylvania-Maryland boundary in the same area.

Iroquois prosperity and prestige during the eighteenth century reached the highest point attained (so far as history knows) by any Indian nation north of Mexico. An English chronicler writing in 1727 draws a picture of an Iroquois tribute-collector at an Algonquian village on the New England coast ("An old Mohawk sachem, in a poor blanket and dirty shirt . . . issuing his orders with as arbitrary an authority as a Roman dictator") that calls up Aztec memories. Although the impressive old Iroquois councilors, sincerely respected by the generations of Europeans who dealt with them, had no magnificence to display other than their simple presence: "The chiefs are generally the poorest among them," wrote a Dutch pastor at Albany in the 1640s, "for instead of their receiving from the common people . . . they are obliged to give."

Times were good: calico dresses and hickory shirts, log houses, barns fat with farm produce. Missionaries and rum came among them and the French never tired of fomenting trouble at home and wars with the "far nations," but all these classic wreckers, while wreaking much havoc, could not succeed in bringing down the Longhouse and its people.

Said Lafitau, writing in the 1700s, "under the uncultured and gross appearances, you will see everywhere among these Peoples a love for their Country engraved in their hearts, and a greatness of soul not only in the face of peril but even proof against unhappiness." And of the Iroquois women: "It is in them that resides all real authority . . . they are the soul of the councils, the arbiters of peace and war."

Vainglorious young men could and did go forth on war parties, sometimes to very distant lands, and the gaudy round of ceremonies and councils continued as before, but the old days of incessant war receded into the past. The old, old men recited their deeds against the Erie or against the French, and taught the young men how to dream a proper death song; but why should the young men take them seriously? In the old days you took your death song very seriously indeed because you fully expected to sing it some day roped up before glistening enemy eyes, as many, many friends of the old men so long ago had done; it was strange (the old men must have thought) that theirs were still unuttered. Sometimes the old men wept when they heard recited the rite of the Great League's founding: "You see the footprints of our forefathers . . . all but perceptible is the smoke where they used to smoke the pipe together."

The union lived, triumphant.

CHAPTER 19

Muskets across the Mountains

The hurricane belt had subsided to soft showers and golden days. But the violent disturbances of its years of storm had sent repercussions bounding across the lakes and forests of the wilderness as far as there were missionaries or traders to record them.

There's no reason to suppose they didn't roll on farther still, toppling ancient societies, uprooting peoples, tumbling together fugitives and invaders, littering the whole middle of the continent with wreckage left by the tumultuous winds of change. Bands of Huron, Erie, Neutral, Ottawa people straggled westward to the upper Mississippi, quarreled with the forest Sioux and were driven back eastward. They joined with other Huron and Tobacco people calling themselves Wyandot, and with Algonquian groups from the eastern St. Lawrence who had adopted themselves into the loose nationality of the Ottawa; they joined and divided again and again.

Some planted villages near the French trading posts of the far Lakes: Michilimackinac, Sault Sainte Marie, Detroit. More and more these dislocated peoples tended to coagulate around distant French forest forts or end-of-the-world French trading towns, little settlements that were Indian in everything but the language.

The aloof people known as the Foxes (the name of a clan mistakenly adopted by the whites as the name of the nation) were an exception and fought off the French, almost the only Algonquian people chronically hostile to the French. But eventually the Ojibwa pushed the Fox people southward to settle with their brothers, the Sauk, in the rich, gorgeous country of lower Wisconsin. Ojibwa, armed with French guns, were said to have driven the Dakota out of Minnesota in a 100 years' war during this period, but recent research raises doubts as to this, and prefers simple fur trade pressures finding expression less in open war than in shifting coalitions of the "upper country" nations that resulted in gradual withdrawal westward of the Dakota. The Cree of the northern forests, armed with trade guns from Hudson Bay and hunger for all the beaver country in the world, assaulted and dispersed the wandering people of the woods to their north and west, raiding northward down the Mackenzie River almost to the Arctic Ocean.

The fierce Winnebago west of Lake Michigan were crushed by pestilence and by a war they provoked with the Illinois. The Illinois, Potawatomi, and Miami, jostled here and there below the Lakes, were subject to Iroquois onslaughts in the 1680s.

For many years afterward displaced Erie and Susquehannock, and Delaware families at last dispossessed of their Pennsylvania lands by European real estate developers operating with Iroquois connivance, and Shawnee bands with their brothers the mystic Kickapoo drifted into the Miami and Illinois country, sometimes settling, sometimes gathering around the French posts that were coming into being along the Mississippi, sometimes traveling southward down the Warrior Trail, while displaced persons from the South passed them traveling hopefully to the North.

The land was filled with wars and wanderers. But in time the exiled bands found new homes and settled, finally, among nations with whom they could live in companionship.

East, south, and north of the Iroquois the turbulence of the Indian-versus-Indian frontier coincided with the frontiers of European settlement. French frontiers were directly affected by the Indian organization of the fur trade. But events and attitudes within the Indian world also had much to do with the subsequent movements of the English colonial frontiers.

The usual picture of land-hungry white settlers irresistibly pushing the Indians back, "clearing the Indians out," is naively oversimplified for any period, and basically wrong for the decisive years before 1800.

In its early phases the progress of the North American frontier, the frontier of actual European presence, was at least as much a creation of Indian politics and attitudes as white pressures. Many forces within the Indian world operated on this far from inexorable advance, sometimes in such obvious ways as an Indian nation encouraging white settlement in order to gain European support and auxiliaries, or storms among Indian states leaving shattered borderlands that invited occupation.

It was no accident that the first frontiers of English settlement to move westward across the Alleghenies, in the mid-1700s, happened to move into the country south of the Ohio, centering in Kentucky, that was, as previously noted, not permanently inhabited by any Indian nation.

The earliest tendrils of the white frontiers, Dutch *boschlopers*, English "long hunters," French *coureurs de bois*, were directed from here to there not only via devious Indian trails but for devious Indian purposes.

White frontiers in North America before 1800 did not expand against the opposition of intact Indian nations. Their direction was determined by circuitous Indian politics for complex Indian aims. The first frontiers in Virginia and New England were the original colonies, tolerated or even welcomed and assisted by the Indian nations. By the time Indian opposition developed, these frontiers were too solidly established to be dislodged.

For after the initial invited penetration, the story, as a rule (as we have seen), quickly changed. But in the subsequent destruction of such penetrated Indian nations, Indian politics continued to play a large part, both for the Europeans and for the Indians allied (for reasons of their own) with them.

The white frontiers moved where these factors directed. White population pressure was only a minor force in determining the course or setting the movement in motion.

But once begun in any area, the seepage of settlement over the border into Indian country became a clamorous factor all its own, unimportant at first but ultimately to become the most explosive ingredient of all, both for the Indian and white worlds.

Many of these frontier settlers were recent immigrants from Europe, too poor to afford a place within the recognized boundaries of the colony, or were shakily established in their settlements by real-estate developers who had contracted to produce such immigrants. The frontier was the low-rent district, the slum of colonial days. From the beginning the frontier also attracted outlaws, runaways, malcontents, younger brothers, freethinkers, and other such undesirables.

Flagrant border-jumpers brought trouble with them, and the region into which they jumped was often a troubled, unstable sector of the Indian world to begin with. When they and their troubles had sufficiently multiplied, a policy of clearing the Indians out came into being automatically. This was primarily a vocal measure, a matter of political agitation: they wanted, of course, the government militia to come and do the clearing out for them.

But their desires were quite often at variance with the policy of the colony's government or the policy of His Majesty's government across the sea. These governing bodies, with sights set on grander strategy, had sometimes if not often done everything possible to keep the settlers from entering the troubled borderlands in the first place.

If the borderers resented the Indians' presence on what they regarded as their potential property, they resented fully as much the rich, bloated, unfeeling, profiteering, tyrannical colonial governors back yonder in their brick colonial mansions, and the bloodsucking Lords of Trade across the sea in their lordly London halls. These fine gentry, lolling safe in their lace and powdered wigs, refused to give white men sufficient protection against the bloody savages because they didn't want to hurt their trade with the savage nations or endanger their dangling war schemes against the distant French, accusations which were frequently true.

Not surprisingly, these quasi-squatter pioneers were more inclined to be vicious than brave, and as far as they themselves were concerned their policy of clearing the Indians out was only exercised against tame Indians or the crumbled remains of previously broken Indian nations among which the new frontier arrival so customarily settled. Making any kind of dent in a still vigorous Indian nation was a job for the troops (with Indian allies) then and later. The frontier settlers' direct effectiveness in advancing the frontier, in the sense of Indian conquest, was never important.

But their indirect effectiveness, in the truly inexorable expansion of their influence on official government policy, was something else again.

And their instinctive hatred for the established order, for the citified and pompous central government that spurned their needs and arrogantly rejected their demands, springing from however small a source, grew to wield extraordinary power. This became the traditional spirit of the border, attitude of the West and of the left wing of the American Revolution.

An early example of this feeling showed itself in Virginia in what has been since known as Bacon's Rebellion. Its leader was a recent arrival in Virginia, one Nathaniel Bacon, distant kin of Francis Bacon. It was touched off by the murder of a settler on the Virginia-Maryland border by a Nanticoke band, which brought out a detachment of Virginia militiamen under Colonel John Washington, great-grandfather of the president (this took place in the summer of 1675).

The Nanticoke band was pursued up the Potomac "with some slaughter," in which several Susquehannock were also slain. Several settlers along the river were then killed in apparently retaliatory Indian "outrages."

This led to a joint Virginia-Maryland expedition against the principal Susquehannock remnant, then occupying, at the invitation of the Maryland governor, an old fort on the Potomac. A half dozen elderly spokesmen came out from the fort to discuss the matter under promises of safe conduct, and claimed the outrages charged against them had been committed by a Seneca war party recently in the area. Whereupon "they were taken away by the

Maryland commander and put to death." (The Maryland assembly later impeached the Maryland commander.)

The rest of the Susquehannock escaped from their besieged fort-village, killed a reported sixty frontier settlers—ten for each murdered councilor—and sent a message demanding damages from Sir William Berkeley, governor of Virginia.

Berkeley, enraged at the murder of the sachems under a flag of truce ("If they had killed my grandfather, my father, my mother, and all my friends, yet, if they had come to treat in peace, they should have gone in peace"), would not field troops against the rampaging Indians.

Young Bacon, already appointed a member of the governor's council, formed an unofficial army and killed a reported seventy Susquehannock ("well nigh exterminated the Indian tribe of Susquehannocks," wrote historian Woodrow Wilson) and then butchered remnants of the peaceable Powhatans at what has been known since as Bloody Run, near the falls of the James River—in fact, modern experts suspect Bacon was principally interested in killing friendly Indians to get their land. (Governor Berkeley had said in 1671, "The Indians, our neighbours, are absolutely subjected, so that there is no fear of them.")

The frontier army then went on to take over half of the whole Virginia colony, chasing out the governor and burning Jamestown before the frontier dander simmered down. This happened in 1676.

It is not unlikely that resentment over Navigation Acts which had brought about lower tobacco profits and higher commodity prices all for the benefit of English shippers may have had as much as Susquehannocks to do with the temper of rebelliousness. A principal figure from another Year of '76, Thomas Jefferson, putting his finger on the spirit of protest against unresponsive centralized rule ("insurrections proceed oftener from the misconduct of those in power, than from the factious and turbulent temper of the people"), suggested more than a century later that Nathaniel Bacon would "no longer be regarded as a rebel, but as a patriot." Some recent scholars, though, have seen Bacon more as an opportunistic demagogue than an early voice of liberty.

But whatever righteous rebellion's other wellsprings, slaughter of Indians was for generations a popular frontier refuge for patriotism.

In sum, white frontiers were set in motion with the considerable assistance, voluntary and involuntary, of forces within the Indian world. Once in motion, any frontier developed a growing force of its own, exerted primarily to impose its policy upon its own reluctant government. One desired feature of that policy was to clear the Indians out, and thus take over the last of the Indian property. This process formed one basic pattern of the Indian story on the white frontier. Sufficiently repeated, it helped eradicate European government, along with eradicating Indian nations.

Frontiersmen sometimes became genuinely industrious about cleaning out the debris of demolished Indian societies caught in the riptide of change— "I've shot and chopped and drowned the critters, I've fried 'em by the houseful and roasted 'taters in their grease," ran the backwoods burlesques—but reality in that brand of murder was rare (except, as we shall see, in California) and of small effect in the ultimate havoc.

Drink and the devil did for the rest, a devil crowned with the three heavy horns of poverty, degradation, and disease. Religion helped by destroying the comfortable elastic world of the old gods and by providing the circumstances for point-blank epidemics among converts crowded in squalid imitation-white housing. There were exceptions to this last, such as thriving mission villages in Pennsylvania, most of them seemingly founded by Moravian missionaries, although unfortunately many of these were destroyed one after another by indignant white settlers or equally indignant non-Christian Indians. Some surviving mission villages, however, were of considerable importance, such as the mission suburb of Goschgosching, a Munsee capital in western Pennsylvania that became the nucleus of Ohio Delawares moving on westward at the end of the 1760s.

Descendants of friend and foe alike shared the common Indian fate within the white world: by about the year 1800 neighboring Connecticut villages were occupied by the few forlorn survivors of the anti-English Pequots, less than 100 strong, and the few forlorn survivors of their tribal brothers and fatal enemies, the pro-English Mohegans, also less than 100 strong.

Some, maybe many, escaped from the long nightmare to the intact tribes beyond the borderlands; Narragansets went to Maine and turned into Abnakis by the hundreds, maybe thousands, after King Philip's War, and the parade of Tuscarora plodding north to join the Iroquois took 100 years to pass.

But one after another of the intact tribes marched to destruction in their turn in the major colonial wars from 1689 to 1763, echoes for the most part of European wars between France and England, but in America fought on the American plan, with as much use as possible of Indian allies.

The brunt of these wars was felt on the frontiers, with enough wanton hatcheting of settlers and burning of farms and villages, enough wives and children carried away into captivity, to madden a people with far less motive for madness than property-minded frontier settlers had.

The stories can still communicate the reality of agony behind the archaic phrases. Wrote a mother, of parting from her six-year-old son, both made captives by "French" Indians at Charlestown, New Hampshire, in 1754:

"The inexorable savage . . . forced him away; the last words I heard, inter-mingled with his cries, were 'Ma'am, I shall never see you again.' The keen-ness of my pangs almost obliged me to wish that I had never been a mother. 'Farewell, Sylvanus,' said I; 'God will preserve you.'" It is good to note that God did, and Sylvanus, although by then as Indian as English, came back when grown to live near his mother in Charlestown.

Typically, though, much of the understandable fury of bedeviled frontier settlers was turned against their own governments, their grievances used as levers to secure various official concessions. One of these was the scalp bounty, sometimes extracted by the radical frontier bloc as a sop for damages claimed from Indian depredations.

Scalp bounties were introduced early by the Dutch, and were adopted at one time or another by most of the colonies. They were much in use in these wars, and could become an expensive business—Massachusetts paid 20 shillings in 1675, £12 in 1703, and £100 in 1722.

Of course, no one could be sure the scalps brought in were the scalps of whatever Indians happened to be enemies at the moment. Missionaries had to keep a frantic watch over their Indian flocks during bounty years—when you could collect hair worth $1,500, as did some Pennsylvania bounty hunters in 1763, simply by hatcheting a score of Indian men, women, and children who plied the basket-making trade in a nearby town.

Here again, in this particular incident, murder of Indians was only a convenient expression of a broader conflict, in this instance a political struggle between poor frontier Scotch-Irish Presbyterians and the wealthy urban Quakers who controlled the Pennsylvania colonial council. The Indian victims here were among the last shreds of the once mighty Susquehannock (now, by the eighteenth century, called Susquehanna), a tiny band inhabiting a village named after one of their ancient tribal appel-lations, Conestoga.

The French used the scalp bounty to have the inoffensive Beothuk of Newfoundland cut off, as the phraseology of the time had it, by the Micmac of Nova Scotia. The Beothuk were a minor nuisance to the French, who offered the Micmac a bounty for Beothuk scalps. After a generation or so not a single Beothuk was left alive, at any rate none who would admit their tribal identity. Some may have escaped across the Strait to join the Naskapi of Labrador.

Those Indian nations left in shambles by the stress of colonial wars were, if within reach, swallowed up and digested by the European frontiers—at an accelerated rate as the frontiers and shambles spread. In each case the cycle of disorder, decay, and fitful extermination was scrupulously repeated, only faster.

The fissures opened in intact Indian nations by the disruptive effects of Indian-versus-Indian wars and European colonial wars are seen in white history as the "opening to settlement" of the trans-Appalachian country, the Ohio country, and the country northwest of the Ohio known as the Old Northwest.

Previous Iroquois conquests (or at least disruptions) in areas of this back country made possible the first tentative entry of English traders and settlers, followed for many years by similar actions or disruptions or pretended disruptions from other major Indian powers, such as the Cherokee.

An early avenue of settlement was through Delaware country in Pennsylvania beyond William Penn's early purchases, some of this falling under Susquehannock claims of conquest in the 1600s. The Six Nations Iroquois, after their pretended conquest of the few surviving Susquehannocks, claimed to have inherited thereby sovereignty over this Delaware country, and by the 1730s were selling Delaware lands along the Susquehanna River to the proprietors of Pennsylvania. The Delawares objected but Pennsylvania sided with the claims of the generous Iroquois land agents, some of these lands being of crucial use to Pennsylvania in a violent boundary dispute with Maryland.

Pennsylvania officials bought land from the Delawares themselves at this period under conditions at times very questionable; the Delawares particularly objected to a slick operation known since as the Walking Purchase. This cheated them out of an immense tract of land running some 100 miles north and west into the interior from a point fifty miles above Philadelphia. Occasional early purchases made by William Penn from the Lenape (Delaware) Confederacy had been based on the stretch of land a man might walk over in a given period, a day or a day and a half. Tradition says (mistakenly, alas) that Penn himself marked out the first of these purchases with a day's walk of twenty miles or so, a leisurely walk "after the Indian manner, sitting down sometimes to smoke, eat biscuit and cheese."

But after Penn's death his policy of fair purchase was revised, by his heirs and his former provincial secretary, James Logan, to a program of taking lands by fraud or force from neighboring Indian communities, with the connivance, more or less adroitly manipulated, of the Six Nations.

In line with this new program one such walking purchase was executed, in 1737, by men specially hired as the fastest walkers available, who clocked sixty miles in the day and a half of the walk, to the indignation of the Delawares—who also protested the legality of the operation on several other counts, including the place and directions involved. Here, say various modern studies, was the chief point of fraud in the notorious Walking Purchase.

The Penn heirs were much in need of more land to sell, and James Logan had a special need of forestland in the region involved, to provide charcoal for an ironworks in which he had an investment. He showed to the Delaware leader, Nutimus, sachem of the Delaware communities at "the Forks" (Forks of the Delaware River), a draft of a 1686 deed for land west of the river, extending "as far as a man can go in one day and a half." The map of this draft, however, appeared to designate land below the Forks, while the land desired by the heirs and Logan was at the Forks and above. Logan insisted that the wording of the draft, which the Indians could not read, referred to land at the Forks and above. On this claim the purchase was based.

A route was prepared before the walk, trees and brush were cleared, horses were provided to carry provisions, boats to ferry the walkers across streams. Only one of the three "walkers" was able to finish the course; Indian witnesses dropped out in disgust. From the farthest point reached a line was run arbitrarily back to the river, not to the nearest point but at a right angle to the line of walk, more than doubling the area thus "purchased." The theft totaled more than 1,200 square miles, enough to qualify as a state, being somewhat larger than Rhode Island.

Logan had unquestionably resorted to "sharp practice," says his biographer, and to answer the continued protests—even war threats—of the Delawares he besought the support of the Iroquois, at a Philadelphia meeting in 1742. A chronicle written a half century or so later says that during one of the "sociable canticoes" accompanying this conference "the subject of the walk was introduced, and the several deeds and writings shown and explained by way of appeal to the high authority of the Six Nations."

The scheduled object of this meeting was to pay the Iroquois for their sales of Susquehanna lands along the Susquehanna River, to which was added a gratuity of guns, hatchets, hoes, and other goods to the value of some £300 over and above the agreed price for the lands, just because the Six Nations were such good friends.

At a formal session on July 12, in the presence of a number of Delaware sachems, including the aged Nutimus and the aged Sassoonan, "king" of the whole Delaware nation, the Onondaga orator Canassatego, "glowing with liquor and good fellowship," delivered a blistering rebuke (text printed by Benjamin Franklin) to the defrauded Lenape:

> Your Cause is bad; your Heart far from being upright. . . . But how came
> you to take upon you to sell Land at all: We conquered you; we made
> women of you; you know you are Women, and can no more sell land
> than Women. . . . This Land you claim is gone through your Guts; you
> have been furnish'd with Cloaths, Meat and Drink, by the Goods paid

you for it. . . . You act a dishonest Part. . . . And for all these Reasons we charge you to remove instantly; we don't give you the Liberty to think about it. You are Women. . . . We therefore assign you two Places to go, either to *Wyomen* or *Shamokin*. You may go to either of these Places, and then we shall have you more under our Eye, and shall see how you behave. Don't deliberate; but remove away.

This act could stand as a latter-day triumph of the Covenant Chain, Governor Andros's neat invention a couple of generations earlier to keep the Indians quiet under the leadership of the Iroquois; Canassatego referred to it in his rebuke: "you are maliciously bent to break the Chain of Friendship with our brother *Onas* [Governor of Pennsylvania] and his People."

The use of "women" as an epithet in Canassatego's speech has received much attention; a recent explanation holds that it merely refers to agreement between the Iroquois and Delaware that the Iroquois would speak for them in foreign affairs. In any case, the Delawares left the council room in "great and silent grief," went to their homes and burned their cabins to signify they would never return, and moved across the Susquehanna to the Wyoming valley.

Although "no doubt there were some land speculators, and those who had conducted the business to such an issue, who enjoyed the triumph with unfeeling satisfactions," it was nevertheless "seriously apprehended that mischief would sometime" result from this "shameful imposition," and in due time grievous mischief indeed did.

But for the moment many outraged Delawares only drifted on westward all the way to the region of the upper Ohio, accompanied by their brothers the Shawnees and remnants of other dispossessed peoples, and there became a nucleus of bitter anti-English (and anti-Iroquois) feeling.

It was also in the 1740s that the Iroquois granted control of the country of the upper Ohio River to the English, and several land-promotion companies were formed to subdivide tracts in this area and sell them off to settlers. English fur traders and explorers of this time roamed as far west as the Mississippi, English trading posts were established on the Ohio and the Allegheny and the Monongahela, and a settlement was planted in 1748 across the first range of the Blue Ridge mountains of Virginia. Virginia was a prime mover in all this, partly to counter western claims by Pennsylvania.

Christopher Gist, a fur trader exploring for a combine of wealthy Virginia land promoters known as the Ohio Company, was at the falls of the Ohio (present Louisville) in 1750. Some of this country, as previously noted, had been regarded by the various Indian nations for a long while as a sort of no man's land, owned by no one—not even the Iroquois.

But now refugees from the Iroquois and the English were plentiful in this region. These "western" Indians encouraged French resistance to the English occupation of their country. The French informed Virginia in 1753 (via twenty-one-year-old George Washington, guided to the French forest forts by Christopher Gist) that if the English wanted the Ohio country they would have to fight for it—as, therefore, they did.

The French and Indian War is often described as the American phase of the Seven Years' War in Europe. It might be more proper to describe Britain's participation in the Seven Years' War as the European phase of the war with France in America; when hostilities broke out between the British and the French on the frontier, George II of England, dreading a French attack on his homeland of Hanover, began the series of treaty maneuvers that led to war between France and Britain in Europe in June 1756.

The immediate cause of the war in America was rivalry between Virginia and France for control of the upper Ohio country, specifically the key point at the forks of the Ohio where the French had built Fort Duquesne (now Pittsburgh). Two British forces sent against this point, Frye's in 1754 and Braddock's in 1755, were cut to pieces by the French and their Indian allies.

The most consequential of these allies were exiled Delawares from Pennsylvania (in the scalp bounties General Braddock offered his troops, the scalp of the great Delaware warrior, Shingas, chief of the Turkey clan, rated by far the highest price, £200, forty times the price for an ordinary French soldier's hair, and even twice as much as was offered for the scalp of the Jesuit missionary among the Ohio Indians).

After Braddock's defeat the entire western border of Pennsylvania, Maryland, and Virginia was laid bare to these Delawares and their friends, who skinned it alive with pleasure. Outposts and settlements were abandoned and the English frontier recoiled, on the average, 100 miles.

The exiled Delawares were eventually appeased by the desperate diplomacy of Conrad Weiser, Pennsylvania's wily interpreter and ambassador extraordinary to the Indians. It had been Weiser's support of shady Iroquois claims to Delaware lands that had helped to cause the trouble in the first place; it was widely believed on the frontier that land frauds such as the Walking Purchase were the sole cause of the "great public distress" of the Indian War ("there could be no doubt but that it was occasioned by the imposition of the walk").

Now the Pennsylvania authorities and Weiser reversed their field and managed to win the cooperation of Teedyuskung, leader of the Delawares still living in Pennsylvania.

(Weiser and his associate, George Croghan, Pennsylvania trader and England's deputy superintendent for Indian affairs in the northern colonies, first tried working on Teedyuskung with liquor, but although Teedyuskung got gloriously drunk with them each night he always had a clear head each morning, with his fantastically accurate memory for each detail of dubious land deals quite unimpaired.)

After numberous conferences, in 1758 Teedyuskung and the governor of Pennsylvania sent the Delaware Turkey chief, Shingas (assured the English price on his head was withdrawn), on an urgent journey to the western Indians in the vicinity of Fort Duquesne to do "all in his power to bring about a peace." Frederick Christian Post, a Moravian missionary, traveled with him, bearing Pennsylvania's guarantee that fraudulent land sales would be corrected.

The mission succeeded in winning enough support from the western Indians to break the French alliance. Post returned in October, 1756, and in November of that same year Fort Duquesne fell to a new English expedition without a shot being fired: the French abandoned the fort before the English arrived.

The Walking Purchase was never rectified; this would have entailed much disruption, and the rowdy Scotch-Irish settlers, if sufficiently annoyed, could have caused more trouble than an Indian war, or, worse, could have driven politicians out of office.

Teedyuskung, much involved in politics as symbolic conscience for the Quaker faction in the Quakers-versus-Proprietors conflict, local production of the eternal Colonial-versus-Britishers alignment, did not insist—there is also some indication that he may have received a sizable "present" from Pennsylvania to drop this particular case.

But Pennsylvania's efforts to straighten out some of the wrongdoing in land sales, even to the point of evicting white settlers, certainly helped in its small way to fire up frontier resentments that would find outlet in the American Revolution.

Various of the Indian nations who had not entirely used themselves up by 1763 were drawn into further debilitating hostilities by the grand Indian alliance on the western border under the Ottawa leader Pontiac; these tribes and fragments of tribes fought a last-ditch campaign to retain the status of sovereign and equal associates they had held in the French beaver trade (by what right could Europeans "give away their country" ceded to England at the close of the French and Indian War?).

A Delaware prophet known as Neolin ("the Enlightened") gave a message from the Master of Life to all Indians to suffer no longer "those who are come to trouble your possessions. Drive them away; wage war upon them. I love them not." French traders stirred up Indian hostility toward the new English intruders and promised (vainly, of course) French support. Land speculators, with their "low, cunning tricks" in gaining control of Indian lands, helped make the English unpopular. The military policy of the English governor-general, the obtuse General Jeffrey Amherst (who, taken aback by the ungentlemanly behavior of some of the enemy Indians, wrote his field commander, "I wish to hear of no prisoners," and "Could it be contrived to send the Small Pox among those disaffected tribes?") was even more effective in creating anti-English feeling among all the native Americans of the Lakes.

Essentially, though, Pontiac's war was in protest against British encroachment in the country of the lower Lakes, with a string of forts hundreds of miles west of the line of settlement—and against settlement itself in more or less instantaneous violation of treaties and agreements. After the French withdrawal from Fort Duquesne settlers swarmed into the Monongahela valley in spite of the treaty negotiated by Shingas and Christian Post forbidding settlement, and in spite of the proclamation in 1761 of the English field commander (Colonel Henry Bouquet) forbidding settlement. More than 200 houses had been built around Fort Pitt (ex-Fort Duquesne) by 1763.

The Seneca, traditionally the only one of the Six Nations Iroquois with a noticeable pro-French faction, were charter members of the Pontiac alliance, but for the most part the alliance was composed not of intact nations but of bits and pieces of many tribes. The country from Niagara to the Illinois had been open as a European frontier for more than sixty years, a situation usually disastrous, as we have seen, to Indian communities.

Even thus fragmented, Pontiac and his variegated army stood off the British for nearly three years, captured nine forts—all the British forts west of Niagara except Detroit and Fort Pitt—and maintained at Detroit one of the longer sieges in American history. British losses were far heavier than losses suffered by the Indians (even though Colonel Bouquet told Amherst he would try distributing smallpox-infected blankets). The war was finally settled only by bribes, conciliation (from Amherst's successor), and promises on the part of the English to restrain settlement, positively, behind a line established by the Proclamation of 1763.

George Croghan had been sent to London with a formula for peace worked out by experienced Indian negotiators but was delayed by shipwreck on the coast of Normandy. ("I Traveld about 140 Miles in france Butt Never See So Much pride and poverty before.") He only arrived in London in February 1764, to find that Lord Hillsborough, the new president of the Board of Trade, had drawn up and announced the Proclamation of October 7, 1763.

Advice that a proclamation should be prepared to quiet the Indians had been put on the table before the Board on the fifth of August; during the following weeks more complete news of the successful uprising of the Indians had been received: "Action must be taken at once." Accordingly the hasty Proclamation, "One of the most important state documents concerning America ever promulgated by the British government," was announced in early October.

The Proclamation stated that "the several Nations or Tribes of Indians with whom We are connected . . . should not be molested or disturbed" in their possession of "any Lands beyond the Heads or Sources of any of the Rivers which fall into the Atlantic Ocean from the West and North West."

Because of the need for haste the Indian boundary line, beyond which no settlements were to be permitted, was not marked out for surveying but was located at the Appalachian divide where the Indians could easily identify it.

The Proclamation continued:

And we do hereby strictly forbid, on Pain of our Displeasure, all our loving subjects from making any Purchases or Settlements whatever, or taking Possession of any of the Lands above reserved, without our especial leave and Licence for that Purpose first obtained.

. . . And, we do further strictly enjoin and require all Persons whatever who have either wilfully or inadvertently seated themselves upon any Lands within the Countries above described, or upon any other Lands which, not having been ceded to or purchased by Us, are still reserved to the said Indians as aforesaid, forthwith to remove themselves from such Settlement.

The Proclamation included the words "for the present, and until our further Pleasure be known," in its instructions to colonial governors forbidding them to issue warrants or patents for any such lands.

British spokesmen did not happen to raise this point of a possible temporariness about the line with Pontiac when Pontiac stated the condition in his treaty that the British were not to regard their possession of the former French forts as giving them title to the country for Englishmen to settle. Pontiac's condition was of course apparently accepted; in fact the British administration did its official best to make the line appear a conspicuous, tangible, and immutable boundary.

And the line was indeed kept inviolate (more or less) by England for almost two years.

Efforts (sort of) to do so infuriated the frontier West, which, as usual, had suffered the most from Pontiac's war, to the point that the border became openly seditious toward the crown, and a noisy and obvious factor in the outbreak of revolution ten years later.

A report in 1765 concerning rebellious frontier residents who had destroyed Indian trade goods and attacked a party of His Majesty's troops added, significantly: "from their conduct and threats since, there is reason to think they will not stop here."

Pontiac's war was clearly a war between equals, for all that nineteenth-century historians settled on the terminology of a "rebellion" or "conspiracy" to describe it, with the implication of an unlawful insurrection of subject peoples against a duly constituted ruling government. The indirect effect of this war, and the complex effects deriving from other Indian-skinning drolleries such as the Walking Purchase, on the gathering tide of American Revolution may also deserve some added historical attention.

With a few exceptions such as the participation of the Seneca in Pontiac's war, the Iroquois, as steadily neutral as their subtle, adroit, and arrant knavery could manage, avoided serious involvement in most of the colonial wars. The French made strenuous efforts in 1754, at the start of the French and Indian War, to win Iroquois support. Quebec and Louisiana were like two gates at either end of a 2,000-mile lane, a lane that had to make a wide, difficult detour by way of the Great Lakes around the Iroquois country. With Iroquois help, the French could have used the waterways of present New York State and the Ohio country not only to shorten, straighten, and reinforce that impossibly long front, but also to build a fence line into the heart of the English colonies.

The Iroquois stuck to official neutrality, neutrality that in itself was of consequence in deciding the outcome of the French and Indian War. Worse, they gave some unofficial help to the English.

An English fur trader named William Johnson had settled in the Mohawk valley and become such a friend of the Iroquois that the English had commissioned him "Colonel of the Six Nations" in 1746. The last two of his three wives were Mohawk girls, the last being Molly Brant, whose young brother, Joseph, became Johnson's special protégé. The most renowned Mohawk war leader at the time of the French and Indian War, one of the four Iroquois chiefs who had been taken on a state visit to London forty-five years earlier, known to the English as Hendrick, was also related to Colonel Johnson by marriage.

There was great Iroquois concern that the French in Canada, aggressively pushing their trade in the Ohio Valley and along the lakes in the north, would attack the Iroquois if the Iroquois persisted in refusing alliance with them. At the end of April 1753, Mohawk hunters had seen a large war party of French

Indians too close for comfort on their northern frontier. Hendrick led a deputation of seventeen Mohawks to New York City less than two months later, in June, and in conference with the governor and council and members of the assembly demanded that plans should be made at once for a united colonial defense on the north. He also demanded that land frauds upon the Iroquois should be redressed, and Indian relations should be taken out of the hands of the Indian commissioners at Albany and turned over to Colonel Johnson. When the New York authorities temporized, Hendrick told them bluntly that the Covenant Chain was therefore broken. "So, Brother, you are not to expect to hear of me any more, and, Brother, we desire to hear no more of you."

This created a crisis of grave dimension both in London and America, and led directly to the famous Albany Congress of the colonies in June 1754, resulting in a plan for union put forward by Benjamin Franklin—rejected or ignored by all officialdom at the time but remembered by history as the first step toward the American Constitution. The Albany meeting itself is remembered by history as the first congress of the American continental colonies— although history does sometimes seem to need reminding that it was held in response to a demand by Hendrick for united action.

Colonel Johnson was later placed in charge of all northern Indian affairs for the English crown, and was given so many bosomy grants of their beauteous land by the Six Nations that he became one of the largest landowners in all colonial America.

In the following year, 1755, the year that Braddock's defeat threw many of the wavering Indian nations into the French and Indian War on the side of France, Colonel Johnson flung a painted war belt among the Six Nations council, in the manner of a war chief, and asked for some of their briskest men as unofficial allies (he also distributed £1,000's worth of presents). Hendrick himself volunteered, and several hundred warriors came with him. Their effect in the battle of Lake George that followed has perhaps sometimes been overestimated—there were 2,000 or 3,000 English militiamen as well as the 200 or 300 brisk Iroquois—but the propaganda value of their presence was undoubtedly important.

At this battle, Hendrick, then an old man of at least seventy, is supposed to have made one of those battlefield remarks that have a way of reappearing down through the ages: "If they [his warriors] are to fight they are too few; if they are to die they are too many." They fought and they died. Hendrick himself was killed, and the Six Nations casualties were exceedingly heavy. But the battle was won, English America was saved, the war could go on to ultimate victory and the finish of France in the New World. Two months after the crucial Lake George action, Colonel Johnson was elevated to a baronetcy.

France's finish was also the finish of the Iroquois as a weight in the balance of diplomacy, there being only the one great power left, England.

But the friendship of Sir William Johnson and that of his successor, Colonel Guy Johnson, could cut both ways, and the Iroquois (most of them) enjoyed an amiable hour of prosperity and peace after the close of the French and Indian War, in spite of continuing cessions of land to Sir William for white settlement.

Sir William placed his youthful brother-in-law Joseph Brant (who had been at Lake George as a thirteen-year-old warrior) in Moor's Indian Charity School, recently opened in Connecticut by the Reverend Eleazar Wheelock. The young man came forth with an education and a religious bent, and assisted missionaries in revising the Mohawk prayer book and in translating the Acts of the Apostles into the Mohawk tongue.

In conjunction with the line of settlement laid down in the Proclamation of 1763 the British Crown took exclusively unto itself the management of Indian affairs. It also reserved to itself the right to purchase or treat for Indian lands, forbidding these dealings in the future to colonies, land companies, or individuals—the United States was later to continue this same policy. In the late 1760s the British government secured permission to go beyond the line of 1763 (by some form of purchase) from such intact Indian nations as the Iroquois, Cherokee, and Creeks, and expanded settlement once again into the Ohio country of broken tribes.

New land-promotion companies were formed, some getting charters and grants from the British Crown, some evading the law by privately "leasing" Indian lands. One such group of speculators, the Transylvania Company (as it was later called) of North Carolina, employed a land prospector named Daniel Boone, who spent six years "in quest of the country of Kentucky" before his employer, Judge Richard Henderson, bought it for the company in 1775, paying £10,000 to the Overhill Cherokees for what was at best a doubtful title.

Indian bands in the Ohio country, under such leaders as the Shawnee Cornstalk, the Delaware Turtle chief Newcomer, and the expatriate Iroquois Logan, son of a famous Iroquois sachem, made occasional objection to the fairly frequent discourtesies of the incoming settlers, the most notorious of these being the unprovoked murder of a little group of Indian hunters and their families by a band of land jobbers led by one "Colonel" Michael Cresap. This name was not unknown in chapters of violence in colonial history, Thomas Cresap having been the chief bullyboy for Maryland in the previously mentioned boundary dispute with Pennsylvania thirty years before.

Several of Colonel Cresap's victims were relatives of Logan or of his Shawnee wife, and Logan, the "Great Mingo" (Mingo being derived from a

Delaware and Shawnee term for Iroquois), led retaliatory raids against white settlers on Indian lands. Real-estate patriots yelled for rescue and Lord Dunmore, governor of Virginia, dispatched troops to defeat some of the "hostile" Indians in a formal war in 1774, thereby incidentally strengthening Virginia's claim to the newly opened country (as opposed to the claims of other colonies or speculators)—which may have been the real reason for Lord Dunmore's formal little war in the first place.

It has been remarked that poorer settlers tended to cross the legal line and take their chances as squatters on Indian lands in order to dodge the prices asked by land speculators. In the case of the Transylvania Company many of the incoming settlers simply ignored the company altogether and settled where they pleased. Numbers of emigrants went all the way across the Ohio into the territories of the broken nations northwest of the river, and the pattern for further Indian "wars" was once more established.

The Proclamation Line of 1763, what was left of it, was tossed to the speculators by the British government in March, 1768; eight months later Sir William Johnson handled the biggest land cession of all, the Fort Stanwix Treaty surrendering Iroquois claims southeast of Six Nations lands in New York and southeast of the Ohio River all the way to present Kentucky. The normal trade winds of land speculation promptly became a tornado, involving British Lord High Poohbahs of banking and politics, and such premature Americans as Patrick Henry and Benjamin Franklin (George Washington had been involved since 1763).

Johnson died in 1774, but his influence remained paramount. Joseph Brant, who had become a leading young chieftain of the Mohawk (Thayendanegea by his Mohawk name), insisted on alliance with the English when the Revolution came over the horizon. Colonel Guy Johnson and the Brants, including Sir William's widow, Molly, succeeded in bringing most of the Mohawk, Cayuga, and Seneca, and some of the Onondaga, into the war on the English side. The Oneida and Tuscarora sided with the Colonies.

Thus, finally, the Iroquois were openly divided against themselves in war. Although its shadow play persisted, it was the end of the Great League as an operating reality. There is perhaps poetic symmetry of a sort in the fact that the American Revolution, with the genesis of which the Iroquois had for so long been indirectly and directly involved, should have brought about the death of the Great League.

Joseph Brant, as a British ally, led his Mohawks in border raids that were seized upon and magnified, according to an early biographer, by the "public writers" until his "name was terrible in every ear . . . associated with every thing bloody, ferocious, and hateful." The idea being that "accounts of such

deeds of ferocity and blood" would keep "alive the strongest feelings of indignation against the parent country, and likewise induce the people to take the
field for revenge, if not driven thither by the nobler impulse of patriotism."
The English poet Thomas Campbell, world famous at the moment, referred
to "the Monster Brandt . . . with all his howling desolating band." A military
proclamation of 1777 signed by Major General Benedict Arnold, in command
of American forces at the time on the Mohawk River, called them "a banditti
of robbers, murderers, and traitors."

The most resounding of the Revolutionary War deeds attributed to the
Monster Brant were the full-fledged battle of Oriskany, New York; the
Wyoming, Pennsylvania, battle and "massacre"; and the Cherry Valley, New
York, raid and "massacre." At Oriskany Brant and his Iroquois participated in
an ambush of a vastly superior American force, both sides suffering heavily—
it was the bloodiest battle of the Revolution—perhaps 100 Iroquois warriors
were killed. At Cherry Valley thirty-some civilians, including women and children, were killed, despite the efforts of Brant and the allied English commander to avoid deaths of noncombatants, and thirty or forty prisoners, mostly
women and children, were taken, later to be exchanged for the families of New
York Loyalists being held by the Americans as hostages.

Brant was not even present at Wyoming, the Indians accompanying the
British on this attack being principally Seneca, not Mohawk. A body of militia was defeated at Wyoming with heavy losses, settlements in the Wyoming
valley were then looted and burned, and the settlers fled to the hills, but there
was no massacre of civilians and no torture of prisoners. The Wyoming attack
was not, as far as the Indian participants were concerned, prompted only by
Revolutionary War considerations: the causes were deep in long-standing conflicts of the Indian-versus-Indian frontier. The Iroquois—or some Iroquois—
had sold land there (in 1754) to a Connecticut combine of land speculators;
Delawares, and other inhabitants (including neighborhoods of Shawnees,
Nanticokes, Mahicans, and Mingos) objected strenuously, among the most
strenuous being Teedyuskung, who made his home in the valley. Pennsylvania
complicated matters in the early 1770s by trying to drive out, with troops, settlers from Connecticut who had arrived in the wake of questionable land sales.

But in the summer of 1778 white squatters and Indian residents alike sal-
lied forth from their principal settlements (site of the present Wilkes-Barre)
to give fight to the invading British and Iroquois. The Wyoming defenders
were routed, and the purely imaginary massacre that followed was given top
atrocity billing in border song and story for a long time to come.

In reprisal American troops laid waste the Iroquois country (starting with
Onondaga towns that had been struggling to stay neutral) as the French had

done so often 100 years before; although now there was more in the way of homes, barns, livestock, orchards and cornfields to lay waste—there is a tradition that sweet corn was first discovered for whites by a farmer-soldier along on this campaign. Of the thirty or so "thriving villages" of the Six Nations, only two still survived by the spring of 1780.

Mohawk and Seneca warriors had kept the score at least even, but after the war the Tory Iroquois lost "over the council table the lands and the political sovereignty that white armies had been unable to seize by force." It was during this time of decline under the influence of hopelessness and whiskey that the Seneca prophet Ganio'dai'o (Handsome Lake) began teaching his precepts of patience and right living in a religion that helped save the Seneca and is still healthy today in the Iroquois world.

Joseph Brant and several Iroquois bands that had served as British allies were given lands on the Grand River, Ontario, and the fearsome Brant returned to his occasional hobby of translating the Scriptures into Mohawk. He also made a return visit to England, where he had been at the start of the Revolution, and where he was a lion of society; he was taken up this time as an intimate friend of the Prince of Wales.

A son of Brant's, in England some years later trying to get back some Iroquois land wrongly taken by Canada, wrote to Thomas Campbell, whose poem celebrating the fictitious Wyoming massacre had not appeared until after Joseph Brant's death, giving the facts on his father's war record, including the incidental fact that he had not even been present at Wyoming. Campbell published a handsome apology, although the poem remained unrevised (world-famous poems, as everyone knows, being unchangeable). In later years, however, praise heaped on Joseph Brant outdid the previous obloquy: "dauntless hero," "noble, generous," "the ideal of the noble red man," "British gentleman-officer and Iroquois warrior-diplomat." One feels that part of the Joseph Brant luck may have been dying in time.

Communities of the Six Nations who had given their loyalty to the "Yankeys" remained in New York. The Seneca, last of the Iroquois to retain their ancestral lands pretty much unbroken, sold most of these in 1797 at the bribe-riddled Treaty of Big Tree to Robert Morris of Philadelphia, who was repaid for financing the American Revolution by being handed this choice land-speculation plum.

The split between the Canadian and New York Iroquois widened during the Indian wars of the Old Northwest that followed the end of the Revolutionary War, and from the early 1800s on there were two Iroquois "great council" fires, one on the Grand River in Canada and one at Onondaga in New York.

The rites commemorating the founding of the League of the Iroquois repeated in their closing lines:

> Now listen
> you who established the Great League
> Now it has become old
> Now there is nothing but wilderness
> Now you are in your graves
> you who established it . . .
> There you have taken your minds and your souls . . .
> What you established
> you have taken with you
> the Great League.

CHAPTER 20

The Road Not Taken

The study of Indian treaties has much to reveal for American history. The revelations, however, fall less on the Indian side of the story than on that of the alien intruder. In his march to the utmost seas he is seen first in the treaties as requesting help, then as a merchant thoughtful of customers, then as a stern but righteous bill collector, and only finally as the landlord.

The newborn United States, like any newborn creature, was most concerned with its immediate security. President George Washington of the brand-new United States of America concluded in 1790 a treaty with the Creek nation of Indians, a considerable achievement of his administration. The "Case of the Creek Nation is of the highest importance," President Washington told the Senate, and "the proposed Treaty is of great importance to the future tranquility of the State of Georgia as well as of the United States." The immediate benefit of the treaty was to secure the peace and safety of the southern border against the activities of the Spanish, then in Florida and Louisiana.

"The fate of the Southern States," summed up the president, "may principally depend on the present measures of the Union toward the Southern Indians."

In the 1790 treaty the Creeks ceded certain lands along the Florida border deemed essential to American security, and the United States government took its solemn oath to guarantee the remaining boundaries of the Creek nation.

But the ultimate objective, so clearly developed in the colonial centuries, was already present in the popular mind. An Indian agent newly appointed by the American secretary of war traveled in 1791 through the territory of the Creeks (highland Georgia and environs) and reported that it "must, in process of time, become a most delectable part of the United States."

The Southeast

The territory was large, some 84,000 square miles, and "remarkably healthy. . . . The constant breezes, which are probably occasioned by the high hills and numerous rapid watercourses, render the heat of summer very temperate; and toward autumn they are delightfully perfumed by the ripening aromatic shrubbery, which abounds throughout the country. . . . The winters are soft and mild, and the summers sweet and wholesome. . . . The country possesses every species of wood and clay proper for building, and the soil and climate seem well suited to the culture of corn, wine, oil, silk, hemp, rice, wheat, tobacco, indigo, every species of fruit trees, and English grass."

But this warm and charming land might give pain to a traveler at present, he reported, since its many resources and natural beauties were "only rendered unpleasant by being in possession of the jealous natives."

In the 1790s that possession was still strong and secure, after generations of high living in the fast company of Europeans.

The position of the Creek confederacy in the Southeast was somewhat similar to that of the League of the Iroquois in the Northeast: a ranking Indian power strategically located in an area of conflict between European rivals. The heart of the Creek country was near enough to early European settlements for trade but not near enough for chronic trouble; the center of the Creek world was 300 miles inland from the nearest early settlements along the coast.

The loose confederacy seldom acted with unity, and there was sometimes serious hostility between the two main divisions of the Upper and Lower Towns, but in general the various Creek towns threw themselves into active, on occasion enthusiastic, alliances with Europeans, more often English than otherwise.

Studies of such tribal nations as the Iroquois and Creeks and the Creeks' northern neighbors, the Cherokee, in their relations with European colonies, have at times made much of the trade motive, the obvious enrichment to be gained from European trade. Motives of all kinds were no doubt present in the alliances with Europeans formed by native American states such as these, alliances of importance in the American background and in colonial history. Indian efforts to open trade with the metal-rich aliens, to control as much of the traffic of trade as possible, even Indian requests for missionaries, were founded on complex objectives, the goods of trade certainly being one.

But the motive often advanced by Indian orators for wanting to establish relations with Europeans was that of learning the Europeans' higher wisdom. The tall and turbaned Creeks as well as the tall and strong-armed Iroquois were, by most accounts, superior people, and it seems reasonable that some of them may have been sincerely motivated by nothing more than a wish to sit at the feet of the people from heaven and learn better things.

Said Yahou-Lakee, Micco ("king" in the English interpretation) of Coweta, principal town of the Lower Creeks, when the Creeks visited James Oglethorpe on the site of Savannah in 1732: "We are come twenty-five days' journey, to see you . . . when I heard you were come, and that you were good men, I knew you were sent by HIM who lives in heaven, to teach us *Indians* wisdom. I therefore came down, that I might hear good things: —for I knew, that if I died in the way, I should die in doing good; and what was said, would be carried back to the nation, and our Children would reap the benefit of it."

And said, on the same occasion, the very tall old Honored Man the English called Long King: "that though they (the Creeks) were poor and ignorant, HE, who had given the English breath, had given them breath also, that HE, who had made both, had given more wisdom to the white men. That they were firmly persuaded, that the GREAT POWER which dwelt in heaven, and all around, (and then he spread out his hands, and lengthened the sound of his words) and which hath given breath to all men, had sent the English thither for the instruction of them, their wives, and children."

This was the reason stated by the Creeks for giving land along the coast and the Savannah River ("where the Savannah bends like a sickle before rolling to the sea") for the founding of the colony of Georgia.

The Creeks had first come into tenuous contact with Europeans in the 1500s, with the Spanish explorations and the early Spanish and French attempts to establish beachheads along the coast of the Carolinas and Florida.

In the first half of the 1600s Spanish missions prospered sporadically, between outbreaks of pestilence and uprisings of the catechumens, among the Timucua and Apalachee of northern Florida, and among the Guale of the Georgia coast. Possibly as many as 30,000 Christian Indians were by 1635 gathered around more than forty mission stations, missions that were by report as rich, gracious, and idyllic as the later and better-known Spanish missions of California.

It seems likely the Creeks would have known Spanish traders by this time—the Cherokee in the mountains north of them, when visited by Virginia traders in 1673, already possessed several dozen "Spanish flintlocks," as well as some Spanish wives.

But English traders from Virginia must also have appeared early among the Creeks: a Creek word for white Americans was and still is *Watcina*, meaning Virginians. After 1670, with the founding of the English colony of Carolina, more English traders and explorers probed through the Creek country toward the Spanish frontier of the Florida missions, and in 1680 Spanish missionaries responded by probing northward through the Creek country toward the English frontiers.

In the military expeditions that naturally followed, a Spanish commander burned four Creek towns, including the important Lower Creek towns of
Tuskegee and Coweta, and the Creeks drew back from the Spanish and reset-
tled nearer English sources of trade.

During the next generation many Creeks, together with some neighbors
known as the Yuchi, who spoke a language unrelated to any other and seemed
to be devoted to fighting, happily joined English slavers in raid after raid on
the Spanish missions. Before 1690 the Spanish abandoned their missionary
activity on the Georgia coast and moved what was left of the converts there
to the region of St. Augustine in Florida.

In 1704 the sadly tamed descendants of the athletic Apalachee were the
principal victims of a crushing English-Creek (fifty English, 1,000 Creeks)
attack on the northern Florida missions: 6,000 head of livestock were
butchered; 5,000 or more mission Indians were captured; fourteen mission
Indians and three Franciscan missionaries were burned at the stake. Captives
taken by the Creeks were bought by the English as slaves, thus rounding out
the efficiency of the entire expedition. The English wanted the slaves for
Carolina plantations, and they wanted to punish the Spanish not only for
being Spanish but for providing in Florida a refuge for runaway slaves—by
Spanish law of the time, any foreign slave became free on reaching Florida.

In Florida at this time the Spanish were experimenting with a Christian
Indian state—no firearms, no white colonies, tiny garrisons only for protection of the missionaries, thirty soldiers for the whole province. The experiment was a grand success for the English slavers and their Creek, Yuchi, and
sometimes Cherokee allies, who reduced the flourishing missions to ruins and
their Christian Indians to colonial slavery. The Spanish abandoned their ill-
met experiment and reinforced Florida as a strictly military frontier.

By the middle 1700s immigrant bands of Yuchi and other peoples from
the Lower Creek towns were moving into the country thus left vacant. They
mixed with the feral survivors of the mission Indians, with runaway slaves of
all kinds that kept appearing from the colonies to the north, and with later
immigrants from the Lower Creek towns. As the years passed an amalgamated
society was formed from all these elements, a fusion of many groups speaking many languages but with dialects of Muskogean, the great language family of the Southeast, gradually becoming the basis of the common tongue. This
new-made tribe spread on southward down the peninsula of Florida and
came to be known as the Seminoles (originally pronounced Seminolees), from
a Creek locution meaning something like "outlanders."

The English, Scots, and French Protestants who settled in the Carolinas
had an unquenchable thirst for slaves. Indian tribes obligingly sold their

occasional war captives (*vide* the Creeks in the Florida raid). Blacks were plentiful, although costly. But anyone could snare for free an Indian or two. Many Indian parents were not only willing but eager to have their children given an education by Europeans, and it was easy to take a child or two away and have the parents' grateful blessing in addition. The child or two duly sold, one later told the parents an affecting tale of a sudden illness, fatal in spite of all one could do, and with a few honest tears another child or two might be picked up on the same visit.

Outright kidnapping of children was simpler and quicker, and therefore deservedly more popular. The large Tuscarora nation of North Carolina suffered from this industry for years and finally, in 1710, sent ambassadors to Pennsylvania asking for permission to emigrate there, for the safety of their children and the children yet to be born. The Pennsylvania commissioners regretted that it could not take them without a certificate of "good behavior" from the authorities who had for so long winked at the kidnapping—i.e., the Carolina government.

In September of the following year, 1711, the Tuscarora solved their dilemma with a savage attack on the North Carolina colonists, opening the war, ironically enough, with the capture and execution of John Lawson, Surveyor-General of North Carolina, the one Englishman of the region who knew the Indians best and felt the warmest affection for them.

"We look upon them with disdain and scorn," he wrote, two years before his death, "and think them little better than beasts in human form; while with all our religion and education, we possess more moral deformities and vices than these people do."

But ironically enough the Surveyor-General, at the very time he was writing, was selling an extensive tract of Tuscarora territory to a European promoter without mentioning the transaction to the Tuscarora—the crime for which they condemned him to death. Swiss and Palatine colonists had been settled on this land just before the uprising, and suffered grievously in death and destruction therefrom.

A military expedition of colonists and Indian allies brought the Tuscarora to terms, but as the expedition felt insufficiently rewarded by North Carolina for its efforts the English commander violated the truce just made with the Tuscarora and trapped a considerable number who unwarily accepted his invitation to a general friendship parley. These captives went to the slave ships and the Tuscarora went back to war, to be defeated by a second expedition the next year, 1713. By this time the Iroquois had offered the Tuscarora a new home in the Five Nations country, and the Tuscarora began migrating northward.

Numerous little coastal tribes who had joined with the Catawba, a South Carolina confederation of two fairly sizable eastern Siouan peoples, in helping the English against the Tuscarora had been promised certain trade preferences as a reward. That these trade matters could be deadly serious is indicated by the national disaster of the Sewee, a little coastal tribe that undertook to open direct trade with England by canoe and lost a portion of its population in the attempt. However, the promise to the little coastal tribes of trade preferences wasn't kept. This led to the mass murder of several hundred settlers by the little coastal tribes, culminating in lengthy hostilities known as the Yamasee War, which was the finish of the little coastal tribes.

The defeated Yamasee, a people living just inland from the Georgia coast, emigrated to Spanish Florida and became Spanish allies (as they had been once before, until 1685, when they had migrated up from Florida to become English allies).

The Catawba went back to being steadfast friends of the colonists, and being the largest nation left in the coastal region now that the Tuscarora had been driven away, received many refugee bands from the shattered little coastal tribes. The far eastern division of the Shawnee who had lived on the Savannah River (the river's name was a variant rendition of "Shawnee"), having chased the Yuchi therefrom sometime about 1680 and performed thereby a "great service" to the new colony of South Carolina, moved out in their turn, drifting northwestward.

This widespread unrest operated in some respects to the benefit of the Creeks, secure in their distant hills. Refugees added to their population, and their prosperity was enhanced by the unhindered growth of European trade.

The Catawba declined with astounding rapidity under the effects of drink, disease, and attacks by any gangs of Shawnee or Iroquois or other Indian juvenile delinquents who happened along. For the Catawba as well as the displaced persons who had taken shelter with them there was no further escape except to the Creeks or Cherokees.

The Creeks waxed stronger, and the Carolina colonies grew in wealth and colonists. By the 1730s upward of 200 ships a year were sailing from Charleston, "laden with the merchandize of the growth of the country"—rice, pitch, tar, turpentine, corn, peas, beans, planks, timber, and deerskins (more than 200,000 a year). "They carry on a great trade with the Indians, from whence they get their great quantities of deer-skins, and of other wild beasts, in exchange for which they give them only lead, powder, coarse cloth, vermilion, iron, strong waters, and some other goods, by which they have a very considerable profit. The great number of slaves makes another part of the riches of this province, there being about 40,000 negroes, which are worth, one with another, £25 each."

Speculators in England began to look with interest on the uncolonized territory just below the Carolinas, "the Most Delightful Country of the Universe," as it was called in a prospectus of 1717.

Its colonization was successfully undertaken by General James Oglethorpe, a wealthy philanthropist, who declared, "In America there are fertile lands sufficient to subsist all the useless poor in England and distressed Protestants in Europe." He established the colony of Georgia as a land of opportunity for imprisoned debtors; it would also serve as a buffer state for the rich Carolinas, and as an obstruction across that beaten path to freedom that was still being taken by so many Carolina slaves running away to Florida. Slavery was prohibited in the new colony (at first), which fit in splendidly both with Oglethorpe's humanitarian sentiments and the idea of an all-white cordon to fence in Carolina's slaves.

The new proprietors of Georgia and the statesmen of England had use for the Creek confederacy, as an instrument of trade and as a line of defense against the Spanish to the south and even more urgently against the French by now ensconced in Louisiana. The French, following their customary policy of vigorous Indian diplomacy, had kept Carolina, Virginia, and Maryland in an endemic state of alarm for years, with recurring rumors of a general attack by "thousands" of French-allied warriors from the Mississippi River tribes.

Since 1703 the English had been endeavoring to form anti-French combinations with the four great nations, Creek, Choctaw, Chickasaw, and Cherokee, located in the touchy southeastern area between the Atlantic and the Mississippi.

The most enduring English success was with the bellicose Chickasaw, who remained pro-English from first to last and were almost as valuable for the English cause in the Southeast as the Iroquois in the Northeast. With Chickasaw country bordering on the Mississippi, the Chickasaw were a never-ending menace to French voyageurs going up and down the river; the French waged a total of five full-dress wars against them from 1736 to 1753 and were soundly whipped each time. One of these, a solid defeat administered at the battle of Ackia (near present Tupelo, Mississippi) against the great Bienville, was called by a perceptive early chronicler one of the most decisive battles in American history, in holding the country of the Cumberland and Tennessee Rivers for the English, a vital sector in the French and Indian War.

For good measure the Chickasaws also handed thundering defeats to the Creeks and Cherokees at various times in major conflicts, although both these nations had the Chickasaw people ridiculously outnumbered.

As far as known history is concerned, unlikely though it seems, the Chickasaw nation, by far the smallest of the four "Civilized Tribes" of

Cherokee, Chickasaw, Creek, and Choctaw, never lost a first-class battle, starting with a whirlwind attack that hastened the march of Hernando de Soto's expedition in 1541, and including the destruction of an Iroquois war party in 1732.

But the Chickasaw, although a useful salient in French territory, were distant from the English colonies; the Choctaw (hereditary Chickasaw foemen, according to report) were generally more friendly to the French than to the English; the mighty Cherokee, in their mountain fastnesses of northern Georgia and the Carolinas, were on the far northern periphery of the theater of action and were inscrutable to boot—"humorsome" was young George Washington's word—in the way of mountaineers. If the Southern English colonies were to stay healthy and grow and if the new colony of Georgia was to survive at all, the continued friendship of the powerful next-door neighbors, the Creeks, was essential.

The Creeks, as noted, were delighted to give it, and to give land as well for the establishment of the new colony. More, a dozen important men from the Creek confederacy and a chief from the Yuchi went to England in 1734 with General Oglethorpe to publicize the new colony, at which they were a huge success. Costumed in scarlet and gold and feathers and fur, moccasin shod, they went to court in royal six-horse coaches for a state visit with George II and his Queen Caroline.

Seven Cherokees of doubtful rank had been brought to England in 1730 by a private individual, and had supposedly agreed to a "treaty" that no other Cherokees ever bothered to take seriously. Moreover, their trip had been clouded by a dubious carnival air.

The Creeks, now that they too had a European colony of their own, showed their ancient Cherokee rivals how such matters should be handled, solemn protocol preceding every step. The only interruption for a commercial was a dignified address by the doyen of the Creek delegation, Tomochichi, said to be more than ninety years old, who asked "a fair and substantial basis for trade; standard weights and measures; standardized prices; favored nation treatment; free repair of firearms; and the prohibition of rum." He also asked for missionaries. With the Indian's comical blindness to property he also observed that the English houses were built to last too long for the short lives of the people who lived in them.

On their return to America the Creeks sent a bread-and-butter letter of thanks painted on the dressed robe of a young buffalo; it hung for years in the Georgia offices of the colony's trustees.

Tomochichi's modest and sensible requests for fair trade practices could not be met, of course, even by colonial officials genuinely willing to try (most did try to effect some kind of controlled system, but efforts and results alike were so spotty as to be all but invisible).

The only really workable trade regulation was that enforced by the Indians themselves in towns harboring traders; since the Indians were ignorant of the finer trimmings of civilized misconduct, this regulation was usually confined to the immediately apparent evil of rum-running. ("Brandy goes off incomparably well," concluded a lyrical eighteenth-century list of "goods that are proper for the savages.")

The English traders that swarmed into the Creek country were not famous for being ideal preceptors of that higher wisdom the simple Indians sought. From the beginning the English trader—more commonly Irish or Scots—was notorious for trickery, vices, brutality, and trouble. As it was put by Benjamin Franklin, "many quarrels and wars have arisen between the colonies and the Indian nations through the bad conduct of traders."

The French, their monopoly system more conducive to a big-business setup with attendant closer control of all trade employees, had a better all around record for fair dealings; but English goods were cheaper and better, to balance the score.

But good and bad, French and English, the traders brought new ideas, and, in the main, the intact nations of the Southeast prospered during the eighteenth century.

Many Indians acquired livestock and adopted improved farming methods. Many took to European clothes and houses. The Chickasaw developed the locally admired Chickasaw horse, a breedy and nervy strain apparently based on a superior stock imported from New Mexico in the Santa Fe trade—an Indian-operated trade in the 1700s. The Choctaw (in keeping with the sturdy, down to earth Choctaw character) developed the Choctaw pony, claimed by its admirers to have more bottom to the hand of height than any other horse on earth, although the better known Chickasaw horse was said by *its* admirers to have stronger "powers of continuance" than any other of the thirty-six "breeds" imported into Virginia before the Revolutionary War (the great Quarterhorse was not imported, but developed *in situ* in Virginia).

In the Indian towns the old ceremonies, the black drink, the busk or green corn festival, the eternal games of chunkey and ball-play went on as ever. The red-painted war post still called young men to battle, and if the battles were fought more and more in the interests of European politics—why not? Obviously the Europeans were on hand to stay, an important part of the future. All in all, that future looked good.

Not that the century was a placid one. The world crackled with change and opened many rifts of unrest. A typical report of 1753 to the governor of

South Carolina gives a glimpse into the daily reality of many such problems, beginning with talk of the end of current trouble between the Creeks and Cherokees: "there came a Coweta Fellow [a Creek war chief] to the Warriour's Camp [Cherokee war chief] and told him that . . . now it was Peace, and his people were ordered to go no more to war against the Cherokees. At which the Estertoe [a principal Lower Cherokee town, on the Tugaloo River] Warriour thanked him, and promised to send through the Nation and forbid the People to go any more to War, and withall gave the Creek Warriour Presents . . . Pipes, Beads, and Tabacco in Token of Peace, and desired he should give them to his Warriours and beloved Men [chiefs and councilors]. . . . Again there is considerable Quantities of Rum imported by the Georgia Traders into the Nation [Cherokee], which if not hindred will certainly be of dangerous Consequence. Several of the Indians . . . complain much of it, and say . . . that if the Traders brings any more and offer it to Saile, they will certainly seize it themselves for they believe the Georgia Traders to be Rogues. . . . I hear likewise that the Emperour [principal chief of the Cherokees] has sold to the Government of Virginia a large Quantity of Land which they say was their Northward hunting Grounds, and that the Emperour had not Power of himself to dispose of any Land. . . . The Indians of this Nation grumble very much as I heard. The Emperour, they say, besides the Price of the Land received rich Presents of the [Virginia] Government. . . . The Little Carpenter [regarded as second chief, at that time, of the Cherokees] is come in, and brought in three or four Cagges of Spirits. . . . There are two French Men at Chote [Echota, an important Overhills Cherokee town just west of what is now Great Smoky Mountains National Park] and Toquo [a neighboring Overhills community; both these towns were on what is now called the Little Tennessee River]. The one is dangerous to be in this Nation. He talks the Tongue, goes to War with them, and in Time may conduct them to his own Nation."

Settlement on the Cherokee frontier had been encouraged by South Carolina since the 1730s, a belt of white setters there desired as a "counterpoise" to the huge slave population on the large plantations toward the coast; a white cordon to the northwest would also help hem in runaways.

War with the Cherokees came in 1760, its climax the taking by the Indians of Fort Loudoun on the Little Tennessee; at the fall of this fort the bantamweight chief Attakullakulla, called by the English the Little Carpenter, ransomed a captured English friend by giving his own gun and the clothes off his back to the warrior who had made the capture.

The new settlers on the Cherokee frontier suffered the most from this war, as usual, and after the war suffered several additional chaotic years of lawlessness from bands of burned out and uprooted survivors.

A vigilante group known as the Regulators responded to the lawless bands with hangings and floggings, which also disciplined the "lower-[class] people"— "most of the low People around had Connection with these Theives," wrote a leading Regulator. The low people were defined as "idle persons," those without a "visible means of getting an honest living," "amoral and apathetic or even hostile to the sanctity of property."

The Regulators also imposed "expulsion of the incorrigible, and work-service for the more tractable offenders." They hanged only "outlaws" and only, or at least almost only, while deputized en masse as Rangers, although they also killed a few "criminals" in skirmishes.

The Creeks in 1752 had been within a hair's breadth of a war with the Savannah colony, brought on by the bill-collecting procedures of a South Carolinian, the Reverend Thomas Bosomworth, who had married a Creek woman of position and influence, Coosaponakesa, known to the English as Mary Matthews. She had been of much help in the establishment of the colony of Georgia, for which Oglethorpe had paid her £200, with a promise of more to come from the British government. When, after nine years, the British government still had not produced any further payment, Bosomworth aroused both his wife and the Creek nation to claims, threats, and menaces that required unusual tact and luck on the part of the Georgia administration to handle. Surprisingly enough, the British government did indeed produce an additional payment, after only seven more years, of above £2,000 pounds, plus a deed to the island off the Georgia coast where the Bosomworths had settled.

A number of Europeans married into the Indian nations of the Southeast, mostly Britishers everywhere except in the western Choctaw towns, where the French prevailed. Traders who were reasonably honorable or able won the absolute trust of their Indian clients, married into leading families, amassed political power as well as wealth; and the rise of an oligarchy composed in large part of such mixed-blood families created an invisible revolution in both Creek and Cherokee societies, and to a lesser extent among the Choctaw. But it was an aristocracy based not on descent but on power—the distinction is important. As said the Choctaw leader, Pushmataha, "I had no father, I had no mother. The lightning rent the living oak, and Pushmataha sprang forth."

The half-European princes who evolved lived by Indian customs but their ambitions were frequently European. Many became personally wealthy in livestock, slaves, and goods. Some became petty tyrants, manipulating Indian custom and law for their own benefit. Some became tribal statesmen of the first rank, of the greatest value to their nations, and of note in American history.

Among the Creeks, favored by their key location ("they have the French and Spaniards to apply to in Case you won't supply them," as a Cherokee reminded the English in the 1750s), personal diplomacy became a constant necessity, with a consequent accretion of real authority attached to those Beloved Men who were of genuine influence with Europeans. This emergence of strong political leaders brought on a struggle for ultimate power between various "chiefs" of the two divisions of the Upper and Lower Creek towns, which at times had an effect on the twists and turns of Indian politics throughout the whole region.

The ascendancy of the chief was a phenomenon that accompanied European invasion everywhere. The Europeans needed a single responsible official to deal with in Indian negotiations; a council wouldn't do. If no real chief existed, as was usually the case, the Europeans often invented one. Sometimes the fictitious power thus invested in these "treaty chiefs" was accepted by the general Indian community and became actual. More often it led to discord.

A lesser conflict also sometimes came into being between full-blood conservative tribal members and mixed-blood progressives, particularly over the incessant question of land cessions to the whites.

The English, French, and Spanish were constantly busy with agitation for this or that course of Indian policy, and with wrangle-making bribes and payoffs to various "chiefs." However, regardless of transient policy considerations, the overriding exigencies of trade and empire demanded that the European colonies persist in a constant effort to sustain "their" Indians. Thus, through all policy vicissitudes the four nations, Creek, Cherokee, Choctaw, Chickasaw, not only survived but flourished.

The English victory in the French and Indian War brought vast changes to the Southeast. At the Peace of Paris in 1763, French Louisiana was divided between England and Spain: New Orleans and the Louisiana territory west of the Mississippi to Spain, and the Louisiana country east of the Mississippi to England. Florida went (temporarily) from Spanish to English control. French settlers here and there up and down the Mississippi crossed to the west side of the river to avoid English jurisdiction, and crowds of Indians went with them: Kaskaskias and Peorias from the Illinois country, Alibamus, Biloxis, ancient refugee Apalachees, and many others from the smaller nations along the lower Mississippi. Natchez remained all but deserted, as it had been since 1729, soaked with blood and bitterness, overgrown by the fragrant southern forest, until the first English plantations appeared—one of the first English houses was built on the sacred temple mound of the old Natchez White Apple village. Spain was rejuvenated as a colonizing power under the aroused administration of the Bourbon Charles III, and brought more prosperity to Louisiana than the region had known under France.

The Indian nations were skillfully wooed, maneuvered, and deployed, and became more valuable than ever to the colonial contenders. Three Cherokee leaders brought to London in 1763, for example, received almost modern superstar treatment, as a bawdy English song of the time recorded:

What a piece of work here, and a d—d Botheration
Of three famous chiefs from the Cherokee Nation.
The Ladies, dear Creatures, so squeamish and dainty,
Surround the Great Canada Warriors in plenty. . . .

For weapons ye Fair, you've no need to petition
Nor weapon you'll want for this odd Expedition.
A soft female Hand, the best weapon I wean is
To strip down the Bark of a Cherokee P—s.

Majority parties in the Creeks and Cherokees stood loyal to England in the Revolutionary War, although the Little Carpenter raised 500 gunmen for service on the American side. Spain regained Florida at the end of the American Revolution, and carried forward an accelerated and increasingly successful campaign to win Indian friends, aided by Indian reaction to the upsurge in American frontiering that came with the defeat of the Lords across the Sea. Important pro-Spanish factions appeared among the Creeks and Shawnees and even among the Cherokees and Chickasaws; and for that matter even among some of the American frontier settlers in the south and west.

But a new and weaker king came to the throne of Spain, and the brief, brilliant Spanish renaissance was over. Napoleon set foot on his star wagon; France took Louisiana back and sold it to the new United States. Spain faded into empty Florida. The few Spaniards left there, mechanically pursuing small-time intrigues with the Seminoles and the Lower Creeks, were no longer El Greco knights or even Velasquez dwarfs but desolate, sun-dazzled, psychologically enchained little figures out of Goya's blackened backgrounds.

In the 1790s, in South America, the last spiritual descendants of the Conquistadors rode away fittingly enough on the last gallop of the champion chimera, with the failure of two final Spanish expeditions sent to hunt again through Patagonia for the City of the Caesars. The pursuit of this particular mirage had been carried on by some twenty formal expeditions and many more private explorations for some 250 years.

With the influx of new settlement into the southern states (colonies no longer) the world of change spun still faster for the four great Indian nations there, who adopted more and more of the fashions and ideas of their white neighbors. A traveler of 1818 reported that 2,000 spinning wheels and several hundred looms had been made and distributed in the Choctaw nation, and that the Cherokee council had promised a set of tools to every young man who would become acquainted with some "mechanical art. . . . Rapidly are they coming into habits of industry."

Among those who did not change to European clothes, quite a few young men took to wearing a long shirt in the manner of a flowing tunic (a "sweep," the Creeks called it in English) which, with the customary headband or turban, was curiously like a costume prevalent in ancient Mexico.

Cherokee women, though, were said to dress "almost universally" in European style, "in gowns manufactured by themselves, from cotton which they have raised on their own plantations." Several years before that time the Cherokee reportedly possessed more than a dozen grist mills, several saw mills, a powder mill, plows, wagons, spinning wheels and looms, thousands of cattle and horses and hogs and sheep, and, wry finishing touch of white acculturation, 538 black slaves.

The Cherokee built roads, schools, churches, and adopted a system of government modeled on that of the United States. The result of all this enthusiastic adoption of new things and new ways was a movement toward an actual new "third world" created of the Indian world and the European world combined, since these modernized Indian peoples retained basic Indian ideas and beliefs as well as language. In return for the world of saws and mills they offered a world of the Indian spirit, a world oriented to community well-being rather than individual competition, a world in which play was taken more seriously than work, religion was practiced with each planted grain of corn, poetry sung with every sunrise.

Among the Creeks, Alexander McGillivray, son of a trader-father and a half-French Creek mother (a famous beauty named Sehoy), had become the most influential leader by dint of tact, diplomacy, persuasion, ceaseless politicking, and a vote in the control of trade goods. A filibustero, one William Augustus Bowles, who strove with might and main and untrammeled imagination to create a pro-British faction in Creek country, was McGillivray's most picaresque rival. His bizarre international career, dashing capture of Spanish forts and American trading posts, and romance fittingly romantic with a Creek maiden, could have been put together by Hollywood except for its ending in Havana's El Morro prison, where Bowles died at the age of forty-two.

President Washington, at his best in managing right moments, succeeded in 1790 in bringing McGillivray (and twenty-six Creek town chiefs) to New York, then the capital of the new American government, where, amid the fanfare of a triumphant reception, the aforementioned Creek treaty was signed.

CHAPTER 21

Along the Trail of Tears

After the 1790 treaty Alexander McGillivray was entitled to receive "salaries" from both the United States and Spain, and remained a partner in a British trading business that imported $200,000 worth of goods a year. He seems to have had a particular interest in the treaty provisions giving him duty-free trade goods.

Such emoluments notwithstanding (he dismayed white officials by turning some of them down), he fought to the end of his life to unify the Creek nation, parry factionalism, and strengthen the rule of the national Creek council against the power of individual leaders, himself included. Georgia legislators honored him (and his trader-father) in 1782 by taking "the extraordinary step of barring any further immigration from Scotland," offering as excuse the loyalty to Britain of Scots traders during the Revolution.

He died in 1793 (his British trading partners immediately laid hands on his personal estate, necessitating later court action from his son and daughter).

His life span is uncertain in the literature; the Hodge Handbook (1906) entry, by Cyrus Thomas, guesses his birth date at about 1739, but later references give c. 1750 or, more recently, c. 1759.

The Creek civil war broke out during the War of 1812 as a result of furious factionalism aided and abetted by American, Spanish, British, and Indian (Tecumseh's party) politicians. The strategic Creek location in an area of conflict between contending European powers obviously brought trouble as well as advantage. But a major cause of this rupture lay in the unilateral American efforts to "civilize" the Creek people. This worthy endeavor included very official action as bill collectors for traders by seizing Indian land—$50,500 ($48,000 of this to the trading company) for four million acres from the Choctaw in the archetype deal, in 1805. This charging the tribe for debts accumulated by individuals was urged by Thomas Jefferson, who believed (rightly) that the Indians' "primitive honesty" would lead them to cede land in payment of the alleged personal debts.

An anti-American party under the half-Scot chief Weatherford opened hostilities by descending on an American force gathered about forty miles north of present Mobile at a place called by gross historical license a fort, Fort Mims. Most of the 350 or so people there—troops of the Mississippi militia and families of settlers with their slaves—were killed. The principal pro-American leader, William MacIntosh, a half-Scot chief of the Lower Creek towns, replied by leading his followers in a massacre of some 200 people of the anti-American party.

Another mixed-blood war captain, Menewa, celebrated for the exploits of his wild and reckless youth when his name had been Hothlepoya (Crazy War Hunter), was now one of the ranking commanders of the "Red Sticks," or anti-American faction. The ensuing Creek War was in at least some part a personal struggle between Menewa and William MacIntosh.

Surrounding states organized militia to march against the anti-American Creeks, and five separate volunteer generals took the field, one of them being an obscure backwoods politician from west Tennessee named Andrew Jackson. Tennessee's Governor Blount "bawled for permission to exterminate the Creeks," in General Jackson's words, and General Jackson's command won the race to exterminate a pretty fair passel of them in the battle of Horseshoe Bend, Alabama, which polished off the Creek War.

Menewa had dug in some 900 Red Stick warriors on a tongue of land surrounded by the Tallapoosa River except for a narrow neck fortified by a breastwork of logs. A number of women and children were in a village at the river's edge.

Indian auxiliaries with General Jackson's Tennessee militiamen were several hundred Creeks under William MacIntosh and Timpoochee Barnard, chief of the Yuchi at that time united with the Creeks, and perhaps 600 Cherokees—and with them a long young white man who had been living with the Cherokee up in Tennessee, Sam Houston.

Before the battle started, General Jackson's Indian guides and "spies" were able to place his 2,000 men so as to surround the Red Stick position on both sides of the River. The artillery—two cannons—was placed to enfilade the breastwork at a range of eighty yards, and opened the engagement with a two-hour barrage. The Cherokee and American Creeks then attacked repeatedly from across the river, burning the Red Stick village in one of the first attacks. When it became clear the Indian auxiliaries could not alone succeed in overcoming the Red Sticks, the main body of militia stormed the breastwork. The remaining Red Sticks were driven to a thicket in the center of the peninsula and the cannon brought up to finish them off in another barrage of several hours.

At length the battered thicket was fired and the few survivors shot down as the flames drove them out. More than 300 women and children were taken prisoner, all captured by the Indian auxiliaries. Of the 900 Red Stick soldiers, only 70 were left alive, and of the 70 only one escaped unwounded—he jumped into the river and got away at the first cannon-shot. General Jackson lost 49 killed (23 of these Indians) and 154 wounded (47 Indians). One of the American casualties was Sam Houston, whose wounds from this battle plagued him the rest of his life.

The Red Stick chief Menewa fell, hit seven times by rifle fire. He recovered consciousness some time after the battle was over, shot a soldier passing nearby and was in return shot through the head, the bullet going in one side of his face and out the other and tearing away several teeth. He came to again in the night, crawled to the river, found a canoe, and floated downstream to a swamp where other Red Stick wives and children had remained hidden.

By the time his wounds were healed the Creek War was long ended, and the Red Sticks' land had been opened to white settlement. Menewa's store, 1,000 head of cattle, and hundreds of horses and hogs, at his town of Okfuskee, had vanished. William MacIntosh had certainly won the contest between them, for the time being. But Menewa was still alive and still very rugged and as far as he was concerned the polls were not yet closed.

The top-heavy victory at Horseshoe Bend brought General Jackson wide recognition and an appointment as major-general in the regular army, which opened the way for his triumph in the battle of New Orleans the following winter that made him a national hero.

Anti-American Creeks escaped to Florida in such numbers that the Seminole population was doubled or tripled. Among the more threatening developments in Florida—regarded by Georgia at least as threatening—was a fort established by the British on Apalachicola River, fifteen miles or so up the river from the Gulf, manned principally by Indians and runaway slaves, known to the Americans as Negro Fort. Jackson ordered the fort destroyed. A gunboat dropped a lucky hot shot in the powder magazine, the resultant explosion killing most of the 300 or so people in the fort.

Such disturbances furnished sufficient excuse for an invasion of Spanish Florida in 1817 by General Jackson that in turn caused enfeebled Spain to cede Florida to the United States.

This was the end of Spain in the Southeast, the end of all rival European pressure in the Southeast. And finally the Indian nations of the Southeast were not needed any more. There were no rival European nations left to buff against. White settlers were all over the back country; Indian trade and Indian middlemen east of the Mississippi were of no further importance—and the easy win in the Creek War revealed that even the stronger Indian nations were too uncertain about fighting to resist anything the whites might decide to demand.

The spirit of the frontier—clear the Indians out—had already become a major force in American land policy when in 1828 it became dominant in government with the election of Andrew Jackson, the embodiment of the frontier spirit, as president.

The idea of dispossessing eastern Indian tribes and resettling them in the "wilderness" west of the Mississippi seems to have surfaced in government councils at the time of the Louisiana Purchase (1803). This expenditure of good money ($15 million, an unheard of amount for the time) to buy a useless wilderness brought violent criticism of Jefferson's administration; Jefferson may have been reacting defensively in espousing an idea of resettling Indians way out there that could offer some use for the newly bought great West along with conveniently freeing eastern Indian lands for European immigrants.

A widespread idea of the "nomadic" character of Indians—an utterly erroneous impression that the settled woodland peoples of the East lived in "a hunter state"—led to a widespread notion that no doubt Indians would troop away westward in "cheerful acquiescence" if offered the western lure of new and better "hunting grounds."

It was true that hunting grounds had become more important in the life of agricultural woodland Indians since the advent of white traders, pelts (in the Southeast, deerskins) being the commonest currency at the trading post.

But under any and all palliative ideas lay the simple itch to possess the land. Jefferson wrote quite frankly in 1803 that the primary purpose of keeping agents among the Indians was to obtain their land, and indicated that he was not particular about the methods used in accomplishing it. The previously mentioned method of traders enticing influential Indians into running up debts that could only be paid by land cessions was followed for long after Jefferson's time (and from long before Jefferson's time, too, for that matter) with elegant results.

The custom of using Indian nations as buffer states dated from early colonial days and well afterward, as in the formal suggestion of Great Britain, in the peace negotiations after the War of 1812, for a neutral belt of Indian nations along the Canadian border in the interest of Canadian national security. Thomas Jefferson and Andrew Jackson and various others in between also alleged national security—requiring American populations along the frontiers—as a pretext for Indian removal, Jefferson instancing the menace of Napoleon in 1803 and Jackson the memory of the menace of England in 1815.

But such removal policies did not decline with the decline of these stated emergencies. Nor, after obtaining Indian lands along frontiers and along routes of communication to frontiers—such as the famous Natchez Trace— did these removers become any less insistent on seizing Indian lands in the interior, where purported national security could scarcely offer any validity at all as an issue.

Possibly the cruelest jest in the long farce of removal pretexts was the frequent official assertion that dispossessed Indians were in fact only being "rescued" from the destructive vices of civilization by being separated from the propinquity of said vices as well as, incidentally, from their lands.

This claim was often stated in public by Andrew Jackson and such of his cohorts as his latter-day secretary of war, Lewis Cass, who having enriched himself on Indian land in Michigan Territory may be presumed to know whereof he spoke when he referred to Indian removal as "this gigantic plan of public charity."

It is not possible, though, to reconcile this expressed concern for Indian welfare with the official actions—from the same officials—bringing immediate wholesale demoralization, destruction, disaster and loss to the Indian nations. Actions speaking more truly than words, these words, no matter how piously declaimed, must be adjudged deliberately false, and the genuine motive for removal being "we may secure a part or maybe getting the whole territory," as Jackson wrote privately to a secretary of war in the midst of such sanctimonious public statements.

There were indeed honest people who honestly felt that removal would be beneficial for the Indian nations of the East. One such was Thomas L. McKenney, superintendent of Indian affairs early in the Jackson administration, who organized a "private" group of likeminded citizens and missionaries into the Indian Board for the Emigration, Preservation, and Improvement of Aborigines in America that campaigned (using funds from McKenney's office) for removal. Some celebrities of the time joined this group, such as Richard M. Johnson, congressman from Kentucky, Baptist preacher, famous for having (maybe) killed Tecumseh in battle, and with all this undoubtedly sincere in wishing to elevate Indians.

Interest in unremoved Indian elevation was also popular. The Reverend Jedidiah Morse had toured Indian communities (mainly in the North) in 1820 urging the acceptance of missionaries and "civilization," defined as dividing their lands into "townships and farms, as the lands of the white people are divided and each man to have a farm of his own, with a title which he can transmit to his posterity." Only by adopting this civilization could Indians be "raised in respectability and usefulness in life" and partake with whites "in all the blessings which they enjoy."

Missionaries to teach such civilization were fortunately available, just at that time authorized by an act of 1819 appropriating $10,000 for their pay—an act, said Reverend Morse, "animating in no common degree." In fact, in the South this appropriation magically turned a total of three missions into twenty-five within five years.

Unfortunately (as shall be seen) these missionaries did not all turn out to be pro-removal.

Indian leaders in the Southeast argued that peaceful coexistence with the whites was perfectly possible and that they should be allowed to remain in a portion of their native lands, where the new third world they were building was predominantly friendly to whites and white ways. White emigrants into the Indian communities were not rare—at the time of Choctaw removal, in 1830, there were enrolled in the Choctaw nation 151 whites, and, in imitation of white ways, well-to-do individuals among the Choctaws also held 521 black slaves.

(Notwithstanding the presence of black slaves and the long woodland Indian tradition of enslaving war captives, some southern Indian communities had nevertheless welcomed runaway slaves and fugitive indentured white servants since colonial times. Hospitable Indian communities had even been known to accept fugitives from debtors' prison, and in some instances to go so far as to pay their debts. One argument used for driving the Choctaw nation out of its homeland was, as stated by Mississippi Senator Thomas B. Reed, that the Choctaws must not be allowed to "convert their country into an asylum for vagabond debtors.")

Non-Indian newcomers to Indian communities found one ironclad prohibition, though, in the midst of their vagabond freedom: they could not sell the land that might be assigned for their use. Herein lay the crucial Indian/white difference.

The thrifty farms of the whites balanced against the "hunter state" of the Indian world was, as has been said, a common argument for removal, and, as has been said, an enormous fallacy. But Indian men among the eastern nations did seem to make an art of loafing, leaving much of the crop work (and crop ownership) to the women, and above all there was that free and easy feeling about land use, that apparent lack of interest in private property. How could people so indifferent to property be anything other than savages?

But as we have seen, agriculture was an ancient institution among the woodland Indians in general, and particularly successful in the Southeast, where a numerous population had sustained itself for century upon century while the bounteous land, like an eternal bride, remained not only bounteous but beautiful. The tobacco and cotton plantations of the whites, on the other hand, had in a brief time laid the land along the coastal plains of the South in ruin, dead-red, eroded, "galled and butchered," and were now reaching for the fertile, virgin soils of inland Indian country.

Pressure from a crowded population of "land-hungry frontiersmen" was even more a fiction in the South than in the North. Even unto the 1840s the open lands of the South were twice those of the North, and the white population only half as great. Precisely the opposite argument was raised at the time: that Indian lands were needed to "encourage immigration."

The white pressure that did exist, even unto the farther southern frontier—Mississippi—was from the start pressure from planters, some among them small "yeoman" planters, others large prosperous operators eager to move bag and baggage, slaves, "mansion house" and all, from the worn-out littoral to the rich Indian-preserved interior.

"Civilization" in white terms meant many other things as well, worshiping the white god, wearing "civilized" clothes, following "civilized" marriage and family customs, but one point never omitted was that of learning to hold private property, abandoning the "savage" concept of group ownership of land. In general the people of the Indian nations were terribly reluctant to accept this change—to destroy tribal ownership of land was to destroy the basic tribal fabric—and many finally preferred to give up their native land and move to a new raw country where they might still hope to preserve such sacred institutions.

The stubborn refusal to allow an occupant of Indian lands to transfer his holdings without the consent of the full nation, the total interdiction against private buying and selling of land, excited an understandable animosity among many white Americans and especially among important and well-to-do planters, where personal profit and speculation were sacred institutions.

Speculation in Indian lands was for generations the prime business of the American frontier. It was intolerable that it should be even hindered, let alone halted, just when King Cotton was hitting his stride with some of the highest, widest, handsomest profits in agricultural history—totally intolerable that "a few naked wandering barbarians should stay the march of cultivation and improvement" as it had been put so neatly by Lewis Cass, a virtuoso of the cliché in an age jam-packed with competition.

Speculation in Indian lands was not only a principal frontier vocation, it was a principal element in white frontier politics both North and South from the inception of the United States, as a Congressional grant of Indian lands in

1787 to the Scioto Land Company bears witness. The grant was made without consulting the Indians concerned and led to years of war and political wrangling exercising a profound effect on an entire generation of frontier history.

On the southern frontier, land developers and plantation owners along with land speculators were the men of power. It was in some part their influence the public officials responded to with Indian removal.

Being human (all too), the politicians did now and then look to their own pockets in the midst of so many immense Indian land grabs. General Jackson himself took flyers in real estate promotion, and gave tips to pals ("I have no doubt ... that in ten years it will gain 1,000 per cent"). But the evidence does not support a supposition that personal gain constituted an important motive for the principal federal officials involved. Political gain, yes; and Jackson particularly, who could seldom see any other side to an issue than his own, regarded Indian removal as an absolute political necessity. His influential constituents said so, and, besides, he heartily agreed with them.

Vast Indian land cessions, in fact the vastest, were made in the Southeast before 1820. Although Andrew Jackson served as commissioner in making some of these huge deals and earned a reputation thereby as an "unscrupulous Indian baiter" willing to use intimidation, deceit, and secret bribes, the basic policy of Indian land acquisition preceded his administration and most of the Indian land of the Southeast was obtained well before he became president.

The Choctaw confederacy, for example, ceded some 2.5 million acres to the United States in 1801, 5 million more during the next four years. Under Pushmataha, best-known leader of the pro-American faction, the Choctaw sent several hundred volunteers to assist the Americans against the Red Stick Creeks in 1812, and 1,000 to join Andrew Jackson at the battle of New Orleans. At this famous battle Pushmataha was a brigadier general (commissioned by the United States) and had personally raised the majority of the Choctaw contingent from the district known as the Six Towns, his own political fief. During the battle the Choctaws carried out a successful flanking movement against seasoned British troops that won high praise from General Jackson. The Mississippi territorial legislature not only voted thanks to Pushmataha and his people for these favors but also voted gifts of a "Rifle gun" and a blanket to Pushmataha and certain of his warriors as symbols of the territory's gratitude. In the warm air of camaraderie created by all this the Choctaw people appeared to hope that they could now live on the remainder of their lands side by side with friendly Americans—indeed they were given an official promise to this effect by the U.S. government in 1816.

But in 1817 Mississippi was made a state, political ambitions were engendered thereby that cooled marvelously the air, and in 1820 General Jackson (wearing his treaty commissioner's hat) extracted from his recent comrades in arms, by the uncomradely but customary means of bribes, bullying, lies, and guile, an additional 5 million acres or so, exciting such jubilation among Mississippi politicians that their new state capital was baptized Jackson in the general's honor.

Modern scholars have not been kind in weighing Jackson's talents as an Indian treaty commissioner: "open intimidation"; "wholesale hidden bribery"; "plundering ... grand larceny"; "provided commissioners could be found with the capacity for the necessary chicanery and intimidation. Fortunately, Andrew Jackson again became available."

At the treaty collecting from the Creeks for the Red Stick defeat at Horseshoe Bend, Jackson demanded $12 million worth (by his own estimate) of "prime cotton land, which would soon enormously enrich southern speculators and planters"—but most of this land came from his Creek allies who had helped win the battle, not from the Red Sticks who had lost. Benjamin Hawkins, agent to the Creeks, wrote repeatedly to Washington expressing his outrage and enjoining Jackson's removal as treaty negotiator, all to no avail.

The Choctaw people were granted a much larger tract of land in exchange for their prime cotton land, but west of the Mississippi, with the stipulation that while those who wished to emigrate to this new land were most warmly invited to do so, those who wished to remain in their reduced homeland would be equally free to stay.

Under preceding administrations, from Jefferson's onward, the notion of Indian removal had been predicated on such voluntary Indian agreement. But voluntary removal simply did not work. The total number of Choctaw people who removed under the foregoing agreement was, over a period of ten years, either eight or fifteen of fifty people, depending on which report you believe—out of a total population of nearly 18,000.

The great change brought by the Jackson presidency was a policy of remove or else.

One of its first pieces of business was passage of what was known as the Indian Removal Bill, which became law in the spring of 1830 after congressional debate of exceptionally hot-tempered style, even for those hot-tempered congressional times. It also became law by the narrowest of margins (102 to 97 in the House), reflecting the considerable size of the opposition. Two opposition measures, likewise defeated by close votes, demanded a guarantee of Indian sovereignty over all lands then in Indian possession, and that Indian lands could be acquired only by a treaty negotiated and accepted by both sides, a revealing comment on the custom of forced "treaties" under the "moderate" policy of the past.

Speakers for the opposition in these debates (all matters of open public record), demolish quite effectively the aforementioned pious pretexts of the Jackson administration, and reveal the Great Removal all too clearly for what it was—pillage of a weaker neighbor. A collection of speeches opposed to the Removal bill, published in 1830, stated in its introduction that the advocates of the bill "trusted only to the power of self-interest and party discipline," and that the opposition "was made in great earnestness, and with every mark of entire sincerity. There was no indication that the concern expressed for the national honor, and the dread of seeing a foul and indelible stain fixed upon the character of the country, were affected or overstated."

Speeches on both sides also give a fairly clear impression that the argument was not merely a sectional conflict—a myth persisting to the present day, particularly in the South. Some northern areas, as shall be seen, later performed a minor league Removal of their own, quite as ugly as the southern model. The opposition to Removal was clearly a very real expression of a moral stand, of importance in the history of the time in itself and in its undoubted relation to the rise of the Abolitionist movement. A famous anti-Removal speech given by Senator Theodore Frelinghuysen of New Jersey on April 7, 8, and 9, 1830, identifying the prime movers of Removal simply as "They who covet the Indian land," became—the speech itself—the hero of a poem by William Lloyd Garrison published three years before the founding of the Anti-Slavery Society. (Garrison was beginning a jail sentence for overfree speech on the day Frelinghuysen began his oration.)

The people of the opposition were numerous, vocal, in dead earnest, and as much the image of the nation as were the pro-Removal people. The congressional victory was far from easy, and far from quick. For years before the introduction of the bill, politicians from pro-Removal strongholds were at work gaining places on committees dealing with land and Indian affairs. By 1830 Mississippi's lone congressman was a member of the House Committee on Indian Affairs, and one Mississippi senator sat on a committee dealing with public land. Pro-Removal forces dominated Indian affairs committees in both the House and Senate by the time the bill was voted. Pro-Removal congressmen also joined with Thomas McKenney's supposedly nonpolitical Indian Board in the activity so familiar today of molding public opinion, or at least bending a little, striving to make it appear that the Removal of the thriving agricultural Indians for the benefit of cotton planters was actually for the good of the Indians, and the great debate simply a disagreement over what was best for our red brothers.

The Indian Removal Bill did not authorize enforced removal of anybody, but only gave the president power to initiate land exchanges with Indian nations living in the United States. However, force was ultimately necessary—indirect and unacknowledged at first, but at length open and direct under any pretext no matter how thin, since otherwise not all the people of the nations would go. Persuasion, harassment, short-of-gun-point coercion, all helped, but could not finish the job.

The states principally involved, Georgia (home of Creeks and Cherokee), Mississippi (created mainly from Choctaw and Chickasaw country), and Alabama (created mainly from Upper Creek and Cherokee country), opened the proceedings—or in some cases had already opened the proceedings—with legislation outlawing tribal governments and placing the Indian nations under the rule of state laws.

This was in violation of assurances granted the Indian nations by treaties with the United States, which had promised protection under federal jurisdiction, rather as army posts or other areas of federal rule are immune from state or local interference. Consequently the Indians appealed to the federal government for the protection promised.

General Jackson and his secretary of war told them the federal government was unable, alas, to comply with its treaty pledges. This was a threat Jackson had been making for years in "negotiating" with Indians—either see it our way or the government may find itself unable to "restrain" local politicians or squatters. Now the threat was reality. State law prevailing within the Indian nations, the Indian lands were wide open for trespass by anyone, including liquor dealers.

This too was in violation of federal law as well as tribal regulations, but again General Jackson and his secretary of war said they simply could not enforce the federal law. Bootleggers crowded into the nations, grog shops bloomed like the blossoms of spring, and large numbers of Indian citizens, dispirited, not surprisingly, by the course of events, went on a drunk that didn't quit until they found themselves either removed or dead.

Actions could now be brought against Indians in the state courts and their goods attached for debt by sheriffs and constables. State laws were enacted prohibiting a court from accepting the testimony of an Indian against a white man, so that a claim, no matter how fraudulent, brought by a white man against an Indian could not be legally contested.

Despite all these persuasions the Indians remained immovable until inducements were added giving allotments of land, to be owned white style, to any and all individual Indians who still insisted on remaining behind when the nations should at last remove. One could, in other words, give up his tribal life in order to keep his home.

This offer had a special appeal for the well-to-do, frequently half-bloods, who occupied improved property of potential value—but it also appealed to a great many full-bloods who intended to take allotments by the whole district and maintain themselves as Indian communities, regardless.

Government officials, though, were sometimes able to circumvent the allotment provisions fairly easily (when the provisions were not abrogated outright by the government, once removal was under way), while allotments that actually did manage to get allotted turned into the finest bargain opportunities for wholesale fraud in all the variegated removal swindles, white squatters and land speculators moving in by the swarm to strip the Indians of their properties by trickery, liquor, or simply lies and force (Choctaw "floats"—allotment rights—figured in real estate deals within deals for years).

Large numbers of Indians, many of whom had been comfortable or even prosperous, took to the woods or the swamps in flight, divested of their possessions and driven from their homes. Occasionally they were divested of the clothes they were wearing by frolicking white men armed with writs or rifles.

Drunkenness, panic, privation, starvation, brought a fine boom in Indian-versus-Indian violence. Crimes of violence by whites against Indians could not ordinarily be brought to court and so are not recorded, but under the circumstances there may have been a few. A renowned Chickasaw warrior and councilor, Emubby, who had served with General Jackson in several campaigns, was killed rather casually by a white man named Jones; the incident got into the papers because of Emubby's prominence: "he had been murdered without any provocation. . . . When Jones presented his rifle at him, he leaped from his horse, opened his breast, and said, 'Shoot! Emubby is not afraid to die.' The wretch did shoot and the Indian fell."

Appeal after appeal to General Jackson and his successive secretaries of war brought the fixed reply that the federal government was not able to restrain either the squatters or the state legislatures, even though it had admittedly bound itself to do so by definite guarantees in previous treaties.

All appeals were referred to a statement of General Jackson's that the matter was not one of right but of remedy. The remedy, in the opinion of General Jackson and his faction, was removal of the Indian nations to the West, where they would be given land grants that would endure, said government spokesmen, "while the trees grow, or the streams run."

It is important to note, again, that this extremist attitude in favor of removal at any cost was by no means unanimous throughout the United States, as the close votes on the Removal bill had made clear—or even throughout the South. There was dissent and plenty of it, some of obvious political origin but quite a bit obviously proceeding from a plain and simple feeling of honest morality.

In the deepest South a newspaper editorialized that "the day of retribution may come" to "visit on some future generations the despotism which the present has exercised over the hapless and helpless Indian." And said a Mississippi planter, "it involves the faith of this whole nation . . . it involves the principle of *right and of justice.*"

The people concerned with honesty and right and justice, though, scaled lighter in political weight, and, when the chips were down, produced less moxie than the people moved by profit, power, and the rabid ethnocentricity of the period: declaimed a Mississippian, arguing that all Indians were inferior to whites, "we have had plenty of Indians in Natchez, and can you show me one who has been civilized by being brought among us?"

Choctaw leaders accepted a provisional treaty of removal in 1830, after a battle royal of behind-the-scene infighting among and between Indians and whites, missionaries, politicians, traders, half-bloods, full-bloods, chiefs and would-be chiefs of the three major Choctaw divisions, and "captains" and sub-captains of the various tribal districts.

Greenwood LeFlore, nephew of the great Pushmataha and previously an arch-enemy of removal, maneuvered himself into a winning position as head chief of the whole nation (an office never before existing among the Choctaw) and principal architect of the removal agreement, earning thereby the "handsome" plantation in Mississippi promised him by the war department for his cooperation. Other chiefs, captains, and subcaptains received extra land grants of value, cash annuities, and government-financed education for their children at private schools and universities in Georgia, Ohio, and Virginia.

The tangled Choctaw tribal scene had included organized persecution, sometimes even public whippings, of pro-removal people, and a marvelously intricate role for religion, mission variety. The spontaneous combustion of the Great Revival at the end of 1828 created an alignment of "hot-gospel" Choctaw preachers and anti-removal half-bloods, with a motto of "Join the church and keep your country." This movement helped convince Jackson and others that the "common Indians" could be brought to favor removal if not for the baleful influence of half-blood leaders and empire building missionaries.

In truth, however, the anti-removal majority and the pro-removal minority in the tribe cut through every sort of category; some of the missionaries were decidedly pro-removal, some with a sincere belief that the Indians would be better off out there in new and untroubled "hunting grounds" and some seeing a better chance for empire building in the West than in the East, some even dreaming of an all-Indian state (possibly under missionary supervision).

But others of the older missionaries, particularly of denominations long established in the Choctaw nation and with an empire already there begun, were said to be a crucial power in the councils and inflexibly opposed to removal.

This may have been one reason all missionaries were barred by the secretary of war from the meeting ground when the removal treaty was presented to the Choctaw nation, the secretary's excuse being that their presence was "improper"—the presumably more proper presence of liquor dealers, whores, and gamblers was permitted, however, "under the assumed protection of the United States government."

Despite such good time prospects, something less than 6,000 Choctaws gathered for the treaty "negotiations"; many of these walked out on the meeting before the treaty was concluded, and most of the Choctaw people over the nation as a whole, says the best evidence, opposed the removal agreement (the nation was "literally in mourning") that was finally signed.

But when new chiefs were elected to protest the treaty President Jackson refused to recognize them; they were perforce obliged to resign and return their offices to the pro-treaty chiefs they had just defeated.

The U.S. Senate added to the confusion by refusing to ratify a "whereas" in the treaty wherein the president avowed the United States could not protect the Choctaws against the state of Mississippi in treaty rights previously promised.

Difficulties were ironed out, more or less, and in November of 1831 the first official contingent of Choctaw exiles, some 4,000 people, started for the new lands they had selected in what were then the western regions of Arkansas Territory. Other parties followed later the same winter.

It happened to be an unusually hard winter. The Mississippi at Memphis was so choked with ice as to be impassable for days at a time to flatboats and most steamboats. There was zero weather and heavy snow in the Great Arkansas Swamp through which the emigrants, some of whom had left their homes destitute, barefoot, and nearly naked, had to struggle. The hardships were endless, the sufferings extreme, the all too frequent deaths most distressing, say the monotonous reports.

Some residents along the migration routes sold food to the under-supplied people at exorbitant prices, squeezing out bits of cash or property that had been smuggled past the deputies and constables. Other residents along the route gave freely of help and supplies and scoured the country to raise more, and wrote indignant letters to their government at Washington, pointing out particularly the animal miseries of old people and young children, and questioning in particular such details as the government policy of issuing one blanket per family to the emigrants instead of one blanket per person.

All difficulties were heightened by lack of funds. Congress had advanced money for the Indian removal, to be repaid by the nations from the public sale of their lands. These funds were transferred to white agents who agreed to "conduct" emigrants to the new Indian Territory for so much a head and of course expected to make a profit; some of these contracts were given as political plums.

Major Francis W. Armstrong, of General Jackson's home town of Nashville, was appointed Choctaw agent and left Washington in November 1831, with $50,000 in cash to meet the expenses of that first winter of Choctaw removal. However, he spent most of the winter at home in Nashville, it being too cold, he said, for him to travel. The Choctaw and their travel supervisors had to make the journey without funds. Major Armstrong arrived with the money at their destination, what was then a western region of Arkansas Territory, in the last days of February.

Major Armstrong was put in sole charge of the rest of the Choctaw removal in following years and was the subject of angry albeit futile complaints from the young Army officers sent along with the exiles to see that treaty provisions were fulfilled.

(Major Armstrong forced the Indians to leave pet dogs behind when boarding for steamboated segments of the trips, and for some odd reason refused to permit his crowded passengers to go ashore at woodyard stops to relieve themselves in the privacy of bushes but stationed men with clubs on the bank to keep the passengers aboard, a situation resulting in the "disgusting sight of a vessel loaded with human beings . . . leaving their evacuations in every direction through the whole range of the Cabins and deck.")

And so removal began. It went on for years, and it developed that the experiences of this first winter were the easiest of all—with the single exception of the Chickasaw migration; the Chickasaws couldn't be entirely defeated, even in this.

Cholera appeared in the summer of 1831, centering around Vicksburg, and came back each summer until 1836, setting up a belt of death that halted most traffic but through which the armies of exiled Indians had to be moved, the federal government and the states concerned being inflexibly opposed to any delays.

Pressures and harassments notwithstanding, the removed people left their homeland with the greatest reluctance. They bore, be it remembered, the weight of time on their eyes; they were descendants of the temple mound people of this region so long before, and perhaps of the burial mound people of still longer before. They had lived for countless generations in this sweet and luxuriant land, and did not share the white frontiersman's restless passion to be always moving on. Likewise the whites could not comprehend the Indians' emotional attachment to a particular place on earth. "They cannot appreciate the feelings of a man that loves his country," so Washington Irving quoted the Creek chief Eneah Emathla. Some watching whites were moved and some amused when departing Indians went about touching leaves, trees, rocks, and streams in farewell.

The conspiratorial treaty politics left an added legacy of distress among the exiled Indians by setting friend against friend and family against family, so that some groups went west carrying dissension with them and feuded angrily for years in their new country, sometimes in all but open civil war. Hostilities had the best of growing seasons as the ignorant and the educated, the good and the bad, those used to high-style gracious living and those from huts in the wildest woods were herded together, reduced to the lowest common denominator by corn likker, degradation, and despair, and driven like cattle, like wild animals. "We were drove off like wolves . . . and our peoples' feet were bleeding with long marches. . . . We are men, we have women and children, and why should we come like wild horses?"

Rotten boats were occasionally hired for river passages, being cheap, but being rotten as well as overcrowded they were sometimes unmanageable and occasionally sank, with most melancholy loss of life (to use a favorite term of the time). A number of emigrant parties lost many of their people, aged and children first, always, from deaths on the march.

The Chickasaw made removal treaties in 1832 and 1834, insisting on provisions by which the government would sell their lands and hold the money for their use, and by which a commission of Chickasaw councilors would pass on the competency of any tribal member making a private sale of property. Even with these safeguards the Chickasaws did not escape unscathed; but as a whole the nation appears to have gotten away with more wealth and in better order than any of the others.

When they moved west in 1837 they took along thousands of their horses, and got a fair percentage of them through—gangs of white horse thieves hanging on the flanks of Indian emigrant parties that had any horses at all were the chief livestock menace; the swamps were next.

Their horse herds made for slow travel. The superintendent in charge of Chickasaw removal wrote: "The Chickasaws have an immense quantity of baggage. A great many of them have fine wagons and teams. They have also some 4,000 or 5,000 ponies. I have used all the influence that I had to get them to sell off their horses, but they would about as lieve part with their lives as part with a horse."

In 1821 and 1823, some years before the big push for removal, William MacIntosh of the Creeks had made treaties with citizens of Georgia ceding

15 million acres of Creek land. He had been supported in these treaties by twelve other Creek chiefs under his control, but opposed by thirty-six chiefs representing nine-tenths of the Creek nation.

MacIntosh was in the pay of the Georgia commissioners, and in 1825, said emoluments being fattened, MacIntosh and his followers signed a treaty ceding the remaining Creek land—10 million acres—to Georgia. These treaties were not only in violation of Creek custom ("Among the Creeks there is no such thing as selling or ceding of lands. *'It is for me, for thee, and for all'*") but also in violation of a specific Creek law that provided the death penalty for any Creek who sold land without the consent of the entire nation in council. MacIntosh was therefore formally sentenced and on May Day 1825, a party of Creeks went to his house and shot him and his son-in-law as well. The formally appointed executioner who killed MacIntosh was Menewa, formerly the Red Stick commander.

The treaty of 1825 was annulled, Menewa went to Washington, vowed loyalty to the United States, and signed a new and supposedly secure treaty by which the Creeks would retain possession of their remaining land.

Governor George M. Troup of Georgia, related to William MacIntosh, was enraged by his murder and became one of the leaders in the subsequent large-scale and extralegal campaign to drive the Creeks out of the country regardless of treaty rights. By 1831 this campaign had progressed to the point that the Creeks were reeling from waves of white squatters, land speculators, and bootleggers who were invading their country under the protection of Georgia and Alabama state laws.

There were 1,500 such intruders in December 1831, according to a protest made by Eneah Micco, principal chief of the Lower Towns. They included "horsethieves and other criminals" and also included men of heretofore respectable position. The president and his secretary of war openly stated that they had no intention of trying to keep the government's treaty promises and insisted on a treaty of removal to the West as the Creeks' only hope of relief.

In 1832 (two months short of the 100th anniversary of their first cordial treaties with Oglethorpe) the Creeks, driven to desperation, finally accepted a removal treaty, with the provision that white intruders were to be removed from their lands for five years while the tribe prepared to depart.

But the treaty also contained a provision giving each tribal member the right to sell his individual selection (or remain on it, if he wished), each sale to be protected from fraud by being subject to approval by the president. Under the new state laws this could mean that the land and property of any individual Creek were now legally up for grabs to the first white man who might present a claim for it, no matter how plainly fraudulent—unless the federal government enforced these protective provisions it had just agreed to. General Jackson and his secretary of war did not enforce these provisions—while enforcing with rigor the provisions of cession made by the Creeks.

If the Creeks had been troubled before by intruders, now they were overwhelmed. Six months after the signing of the 1832 treaty, the Creek council said in a memorial to the secretary of war: "Instead of our situation being relieved as was anticipated, we are distressed in a ten fold manner—we are surrounded by the whites with their fields and fences, our lives are in jeopardy, we are daily threatened. . . . We have for the last six months lived in fear, yet we have borne it with patience, believing our father, the President, would comply on his part with what he had pledged himself to do."

Creek people were driven into the forest and swamps, their crops and homes were seized; many were reduced to starvation. Said newspaper stories of the time: "To see a whole people destitute of food—the incessant cry of the emaciated creatures being *bread! bread!* is beyond description distressing. The existence of many of the Indians is prolonged by eating roots and the bark of trees . . . nothing that can afford nourishment is rejected however offensive it may be." "They beg their food from door to door . . . it is really painful to see the wretched creatures wandering about the streets, haggard and naked."

White speculators had their capital in Columbus, Georgia, across the Chattahoochee River from Coweta, the capital of the Lower Creeks. A leading business, of course, was fraudulent certification of land titles, but a thriving sideline was grabbing title to the property of Creeks who died, since state laws provided that only a white man could administer the estate of a deceased Indian. These businesses sometimes assumed the rather jolly air of a mass sports event, and while a U.S. marshal said they attracted "some of the most lawless and uncouth men I have ever seen" they also involved "men of every degree," as another investigator reported. A special agent wrote to the president: "A greater mass of corruption perhaps, has never been congregated in any part of the world."

The capital town of the lower Creeks eventually taken over by these whites became the present Phenix City, Alabama, honored in the twentieth century with a journalistic reputation as the "most lawless" town in the country.

Legal aspects of the situation received much national attention. Georgia claimed technical justification for its aggressive actions on the basis of an agreement (the Georgia Compact) worked out in 1802 by Albert Gallatin, then Jefferson's secretary of the treasury, establishing the boundaries of Georgia in the wake of the notorious Yazoo fraud. (This was a sale to four land companies, made in a sea of bribes and corruption, of a huge grant of "western" lands; new legislation annulled it within a year but court actions kept it very much on the scene.)

One provision in this famous Georgia Compact stated "That the United States shall, at their own expense, extinguish, for the use of Georgia, as early as the same can be peaceably obtained, on reasonable terms, the Indian title to the county of Talassee, to the lands left out by the line drawn with the Creeks [in 1798], which had been previously granted to the State of Georgia, both which tracts had formally been yielded by the Indians; and to the lands within the forks of Oconee and Ocmulgee rivers, for which several objects the President of the United States has directed that a treaty should be immediately held with the Creeks; and that the United States shall, in the same manner, also extinguish the Indian title to all the other lands within the State of Georgia."

This final phrase, with its curious air of a copyist's error or a spurious addition, caused the enormous subsequent trouble in seeming to lend legality to Georgia's efforts to drive all Indians from its borders, and, on the authority of that very odd and tiny phrase, seize the entire vast territory still left to the Creeks, Cherokees, and any other Indians living within Georgia's boundaries.

The troublemaking little phrase was doubly odd, since no Indian nations were signatories of the Compact, and since it was in direct contravention of previous treaties between the United States and Indian nations of the region, such as the Creek treaty of 1790, just twelve years earlier, in which the "United States solemnly guarantee to the Creek Nation, all their lands within the limits of the United States."

An error of this magnitude would seem unlikely, to say the least, for Albert Gallatin, "the father of American ethnology."

Georgia had also, by that time, established a reputation for unscrupulous behavior toward the Indians, and open hostility toward federal authority—refusing for example to "accept" the Creek treaty of 1790. An adverse Supreme Court decision in 1793 was answered by the lower house of the Georgia legislature with a bill ordering that any person, federal marshal or otherwise, executing any process issued in this case should be guilty of felony and immediately hanged "without benefit of clergy."

Laws were not only introduced but passed in Georgia within the next few years stripping wealthy Indians of their property (thus fulfilling the common prophecy that Indians could not prosper in the white world) on excuses ridiculously racist even for the period—for example, if an Indian employed a white man as overseer on his plantation, as some did, said plantation was to be "confiscated" by the state, as some were.

Of moment in this connection was the case of Corn Tassel, a Cherokee accused of murdering another Cherokee, seized and tried by a Georgia court even though the crime had occurred within the jurisdiction of the Cherokee nation. This was in violation of treaties between the Cherokee and the United States, and the Supreme Court promptly granted a writ of error on the ground that Georgia's action was unconstitutional. Georgia responded by hanging the accused man.

Successful defiance of federal authority in this open and very public disinheritance of the southern Indian nations played a part in the contemporary rise of the nullification movement in South Carolina, a states' rights movement to nullify a federal tariff, an early distant drum announcing the Civil War.

South Carolina "welcomed Georgia as an ally," anti-Jackson newspapers proclaimed the Union in danger, and John C. Calhoun, Jackson's vice-president at the time, reached his troubled decision to assume the leadership of the Nullifiers.

Georgia followed this easy victory by arresting a number of missionaries for transgressing a law forbidding whites to dwell among the Indians without a license—the license requiring an oath of allegiance to the state of Georgia.

Two of the missionaries, one of them the famous Samuel A. Worcester, fought the case through to the Supreme Court. The decision, delivered by Chief Justice John Marshall, found the Cherokee nation "occupying its own territory, with boundaries accurately described, in which the laws of Georgia can have no force, and which the citizens of Georgia have no right to enter but with the assent of the Cherokees themselves or in conformity with treaties and with the acts of Congress. The whole intercourse between the United States and this nation is, by our Constitution and laws, vested in the government of the United States. . . . The Acts of Georgia are repugnant to the Constitution, laws, and treaties of the United States. . . . They are in direct hostility with treaties, repeated in a succession of years, which mark out the boundary that separates the Cherokee country from Georgia; guarantee to them all the land within their boundary; solemnly pledge the faith of the United States to restrain their citizens from trespassing on it; and recognize the pre-existing power of the nation to govern itself." The decision was wildly celebrated by the Cherokees.

However, President Jackson refused to execute the decision of the court. The state of Georgia also refused to carry out the court's order.

However, the two missionaries only had to do a year in prison instead of the four years at hard labor called for by their sentence.

General Jackson's pronouncements repeatedly invoked the principle of states' rights, insisting, in contravention of numerous previous Indian treaties, that the states must have jurisdiction over the Indian people within their borders ("*Sir, the sovereignty of the States must be preserved*"), although, on occasions dealing with other than Indian matters he announced himself stoutly opposed to that principle ("Our Union, it must be preserved"). When illegality could not be denied, he asserted that the federal government was simply too feeble to enforce federal law in the states of Georgia, Alabama, and Mississippi.

But when it came to the South Carolina Nullifiers ("This abominable doctrine that strikes at the root of our Government and the social compact, and reduces every thing to anarchy, must be met and put down or our union is gone, and our liberties with it forever"), Jackson reacted with his customary flaming vigor ("treasonable conduct . . . positive treason. . . . I will meet it at the threshold, and have the leaders arrested and arraigned for treason"), sent General Winfield Scott and heavy troop reinforcements into South Carolina and a naval force to anchor off Charleston, and avowed that if need be he would arrest and execute not only John C. Calhoun but every member of Congress from South Carolina who had taken part in the nullification proceedings.

It seems painfully obvious now that General Jackson's administration zealously shared the desire of Alabama, Mississippi, and Georgia to seize the Indian lands, by illegal means if necessary—what is even more painful, however, is that this was equally obvious then. Wrote Frances Trollope (mother of the British novelist) in 1831 after a three-year stay in America, "You will see them one hour lecturing . . . on the indefeasible rights of man, and the next driving from their homes the children of the soil, whom they have bound themselves to protect by the most solemn treaties."

Some aspects of the situation are of particular historical interest. For one example among many: an Alabama citizen named Hardeman Owen, a tough boy noted for his exceptional thoroughness in beating up Indians when chasing them off their lands, made an unsuccessful attempt to murder a U.S. marshall from Fort Mitchell, Alabama, ran Owen down and killed him when he fired upon them. An Alabama grand jury then returned warrants against the soldier who shot Owen, the other soldiers and officers present, and the federal marshal who had called out the troops; and a court ordered the arrest of the commander of Fort Mitchell.

Alabama's objection was to federal officers who had molested white intruders in the Creek country. Some U.S. marshals had made a nuisance of themselves, and incidentally broken state laws, by making individual efforts to enforce the protective provisions of the recent treaty.

Francis Scott Key was sent to Alabama to calm matters, and Alabama at length dropped the indictments and the Star-Spangled Banner could return to its wave.

Such incidents, and encouragement from the highest government sources for the idea that in Indian affairs state jurisdiction could take precedence over national jurisdiction guaranteed by treaty, very possibly added a few states' rights vineyards besides South Carolina's to the grapes of wrath that would be harvested a generation later in the Civil War.

In spite of pressures and harassments the Creeks delayed their departure for four of the five years allowed them by the removal treaty, being unable to agree on the specific lands of destination.

During this time the situation of the Creek people did not, of course, improve. Individual allotments were "floated off" to worthless tracts while reserves of value went to speculators; forged receipts and signatures, fraudulent impersonation of rightful owners, were approved by officials, and acts of violence against Creek allottees went officially unobserved

When a resistance movement against their sufferings spread among some of the Creeks (the "Creek War of 1836"—several houses, a mail coach, and a boat were set on fire), both Alabama and Georgia hastily organized militia companies and Secretary of War Cass sent Brevet Major General Thomas S. Jesup to the Upper Creek country to command regulars and militia "for the suppression of hostilities."

The secretary of war also suspended fraud inquiries so instantaneously that some contemporary wiseacres suspected the war was "a humbug . . . devised by interested men" to stop investigation of their profitable business activities.

General Jesup's orders read: "Your efforts will be directed to the unconditional submission of the Indians. As fast as this is effected, and, as any portion of them can be collected, they must be disarmed, and sent immediately to their country west of the Mississippi." Any not at the moment hostile would probably become so "unless prevented by a timely removal." Those who were truly friendly should be treated "with the kindest attention" but General Jesup was "to send them off as speedily as practicable by a military force if necessary."

Menewa, in obedience to his promise of loyalty, joined this army in rounding up insubmissive Creeks, as did nearly 2,000 other Creek warriors.

The captured "hostiles" were started west in a double-file procession, manacled and chained together, eighty-four-year-old Eneah Emathla, supposed to be the leader of the hostiles, among them. "I was informed . . . that he never uttered a complaint," said a reporter in describing the first leg of the march.

Subsequent marches, as all the Creeks were thoroughly removed, produced a saga of unspeakable suffering, only surpassed by the later epic of the

Cherokee. Profiteering on the supplies (or lack of same) for the thousands of people herded westward under military control seems to have been the principal difficulty—this brought deaths of more than 25 percent among a group of 600 Creek people removed, under otherwise favorable conditions, at the end of 1834. Such a mortality rate might seem to support stories of a much higher rate under unfavorable conditions.

White heroes of officialdom were not plenty (in a favorite word of the time) but there were some, such as Lt. Joseph W. Harris of New Hampshire, an 1825 West Point graduate. He wrote in the stormy air of the 1834 cholera epidemic (he had cholera himself at the time), "I am not much of a physician and feel that I am but a poor prop for these unfortunates to rest upon—but I have done and will do my best." Lieutenant Harris's best, in the full story, was resplendent with humanity and valor, although not always according to the regulations. He kept on giving his best in the work of Indian removal until his death in 1837 at the age of thirty-two and may have received his Order of Merit from Higher Headquarters later.

And so the nations departed.

The Cherokee resisted with extraordinary tenacity in the face of concerted oppression that mounted year by year. (It had its entertaining incidents—the Cherokee leader John Ross, evicted from his Georgia mansion and living in a dirt-floored log cabin across the line in Tennessee, received as a guest there John Howard Payne, the author of "Home, Sweet Home." The Georgia State Guard happened to cross the state line at that time to abduct Ross and kidnapped Payne too as a suspicious character; he was held in a Georgia jail for twelve days.)

President Jackson's message to Congress in December 1835 described the removal of the Indians, carried out in "a spirit of enlarged liberality." The Indians were, he said, removed "at the expense of the United States," annuities were paid "in all cases," beneficial arrangements of every kind had been made for their physical comfort and moral improvement.

As we have seen, this description did not quite fit the facts. For a very minor detail, the expenses paid by the United States were actually to be paid from sale of the Indian lands. But the fantasy of what kind, good people we were could comfort troubled people in Jackson's party and, if taken at their face value (however difficult it might be to keep a straight face), could be of convenience to patriotic nineteenth-century historians.

The Cherokee (and the uneasy moderate segment of the American public) had constantly been assured and reassured by the Jackson administration that removal by force was not at all contemplated ("NOTHING OF A COM-PULSORY COURSE, TO EFFECT THE REMOVAL OF THE UNFORTU-NATE RACE OF PEOPLE, EVER HAS BEEN THOUGHT OF BY THE PRESIDENT"); just as the Cherokee had been assured by the most solemn previous guarantees that lands not ceded would be secured to them "forever" and "the authority and power of the United States were solemnly pledged to protect the Cherokees from intrusions and trespasses" and "from all encroachments upon the lands not ceded."

From George Washington onward ("Rest, therefore, on the United States, as your great security against all injury") principal officials of the federal government had personally reiterated these pledges. The government had repeatedly stated that these treaties were law of the land and, as President Washington had said, could not be annulled by any later president. All these assurances were systematically and openly broken, although never openly repealed, and still the Cherokee hung on.

"It is impossible to conceive of a community more miserable, more wretched," said Henry Clay, adding that even "the lot of the African slave is . . . far preferable" since the "interest of the master prompts him to protect his slave."

John Ross continued to seek legal means to save his people, suggesting in 1835 that the dilemma of Georgia's claims (illegal or not) could be solved by the United States buying the land of the Cherokees in Georgia and granting them "a sufficient portion of it in fee simple" and also giving Cherokee people full citizenship to protect them against discriminatory state laws.

But the Jackson administration insisted on nothing less than total removal, and in that same year (1835) obtained an openly fraudulent removal treaty (backed by fewer than 10 percent of the total tribal population), railroaded it through Senate ratification (by a margin of one vote), and the following year, for fear that this Treaty of New Echota "would not be carried out by the mass of the Cherokee nation" assigned a military force to the Cherokee country with orders "to reduce the Cherokees to submission if they should begin any hostilities."

Two years later, at expiration of the time allowed by this false treaty for the Cherokee people to get out, the Eastern Division of the U.S. Army was ordered to the Cherokee country "with a view to the fulfillment of the treaty." The Cherokees were gathered in concentration camps from which at last they departed westward on their own—with the exception of a few hundred who hid out in the Great Smokies, where their descendants now live (and put on an annual anti-Removal pageant for tourists).

The Cherokee, having resisted longest, suffered the most, a staggering portion of their entire population dying along the route of "The Trail of Tears." This has usually been reckoned at about 4,000 deaths but a recent careful study gives a figure of more than 13,000—crazy, but maybe insanely real.

Furious division went west with them, resulting eventually in the murder of the leaders of the splinter party that had agreed to the removal treaty. At the report of the first of these murders General Jackson, angered, announced that "The government of the U.S. has promised them protection, *it will perform its obligations* to a tittle." But even in this most earnestly intended instance the government did not perform its obligations, and occasionally violent feuding went on for years.

In the midst of these difficulties the difficult work of Cherokee national reconstruction was patiently, if painfully, carried on. It was during this time that John Ross, beset by a local military commander partial to the small pro-treaty party, exhibited the best of his political skill, which was very good indeed, and the Cherokee people exhibited the seemingly superhuman staying quality of an almost but not quite murdered Indian nation.

Thomas McKenney, superintendent of Indian affairs whose pro-Removal work had been faithful and effective, finally had too much, revolted, and was promptly fired. He published his *Memoirs* ten years later, stating bluntly that the gunpoint-removal of the Cherokee "proceeded from a fraudulent act, connived at by the Executive of the United States." Since McKenney himself had been involved in the preliminary conniving, and was a religious man, he spoke of divine justice, of atonement, of a day of retribution as "an accumulation of wrath!"

Perhaps an inspired prediction—the greatest explosion of wrath in the history of the country then gathering so near at hand.

An effort was made to include the Seminole of Florida in the general removal from the South—this brought on war, which lasted until 1842 formally, simmered along informally for quite a while longer, cost the lives of 1,500 American troops, and the stupendous (for the times) total of $20 million in military expenses.

Its most publicized feature was the capture of the young Seminole chief Osceola by the American General T.S. Jesup, then fresh from the triumphant removal of the Creeks. When the much-wanted Osceola agreed to a conference under a flag of truce, General Jesup sent an officer to the appointed place, seven or eight miles from St. Augustine, and while the meeting was taking place had the conference ground quietly surrounded by a body of troops, who

at a signal made Osceola and his party, thirteen other chiefs, ninety-five altogether, prisoners.

This opened a program of treacherously taking captives under a flag
of truce.

The son of Philip, principal chief on the St. John's River, was captured
when he came to St. Augustine under a flag of truce to consult his prisoner-
father about the future policy of his band. A group of Indians was invited
to gather under a flag of truce to hear important news the general had from
the president; 513 assembled Seminoles were captured. A Cherokee peace
mission to Florida brought in a leading Seminole, Mikanopy, with eleven
other chiefs and a group of warriors, under a flag of truce—to be imprisoned instanter. The shocked John Ross wrote to the secretary of war, "I do
hereby most solemnly protest against this unprecedented violation of that
sacred rule."

But unfortunately it was the only strategy that worked. Said General
Jesup, in a report of 1837, "No Seminole proves false to his country, nor has
a single instance ever occurred of a first rate warrior having surrendered."
Jesup had previously urged (in vain) that the government should give up
insisting on Seminole removal, prolonging "a useless war without any hope
of a satisfactory conclusion."

Osceola died in a military prison not long after his capture. The painter
Catlin interviewed him during his imprisonment and wrote that he "seems
to be in great distress of mind."

Some of the Seminole women (as some of the women of the Red
Stick Creeks had done) killed their small children to free themselves
to fight beside their men. The war developed into a game of hide-and-seek in
the swamps of the Florida Everglades; as General Jesup had observed, it was
obvious that it could never be won by either side.

Peace was finally offered on quite honorable terms worked out by Army
Colonel Ethan Allen Hitchcock, who during the war wrote, "Five years ago I
came [to Florida] as a volunteer, willingly making every effort in my power
to be of service in punishing as I thought, the Indians. I now come, with the
persuasion that the Indians have been wronged."

(Colonel Hitchcock was later, in 1841, sent to Indian Territory to investigate frauds connected with the Removal; his report was not made public and
has disappeared from official files.)

However, resistance on the part of influential whites to peace with the
Seminoles (determination of owners to recapture fugitive slaves living among
the Indians may have been a subsurface war aim) caused the fighting to drag

on and on, successive generals seeing something that looked like light at the end of the tunnel but never reaching it. Army losses were continually higher than Indian losses, "humanitarians in the North" set up a "howl of protest" over such military expedients as the use of fighting bloodhounds, until at last in 1842 ("after some hesitation lest the honor of the country and the gallantry of the army be compromised") President Tyler simply declared the war at an end.

In 1858, after further scattered and rather futile military operations, an army colonel declared it at an end for the second time. Most of the Seminoles eventually moved west to Indian Territory, but several bands remained in the region of the Everglades and are still there, having resisted, through the nineteenth century, all inducements to emigrate.

The ever-faithful American allies among the Creeks and Cherokee, who had made possible the Horseshoe Bend victory that had launched General Jackson's national career, came off in the removal no better than the ancient hostiles. Ex-hostiles such as Menewa, who had become steadfast American allies (Menewa adopted the army uniform of an American general), fared no better than the implacable anti-Americans who remained implacable.

Several hundred Creeks, including Major David Moniac, a Creek graduate of West Point, "volunteered" for service with General Jesup against the Seminoles (only after the volunteers volunteered would Jesup release money from the Creek annuity to pay alleged debts, making it possible for the departing Creeks to save some of their belongings from claims of creditors). The volunteers served with the understanding that their families would be protected until their term of enlistment ended and they could proceed with emigrating to the West. While they were in Florida, however, citizen companies from Alabama and Georgia overpowered the federal agents assigned to protect the waiting families, seized whatever property was loose, made a number of the families prisoners on various charges, and clubbed to death with their muskets a ninety-year-old Creek who foolishly tried to prevent the rape of a fifteen-year-old girl.

Volunteers returned to find the last of their possessions gone and their families already sent on west.

The terms of the Creek treaty permitted individual Creeks to elect to stay in their native land (if they were willing to brave continued persecution by the states) and quite a few meant to do so. These provisions, though, were abrogated by the government and all Creeks were forced to leave, including Menewa, who had received a personal promise from high authority to the contrary. On the night before he left he went back to his town of Okfuskee and spent the night alone. He said to an old white friend the next morning, "Last evening I saw the sun set for the last time, and its light shine upon the tree tops, and the land, and the water, that I am never to look upon again." Then he walked away. He was an old man, and had been many times wounded. But those who believe that Indians don't cry haven't looked over the official reports of the Great Removal.

And so the nations were gone from their warm and charming land. But something more had happened than the mere uprooting of 60,000 (or 80,000?) or so people from their homes. The frontier spirit had clearly paraded the black horse of its evils coupled to the white horse of its virtues. Natural resources—in this case, people—had been exploited, with a particularly vicious cruelty, in an open conspiracy involving the president of the United States and a considerable segment of its population. Young America, in short, had been told a most effective bedtime story of crime without punishment. The nation, in short, had been exposed to quite a spectacle of dirty business, and it is reasonable to suppose the sinuous folds of the young American mind had picked up a new wrinkle or two.

CHAPTER 22

A Man for All Seasons

A subject such as the Great Removal deserves an epic, and, for history, a symbol. Both of these might be found in the story of Sequoya.

Sikwayi, in English usually spelled Sequoya, was a Cherokee Indian famous in his time for inventing a set of letters by which the Cherokee language became a written language, first of the many North American Indian languages to be put in writing with a really workable alphabet of its own.

This was an astonishing single-handed achievement, and becomes still more so when we find that Sequoya was quite unlettered, spoke only Cherokee, and could not read or write any other language. It becomes something of a miracle when we realize that the form of writing he worked out was so simple and easy that seldom or never in all history has a whole people been able to learn so rapidly to read and write.

Very little is known of Sequoya's early life. He was sometimes said to be part white although there is no evidence for this other than occasional mention in secondary literature that his father or grandfather was white—his white man's name was George Guess. But his upbringing was all Indian. As a child he lived in Cherokee towns along what is now the western boundary of the Great Smoky Mountains National Park, in or about the present Monroe County, Tennessee. Grown up and married, he followed the usual Cherokee custom in establishing a new home near his wife's family. This was in the Cherokee towns on Wills Creek below Fort Payne in what is now De Kalb County, Alabama, some forty miles below the three-corner junction of the modern states of Alabama, Georgia, and Tennessee.

He was lame from a game leg, evidently caused by a knee injury in childhood. He lived, as did most Cherokees of the period, in a farm cabin not particularly different from the farmhouses of white settlers in that frontier area, and in keeping with the way of life of the country (then and now) did some hunting and some trapping and some farming and kept some stock.

But mainly he made his living as a silversmith, turning French and English coins into bit-rings, spurs, spoons, ornaments. He had a talent for drawing (using dressed deer-skins for canvases) and was clever with his hands—while still a boy he made wooden cream-separators of an improved design that became locally popular, and when in later life he wanted a set of blacksmith tools he made them himself, hammer and tongs and drills, and built his own forge furnace and bellows in the process.

As a silversmith he was unusually gifted, according to tradition, although no known examples of his craft are around today to prove it. Should any turn up authentication would be easy—a challenge for antique dealers in the region—since he signed his silver work with his English-language name, George Guess. A friend, Charles Hicks, an educated Cherokee who eventually became a principal chief of the Cherokee nation, wrote out the name for him and Sequoya made a die of the signature with which to stamp his work.

Sequoya was born at a time, a few years before the American Revolution, when the Cherokees still followed their ancient ways in a climate of independence and assurance. After the War of 1812—in which Sequoya, like many Cherokees, fought on the side of the new United States under General Andrew Jackson—traders, missionaries, and settlers began appearing in increasing numbers throughout the Cherokee country and the countries of neighboring tribes. It seemed the Indian nations of the Southeast were to be rapidly Americanized. As has been noted, the populations of these nations for the most part accepted this prospect not only willingly but with enthusiasm. Many, especially among the Cherokee and the Creeks, had intermarried with the whites, some spoke and wrote English, French, or Spanish, and several scions of aristocratic Indian families had been educated at the early American colleges of the day. There were, to be sure, conservatives who resisted all this newness, but the prevailing spirit was rambunctiously on the side of Progress.

This spirit was made most dramatically manifest by Sequoya's creation of a written Cherokee language.

There is a story, published during Sequoya's lifetime and possibly well founded, that Sequoya picked up a taste for liquor that overwhelmed him, turned him into an alcoholic and his family life into a shambles, until by a desperate effort of will he broke the habit and substituted for it the spirit of apostolic fervor that thereafter ruled his character, and that first planted in his mind the idea of inventing a written language for his people.

Whatever the motivation in his inner life, the decision to create a Cherokee written language, to overcome at one great leap the most notable difference between the white and Cherokee worlds, was only one more point, although perhaps the highest point, in the acceptance by his people of the white man's way.

Sequoya was of middle age when he began this seemingly impossible task. He began, someone reminisced later, by scratching marks on a whetstone like the marks on the pages of books, and arguing that of course such marks could be made intelligible in any language if simply the same marks always stood for the same words.

He set to work, in the following weeks, months, years, designing such marks or letters, sketching them on bits of hide or paper, using letters from an English-language spelling book as some of his models, and making up additional characters of his own devising. At first he conceived of a different letter to represent each word in the Cherokee language. When he saw this would require countless thousands of letters he changed his approach and tried using a different letter for each different sound or syllable.

Since he knew nothing whatever of such abstract intellectual matters and, as has been mentioned, could not read or write any language, including English, his task must surely have seemed so unlikely as to be ridiculous.

But finally, after ten years or so, he completed a total of eighty-six characters or letters standing for various sounds that could, in various combinations, express any word in the language. He taught this alphabet to his little daughter, Ahyoka, and then appeared before a gathering of important persons from his mother's clan, including two of the chief men of the Cherokee nation, to give a private demonstration.

Tradition says it was generally believed by then that Sequoya was a little nutty. Tradition is here on shaky ground, Sequoya having been one of fifteen Cherokee leaders forming an important treaty delegation in 1816, in the midst of his work on his letters, and supposed lunatics are not customarily favored for such appointments.

But it is reasonable to imagine that these witnesses may have assembled reluctantly, prepared for an embarrassing session. One of them, a cousin of Sequoya's named Agili, a well-educated man known to the whites as Major George Lowrey, said (as quoted in a later reminiscence), "Well, I suppose you are still engaged in making marks." Sequoya admitted that was so, and said blandly, "When a talk is made, and put down, it is good to look at it afterwards."

Was the talk really written down, Agili inquired, or did Sequoya only keep it in his memory, and imagine that he read it from his alleged writing?

"I read it," Sequoya said firmly, and proceeded to prove it by letting the witnesses send messages back and forth between him and Ahyoka. Words dictated to Sequoya he put in his writing and had the written message taken to Ahyoka, some distance away, out of sight and hearing, who read the words exactly as they had been spoken. Ayhoka in her turn wrote messages that were carried back to Sequoya, who read them word for word. The relatives who had come to scoff remained to marvel. An uncle remarked in amazement that Sequoya must have been taught by the Great Spirit. Sequoya, with the sharp matter-of-factness of any scientist, answered that he had taught himself.

This was in the early 1820s. The syllabary was made public, and, said a missionary, "In a little over a year, thousands of hitherto illiterate Cherokees were able to read and write their own language, teaching each other in cabins or by the roadside. The whole nation became an academy for the study of the system."

Everybody went to school—grandchildren taught grandparents, warriors taught wives, medicine men taught traders. Everybody learned, practicing their letters by painting Sequoya's alphabet on their cabins, carving letters on trees or fences, scratching them on pieces of bark or board or buckskin.

Everybody learned, and learned with fantastic speed. Contemporary records attest to the veritable fact that a week or so, or even three or four days, was enough for the average Cherokee to begin to read and write in Sequoya's syllabary. A typical report by a white observer says, "Young Cherokees travel a great distance to be instructed in this easy method of writing and reading. In three days they are able to commence letter-writing and return home to their villages prepared to teach others."

This mass rush of instant learning appears to be unique in history.

The basis of the Sequoyan system is phonetic spelling reduced to its utmost simplicity. If in English a single letter, say "§", stood for the sound "ood" wherever it might appear, we could write "would" or "could" or "hood" with only two letters, "w§" or "c§" or "h§" and so on for many similar words; and if the common English word termination "ing" were expressed in the single character "Δ" we could then spell "sing" or "ring" with only two letters, "sΔ" or "rΔ" or such a word as "pudding" with only three letters, "p§Δ"—and we too w§ be findΔ ourselves becomΔ g§ st§ents, brΔ instant learnΔ into play.

The Cherokee language must not be imagined easily teachable, by the way, from some notion that it is "primitive" or "simple." The languages of "primitive" peoples are never simple, but on the contrary are likely to be more complex, poetic, abstract, and sophisticated than the more streamlined workaday languages of technically advanced societies.

Cherokee, a rather distant relative of the Iroquoian language family, is regarded as a very tough language to learn, and the variant dialect that was spoken and written by Sequoya (which among other changes substitutes "l" for "r", making the word "Cherokee," for example, sound something like "Tsalagi") tougher still. A historian of Moravian missionary work among the Cherokee wrote that the first ten years of the mission were "practically barren of results" because the missionaries could not speak at all to the Indians except by gesture. A missionary linguist assigned to learn the Cherokee language spent several years assiduously trying, found "nine modes, eighteen tenses and three numbers" but with all his study could not "express himself to the comprehension" of Cherokee people.

Sequoya's alphabet was made official in 1825 by the General Council of the nation, meeting at the Cherokee capital of New Echota (in what is now Gordon County, Georgia). At the same time the Council voted to establish a government printing office for Cherokee publications—a resounding first in the history of the Indian world.

The Reverend Samuel A. Worcester, then a young missionary destined to become, as has been noted, much better known, was largely responsible for the establishment of this press, first arguing the Cherokee General Council into appropriating funds for it, and then arguing the American Board of Foreign Missions into providing help in the complicated business of obtaining the necessary specialized equipment. Some of the missionaries objected to the use of Sequoya's alphabet for religious purposes because it was "Indian" and because it was also being used by the Cherokees' own priests to record "heathen incantations." Young Dr. Worcester, who had seen Sequoya's language in action, changed their minds by pointing out that with no other written language in the world "can the art of reading be acquired with nearly the same facility."

A flat-bed press of a "very superior kind" was ordered from Boston, and at the foundry of Baker and Greene, in Boston, punches were cut and types cast "after the model of Guess's alphabet." Press and type were shipped by water and in late January, 1828, completed by wagon the last leg of 200 miles from Augusta, Georgia, to New Echota, where on February 21, 1828, the *Cherokee Phoenix*, a weekly newspaper printed part in Sequoya's writing and part in English, began publication.

The first official use of Sequoya's language was in a translation from English to Cherokee of the previously published laws of the Cherokee nation; one of the two official translators was Sequoya's once skeptical cousin, Major George Lowrey.

Other Cherokee language presses were later established in the western Cherokee country (Oklahoma), and in the course of years printed millions of pages in Sequoya's characters, ranging from religious tracts and Bible translations and Cherokee history to newspapers, legal documents, a very popular annual almanac, and even fiction written by Cherokee novelists.

Missionary fears of the "heathen" use of Sequoya's language were well founded. Medicine men adopted it very readily for recording rituals and sacred lore, formulas that had been "handed down orally from remote antiquity," wrote one eminent ethnologist, "until . . . the invention of the Cherokee syllabary enabled the priests of the tribe to put them into writing . . . such an exposition of the aboriginal religion could be obtained from no other tribe in North America."

In later years publications in other Indian languages followed the Cherokee lead but most of these were in the English alphabet, so that readers had to first learn to read English letters, a considerable obstacle.

Cherokee newspapers maintained a wide and lively readership for many years—partly also because they were distributed free at the expense of the nation to all who could not read English.

Sequoya had moved west to Arkansas with a community of independent Cherokees before the expulsion of the "Civilized Tribes" got up steam in the South, and in fact several years before he finished his syllabary. He returned temporarily to his old Wills Creek (Alabama) home among the eastern Cherokees to give the demonstrations that introduced his system of writing, then in 1829 moved further westward with the Arkansas community into what is now Oklahoma.

He was honored in both his countries, East and West; as more concrete appreciation, the Cherokee nation presented him with a commemorative silver medal.

After the arrival in the West (Oklahoma) of the last embittered survivors driven from their eastern homeland, Sequoya joined with others of good will in laboring to bring the people back together. Although a lifelong friend of important Cherokee political figures, such as John Ross, Sequoya was not himself a working politician. But his name was known to everyone, and the several political factions of the divided nation were inclined to accept the evident tolerance he felt toward all. He was, therefore, elected president of the western Cherokee during the difficult time of reconciliation. The president of the eastern Cherokee for the same period was another nonpolitician much identified with Sequoya's language—Major George Lowrey.

The acculturated third world offered by the Cherokee having been rejected by the whites, Sequoya adopted a new mission: peace and understanding among all Indians, later to lead to peace and understanding among all peoples. The first step toward this objective was, of course, to be by means of language.

By this time, at the beginning of the 1840s, Sequoya was an old man, seventy or so. His principal livelihood came from a salt spring he owned. He had never profited from his syllabary. The American government had given him a grant of $500 in recognition of the benefits he had wrought, but thumbing up the money to pay this had been delayed by more compelling matters so that after six years he had received in bits of cash and bits of merchandise a total of $389.75, by which time the government gave up the unequal struggle and left the rest unpaid. But he was a patriarch in his family and an elder in his nation, and the written language he had created was more than ever his vocation and his passion.

A legend grew up of his ceaseless travels over all the West, leading a pack-horse loaded with Cherokee literature—primers, spelling books, almanacs, newspapers, histories—searching out the most distant communities of Cherokee people, traveling to spread the word, the written word. He searched as well (so says the legend) among other Indian tribes, even unto the "wildest" (where, says the legend, he was always welcomed with "uniform kindness"), searching for some means of building a universal Indian language, of constructing with words a road to a true new world, a world of truly understanding one another.

The Indian West of that day was in a state of great turmoil, flooded with Indian refugees from the East, an East wrapped in the thunderclouds of the white frontier. Sequoya as peacemaker would certainly have had plenty of business.

But few records of such activities remain, only the tradition of his role as an apostle of pan-Indianism and peace, urging the invincible force of peace against wrongs no matter how unfair.

Dressed in Cherokee costume—a tunic, unornamented moccasins and buckskin leggings, and a shawl wound in a turban round his head, the turban being the commonest Indian headdress in the Southeast, he was, if the legend is to be believed, a sort of Johnny Appleseed of the word, everywhere converting strangers into brothers, tirelessly inquiring among all the multitudes of Indian languages and Indian peoples for a common ground, a common understanding.

John Howard Payne, who spent an evening with Sequoya in 1840, wrote of him, "His air was altogether what we picture to ourselves of an old Greek philosopher."

We do have an account of one of Sequoya's western journeys, printed in the June 26, 1845, issue of the *Cherokee Advocate*, a weekly newspaper published in the western Cherokee capital of Tahlequah, Indian Territory. The story was told by one of his companions on this trip, a man named Oo-chee-ah (meaning "The Worm").

Sequoya set out from his home in Skin Bayou District, Indian Territory, in the summer of 1842 with The Worm and several other followers, one of them his son Tessee Guess, to try to find a village said to have been established by Cherokee emigrants in Mexico.

The long trip took the little party across the Republic of Texas, the long way across, from the far northeastern corner to the far southwestern corner, at a time when the old wild West was an even older and wilder West. Texas, in that year of 1842, was a hostile land crowded with hostilities, on a shooting acquaintance with seemingly everyone—Indians, Mexicans, traders on the Santa Fe Trail, even with the U.S. Army; a land of a few frightened towns and endless empty space all held together by its only visible asset, Sam Houston. The Raven (Houston's name when he had lived among the Cherokee) was a longtime friend of Sequoya's, and an ardent admirer of his wonderworking alphabet.

Riding horseback and leading pack horses, living off the land as they traveled (venison, wild turkey, wild honey), Sequoya and his party moved south "at a moderate pace through the prairies" for fifteen days from Sequoya's home to the Red River, the boundary line of Texas, and then four days westward to the Indian villages that then existed in the neighborhood of the present Wichita Falls, "Wacoes, Caddoes, and Wichetaws" living there in neighboring villages, although, said The Worm, they spoke different languages. The Worm knew the country and some of the trails, and a hatful of Indian languages as well as enough English and Spanish to get along.

During this part of the trip Sequoya fell ill, with a cough and a "pain in his breast, which extended to different parts of his body." From the Waco village he sent all his companions back home except his son Tessee and The Worm, since he did not feel well enough to be responsible for a large group. His words in dismissing these young men were, as reported by The Worm: "My friends, we are a long way from our homes; I am very sick, and may long remain so before I recover. Tomorrow, therefore, I wish you all to return home but my son and The Worm, who will journey on with me. I wish you to consent to my proposal." The young men obediently "acceded" to this request, said The Worm, "and took leave."

The head man at the Waco village, a chief "called by the Cherokees, Ootill-ka, or the man who has a feather in his head," held a conference with Sequoya which may have been typical of the talks with which Sequoya was greeted on his travels. After stating that "he was very sorry to find the old man so sick, and that he would take him to his lodge, where he could take care of him" and "would not talk much to him, for fear of wearying him while sick," the chief installed Sequoya in a lodge set apart for him and gave him repose and "busied himself providing such nourishing food as he could eat."

When later in the day Sequoya seemed to feel stronger, the chief took a seat near him and talked of the peace and friendship existing among all the neighboring Indian communities. The following day, after a further talk with Oo-till-ka, and ceremonial presentation to the chief of some tobacco, Sequoya and his two companions journeyed on.

At a stream where Sequoya stopped to bathe, he confessed that he was "afflicted still with pains," and said to The Worm, "My friend, we are here, in the wilderness; do not get tired of me. I desire to reach the Mexican country. You know the course. . . . You will not get tired of me, altho' sick?" The Worm assured Sequoya "of my willingness to go with him."

Again they trended southward, and after twenty-one days' travel across many water courses and country sometimes wooded, they heard, while encamped on a river, the report of guns and then a drum. "In descending the river to discover who were so near us, we came upon a road along which some persons had just passed. . . . We then took the road and when we overtook them, found them to be Shawnees, and with whom we encamped that night."

The next morning the Shawnees helpfully directed them toward the "country of the Mexicans." They pointed out the same route, Sequoya noticed (said The Worm with some pride), that The Worm was already following. The Shawnees were on a hunting trip and told Sequoya that if in the Mexican settlements "he found anything interesting, they would be glad to hear it on his return."

After another week's travel Sequoya and his two companions stopped to camp at "a very beautiful, bubbling spring." Even before they dismounted they noticed bees coming to the spring, upon which Sequoya said that "we are neither runaways nor in such a hurry but that we can stop and look for some honey." Tessee Guess found the bee tree a short distance away, and they camped two nights at the spring. But on the second night their horses were stolen by some "Tewockenee [Tawakoni] Indians"—a people who lived with the Wichita.

Left afoot, Sequoya "requested us to take him to some safe hiding place; to secrete our effects in the tops of trees, and . . . proceed directly to the Mexican settlements, where probably we could obtain other horses."

The Worm and Tessee Guess went on that evening, leaving Sequoya alone. The next day, after crossing "a river called Mauluke" on a raft, they heard "the reports of many guns . . . in the direction of our route." The Worm and Tessee hurried on, cleared the mountains, came on a town in a prairie, camped for the night out of sight of the town, but "did not sleep much as the firing of guns was kept up throughout the night. The place was San Antonio."

In the morning the two Cherokee explorers went into San Antonio, where "we were not perceived by any one until we got in some distance, when we met with two soldiers, who shook our hands friendly and requested us to follow them. We did so, until met by an officer who, inviting the soldiers and ourselves to follow him, conducted us around a considerable portion of San

Antonio to a store, where the people were drinking. The officer having entered the store for a few seconds, he told us to follow him to the quarters of the commanding officer, and informed us that we were then in a situation where we could do nothing, intimating that we were prisoners."

The commander of the town was at first unfriendly, telling them that Cherokees were enemies of the Texans and they would have been shot on sight except for "the *caps*" (turbans) they were wearing, "which alone saved us, as the neighboring tribes go with bared heads."

After some conversation, however, the officer became friendly, and although he said he had no horses to lend gave them passports and also a good axe with which to get honey, and warned them to be extremely careful in traveling on, since the country was full of wild and hostile Indians.

The two adventurers left the town, feeling lucky to escape, and warned to the last by the soldiers to be on the lookout against Comanches. They returned to Sequoya, installed him safely in a cave with a supply of honey and venison, and again set out for Mexico, this time avoiding San Antonio.

On the third day after leaving Sequoya they suddenly saw three horsemen coming upon them at full speed, a doubly fearful sight for it was a wild and windy day. They ran for cover to a cedar thicket, threw down their packs, and prepared to defend themselves, The Worm shouting to the horsemen in the Comanche language, asking if they were friends.

"They said they were, and immediately threw down their lances and arrows, and came up and shook hands with us, and said as we are friends we will sit down and smoke the pipe." The Comanches told them that they had supposed them to be Texans because they were wearing "caps" until they got near enough to see they were also wearing feathers in their turbans, the feathers having come from a turkey young Guess had shot not long before.

After smoking, the Comanches went to get their women "whom they had left, upon discovering our tracks." They said that the way to Mexico was rough and mountainous but as they were heading that direction themselves they would show the travelers the best route.

The Worm and Tessee traveled with the Comanches for three days, and then, following their directions, went on alone fourteen days farther to reach the first Mexican town (Matamoros).

"Before reaching the town we came to a river that we could not cross and had to encamp. Not being aware whether we were near any habitations or not, it caused us so much anxiety that we could not sleep—when some time in the night we heard a drum."

In the morning a mounted Mexican appeared on the opposite bank of the river and told them there was a ferry lower down; they crossed at the ferry, and an officer went with them to the town, about six miles distant. The alcalde of the town (where "many of the women were very pretty") told them there was indeed a Cherokee village, some thirty miles away.

He also questioned them closely, with the obvious suspicion that they might be spies for the Texans, and told them the Mexicans had recently defeated the Texans in battle and taken 300 Texans prisoner.

The two Cherokees thought this an unlikely tale; it was, however, a fairly accurate report of the Mexican capture of the 300 Texans (ostensibly traders) sent in the summer of 1841 on an ill-fated expedition to Santa Fe, New Mexico, then a part of Mexico.

During the months that Sequoya and The Worm were wandering around southwestern Texas, Mexican troops sacked several Texas towns, including San Antonio (twice), and the inhabitants of south Texas fled eastward in panic, creating what came to be called the "runaway scrape of '42." On Christmas Day 1842, a Texas force of more than 200 volunteer soldiers was captured at the Mexican frontier town of Mier, not more than 100 miles up the Rio Grande from Matamoros; the prisoners taken at Mier made an unsuccessful attempt to escape for which every tenth man was shot, the victims chosen by a drawing of black beans, an incident immortal in Texas history.

The two Indians, though, were shown every courtesy (including a couple of Texas ears strung on a stick). They were conducted by an officer "into two or three houses, in each of which he gave us to drink of ardent spirits, which he called whiskey, but which tasted very different from any we had ever before drunk," and were served a dinner so highly seasoned with pepper that they could only eat it with difficulty, "through politeness." They were thereafter given meals "that an Indian could eat" and without cost, by a resident who said he would not charge Cherokees anything for "he had been much among them without any expense."

The next day they were taken by a Mexican guide to a town The Worm called "San Cranto," thirty miles or so distant; and ten miles farther on (after passing through a small settlement of runaway Negroes, "some two or three of whom I met with spoke the Cherokee language") they found the Cherokee village, under the leadership of a man named Standing Rock.

"Our brothers were very glad to see us," related The Worm, "and gave us a warm welcome to their little village. Being soon apprised that we came to obtain assistance to convey in the aged Sequoyah, who was very anxious to visit them, they declared their readiness to afford us company."

After a couple of days rest they started back for Sequoya, with a borrowed horse and with supplies, accompanied by seven men from the Cherokee village, and reached the cave after eighteen days travel.

There they found Sequoya gone, and a letter (in his language, of course) bound to the limb of a tree. The letter said a flood had driven him from his cave and swept away his store of provisions, and so he had decided to go on in the direction of Mexico. The letter was dated only four days before, but "great solicitude was felt by us" for Sequoya's safety and survival, as "he had no gun . . . but relied upon our rifles."

They found his tracks, easily identifiable because of his lameness, and "tracked him to the river, saw where he had sat down, followed down the river and came to a raft he had crossed on; we crossed at the same place, came to one of his former camping grounds, and saw where a horse had been tied; feeling confident that he must have obtained a horse by some means or other, we followed on very fast to another camping ground, where we saw bones, which assured us that he had obtained food likewise. There were many speculations, how he had come by the horse and provisions, some surmising one thing and some another. From the constant rapidity with which we pushed on, and our long journey, the Mexican horse as well as myself began to get tired."

But the next evening Sequoya was discovered, camped in "the centre of a thicket in the forks of the river . . . seated by a lonely fire."

He had with him a horse and plenty of provisions, and explained that he had met some Delawares, who camped with him and "gave him some of their victuals and partook of his honey." The Delawares then said to him, "Come, let us now return to our own villages, we will take you to your own door." Sequoya replied, "No, I have sent forward two young men to the Mexican country, whom I shortly expect back; I am anxious to visit that country. Go with me there. We will shortly return to our own country." The Delawares could not go with him, but took a letter he wrote to deliver to his home, stayed with him until they had "killed for him some meat," and, since he was aged and crippled, gave him a horse to ride.

After resting a few days, the Cherokees all now returned to the Cherokee town in Mexico, where, and all along the way, "Sequoya received the kindest hospitality."

He was given the best of care by the village chief, Standing Rock, but his illness did not improve. In the month of August 1843, "in the town of Sanfernando" (San Fernando, state of Tamaulipas, Mexico), Sequoya died.

He had saved his papers from the flooded cave—"While sick, and at other times when not traveling," The Worm said, "he was constantly writing." These writings were buried with him. The site of his grave is unknown.

That it ended with Sequoya's death is doubtless the reason the story of this trip was preserved. Possibly the picture it gives of his travels may be in some respects representative of others of his missionary journeys.

Before news of his death reached Indian Territory, a notion somehow arose that Sequoya had run out of money and was destitute in the Mexican Cherokee village. The U.S. Commissioner of Indian Affairs had a messenger sent from Indian Territory to Tamaulipas, Mexico, bearing $200, but he met on the way a party of Cherokees from Mexico who told him Sequoya had died. In the meantime the Cherokee nation had taken quick action to grant to Sequoya an annual pension of $300 dollars. The grant provided that upon the death of Sequoya "the same shall be paid to his wife, Mrs. Sally Guess, annually during her natural life." The records show that it was paid, punctually, and after her death payments were continued to members of Sequoya's family until 1898, when the United States took charge of Cherokee tribal affairs.

In the manner of the best of myths, Sequoya was transfigured after death into a tree, Sequoia, the generic name for the giant California Redwood and the related Big Tree (Sequoiadendron)—one of the rare instances of botany choosing most aptly in thus bestowing the name of the Cherokee teacher on these most impressive of living things. The Hungarian botanist, Ladislaus Endlicher, proposed the name—with the Latinized spelling of Sequoia—only four years after Sequoya's death. Several years later the English botanist, John Lindley, argued instead for the name *Wellingtonia*, saying that the greatest living thing should be named for the greatest living man, the Duke of Wellington. After some debate, during which the genus *Sequoia* became widely known in England as *Wellingtonia*, the argument was decided by the French Société Botanique, in favor of Sequoia.

Skin Bayou District is now Sequoyah County, Oklahoma. Sequoya's loghouse home there has been maintained since 1936 as a public monument. His statue stands in the Hall of Fame of the Capitol, Washington, D. C.

The world's most complete collection of the *Cherokee Phoenix* is one of the treasures of the British Museum. Valuable collections of other Cherokee publications are preserved today in a number of libraries and museums. Some publication in Sequoya's syllabary still continues, in periodicals produced by Cherokee organizations.

The third world Sequoya and his people had offered, a world of community rather than profit, and Sequoya's vision of language as a means to peace and understanding, came at a turning point in American history that turned against both his third world and his vision. But the vision remains, permanent in his language. The road may some time turn again.

Death and Dispossession
in the Heartland

The Great Removal from the Old South was matched by a Lesser Removal from the Old Northwest, but lesser only in the sense of driving out smaller numbers of people.

In certain unhealthy respects, in the part played by speculation in land, in gigantic swindles by traders and "treaty" makers, even in incidents of atrocity, the North easily equaled the South.

By 1810 a total of some 29 million acres had been cleared (or almost cleared) of Indian title across Indiana Territory and over much of present Illinois, much too much for legitimate settlers but a feast for the speculators.

William Henry Harrison, governor of Indiana Territory in the early 1800s, "held treaties with factions, with isolated bands; in short [says the principal authority for this area] with any Indians over whom he could exert a temporary influence, quite in defiance of Indian usage, which required the consent of a general council." The conduct of Governor Hull of Michigan Territory was "scarcely less reprehensible than that of Harrison."

Throughout this time in the Old Northwest, Indian traders received, as a special provision of such land-sale "treaties," payment for debts claimed against Indian leaders or communities. This practice diverted to the traders a total of more than $2 million Indian money between 1825 and 1842, when the U.S. Senate, questioning the legitimacy of many of these claims, refused to ratify their inclusion in subsequent treaties. A considerable share of this enormous sum went to the American Fur Company, recipient of so many signal favors from Lewis Cass (territorial governor, secretary of war) that their warm friendship has been a subject of remark by historians ever since.

Land as well as cash was transferred to trading companies or other interested parties by these treaties, often reserving special allotments of choice land for tribal leaders, which allotments were then passed on, by prior agreement, to the white creditor or land speculator.

Government Indian agents sometimes thus enriched themselves from treaties they themselves helped negotiate, one such being U.S. Senator John Tipton of Indiana, ex-government agent for the Potawatomi and Miami people whose rich lands north of the Wabash were the last big plum of the area. In this way "valuable lands in the regions east of the Mississippi passed by hundreds of thousands of acres to speculators, without ever having been part of the federal domain."

Speculation in Indian lands, as has been noted previously, was the principal frontier profession. It should be emphasized that such speculators ("Tipton, like most contemporary Hoosiers, speculated in land to the extent of his means") were not exceptional but typical, although Tipton to be sure was a much bigger winner than most. A recent study of Midwestern pioneering concludes, "On the mid-continent frontier, then, almost all the early comers to any area were speculators first and homeseekers second or not at all."

The Indian wars of the Old Northwest that broke out after the American Revolution sprang more from such treaties and questionable grants—beginning with the completely illegal congressional grant to the Scioto Land Company in 1787—than from the British agitation usually blamed by American politicians at the time.

Little Turtle, a Miami, in command of combined Indian forces, opened these wars with victories over two American armies in the years 1790 and 1791 but met the inevitable defeat in 1794 against a third American army, under Mad Anthony Wayne, who then forced from the Indians the Treaty of Greenville. This pact was "so framed as to be productive of the very evils it sought to avoid"—that is, collisions between Indians and whites.

Indian despair and further extortionist treaties flourished side by side in the Old Northwest between 1794 and the final Indian military convulsion in the region, the unsuccessful resistance raised by the Shawnee chief Tecumseh in 1811.

Tecumseh waged a well-organized campaign to engage every border nation or remnant thereof from the deep south of Florida to the far north of the upper Missouri River, his objective being to hold the Ohio River as a permanent Indian boundary line. Above all he argued that the land, especially

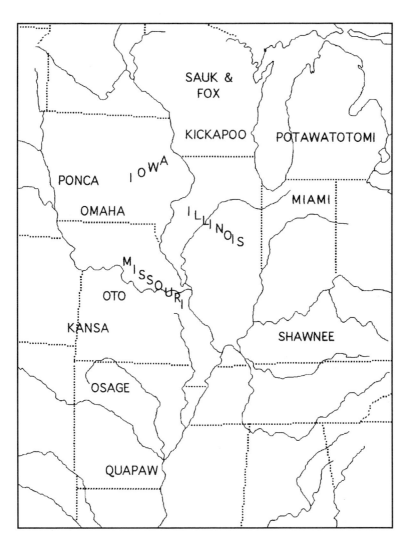

The Central United States

the Ohio Valley, belonged to all tribes in common and that no portion could be sold or ceded by any single nation without the consent of all.

He made amazing progress in four short years in constructing the basis of a genuine pan-Indian union, assisted by such continuing outrages on the part of white Americans as the second treaty of Fort Wayne in 1809, the last and perhaps the most unjust of the series engineered by William Henry Harrison. This one ceded a large tract of Shawnee land on the Wabash but overlooked the formality of securing even a single Shawnee signatory.

Tecumseh and his allies tended, not surprisingly in the light of these American-made "treaties," to be pro-British as the War of 1812 came into view, and in the summer of 1811 Harrison called a council at Vincennes with the hope of persuading the Indians to remain neutral. (When the warmly disliked Harrison offered Tecumseh a chair saying, "Your father offers you a seat," Tecumseh is said to have exclaimed in indignation, "*My father! My father!* The sun is my father, and the Earth my mother; she gives me sustenance, and I will rest on her bosom!" whereupon he seated himself on the ground "with as lofty and commanding an air, as if the green sward beneath him had been the throne of the Caesars.")

Tecumseh later, after a speech of "impassioned eloquence, which has rarely been equaled, and never, perhaps, surpassed, by any native orator," broke up the meeting, accusing Harrison of falsehoods.

Harrison subsequently chose a time of Tecumseh's absence to lead troops against his headquarters, the large Indian village of Tippecanoe on the banks of the Wabash (at present Lafayette, Indiana). Tecumseh's brother, Tenskwatawa, called the Prophet (one of the many messiahs springing up among a people beginning to feel the tremor of the world's end), ordered an overhasty attack instead of playing for time until Tecumseh's return. Losses were about even (and heavy) on both sides, but the Indians were forced to retreat and the Prophet was discredited, with some resultant damage to Tecumseh's overall campaign.

His vision of a total Indian confederation died in the War of 1812, in which Tecumseh, leading some 2,000 warriors and commissioned a British brigadier general, fought as subordinate to an inept English commander and was killed at the Battle of the Thames, October 5, 1813. There is a story, perhaps apocryphal, that he had a presentiment of death before the battle and discarded his general's uniform for Shawnee buckskins.

After the fighting came the profiteering. This went on for years of land cessions and removal treaties that became more and more mere imitations, making use of artificial treaty chiefs speaking in the name of nations that had become little more than memories. The paper storm of these purported agreements rolled all the way west to the Mississippi, driving the scattered survivors of the nations before it or leaving them here and there as islands of paupers, and rarely meeting resistance.

A string of treaties negotiated by Keokuk as chief of the Sauk people (which he was not) giving up the Rock River country of the Sauk and Foxes did bring a show of something the authorities construed as resistance from Black Hawk, the legitimate leader of an important Sauk band. (When Keokuk announced in council that the U.S. government had made him supreme chief of the Sauk, Black Hawk, so they say, struck him across the face with his breechclout.) In any case, Black Hawk's reluctance to keep his village west of the Mississippi in obedience to the terms of Keokuk's agreements brought on some excitement and the shooting up of Black Hawk's fleeing people by the military. This holiday excursion of the frontier militia took place in 1832. It is embalmed in the history books as the Black Hawk War, a rather raggedy example to serve as the last of the Indian wars of the Old Northwest.

No resistance was even alleged in the case of the Potawatomi a few years later; rather it was the impatience of white squatters on their land demanding the final removal of the Indians. The few bands left in Indiana of the once powerful Fire Nation (Potawatomi: "People of the place of the fire") promised in treaties "extorted from them under duress or when they were too intoxicated to realize what they were doing" to get out of Indiana by 1839, but in the summer of 1838 Senator Tipton, alarmed, so he said, by threats from the impatient squatters, received authority from the governor to raise an armed force to "police the frontier and, if possible, to secure the consent of the Indians to their own removal." He gave this authority a splendidly cavalier interpretation in assembling the Potawatomi people under pretext of holding an important parley, and then without any adequate preparation marching them all off westward as military prisoners. Seven or eight hundred people were thus kidnapped.

Forty-nine, mostly children, died within the first two weeks; at one time on the nightmare march some 300 were incapacitated with illness. They were turned loose in their new lands west of the Missouri where "they found no welcoming homes or cultivated fields such as they had left in the Wabash country."

Indiana's last big plum, previously mentioned, was a rich tract around present Kokomo, ceded in 1840. Peshawah, better known to the whites as Jean Baptiste Richardville, a principal chief of the Miami, was "showered" with individual reserves of land that by 1838 totaled nearly forty-five sections, and in the crowning final treaties extorted from the Miami during the next two years was bribed with more than $30,000 in cash and additional individual lands. Other favored Indian leaders in the region received appropriate benefits.

The cash went to the trader's barrelhead and the individually reserved lands to the powerful trading houses and speculators such as Tipton, who with his trader accomplice was so fearful that other traders might outbid them for control of Richardville's reserves that "all rules of fair play were abrogated." The little community of Russiaville near Kokomo is said to be Richardville's memorial, his French-accented name having been transmogrified into Hoosier Rooshaville.

Some of the banished nations, including the Potawatomi bands driven out of Indiana, were barely given time to pause in the new lands that were to be theirs "forever" before the paper storms of the speculators were upon them again—the Indiana Potawatomi were forced to "re-cede" their new reserve in eastern Kansas and go on farther west only a few years later. Two series of new treaties, in the middle 1850s and the 1860s, were wrung from most of the "intruding" Indians for their reservations in what turned out to be the valuable country of eastern Kansas. Lands ceded under the first series were seized in the good old way for Indian debts or under the newer pretext (wholly illegal) of tax delinquency. The second series provided as a rule for the specific purchase of specific reservations, often naming the prospective purchaser and the price of purchase—the purchasers in the 1860s being railroad groups.

Railroad promoters spared no punches in competing for influence with the Indian Office and for influence in the Senate for ratification. The Indian lands, thus bought for a token price, were preferred to the wholly free grants of land made so generously by Congress to the railroads, since the Indian reserves were not affected by the alternate-section provision of the congressional grants.

Wide-open corruption eventually reached a point even the Grant administration could not stomach, and Congress in 1871 passed a law ending the Indian Office's control of the Indian-treaty racket and taking unto itself all future acquisitions of Indian lands.

By this time railroads already possessed one-fifth of the state of Kansas; and roughly half of Kansas's total 52 million acres had gone, via various dodges outside restrictions of the general land laws, to speculators large and small—the best half, needless to say. Legitimate homesteaders got the dusty slim pickings left over. (Wrote Horace Greeley on a visit to Kansas in 1859: "As to the infernal spirit of Land Speculation and Monopoly, I think no State ever suffered from it more severely than this.")

As a local official once explained to me, "That was when they were processing the Indians out of here."

The nations beyond the Mississippi intruded upon by the exiled peoples of the East were, most of them, made up of communities similar in some respect to those of the eastern woodlands, similar in other respects to those of the great plains farther west. The Caddoan tribes of east Texas and adjacent country were farmers, villagers, mound builders, sometimes guarding sacred fire in their temples, but their dome-shaped houses were usually of grass. Other westward representatives of this group, such as the Wichita—residents of the Quivira found by Vásquez de Coronado in 1541—were village farmers but also part-time buffalo hunters of the plains.

The Siouan Quapaw (also known as the Arkansa) were prairie Sioux who nevertheless built forest-style stockades around their towns. The Siouan Osage of present Missouri, one of the most powerful of the trans-Mississippi nations, lived in a country of prairie and cross-timber woodland and were prairie Sioux in their clan divisions but southeastern woodland in their arrangement of peace and war moieties. Both the Osage and the Quapaw were famous for the bow wood of Osage Orange that came from their country; the name Ozark being an Americanization of the French *Aux Arcs*, "at the (place of the) bows."

The Kansa, relatives of the Osage and Quapaw, as well as of the Omaha and Ponca to their north, were prairie villagers, familiar during the mid-nineteenth century to traders along the eastern stretches of the Santa Fe Trail, the men always recognizable by their distinctive haircut: the head shaved or plucked except for a lock at the back.

The Pawnee, living at the borderline of prairie (tall grass) and plains (short grass), a Caddoan nation, became one of the Great Plains tribes in our western history.

Three related Siouan groups ranged northward of the Kansa: the Missouri, Oto, and Iowa (this last name said to derive from the Dakota term *Ayuhwa*, meaning "Sleepy People"), all three small tribes of, probably, no more than 1,000 or so souls each in their best days. The Missouri were almost destroyed in a war with the Sauk in 1798, and in the early 1800s suffered a disastrous defeat from the Osage, which ended the tribe as an independent unit, survivors going to live with the Oto and Iowa.

North and west up the Missouri River began the country of the Sioux par excellence, the various divisions of the Dakota. But far up the Missouri, deep in the short-grass plains of modern North Dakota and environs, were three tribes of village people stubbornly clinging to many of their village ways, farming and living in earth houses. These were the Caddoan Arikara, along with an emigrant group from the Skidi Pawnee, and the Siouan Hidatsa and Mandan. Very well known to early fur trappers, traders, and explorers along the upper Missouri, these three nations were almost wiped out by the terrible smallpox epidemic that came up the river in 1837. Some accounts say there were only 30 to 150 people left alive in the two Mandan towns out of a pre-epidemic population of some 1,600.

To the west of all these nations there were still others, seemingly endless ranks of tribes, each with its own territory and its own way of life, stretching across the seemingly endless western plains and mountains; when Lewis and Clark made their flea-plagued three-year trip to the Sea of the West (1804–1806) they met these differing peoples all the way. They were in fact guided by one of those distant people, a Shoshoni girl from the Rocky Mountains named Sacagawea who left an enduring image in a very literal sense: there are said to be more statues erected to her than to any other woman in American history.

CHAPTER 24

Through the Lookinglass III

The New World story may be of importance beyond Indian history. It might be well to pause here and consider some aspects of this point.

Columbus's first announcement of his discovery, written on shipboard homeward bound in February 1493, was published in Spain during the following summer; in a Latin translation meant for learned scholars, it went through nine editions from 1493 to 1494, and before the end of 1493 was published in 68 metrical stanzas of Italian verse, meant to be sung in the streets (the news magazine for the illiterate). That version also appeared in a number of popular editions. The Florentine humanist Poliziano (Politian to the English) was far from alone in instantly seeing Columbus's New World as a great and beneficent influence "in the whole life of man."

Ego statim atque ad mare illud perueni prima insula quosdam Indos violenter arripui: "As soon as I had landed on the first island that I encountered in that sea I had several Indians taken prisoner" and the people of the New World were thenceforward Indians. Columbus had brought back six of those *quosdam Indos* with him; they were a "well-formed people and of a fair stature . . . very comely" and created a sensation, especially among the Spanish ladies.

The many editions of these first reports were followed by a struggle between Spain and Portugal in the Papal court over ownership of the discoveries. Portugal was the great name in exploration, her position supported by three papal bulls and the formal Treaty of Alcaçovas. But the Discovery was Spain's, as was the newly elected pope, the Borgia pope (father of Cesare and Lucrezia Borgia), the Borgias being an Aragonese family. The dispute was finally settled in 1494 by the Treaty of Tordesillas on the "Partition of the

Ocean Sea," which gave Portugal what turned out to be the hump of Brazil, and Spain everything else.

This division was the first American matter to occupy Europe's leading statesmen. There were to be many more; the New World and its people so easy to plunder became a world-class star almost overnight. Much has been said about the fatal changes brought to the New World by the Old. Our subject here will concern the changes, less immediately obvious but no less prodigiously effective, brought to the Old World from the New.

Rich America, as Spain's treasure trove, played a role of many sides in the Reformation; in the fur trade so important at the time to England, France, and Russia; in the rise of English and Dutch mercantilism; in the foundation of international law, as laid down in the lectures of Francisco de Vitoria at Salamanca in 1539 and in the great debate between Las Casas and Sepúlveda at Valladolid in 1550.

All European political life after 1492 was to some degree altered by the presence of the New World and its peculiar people.

The New World wrought direct changes in the Old with the spread to Europe of potatoes and maize, tomatoes and rubber and tobacco, chocolate and peanuts and popcorn and chewing gum, and countless other agricultural items and medicines (such as quinine).

Some authorities believe that syphilis also came to Europe from the New World, but others believe the opposite, that it was merely one more in the catalogue of diseases brought from the Old World to the New. A recent theory suggests neither view (or both) may be correct, and that venereal syphilis may have developed in any urban environment from various other manifestations of treponemal infection (there are many) that were worldwide from the earliest times, a "dialogue" between such a "biological gradient" and its changing environment "that has run continuously from the Old Stone Age." A later discussion concludes that the "field is still wide open for those who wish to theorize" concerning the origin of the disease.

Indirectly, the peculiar character of the American Indians and their way of life became profoundly operative upon the European soul, an operation that, in all its far-reaching ramifications, still goes on.

Gold and spice and azure jewels filled the minds of the first Spaniards in the New World, but, curiously, it is the life of the lovely people that most fills the Spanish reports. One could almost imagine that the beautiful (and nude) island girls who came forth dancing and singing in welcome at Caribbean towns were the fabled dryads, the wood nymphs sung by ancient poets, so said Peter Martyr of Anghiera, first historian of the New World. Simple childlikeness was transfigured into unearthly poetry when the

Spaniards broke their way into the marvel-filled civilizations of the mainland, and the Maya sang of their coming (in the Book of the Jaguar Priest of Tizimin): "They are agitated by the drums. The Bat is awakened by the drums. The four Bacabs ride to earth on the back of a green rainbow. One by one the stars fall." The bearded invaders thrust with their swords and were pierced in return by words: "The warrior will employ his prowess on nobody. When they are taught about the abundant life, they will have compassion on the fields. They will have compassion on the mountains."

The poetry and the strange new life seized on the unconscious imagination of Europe and remained a living force long after the plunging swords had crumbled into rust.

"I wolde think their life moste happye of all men, if they might therwith enjoye their aunciente libertie," to quote the language of Peter Martyr's first English translation (1555), speaking of the Indians. "Emonge these simple sowles, a few clothes serue the naked: weightes and measures are not needefull to such as can not skyll of crafte and deceyte and haue not the vse of pestiferous monye. . . . So that if we shall not be ashamed to confesse the truthe, they seeme to lyue in that goulden worlde of the whiche owlde wryters speake so much: wherein men lyued simply and innocentlye without inforcement of lawes, without quarrelinge Iudges and libelles, contente onely to satisfie nature . . . "

Amerigo Vespucci spoke repeatedly of the extraordinary New World liberty: "They live amongst themselves without a king or ruler, each man being his own master. . . . nor do they obey anyone, but live in freedom . . . They have neither king nor lord . . . Neither the mother nor the father chastise their children, and it is wonderful that we never saw a quarrel among them . . . They have none of the riches which are looked upon as such in our Europe and in other parts. . . . no private property, because everything is common . . . and no king! They obey nobody, each is lord unto himself."

The Calvinist parson Jean de Léry, in Brazil in the 1550s, wrote, as by then so many others had reported, "They have neither kings nor princes, and consequently each is more or less as much a great lord as the other." The Spanish historian José de Acosta, wrote in the 1580s after a number of years in Peru, "Surely the Greeks and the Romans, if they had known the Republics of the Mexicans and the Incas, would have greatly esteemed their laws and governments." He summed up the social structures: "A number of the peoples and nations of the Indies have never suffered Kings nor Lords of an absolute and sovereign sort. They live in common and create and ordain certain Captains and Princes for certain occasions only, during which time they obey their rule. Afterward, these leaders return to their ordinary status. The greatest part of the New World governs itself in this fashion."

Sir Thomas More's *Utopia* was placed in Vespucci's New World, and although his busy republic with its rigorously enforced equality scarcely resembles any reported American society alive or dead, the absence of pestiferous money and mine and thine ring familiar bells.

Early accounts speaking less favorably of the New World people were, in France, less numerous, but often highly sensational, particularly when featuring cannibalism. "I have seen a man eat his children and wife," said one of Vespucci's best sellers in French.

But all such counter attractions could not compete with liberty and equality in capturing the interest of the leading minds of Europe.

Pierre de Ronsard, the most admired poet of his time in France, described in a famous poem of the 1550s the New World liberty, where the people knew not the names of Senate or King, where there were "none of the lawsuits engendered by the words Thine and Mine.... Live, happy people, free of care and troubles,/ Live joyously, I would that I could live as well."

Michel Eyquem de Montaigne published in various of his essays in the 1580s what have become the most quoted remarks of his century on the New World people, who live in freedom "without rule . . . without ruler," clearly not inferior to us in wit and reasoning, witness the "astounding magnificence of the cities of Cusco and Mexico" and the beauty of their works of art. He wrote, in line with a tradition followed by many later writers, "Those who return from this new world, discovered in our parents' time by the Spanish, can testify to us how these nations, without judges and without laws, live more legitimately and more orderly than our own, where there are more officers and laws than anyone and anything else." He wishes Plato and Lycurgus could have known of them, for it seems to him their society surpasses anything philosophy has imagined in dreaming of a just and happy human condition. If he might live under such sweet liberty, said Montaigne, "I assure you that I would very willingly paint myself all over and go naked."

"It is a nation, would I answer *Plato*," so reads his essay "Des Cannibales" in its first English translation (1603), and subsequently follows the points made by Peter Martyr so many years before, "that hath no kinde of traffike, no knowledge of Letters, no intelligence of numbers, no name of magistrate, nor of politike superioritie, no use of service, of riches or of povertie, no contracts, no successions, no partitions, no occupation but idle . . . no use of wine, corne, or mettle."

Shakespeare, in writing *The Tempest* (written while the 1603 translation of "Des Cannibales" was a hot new publication), gave in act 2, scene 1, to the honest old counselor Gonzalo a speech on the ideal commonwealth that, as has been often remarked upon, included word for word various of Montaigne's (and thus of Peter Martyr's) above phrases:

I' the commonwealth I would by contraries
Execute all things: for no kind of traffic
Would I admit, no name of magistrate;
Letters should not be known; no use of service,
Of riches, or of poverty; no contracts,
Successions; bound of land, tilth, vineyard, none;
No use of metal, corn, or wine, or oil;
No occupation; all men idle, all;
And women too; but innocent and pure;
No sovereignty. . . .

Maybe Alcaeus could be paraphrased to say words change the world, not kings nor empty wars.

Reports from the New World, so often dwelling on that marvelous liberty—even when dealing with obviously stratified societies, such as those of the Aztecs or Incas—were reproduced in works of all kinds, by "cosmographers," general historians, travel writers, clerics, politicians, soldiers, explorers, colonists armchair and real, even in a treatise that made the first use of the term "political economy" (Antoine de Montchrestien 1615): "They hold that the earth belongs to no individual, any more than the light of the sun. . . . They are born totally free and therefore are little given to work."

Reports expressing a proper indignation at certain disgraceful New World behavior also sometimes went a bit far and perhaps oversold. Vespucci again: on the beautiful and insatiable women who gave their presumably helpless male victims the juice of "certain herbs" or spider bites that would petrify the penis which they would then assault so cruelly that some poor devils lost "the virile member, and also the testicles."

André Thévet, a sixteenth-century geographical writer who had actually been to Brazil, although as briefly as possible, made much of the fact, as did Vespucci before him and many others afterward, that since among the Americans each is as much a great lord as the other and that among them there are no riches, "their motive for war is certainly ill founded, solely from desire for some vengeance, without any other reason, quite as among brute beasts."

One of the more extreme anti-Indian publicists ("God never created a nation so full of vice and so lacking in any virtue"), historian Francisco López de Gómara, praised so fulsomely the conquests of Fernando Cortés that he provided pro-American Montaigne with the angry indignation in Montaigne's explosive condemnation of the fair cities destroyed, the goodly nations massacred, the best part of the world overthrown for the commerce of pearls and peppers ("oh, mechanical victories, oh, base conquests!").

One of the most quoted statements of the seventeenth century, from the missionary Jean-Baptiste Du Tertre on the island of Saint-Christophe in 1651, dealt with Caribs, the original evil cannibals of Columbus's reports: the "Savages of these isles are the most content, the happiest, the least addicted to vice, the most sociable, the least false and the least tormented by sickness of all the nations of the world. Because they are such as nature produced them . . . they are all equal, without anyone recognizing any sort of superiority or any sort of servitude. . . . No one is richer or poorer than his companion . . . they live, all, at liberty."

As the religious wars in Europe got into high gear, in the 1630s, these reports on the butchered New World were given still more attention in serving as attacks on the Spaniards, the Spanish being the leaders and financial backers of the Catholic forces in Europe. One of the most influential of these attacks was the translation into French and Latin by Urbain Chauveton (dating from 1578 to 1579) of Hierosme Benzoni's (originally Italian, 1565) *Histoire Nouvelle du Nouveau Monde*. Gómara is singled out for specific criticism in this work, for writing from hearsay; Benzoni had spent fourteen years in America. Avarice, says Benzoni/Chauveton, is the idol of the Christians while the Indians are neither avaricious nor rich; from avarice the Spaniards desecrated the "singular gift of God" that was the New World.

One of the most influential of all works on the New World before the time of Rousseau was published at the beginning of the eighteenth century (1703), the work of a young French officer in Canada, Louis Armand de Lom d'Arce, baron de Lahontan. That Lahontan's conversations with a wise Canadian Indian happened to attack the Europe of Louis XIV, which Lahontan happened to wish to attack, did not detract from the effectiveness of the concomitant picture of New World life, liberty, and happiness presented by the Huron philosopher, Adario.

Some day, says the author, "that Anarchy may be introduced among us that exists among the Ameriquains, of whom the least feels himself more than a Chancellor of France." Adario seconds the hope that an equality of wealth might gradually appear in Europe, "and that at last you will detest this greed that causes all the evils one sees in Europe, and thus having no *thine* nor *mine* you will live with the same felicity as Hurons. . . . Would one see classes and distinctions among men if there were no *Thine* and *Mine*? You would all be equal, as are the Hurons."

In answer to the charge of Indian indolence, Adario says, "What have we in the world dearer than life? Why not enjoy it?" The author agrees that the

Indian "Nations which have not been corrupted by the presence of Europeans have neither *thine* nor *mine*, neither Laws nor Judges nor Priests," and in all this are wise and reasonable, since private property "is the sole source of all the disorders that trouble the Society of Europeans."

Echoes of Lahontan are found, says his modern editor, among "the most daring thinkers of the eighteenth century," including Diderot, Swift, Rousseau and Voltaire; the philosopher Leibniz found in Lahontan "evidence refuting the speculations of Hobbes" and showing that man in a state of nature was not bad but good, and that it was "pursuit of a better and happier life, by mutual assistance, that led to the foundation of Societies and States."

The hit play in Paris in 1721, Delisle de la Drevetière's *Arlequin Sauvage*, was in many respects a direct dramatization of Lahontan. "In my forests I knew neither riches nor poverty. . . . I want to be a free man, nothing more," says the American Indian hero, while the Paris public cheers.

With Rousseau and the French Revolution this set of ideas joined the property of the world in general, and historians have tended to ignore the many centuries of its New World beginnings, from the civilizations of the Andes to Lahontan's Hurons.

But a divergent line of European thought occupied with the problem of property was not altogether unaware of the shades of Montaigne's previously cited Indian tourists.

Lewis Henry Morgan, one of the first American anthropologists, was a longtime student of the Iroquois and unmuddled by Romantic notions of an Indian golden world, but the propertyless society of the New World gave him a theme he felt was important. He wrote in his most ambitious book, *Ancient Society*: "Since the advent of civilization, the outgrowth of property has been so immense . . . that it has become, on the part of the people, an unmanageable power. The human mind stands bewildered in the presence of its own creation. . . . A mere property career is not the final destiny of mankind, if progress is to be the law of the future as it has been of the past. . . . The dissolution of society bids fair to become the termination of a career of which property is the end and aim; because such a career contains the elements of self-destruction. Democracy of government, brotherhood in society, equality in rights and privileges, and universal education, foreshadow the next higher plane of society to which experience, intelligence, and knowledge are steadily tending. It will be a revival, in a higher form, of the liberty, equality and fraternity of the ancient gentes."

This was published in 1877 and used by Karl Marx and Friedrich Engels as a corroboration of Marx's materialistic theory of history. Marx was especially impressed by Morgan's basic point, that primitive society is organized on a structure of family relationships while modern society is based on property relationships, and made notes for a book on Morgan's researches but did not live to write it. Engels did so, in his *The Origin of the Family, Private Property, and the State in the Light of the Researches of Lewis Henry Morgan,* published in 1884, in which he described the notion he had gathered of the Indian way of life—a restatement of the old familiar pattern: "And a wonderful constitution it is . . . in all its childlike simplicity! No soldiers, no gendarmes or police, no nobles, kings, regents, prefects, no judges, no prisons, no lawsuits. . . . There cannot be any poor or needy, the communal household and the gens [related family groups] know their responsibilities towards the old, the sick, and those disabled in war. All are equal and free—the women included. . . . And what men and women such a society breeds is proved by the admiration inspired in all white people who have come into contact with unspoiled Indians, by the personal dignity, uprightness, strength of character, and courage of these barbarians."

Not surprisingly, the leveling idea of liberty pure and simple ran first through some regions of America before making its tour of Europe. In the colonies that became the United States this idea manifested itself in Indian costume in the several pseudo-Indian political, military, and fraternal societies organized from the mid-1700s onward. The best known of these was the Tammany Society, taking its name from the Delaware councilor Tamanend and calling its different lodges "tribes," its officers "sachems," and its meeting place the "wigwam." It came into prominence after the Revolution, dedicated to "the independence, the popular liberty, and the federal union of the country" and earned a fair share of credit for the eventual triumph of such ideals in the United States. It was also of some influence in helping to secure the 1790 treaty with the Creek Indians that bolstered at the time the security of the southern borders of the new United States. It was after the Civil War that the Tammany Society degenerated into the New York City political machine familiar, and not quite so admirable, into modern times.

In certain basic respects the New World and the Old World views of society were most clearly opposed in areas of the United States colonized principally by a people to whom diligent labor, thrift, the making of money, became the highest virtues. Time, people, woods, streams, fields were all to be measured by the yardstick of profit. In Protestant America this principle emerged as the ruling ethic; its aim, in the words of the economist Max Weber, being "the earning of more and more money," gain, profit, acquisition, that was thought of "purely as an end in itself."

Railed Cotton Mather of Indians, writing in the 1690s: "They are *Sluggards* to a Proverb; they are for any way of Living rather than Work. . . .

They are abominably indulgent unto their *Children*; there is no *Family Government* among them." And he demanded of his Puritan audience to "Enquire, Sirs, how far we have *Indianized* in every one, but especially the last of these *Evil Manners*." During the colonial wars European captives frequently Indianized to the point of refusing to part from their captors and return to "civilization" when they had the chance. This was a subject of indignant remark by generations of uncaptured Europeans. Said the historian of an Ohio Valley Campaign in 1764, when a number of white captives had to be forcibly repatriated: "For the honour of humanity, we would suppose those persons to have been of the lowest rank, either bred up in ignorance and distressing penury, or who had lived so long with the Indians as to forget all their former connections. For easy and unconstrained as the savage life is, certainly it could never be put in competition with the blessings of improved life and the light of religion, by any persons who have had the happiness of enjoying, and the capacity of discerning, them." But a surprising lot of white captives opted for it, nevertheless. What did it profit a man to work the fat off his back for the blessings of improved life, when the twinkling stars were equally bright for everyone lost in the dark? Indian life may have had an edge in the pursuit of happiness precisely because it would not race.

In this collision of rights of way the Indian attitude was more than troublesome, it was downright sacrilegious.

Sometimes the heterogeneous colonists quarreled bitterly among themselves but in the last analysis they could make common cause since in the last analysis they were all after the same thing. Frontiersmen became as Indian as white in many ways, and in deeper ways than simply borrowing such gadgets as snowshoes or canoes, but as a rule they never forgot the basic objective of their life—profit, property.

Spain was more successful in transforming the Indian peoples into a familiar peasantry, absorbed into church and state in such numbers that what is now called Latin America could almost equally well, with a few regional exceptions, be called Indian America. In much of Protestant America the Indian nations were stamped out to the point that a nineteenth-century synonym for the Indian race became the Vanishing American—which has turned into a particularly fallacious image, American Indians being the fastest growing ethnic group in the United States at present. The ultimate conflict in points of view may well have underlain this fallacy, and underlain the series of Indian images created by the white mind in response to this conflict.

The noble savage gave way to the bloodthirsty savage, reeking with gore. An 1837 volume entitled "Indian Anecdotes and Barbarities. . . . Being a description of their customs and deeds of cruelty, with an account of the captivity, sufferings and heroic conduct of many who have fallen into their hands, or who have defended themselves from savage vengeance; all illustrating the general traits of Indian Character" describes a massacre at Schenectady in 1690: "They ravished, rifled, murdered and mutilated the inhabitants, without distinction of age or sex, without any other provocation or excitement than brutal lust and wantonness of barbarity. Pregnant women were ripped open and their infants cast into the flames or dashed against the posts of the doors!!"

The insensate barbarian gave way to the Red Brother asking Guidance of the Missionaries, the whiskey-begging beetle-eating derelict of the jaundiced, the culture-index cipher of the scientists. Some of the imagined images left a pronounced impression on the American character (the psychiatrist Jung is reported to have said he could detect an Indian streak in all his American patients).

Many of the images had an even more pronounced effect on the fate of the Indians. Town-dwelling people, rich in culture and cornfields, were transfigured in the popular (and political) mind into nomadic hunters. Well-meaning citizens, good people, had to keep reminding themselves that the dispossessed Creeks or the outlawed Sauk and Foxes of the synthetic Black Hawk "War" were savages.

But, at the same time, some sections of public opinion turned the Creeks and their neighbors into romantic heroes. And the reaction of many people in the North to the methods of Indian removal in the South added fuel to the heated reform movements of the epoch, among these the militant American Antislavery Society (launched in 1833), the Abolitionist movement.

The North had its full share of practical men, of course, but while Illinois militiamen were shooting Sauk and Fox people ("It was a horrid sight to witness little children, wounded and suffering the most excruciating pain, although they were of the savage enemy"), the Sauk and Fox leader Black Hawk was becoming a national celebrity. At the end of the "war" in 1832 he was taken after his capture on what can only be described as a triumphal tour of the cities of the East (and his bones were stolen for exhibition after his death in 1838). He was compared, in an epic poem written in his honor, "As soldier, patriot, soul magnanimous," with Napoleon and Wellington

And sure they had no better cause,
Than fight for country, kindred, laws!

The mid-nineteenth century found its Indian heroes in factual accounts as well as in Fenimore Cooper fiction, in the past as well as the present, in biographies, novels, dramas dealing not only with such superstars as

Tecumseh, Pontiac, King Philip, Moctezuma, but with relatively obscure Indian leaders of long before, such as Big Mouth the Onondaga. What is by many regarded as the best book by America's best historian (*The Oregon Trail*) was undertaken by Parkman in 1846 simply for the purpose of "studying the manners and character of Indians in their primitive state." The last work of the age's most enduring sage, Thoreau, a work left unfinished at his death, dealt with Indians.

Indian images in the public mind are possibly seen most clearly through some minor luminaries of the time. One such, much celebrated in Washington during his visit there in 1821, was the intrepid young Petalesharo, son of a chief of the Skidi Pawnee. The Pawnee had in earlier centuries moved up the west bank of the Mississippi and the Missouri to Nebraska and beyond, and retained a showy collection of what seemed to be temple-mound religious practices from the southeast, splendid with symbolism and poetry, and culminating, at least among the Skidi Pawnee, in a splendidly gruesome human sacrifice at the time of the summer solstice, an arrow-shooting sacrifice reminiscent of similar rites pictured in pre-Columbian codices from deep in Mexico. Petalesharo put a stop to the practice by rescuing an intended victim, a Comanche girl, in the best last-minute tradition ("Who was it that intrepidly released the captive maid? It was the young, the brave, the generous PETALESHARRO"), dramatically defying priests and thunderbolts and the assembled faithful.

A figure of the Washington social season of 1826 and 1827 was an Ojibwa confidence woman, Tshusick, who ran a sanctimonious racket on high government officials and their ladies, including the lady of President John Quincy Adams. A contemporary, Eleazar Williams, a Christianized Oneida called by a biographer "the most perfect adept at fraud, deceit, and intrigue that the world ever produced," was alleged to have looted the Oneida and several missionary societies of thousands of dollars during the 1820s (while moving most of the Oneida against their will from New York to Green Bay, Wisconsin, into the bargain), and turned up in the 1850s as the pretended Lost Dauphin of France, son of Louis XVI, immediately gaining a large claque of white followers.

Obviously, in areas mystical and romantical a certain cachet attached to being an Indian, and it is not surprising that Indian-model mumbo jumbo played a part in the founding of various religious sects during the period. The Book of Mormon, adopting the then-current theory that the Indians were remnants of the Lost Tribes of Israel, dubbed them Lamanites, and offered a history for their movements from 600 B.C. until after the Resurrection, when Christ appeared to them here and there under the guise of Viracocha, Kukulcan, or Quetzalcoatl. The sects of the Shakers and the Spiritualists gave quite a bit of attention to Indians, generally regarding them as virtuous and mystically powerful simply because they were Indians, in contrast to the wicked (fallen) Lamanites of the Mormons. A natural counterpart to the virtuous Indian mystic was the Indian herb doctor (sometimes quite a good doctor indeed), forerunner of the Kickapoo Medicine Show of a generation or two later.

In the different images the Indian was sometimes wondrous wise, and a virtue attached itself to Indian wit as well as to Indian yarbs and roots. When a Jesuit priest reproached an Algonkin priest with the immorality of his people saying, "You don't even know which of the children around you are your own," the old Indian replied, "I will never understand you Frenchmen—you love only your own children, but we love all children." When a Dutch pastor told some Iroquois that in his sermons he reminded the Christians each week "that they must not steal, nor commit lewdness, nor get drunk, nor commit murder," the Iroquois (puffing on their long tobacco pipes) said he did well but asked in pretended amazement, "Why do so many Christians do these things?" A Seneca sachem, objecting to Christian missionaries among his people, said he had been to Buffalo and seen how the white people lived, and they needed missionaries more than the Seneca did. These and other bright sayings from the past were given wider than usual circulation in the mid-nineteenth century, almost for a time threatening to replace the dominant but spurious wooden image of the dour and humorless Indian with one a little nearer to reality; although in reality the favorite ironic wit of the Indian was not always so virtuous and, like old Chaucer, was frequently too graphic for our wincing modern ears.

But in the differing images a romantic virtue sometimes clung even to Indian savagery, so that London street brawlers of the eighteenth century proudly called themselves "Mohocks," as Parisian toughs of a later period took the name Apaches. And a real honorary Mohawk, the English Duke of Northumberland who had been adopted into the Mohawks as a warrior during the Revolutionary War, wrote in 1806 from England to the Mohawk leader Joseph Brant: "There are a number of well meaning persons here, who are very desirous of forming a society to better (as they call it) the condition of our nation, by converting us from warriors and hunters into husbandmen. Let me strongly recommend it to you, and the rest of our chiefs, not to listen to such a proposition."

In the various images a certain scientific virtue even attached to strong-stomached primitivism (the long fingernails of an old Montagnais woman scraping a greasy pot, and the professionally long fingernails of the official Choctaw bone-pickers who cleaned the bones of the dead for burial; and the Creek Honored Men vomiting with punctilio the black drink), for the age was intellectually elevated as well as refined.

Intellectual curiosity probed Indian mythology, legend, folk history; a scholarly treatise accidentally transferred the name of the great Iroquois political reformer Hiawatha to the story of the Ojibwa demigod Manabozho, and the accident was sealed in marbled meter for posterity in Longfellow's poem (would it have been as deathless under its right name of Manabozho?).

The nineteenth century became intensely concerned with costume everywhere in the precincts of triumphant western "civilization"—naked savages were savages because they were naked. In the United States the Spanish records of American antiquity were forgotten; all indigenous peoples of the hemisphere took on the look of Catlin drawings from the trans-Mississippi plains.

As the Vanishing American vanished from the eastern states he acquired an air of nostalgic fable, bathed in the rush of poignant affection that one feels for the dying. Sang Lydia Sigourney ("The Sweet Singer of Hartford"), America's most popular female poet of the first half of the nineteenth century:

Ye say that all have passed away,
The noble race and brave
That their light canoes have vanished
From off the crested wave;
That 'mid the forests where they roamed,
There rings no hunter's shout;
But their name is on your waters,
Ye may not wash it out.
. . . Ye say their cone-like cabins
That clustered o'er the vale,
Have disappeared as withered leaves
Before the autumn gale;
But their memory liveth on your hills.

Indian images of the time emphasized tribes melting away at a touch, or skulking savages being eradicated like other agricultural pests. The war was over, the conquest won, and a curious blindness blacked out the long and important Indian role even in the North American story, relegating it to a minor, if colorful, bit of business.

The central mystery of the Iroquois, their tremendous staying power that had been so influential in the course of events, was obscured by the fictional sideshow of Joseph Brant's howling desolating band. The similar staying power and historical importance of the Chickasaws and Choctaws and Creeks and Cherokees was lost in the emotional sideshow of their removal.

But the jumbled Indian images did occupy the popular fancy to an amazing degree in literature, laws, and the practice of the comfortable nineteenth-century morality.

In the official image the Indian problem was a purely economic matter to be handled as economically as possible. The starched missionary image saved the Indian child and killed the Indian poet and created pious, if rather childish and indolent, Christians of the second class. Academicians, always correct and seldom right, created a rattle-shaking taboo-conditioned automaton that had nothing whatever to do with the stagey ghosts of Those Who Have Gone to whom the sentimentalists strewed memorial garlands, using thank as the past tense of think.

An image popular in the West late in the nineteenth century was that of unfairly favored economic rivals, perhaps because of the free beef (or sort of facsimile thereof) furnished some Indians who, confined on reservations, otherwise had no food. "I have shot one of those damned Government pets," said a South Dakota rancher who with a couple of companions had fired from concealment on two Oglala families passing in wagons (the three dry gulchers were promptly acquitted by a jury of their neighboring peers).

But all the tumbled phantoms of all the jumbled images could not bridge the gulf to a comprehension of the Indians as people to be taken seriously, as people who were an integral part of the national history and their own incomprehensible world part of the national life.

Arresting as the images (some of them) were, the public could comprehend the practical necessity of the removal of the eastern nations, tragic and not quite legal though it might be. (Or the practical necessity of taking from the western Indians anything of value they might accidentally possess, such as the Black Hills.)

Practical men, at least, could comprehend the need and condone the conspiracy, as practical men before and since could condone other instances of rapacious exploitation of America's natural resources; the curious schism in the American character between private right and public wrong was not born with the dirty business of the Great Removal, although it received a resoundingly helpful whack therefrom.

The tragedy of the exiled "Civilized Tribes" brought sympathy, and the long and heroic resistance by the Creek and Cherokee people to a persecution that should have crushed an ordinary people in six months brought admiration; but even the most outraged idealists could not perceive the other side of the tragedy—the costly loss to the states of Georgia, Alabama, and Mississippi of such potentially superior citizens.

"Why should you take by force from us that which you can obtain by love?" old Powhatan had asked.

But the old men were long gone, while wild roved an Indian girl, bright Alfarata, where sweep the waters of the blue Juniata, and she was swift as an antelope through the forests going and loose were her jetty locks in wavy tresses flowing, and it would be a safe bet she'd never pounded hominy. But what difference? Phantoms live on memories, not food. Phantoms looked from the Alabama hill that broke Menewa's heart, and danced a solemn step or two in the busy streets of Plymouth, among the phantom lodges of Patuxet, and phantoms grinned at phantom jokes in a thousand phantom councils. Phantoms settled down to live in the names of the land, as the Sweet Singer said; but also, far more than most Americans suspected, in the heritage of the New World liberty in their past and their future.

CHAPTER 25

Under the Northern Lights

The French explorer La Pérouse said in 1786 of the Tlingit people at Yakutat Bay, Alaska, farthest north of the Northwest Coast people, that they "bargained with as much skill as any tradesman of Europe." Perhaps with even more skill (or command), for in its earlier years the maritime trade was controlled by the coastal Indians with an independence French *commerçants* would have envied. The rare foreign ships were no visible threat and their trade goods, especially iron (for knives), and guns were good to have but scarcely essential. The seal and, above all, the sea otter pelts sold by the natives created, on the other hand, a fabulously desirable trade with China for the Europeans and, later, the Yankees. Some present day scholars are inclined to agree with the complaints of outraged shipmasters (and their backers) that they were simply exploited by the hard-fisted Indians, although such a backer as the European-Yankee John Jacob Astor seemed to find the risk worth taking.

Westering trade and exploration by sea far outstripped that by land, and the exotic faraway tribes of the northern coast of the Pacific were generally known to eastern America while the nations of the plains and mountains in between remained no more than shadowy names. New England deepwater sailors of 1800 knew the outlandish whale-hunting Indians of Nootka Sound better, no doubt, than they knew the Indians of New England.

The fur-clad peoples of the farther North had been known to English explorers since Elizabethan times: whalers, fur traders, and missionaries had kept the acquaintance going for 270 years when in 1848 the great Arctic expedition of Sir John Franklin vanished into thin air and turned the eyes of the world on the land of the Eskimos. Thirty-eight relief expeditions were sent out in the next ten years (it was later discovered that Franklin's large party had perished, to a man, of starvation); 7,000 miles of unknown Arctic coastline were incidentally explored; and the Eskimos (more often called Inuit nowadays, their own name) were solidly and permanently implanted in the consciousness of America and Europe.

Due to their distinctiveness the Inuit probably remain among the most widely known of all America's native peoples. European provincials who may never have heard of the Iroquois or the Aztecs are likely to know about Eskimo igloos and dog sleds.

Nevertheless, in spite of the exhaustive ethnologizing and publicizing they have so long received, the Inuit are still, in a sense, semiconcealed, hidden by the fearsome unfamiliarity of their country. One can picture the people but not the life, the life of long dark winters and incredible cold, the hardships and the dangers. It is particularly difficult to conceive of this bitter, anxiety-ridden life bringing forth a people usually described as placid and rather jolly, a people whose past reveals, within the limits imposed by their harsh if vivid world, several cultures of spectacular richness.

One further uniqueness, as far as European views of the Inuit are concerned: long before the early Greenland whale fisheries, long before the first voyage of Columbus, Eskimos and Europeans commingled in an association that lasted for centuries—in Greenland.

The Norse, Irish, and Vikings who settled in Iceland from about A.D. 850 to 1100 planted colonies on the coast of Greenland, the far eastern frontier of the New World and the Eskimo world. In contrast to their brief and dreamlike trips to the coast of North America, Norsemen established permanent settlements in southwestern Greenland and lived in some contact with the Eskimos there for "about five" centuries. These settlements were finally either wiped out by the Eskimos or abandoned, but until the mid-1300s, if not somewhat later, they remained in fairly frequent contact with Europe. But the two peoples met, so to speak, incognito, neither quite realizing that the other was from a different world. Europe was unaware, and the Inuit were unimpressed.

A few words of Old Norse or Old Icelandic origin found their way into Greenlandic Eskimo speech, a few hammers were made of church-bell metal, a few tubs were coopered (with hoops made of the corset whalebone known as baleen), and a few Greenland Eskimos of the time learned to write a few lines in medieval runic rhyme. Otherwise, to the New World natives of Greenland the generations of intruding Europeans were as if they had never been.

This long and bootless association reveals something of the difficulty of transferring elements from one culture to another, and something of the difficulty of discovering a New World before the discoverer is ripe for the event.

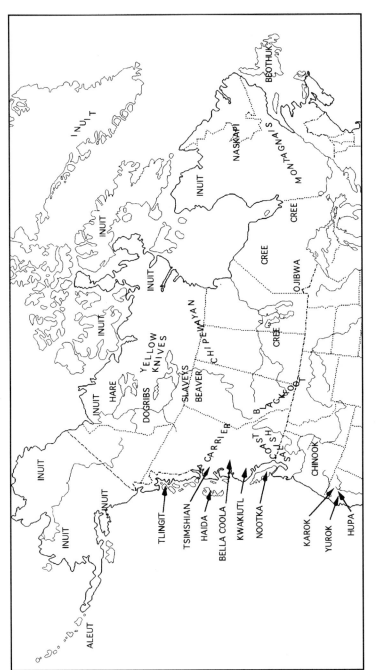

Canada and the Arctic

The possibility of very early inhabitants of the far North some 25,000 years ago or more has been mentioned, and evidence of human presence has been turned up in a number of Arctic sites dating to later post-glacial times, 11,000 to 8,000 years ago, when the wild flooding that may have wiped out much earlier evidence had ceased. Archeologists debate whether any of these people were ancestral to the Inuit.

However, residents in the Aleutian Islands, inhabiting the Anangula village site on an islet now off the shore of Umnak Island, roundabout 8,000 years ago, and possibly even using boats at that early time, are regarded as probable ancestors of the Aleuts (pronounced Alley-oots), kinfolk of the Inuit.

Artifacts from these early sites are dominated by a blade culture, flakes struck from flint cores, which had been the ruling industry in Siberia for many thousands of years. Several other distinct technological varieties have been identified in the subsequent thousands of years, as the New World microblade business became distinctly American, and by 6,000 years ago or so a difference had clearly developed between coastal people and inland hunters. Undoubted Eskimo presence (if it had not been there all along) emerged in northern Alaska and along the Bering Sea something more than 3,000 years ago. Even this relatively recent date gives them a fairly respectable antiquity, longer than the Romans have been in Rome or the French in France, pointing up once more the vast scale of time in the New World story.

The Inuit are not classified by anthropologists as Indians, nor do they regard themselves as Indians. They have an Asiatic look but are a physical type unto themselves, average in height, plump, massive-faced, narrow-nosed, longheaded. The name Inuit means as usual The People; the name Eskimo may have come (most Eskimo people deny it) from an Algonquian word meaning "raw-meat-eaters" or maybe, some students have suggested, from a term applied by early French missionaries meaning "the excommunicated." Norsemen called them *skraelingar*, meaning "little people." Most of their Indian neighbors gave them the usual Indian appellation for Others, some term meaning something such as "snakes" or "enemies"; the central Eskimo retaliated by calling the Cree and Chipewyan people south of them *itqilit*, meaning "lousy."

Eskimo-Aleut is a language family all its own, the two branches, Eskimo and Aleut, only distantly related, evidently having divided long ago from a common progenitor. Occasional loan-word parallels hint at contacts in bygone ages with Finnish, Lapp, Pequot, even the Aztec Nahuatl, among others, but no real kinship has yet been established. Hypothetical connection with Ural-Altaic (Finnish, Lapp, et al.) may be regarded as "less controversial" than other guesses. More intriguing is a suggestion that in its Asiatic beginning

Proto-Eskimo-Aleut might have been a form of Proto-Indo-European, parent language of Sanskrit, Greek, Latin, German, English, and a galaxy of more or less cultured tongues—thus the English word "ignite," for example, from the Latin *ignis* meaning "fire," might have stemmed ultimately from the Eskimo *ingneq* meaning "to make fire by twirling a stick in a block of wood." But all the various hypotheses are only suggestions. Eskimo-Aleut remains officially unrelated to any other language, and is likely to continue remaining so for a while.

The Eskimo branch of the Eskimo-Aleut language contains two subgroups, Yupik in southwestern peninsular Alaska made up of five related languages, and Inuit-Inupiaq, a ribbon of closely related dialects running across Arctic Alaska and Canada to the coasts of Greenland.

For this swing of 5,000 miles across the Arctic and sub-Arctic seacoast, islands, and tundra, from Siberia across Alaska and the immense reaches of the north of Canada to Greenland, the isolated villages of the Inuit were the only sign of man.

Their total population in this enormous area perhaps never exceeded 100,000, perhaps seldom exceeded 50,000. There were no tribal governments, no real village governments, and consequently no war and no law, other than observance of custom and taboo. (Murder was punished by the victim's relatives, if they felt up to it.) The real unit of government was the family.

There was a striking uniformity among the people, the Inuit people (Aleuts excepted), over all this great area; a similarity in the way of life, allowing for differences arising from variations in the food supply; and, as noted, a quite remarkable similarity in language—Aleut, as distantly related as Russian to English, again excepted. More, there is a remarkable similarity down through the centuries—the rise and fall of both Eskimo and Aleut culture follows a curve so slow as to be almost imperceptible unless it is measured from stations 1,000 years apart.

In some regions it has been difficult for archeologists to detect much real change at all: Aleut culture of 2,000 B.C. was apparently not very different from that of A.D. 1700. In other regions periods of gradual cultural development have been distinguished, reaching a high point (and a brilliant one) not long after the time of Christ.

Investigators divide the Eskimo into geographic groups for purposes of identification, but the basic Eskimo division is between the whale and walrus and seal hunters of the coasts and the caribou hunters of the interior (some groups hunt both at different seasons, still today as 2,000 years ago). And the basic question in Eskimo ancient history is which came first, the coastal or the inland way of life. A Danish scholar argued some eighty years ago that the inland life, more "primitive" than the coastal life, was the original, a belief that still has many takers, but a definite answer is not yet agreed upon.

Further unanswered questions concern how much of the Inuit way of life came from Asia and spread eastward over the Inuit New World, and how much originated in America and, sometimes, spread back to Asia. The famous vaulted snow house, never observed in Asia, would seem to be one of the unquestioned Inuit inventions. (*Igdlo*, incidentally, source of the familiar "igloo," is the word for any house, whether built of stone, snow, sod, or wood, from northern Alaska to Greenland; "snow igloo" is *igluvigac*. The snow house, which could be built in an hour or two, was often only a temporary shelter.)

Some specialists trace lines of cultural influence from the south, involving such long-ago people as the Great Basin hunters of the great-horned buffalo, or Great Lakes tribes of Old Copper times.

In a very general sense the earlier Eskimo cultures so far accepted as Eskimo by all authorities appeared to be somewhat more elaborate toward the west, more simplified toward the east, until, after a further 1,000 years or so, new higher-culture developments in the central Arctic fed back westward, leveling out the coast to coast basic uniformity.

But even in the somewhat varying earlier cultures many of the familiar Eskimo elements are already present: boats made of skins sewed over wooden frames, the decked one-man kayak and the larger open umiak; sleds with runners of bone or ivory, probably from the first for use with dogs (according to observed custom of later times, the dogs were hitched tandem in the west, fanwise in the east); ivory snow goggles, at first with round holes, later with slits; hobnails of bone or ivory for lashing to your boot soles in working your way over ice, very similar to the crampons of the modern mountaineer; ice scoops and ice picks; plugs to stop up the wounds of animals and save the precious blood; specialized fishing gear; specialized harpooning gear for use with floats of inflated bladders; specialized bird-catching gear; bows and arrows for hunting musk ox, caribou, and other big game; and usually the blubber or seal-oil lamp, center of the coastal Eskimo household from time immemorial. This, the only lamp known in the Americas, was at first used, it seems, only for light, later for heat and cooking. Traditionally its small, smokeless (if properly trimmed) flame was the only heat in Eskimo homes of woodless country—where the temperature could settle down and stay a while at -50° or -60° F.

This lamp might possibly have been an instrument of pollution in the otherwise sparkling Arctic atmosphere: it was kept burning continually, tending it was woman's work—and nasopharynx malignant tumor was found to be surprisingly prevalent among Greenland Inuit, twenty-five times the rate among Danes. A young Greenland woman died some five centuries ago from this; her mummified body was found recently, entombed among rocks along with five other women and two children, all the bodies and clothing in excellent condition—soot in the lungs of one of the women was as heavy as for an urban dweller of the present. From tending lamps, so the experts guess. The leader of an American expedition in the Arctic in the 1850s (in search of Sir John Franklin) wrote of their problems with soot-bearing Eskimo lamps—although the most troublesome by far were lamps that had been improved with civilization's latest gadgetry.

A flowering of the microblade industry 4,000 years ago on the Alaskan west coast, known as the Denbigh Flint Complex, is widely regarded as a founding cornerstone of Eskimo culture. Archeologists have settled on various broad divisions for later ancient Inuit cultural traditions, usually turning on certain differences between the communities fronting on the Arctic Ocean and communities of Pacific coast Inuit and Aleut communities, although with many correspondences and connections in between. Best known in these (all pretty much climaxing in the centuries between A.D. 1 and 1000) are the Aleutian tradition, the Kachemak Bay tradition in the Kodiak area, the later Norton tradition in Alaska followed in northern Alaska by the Ipiutak, Dorset in northern Canada and Greenland, and early Thule across the entire Arctic coast from Greenland to the Bering Sea.

All produced decorative work in bone and ivory, sometimes of a high order. Possibly the finest of all Eskimo carving and engraving is found in the exquisite ivories of the Ipiutak culture, where the dead in their log tombs were furnished with artificial eyes of inlaid ivory, mouth-covers and nose plugs of carved ivory, and accompanied by elaborate ivory masks, fantastic carved animal figurines, carved ivory spirals and chains. These last are believed to represent imitations of the metal chains and swivels hung as magic gadgets to the gowns of shamans far to the west in Siberia. The artificial eyes resemble, so some students point out, jade eye-amulets of Han dynasty times (206 B.C.–A.D. 220) in ancient China.

Pottery was evidently introduced during this time, and—probably the one great revolutionary event in coastal Arctic history—the virtuoso profession of whaling from an open boat was developed.

During this time, so say some Inuit, another race lived among them, a most revolutionary event with mighty ancestors, men so powerful one of them alone could haul a walrus across the ice as easily as an Inuk (Eskimo man) could drag a seal, people known as the Tunnit or Tornit. For some reason they went away, but "so greatly did they love their country, that when they were leaving, there was a man who, out of desperate love for his village, harpooned the rocks with his harpoon and made the stones fly about like bits of ice." There are (possibly) some indications that the Tunnit may have been historical, maybe the bearers of some culture change, but if so who they were or where they went is not known.

There may have been non-Inuit groups in the Arctic past of this period: some features of the Dorset culture are thought to hint at the now extinct pale-skinned Beothuk Indians of Newfoundland.

Among the Inuit themselves there may have been varying peoples; the inland and coastal groups may once have been distinct in physical type. The Aleuts are so different that it is almost possible to think of them as, in earlier times, a separate people, but it is more likely their differences resulted from continuing new groups arriving via the Kamchatka peninsula.

In various respects the ancient way of life changed in the centuries after about A.D. 1000. The quality of art, while still impressive, nevertheless exhibits a definite decline. Tools and weapons became more specialized. There were a few further innovations—such as pipes and tobacco—that traveled around the world after the discovery of America to reach at last the Inuit via Siberia in the 1700s and 1800s. But essentially the pattern of living remained the same.

Winter houses were built, often over a dug-out floor, of whatever was available, driftwood, whalebones, stone, sod, or snow. The domed snow house was rare in Alaska, more typical of Canada, where modern explorers have visited vaulted halls of snow roomy enough for dancing parties of sixty people, and noted that the roaring sheet-iron stoves in use today—their rusty chimneys elbowing out through the domed snow ceilings—did not melt the well-built walls or roofs.

Summer dwellings were sometimes skin tents, conical in the western regions, ridged in the east. Clothes were tailored from skins of large animals (such as bear, caribou), boots from sealskin. Sea-mammal gut was stretched for skylight panes, and also used for waterproof coats—a man hooded with it and lashed watertight in his kayak might drown but he would not get very wet. A principal piece of furniture was the drying frame, for drying the constantly wet clothes. A winter sport, next to sex (in which the Inuit by report have always taken a frank and enthusiastic interest), was gymnastics performed on stretched sealskin ropes.

In the winter, seals were hunted at the ice edge or breathing holes, a freezing job, waiting motionless for hours with harpoon ready; in the summer they were harpooned from kayaks in the open sea. Kayakers became desperately expert at handling their swift and maneuverable craft, but even so Arctic waters are wild and dangerous, and it is not surprising that one of the Eskimo words to travel farthest among neighboring people is *pivoq*, meaning "he lost his life by upsetting in his kayak." In the summer the whalers put out in their umiaks (which were occasionally rigged with grass-mat sails), sometimes operating almost out of sight of land.

Inland people hunted caribou in the spring and fall, at the migration of the herds, and in between lived on salmon. Here, starving times were common. They had no oil or blubber; their lamps were made from caribou tallow with a wick of heather, and were all but heatless.

Seaside villages sometimes moved inland to hunt the caribou, a time of holiday:

> Glorious it is
> To see long-haired winter caribou
> Returning to the forests . . .
> While the herd follows the ebb-mark of the sea
> With a storm of clattering hooves.
> Glorious it is
> When wandering time is come.

The song may be old; no one is sure. It was sung for and translated by the late Knud Rasmussen, one of the greatest of interpreters of the Eskimo mind and poetry, a poetry which in his hands at least shimmers and flames like the northern lights. Rasmussen, already well known as an Arctic explorer, established, with Peter Freuchen as storekeeper, the trading post of Thule among the Polar Eskimo of northern Greenland in 1910—it was this Thule that gave its name to the most widespread Eskimo cultural tradition so far unearthed. But Rasmussen's poetry has outlived his science.

> The lands around my dwelling are
> now more beautiful
> from the day when it is given me to see
> faces I have never seen before

is another Rasmussen translation, from an impromptu Iglulik song of greeting that points up the immensity of loneliness in much of the past Inuit world, where the tiny settlements of a dozen families or so might not see a stranger every year.

Could this aloneness have something to do with the hyperbolic Eskimo hospitality? The host is so ashamed of his wretched dwelling, of the food he is offering you that is so unworthy because he is such a worthless hunter, of his useless wife who can do nothing right (all these being famous for excellence).

But there is a note in this that rings a little bell of memory for anyone who has lived, say, in a traditional neighborhood in Japan. Perhaps an echo from very ancient Asia could also be involved.

Early accounts of Inuit life are sometimes contradictory. Each community living quite independently might lead to certain periodic variations, even among a people of notably uniform ways. A report of the 1850s pictures coastal Inuit people of northwest Alaska as suspicious and aggressive, unlike the usual peaceable and friendly image. But frequent mentions of whaling crews in the vicinity might offer a clue as to why—or the trading ships from Asia that came in the summer, four or five a year.

Trade was, of course, exceedingly important to the isolated Inuit communities, and its network could embrace a considerable area. Goods brought by the trading ships from Asia—Russian kettles of iron and copper, women's knives, double-edged knives, tobacco, beads, tin—were traded at Kotzebue Sound on the Alaskan coast to Inuit people there who traded some of the purchased goods the following summer at Point Barrow in the north, for goods the Point Barrow people had received from the eastward the year before and for the Barrow people's own goods from the sea: whale or seal oil, whalebone, walrus tusks, hide thongs, seal skins. The Point Barrow people then traded some of their new acquisitions the next year to people of the Mackenzie delta for wolverine and wolf furs, Inuit lamps, English knives, beads, guns and ammunition. These goods, or some of them, made their way back westward, eventually back to Kotzebue Sound and on across the Strait to Siberian Eskimo people on the Chukchi Sea. A double-edged knife might take a half dozen years to arrive at Winter Island far to the east, and a Copper Eskimo stone lamp might rest a year with each new purchaser to take up to nine years to reach the Chukchi. Inland people, such as hunters living on the Colville River, participated along the way, along with the seacoast customers.

The sea people, though, lived a life fundamentally richer in provisions and goods, and especially richer in taboos. Illness, misfortune, or lack of success in hunting seal or walrus was certainly caused by some broken law that had thrown the world out of balance. An angakok, a shaman, would find out what had gone wrong and correct it. Had the sick woman's husband perhaps speared a salmon at a time when this was taboo? Then of course the salmon were offended and would not let themselves be caught. Or perhaps a sin had floated down to the bottom of the sea, to fall like dirt in the hair of the great goddess known as "She Down There"; her name among the Central tribes was Sedna, her West Greenland name Arnarquagssaq. Then, of course, she was indignant and was keeping the fat creatures of the sea out of reach of those on land, and the angakok would have to make a spirit journey down to her and square things. The shaman, common among many Indians as well as among Siberians, was particularly popular among the Inuit. Women could be shamans, maybe better at the job than men. They performed magic, secured revenge, cured illness, sometimes by a method widely known among the peoples of both North and South America, sucking out the illness and spitting forth a pebble or some such object to prove it.

The ages passed, and the Inuit moved with the same age-old acts and gestures through the summers as fleeting and brilliant as flights of ravens and wild geese, through the winters of interminable night, when they harnessed their sled dogs by the green light of the aurora. Perhaps the ancient life of men in caves still lived in their names for constellations: the Caribou and the Wolf (in the Big Dipper region of the sky); the Pleiades were "Branches on Antlers." And a magic song ran

> I will take care not to go toward the dark
> I will go toward the day

It will bear repeating that Eskimos are regarded as distinct from Indians, and that Indians (far outnumbering the Eskimos) also inhabit some regions of the North. In the hundreds of miles of tundra and thousands of miles of great black forests inland from the Inuit, in a huge land encompassing nearly half of all Canada and much of interior Alaska, there lived almost numberless bands of Indian people. For the most part they were of two basic language stocks, Algonquian on the east and south, Athapaskan on the west and north, but all lived by hunting, fishing, and gathering, and led therefore similar lives.

Big game, depending on the season and the place, was moose, caribou, bear, deer, and for those in mountain country sheep and goats. Small game was everything else. Summer travel was best by canoe (sometimes of birchbark) on the almost numberless lakes and streams; in the winter snowshoes, of a great variety of styles, became a necessity for many.

The largest area of their land, the Canadian Shield Subarctic, had been tremendously glaciated in past ages. Its lakes and waterways occupied depressions left by mountain ranges of ice; its rivers had not cut their channels through time but meandered like trickles (frequently rip-roaring trickles) on a window.

Slain animals were honored by placing antlers and skulls above the meat racks; some propitiated with especially solemn ceremony the soul of a slain bear, as among some Eskimos and many other hunting people, and for that matter as among the Ainu of Japan and as among some Old World Paleolithic men of more than 50,000 years ago.

They lived near neighbors with hunger; literal starvation was in winter never very far beyond the horizon. Most were subject to food-saving customs of infanticide and abandonment of aged parents. The hard life was especially hard on women. In addition, some groups, such as the Athapaskan-speaking Chipewyan, had a reputation for treating their women harshly. Others, such as the Algonquian-speaking Cree, were said to be particularly kind to women (and even to orphans). Cree women (possibly as a result) were famous for their beauty.

Below the vast country of the Cree the other great Algonquian-speaking division, the Ojibwa (Chippewa), along the present U.S. boundary in the Great Lakes region, its northern bands hunting moose, its southern bands harvesting wild rice (both made maple syrup), became the best known Indian nation in America in the mid-nineteenth century, due to the use of its literature in the famous poem that, as has been mentioned, mistakenly named an Iroquois as protagonist, Hiawatha.

The Athapaskan-speaking people of northwestern Canada and interior Alaska, some of them still today the least-known Indians of North America, are divided by ethnologists into (usually) twenty-one main tribes, Chipewyan much the largest. These were not tribes in the customary sense of the word, but quite unorganized groups of scattered bands more or less alike in speech and ways of life. With the coming of Europeans and the fur trade, bringing trading posts into Indian country, a basic reorganization took place. The primary concern was no longer merely a search for game as daily food. The primary concern over all the fur trade area became finding and gathering what the trading posts wanted to buy: furs of beaver, sealskin, blue fox, whatever the region offered.

This meant establishing a trapping territory, within a hunting territory furnishing enough game to flesh out the trading post's flour and sugar and tea. It also meant returning to this same territory each year, and making some effort to conserve its resources, both of fur and of game.

Groups broke up and re-formed, sometimes with violence, invasion, fighting, deaths, in accordance with this principle, and formed coalitions and waged guerrilla warfare for control of routes to the trading post and to maintain middleman contact with the trader.

The different peoples were named and renamed by the traders' reports. Thus some Chipewyans trading at Lake Athabaska were known as Athabaska people, and thus Alexander Mackenzie, with trading headquarters at Lake Athabaska, spoke of them as Athabaska Indians in his account of a journey across the continent in 1789 and 1793. Albert Gallatin, "synopsizing" North American Indians in 1836, then took from Mackenzie's use the term "Athapascas" for all the language-related people of the western Subarctic, and John Wesley Powell, classifying North American Indian languages in 1881, then took the name for the name of their language—the most widely distributed of all Indian language families in North America.

Oddly enough, there seem to have been more Algonquian-speaking Cree people than Athapaskan-speaking Chipewyan people around Lake Athabaska in Mackenzie's time, and the name does not seem to come from any word in the Athapaskan language.

Large groups of northern Athapaskan hunters lived in and about the valleys of the Yukon and Mackenzie Rivers, sometimes occupying very extensive country (the Mackenzie River system being the second longest in North America). One such group, in a number of divisions, was the Kutchin—one division was known in earlier times as Yukon Flats Indians.

Divisions of another group, the name of each division terminating in –tine (Athapaskan name for themselves, the same word as Diné or Indé, meaning "the people"), included the Hare people, a traders' translation of their name, Kawchottine, meaning "the great rabbit people." They were said to survive the winters on the white hare called snowshoe rabbit by the unlettered, which mysteriously vanished for a season every seven or every nine years (specialists debate), bringing very real starving times.

The Thlingchadinne (–tine in still a different spelling) lived southeast of the Hare; their name, "dog-flank people," was said to refer to a myth of a dog ancestor (totem?); traders called them the Dogribs. East of the Dogribs, south of the Copper Eskimos, were the Tatsanottine, "copper people," from the copper tools they made out of the native metal near Coppermine River; the traders' name here became the Yellowknife. Southwest of the Yellowknives were the Etchaottine (meaning unknown), a group said to have been much victimized by the Cree in early fur trade times. Traders adopted the contemptuous Cree name for them, Slave people, or, in more genial traderese, Slaveys. They were noted for treating their women with much kindness, men even constructing the lodge and bringing in firewood; they were also eccentric for refusing to abandon or kill their aged and infirm parents, at whatever cost in trouble or food supply. South of the Slave country's Great Slave Lake the Tsattine ("beaver people") also had a history of fur-war suffering at the hands of the Cree. (The Cree had guns first, from the early traders far to the east on Hudson Bay.)

West of the Beavers an unorganized group of bands called the Sekani had also experienced neighborly aggression from both Cree and Beavers; to their south were the Carriers, Athapaskan-speakers but with manners and customs picked up from the Northwest Coast nations at their western elbow. They did retain the law from which their peculiar name derived—requiring a widow to carry along in a basket for three years the ashes of her dead husband.

The land of the Cree in their several divisions stretched over an enormous area, around the southern shores of Hudson Bay to James Bay and well beyond into northern Quebec; much of their territory west of James Bay may have been seized during the great rearrangement of peoples brought on by the fur trade. Eastern neighbors of the Cree were two other Algonquian-speaking nations, so similar in most ways that they might be considered one people with two names, the Naskapi to the north, into the interior of Labrador, the Montagnais below them, all the way south to the gulf and river of St. Lawrence.

The featured role of the Naskapi-Montagnais in some backing and filling of ethnological theory in recent years—did they or did they not practice from ancient times a privatization of property—has been previously discussed.

The private possession of wealth and ostentatious display of its accouterments were certainly a desire, if not an obsession, of the people at the opposite end of the continent from the Naskapi-Montagnais, the Indians of the remarkable Northwest Coast culture.

One most noticeable difference between New World and Old World literature is the absence in the New of tales of sudden treasure—genre of Ali Baba, Aladdin, the numerous Jack tales—absent everywhere in the New World except on the Northwest Coast. There, Komogwa, master of all riches, and a number of similar deities figure prominently in religion, folklore, and proper thinking. Even, among some Northwest Coast peoples, the mythology of earthquakes was associated with riches, as in ancient Japan.

The Northwest Coast people are equally marvelous on several other counts. They produced a genuinely high culture (ranking with that of the Pueblos of the Southwest or the temple-mound people of the Southeast) without benefit of either agriculture or pottery, customarily the chiefest handmaidens of cultural progress. Alone among such high cultures of North America it was uninfluenced by the ancient civilizations of Mexico and points south; its ultimate affinities were more with northeastern Asia, although the Northwest Coast people vigorously disguised borrowed elements into their own highly individual patterns. Almost alone among such high cultures in the New World, it seemingly reached its zenith after contact with Europeans, rather than some centuries or millennia before (possibly with an assist from the steel wood-carving tools brought by the Europeans).

But the Northwest Coast trait most unusual among American Indians was the inordinate value placed on private property, on the acquisition of private property, the purpose being a bizarre and inordinately pompous display of personal munificence in throwing it away.

In its purest form the Northwest Coast way of life was seagoing, and fishing (salmon, cod, halibut) its mainstay. Roots and berries in the tall, lush, coastal forests furnished variety, camas root first of all, and cranberries and blueberries, and the Saskatoon berry that contains three times as much iron and copper as prunes and raisins.

Food was abundant, and easy to come by. Work in the spring and summer laid up enough for a year. The mild, idle winters were for luxury, a luxury that spawned fantastically intricate systems of ceremonials; of clans and the groups of clans known to the anthropological trade as phratries; of secret societies; a limitless wealth of decorated blankets, baskets, and boxes; an outpouring of fantastic wood carving; and a fantastic elaboration of social climbing.

Related families lived together in gabled plank houses with the house posts and door poles carved and painted with the family crest—from which developed the wooden memorial monuments we call totem poles.

Trees were hollowed out by fire and adze into great sixty-foot canoes of admirable workmanship, bounteously adorned with carving, "carved in grotesque figures and remarkably well handled," in the expert testimony of a British sea dog, Captain Sir Edward Belcher, R. N. (whose name adorns several spots in the Arctic map), referring to some Tlingit crews he saw in action in 1837.

A few of these people, notably the Nootka of Vancouver Island, used their barbaric longboats for harpoon whaling, the real McCoy, in which the whale was harpooned again and again and finally killed with a thrusted lance and then towed to shore.

Slat armor was worn in warfare, along with wooden helmets and (maybe) terrorizing carved masks. Mustaches and occasional beards were in fashion among some tribes, as among some Eskimos.

Slave raids and the resultant slaves were common; in ultra-rich villages slaves were said to make up nearly a third of the population; a Nootka chief of the early 1800s had "nearly fifty male and female slaves," reported an American captive.

Social classes (above the slaves) were divided into commoners and nobles, with here and there, as among the exceptionally powerful chiefs of the Haida of the Queen Charlotte Islands, a sort of embryonic royalty.

These were an emotional people, much given to weeping, melodrama, and soaring imagination. Mighty spirits, beings of boundless power, walked the earth—at least in the stories told in the winter, when the North Wind smoothed the sea:

Something wonderful came in and stood there. His
large eyelids were too powerful to look upon. Where he
placed his foot he stood for a while. When he took
another step the earth and the house shook.

The Northwest Coast way of life extended from the Tlingit in the north,
along the islands and coasts of southern Alaska (centered in the region of pre-
sent Sitka, the name of a Tlingit division), down through the Haida,
Tsimshian, Kwakiutl, Bellacoola, Nootka, and the Coast Salish of present
British Columbia and the Salish and Chinook of Puget Sound and the lower
Columbia river, to the Yurok, Karok, and Hupa of northern Calfornia.

Ways of doing things of course varied a great deal throughout this
immense distance. It was for a long time supposed that the heart and high
point of the Northwest Coast spirit was toward the north, with the Tlingit and
Haida its best models for certain aspects, the Kwakiutl or Tsimshian or Nootka
for others. Recently, though, a resistance movement against regarding some
cultures as "marginal" and others as "central" within a given culture area has
been gaining ground among the specialists.

Tlingit and Tsimshian people made the famous Chilkat blanket, woven
from cedar bark and the hair of the wild mountain goat into a mystic design
that was imbued, so they say, with the power of speech. The Tsimshian were also
the great traders, dealing in copper from the north and captured Salishan slaves
from the south, otter skins from the Haida, dentalium shells (a kind of West
Coast wampum) and candlefish oil from anywhere. Among the Tsimshian's
inland neighbors, the Athapaskan-speaking Carriers, ownership of a Chilkat
blanket signified a successful man (as evidence of Tsimshian salesmanship).

The Kwakiutl were (although connoisseurs argue) the premier wood
carvers, and apparently originators of the secret societies, each paying dramatic ceremonial homage to its protective supernatural patron, that spread
throughout the Northwest Coast.

Most of these national names meant, as usual, "people," and the Northwest
Coast styles spread over many varying peoples speaking varying languages.
These webs of language, large and small, became more complex and tangled
toward the south, approaching the Babel of tongues that was California. One
of the first great men in linguistics, arguing that language and culture have
nothing to do with each other, used the neighboring Yurok, Karok, and Hupa
of California as an example: each speaking a separate language, each of these
languages from a different North American language group, and yet all three
tribes very much alike in being typical of their culture area, that of the
Northwest Coast—which barely reached far enough south to enclose them.

The Columbia River region was another great aboriginal crossroads, similar to the lower Mississippi, and the language of the Chinook people there was used as the basis of a trading jargon spoken far and wide over the Northwest, eventually from California to Alaska. In the meantime, (perhaps to prove that all language is vain) the Chinook themselves merged with another tribe (the Chehalis) and dropped their own language entirely.

But the Chinook jargon remained very much in business. One of its minor accomplishments was *hootchinoo*, "liquor," from Hutsnuwu, Alaskan tribal name associated with liquor-making, giving us "hooch" in slang. A major contribution changed Nootka *patshatl*, "giving," into "potlatch," the headline feature of the Northwest Coast ceremonial action, a feast staged to celebrate any occasion, in which gifts were given out and wealth was thrown away, all redounding to the fame of the giver.

Potlatches became contests of squandering between rival clan chiefs. Precious oil would be thrown on the fire at a "grease feast" until guests were singed by the flames, and an opulent chief might kill a valuable slave with the special club known as a "slave killer" and contemptuously fling the slave's scalp to his opponent, or might break and destroy an even more valuable "copper" (plates of wrought copper, regarded as very high-priced currency), an act roughly equivalent to lighting a cigar with $1,000 bill.

Some potlatches were minor affairs and some even clowning imitations, but the real ones, the great ones, were carried out with intense formality, the rivals singing songs of insult:

"What will my rival say again, that 'spider woman,' what will he pretend to do next? . . . Will he not brag that he is going to give away canoes, that he is going to break coppers? . . . Do you know what you will be like? You will be like an old dog, and you will spread your legs before me when I get excited. You did so when I broke the great coppers 'Cloud' and 'Making Ashamed,' my great property. . . . This I throw into your face."

The humiliated loser sometimes sailed off to war and deliberately threw away his life, out of sheer chagrin. More importantly, the entire clan or social group of the potlatcher won or lost face as a result of these contests, and the whole group more or less participated to make the really grand potlatches possible, a spur to industry that may have played its part in the growth of the Northwest Coast culture.

The Kwakiutl complicated the potlatch system with a practice of involved loans and repayments, purchases and re-purchases, frequently connected with a position in the *numaym*, a property-owning social group perhaps vaguely reminiscent of the group of retainers attached to a noble house in medieval Japan. One could marry into the numaym, sometimes leading son-in-law and father-in-law into complex deals that would frazzle a Hollywood agent.

Obviously, among the Northwest Coast people wealth was, as said an early authority, "considered honorable, and it is the endeavor of each Indian to acquire a fortune." The objective, though, being "not so much the possession of wealth as the ability to give great festivals."

The idea of gaining prestige by giving away things of value is a thread noted before (as among the Iroquois chiefs who kept themselves poorest of all by constant giving) in the basic fabric of Indian life, and the specific idea of a public giveaway in celebration of some specific event, a naming, a coming of age, a grief at death, existed in a number of Indian societies that exhibited no particular interest in wealth as such.

As in some other Indian groups the Northwest Coast notion of property also extended to a variety of intangibles, possessions that could not be so freely given away and remained individual possessions until (often) bequeathed as individual inheritances. Thus in some Northwest Coast communities, titles or memberships in certain religious or social orders, professions such as carving or boatbuilding or maskmaking, ownership of certain songs or dances, might be handed down from the mother or the father (or the father-in-law) depending on the custom of reckoning descent. It was the obsessive accumulation of wealth, sometimes including the use of interest (possibly picked up from trading-post practice), and the obsessive sacrifice of the wealth that appears to be unique.

Besides the difference in the objective of riches there was an odd difference in the picture of riches, not easy to analyze. The Haida song (very freely rendered) previously noted may bear repetition as an example:

> a rich woman
> cedar bark and slaves within reach
> sitting above a dish of steamed halibut
> eating with a spoon
> but a powerful spirit entered and stood there, the house shaking, and then
>   cut her through and buried her bones and wore her skin and became
> a rich woman
> cedar bark and slaves within reach
> sitting above a dish of steamed halibut
> eating with a spoon.

Young men and women of many Indian nations went alone into the forest to fast and pray and seek a guiding vision, but on the Northwest Coast the right to do so and sometimes the blessing of the vision as well (transformed into the ritual of a secret society) became an item of property to be inherited.

Membership in a secret society brought high prestige as well as high drama. The drama was the keen clear note of fearful life unchanged from ancient ages: for here again the cult of the Bear appeared, and the cult of the Cannibal, echoes from the dawn of man.

Sang the people, while the Bear dancer danced and juggled glowing coals and threw them among the onlookers, sometimes setting fire to their cedar-bark clothes, and while the Bears of the Bear Society, wrapped in their great black bearskins, angrily clawed the earth:

> How shall we hide from the bear that is moving
> all around the world?
> . . . Let us cover our backs
> with dirt that the terrible great bear from
> the north of the world may not find us.

The initiate of the Kwakiutl Cannibal Society fasted in the woods until, emaciated and hysterical, he appeared for the frenzied dance of initiation.

He was lured into the house of the Society by a naked woman, dancing backward, enticingly, holding in her outstretched arms a corpse.

The Cannibal dancer followed her step for step, trembling, drawn on as if against his will, and in the house was seized with wildness and bit flesh from the arms of the communicants around him, and in ecstasy he danced, while the people sang for him:

> Now I am about to eat,
> My face is ghastly pale.
> I am about to eat what was given me
> by Cannibal
> at the North End of the World.

The ceremony ended with a ritual feast of dog, stand-in for human flesh in mock-cannibal performances in a number of Indian societies.

But anyone could see spirits in secret dreams, and the spirits could be prayed to. Toward the southern periphery of the Northwest Coast world, below the present Canada–U.S. boundary, this spirit dreaming was of much moment; and reverent young dreamers deep in the cathedral forests of Douglas fir or towering Redwood prayed, with all the devotion of their beings, "I want to be rich."

The fur trade was the great bringer of technological civilization— in this case it should certainly be "civilization" in quotes—to the great majority of the people of the North, Indians and Inuit alike. Its chief apostles were the agents of the "Governor and Company of Adventurers of England Trading Into Hudson's baye," organized in 1670 to compete with French *coureurs de bois* for the prime "oiled beaver" (skins worn next to the body for a season, hair side in) of the Cree and their northern neighbors.

The other great English fur combine, the North-West Company, began to get under way in the 1770s; in 1796 it split temporarily into rival factions that spent no less than 195,000 gallons of liquor on the Indians during a two-year trade war. The inevitable conflict between the North-West Company and the Hudson's Bay Company reached a bloody climax in 1816, with a veritable war on the Red River of Canada; the two companies merged five years later.

Epidemics of the newly arrived Old World diseases took a terribly heavy toll, among hunting people whose food ceased when they fell ill. A comparatively lucky group was described by David Thompson (trailfinder for the North-West Company) in 1781: "we went up the bank to the camp and looked into the tents, in many of which they were all dead, and the stench was horrid; those that remained had pitched their tents about 200 yards from them and were too weak to move away entirely, which they soon intended to do; they were in such a stage of despair and despondence that they could hardly converse with us, a few of them had gained strength to hunt which kept them alive."

Throughout the North the survivors, says a medical historian, were a "mere handful" of the original populations. The people were consumed, wrote Alexander Mackenzie in 1793, "as the fire consumes the dry grass of the fields."

As has been described, the hunting economy of the northern forests was altered to a commercial fur-trapping economy, and the winter supply of game was altered to flapjacks (potato chips and pop added today) from the H.B.C. or "the Bay" (Canada's names for the Hudson's Bay Company) trading posts. Caribou, butchered by the herd for their hides in the nineteenth century, virtually disappeared from some parts of their range. "High wine," virtually (I can't resist the irony of adverbial virtue in these iniquities) straight alcohol, to be diluted (plenty) by the trader, disrupted the people, the families, the hunting, and every aspect of life possibly even more deeply than the incredible numbers of deaths from disease.

Missionaries and whalers contributed to early European influence in the north country. The Moravian United Brethren, after much difficulty and some loss of life, established in 1764 a noteworthy mission among the Labrador Eskimos. Danish missionizing in Greenland, begun in 1721, led to trading posts and Danish colonization. Nineteenth-century whalers summered so regularly with the Polar Eskimos that their local nickname was *upernagdlit*, "sign of spring." New Bedford whalers working Hudson Bay were frequently crewed by Aivilik Eskimos of the bay's far northwestern shores. Greenland Danes thought this habit of working together put whalers and Eskimos on good terms, helping to bring better results in the eastern Arctic than the disastrous record hung up by European invasion in Alaska and the West.

The foggy, raw, and windy climate of the Aleutians and the southwestern coast of Alaska, while often defined by its denizens as miserable, is much less rugged than that of the rest of Eskimo country. ("It doesn't rain in the Aleutians, it rains in Asia and blows over," said the GIs of World War II.) The Inuit here have certain marked differences in dialects and styles of life (the Aleuts, as already noted, are such extreme variants they scarcely pass for cousins), so different that two broad Inuit divisions have been suggested: Arctic Ocean Eskimo and Pacific coast Eskimo, with the breaking point in the vicinity of Norton Sound in Alaska. Coastal Inuit below this point were still kayakers, of course, and some were whalers, but the more usual food for some villages became salmon and birds, and an un-Eskimo interest in social status and costume hats appeared, reflecting the Northwest Coast people next door to the south.

In the Aleutian Islands and Alaska, the fur trade came from Russia, led by the freebooting Siberian frontiersmen called the *promyshlenniki* (the word means "traders") who killed with true frontier abandon whatever they found on the beaches—seals, the six-foot Bering Sea king crabs, or the artistic, "mild, polite, and hospitable" Aleuts. Some organization was imposed on the carnage when the Russian American Company was given a fur monopoly by Russian imperial decree in 1799—by that time the Aleuts were said to have been reduced to one-tenth of their pre-promyshlenniki population. The survivors were put to work as sea-otter hunters and voyaged under Russian command as far south as Santa Barbara in southern California. Eighty Aleut sea-otter hunters helped colonize the Russian post of Fort Ross in northern California in the 1820s.

A Russian base was established among the Inuit on Kodiak Island during the bloody promyshlenniki times, and many years later (1799) a fort on the Alaska mainland at what is now Sitka. The first edition of this was destroyed rather promptly by the Tlingit, and only re-occupied a couple of years later with the help of a Russian naval vessel passing by on a round-the-world tour. But casualties in this were heavy—dozens of Russian dead, and more than 100 of their Aleut laborers killed.

A Russian post was founded at Norton Sound, on the Bering Sea, in 1832, and in its contacts with the Eskimos there, and with the remaining Aleuts, the

Russian company did make some real effort to look after their welfare; the health of the fur trade, after all, depended on the health of the local people gathering the furs. It is reported, for example, that syphilis first reached Norton Sound not from the Russians, but from an American telegraph crew in 1866.

The Russian advance into the New World brought a hurried response from the Spanish in a voyage up the Northwest Coast to Alaska in 1773 and 1774. Thereafter trading ships of various nations called with increasing frequency at Nootka Sound on Vancouver Island. Fast and loose trade with the Nootka people resulted in several savage massacres—a Yankee vessel, the *Boston*, was attacked and destroyed in 1803 (a year after the Tlingit destruction of the Russian fort in their country). Another ship, the *Tonquin*, suffered a similar attack in 1811, these earning for the whale-hunting Nootkas a well-deserved reputation as dangerous customers. But this didn't keep further trading ships from undertaking the long journey from Boston, all the way down to the tip of South America, through the difficult straits there, and all the way up the Pacific coast of both Americas. It was this continuing trade that brought the influences that revolutionized Northwest Coast life, that brought new foods (delicious potatoes!), and that brought the previously mentioned steel tools, sending the art of the Northwest coast into a most glorious sunburst—but that came at sunset.

The Russian advance from the north and west also brought a response in Alexander Mackenzie's transcontinental journey, and in the arrival of Lewis and Clark at the Pacific twelve years later, in 1805, and the subsequent establishment of English and American trading posts roundabout the lower Columbia River. In the 1830s American and Canadian missionaries appeared in Oregon, and in the 1840s settlers; the world of the Northwest Coast, its potlatches and its arrogant nobles, entered upon the days of its decline.

The Crimean War (raising justifiable fears that Great Britain might lay hands on Russian possessions in America) set Russia to dickering with the United States for the sale of Alaska. The sale was finally made at a price of $7,200,000, one ninety-fourth of the amount since taken out of Alaska in gold alone.

Transfer took place on Friday, October 18, 1867, at Sitka, where American officials and troops arrived by a steamer which also brought one Hayward Hutchinson, a Baltimore business man who did a little business that day with representatives of the Russian sealing monopoly. Back in San Francisco he helped organize the Alaska Commercial Company, which obtained from the Grant administration in 1870 a monopoly lease of the Pribilof Islands with their priceless seal fisheries.

Military occupation of Alaska continued for ten years, to the detriment (sources seem to agree) of the native people. A young army officer's journal: "Phillipson's account of the 'old times' under the Russian government.' They was the most 'appiest people I ever see....' Contrast now.... Drunkenness, squalor. Debauchery, prostitution, stagnation." A standard history of Alaska, published in 1886: "At no period in the annals of Alaska were there so many Indian émeutes as during the few years of the [U.S.] military occupation; at no period were lust, theft, and drunkenness more prevalent among Indians and white people alike. After the withdrawal of the troops in June 1877, disturbances among the natives became fewer in number and less serious in character."

The Alaska Commercial Company, during the twenty years of its lease, netted many millions of dollars for its few (sixteen in 1872) stockholders and left the seal herds marvelously depleted. It claimed, however, to have improved the lot of the Aleuts who lived on the Pribilof Islands. Missionaries claimed otherwise. The company was the subject in 1876 of a congressional investigation that got nowhere; a U.S. Treasury agent stationed in Alaska to guard the public weal against overexploitation happened also to be the company's Superintendent of Seal Fisheries.

Would-be competitors kept the company under a fairly constant fire for years, charging in effect that Alaska was maintained as its private pork barrel and subjected to merciless plunder. Since the company controlled Alaskan trading posts and shipping, and thus exerted almost total control over travel in those parts, the charges were difficult to investigate.

With authoritative statistics in short supply, stories spun from fancy had a field day. Rumor related that whiskey, prostitution, and disease, liberated from the more rigid controls of Russian times, now left the Eskimo people dying out. There were official reports that whole communities were found dead from starvation as a result of the new institution of the summer drunk. Unofficial opinions from some hunters opined that the breech-loading rifle had done for the caribou and seal, leaving nothing for anyone, even if sober.

It is, of course, not possible to judge these reports from an Eskimo point of view, no matter how earnestly the best ethnologists may try to do so. Information is overwhelmingly from the intruders, and consequently alien. There was some factual evidence; later specialists have calculated that the Inuit population in Alaska may have been reduced by as much as half during these times, culminating in the 1880s. But most communities remained, and found hunting and fishing enough to continue their seasonal round of activities more or less unchanged.

It was at this epoch that an American Presbyterian missionary, Sheldon Jackson, set up shop in Alaska as superintendent of education. He wanted to save the Eskimos not only from starvation but from savagery as well—tales of subhuman primitivism among "natives" everywhere were also much in vogue at the time, especially in the literature of missionaries.

Arctic old timers (anyway, relatively old timers) talked to him of the Chukchi of Siberia who appeared to be downright prosperous with their herds of tame reindeer. This produced an idea that would even bring some education in the white man's profit-oriented ways, and Sheldon Jackson devoted years, the rest of his life, to a reindeer dream for the Eskimos of Alaska. Some were procured from the Chukchi, before Russia banned reindeer export in 1902, and many more from northern Norway and Finland, with Lapp families coming along as instructors. Small herds were given or loaned to a number of missions operating schools, some Eskimo youths went through the long apprenticeship to learn the herding business, a few bunches of immigrant reindeer went into Inuit hands. After years of haphazard results the reindeer experiment dwindled away. Devoting the community to following its herd interfered with all other community activity and custom, Inuit custom that in the long run prevailed, it would seem, in saving the Inuit of Arctic Alaska.

CHAPTER 26

Golden Hills, Crimson Blood

The land ran down in golden hills from the mountains to the sea, with green groves of oak in the folds between and poppies red on the slopes in their season. A little river, dry for half the year, curled along the bottom of the valley. This was the site of the present Los Angeles, and in the year 1602 there were probably a couple of dozen villages scattered here and there over its area, impermanent-looking clusters of mat-made huts and trash and tumbled baskets.

People probably related, in any case speaking the same language (a Shoshonean tongue), also lived on a couple of islands off the coast, the nearer now known as Santa Catalina or, in song and tourist promotion, as Avalon.

Three Spanish ships, commanded by a Basque navigator named Sebastian Vizcaino, put in at the nearer island on Santa Catalina's day (November 25) of the year 1602, and the diarist of the expedition wrote of the people who lived there: "*The women are very beautiful* and virtuous, the children are fair and blonde and very merry."

Some three weeks later the same little fleet explored an excellent bay 325 miles up the coast, which Vizcaino named after the Count of Monte Rey, the New Spain viceroy who had sent out the expedition. The crews of the three ships were riddled with scurvy, and sixteen men had already died since their departure from Acapulco, Mexico, seven months before; the explorers were scarcely in a condition to look at this particular new world (perfumed by a dead whale washed ashore, upon which bears fed by night) through rose-colored glasses.

Nevertheless, the Carmelite friar who was keeping the journal of the expedition wrote that the people of Monterey Bay were "affable, generous Indians, friendly to the point of giving whatever they had; they much regretted the Spaniards' departure, because they had so much affection."

The people of the California coast had been encountered now and then by other Europeans—English pirates, Manila galleoneers, previous Spanish explorers—for at least sixty years before the time of Vizcaino, and in general had been described as friendly, frank, handsome, lightskinned, of good stature and extraordinary strength. They could stride along for a mile carrying a weight an Englishman could scarcely lift, wrote a companion of Francis Drake's in speaking of the people north of San Francisco Bay; and he added that they were marvelous runners. Vizcaino in a letter to the Spanish king spoke of the plank canoes used by some of the southern California coastal and island people "in which they go to sea with fourteen paddle-men of a side, with great dexterity—even in very stormy weather," dashing over the water with such speed "that they seemed to fly."

The life described by these first foreign observers—the nearly naked men occasionally dressed in skins and the women in "aprons" of rushes, the fishing and food gathering, the multitudes of baskets (and the little round basketry hats of the women, resembling so exactly the caps of the acorns they so much used), the dancers with belts of deer-hoof rattles, the sweathouses in which the men sweltered of an evening before plunging into a cold stream for a bath—had been going on basically unchanged for a very long time.

In many material aspects this life of most of the California people was exceedingly spare and austere, "primitive," as the terminology used to have it, more primitive than that of any other region in the area of the United States with the exception of the Great Basin—the Nevada-Utah deserts—next door east.

Over most of California there was no agriculture; the people were technically at the bottom of the standard anthropological scale, hunter-gatherers. The gathering, however, was easy: grain, seeds, nuts and berries of all kinds; grasses of some two dozen genera were threshed for grain, as were multiple members of the aster family, such as dandelion, goldenrod, sunflower. Sweet clover was particularly desirable. Acorns furnished the main crop where oaks were plentiful, acorn flour made by a quite intricate process of pounding the acorns and leaching out the tannic acid. Mesquite beans took the place of acorns in the desert, pine nuts on the mountain slopes. In some areas the California buckeye, containing knockout drops (of hydrocyanic acid) so powerful that it was sometimes sprinkled in streams to stun fish, was preferred over the acorn, after its poison was removed (another intricate process). There was game in abundance, and fish and shellfish on the rivers and coasts.

There was only scarce and as a rule rather crude pottery; no general wealth of art (although some splendid special), except in basketry; few elaborate dance

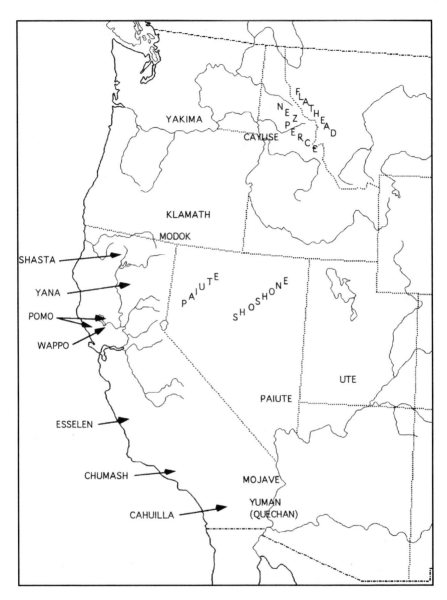

Western United States

costumes, no carved and painted masks; no leagues and confederacies and formally organized governing councils.

Good living made for heavy population, and California was more heavily populated than any other region north of Mexico. And there is a frequent supposition that good living and dense population bring material progress. But ancient California does not bear this out in the least.

The people there were mostly in small or medium-sized groups with a bewildering variety of backgrounds and languages. Each group usually inhabited a country marked out with some precision and regarded as having been forever theirs. Most seemed to assert they had sprung from the soil where they lived; there were comparatively few migration legends.

Evidence appears to indicate a tranquil sameness century after century, penetrating enormous depths of time. It is necessary to set up stakes long ages apart to catch the slow motion of change, as with the Inuit and Aleuts. Some specialists have thought it possible the California past remained so static because the people deliberately preferred it that way (as has been mentioned previously in connection with the ancient Archaic), their life having attained a comfortable balance with the pleasant environment.

All this applies to material matters. It is possible some, maybe many, of the varying peoples might have occupied much of their leisure with spiritual matters, perhaps specifically with religious contemplation. The dream-songs of Yuman-speaking people in eastern California are still today noteworthy in American Indian literature; the surrealism of some of the Mojave song-cycles, requiring several days and nights to perform, has been much studied. In southern California the toloache ritual, a religious initiation involving visions brought on by the narcotic Jimson weed, may possibly have originated on Santa Catalina Island. California may have been, even prehistorically, a religious seed-bed.

Or perhaps the people were merely content with drifting and dreaming on their sunny oceans of time. Maybe the principal occupation was being very merry.

But bents of spiritual or religious thought, if present in prehistoric deeps of time, may have been ancient indeed, for the oldest tribes in California were possibly descendants of groups of the earliest people to enter the New World so long ago.

Likely candidates as descendants of the most ancient ancients were people speaking the dozens of related languages now gathered into the language family called Penutian, Wintu and Patwin tribelets in the Sacramento valley, Maidu and Miwok along the lower slopes of the Sierra, with occasional Miwok extensions to the coast, the Yokuts in the San Joaquin valley, or the Costanoans scattered along the coast from San Francisco Bay to below Monterey. Or the people of the language family now called Hokan, including the Chumash of the coast and islands around Santa Barbara (Vizcaino passed by there on Santa Barbara's day, December 4); the Pomo, along the coast north of San Francisco Bay with extensions inland to the twenty-mile-long Clear Lake; the Shasta, north of the mountain of the same name; and the Salinans, who ranged the highest coast line in the world, the coastal mountains south of Monterey now known as the Santa Lucia mountains (Vizcaino passed by there on Santa Lucia's day, December 13).

It is thought that newcomers spread into California from the north and from the southeast in the thousand years between 500 B.C. and A.D. 500. In the north some of these may have been such Athapaskan-speaking peoples as the Hupa, of the picture-postcard Hoopa valley on the Trinity River; and in the south groups such as the Cahuilla of the mountains and deserts east of modern Riverside, and the aforementioned people of the region of present Los Angeles, these speaking Shoshonean languages.

There was occasional gardening of sorts in some of the communities; and in what is now called Owens valley, east of the Sierra Nevada, the Paiute people along Bishop Creek practiced their extraordinary (extraordinary because unique) irrigation of large tracts of wild grasses and grass nuts. "Their ditches for irrigation are in some cases carried for miles, displaying as much accuracy and judgment as if laid out by an engineer, and distributing the water with great regularity," says an account of 1859. Some of the ditching is still in use today, one still known locally as Paiute Ditch.

But full-scale agriculture in California was practiced only by the Yuman peoples, such as the group now called the Quechan, living along the Colorado River bottoms in what is now the far southeastern corner of the state. His country was abundant in "maize, beans, cotton, tobacco, watermelons," wrote Quechan "Captain" Salvador Palma to the Spanish viceroy in 1776, and indeed, said early European explorers, Yuma crops were among the finest yet seen in the New World.

But even so the Yuman peoples were solidly Californian in their neglect of material goods ("the tallest and most robust people that I have seen in all the provinces, and their nakedness the most complete," said a Spanish explorer) and in their preoccupation with religious ideas. Songs, the "dream-songs" of Yuman-speaking people, are, as has been mentioned, still today outstanding in American Indian literature, consisting of intricate surrealistic patterns improvised on a theme that frequently seems to be only a foundation for this rich decoration. Related people speaking Yuman dialects—but not farmers—lived in the Mojave Desert of California, as well as in the region of present San Diego, and down most of the peninsula of Lower California.

All these different people and many more had become settled by about A.D. 1200 in their diverse little homelands.

During the same long epoch, from about A.D. 500 onward, other broad, gradual changes took place. The Northwest Coast culture reached down from the north to seduce a few river and coastal groups below the present Oregon boundary and perhaps to communicate the worship of the raven to the Santa Barbara country, where it became the worship of the giant California condor. And from someplace the Chumash seamen of the Santa Barbara coast learned to make their unusual plank boats, the pine planks joined with lashing of sinew and caulked with asphaltum. These plank canoes were not made by anyone else in North America, and were only known elsewhere in the hemisphere at a spot on the coast of Chile.

Among such people as the Pomo the art of basket-making reached a phenomenally high point, producing extravagant work dripping with feathers and beads. At Drake's Bay in 1578 these people showed Drake one of their famous feather baskets "so well wrought as to hold water." Virtuoso examples exist of tiny baskets the size of a pinhead, made with stitches too minute to be counted with the naked eye.

The lingering development of California societies brought, in time, refinements and new religious ideas, oddly localized. The rich ceremonialism of the Northwest Coast was fairly well limited in California to the few northern groups that had most fully absorbed Northwest Coast ways—particularly the Karok, Yurok, and Hupa. The Yuman chants remained important only to the Yuman desert peoples of the southeastern regions, centered along the Colorado River. The *toloache* initiation ritual was centered in southern coastal areas.

Feather-veiled Kuksu dancers, the "big head" dances of the Kuksu secret society, principal wintertime events to some communities of the great bloc of Penutian-speaking people of central California, including Patwin, Maidu, Miwok, and others, were ignored or only haphazardly copied by some neighboring communities. The Patwin, possible originators of the cult, did not pass it along (in aboriginal times) to their own brothers, their closest neighbors to the north, the Wintu. The Kuksu center among the Maidu appears to have been in the northwestern division known as the Konkow. The "mountain Maidu," northeastern communities, performed the dances but did not organize the Kuksu society. On the other hand some speakers of alien tongues became rather faithful converts, such as the Esselens and Salinans of Big Sur south to the headwaters of the Salinas River, and the Pomo of the redwood forests along the north coast and inland to the hills enclosing Clear Lake, all these people of Hokan languages.

Singing protectively over the adolescent girl and forcing her to hide her dangerous eyes so she would not wither trees or drive away the game were more or less universal, as such customs were practically universal over all western North America.

Annual rites to renew the world (with sometimes a New Fire ceremony) were in California most prominent in the northwest. Periodic rites of public mourning for the dead were mainly reported from central and southern regions. Often, at such a "cry," or simply at a funeral cremation, quantities of baskets and other valuable goods were burned (although sometimes articles were swapped or sold before the fire reached them).

Annual mourning rites (for nations as far apart as Maidu and Ojibwa) could fall near enough to Halloween or to the Mexican Day of the Dead or to the All Saints' Day and All Souls' Day cemetery observations of western Europe for a missionary connection to be suspected, but there are too many aboriginal indications. Connections with the pre-Columbian death cult in the Southeast, and thus indirectly with Aztec Mexico, could be more likely; more likely still fears and griefs rooting back to the birth of social life, properly including therefore endless varieties of mortuary customs. The highly cultured Huron people, for instance, celebrated a great festival of the dead every eight to twelve years at which the recent dead were re-interred, with much display and many grave goods (some of which were ceremoniously presented to kinfolk or officials); conceivable similarities may be found to the ways of the Chincheros people on the coast of Peru so many thousands of years before.

Song cycles and dance cycles were sometimes based on voluminous, dreamlike creation and animal myths maybe composed directly by unknown Homers among the mystical, mythmaking Californians. Or perhaps group ceremonies that evolved into seasonal dance cycles grew out of shaman-versus-shaman contests in which they tried to out-wizard each other. Ground-painting ceremonies doubtless came from the Southwest of the Pueblos. The bear dancers (who really turned into bears), and the dying god here and there in the theologies, and the spirit-impersonators of the Kuksu societies reminiscent of, among others, the Kachina dancers of the Pueblos, may also have been importations from other elsewhere.

But on the whole, imported ideas were not clearly evident. In a very general sense the California religious ideas, dark, obscurantist almost as if consciously artistic, were growths from the California soil.

Spain left the upper California coast more or less unattended for 166 years after the voyage of Vizcaino in 1602 and 1603. During that time the Spanish frontier of missions and mines, Indian vaqueros and leather-jacketed border soldiers, crept laboriously up through northern Mexico to New Mexico, eastward into the "kingdom of the Texas," westward into southern Arizona and the desolate peninsula of Lower California.

As swollen Spain grew older and more tired the movements of such expansion became more and more reflex responses to alarms real or imaginary: to the menace of the French in Louisiana, or of the Illinois French working their way westward to the Rocky Mountains, or of the Canada English working their way westward to the Pacific. In the middle of the eighteenth century the new threat appeared of the Russians in the Aleutians and Alaska, seemingly ready to swallow up the whole Pacific coast. This coincided with the Spanish colonial renaissance under Charles III, when for a brief generation new vigor surged through the veins of the Spanish empire. The Spanish occupation of California, "Upper California" as it was first called, resulted.

In the spring of 1769 Spanish frontiersmen, priests, soldiers, and Indian allies were at San Diego, and in the spring of 1770, after many difficulties, a Spanish expedition was at Monterey "to occupy and defend the port [in the oft-quoted ironic remark of the expedition's commander] from the atrocities of the Russians."

In the next fifty years or so twenty-one mission stations were planted from San Diego to Sonoma, accompanied by six tiny garrisoned presidios and settlements of colonists. The missions gained their sustenance from Indian lands and Indian labor, and in return undertook to educate the Indians in the ways of Christianity and Spanish civilization and thus prepare them to become responsible colonial subjects.

The "Mission Indians," the people of about 700 miles of mainly coastal country, were only a fraction of California's total Indian population, and of these only a fraction became Christian. Converts numbered 21,100 in the missions' best year, 1820.

They lived in large pueblos at the missions, laboring at every trade from adobe making to soap making, sheepherding to pigeon tending. They were restrained from going back to the "monte"—back to their old free life—although groups would now and then be given a few weeks off to gather wild fruit in the woods and the hills, both literally and figuratively: figuratively in proselyting for new converts or coaxing runaway neophytes to return. Discipline was maintained by such corporal punishments as shackles, hobbles, stocks, imprisonment, or flogging—although no more than twenty-five lashes a day; and women, says a report of 1800, were only rarely flogged.

Runaways were a constant problem, and the terrible death rate ("sickness and death dealt unsparingly among them," in the words of one observer) a greater problem still: on the basis of mission records the total loss to the

Mission Indian population between 1769 and 1833 has been estimated at seventy-two percent.

In the main the myth-shrouded world of the California coast people, idle and merry, appeared to collapse almost at the first toll of a mission bell. There were a few armed revolts but none of much consequence—these people were hopelessly simple when it came to making war. Indeed the superior Chumash, the matchless artists of the coastal country (their prehistoric rock paintings among the world's finest), were rated by some early writers as "dull of intellect" because of their low grade "progress in warfare," although defended by another local authority on the basis that the Chumash "scarcely understood the use of arrows" not because of stupidity but merely because their "life was gentle."

Resistance, where it occurred, tended to emphasize such passive measures as the persistent abortions practiced by the sullen women (Chumash here too) of a mission district near Santa Barbara, as noted in a report of 1810. Abortion and infanticide presumably played some part in the spectacularly low birth rate at the missions—29,000 in a cumulative total from 1769 to 1833 (and of those born, some three-quarters died in infancy), as against 62,000 deaths in the same period.

It would seem that the collapse of their world changed the very look of the people. Travelers during mission times describe Indians markedly different in appearance from the tall, candid, handsome natives seen by the early voyagers 200 years before: the Mission Indians are invariably pictured as short rather than tall, dark rather than fair, and above all dirty and spiritless.

The motivation of the describer may have played a part in this—early explorers, eager to encourage further expansion, exploration, missionizing, often larded their reports with praise of the new country and all its works, while later observers, usually foreigners having an irritable time of it with everyone, just as often found all they encountered, including the people, detestable (as irritable foreigners, including Americans abroad, are still inclined to do).

In reality the Costanoan people of part of the coast undoubtedly were short and dark, but the Chumash were undoubtedly not and the Yuman people of still another part of the coast were known for tallness ("man size" was an average six feet), as well as for darkness of color. Maybe crowded living, heavy new clothes, drudging labor, altered diet, suppression of the cleansing sweathouse, helped make the people dirtier and less cheerful, and maybe suppression of such pagan (but incidentally bleaching) cosmetic aids as washing the hair with urine, or plastering the hair and face with mud or clay for several hours—to give gloss to the hair and kill vermin—made the people darker. Maybe shrinkage of the spirit made them shorter.

A European artist writing of San Francisco Mission in 1816 quoted a mission Father describing the natives as "lazy, stupid, jealous, gluttonous, timorous; never have I seen one laugh, never have I seen a single one look you in the face. They have the air of taking interest in nothing."

The missions flourished mightily, however, in a material sense, with an easy commodity prosperity that combined with the stringent discipline to produce a society of closed minds and open hands, a plump insular society almost hermetically sealed off from the rest of the world, especially after 1781 when the people along the lower Colorado River closed the overland route between Mexico and California.

Thousands of horses and hundreds of thousands of cattle and sheep grazed on the millions of acres of mission lands, and crops of wheat, corn, and beans ran to 120,000 annual bushels. Mission storerooms were treasure houses of wine, leather, wool, oil, and other such riches.

Given enough time such going concerns might still have transformed the Mission Indians, shrunken spirits notwithstanding (and even shrunken population—the general mission population did appear to be making a slight actual upturn along toward the end) into the solid basis of a Hispanicized native people in the typical Spanish colonial pattern.

But time ran out for Spain while the colony of California was still an unassimilated frontier. The missions were in business, on the average, only a bare half century. In the early years of the nineteenth century a wind of revolt, born of the American and French Revolutions, ran round the world. Rather suddenly, the 300-year-old Spanish empire was blown apart. Between 1811 and 1825 most of Spain's New World colonies won their independence. Mexico became an independent kingdom in 1821 and a republic only three years later. In California, for the moment remaining a possession of Mexico, revolution first made itself felt in the destruction of the wealthy missions, which were secularized in the middle 1830s.

Theoretically this secularization was supposed to give the mission lands back to the Indians, thus making the Mission Indians a self-sustaining people. In practice, the missions were carved up to form the great California ranchos ("a wild carnival of looting"), and the Mission Indians were scattered like quail. Many, especially among the people who had been brought from the inland valleys, returned to their homes and tried, for the time, to resume their ancient life. Other survivors turned into peons on the ranchos or free-lance vagrants about the coastal settlements.

This was California's pastoral interlude, this Mexican epoch of the great ranchos, when the rancheros and their enormous families and a few handfuls of urban families, some 4,000 people all told, lived a gracious, leisurely life, a life of music, horses, abundant love-making and ever-ready prayers, an idle, merry life, in fact, preoccupied with games and religion, over the bones of the thousands of coastal Indians who had lived their idle, merry life, preoccupied with their games and religion, on the same rivers and coasts and town sites so short a time before.

A few old people, both Indian and white, could easily have still remembered in the 1830s the first meetings forty or fifty or sixty years before; it must have seemed to them that only a moment had passed since the Indian had looked up, all nature teeming in the prism of his eye, to welcome the strangers and their gods.

Recruited from both ex-Mission Indians and gentiles (wild Indians) the Indian peons worked as tanners, saddlers, farmhands, and above all as vaqueros. On California ranches unto recent times a Spanish-speaking cowboy who wanted to lay claim to being a top hand stated the proverbial boast, "*Me crié entre los Indios* (I was raised among the Indians)." A British travel writer described a California Indian he met on the Santa Fe Trail in the 1840s as "a young centaur, who handled his lasso with a dexterity that threw all the Mexican exploits I had previously seen into the shade."

For the most part, though, the Indian peons, relegated to a servile status seldom better and sometimes worse (they had no cash value to their master) than that of black slaves in the American South, did not share too well in the gracious living of the period.

The distribution (to deserving politicians and their kin) of the immense mission spoils was only being completed at the time of the American conquest of California in 1846, during the Mexican War. The discovery of gold came two years later, the stampede of the California gold rush followed, and by the autumn of 1850 California had become a full-fledged American state.

The non-Indian population jumped from 10,000 in 1845 to nearly 93,000 in 1850, according to the federal census of that year, or to some 160,000 according to a claim by the state government after a census of its own in 1852.

The population of Indian California before the arrival of any Europeans is estimated to have been something more than 300,000 people. The epidemics and the attrition of Spanish and Mexican times may have reduced this figure by 1848 to something like 175,000, most of these in the mountains and interior valleys where they had not yet fully enjoyed the experience of white "contact."

The newly arrived gold rushers and companion pioneers killed these people off in what seems to have been the biggest single spree of massacring in U.S. history. Some guesses say there were perhaps as many as 100,000 still left by 1851, perhaps 30,000 by 1859. A fairly dependable count in 1880 gives no more than 20,000 left at that time. These may have dwindled away to still somewhat less by the end of the century.

The thousands of newcomers to California brought with them the Indian policy of the American frontier—clear the redskins out. The California Indians obligingly furnished depredations, occasionally killing or robbing the bearded miners or isolated settlers or driving off livestock.

The California Indians were, as a whole, even more obliging by being so far from formidable in a fight. Whooping bands of the new California citizens formed companies of Indian fighters and butchered Indians with abandon in a long series of Indian "wars" that are all regarded as illegitimate by modern California historians.

However, the Indian fighters asked and received pay and expenses from the government, a point that became increasingly important as the diggings played out and times grew hard. The U.S. government reimbursed the state of California $924,259 between 1850 and 1859 for this sort of semi-pro Indian killing, exclusive of the expenses of the U.S. Army in policing California Indian country and suppressing "uprisings."

Prostitution and venereal disease ran rampant among gold-country Indians, and gang rapes of Indian women became so flagrant that the press put aside proper prudishness and took cognizance. Indians of California had no police protection, were not permitted to testify in court, could not bring a damage suit or accuse a non-Indian of any legal infraction, could be picked up and jailed indefinitely without warrant, bail, or any charge (or could be sold at auction by the court), held no property rights, and could be driven away wherever a non-Indian wished to prospect or settle.

The first California state legislature passed in April 1850 a law entitled an Act for the Government and Protection of Indians, which was in reality a thinly veiled authorization for whites to hold Indian slaves. This may have been essentially the work of pro-slavery elements in the new state—their political party was called the Chivalry—as a move in the free-state/slave-state bargaining of the epoch (California's constitution, just enacted, prohibited slavery in the state). Slavery itself seems therefore to have been the objective of the new law, rather than Indians, who were in comparison of only minor interest.

As evidence of this, even an Indian's life was of no interest whatever to the new society. No non-Indian, "of whatever ethnic origin, could be held responsible for the death of a native, nor could any legal action be taken against him."

Massacres of Indian people took place anywhere and upon any pretext. One that appears to deserve a reasonably serious look more than most, not having been carried out by the boys from the corner saloon but by the U.S.

Army, and in retaliation for the murder undoubtedly by Indians of two white men, took place on an island in Clear Lake in 1850. Abundant evidence, however, indicated the two white men were guilty of numerous criminal acts, including murder, against the Indians who finally attacked them. Further abundant evidence indicates that the Indians who killed the two white men were not among the band of Pomo people shot to pieces by the troops on what was known afterward as Bloody Island.

Some outrage was expressed at the time over the Army killing these people without regard to age or sex; but some defenders of the military asserted only warriors had been killed, although admitting that some women may have drowned in trying to escape. Since the assault was begun with mountain howitzers, and shellbursts are not noted for respecting such distinctions, it is not possible to believe sex and age were carefully considered.

A Pomo interpreter, born in the 1860s, wrote out years later an account of this incident based on statements of survivors he had heard during his life. One "old lady a (Indian)," told of hiding in the tules and seeing men, women, and children killed indiscriminately; one wounded woman holding an infant was not far from her, and she "heared the woman say, O my baby," when two soldiers running past stabbed them. But another survivor saw other soldiers rescue a little boy about three years old from beside his dead father, wrap him in blankets and give him food and take him to safety by the fire. One old man who had been a youth at the time "said he sat down under a tree and cryed all day." The dead, by most guesses, totaled more than 100. Two of the soldiers were wounded.

With this sort of background, an obituary a few years later (1858) of a Sacramento Valley citizen could read, "Bill was a terror to the Indians, having killed a great many in his time; some of whom, as he said himself, he shot to see them fall."

A good many voices were raised against this behavior, but they were not the ruling voices. From Clear Lake itself a correspondent wrote to a newspaper in 1859 of a "willful murder" in three savage dogs being set upon "an old Indian and his squaw . . . engaged in the harmless occupation of gathering clover . . . they tore and mangled the body of the squaw in such a manner that she died shortly after." The old man survived, although badly bitten. But the dogs, said the correspondent in angry irony, were only set on them "for fun, and they were only Diggers!"

Prevailing opinion held that the "Diggers," being so hopelessly alien, were hopelessly stupid. The alienness, as expressed in regard to a group called the Wappo who lived in and about the north end of what is now known as the Napa valley, included "their kindness," their "self-effacing behavior." "They spoiled their children." "They held firmly to their lands and families; however, property was essentially a disfavored concept. Private ownership almost implied piracy or seizure. One owned something only at the expense of someone else. . . . In most situations to force anyone to do anything is immoral." The Wappo may have been a rather extreme example of these excellent qualities—the name was derived from Spanish *guapo*, meaning excellent, in modern everyday Spanish a *guapa* is a *real* good-looking woman—but nevertheless, concludes the specialist quoted here, "these were in part attributes found widely in California." And, perhaps especially alien to a people suffering the fits of gold fever: "Life moved in a leisurely way with few excitements."

Or, among the Pomo, say other specialists, government was "achieved" through good behavior, consensus "as to what constituted appropriate behavior in all situations."

But to laborious whites, the Indian men spent hours in the sweat lodge, endlessly gambling or simply loafing. The women made endless social bees of leaching acorns, gathering clover or manzanita berries or the like, digging "Indian potatoes." The only thought really stirring to all seemed to be the prospect of a "big time," a gathering for fun and games or for certain ceremonies. Drunkenness of various hues became occasionally noticeable after the arrival of gold rush civilization.

Traditional tales about magic lizards or super slick Coyote (a country cousin of Till Eulenspiegel) seldom contained uplift—examples from the Wintu of northern California: the animal hero beats his wife so much he gives her warts; the animal hero spying on girls swimming sees one so young she is just entering puberty, and dives into the water and swims between her legs and rapes her; a neglected wife disguises herself to obtain sex from her magic animal husband, who is not amused when he learns of it and beats her until his wrist hurts. Are these all for big laughs? (Why are the women laughing?)

But from a division of the Wintu, also victims of massacres in those days, comes a little poem that is among the most quoted masterworks of all Indian literature—a few brief words speaking of the North Star:

The stars shining in the sky are my hair
the round rim of the earth which you see
binds my starry hair.

Neighbors of the Wintu in the Mount Shasta region, the Yana, for long believed a mysterious people with a language all their own but later placed in the Hokan language family, were, so pioneer tales attest, subjected to an exceptionally thorough massacre in the mid-1860s. Two white women were murdered, maybe by outlaw "Mill Creek Indians," fugitives from different tribes who had associated themselves with the Mill Creek Yahi band, southernmost cousins of the Yana.

Local people telling the story a generation later, in the 1890s, explained that in the 1860s there was a floating population of unsuccessful gold diggers in northern California who "had no use for Indians" and were "ready to kill them on slight provocation." The few settlers who lived among the Yana in friendship, and hired them to work on their ranches, were "overawed" when a couple of parties of white men, assuming the Yana were guilty of murder, set out to kill every Yana in the country. Yana men working for white ranchers at harvesting, men threshing hayseed in a barn, were killed without preamble (and their pay, if they had any, taken from their pockets). Women working in ranch houses, children playing games, all were slain on sight. Said the leader, shooting a child, "Nits will be lice."

A few were saved. One story told of a white woman throwing a quilt around three Yana women working in her house and standing in front of them, holding the ends of the quilt. "If you kill them you will kill me," said she—she was, as it happened, big with child, requiring "a deed too ghastly for even such heroes."

Says a modern specialist, "after this period only remnants of the Yana people survived."

Kidnapping of Indian children to be sold as servants or laborers was quite frequent. One recent authority, in a careful estimate from such records as exist, put the figure at something near 4,000 California Indian children stolen in the years from 1852 to 1867, "not counting women taken for concubinage or adults for field labor." A Sacramento newspaper stated in 1862 that some "pestilent" characters were killing the Indian parents in order to seize the children for sale, the price running from $30 to $200 per child.

It was not good to be a red man, or woman or child, in the new world of California established in the 1850s and 1860s.

And yet, as noted, there were many who spoke for the Indians, not only on the grounds of humanity but on the perhaps more telling grounds of economy. An official report to Congress in 1850 summarized that it was "*cheaper to feed the whole flock for a year than to fight them for one week.*" Said Benjamin D. (Don Benito) Wilson, ex-mountain man who had become a prosperous rancher in southern California, "None here but see and lament their sad condition . . . Humanity, not war, is the true policy for them."

Southern California, relatively untouched by the swarms of immigrants hotfooting it for the northern gold fields, was inclined to be less bloodthirsty about extinguishing all the Indians in sight. There were troublesome, half-wild Indians in the deserts not far distant from Los Angeles, but a reasonable peace was enforced by such peacemakers as Don Benito Wilson and Juan Antonio, noted chief of the still consequential Cahuillas (although Juan Antonio opened his career by leading Cahuilla forces allied to Mexican forces in a full scale massacre of ex-Mission Indians from San Luis Rey, suspected of murdering a group of Mexicans; guesses as to the number of Luiseño dead ran from 33 to 100).

The debauched ex-Mission Indians of Los Angeles furnished a revolving slave-labor force for years, regularly arrested for drunkenness on Saturday night in Nigger Alley and bailed out on Monday morning for $2 or $3 a head (paid to the court, not the Indian) by anyone who could use an Indian for a week's work. "I wish you would deputize someone to attend the auction that usually takes place on Mondays and buy me five or six Indians," wrote a ranch foreman to a Los Angeles associate in 1852.

The *aguardiente* sold to the Indians was real firewater, being sometimes mixed with corrosive acids, and gave rise to wild weekly jamborees in which Indian people of all ages and sexes brawled tooth and nail. "Those thousands of honest, useful people," wrote a Los Angeles resident of the 1850s, speaking of the local ex-Mission Indians, "were absolutely destroyed in this way."

Eventually, most of the surviving California Indians were placed on tatterdemalion little reservations (many of which grew steadily littler), there to finish dwindling away in comparative peace. They didn't vanish, quite, although many once-populous stocks became extinct. They were sacrifices, said a government inspector in 1858 (he meant it ironically, but the notion was all too common) for the "great cause of civilization, which, in the natural course of things, must exterminate Indians."

But mass extermination by the gun still went on, here and there, into the 1870s—an old-timer with a Mark Twain touch recalled years later an incident of 1871, when some ranchers in the Sacramento valley found a steer wounded by Indians (a group of Yahi people), trailed the Indians with dogs, cornered them in a cave, and killed "about thirty. . . . In the cave . . . were some Indian children. Kingsley could not bear to kill these children with his 56-calibre rifle. 'It tore them up so bad.' So he did it with his 38-calibre Smith and Wesson revolver."

The frontier process in California was on such a fast track that the California people seem hardly to hear the mission bell before they are gone. An aged Indian could have experienced the whole story, from the first appearance of Spanish colonizers to the destruction of the 1850s, in a single lifetime.

One island woman from San Nicolas, farthest offshore of the Santa Barbara Channel Islands, did even better in living the full circle of the drama.

In her time she had seen the Russian and Aleut sea-otter hunters bring death and carnage to the island, and later press gangs from the missions rounding up and taking away any islanders who could be caught.

In 1835 Mexican authorities removed the last of the natives still living on the island, and the woman was left behind when she ran back from the boat to find her child, who had been overlooked. The boat departed, and, although there was some talk of returning for her, no one really wanted to bother.

The child died after a time and the woman was alone and forgotten on the island for eighteen years. She had the houses of her people to live in, houses made of the ribs or jawbones of whales, walled with skins. There were fish, seals, birds, shellfish, and roots and berries for food, and the island's ancient gods belonged to her alone. The island is wrapped in incessant winds and fogs, heaviest in the summer when the seal cubs cry like babies. Bird-skins furnished warm and delicate gowns.

She was found by hunters and taken into a Santa Barbara that had become an American town, and efforts were made to locate some of the remnants of the thousands of Chumash and Santa Catalina Pepimaros who had inhabited the other offshore islands not so many years before. A number were turned up and brought to see her, but no one could understand her language.

She was good humored and frequently sang and danced, but something in the strange new world, possibly its food, possibly her multiform isolation within it, was too much for her and she died within a few months.

CHAPTER 27

From Sacajawea to Chief Joseph

The rainbearing west winds that sweep into California from the Pacific meet their finish when they hit the Sierra Nevada, the great wall separating California from the ordinary world. Eastward, rainfall remains diminished all the way to the famous Hundredth Meridian at Dodge City, Kansas; the dryest areas, known as the Great Basin, are centered in Nevada and Utah. Here in pre-Columbian times lived a number, evidently a rather large number, of bands of hunter-gatherers apparently preserving ways of life that had existed with pretty much no change at all for unnumbered thousands of years.

Each group roamed forever over a given territory around a recognized central site, picking a living—an immensely knowledgeable one—from the pastel deserts and the brilliant, flowery, barren desert mountains. They hunted and snared game large and small, from deer and antelope to grasshoppers and birds, gathered wild seeds and fruits, and made some use out of nearly every object within their horizon.

The usually unorganized bands are customarily identified by anthropologists on the artificial basis of language, as in California and the Subarctic of Canada. Most of those within the Basin country proper spoke some Shoshonean tongue, as did so many in neighboring southern California, and most had a Shoshonean look—short-legged and dark-skinned. The people known specifically as the Shoshoni occupied a great arc of country all the way from the Panamint Mountains and Death Valley in California through a wide swath in Nevada and contiguous belts in Utah and Idaho and on into the heart of the Rocky Mountains in Wyoming.

Some of the desert Shoshoni, such as the Gosiute of the shores of the Great Salt Lake, were abysmally poor; some of the Rocky Mountain Shoshoni were gorgeously rich and showy, as befitted people living in some of the most gorgeous and showy mountain country on earth, that of the Grand Tetons. Shoshonean languages are included in the large language family called by anthropologists Uto-Aztecan; the Utes ranged up and down Utah and east-ward into the Colorado Rockies. The people known as the Paiute (sometimes said to mean "true Ute") inhabited parts of Nevada and its borderlands, a huge tribe made up of a great many independent bands, divided into North and South Paiute by present students. Their irrigation of wild grasses, unique in the world, has been mentioned. The religious wave that came from one of their communities and spread over much of the American West will be dis-cussed later. A mountain branch of the Paiute, in Idaho and Wyoming, were known as the Bannocks.

Around the edges of the Great Basin there were some peoples of non-Shoshonean language who seemed in various respects to resemble Basin types. Such were the Washo, of the region between present Reno and Lake Tahoe, and the conspicuously fierce Klamaths and Modocs of the California-Oregon border. The Klamaths made the most beautiful and warlike arrows he had ever seen, said Kit Carson, and their bows could send those arrows, said a vera-cious missionary, clear through a horse.

Most of the dwellers in the limitless mid-Basin deserts were chronically poor and correspondingly weak. They made a little trouble, but not much, when miners and ranchers moved into their country. In the end they usually attached themselves to ranches or towns as casual laborers or beggars, and thus remained on the sunburned native soil where they had lived for so many generations.

But in the far western reaches, in the 1830s to the 1860s, Paiutes and friends raided California ranchos in great horse-rustling operations, fought a pair of formal little battles with the whites at Pyramid Lake in 1860, and gained western-story remark by making elegant horse-race pursuits of such desert interlopers as Pony Express riders and stagecoaches.

Some of the Northern Shoshoni of the Rocky Mountain slopes became horse people, and sometimes very good horse people—one migrating branch, known as the Comanche, produced perhaps the finest horsemen and the most redoubtable warriors in America, in the opinion of some experts who had had the hair-raising pleasure of their acquaintance in hostilities.

Lewis and Clark's providential and beloved girl guide Sacajawea came from the Shoshoni of the Rocky Mountains, having been captured in 1800 by Minnetarees (a name applied to both Atsina and Hidatsa people) in Atsina country on the plains and having wound up, by a set of curious chances, at the Hidatsa towns on the Missouri far to the east three years later, at the moment Lewis and Clark were in the neighborhood preparing to head west.

The historical importance of this happy accident can be overestimated; maybe the Lewis and Clark expedition could have made it to the coast anyway, without her services as interpreter, and without the horses she was able to get from her people when they reached the Shoshoni, and maybe Clark's party (Clark knew her as "Janey") could have extricated itself anyway from the Montana mountain passes on the way back without her help, and maybe subsequent constant friendship of the mountain Shoshoni for Americans, with its effect on far-western colonization and American possession of the Oregon country, would all have come to pass anyway. On the other hand, maybe not.

It is evident that Sacajawea had no sense of directing destiny. Meriwether Lewis said of her, "if she has enough to eat and a few trinkets to wear I believe she would be perfectly content anywhere."

The destiny of western America received a few other nudges from people around the Great Basin who were quite innocent of any such intention, as so often seems to be the case in the making of history.

Ceremonial organization among the Great Basin people seems to have been relatively slight; the food supply did not encourage large gatherings. A highly individualized sort of shamanism was common, in which dreams were sung. This does not mean the religion may have been less powerful or the dreams less moving than others; the most influential spiritual voice in history, among Indians of the United States, was to come from the mid-Basin, with Wovoka—of whom more in good time.

Far northwest of the Basin, westward of the mountain Shoshoni, ranging over most of central Idaho and the eastern sections of Washington and Oregon, there lived a number of tribes speaking various related languages now known collectively as Shahaptian. These included the Nez Perce, most easterly of the group, centering in Idaho and the Snake River country where Oregon, Idaho, and Washington come together, and the Palouse, the Walla Walla, and the Yakima, these the most westerly, living along the Yakima River westward of the great bend of the Columbia.

All these had been river people but they took enthusiastically to horses when horses became available. This was probably in the very early 1700s; the horses probably came from the Spanish settlements of New Mexico and were probably passed along to this upper country by the Northern Shoshoni.

By the early 1800s the Nez Perce (the French name, *Nez Percés*, is Americanized to Nezz Purse in their country) were more skillful than Virginia hostlers at handling horses, so said Americans who had seen both. They had already become identified with a famous breed developed in the region, the Appaloosa horse—the name coming no doubt from the neighboring Palouse. A small, distantly related tribe living south of the Yakima, known as the Cayuse, built up such a trade reputation as horse-dealers that "cayuse" became another name for horse among early Oregon settlers, possibly with opprobrious overtones, as was for a time "Navvy" (Navajo horse) in the Southwest.

All these were warlike people, and of them all the Nez Perce were the most numerous (Lewis and Clark guessed their population at 6,000) and most powerful.

Like the Shoshoni, not only were the Nez Perce friendly, hospitable, and helpful to Lewis and Clark in 1805 and 1806, but also to the other Americans who passed through their country during the next fifty years, and whose name in that time became legion.

The stubborn, although sometimes sorely tried, Nez Perce friendship for Americans—through all those fifty years, and more, not one American lost his life at Nez Perce hands—was of considerable influence, due to their position of leadership in the region.

The Nez Perce were minor instruments of history in still another manner, which came about in the following way. In 1825 Canadian fur traders arranged to have two deserving Spokan and Kutenai youths sent to the Red River of Canada for schooling. The Kutenai and Spokan were neighbors living to the north of the Nez Perce. Later, three Nez Perce youths also attended the Red River Mission School.

Apparently the Nez Perce became increasingly interested in obtaining the advantages of formal education for their young men, and some Nez Perce people visiting St. Louis in 1831 asked this boon of General William Clark (of Lewis and), then governor there. Somehow the story of their request got a little twisted in the telling, and the deputation of distant Indians was represented as coming all this way to seek the white man's religion. As a matter of fact there had been Christianized individuals here and there among the Nez Perce and their neighbors since before 1820, due to the amateur missionary work of Christianized Canadian Indians (particularly Iroquois from Caughnawaga, a settlement of Catholic Iroquois in Quebec) who came to the far West in fur-trapping brigades.

On the other hand, a request for teachers and a request for missionaries were one and the same thing, there being no other kind of white teacher known to trans-frontier Indians anyplace in the hemisphere.

In any case, the tale of the "Four Wise Men of the West" journeying so far to deliver their appeal for "The Book" of the white man was widely reprinted, and the eastern religious press became much exercised. The missions to

Oregon of the Reverend Jason W. Lee (1834), Dr. Marcus Whitman, the Reverend H. H. Spalding (1836–1837), and others followed, with some effect on the opening of heavy American emigration to Oregon during the next ten years.

This migration, installing the nucleus of a settled American population in Oregon, became a factor in settling the dispute between the United States and England on the boundary of the Oregon country. The entire country in question, between the Columbia River and the 49th Parallel, was turned over to the United States when the boundary matter was concluded in 1846.

Among most of the people of the far Northwest, fishing was usually the mainstay of life—Lewis and Clark in October of 1805 found the broad Columbia almost continuously lined with fish racks and bands of salmon fishers.

But toward the east, toward the sweeping Rockies and the starry winds of the Great Plains, the coming of the horse brought change; hunting became more important, especially the annual buffalo hunt, and clothes and customs took on some of the dash and flamboyance of the wild horsemen beyond the mountains. A lodge became a tipi, full-dress fringed skins and feathered war bonnets came into fashion, and flowered bead designs blossomed on anything that would hold still to be stitched.

Such were the Nez Perce and their neighbors, the Bannock to their south and the Flatheads to their northeast, centering on Flathead Lake in present Montana.

The Flatheads were, in their own name, the Salish; the name was later applied to one of the largest language families of the Northwest, Salishan. The Flatheads did not flatten their heads but left them as nature made them. However, an undeformed head appeared flat on top compared to the tapered skulls of various Salishan and Chinookan people farther west who did practice ornamental skull deformation. Hence the misnomer, applied to the Flatheads by these richly cultured neighbors who thought of a pointedly deformed skull as a mark of proper upbringing, of having been "well-cradled."

Most of these tribes of the Northwest plateau country—Lewis and Clark counted twenty-five along their route through the area—provided valuable help and instruction for the first American settlers. The beginning of permanent American settlement in Oregon, the trading post of Astoria, was set up by an expedition that labored its way westward in 1810–1812 and would have perished three times over if not for Indian provisions and Indian guides— some of these guides showed the whites for the first time what was later to become the vital Farewell Bend of the Oregon Trail.

But it was when waves of settlers began arriving, a generation after the Astorians, that Indian friendship was most decisive. The Nez Perce and the Northern Shoshoni, as mentioned, were distinguished in this regard—Washakie, the illustrious war chief of the Eastern Band of the Wyoming Shoshoni, was given a memorial of gratitude signed by some 9,000 emigrants, having helped them cross difficult fords or recover strayed stock, and having kept his people out of quarrels even when an occasional surly emigrant seemed bent on same.

But, in general, the first settlers to the Oregon country were not looking for trouble with anyone (unless it might be with the British); they were looking for a promised land of corn and wine, green grass and fertile loam—Beulah Land they called it in their hymns, after the land of heavenly joy described by the Pilgrim in his Progress. They were for the most part earnest, honest, pious people, and they met the Indians' friendship with a friendship no less genuine in return. Perhaps as many as 10,000 came to settle in the Oregon country in the early 1840s, mostly in the Willamette ("pronounced WillAMette, GodDAMmit," as said the residents) Valley, with a few in the valleys of the Columbia and the Cowlitz and on Puget Sound.

If the river tribes restrained themselves from any grave objections to this invasion of "Bostons," as they called the settlers, the Americans likewise invoked patience when a Klickitat passerby stopped at a farmhouse to demand a prepared meal, or a few roistering Smackshop Chilluckittequaws requisitioned an ox or a horse, or a drunken Chinook stopped respectable people to shout in the jargon, "*Nah, six, potlatch blue lu!*" ("Hey, friend, give me whiskey!")

The first real trouble came in 1847, with the destruction of the Whitman mission among the Cayuse (whose own name, Wailetpu, was incorporated in the name of the Shapwailutan language family, which includes the Nez Perce and many other people of the region) and the murder of twelve Americans there, including Dr. Whitman and his wife. The subsequent deaths from measles of two little girls among the surviving women and children—Mrs. Whitman was the only woman killed—are usually added to the total.

The immediate causes of the Whitman massacre are not clear. The Cayuse are said to have been increasingly resentful of the missionaries as more and more Bostons swarmed into the country, believing that the missionaries were in league with the Bostons to dispossess the Indians entirely. Bitter competition between Protestant and Catholic missions caused angry controversies among the Indians, making for quarrels, grudges, and high feelings. A measles epidemic just before the murders—killing perhaps 200 Cayuse people in only a few anguished weeks—helped to overheat the atmosphere, and may have given rise to malicious rumors of witchcraft or evil-evoking shamanism.

Settlers formed a volunteer army and exacted preliminary revenge, and Congress was importuned for military protection. To make peace the Cayuse (in 1850) turned over to the Oregon authorities five of the Whitman murderers, or five Cayuse men who at any rate played the part for the sake of saving the rest of their people. They were duly tried and hanged in Oregon City.

The early 1850s brought a surge of new population to Oregon, much of it consisting of ex-gold rushers from the California diggings looking for fresh bonanzas. The political machinery of organized territorial government got into high gear. Washington was set up as a separate territory in 1853, under Isaac J. Stevens, who had a strong anti-Indian reputation, as governor. U.S. Army troops were on hand as a result of the alarms of the Cayuse War, and were regularly augmented thereafter.

The frontier process of Indian disposal got under way with the customary councils big and little, the treaty chiefs of dubious position, the usual stubborn bands that refused to obey the treaty chiefs' treaties, the usual hostilities to force them to do so. There was the usual reluctance on the part of some tribes to make any land-ceding treaties at all, and the consequent overrunning of their country by unauthorized squatters and the consequent hostile incidents and the consequent wars.

The famous Nasqualla orator Leschi spoke during this period of the "polakly illeha," the land of darkness the white people were preparing for all Indians, where "the sting of an insect killed like the stroke of a spear, and the streams were foul and muddy, so that no living thing could drink of the waters."

There were numerous sizable operations involving the military, as well as countless volunteer "wars" on the California model, with attendant expense accounts billed to the government.

One of the least illegitimate of these volunteer activities was the brief foray against the Rogue River Indians of southern Oregon in 1853, resulting in the "purchase" of the entire Rogue River valley, more than 2 million acres, for a price of $60,000; $15,000 of this was to go to settlers for claims of war damages, $45,000 to the Indians, to be paid in annuities of approximately $2.75 per Indian for sixteen years. There was also an added bill to the government of $258,000 for the five weeks' service of the 200 to 500 volunteers involved.

The Rogue River country was left far from pacified by this expense; an outbreak in 1856 cost the lives of many officials and innocent settlers, extensive military operations, and the near extermination of a number of the groups known collectively as the Rogue River Indians.

The increasing helplessness of the Indians led to the usual corresponding increase of lawlessness on the part of opportunistic whites, which goaded further desperate acts of retaliation or resistance ("wars") into being. Military commanders, sent to Oregon to protect American settlers, found they had to spend much of their effort vainly trying to protect the Indians, and wrote repeatedly to higher headquarters that outrages by white men were responsible for the disturbances. These outrages were sometimes deliberately intended to keep the hostilities burning, due to a quite sincere belief in many quarters (and an eye on profit in others) that the Indians should be wholly exterminated.

The basic thought on Indians expressed in a journalistic history of San Francisco published in 1855—"Apart from sickly sentimentalism and Rousseau-like theories, the sooner the aborigines of California are altogether weeded away quietly, the better for humanity"—was echoed by many popular and practical leaders in Oregon. "Let our motto be extermination, and death to all opposers," said a newspaper in Yreka, a trading town in the California-Oregon border country—whose merchants, incidentally, sold goods to a volunteer Indian-chasing expedition in 1854 at such exorbitant prices that the commanding general on the Pacific coast sent a protest to Washington against paying the expedition's expenses, alleging that the entire project was unnecessary and had only been drummed up as a speculation to benefit the suppliers.

The exterminators were noisy and given to ever wilder xenophobic visions—saloon orators as well as the official newspaper of the Know-Nothing Party in Oregon called for the extermination of all Catholics as soon as the savages were finished off. They also committed quite a bit of personal exterminating in their own small way—three unauthorized squads in one sector of Oregon killed between twelve and eighteen savages per squad in less than a week in 1853, in each case by inducing the savages to lay down their arms under pledges of peace and then shooting them.

But it should be pointed out that, as in California, a reasonable proportion of the Oregon and Washington settlers seems to have felt sympathy toward the Indians, sometimes when such an attitude was so unpopular as to be dangerous. There were members of volunteer companies who denounced with considerable fervor the killing of Indian women and children. There were farmers who hid Indian friends in their houses when the troops or the volunteers were on the warpath—and Indians who did vice-versa when the Indians were uprising, and at least one farm woman who (in a preview of the similar report during the Yana massacre) was reported to have told the volunteers they would have to kill her first to get at the Indian women and children sheltered in her house.

However, as in so many other pioneer settings, the anti-Indian people were more actively interested (and motivated) in removing the Indians than the just and peaceful people were interested in peace and justice. As a result, the peaceable part of the public was not as a rule the dominant group.

A great treaty-making council was held in the rainy spring of 1855 with the tribes east of the Cascades. It took place on an ancient council ground of the Yakima in the Walla Walla Valley, and was attended by 4,000 or 5,000 people of the Yakima, Nez Perce, Walla Walla, Cayuse, Umatilla, Palouse, and eight other tribes of the region. There was much talk about land cession and confinement to reservations; most of the Indian spokesmen were opposed to both ideas.

A Cayuse orator said, "I wonder if the ground has anything to say? I wonder if the ground is listening to what is said?"

Support for the treaties desired by Governor Stevens, who had been appointed a U.S. treaty commissioner, came principally from an influential bloc of the traditionally pro-American Nez Perce, under a leader known as Lawyer. Lawyer stated that he was in favor of a treaty because his father had agreed with Lewis and Clark to live in peace with the whites. Lawyer's political foes murmured that he was after the appointment as head chief of the Nez Perce, an artificial office created some years previously by the missionaries.

Kamaiakan, a Yakima leader, headed the opposition, even though the U.S. commissioners offered to make him supreme chief of all the nations gathered there. But at last each tribe of the fourteen present was permitted to select its own favorite home valley as a reservation, and on these terms the treaties were signed. Charges and countercharges of duress, deceit, and treachery in connection with the treaties came in later years, but they were academic—for war broke out within three months after the council, the major and decisive conflict in the Northwest.

Miners and settlers did not wait for tribal and congressional ratification of the treaties before streaming into the treaty lands (gold strikes in the Colville and Coeur d'Alene countries spurred them on), and the Yakima and a half-dozen neighboring tribes decided almost unanimously that they did not want to ratify the treaties at all.

White squatters were attacked, an Indian agent was killed, and Governor Stevens called out the troops. The war lasted for three years, spreading to engulf people as far away as the Haida of British Columbia and some members of the Duwamish League of Puget Sound—although Chief Seattle of the Duwamish League remained a strong American ally. It featured innumerable actions by irregulars of both sides, two Indian victories over regular Army troops, two naval engagements (an attack of Yakimas and their allies on river steamers, and a hot assault on the town of Seattle fought off by a naval force then in the harbor) and ended with the defeat of the Indian forces by somewhat more than 700 artillery, cavalry, and infantry Army troops.

Two or three dozen of the Indian leaders were hanged. Kamaiakan, wounded, escaped to Canada.

Wars continued, official and otherwise, and raids and retaliations, but for most of the tribes of the Northwest there remained only the final phase of decay and dissolution.

Sometimes, though, they decayed hard, as in the case of Captain Jack and his band of Modocs. By 1870 this was, according to some accounts, a degraded band that hung around Yreka getting drunk and selling children when it wasn't out in the countryside terrorizing honest farmers. According to other accounts, Jack carried letters from prominent Yreka citizens testifying to his good conduct and good faith with the whites.

Captain Jack as he was known to the whites (his Modoc name was Kintpuash) preferred the Lost River country south of Upper Klamath Lake to the Klamath reservation on the lake where all the Modocs were supposed to go, and where about half of the tribe was already installed. The Lost River country was his home, Kintpuash said, and besides that he didn't like the Klamaths and couldn't live with them.

But settlers wanted the Lost River country too, and they didn't want Kintpuash and his people as neighbors. When troops came in 1872 to remove him by force to the reservation, Kintpuash and his band killed as many soldiers and settlers as they could and then took up a position in the lava beds (now a national monument) south of what is today called Tule Lake, just below the California line. More troops were summoned, and still more, and were joined by Indian scouts and allies—some of them Modocs from the Klamath agency—until after seven months more than 1,000 men were in action against Kintpuash and his handful of followers.

The Modoc band consisted of perhaps 250 men, women, and children. Perhaps seventy or eighty of these were men of warrior age—several of the men were well known to the whites, under such monikers as Humpy Jerry, Shacknasty Jim, or Curly-headed Doctor. Attack after attack was trapped and badly hurt in the nightmare lava beds, total Army casualties running to over 100 killed and wounded. A peace conference was arranged, and Kintpuash broke up the proceedings by killing out of hand the president of the peace commissioners, and Army commander of the Department of the Columbia, the noted General E. R. S. Canby—Kintpuash wore General Canby's uniform in some later engagements. A Methodist minister was also murdered, and the other peace commissioners barely escaped with their lives.

The nation was shocked by this cold-blooded treachery; President Grant demanded commensurate action from his commander of the Army, and his commander of the Army, General William Tecumseh Sherman, replied, "You will be fully justified by their utter extermination."

Field guns were finally brought up and the Modocs were shelled out of their lava beds and at last, in scattered groups, hunted down and forced to surrender.

Kintpuash and three of his lieutenants were hanged, and that was the end of Captain Jack (except that his severed head, and the heads of his three executed companions, were sent by the U.S. Army to Washington for the "anatomical" collection of the Surgeon General, whence they were later transferred to the collections of the Smithsonian Institution).

The rest of Captain Jack's remaining band, thirty-seven men and 111 women and children, were sent to Indian Territory. A generation later, in 1909, those still surviving were permitted to return to the Klamath reservation if they wanted to.

Among the Nez Perce (distant relatives by language family to the Modoc and Klamath), so constant in their American friendship, there lived a man of importance named Joseph, the name having been given him by the Reverend Spalding, whose school Joseph had attended. Joseph was the son of a Cayuse father but his wife was Nez Perce, and he had been at the great Walla Walla conference of 1855 as one of the Nez Perce spokesmen. The treaty he signed there reserved for his Nez Perce band what it claimed as its ancient home, the Wallowa Valley along the Snake River at the mouth of the Grande Ronde, crossroads of the present boundaries of the states of Oregon, Washington, and Idaho. After 1855 the Nez Perce stuck to peace and American alliance while all Oregon was on fire with war, rescued a body of American troops in 1858, and refused entanglement in troublemaking plots at the opening of the Civil War. In 1863 a new treaty was negotiated, in which Joseph's band did not participate, which ceded the Wallowa Valley to the government for settlement.

Joseph protested that the other Nez Perce people who had made this cession had acted without authority, and in violation of the previous treaty of 1855. He and his band stayed in the valley, although white settlers started moving in and the usual unavoidable hostile incidents occurred.

In 1871 Joseph died and the leadership of his band went to a son named Hin-mah-too-yah-laht-ket (Thunder Rolling in the Mountains), who was known to the Americans as Young Joseph, and later as Chief Joseph. The Nez Perce are so often described as noble, handsome, brave, truehearted, and in general excellent in all respects, that it seems possible they really may have been, J. Fenimore Cooperesque though the presumption may be. When it comes to Young Joseph the paean reaches crescendo. He was, so they say, of wisdom, eloquence, and goodness immeasurable, and in his pictures as a young man he is obviously no mountain Indian, but a figment of Sir Walter Scott's imagination, or more likely George Sand's.

In the spring of 1876 a man of Young Joseph's band was killed by a settler in the course of one of the unavoidable hostile incidents—all of which the Nez Perce had so far endured without retaliation. Young Joseph said of this murder: "As to the murderer I have made up my mind. I have come to the conclusion to let him escape and enjoy health and not take his life for the one he took. I am speaking as though I spoke to the man himself. . . . I pronounce the sentence that he shall live."

The government offered allotments of land to be owned white style by individual Indians who might want to try staying on in their home as small farmers among white neighbors. But Young Joseph and his people were horsemen, with wealth that they very much cherished in their herds of horses, many of them the blue Appaloosas with five-finger-spotted rumps that had become traditional Nez Perce war and hunting horses, and the twenty acres offered under the allotment plan to each Indian man was far from enough for a stockman.

The Indians wanted to stay in the valley as a community because they were a community and because the valley was their home. Political influence in Washington, however, was more responsive to those who wanted the Wallowa Valley turned over to white occupation.

The Department of the Interior, however, decided in 1873 to declare the Wallowa Valley a reservation and pay the eighty-seven squatters there $67,860 for their improvements, a solution that in 1875 Congress refused. This, says the best authority on the matter, sorely disappointed the squatters, "who had settled for the purpose of being bought out. If a man discover where a reservation is to be located, he cannot do better financially than locate upon it."

Local party politics seems to have been chiefly involved in the congressional refusal; the governor of Oregon particularly seemed intent on this unjust and arrogant action. Missionaries, also, were engaged in fighting the Dreamer religion that had many communicants in Joseph's band; one missionary at least recommended that the Indians be brought within "Christianizing influence" even "if force were necessary."

In opposition a military report of August 1875, said the white population was less than that of a year before. "Since the valley was restored to settlement, three families have disposed of their improvements for a trifle, and moved away; nor do I believe any others have come in. . . . This shows how the white people who reside here regard this valley. On the other hand, the Indians love it."

General O. O. Howard supported this opinion, but even so Howard, serving on the Commission of 1876 to study and decide the issue, apparently went along with the other three members of the commission in voting to drive Joseph's band out of the unwanted (by white settlers) Wallowa Valley. The commission decision was thus directly responsible for the ensuing war. In his later public writings about Chief Joseph and the Nez Perce, Howard does not mention his part in the commission.

To avoid a hopeless clash, Young Joseph at last agreed to take his people out of the valley and settle on the Lapwai reservation, as the government commanded. This was in the spring of 1877. Unfortunately some white neighbors grabbed the chance to make away with several hundred of the Indians' horses while the Nez Perce were preparing to move. The departing people, already heartsick, homesick, and outraged, were driven to an anger that could no longer be restrained. In a night and a day of vengeance a party of a few young men murdered eighteen settlers, and out came the troops.

After seventy-two years of peace, the Nez Perce were at war. Joseph, who had said, "rather than have war I would give up my country . . . I would give up everything" no longer had a choice.

It happened that among the troops there was a twenty-five-year-old West Pointer, one Lieutenant Wood, who later, under the name of Charles Erskine Scott Wood, became one of the finest writers in America. The picture of Indian fighting scribbled in his journal might be dull but was probably real: "hot stifling march across a dry prairie. No breakfast no water, men fainting and falling by the wayside." But, the next day: "the afternoon march and camp on the prairie, grass to our knees, rolling hills."

And his first Indian battle: "The advance, more rains, Indians speckling the hills like ants. Firing. Sudden feeling of intoxication on hearing the shots nervous eagerness for the fight." But the fight was over. The ants speckling the hills and the distant slam of the shots was an Indian battle.

In several such battles the American commander, General O. O. Howard, was outmaneuvered, suffered heavier losses, and could gain no advantage though superior in mobility, firepower, and numbers. It appeared that the young Chief Joseph might have unusual military talent.

He certainly did, said the Army officers who opposed him.

He decided to lead his band—400 to 500, with at the most something between 100 and 200 effective warriors—to safety in Canada, and for four months he fought his way through and around Army units (with their Indian scouts) that were rushed in from all sides to head him off, fought a running campaign of over 1,000 mountain miles that has been compared to the Anabasis of Xenophon's Ten Thousand Greeks, conducted with a magnificent generalship that has been compared to Napoleon's best.

The question has been raised in recent studies as to how much of the credit for this campaign should go to Joseph and how much to the leaders of smaller bands or other chief men present during the march—the lean Looking

Glass, famous warrior, who joined along with his band after Joseph's first startling victory had been achieved; or White Bird, who at the last moment did succeed in reaching Canada with about 100 followers; or Joseph's brother, Ollokot, leader of the warriors in Joseph's band, "he who led the young men," as Joseph spoke of him, or others among the ranking men.

Even with written records the same sort of question is raised in studies of Napoleon, assessing the exact contributions (or errors) of such as Marshal Ney. Without records from the Nez Perce headquarters it will never be possible to assign credit with any exactness.

Nor is it possible to assign exact commands to the various principal men. Indian rank and authority are slippery matters at best, when it comes to defining them in traditional European terms. The custom of separate peace and war chiefs, common among some Indian peoples, was not followed by the Nez Perce and neighboring people of the Columbia River plateau region, or by the people of the neighboring Great Basin area and the California region. Authority here was instead likely to be rather informal.

Contemporary comment associates the aura of principal authority with Joseph. He may thus be regarded as the inspired tactician of the march of his people, or, if one wishes, simply as the symbol of their inspired spirit.

A history of the Nez Perce written in 1880 by James Reuben, a member of Lawyer's band, states:

> In 1863 another treaty was made
> in which Lawyer and his people consented
> but Joseph and his people refused
> to make the second treaty.
>
> from that time Joseph's people
> were called None-treaty Nez Perce.
>
> The treaty Nez Perce number 1800
> None-treaty numbered 1000.
>
> 1877 Government undertook to move Young Joseph
>   people on the Res.
> At this date Young Joseph was the ruling chief . . .
>
> Joseph and his followers broke out
> and there was Nez Perce war bloody one
> nine great battles fought.

The compiler of this record, James Reuben, was a nephew of Chief Joseph and son of Reuben, Lawyer's successor as chief of the Upper Nez Perce (Treaty Nez Perce). He was one of several Christianized Nez Perce scouts who served from time to time with General O. O. Howard's forces against Chief Joseph's band. Nevertheless, he went to live in exile with Chief Joseph's surviving people in Indian Territory, where he occasionally acted as interpreter. It seems likely the contents of his history would have been read to and approved by members of Joseph's community, including Joseph himself. (To an interviewer who asked Joseph if he bore ill will toward James Reuben, Joseph "answered promptly, 'No, a war is a thing where there are two sides.'")

Military sources disagree with James Reuben in counting twelve engagements during the war, not nine as Reuben had it, raising the interesting question of how Indians may have differed from Europeans in defining battles.

Joseph and his people dealt with four different Army columns, cut off pursuit by a daring night raid that left the pursuers without transport animals, or by an adroit feint that turned the pursuing columns around to run into each other, or simply fought and outfought the enemy with the handful of dazzling Nez Perce cavalrymen. "They rode at full gallop along the mountain side in a steady formation by fours, formed twos, at a given signal, with perfect precision, to cross a narrow bridge, then galloped into line, reined in to a sudden halt, and dismounted with as much system as regulars," said an Army general.

The Nez Perce were hurt several times by heavy casualties—eighty-nine killed in one engagement, fifty of those being women and children. But they continued to march, and they continued to fight.

They practiced one notable novelty, novel for either red or white warriors, in the warfare of the time and region. Joseph had reportedly ordered no scalping in the battles that he was to command, and—from his people—there was none.

The war they fought, said General William Tecumseh Sherman, was "one of the most extraordinary Indian wars of which there is any record. The Indians throughout displayed a courage and skill that elicited universal praise; they abstained from scalping, let captive women go free, did not commit indiscriminate murder of peaceful families, which is usual."

General Nelson A. Miles, whose column finally cut off Joseph's retreat, was quoted as saying, "In this skillful campaign they have spared hundreds of lives and thousands of dollars worth of property that they might have destroyed," and was moved to add gratuitously that Joseph's Nez Perce "have, in my opinion, been grossly wronged in the years past." One gross wrong may be attributed to General Miles himself, who endeavored to make Joseph a prisoner during discussions under a flag of truce, a tactic that, as we have seen, was used fairly often by the forces of civilization. In this case it failed, but it delayed the Indian surrender for an extra added three days of needless suffering and casualties—Looking Glass was killed by a stray bullet on the last of these three days; Too-hul-hul-sute and Joseph's brother, Ollokot, had both fallen in the preceding final battle.

Joseph had "led his tribe—men, women, and children, sick, wounded, maimed, and blind—through the Bitter Root Mountains, twice across the Rocky Mountains, through the Yellowstone National Park, across the Missouri River, to the Bear Paw Mountains, where, on Eagle Creek, within thirty miles of the Canadian line, he finally surrendered, October 5, 1877," wrote young Lieutenant Wood (grown older) some years later, in a letter recounting the saga and its conclusion. Lieutenant Wood had been made General Howard's aide-de-camp and so was in at the finish, which came with the arrival of Howard and his additional forces at the end of the above-mentioned three days' standoff.

C. E. S. Wood's letter continues: "on the evening of a wintry day, the prairie powdered with snow, and a red and stormy sun almost at the horizon, Joseph surrendered, his people coming out of the burrows they had made in the hills, and where they had been living without fires, subsisting on the flesh of the dead horses. . . .

"In the final attack, a surprise by General Miles, Joseph's little girl, about eight or nine years old, and of whom he was very fond, fled in terror out on the prairie, and at the time of his surrender she was supposed to have perished from cold and starvation. As a matter of fact, she was afterwards found among the Sioux as a prisoner or slave, and was restored to Joseph; but with little effect, as his express condition of surrender—that he should be allowed to go back to the reservation which had been provided for him—was broken by the government, and he and his people were sent to the malarial bottoms of the Indian Territory, where all of his own children (six) and most of his band died. [An error, for the lost little girl did survive and grow up, although separated from her father.]

"At the time of the surrender, the able bodied warriors were surprisingly few, in contrast to the number of sick, aged, and decrepit men and women: blind people, children, babies and wounded that poured out of their burrows in the earth as soon as it was known that they could do so with safety.

"Joseph came up to the crest of the hill, upon which stood General Howard, General Miles, an interpreter, and myself. Joseph was the only one mounted, but five of his principal men clung about his knees and pressed close to the horse, looking at him, and talking earnestly in low tones. Joseph rode with bowed head, listening attentively, apparently, but with perfectly immobile face. As he approached the spot where we were standing, he said something, and the five men who were with him halted. Joseph rode forward alone, leaped from his horse, and, leaving it standing, strode toward us. He opened his blanket, which was wrapped around him, and handed his rifle to General Howard, who motioned him to deliver it to General Miles, which Joseph did. Standing back, he folded his blanket again across his chest, leaving one arm free, somewhat in the manner of a Roman senator with his toga, and, half turning toward the interpreter, said:

"'Tell General Howard I know his heart. What he told me before, in Idaho, I have it in my heart. I am tired of fighting. . . . My people ask me for food, and I have none to give. It is cold, and we have no blankets, no wood. My people are starving to death. Where is my little daughter? I do not know. Perhaps, even now, she is freezing to death. Hear me, my chiefs. I have fought, but from where the sun now stands, Joseph will fight no more forever.'

"And he drew his blanket across his face, after the fashion of Indians when mourning or humiliated, and, instead of walking towards his own camp, walked directly into ours, as a prisoner.

"After long delay, and when his band was reduced to a comparatively small number of people, he was [in 1885], with the remnant of his tribe, allowed to come north from the Indian Territory—not to his old ground in Idaho, but to Northern Washington. No supplies were provided for them. They marched from the Indian Territory to their new home, and arrived on the edge of winter in a destitute condition, experiencing great suffering. . . .

"I think that, in his long career, Joseph cannot accuse the Government of the United States of one single act of justice."

The above version of Joseph's surrender speech was written from memory, although it was Lieutenant Wood who took down the original at the time, in his capacity as General Howard's aide. The speech has become famous and has been many times quoted, in almost as many different versions.

CHAPTER 28

Buffalo Indians and Pony Soldiers

Buffalo Bill's Wild West Show, after four years as a roadshow hit in the United States, went to London in 1887, the "most thoroughly howling success" America had ever sent abroad, said one critic. It was an equally smashing success at the Paris World Fair in 1889, where it had to compete with the sensational debut of the Eiffel Tower. By the end of 1892 all Europe had become familiar with the show's slam-bang finale, a staging of Custer's Last Stand. The wild riding of the Indians therein stamped an image on the public mind that still prevails over much of the Old World as the picture of the American Indian—feathered war bonnets breakneck on horseback. In fact, to much of the world the Indians of the great plains of the American West *are* the American Indians, none others need apply.

It isn't easy to keep in mind, especially in the public mind, that the horse didn't join the American Indian, any American Indian, until brought by the European invaders.

The prehistoric horse was born in the Americas, many millions of years ago, but for some reason became extinct in the New World at the close of the Ice Age. However, horses had long before spread to the Old World, possibly across the occasional Siberian land bridge. Thus the horses brought by the Spaniards to the New World were, fairly literally, coming back home. Perhaps they knew it. In any case, they went forth and multiplied at an astonishing rate.

For horseless South America the principal early center of distribution was Peru, where horses first arrived in 1532. By 1535 they had entered the horse heaven that was to become Argentina, and by 1600 streamed over the Argentine pampas in herds too vast to count. The varying peoples there, and

412

the people of the rolling, scrub-covered country adjoining on the north, known as the Chaco, became intense horsemen and utterly revolutionized the ways of their world in the process.

Horses appeared in Mexico in 1519, ten stallions, five mares, and a foal, brought by the soldiers of Cortés. They spread so rapidly among the native people that in 1594, beyond the Spanish frontier in northern Mexico, the chief of a village of Laguneros Indians rode out on horseback to welcome a venturesome Jesuit, the first missionary to appear in those parts. The exploring padre duly reported his cordial reception, in no wise making anything remarkable of the mounted chief. Obviously there was nothing extraordinary—in the 1590s—about wild Indians owning and riding horses.

Above Mexico the horse frontier jumped to northern New Mexico, to the heel of the Rockies, when Oñate's colonists drove up thousands of head of assorted livestock in 1598. The Santa Fe country remained for generations the chief dispersal point north of Mexico for the new American horse. Spanish officials now and then made efforts to enforce security regulations against letting Indians learn the use of horses, but the *mayordomos* at ranches and missions had to reply that there were only Indians available to work as vaqueros. The Indians learned. The secret plans of the manipulation of that ultramodern weapon, the horse, must have been stolen many times over by amateur Indian secret agents. And having learned, Indians liberated horses by the bunch, by the herd, from the ranchos of Chihuahua and New Mexico.

The Pueblo revolt of 1680 threw all the horses in New Mexico on the open Indian market for a dozen years, and from this point on (if not before) the horse frontier left the white frontier years behind. Bartered or stolen from band to band, ridden on terrorizing raids that covered hundreds of miles, galloped into hitherto unknown lands on wonderfully rich hunting trips, driven in herds to distant nations by Indian merchants, horses fanned out over the West, their hoofbeats a flourish of drums announcing a marvelous new life. The sun-cracked wastes of Utah were too poor in graze and water to invite a man to keep a horse but the Utes of the Rockies' western slopes took to horses and passed them along (perhaps unintentionally) and by the 1690s (if not well before) horses were being introduced among the Northern Shoshoni of Wyoming by someone, spies or tradesmen or exiles from horse-owning bands, who could teach the mysteries of their management.

And now, with Shoshoni war feathers tied in their flying tails and with Shoshoni bowmen on their backs, horses trotted out of the mountains to sweep across the high plains, the seemingly endless plains that stretch from the Rockies to the Mississippi valley prairies, in pursuit of the antelope, the buffalo, and the constant Shoshoni foe, the bold-hearted people of the northern plains known as the Blackfeet.

A populous and powerful new horse people threw the central plains into a turmoil of warfare with their appearance in the early 1700s; they were a branch of Shoshoni people known to the Louisiana and Illinois French as the Padouca, later so famous as plains horsemen nonpareil, the Comanche. Their presence beyond the mountains east of Santa Fe was noted very early in the 1700s; in 1724 they met in a great peacemaking council with the French explorer, Etienne de Véniard de Bourgmont, and with leaders of a half dozen nations of plains and prairie peoples, Missouri, Kansa, Osage, Oto, Iowa, and Pawnee. This took place in what is now Kansas, very much in the region of the Quivira reached by Vásquez de Coronado nearly 200 years before. Identification of the Padouca at this council as Comanche seems quite secure; some recent confusion with Plains Apache is rather clearly in error.

La Salle in the Mississippi valley in the 1680s found horses and horse savvy among Caddoan people in what is now east Texas, evidence of considerable long distance commerce in horses antedating by many years the Pueblo revolt of 1680 and its consequent open market, as was likewise indicated by the horse polity among the Padouca (Comanche) in the early 1700s. The Pawnee were spoken of at an equally early period as horse traders. The Comanche who met with Bourgmont were also obviously horse traders, being in constant need of replenishing their horse supply since, as they explained to Bourgmont's people, they got no colts from their mares due to furious running of the mares during buffalo hunting. Clearly they had known horses long enough to gain much expertise but not yet long enough to learn even the basic points of handling gravid mares.

The Comanche, developing into such dedicated horse people, would naturally tend to move toward where the horses were, and the main stream of this trade, before and after 1680, seems to have been across the plains eastward from Santa Fe. Why the Plains Apache, resident for centuries on this particular main street, did not precede the Comanche, Kiowa, and others of neighboring areas in becoming horse specialists, is a puzzling question; they traded in horses as early as the 1690s (if not before) but never were noted as horse Indians, and well into the 1700s bands that appear to be Plains Apache are described as still on the horse/dog fence for travois transportation.

Trudging foot people of the plains who did not have horses were of course thrown into panic by enemies transformed into centaurs nine feet tall who could dash upon their victims with the speed of the screaming wind. Mounted Shoshoni were attacking Piegans (the southern division of Blackfoot people) by 1730, according to the recollection of a Piegan senior citizen more

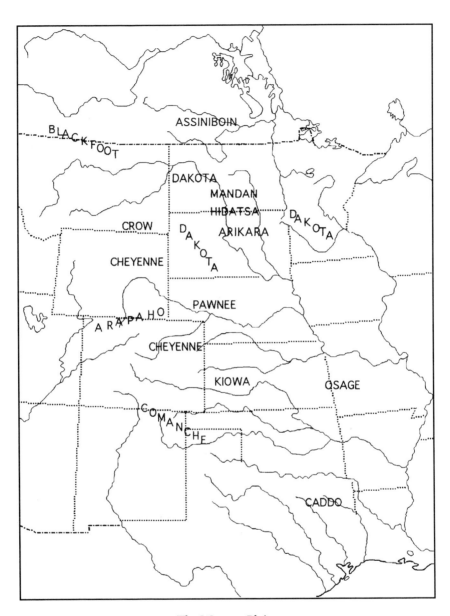

The Western Plains

than half a century later; the Blackfeet asked for help from the Cree and Assiniboin to their east, who came and defeated a Shoshoni war party with the aid of another black magical new weapon—the gun.

The horse frontier, moving in from the south and west, and the gun frontier, advancing from the east, met on the great plains in a spectacular union and created the figure that has obsessed the world ever since as the archetype of the American Indian, the feather-streaming, buffalo-chasing, wild-riding, recklessly fighting Indian of the plains. This figure, shaped by the European's horse and gun, decorated from war bonnet band to moccasins with the European's beads, only reached full glory when the untouched Indian world was all but a memory. The Plains Indian was a late, last flowering of the ancient cultures already vanished or reduced to wreckage over most of the hemisphere. He was less sheer Indian, being so much altered by the breath of the European frontiers, than almost any of his predecessors down through the ages of Indian history, from the ancient Nazca and the Olmec and the Maya to the Anasazi and the Hohokam and the Iroquois of Deganawida.

But in some other respects the Plains Indian is an excellent happenchance choice as a universal Indian symbol. In his exaggerated world he intensified a whole palette of more specialized Indian colors common to other Indian groups although by no means to all: warrior societies and elaborate codes of combat, fear of sex and grief for the dead and emotional excesses deriving from both, sacred objects and sacred rites deriving from inspired visions or dreams, and the omnipresent sacred power to be sought in visions and dreams. In all these respects and many more the Plains Indian was the Indian carried to extremes.

Finally, the boundless land in which he lived, confined only by the wide and starry sky, underlined the pervasive notion of Indian freedom.

These modern Plains Indians sprang from many different roots, from hunters and farmers who had entered and lived in and about the plains for untold generations, as well as from the diverse bands and nations that had poured into the plains in relatively recent times with the storm fronts of the horse and gun.

It was long believed that the plains were generally without inhabitants before the horse (with which to chase the bison) and the plow (with which to farm the grasslands), but archeologists now present evidence of buffalo hunters established in the plains more than 10,000 years ago at least, and possibly much more. Mountains of bones from the herds they stampeded over cliffs or into ravines have been found from Texas to Canada, sometimes in such quantities that present day Indians have made a business of selling the bones to be turned into commercial fertilizer.

The people mixed and changed, came and went, during that immense passage of time, and so did the world around them. From about 5000 B.C. to about 2500 B.C. the weather was warmer and dryer, and there seem to have been fewer animals and fewer people on the plains; in the times following this Altithermal the evidence of human and animal abundance seems to increase. Eventually villages of farmers appeared not only along the river courses but also along small streams and creeks in the less arid regions of the high plains.

Some of the typical plainsmen for many hundreds of years may have been farmers who hunted as a sideline. Some ancient peoples along the eastern marches of the plains were clearly connected with the great Hopewell culture centering in the Ohio valley far to the east, and there centering some 2,000 years ago in time. Apart from the villagers, buffalo hunters continued to follow the herds; new hunters came and went, mixed and changed. They left stone tipi rings, "medicine wheels," pictographs, boulder alignments, in countless numbers; it has been suggested that some of these may have had something to do with astronomical observation.

The plains were long a frontier, long before any Europeans appeared, between the two different farming worlds, the Indian worlds to the east and the west, worlds actually quite different from each other although their farming economies were founded on the same basic crops: corn, beans, and squash. In the corn-pounding, hominy-boiling towns to the eastward the farm was principally woman's work and the holy places were summits of mounds or pyramids raised to the heavens, while in the corn-grinding, tortilla-slapping towns to the westward men worked the farm fields as a rule and the holy places were more likely to be underground, in the kivas.

In subsequent times farming gave way over most of the plains country to a return to nomadic hunting; some peoples who had once grown corn and made pottery forgot how to do both, and devoted their lives to hunting the inexhaustible buffalo.

Among the historic nations of known location the Blackfeet (a literal translation of their own name, Siksika, possibly referring to black-dyed moccasins) are regarded as the ancients of the northern plains. Their language, a much-altered Algonquian variant, had evidently been separated for a long period from other Algonquian languages to the east. In the not too distant past they appear to have expanded westward over the Alberta-Saskatchewan plains and later, maybe at about the time they acquired horses, southward into what is now Montana, thrusting out a people then living in the plains in the region of the present Canadian boundary; these were the Kutenai, a tall, estimable people speaking a language unrelated to any other, who gradually moved westward across the Rockies and became northern neighbors of the Flatheads and Nez Perce.

The Siksika, by the time whites became familiar with their country, dwelt along the eastern base of the Rockies throughout Montana and far up into Alberta, to the edge of the black northern forests that begin beyond the North Saskatchewan River. Known collectively as the Blackfoot Confederacy they were a numerous (estimated 15,000 in 1780) people divided into three tribes of common descent, common language, and (sometimes) a common front against a common enemy. These three tribes were, in the farthest north, the Siksika proper; below them to their south the Kainah or Bloods (possibly from a former name for themselves, "Blood People," or possibly from their sacred face paint of red earth); and farthest south, generally below the present Canadian border in Montana, the Piegans ("Poor Robes"). On the north a small Athapaskan-speaking tribe, the Sarcee or Sarsi (Blackfoot for "No-goods") allied itself to the Siksika in later years.

East of the Piegan another group speaking a highly aberrant Algonquian language roamed the plains of Montana and Canada between the Missouri and the Saskatchewan—these were the Atsina, brothers of the Arapaho of the Wyoming plains from whom they had separated perhaps as recently as the seventeenth century. They may have been in the plains country, somewhere, well before that time.

Misreading the sign talk, early traders often called the Atsina by the names of Minnetarees or Gros Ventres—which same names were also applied to a totally unrelated tribe speaking a Siouan tongue, the Hidatsa, village farmers along the Missouri River in what is now North Dakota. The Hidatsa may well have been survivals of the plains farmers of earlier times, and so also old residents of the plains; they were neighbored on the north and south by a few other villages of plains farmers, the Siouan-speaking Mandan upriver from them and the Arikara, an offshoot of the Pawnee, down the Missouri to the south. Earthlodge villages in the easterly regions of the plains, dating to pre-1500, are identified by archeologists as Pawnee, carrying associations from the temple mound people of the Southeast.

A part of the Hidatsa who called themselves the Absaroke, meaning Crow-people or Bird-people, left the Hidatsa towns and traveled westward to settle in the country of the Yellowstone and its southern branches of the Powder and Big Horn rivers. They stopped farming and building earth lodges and making pottery and became hunters living in skin tipis. This evidently happened several centuries ago. The change entailed all manner of accompanying change in social structure and habits, in rites, in the very teleology of life itself; the Absaroke became model people of the plains; they are known to history as the

Crows. Their country ran so much to mountains that they are sometimes spoken of in the two divisions of Mountain Crows and River Crows.

These groups were the principal known inhabitants of the high plains north of Kansas before the coming of the horse and the gun. The gun frontier brought in new peoples from the east, who seized on the horse and became thoroughgoing plainsmen almost, one gathers, in a single generation. In the northeast a part of the Cree, snowshoe and canoe people when they were at home in their Canadian forests, pressed into the prairies and then the plains with Hudson Bay Company guns, looking for beaver, and became the Plains Cree. They drew along friends from southern Ontario, the Assiniboin, a sizable tribe that had separated in recent centuries from the great Siouan-speaking nation known as the Dakota. The rest of the Dakota and the Algonquian-speaking Cheyenne moved out of the forests of the upper Mississippi country into the plains; both had been farming people as well as hunters, decorous and valorous, and were clearly of a high order in character, intellect, and ability.

The Cheyenne crossed the wide Missouri into the short-grass plains and in the unlikely space of perhaps fifty years or so roundabout the last quarter of the eighteenth century and the first quarter of the nineteenth transformed themselves into horsemen, constant buffalo hunters, magnificent warriors, in short into Plains Indians of the first class. They divided, at length, into two groups, the Northern Cheyenne around the headwaters of the North Platte and the Yellowstone, and the Southern Cheyenne headquartering along the plains of the Arkansas within sight of the southern Colorado Rockies.

The Dakota, who formed a true confederacy (the word means "allies," language variation changed it to Nakota among the Yankton and Lakota among the Teton), were made up of seven tribes—their own name was *Ocheti shakowin*, "the seven council fires." Some of these tribes, such as several known collectively as the Santee, remained on the edge of the eastern forests and adjoining high-grass prairies and remained semi-agricultural. Others, such as the Teton, moved into the plains in the 1700s and within a century or so were known the world over as the very embodiment of Plains Indianism—the famous Sioux. The French coined the name Sioux from an Algonquian term meaning "enemies"—in fact, in its full original form, referring as usual to "serpents." Out of all the different Siouan peoples the Dakota have usually been designated specifically as the Sioux, somewhat as the Five Nations Iroquois became the specific Iroquois.

The Sioux spread clear across the plains into the country of the Crows, who resisted their invasion and became their inveterate enemies; the Crows were so seriously threatened by the huge nations of the Dakota, pushing in from the east, and the Blackfeet, pushing down from the north, that early observers thought (in the 1830s) they were facing extermination. At the height of Sioux power, the Northern Cheyenne were bordered on the north by the Oglala, the most westerly and one of the most renowned of the Teton subdivisions, which were also seven in number. Dakota territory included much of the area of the present states of the same name, extending south into Nebraska and east into Iowa and Minnesota.

For all the people of the plains, newcomers and old residents alike, the horse brought a miraculously changed life. Before the horse, families moved their possessions from place to place with the help of dogs, dogs bearing little packs or dogs dragging the A-shaped frame of trailing sticks across which baggage was lashed, the contraption named by the French a travois. Possessions, therefore, could be neither many nor heavy. After the horse, lodge poles could be as long as thirty feet, tipis (a Dakota word) could be made of as many as eighteen or twenty dressed buffalo hides, enclosing a room some fifteen spacious feet across crammed with furnishings, riches, and relations.

After the horse, buffalo could be found miles away, chased down on the run, although by the numbers to a certain extent, since the formal hunt as a rule was regulated, like camp life, by a police society.

After the horse, dried meat and the everlasting *pemmican* (dried meat pounded up with suet, marrow, and maybe some such added flavoring as wild cherries) could be kept and moved by the ton. One could own and carry along a wealth of buffalo robes, pots, skin bags and rawhide traveling trunks (*parfleches*), tools, new clothes, spare time, and new delights.

The custom Vásquez Coronado had noticed in 1541 of Plains Indians trading buffalo robes for the corn and beans of farming villages could be extended: traders could go miles farther for special foods, such as mescal, or for luxury importations, jewelry or rare furs or the beautiful Nez Perce bows, made of the horn of the wild mountain sheep.

The Mandan, Arikara, and Hidatsa towns became trading centers for horseborne commerce and entered upon a century of prosperity.

Better still, there was time for war, and horses gave it method as well as purpose. A man's fortune was counted in horses; a young man's future depended on horses. Horses became a common booty of war, the capture of horses a prime objective of war.

War's other aspects, fighting and the danger of death, were gradually bound around with as much ceremony as a Japanese tea party. Elite soldier societies multiplied, each with special costumes, special grades, special manners, special sacred rites, special taboos. Wars called for fancy tricks, fancy riding, fancy fighting, as war songs called for fancy drumming. Two of the three finest feats of war were to capture by stealth an enemy's best horses, the valued stallion or fleet hunters he kept picketed close beside his lodge; or to touch an enemy's body in battle—this last, called via the French counting "coup," gave rise to rigid, complex, and jealously administered systems of war honors. A man of war introduced himself on a public appearance by recounting his deeds in battle, reciting his coups. Soldier societies and coup systems existed elsewhere in the Indian world, some of the elsewheres very far removed in time as well as in space, but in the plains they appear to have attained unusually elaborate development.

All its decor notwithstanding, Indian-versus-Indian war on the plains was not as a rule serious to European eyes. Raids back and forth by handfuls of self-appointed soldiers bent on grabbing a few horses or a captive or two couldn't seem much of a war to a veteran of, for example, Malplaquet (20,000 dead).

But the plains on fire from end to end with the little Indian-versus-Indian fights that never really ended did effectively hinder or even halt travel and trade, and trade was indeed a serious matter.

To the French company that owned the plains during the first half of the eighteenth century, trade was in fact the only thing that mattered. The trade of its dreams would be trade with New Mexico, erroneously supposed to be rolling in all the storied riches of New Spain. These dreams were the dreams, though, of the company's directors, who were in Paris. The company's managers in the field, while of course loyal and true blue through and through, could harbor other ideas.

A French advance man of Bourgmont's time, Bénard de La Harpe, had actually opened a back door to New Mexico through Spanish missionaries on the northern edge of Texas in 1719 (the official Spanish position that the French were only an encroaching enemy was not always fully shared by Spain's managers in the field, religious, commercial, or both). But La Harpe's enthusiasm for a French base in this place or that beyond the frontier aiming at "the commerce that could be initiated with the Spaniards of New Mexico" was not shared at all by the French colonists of Biloxi or Mobile or New Orleans, who saw in such an incipient commercial center only potential business competition. Their warm regard for their own present profit against somebody else's potential profit was naturally supported by their leading citizen, the French governor of Louisiana, who was the company manager on the scene. La Harpe's dreams, not surprisingly, expired in conference.

Bourgmont's contract with the company in 1724 promised him a patent of nobility as well as money if he could succeed in calming the fighting against the Padouca and thus make smooth the way to New Mexico.

Bourgmont's efforts to bring peace to the plains would have to begin, however, with the repatriation of Padouca captives sold as slaves to the French, and would have to conclude with an end to all the Padouca slave trade. But the French colonists in Louisiana and the Illinois were not at all eager to give up their "fruitful commerce in padouka slaves and horses." Consequently the governor of Louisiana and the commandant at the Illinois tried, as well as they could, and none too discreetly, to sabotage Bourgmont's project. Why does the Louisiana governor, asked Bourgmont in a letter, "oppose a peace that could procure so much advantage for the Colony?"

Bourgmont was equal to the challenge and in spite of the peculiar politics brought peace to the Padouca and their foemen across the plains, and in fulfillment of the final step of his contract escorted a deputation of five "chiefs" (he wanted ten but the company economized) to Paris, where they went hunting with the youthful Louis XV, and a newspaper quoted one as saying that perfumed Paris ladies smelled like alligators.

As can be seen in this situation, disunity among Indian nations, so often instanced by historians as a crucial factor assisting European conquest, could at times provide an obstacle to European expansion. Historians have given less attention to the chronic hostility between the several European nations, delaying New World conquest by gathering Indian allies to wage destructive war on each other's establishments. Less notice still, in the large view, has been bestowed on the incessant and sometimes violent discord within the European nations themselves between rival commercial factions, rival political factions, and rival religious factions.

Bourgmont's considerable achievement in making peace on the plains and smoothing the way to New Mexico—the New Mexico settlements were twelve days from their customary village, the Padouca said, and they would be glad to guide the French there—came to absolutely nothing, due to such chaotic conditions both in France and in the colonies. Even Bourgmont's valuable geographic report, while it found its way into the archives for the use of future historians, was lost, ignored, or suppressed by officials on the scene. It is gratifying to note that Bourgmont did receive his grant of nobility in December 1725, although he then ran into difficulties trying to collect from the company for expenses he had advanced in bringing the Indian delegation to Paris.

Clearly the Europeans' serious and businesslike business and war were not always logical. For the Plains Indians, logic was totally in control—war and every other activity were pursued to keep the group and the world around it in healthy balance with its accompanying spirit world. The leader of a war party was usually guided by the auguries of dreams (as among the ancient

Greeks), and a sacred symbol, inspired by a vision or a dream or religious practice, was carried along, sometimes like a banner, sometimes like a secret weapon. In this life, where a man was expected to die young, and many did, the rare boon of long life could only come from divine protection, a supernatural power granted, along with directions for its use, in a vision or dream.

For, above all, the new world of the horse brought time and temptation to dream. The plains are afloat in mysterious space, and the winds come straight from heaven. Anyone alone in the plains turns into a mystic. The plains had always been a place for dreams, but with horses they were more so. Something happens to a man on a horse in a country where he can ride at a run forever. It is quite easy to ascend to an impression of living in a myth. He either feels like a god or feels closer to God. There seems never to have been a race of plains horsemen that was not either fanatically proud or fanatically religious. The Plains Indians were both.

Sacred bundles and sacred objects, often associated with visions and dreams, operated for the welfare of the group as a whole, as long as the rules were carefully followed, as long as devoted attention did not lapse—as long, for instance, as the owner of a Blackfoot pipe bundle sang the correct ritualistic songs in the correct number of sets on the special occasions when the bundle was opened, and observed the prescribed taboos.

Sacred objects were owned by people of piety and consequence; sometimes their power was transferable, and their buying and selling constituted one of the uses of the new wealth that came with the horse. But everyone could dream. Any man dreamed of the horse he would capture, and of what sort of feathers to wear in his hair, and the paint to put on his face, and the foe he would kill, and the girls he would marry, and the pattern to put on his shield, and the way he would die.

With horse prosperity entire tribes could gather every year or two or three for observances of the greatest importance, when the tribe was reunited and renewed. Such observances took many varied forms with different peoples, but one principal appeal to visions and dreams, the Sun Dance, was common to many of the people of the plains. It differed from place to place and from time to time and, sometimes, even between two different priests. But essentially it gathered together many rites of preparation that culminated in the ceremony of the dance, which continued for several days, usually between two and four. The participants (male) were expected to fast and, at intervals throughout the entire dance, to take their places and stare fixedly at the top of a central pole, where some mystic object was fixed to represent the sun in its nest of thunder. The Sun Dance was (and is) scarcely a dance; the communicants stood more or less in one place, shuffling a little forward and backward, to the drumming of special Sun Dance songs. They held eagle-bone whistles in their mouths, to sound with each breath. For some, a vision might finally be granted. Some, in fulfillment of a vow or to wring pity from the watching spirits, tortured themselves by running skewers through the muscles in their chests or backs and swinging from thongs until the skewers were torn loose.

The Creator, the Old Person, God by whatever name, spoke through visions and dreams over much of the Indian world; it was merely typical of the plains people to go to extremes in this conversation. These were people of emotional excesses. Blighted love, or sometimes nothing more than a scolding from her mother, might drive a girl to suicide. Humiliation could make a man decide to embrace death by single-handedly charging an enemy war camp. Death was properly a matter of magnificent emotion. Mourning brought wild excesses of grief. The third great feat of war was bravery in rescuing a dead body from the enemy, so it could not be mutilated.

In general there was a considerable sameness among the people of the plains, regardless of the diversity of their origins. All lived in the same dream-haunted atmosphere. Whites sometimes claimed they found the Plains Indians all alike in looks, but the physical variety ran from tall to short and lean to fat. The Comanche were reported in the early days to embody in themselves two extremes, the handsomest of people on horseback, awkward and homely on foot. They were surely unsurpassable as horsemen in elegance and ease, said the painter Catlin in the 1830s, but rather low in stature, "often approaching to corpulency . . . heavy and ungraceful. . . . A Camanchee on his feet is out of his element . . . but the moment he lays his hand upon his horse, his *face*, even becomes handsome, and he gracefully flies away like a different being."

There were also considerable gulfs of difference extending far deeper than looks or styles, rich and varied as these last were. Such deeper differences might be represented at one end of the spectrum by the relatively earnest and austere Cheyenne, very much concerned with living up to a standard of high-minded and responsible behavior, and at the other end of the spectrum by the relatively free and easy Blackfeet. A trader among the Blackfeet in the era around 1800 wrote that they were the "most independent and happy people of all the tribes E. of the Rocky mountains. War, women, horses and buffalo are their delights, and all these they have at command."

By 1800 French traders had been in the Great Plains for a century. La Salle on the Mississippi in 1682 heard news of two Plains Indian nations called the Gattacka and Manrhoat, now identified as (probably) the Kiowa Apache and the Kiowa. In 1706 a Frenchman all the way west across the plains, in what is now eastern Colorado, left proof of his presence in being killed there by Apaches; he was with, although lagging riskily far behind, a band of Pawnees the Apaches believed to be marauders, and was lagging behind because of his pregnant Pawnee wife. The Apaches took her hair but not the man's, he being bald. He was wearing a red cap, a *coureur de bois* to the life, and armed with a shotgun; his wife was carrying a kettle. He was nothing new to the Apaches; they had at that time guns, hatchets, and other trade goods from Frenchmen and Pawnees to the eastward, astoundingly early though it was—a generation before the birth of Daniel Boone—for European trade and traders to reach so far across the continent. Back east, a very long way back east, English exploration was just working its way into the Blue Ridge Mountains.

The free-ranging coureurs de bois, much criticized by missionaries and other duly constituted authorities, were the first Europeans to see most of North America above Mexico. How far "into the unknown west," said Canada's leading businessman of the 1690s, "these freebooters of the wilderness penetrated may never be discovered."

A Spanish military expedition that was sent east from Santa Fe in 1720 to find the encroaching French was destroyed by Pawnees; thereafter the French openly made the plains their own. A formal French expedition was at the Mandan towns in 1739, noting the riches of commerce there and gathering information from horse-owning plains people. Some of the same explorers came within sight of the South Dakota Black Hills four years later.

France's official fur-trading organization was dismantled by the defeat of France in the French and Indian War, but the French wilderness mechanics, the voyageurs and coureurs de bois, remained; they, and the Indians they had such a knack for getting along with, hired out their talents to English and Scottish masters and were the muscles of the two great English fur-hunting combines. Well before the end of the 1700s French traders had reached the Rocky Mountains by nearly every important river between the Saskatchewan and the Red. For much of the 100 years thereafter French or Indian-French assistance was present in successful dealings with the nations of the northern Rockies and the upper plains.

Six veteran Frenchmen and two Indians accompanied Alexander Mackenzie on his trail-breaking journey to the Canadian Pacific in 1793, and five Frenchmen crossed the plains with the Lewis and Clark expedition in 1805—not counting the infant Jean-Baptiste Charbonneau, born to the Shoshoni girl guide, Sacajawea, two months before the start of the trip.

Lewis and Clark opened the way for a new specimen of foreigner in the plains and the "Shineing Mountains," as Captain Meriwether Lewis referred to the Rockies. This was the American trapper, the "free" trapper, the mountain man. The mountain men became a byword for knowledge of the wild Far West and solitary survival therein; a few who survived gained fame in specialized circles as guides for later western explorers. One of the most remarkable, so much so that some students have thought him wholly legendary, was Sacajawea's son Baptiste, who was educated at the court of a European prince and returned to the Rockies to whack out a monumental mountain-man career, packed with the history of westward-rolling America, and at last went home to his mother's people, the Northern Shoshoni, in their Wyoming country of the Wind River Mountains.

The mountain men lived and worked with the Indians and constituted, in effect, a small, scattered tribe of their own, so far from the life of the "States" they were scarcely recognizable as white Americans. With one implacable exception the Indians usually dealt them more hospitality than hostility, the friendliest being the Northern Shoshoni, or Snakes, as the mountain men called them, using the name given them by the Sioux and the French.

One of the few large-scale Indian battles the mountain men encountered took place in the valley of the Little Snake River, almost on the present Colorado-Wyoming line, in the summer of 1841, when some thirty trappers, captained by a mountain veteran named Henry Fraeb, along with a number of Shoshonis, were attacked by a large war party of several hundred Cheyenne, Sioux, and Arapaho—for what reason is not known.

The mountain men forted up behind killed horses and mules and logs and withstood charge after charge throughout the day, the plains warriors galloping up furiously to within ten or fifteen yards while Fraeb yelled constant warnings to his men to hold their fire and shoot carefully in turn, so there would always be some loaded rifles. The mountain men knew their business and were able to maintain a steady fire from their heavy Hawken rifles, slow to load but very deadly. Each charge broke with a vicious flurry of arrows, as the army of attackers wheeled and dashed off, gathering up their dead and wounded on the way.

At the end of the day, the Cheyennes and their allies stopped fighting and went away. By then Old Fraeb had been killed, and, said one of his men years later, "he was the ugliest looking dead man I ever saw, and I have seen a good many. His face was all covered with blood, and he had rotten front teeth and a horrible grin. When he was killed he never fell, but sat braced up against a stump, a sight to behold." Several other trappers were killed in the same fight, commemorated by the trappers in strewing the names Battle Creek and Battle Lake and Battle Mountain over the vicinity, and calling the mountain just south, where they and the Shoshonis had sent their women to hide, Squaw Mountain.

The one implacable enemy of the American trappers in the early days was the Blackfoot confederacy. Principal source of the savage Blackfoot hostility may have been the Canadian companies on the Saskatchewan, where the Siksika people traded. Some witnesses, at least, believed it was considered a legitimate business tactic, in the fur trade, to urge one's Indian clients to kill off the competition. The Blackfeet did so with joyous application, and their very name was enough to make a mountain man swallow hard and think serious thoughts of his hair.

Since the Blackfeet were the most powerful nation north of the Missouri, they effectively deflected for some years American drift to the north. Finally, in the 1830s, American traders made some progress at winning Piegan trade from the Hudson Bay Company, and some progress at making peace (with a great flow of rum), although trapper killing still went on. But most of the trade of the Piegan and their Atsina allies, controlling the country that is now northern Montana east of the Rockies, did find itself in American hands by the late 1840s.

The mountain men, by this time, had largely vanished from the trapped-out beaver streams. Their place, in the plains and the Rockies, was being taken by trains of West Coast-bound overland emigrants. The frontier stole in from the east like dusk, and by the 1840s the nations of the plains had already felt its touch, in the form of whiskey, plagues, syphilis, and a bewildering increase of war.

In the 1830s the Southern Cheyenne and Arapaho fought the Comanche and Kiowa along the Arkansas River. To the north, above the Platte, the Sioux and the Northern Cheyenne were at war with the Crows. Many of the people of the farther plains were hostile to the Shoshoni, who ranged down from the mountains, and to the Pawnee, who ranged westward from the eastern reaches of the plains.

The "intruding" eastern Indians, Delawares, Shawnee, Potawatomi, and many others, driven west of the Mississippi, were fearful adversaries, expert with firearms at a time when the plains people had few guns, when they "would pay a good price for a barrel hoop to convert into knives and daggers," as a mountain man remarked of the early 1840s. The eastern intruders were sometimes attacked on sight, as numbers of fleeing survivors of Black Hawk's band were later "cut off" by the Sioux after they had reached the Mississippi's west bank.

Some of these many hostile confrontations were conducted with propriety and a regard for the laws of tradition, but some were not. Such Cheyenne celebrities as Little Wolf, chief of the Bow String soldier society, and White Antelope, one of the chiefs of the Crooked Lance society, won great fame fighting Comanches and Pawnees in the most honorable and decent manner.

But in 1838 a group of Bow String men whipped with their quirts the aged and respected keeper of the Medicine Arrows, the Cheyennes' most sacred possessions, in order to force him to perform the requisite ceremonies so they could go to war. This was an unheard-of thing. The chief of the Dog Soldiers, the principal Cheyenne soldier and police society, killed another Cheyenne in a drunken brawl. This was an unheard-of thing. He had to go into exile along with all his relations. As a result of these blasphemies the Cheyenne suffered bitter defeats at the hands of Kiowas and Comanches, until a peace was made between them in 1840. Thereafter the Arapaho and Cheyenne people made the Utes, westward across the Rockies, their grade-A enemies.

The incessant simmer of hostility was bad for trade and travel, as in Bourgmont's time more than 100 years before.

In the early 1840s five Blackfoot chief men took a three-year trip to see the world, traveling from the Alberta plains down the eastern curb of the Rockies all the way to Taos, along the Old North Trail—the very, very old North Trail, possible main route of the first people to enter North America so many thousands of years ago. Stretches of it were then still rutted by travois and marked by countless generations of travelers, in particular by the tipi circles of stones previously mentioned. In my New Mexico childhood old-timers held a kind of folk belief that these marked lodge burials: the practice of honoring a great and good man by leaving his body propped up in his lodge to receive death, the tipi weighted with stones around the edges to resist as long as possible the whipping wind of the plains. The five Blackfeet may have been the last Indian tourists to travel the Old North Trail in peace.

Especially, wars bothered the trade and travel of Americans, filling the country with excitable war parties that menaced emigrants and sometimes stole anything not tied down. American troops were marched into the plains several times in the 1830s and 1840s, to the delight of the Indians, who admired the show of color and guns and, most of all, the soldiers' swords. "Big Knives" was the polite name for white Americans among the plains people, as it was among many other Indians over the United States, and a saber was much valued by Plains Indians as a weapon.

In 1849 two military posts were established along the Platte, and in 1851 ex-mountain man Tom Fitzpatrick ("Broken Hand"), appointed U.S. Indian Agent, held a great council near the farthest west of these, Fort Laramie, a converted fur-trade post at the mouth of the Laramie River on the North Platte. The council encampment was at Horse Creek, thirty-seven miles east of the fort, and was the scene of the greatest assembly of Indians in plains history, or at any rate the greatest assembly since Bourgmont's great Padouca council of 1724, where the Padouca people alone had numbered "several thousand."

The number present at Broken Hand Fitzpatrick's 1851 council was estimated at from 8,000 to 12,000 people, representing Assiniboin, Atsina, Arikara, Crow, Shoshoni, Sioux, Cheyenne, and Arapaho people, some of these not accustomed to meeting except in battle. All agreed on a general peace (Pawnees tacitly excepted, no Pawnees being present) and promised to be more considerate of emigrants, whose covered-wagon trains had by then been familiar along the Oregon Trail for ten years and during the previous two summers had filled all the westward trails to overflowing, rushing to the gold in California.

The United States promised to keep troops in the plains, ostensibly to protect the Indians from white depredations, and the Indians authorized the building of roads and forts in their country—a point vividly protested later on by some of the membership, and a point fairly sure to result in Indian-white collisions, as had been clear at least since Mad Anthony Wayne's malignant Treaty of Greenville back in the Old Northwest nearly sixty years before.

Three years later, ten miles or so from the scene of this famous peace council, the wars of the United States against the Plains Indians had their not-so-grand opening.

The immediate cause was a dilapidated emigrant cow, allegedly abandoned, and killed by a Minneconjou Sioux for the hide. The emigrant put in a claim at Fort Laramie for damages. Spokesmen from the Sioux camp offered ten dollars, the emigrant demanded twenty-five. The Sioux wouldn't or couldn't meet his price, and a lieutenant took thirty-two men and two howitzers and went to the Sioux camp, several miles down the river from the fort, to drag out the cow-killer. There were many lodges of Oglala and Brulé people, and among the Brulés a few lodges of Minneconjous, summer visitors from the Missouri; all these were divisions of the Teton Lakota. Man Afraid of His Horses, the Oglala leader, was present and tried to pacify the lieutenant, as did the leader of the Brulés, Conquering Bear, who was considered a "good old man" by Americans who knew him. But an argument developed, and the lieutenant had Conquering Bear shot down on the spot. In the fight that followed, the lieutenant and all his men were killed.

This was not the first blood spilled between the plains people and the soldiers who had come to protect them. The summer before, a detachment of Fort Laramie troops had killed three or four Sioux in a regrettable misunderstanding, which the Sioux had recognized as such. But this was the first blood of American soldiers.

The American public (or at least some of its vocal segments) clamored for retaliation, which was provided the following summer, in 1855, when an army of 1,300 men marched into the plains from Fort Leavenworth and destroyed a Brulé village near the forks of the Platte, killing eighty-six. The number—unpublished—of women and children among the eighty-six brought a protest from General Winfield Scott at higher army headquarters back east. But at a conference in the spring of 1856, the properly humbled Brulés promised to turn over the man who had killed the cow.

In that same year (1856) an argument with a band of Cheyennes over a stray horse led to an attack by troops on an unsuspecting Cheyenne family, which led to the death of a stray trapper who had had nothing to do with the military attack. That, in turn, led to an army attack on some innocent and astounded Cheyennes, killing several of them and seizing all their horses and property, which, in turn, brought a Cheyenne attack on two wagon trains, killing seven people, including a woman and two children.

This tragicomedy dragged along until the summer of 1857, when Colonel E.V. Sumner set out with a strong force to put a stop to it. On a July day in a handsome plains setting along the Solomon River, in present Kansas, he met the flower of the Southern Cheyenne in one of the few real picture-book battle scenes in all Indian history. Everything was as it should be; some 300 mounted warriors drawn up in battle line singing their war songs, all in their full war costumes, colorful as fireworks; and they had all had time for all the necessary pre-battle ceremonies. Their great medicine man, Ice, had picked the battleground for them, and seemed to be certain that he had been granted the spiritual power to render the soldiers' bullets harmless. Accordingly, the Cheyennes, although outnumbered, were confident of victory. But Colonel Sumner charged with cavalry, and curiously enough decided to make the charge with the saber, possibly the only instance of a full-fledged saber charge in all the plains wars. No medicine had been made against sabers. The Cheyenne warriors fired a hasty flight of arrows, and fled. Losses on both sides were small, but there was no question as to who had won. A peace was made the following spring.

But war had settled down to stay. Peace, from now on, would only be in intervals that could not last, like sunny days in winter. Everyone believed each time—anyway, they said they did—that peace this time was forever. The whites assured each other they had solved the Redskin problem at last and held foot-stomping jamborees to celebrate. The Indians rejoiced in their lodges and invited each other to company dinners, high-spirited social dances abounded, and young warriors became young dandies, dripping rich habiliments and waving turkey-feather fans and contriving elaborate strategies to get a word with their girls by the light of the moon. But then the whirlwind of hostilities would spring up again, spin to a bloody climax and stop with an uneasy jolt at still another peace. As the frontier reached out to envelop the plains the intervals of peace grew briefer and more clouded, the rings of war more distended and more violent.

Cherokee gold rushers had seen placer deposits in the Rockies on their way to California in 1849; in 1858 they returned with other prospectors and discovered gold in Cherry Creek at the foot of the Rockies, near present Denver. The Pike's Peak gold rush got under way the following summer, pouring an estimated 80,000 Pike's-Peak-or-Busters into the plains during the next three years. Other mining strikes followed. Some of the Plains Indians seriously thought the crowds of would-be prospectors rushing hither and yon to new strikes real or fancied were people who had gone insane by the bunch.

Town founders and real estate promoters came along with the mining camps, settlers followed after, and within less than a decade railroads were appearing on the buffalo plains. The frontier wrapped its coils around the Indians of the plains and in due time swallowed them up.

Basically, the story is no different from the penetration and destruction of Indian nations elsewhere. There were the treaties, the dissensions and factions within the Indian nations, the enforced new treaties, the disputes swelling into new wars. There were then the wars, the clarion call for extermination and piece-meal attempts at same, and the long, agonizingly long, diminuendo ending.

The wars were founded on very much the same elements as in the Indian wars that had gone before. At bottom there was pressure for property—time after time agreements on the location of reservations were upset by mining, railroad, or land-speculation interests that were able to bring sufficient influence to bear on the government. Orders went out to persuade the Indians to accept revised treaties and revised reservations. The Indians often had to be persuaded by force. Each of these occasions broke a solemn promise of the United States and led to a chronic Indian distrust of anything marked "USA." General George Crook, the most experienced of western Indian-fighters, summed up this process: "Greed and avarice on the part of the whites—in other words, the almighty dollar, is at the bottom of nine-tenths of all our Indian troubles."

There were the usual subsidiary causes, such as the refractory bands, sometimes making up the majority of a tribe, that denied the authority of treaty chiefs; wild warriors who would not be controlled; gangs of bootleg traders, buffalo hunters, prospectors or amateur Indian killers who would not be controlled either and who overran Indian lands in defiance of government orders to stay out and keep the peace.

Said the superintendent of Indian affairs for Montana in 1869: "Nothing can be done to insure peace and order till there is a military force strong enough to clear out the roughs and whisky-sellers in the country." Five years later the Canadian North West Mounted Police were organized specifically to put down this whiskey trade north of the border; 150 "Mounties" ended it in less than three months, to the indignant protests of its Montana proprietors— but it was not thus ended, of course, on the American side of the line.

There were also some new trouble spots that attained prominence in the plains wars. The Bureau of Indian Affairs was transferred to the Interior Department from the War Department in 1849; conflict between its agents and the Army became frequent and sometimes serious, an occasional conse- quence being the dishonoring of Indian peace or surrender terms when one department triumphantly succeeded in overruling the other.

"Indian rings" of crooked officials and crooked suppliers made graft a big business, while Indian families imprisoned on reservations suffered concen- tration-camp privation, ate their gaunt horses or the bark of trees, and some- times starved to death by hundreds. Large numbers of Indians were shifted from this reservation to that, perhaps many miles from their homes into what was to them a foreign land, by whatever clique of whites happened to get momentary control of Indian matters—"I think you had better put the Indians on wheels," said one weary chief.

The disappearance of the buffalo is sometimes emphasized as a cause of war on the plains, maybe too much so. As early as the close of the 1830s, when the buffalo could still darken the earth and their gigantic mirages fill the sky, numbers of Indian leaders foresaw the finish of buffalo hunting. The ques- tion was not if the buffalo would vanish, but when. Some thought soon, some thought not for 100 years. The former sometimes associated themselves with the treaty factions with the thought of making a deal for the sale of land and mineral rights that would subsist their people through the coming time of change. But the buffalo motive is further diminished by the fact that in Canada the Blackfeet, Bloods, Plains Cree, and Assiniboin, buffalo people from horns to hocks, made no war to save the buffalo.

The only major Indian war in British Canada's history was not primarily an Indian war at all, but was styled by Canada a rebellion, and had strong over- tones of religious strife, pitting Protestant Ontario against the Catholic Métis of the Red River of the North. The Métis were mixed-blood French-Indian plainsmen, at that time mostly French-Cree and French-Assiniboin. Under the mystical Louis Riel they made a noble effort in 1870, with an epilogue in 1885, to set up an independent semi-Indian state in Canada's great plains, and lost.

So much for the prosaic motivations behind the Indian wars of the plains. In reality, like so many other Indian wars, they were dismal, dirty, and need- less. But their reality has been largely forgotten, if it was ever perceived to begin with. The wars of the plains entered immediately into our folklore, and there they will remain, no doubt, until the end of time. In our folklore they are all Indians and all Indian wars in one gaudy package. As the Plains Indians were amalgamations of other Indians of the eastern forests and the western mountains, and, with their horses and guns, were in part the white man's creation, so the folklore of their wars is an amalgamation of all such folklore from every point of the continent.

It is in the Plains Indian as the classic Indian warrior, as hyper-Indian, as the mythic Indian carried to extremes, that the folklore of the plains revels most. Never were such brave knights, such reckless horsemanship, never such tragic nobility, and when a general said, as a general did, that they were good shots, good riders, and the best fighters the sun ever shined on, one can see the mist of emotion in his eyes, and he'll shoot the man who doesn't bare his head.

And above all, never was there such rainbow color brought to combat— the painted shields and war-horses, the painted eyes and bodies, the buffalo hats, the lynx-skin headdresses with an eagle feather for each slain foe, the rippling war bonnets, sometimes trailing down to the heels, the jewel-work of beads and porcupine quills, arrow quivers furred with the magic skin of the otter, hearts made strong by dreams that came in the form of songs.

The wars of the plains are America's *Iliad*. It is sung in the jagged rhythm of a wild Sioux charge. It is all poetry, for poetry is really made of blood and not of daffodils. It will outlive sober history and never quite die, as poetry never quite does. Red Cloud and Sitting Bull and Roman Nose will, very likely, still touch a light to the spirit as long as America is remembered.

The Minnesota Sioux, the four Dakota subtribes known as the Santee, had signed a treaty in 1851. They felt cheated by the treaty and cheated in their reservation life, and in the summer of 1862 they tried to kill all the whites in their country, under the leadership of one of their chiefs, sixty-year-old Little Crow. They murdered some 700 settlers and killed 100 soldiers before they were driven out of Minnesota to join the other Dakotas on the plains. Several dozen Santee chiefs and warriors were hanged. Fugitive Little Crow, foraging for berries, was shot by a farm youth.

The Sioux of the plains were asked to sign a treaty in 1865 to permit passage from Fort Laramie along the Powder River to the gold fields of Montana. Red Cloud (named for the red meteor of 1822), greatest of Oglala warriors, refused to sign and refused to cede. When the troops built forts along the trail, Red Cloud with his followers and Cheyenne allies closed the trail to supplies and held the troops under a virtual siege for two years at Fort Phil Kearny, at the foot of the Bighorn Mountains in what is now northern Wyoming.

There was a famous fight along this trail one December day in 1866 when Captain William J. Fetterman, who was reported to have said, "Give me eighty men and I'll ride through the whole Sioux nation," rode forth with eighty-one and was decoyed by a daring party of ten picked warriors—two Cheyennes, two Arapahoes, and two from each of the three Sioux divisions present—into ambush and annihilation. There was another famous fight the next summer when Red Cloud's finest cavalry stormed down to make meat of a wood-chopping detail from the fort—thirty-six men. Thirty-two managed to reach the shelter of a wagon-box corral and, armed with new breech-loading rifles, fought off repeated and suicidal charges throughout the day; twenty-nine were still alive and fighting when relief arrived from the fort.

But Red Cloud could not be pushed aside, the trail could not be used, and in 1868 the government at last surrendered. The forts were dismantled, the troops moved out, and the Powder River country, including the Black Hills, was reserved to the Dakota forever.

Red Cloud signed the concluding treaty, and true to his word never again made war on the whites; he only tried to avoid them, and counseled his people to do the same. If you wished to possess the white man's things, he said, "You must begin anew and put away the wisdom of your fathers. You must lay up food and forget the hungry. When your house is built, your storeroom filled, then look around for a neighbor whom you can take advantage of and seize all he has." He was a voice of legend; when he recited his war deeds it took a long time, because he had counted the incredible total of eighty coups; once he had returned from the Crow wars with an arrow driven entirely through his body, projecting front and back.

Peace lasted very pleasantly through the early days of Denver for the Southern Cheyenne and Arapaho even though troubled by emigrant traffic (the wandering Cherokee Forty-niners established a new main route westward through Colorado before they left the country, the Cherokee Trail, that after 1862 replaced the South Pass road as the most traveled highway). A large party of Arapaho camped in the heart of Denver during the town's first couple of years around the turn of 1860, and left the women and children there while they went to make war against the Utes, for all the world like pioneers.

Then came a treaty in 1861—only a few chief men could be induced, with great difficulty, to sign, and some of these later claimed they had been misled as to what they were signing. The treaty ceded most of Southern Cheyenne and Arapaho territory, but worse than this it contained a clause later construed by government officials as permitting a railroad through what Indian lands were left.

A railroad meant a chain of white settlements, and this meant an end to the last of their country, and the Cheyenne and Arapaho general public at length forced a number of the treaty chiefs to repudiate the treaty, under pain of death. White politicians regarded this as hostility, and the refusal of some bands and soldier societies to sign the treaty at all was regarded as hostility.

But peace dwindled along until the spring of 1864, when the Reverend J. M. Chivington, colonel of Colorado volunteers, reported that Cheyennes had stolen some cattle from a government contractor's herd. The report was suspect at the time and later—old mountain men said that whenever a greenhorn lost a stray he blamed the Indians—but Colonel Chivington took stern and instant measures, troops attacked families of amazed Cheyennes, the Cheyennes attacked families of unsuspecting settlers, and another war was on.

Using the most eloquent persuasion, Colorado's governor managed by autumn to get some of the alarmed Cheyennes to come to Denver for peace talks. The Cheyenne peace party was headed by Black Kettle and the distinguished war chief White Antelope; they talked to the governor and, on the advice of the military commandant at Fort Lyon, established their village on Sand Creek, thirty miles from the fort.

The village was then destroyed in a stealthy, sudden attack by Colonel Chivington and a force of something between 600 and 1,000 troops, mostly volunteers. Colonel Chivington was reported as saying, "Kill and scalp all big and little; nits make lice." The boys, as his reports refer to his soldiers, did so with enthusiasm.

(The war cry, "Nits make lice," was also reported, it will be remembered, from the Yana massacre in California, also in 1864.)

Black Kettle ran up both an American flag and a white flag, but the boys were having too much fun. They butchered any Indian in sight (except for some Cheyenne men who managed to fort up on the creek bank, and who had rifles). Black Kettle's wife was shot down, and passing soldiers fired seven more bullets into her body; she had nine wounds, but lived. Another old woman was scalped but came back to life and was trying to walk but she couldn't see, for the skin of her forehead had fallen over her eyes. A child at the toddling stage brought merriment to some of the boys, testified an Army major later, as they took turns trying to bring it down at seventy-five yards; one finally did. A lieutenant, testified another officer, shot and scalped a captured group of three women and eight children, one after the other, while they begged for mercy.

Black Kettle escaped. White Antelope refused to run. Some accounts say that he tried to talk to the troops and some that he stood in front of his lodge and folded his arms and sang his death song. It was a good death song, and has been remembered. It went: "Nothing lives long, except the earth and the mountains." He sang until he was cut down by bullets and died. He was some years past seventy at the time.

Perhaps 200 Cheyenne women and children were killed at Sand Creek, and perhaps seventy men, and an estimated forty or so Arapaho people who were with the Cheyennes; but there was a great deal of dispute among the boys as to the number of dead, and the figures are not necessarily accurate. The boys went back to Denver and exhibited scalps and severed arms and legs in a theater. White Antelope's scrotum was later made into a souvenir tobacco pouch.

The boys had reason to be proud. This was probably the greatest victory, measured by Indians killed, the whites were to record in all the Indian wars of the plains.

Not all Americans were proud of the boys. An old mountain man named Kit Carson spoke of them as cowards and dogs. A story was current that the volunteers had staged this Indian "war" to keep from being sent into Civil War action in the east. Nor were all the settlers jubilant. The Cheyenne plains went up in flames during the next three years; in two summer months alone 117 settlers were killed and their women and children (unlike the civilized treatment of nits) dragged away as captives, in dozens of widely separated raids.

A government commission reported, four years after Colonel Chivington's victory: "It scarcely has its parallel in the records of Indian barbarity. . . . No one will be astonished that a war ensued which cost the government $30,000,000 and carried conflagration and death to the border settlements."

There were many men of valor among the valorous Cheyenne, including such leaders of exalted rank as Little Wolf and White Antelope. But none, probably, was more famous at the time to the ordinary public both Cheyenne and white than a hook-nosed 6-foot 3-inch warrior named The Bat. The Americans called him Roman Nose, translating thus his warrior name of Woqini (Hook Nose). Roman Nose was idolized by the young men and was especially famous because he was invulnerable in battle. He had a magic headdress, made for him by Ice, the medicine man, from a vision Roman Nose had seen during his vigil and fast, a headdress with forty eagle feathers set in a tail so long it nearly touched the ground even when Roman Nose was mounted, and while he wore it bullets and arrows could not touch him. He proved this time after time, riding at a leisurely lope up and down in front of the enemy, while all the enemy shot at him and missed. This always inspired the other Cheyenne warriors.

The war bonnet required elaborate ceremonies at each donning and was surrounded by various taboos, one being that Roman Nose must never eat anything taken from the pot with an iron instrument, fork or knife. If he broke this taboo he broke the war bonnet's medicine, and long rites of purification would be necessary to restore it.

It happened that in the summer of 1868 a company of fifty experienced plainsmen, enlisted in the Army as scouts, was trapped by a large number of Cheyenne, Sioux, and Arapaho warriors. Shortly before this battle started, Roman Nose was a guest in a Sioux lodge and the hostess, unaware of his taboo, took food from the skillet with a fork. Roman Nose did not learn of this until after he had already eaten (folk memory says the food was fry bread).

When the fight began he did not go to it, until the chiefs came to him and said the warriors needed him; one said, "All those people fighting out there feel that they belong to you." Roman Nose said a taboo had been broken, but he painted himself and went through the ceremonies of getting out the war bonnet and putting it on, and got his horse and rode at the enemy. He was shot from his horse and brought back to the lodges where he died at sunset.

The Cheyennes made a few more desultory attacks, principally to recover bodies of their dead, then ceased their attacks and went away. The company of scouts had fought from an island in the bed of the Arkansas River, now named on maps Beecher Island after the company's lieutenant, who was killed there.

Occupation forces fighting guerrilla resistance are at a disadvantage, since they cannot often lay hands on the guerrillas. If their government, or the spirit of the public back home, will stand for it they prefer the hostage tactic—executing all the people of a hostage town in reprisal for acts of guerrilla warfare. When the War Department gained the ascendancy in its incessant conflict with the Indian Bureau it sometimes used this method. Unfortunately such villages chosen for destruction, in the plains wars, were likely to be strongholds of pro-American peace party Indians endeavoring to be friendly, since such villages were likely to be the nearest ones available.

Black Kettle had made unceasing and increasingly successful efforts for peace since the Sand Creek massacre, believing there was no other hope of survival for his people. In the winter of 1868 his village, which was then lodged on the Washita River in Oklahoma, was treated to its second stealthy and unexpected attack by Army troops, who were under orders to destroy a village and hang all the men and take all the women and children prisoner.

Something between thirty-eight men, women, and children (Cheyenne figures) and 103 warriors (Army figures) were killed, and this time Black Kettle was killed too. But men from nearby Arapaho, Kiowa, and Comanche villages came to the rescue, and the American commander prudently withdrew, leaving behind a detachment of nineteen troopers who had gone prisoner-catching—all nineteen were slain.

The American commander was Lieutenant Colonel George A. Custer, and this was his first major engagement with Indians. It might be called Custer's first stand.

The following winter the same Lidicesque technique of destroying a village as a lesson to the out-of-reach resistance was used by the military in northern Montana, on the Marias River, where a village of Piegan people, selected either at random or by mistake, was destroyed in a stealthy dawn attack. It developed that the village was that of the Piegan chief most noted as friendly to the whites, Heavy Runner. He was reportedly shot dead as he walked out to stop the troops, holding his hands above his head and waving his identification paper.

It also developed that the casualties were overwhelmingly women and children, and that there had been no resistance—the four companies of cavalry involved lost one man killed, and another trooper broke his leg when he fell from a horse. It also developed that the village was in the midst of a small-pox epidemic at the time.

These developments brought some rather angry criticism from the eastern press. General Phil Sheridan replied with the hostage-killing philosophy in a nutshell: "If a village is attacked, and women and children killed, the responsibility is not with the soldier, but with the people whose crimes necessitate the attack." The rearward frontier, back far enough or heavily settled enough to feel safe and sound, with its general notion that extermination would be good for business, generally approved. The people in the forward areas, without even the cranky little voice of a small town newspaper, were generally not heard from.

The plains wars reached their climax in the 1870s, after the discovery in 1874 of gold in the Black Hills. The Sioux had to be persuaded to sell out, the Black Hills having been guaranteed to them forever by the most recent treaty. The persuasion was a difficult job. It required many columns of troops assisted by many scouts—Pawnees and Crows and Shoshonis who had joined the white soldiers to fight their old plains enemies.

In this war Red Cloud remained apart. The Sioux and their allies came gradually under the influence of two powerful and very different personalities. One was Crazy Horse, an Oglala warrior famed for his boldness, who had led the decoy party that had beckoned Captain Fetterman and his eighty-one men into the hereafter. The other was Tatanka Yotanka, Sitting Buffalo, known to the Americans as Sitting Bull. There was a fashion for some years among western historians of belittling Sitting Bull's importance; recent scholarship seems to have restored him to the place of eminence he held in his own day. He was a dreamer of visions, a seer of the future, and war chief of the Hunkpapa division of the Teton Lakota. He was also one of the most profound and idealistic statesmen in Indian history.

In June of 1876 the main body of unpersuaded Sioux was found by General George Crook, leading 1,200 or so soldiers. A more or less equal number of warriors attacked him, everyone fought well, there were many individual acts of courage, it was a long and violent and well handled battle, the classic battle, perhaps, of the plains wars, but the ground kept growing Indians, and Crook at length had to withdraw and limp back to his base of supplies to await reinforcements. The battle was fought among crabapple blossoms in the valley of Rosebud Creek in southern Montana.

The Indians moved across the ridge to the next river west, the Little Big Horn, and established a large camp, made up of Crazy Horse's people and Sitting Bull's people and allies from the other Sioux divisions and the Cheyenne. Eight days after the battle with Crook, this camp was attacked on a Sunday afternoon by a regiment of cavalry. The attack was defeated. Crazy Horse himself, shouting, "Today is a good day to fight, today is a good day to die," led a rush that cut off half of the attacking forces. Every man in this surrounded group of cavalrymen was killed in a desperate, blazing fight that lasted less than half an hour.

The attacking force had been the elite Seventh Cavalry, organized for the specific purpose of whipping the Plains Indians, destroyers of Black Kettle's camp on the Washita. It had been led by Lieutenant Colonel Custer, who died in the battle along with more than 260 of his men.

This battle was, and has remained, the sensational moment of truth in the wars of the plains, at least for the Americans. It was the kind of resounding defeat that simply could not be handed to a modern nation of 40 million people by a few scarecrow savages. Especially not in the very middle of the great centennial celebration—the first report appeared in eastern newspapers on the morning of July 5, 1876, and caught the country smack in the act of congratulating itself on its first 100 years.

The sea of literature on Custer's last stand could sink a battleship, which might not be a bad use for much of it. Excuses cover every possibility, unto such psycho-bizarrerie as an explanation that Custer was a natural-born loser, being an immature phallic narcissist.

But the defeat was, in actual effect, the end of the wars of the plains, and Crazy Horse and Sitting Bull lost by winning. Troops harried their people without mercy, forts were established in unceded territory, and the Indians had no means of keeping a standing army in the field indefinitely. Separated into small bands they were hunted down or, as was Sitting Bull with his followers, driven into Canada.

The ending went on and on, like the dying wail of a death song. It went on for years, while the poetry and the romance evaporated, and these were seen to be not knights and paladins after all but only bedraggled scurrying creatures rather like fugitive convicts. So they were turned over to jailers who knew how to handle tough prisoners, and the greatest of warriors is nothing more than any other weak-stomached man when he has nothing to do but crouch under guard and watch his people starve—as some 600 Montana Blackfeet died of "sheer starvation" in the winter of 1883.

But it was at this time, when the glitter and nobility had vanished, that the more unreasonable feats of valor and fortitude took place, performed by defeated people only in response to their own individual summons. There were more of them than there were battles in all the wars put together. Some became famous, some did not.

In a time of tension on the plains Few Tails, a man of consequence among the Oglala, was shot and killed by white men for no reason other than being Indian; his wife, Clown, was wounded, one bullet in the leg, one bullet in the breast. They were off the reservation, with a proper official pass for so being. Clown revived after some hours, escaped on one of the horses from their wagon team, and went to a house of white people she thought were friends—they ordered her to go away. She passed by a store where she had often traded but after the previous rejection by supposed friends she was afraid to enter. Thereafter traveling only at night, with no provisions, she covered 100 miles to the Pine Ridge Agency in seven days, arriving more dead than alive. But there her wounds and exhaustion were treated. Eventually she recovered. If her incredible ride doesn't sound incredible try it some time, 100-mile trail ride, moving only at night, with no provisions other than two bullets in your body. She had also, of course, the memory of her husband's murder for company.

In an obscure little police action a young Sioux, wearing a trailing war bonnet that is somehow comical, like his father's hat, paraded up and down and said to the soldiers, "I am a soldier walking on my own land. they have already killed my grandmother. I will give up my gun to no man." A moment later he fired into a truce party of the soldiers led by General Miles. His uncle said sadly, "My friend is young." Then the uncle too fired directly at General Miles. Both young Sioux and uncle were dead in a few minutes. Someone knelt and took careful aim and shot the young man through the forehead, the bullet cutting the war bonnet's brow band. They were scalped and left to stay forever in their land. It was all so obscure the name of the young Sioux is not even certain; He might have been called Ankle, or Big Ankle.

But to Indian people of the vicinity this gesture so utterly futile was and still is memorable. The uncle, and leader of the band attacked by the troops, was named Lame Deer. The action took place in early May 1877, on the banks of what was then called Muddy Creek and is now called Lame Deer Creek, near the present village of Lame Deer, Montana, center of the Northern Cheyenne reservation. Lame Deer's grave is on the hilltop above. White Bull, a Cheyenne scout with the U.S. Army, took the scalps of the two men and recounted their bitter story to George Bird Grinnell, historian of the Cheyenne.

Well, it all ended. Through the years it wavered away and ended. The New York *Herald* was still calling for extermination in 1879, saying editorially, "The continent is getting too crowded." But no one really took that seriously any more. Starvation, disease, and tough prison wardens were just as effective anyway, and there were the sentimentalists who kept insisting that sooner or later some of the Red Men might actually be civilized. Many of these good people, entirely sincere in the belief that Indians could only be saved by replacing their tribal union with the religion of individual profit (a belief still very much in operation), joined with other good Americans in the land-speculation business and turned the so-called Allotment Act into law in 1887. This distributed fragments of reservations to Indian farmers as small family-sized farms and, upon a token payment, opened the vast acreage left over to white settlement. The process dwindled away after the first big winnings, having by then lifted some 90 million acres, roughly two-thirds of the remaining Indian land base in the United States, out of tribal pockets.

And there was whiskey. That Indian trade whiskey, said Charley Russell, the old Montana cowboy turned world-famous painter, you could be shot and killed, and you wouldn't die until you sobered up. So if you never sobered up you were bound to be all right.

Sitting Bull and what was left of his band returned, having been promised amnesty and security, and in 1885 Sitting Bull joined Buffalo Bill's Wild West Show for a summer tour, rather as if Kaiser Bill (the First) had joined a circus for a while. After the wild finale he sold his photograph (signed) for a dollar a copy, from the tailgate of a wagon. The money he got for this, said Annie Oakley, was passed out to the raggedy small boys who swarmed over the circus grounds at each stop of the show. At the end of the tour Buffalo Bill made him a gift of a trick gray horse Sitting Bull much admired. The horse would sit down and hold up a hoof to shake hands.

The breakup of the great Sioux reservation by the treaty of 1889, for which General Crook was used as figurehead, was only managed by keeping the Sitting Bull faction out of the proceedings.

At the very end of the long ending the messiahs appeared. One was a Nevada Paiute named Wovoka. An older Paiute messiah a generation earlier had announced a similar revelation that had aroused some interest in dreamer cults in the Northwest; Wovoka's vision was borne eastward into the plains. His religion was called the Ghost Dance by whites, because it preached that the ghosts of their forebears were on hand to help living Indians in their hour of extremity; it was based on peaceful endeavor.

A great revival founded on Wovoka's preaching spread among the emotional people of the plains; the theme of peaceful endeavor was revised here and there into a theme of hostility, and the authorities were much disturbed by all the excitement.

Sitting Bull was killed in the process of being placed under precautionary arrest by order of the Indian agent at Standing Rock Agency. The surprise arrest was attempted at night, an hour before dawn, December 15, 1890, by nearly fifty Indian policemen (appointed from anti-Sitting Bull factions), neatly bringing on a fight in which seven of Sitting Bull's band were killed and six Indian policemen. Sitting Bull himself was killed instantly by the police at the first hostile shot. His seventeen-year-old son was then dragged out of the house by the police and shot. The gunfire made the trick gray horse think the show was on; he sat down in the midst of the crossfire and raised his hoof, perhaps in admonition.

It was widely believed at the time—and so reported, from whites and Indians at the Standing Rock Agency as well as by the New York *Herald*—that the arrest was intended to be a prelude to Sitting Bull's murder.

Sitting Bull was buried in quicklime, allegedly to keep sideshow impresarios from stealing his body for exhibition; or there might have been some fear of his people making use of it to rouse a sense of loss. Or perhaps a fear that the Ghost Dancers might bring him back to life.

Crazy Horse had died a dozen years before, in 1877, bayoneted by a soldier while being held a prisoner.

With the U.S. Army, under the very zealous General Nelson Miles, regarding all Ghost Dancers as hostiles, Red Cloud's "friendly" reservation, Pine Ridge, became a haven of safety. In the ultra high tension days following Sitting Bull's murder, the two principal Ghost Dance leaders in the region, Kicking Bear and Short Bull, went to Red Cloud's with all their numerous following. The aged Red Cloud also invited the Big Foot Minneconjou band at Cheyenne River to come and visit; this small band was said to have included

Ghost Dance converts; they set out, something between 250 and 350 people, mostly Minneconjous, accompanied by a few Hunkpapa families, a couple of days before Christmas 1890.

Miles and his field officers appear to have regarded this band as particularly fearsome, for no recorded reason. It was far smaller and certainly less avowedly Ghost Dance than the bands of Kicking Bear and Short Bull, which had returned to Pine Ridge unmolested. The military may have received reports that some families of Sitting Bull's band, having fled from their homes after Sitting Bull's murder, had joined Big Foot's band; the generals may have feared some response to the murder.

In any case, orders went forth to make the Big Foot people prisoners and ship them out of the "war zone."

Various Army units then indulged in a series of Keystone Cops misunderstandings, which they reported as Big Foot cunningly giving them the slip. (Big Foot had fallen ill with pneumonia en route to Pine Ridge, slowing the band's traveling, which was pretty cunning.) Four troops of the Seventh Cavalry finally found them after five days, only some twenty or thirty miles from the Pine Ridge Agency.

The Indians camped overnight (hoisting a white flag as a "sign of peace and a guarantee of safety") in the center of a ring of troops, the number of soldiers doubled to nearly 500 during the evening, plus three reporters, plus the trader from Pine Ridge with a barrel of whiskey. The officers held a well-lubricated party until late in the night, to celebrate the Big Foot capture. Enough personnel stayed sober to set up four quick-firing Hotchkiss cannon and sight them in on the Sioux camp.

In the morning the troopers formed a rough hollow square with the Indian camp in the middle, and the Sioux men were called out from the others to be disarmed. Guns turned in were too few, so the Indian tents were searched, women and children and belongings turned out, and every kind of possible weapon—knives, antique tomahawks—appropriated. The men were then required to open their blankets to be personally searched. At this point a disturbance took place. It is said someone fired a shot, or several shots, at the soldiers.

In any case, the surrounding troops opened an intensive fire at point-blank range upon the surrounded Indians. Most of the warriors were apparently finished off first, although some desperate resistance evidently took place, for twenty-five troopers were killed and thirty-nine wounded. Or wild shots, especially from the cannon, may have caused some of the Army casualties. The quick-firing Hotchkiss gun employed an explosive shell that could kill people by the group, or blow a hole six inches wide through flesh and blood, and one of the dead troopers (an officer, the only commissioned officer killed) was hit by a "bullet" that carried away the top of his head.

Piston-operated quick-firing guns and recoil-operated machine guns were being tried out in this period by the military of the technocratic nations, the civilized nations in nineteenth-century language, to learn lessons that would be of value in the next real war. General Staff discussion of the performance of such new weapons in cutting down hordes of poorly armed "natives" from Africa and India to the islands of the ocean sea sometimes reached the press, resulting in such comment as Hilaire Belloc's

how fortunate that we have got
the Gatling gun and they have not.

In the destruction of Big Foot's band the shooting went on as long as anyone, man woman or child, remained to be shot at. A few got to cover in a dry ravine and escaped. Some of the women were pursued as far as a couple of miles or so over the plains before they were caught and killed.

There has been debate, as there was after Sand Creek, as to the total number of Indian dead. Big Foot's band at this time consisted of about 100 men (reports ran from 73 to 120) and possibly 250 women and children; estimates of the dead ran as high as 300; the military commander of the department stated there were no fewer than 200.

Information from the Indians is of course disconnected. Later memories from a surviving warrior, Dewey Horn Cloud, may or may not have been typical: he lost his mother and father, two brothers, and his wife—a twenty-five-day-old baby girl was still nursing at her breast when her body was found. The infant died within a few months.

A civilian burial detail (at two dollars a corpse, plus souvenirs) came out but only after several days, a blizzard having intervened, and it was assumed relatives and friends from Pine Ridge had removed by then a number of bodies. The burial detail found 146.

Dr. Charles Eastman, Santee Sioux graduate of Dartmouth and the Boston University medical school and government physician at the Pine Ridge Agency, came out with the burial detail. He described dispassionately the way young girls, having run a distance away, had knelt and covered their faces with their shawls so they would not see the pursuing troopers coming up to shoot them.

Some of the eastern press expressed outrage, but so also did General Miles: "the dispositions of the 400 soldiers and four pieces of artillery were fatally defective; large numbers of troops were killed and wounded by fire from their own ranks, and a very large number of women and children were killed in addition to the Indian men."

But in the following inquiry all the people involved said they had behaved with utmost correctness. It was true that the Army scout and interpreter, John Shangreau, had told the officers that if they tried to take the guns and horses of the Indians—evidently Big Foot and his band had not quite realized they were supposed to be prisoners—it would bring on a fight and "you will kill all these women and children." But the officers had orders, repeated orders, to dismount and disarm the band and if they resisted to "destroy them."

Possibly the papers could be blamed. They had been told a Sioux outbreak was in progress, but nothing was happening.

It took place on Wounded Knee Creek in South Dakota. Many years later Stephen Vincent Benét wrote a poem in which he mentioned Wounded Knee, although there is no reason to suppose he was thinking of this incident. The last lines go,

> I shall not rest quiet in Montparnasse . . . I shall not be there. I shall rise
>   and pass.
> Bury my heart at Wounded Knee.

They gathered up the frozen dead—the Indian dead—in wagons at Wounded Knee, and buried them all together in a communal pit.

Families at Cheyenne River and Pine Ridge still remember a line from Dewey Horn Cloud's later testimony: his dying mother, in the famous Wounded Knee ravine, said, "My son, I am going to fall down now. Pass by me and go on."

The Last Stronghold

A Mescalero Apache song, the Dawn Song from the Gotal Ceremony:

The black turkey in the east spreads his tail
The tips of his beautiful tail are the white dawn

Boys are sent running to us from the dawn
They wear yellow shoes of sunbeams
They dance on streams of sunbeams

Girls are sent dancing to us on the rainbow
They wear shirts of yellow
They dance above us the dawn maidens

The sides of the mountains turn to green
The tops of the mountains turn to yellow

And now above us on the beautiful mountains
it is dawn.

"Apache" is one of the handful of American Indian tribal names known generally all over the world, as witness the Apaches—street toughs—of Paris in the epoch of 1900, and their famous "Apache Dance."

History limits Apache people to the Southwest of what is now the United States, and to northwestern border regions of Mexico. They were in no sense

a single nation or confederation, but, in pre-reservation times, groups of loosely organized bands, united by their common language, Athapaskan.

Their name for themselves was (and still is) Inde, Nde, meaning as usual The People. They came from the great Athapaskan hive in what is now far northwestern Canada and neighboring Alaska, drifting southward, probably along the flanks of the Rockies, in a long slow migration that may have taken centuries. They were following the buffalo in the southern plains when the Vásquez Coronado expedition entered there in 1541.

Wherever they appeared as they moved along they were invaders, sometimes at peace as traders, sometimes at war as raiders.

For several hundred years they were borderland traders familiar to various towns of the Pueblo civilization, and, eventually, familiar to the mine-and-mission Spanish colonial frontier.

A Spanish missionary of 1630 wrote that the Pueblos were "surrounded on all sides by the huge Apache nation." Those who followed the buffalo, called by the Spanish the Vaquero Apaches, tanned buffalo hides in a number of special ways, "some leave the hair on them, and they remain like a plush velvet, and serve as bed and as cloak . . . others they tan without the hair, and thin them down, of which they make their tents and other things. . . . And with their hides they trade through the land. . . . At which point I cannot refrain from telling one thing, somewhat incredible, however ridiculous. And it is that when these Indians go to trade and traffic, the entire rancherias go, with their wives and children, who live in tents made of these skins of buffalo . . . and the tents they carry on pack trains of dogs, harnessed up with their little packsaddles. . . . And they are accustomed to take 500 dogs in one pack-train, one in front of the other, and the people carry their merchandise [thus] loaded, which they barter for cotton cloth and for other things."

But tales of warfare were also common, in speaking of Apaches. Ancient Pueblo tradition, with typical Pueblo dry humor, spoke of sessions of evening talk as "Apache-killing."

Apache people of central and southern Arizona found their principal foe, irreconcilable generation after generation, in the Piman people of this region, the O'odham (their own name, meaning of course The People), settled there for some 8,000 or 9,000 years.

Apaches centering in northeastern Arizona were on terms of frequent hostility with such nearby people as those of Zuñi and the later people of Laguna (founded 1699). The word Apache came originally from a Zuñi word meaning "enemy," first specifically bestowed as a name, it seems, upon the specific invaders who took over the lands of an abandoned Tewa pueblo called Navahu.

Or so at least it sounded to the ears of the early Spaniards. In time the name Apache was applied by extension to other related peoples all over the Southwest.

Apache bands were prominent among the wild tribes that halted, in the 1650s, the movement of the Spanish mission frontier northward from Sonora toward what is now Arizona. In the 1680s and for some years thereafter the Jesuit explorer, Padre Eusebio Kino, located mission sites in the Gila River country among the Piman people there, although the surrounding Apache country—Apacheria—remained risky territory.

This Spanish frontier was given a boost in the 1730s by discovery of silver in the Altar valley, below present Nogales, the area then known as Arizonac. But no veins were found and the surface workings played out within a few years—phenomenal surface workings though they were—producing huge nuggets of almost pure silver up to two tons in weight. No bulwark of mining towns resulted and the problem of the Apaches remained.

Nearly a century after Eusebio Kino another religious explorer of the Southwest, Fray Francisco Garcés of the Franciscan order, trying to work out a trail from California to Santa Fe far enough above the Gila River to be reasonably free of the danger of Apaches, chanced a visit to the Hopis, or the Moquis, as they were generally known at that time, in what must have been a rather wan hope of getting their cooperation. The Moquis had not welcomed missionary priests for many years, since murdering the Spanish missionaries among them during the general revolt of 1680.

Fray Francisco Garcés, however, was famous not only as an explorer but also as a diplomat among the Indians. He "appears to be but an Indian himself," said a fellow-priest. "He sits with them in the circle, or at night around the fire, with his legs crossed . . . talking with them with much serenity and deliberation. And although the foods of the Indians are as nasty and dirty as those outlandish people themselves, the father eats them with great gusto and says that they are good for the stomach and very fine."

But at the principal Moqui pueblo of Oraibi no one at all spoke to him, a sign so sinister the three Hualapai guides with him were alarmed and disappeared. Fray Francisco sat beside his saddle in the village plaza and waited throughout a hot midsummer Tuesday and a hotter midsummer Wednesday. Wednesday evening he succeeded in giving a youth a present, surreptitiously, as payment for undertaking to deliver a note to the Franciscan missionary at Zuñi, Fray Silvestre Veléz de Escalante. The note recommended exploration of a Santa Fe-California route keeping above the Moqui towns. On Thursday the people stopped ignoring him and gathered in a crowd, and Fray Francisco expected that now he would be put to death. Then four chief men came and told him to go away at once. His mule was brought and he went away.

The Moquis, connoisseurs of patience, may have been impressed by his two long days of sitting there, in patient silence, beside his saddle.

The final day of his failure at Oraibi, Thursday the fourth of July 1776, might reasonably be designated as the opening of modern Apache history, modern in the sense that more is known of it for the subsequent periods.

By the end of the 1700s most Apache groups had been so long established in the mountains and mesas, plains and deserts, of the Southwest that they believed it to be their native homeland.

The Apaches de Navahu had long ago become a distinct people, so long ago the alteration had been forgotten. Now they were the Navajo (the Spanish and still the preferred spelling), of distinctly different lifeways, no longer reckoned a branch of the Apaches. They dwelt to the northwest of the central Pueblo world, in what is now northwestern New Mexico and northeastern Arizona.

Westward and southward from the Navajo country, along the upper waters of the Salt and Gila Rivers and in the mountains of eastern Arizona, was the domain of various Apache groups, such as the Tonto Apache bands between modern Flagstaff and Roosevelt Lake and the White Mountain Apache in and about the midsection of the present Arizona-New Mexico line. These, together with the Cibecue and San Carlos people, are sometimes referred to nowadays as Western Apaches.

Further south, in southeastern Arizona and southwestern New Mexico, were, among others, the Chiricahua of the Arizona mountains of the same name, and the Mimbreños of the Mimbres Mountains in southwestern New Mexico; both figure in much of the literature devoted to Apaches, the Mimbreños sometimes regarded as an eastern Chiricahua band.

In southern New Mexico were Mescalero Apaches, in a number of divisions, a name that came from the Apache custom of roasting mescal (agave) to make a famous dessert; Mescalero people were assumed to have been in the business of trading mescal with unfortunate Pueblo urbanites who didn't have any.

Apaches in what is now Arizona, excluding the Navajo, were all more or less similar, it is believed, in their aboriginal way of life: something like a fourth or fifth of their food coming from patches of corn, beans, and other such staples, and the rest from hunting and intensive gathering of wild foods. These included mescal, acorns, and a bushel or so of other items led by piñon, cactus fruit, yucca, sunflower, mesquite, saguaro, pigweed (the family of this latter, amaranth, is reported a profitable farm crop at present).

Those Apache groups east of the Rio Grande, some occupying areas in the plains of west Texas, clung more persistently to buffalo hunting as one of their basic traditions.

Quite a distance north of Mescalero country, in northeastern New Mexico and the mountains of the present Colorado line, were the Jicarilla Apaches (pronounced Heekareeya, a word meaning "little gourd" or "gourd cup" in New Mexico Spanish of the seventeenth century). New Mexico folklore used to maintain that the name came from little cup-shaped baskets made by Jicarilla women, but modern ethnographers now look askance at this. It has also been suggested the name may derive from a gourd-shaped hilltop in their country. Natural features or plants seem to provide most of the names for Apache groups, rather than the animal totems of so many other Indian traditions: the two principal Jicarilla divisions that also appear to fulfill the function of ceremonial moieties, Llanero and Ollero ("Plainsman" and "Potter") or this second name is sometimes given as Hoyeros ("Mountain people"), bear names that apparently refer to habitat or way of life.

Jicarilla territory in Spanish times extended westward toward the Navajo, and on the north, above the present Colorado line, bordered the ancients of the southern Rockies, the Ute. For centuries Jicarilla people were in fairly regular contact with the pueblo of Taos and became in a formal manner almost kinfolk of the Taoseños, each making a point of attending the other's ceremonies.

The total population of all the Apache groups—always excluding the Navajo—has been estimated at between 5,000 and 6,000, in prehistoric as in early historic times. Their population is much larger today, despite a notion current in some foreign lands that Apaches somehow vanished with the onset of "civilization."

During their slow prehistoric migration southward, Apaches (probably including Navajo forebears) were among the most important occupants of the great plains; at various periods in the old pre-horse times, from the 1300s to the 1700s, they may have constituted the strongest force in the southern plains.

They were sometimes enemies, sometimes allies, of the terrible Tonkawas of Texas, a plains people with a ferocious reputation, supposedly dreaded by all and therefore assiduously wooed by both the Spanish and the French. The Tonkawa were cannibals, it was said—a common epithet for foes, as was Big Cannibal a common ogre in songs and poems. One recalls the original Narraganset meaning of the name Mohawk ("man-eater"), or the famous Kwakiutl Cannibal Society at the opposite end of the continent. Some contemporary European colonists were willing or even eager to accept these epithets literally, as are some historians of the present day, finding in them a useful touch to heighten the exoticism of the Other. We can be fairly sure that in some sufficiently distant future our own society will be supposed cannibalistic, from erudite study of the reception of the Eucharist in the act of Christian communion.

An Apache captured and adopted by the Tonkawa became their most noted chief, and in 1782 brought about a great Apache-Tonkawa conference for the purpose of uniting the two peoples to fight the Spanish. More than 4,000 Tonkawas and Apaches gathered for this meeting—and to trade horses for French guns. The pact of unity failed to go through, and a couple of years later the Spanish succeeded in seizing the naturalized Tonkawa chief by treachery and put him to death. The Spanish called him El Mocho (the cropped one), due to the fact that he had lost his right ear in a fight with the Osage.

This Apache-Tonkawa convention was one of the last high points of Apache presence on the southern plains. During the 1700s new people were moving in from the north, Comanches and Kiowas. Said an eighteenth-century Spanish missionary in Texas, the Comanches were "far superior to all others in number, extent of lands, modesty of dress, valor . . . and hatred for Apaches." The old name of Padoucas, prominent in the literature of the southern plains until the late 1700s, is associated by most authorities with the Comanches but by some others with the Apaches, attesting the duration and confusion of their entanglements. At last the Apaches of the plains, most of them, withdrew to the plains' western margins.

This marginal country may have been the center of gravity for the wide-ranging Apache people since their first appearance, with extensions eastward across the southern plains and westward as far as present Arizona. A string of towns within this marginal area, the Tano pueblos, southernmost of the Rio Grande pueblos, had been devastated in or near the year 1525 by a war of hurricane pitch, believed by some specialists to have been waged by Apaches.

One Apache group stayed on the plains—the people known as Lipan Apaches, closely related, it was said, to the Jicarilla Apaches. They remained pretty much in the Llano Estacado, the Staked Plains, in west Texas and eastern New Mexico, which kept them in chronic conflict with Comanches.

The Lipan were by no means unremittingly hostile to whites during that time; there were intervals of peace and even of alliance. Lipan Apaches in Texas even accepted Spanish missions—briefly—in the eighteenth century and on a number of occasions allied themselves with Spanish troops against the Louisiana French or other occasional enemies of the southern plains. The perilous exposure of their anti-Comanche position may have had something to do with this politicizing.

But in general Apaches remained unbeguiled; wild and untamed, in the usual sense of the words in that time, which is to say independent.

Apaches lived for more than 200 years on the frontier of European colonial settlement and throughout all that time remained generally independent, which seems to be a record unequaled by any other Indian people on the continent.

Since they came to be regarded as a lost cause anyway, Spanish and later Mexican administrators had no compunction about playing them false in negotiations or promises, if anything was to be gained thereby. Apaches responded to such perfidy, naturally, with renewed hostility. Each side raided the other now and then for slaves and loot, in which the Apaches, being past masters of the art of the raid, undoubtedly kept the score more than even.

The important point is that Apaches, in this long relationship, were not at all strange mountain hawks wide-eyed at the wonders of a town, and savagely simple in their contact with white people. They had had long experience in dealing with whites, while still contriving to keep themselves apart and free.

Comanches, as earlier recounted, sprang from mountain Shoshoni who came down into the plains with the acquisition of the horse. Mystically certain of their superiority, in the way of born horsemen, Comanches couldn't quite help (so it seemed) regarding other people, white and red, as inferior beings. This may have contributed to their success in trade and war. With an estimated seventeenth century population of some 7,000 the Comanches must have considerably outnumbered the Apache families on the plains, and were more than three times the strength of their constant allies, the Kiowa.

Kiowas present something of a puzzle in their early history. Their traditions, and some documentary evidence, place their earliest appearance in our history at the headwaters of the Missouri River, in the mountains of present Montana. They were friends of the Crows in that area during the 1700s, and at the end of that century drifted southward to the Arkansas River, where they effected their alliance with various Comanche divisions and thereafter occupied the plains eastward of northern New Mexico. An Athapaskan-speaking band that entered the southern plains with the Kiowa came to be known as Apache because of their language, and were called the Kiowa Apache. Alien in tradition and culture, they were nevertheless a fully accredited band of the Kiowa nation, with a designated place in the camp circle.

Many students feel sure the Kiowa must have come originally from the southern plains—long before, so long ago the memory had died out of their remembrance. This belief is based in part on the kinship of the Kiowa language with the language of Taos people—a kinship deformed and wasted away by age (hence the supposed difficulty of the Kiowa language: nobody can learn Kiowa, it only sounds like chunking stones in the water, said an old mountain man who could talk a number of other Indian languages)—but the kinship is nevertheless fairly definite, according to some recent studies.

It is of course easily possible that at some unknown time in the past a people had emigrated to the plains from the Pueblo world, perhaps even from the Taos region. Remains of farming settlements of centuries ago in and about what is now the Oklahoma and Texas Panhandles are thought by some archeologists to echo Pueblo ways, even unto houses built with stone slabs in apparent imitation of Pueblo architecture.

Speculation has sometimes linked these archeological unknowns with ancestors of the Kiowa people, midway in a long metamorphosis from corn-growers into plains hunters. While thus speculating, it might be permissible to speculate further that these émigré villagers might have begun moving north during the long drought periods of the middle 1400s. Callously abandoned by the gods of corn and rain, they might have turned finally away from farming during that same bitter time. Early names for themselves, remembered by Kiowa people from what are felt to be ancient times, include such as the "Kwuda," the "going out" or "coming out" people.

The Kiowa were generally acknowledged as among the most eloquent in the sign language, the international language of the plains by which Plains Indians from different language groups could converse with remarkable precision. A similar sort of communication with signs made by the hands existed here and there elsewhere in the Indian world, but it seems to have reached its most finished form on the plains. There may have been some relationship between the perfection of this sign language and the very ancient use of signals on the plains: signals of smoke, signals of fire, or signals made by waving robes or by moving in a circle or back and forth.

On the level high plains, where you can see forever, such signals would be a natural development. Their use was noted by the first white men to enter the Southwest, in the 1540s. In later years the Sioux worked out a system of signaling with mirrors, and troops were sometimes only aware of the presence of Sioux around them by the flickering of this mysterious heliograph on distant bluffs and ridges. The Sioux are also said to have signaled at night with fire arrows.

Much of the paraphernalia of Plains Indian signaling, but principally the heliograph, was adopted by the army of the United States (and later by the British Army) and used in early operations of the Signal Corps.

Comanches and Kiowas took over the southern plains in uneasy times. The dust raised in the east by the French and Indian War rolled across the Mississippi and far out on the plains during the late 1700s. Spanish Louisiana, wanting buffers against the mighty Osage, coaxed Indian colonists westward from the lower Mississippi into the Caddo country on the eastern edge of the great plains; such strong Caddoan people as the Pawnee, Wichita, and the Kadohadacho Confederacy welcomed the immigrants more or less peacefully, but the Siouan Osage took umbrage, formed war-making alliances, and fought.

A Cherokee band moved west of the Mississippi in 1794, after killing a number of white men to announce the reason why. The band was headed by a leader named Bowl, a warlord of repute; refugees from several other tribes later joined, and in the 1820s the augmented band went to Texas. There the Mexican government gave Bowl and his people a grant of land between present Dallas and Houston.

After Texas was broken free of Mexico by its American colonists in 1835, Sam Houston made an effort to protect Bowl's Cherokee band, but most of the new rulers of Texas were opposed to leaving any part of the country in the possession of any Indians. Sam Houston's successor as president of Texas was the ex-private secretary of Governor Troup of Georgia, of Creek and Cherokee expulsion notoriety, and the policy makers of Texas thereafter were usually dedicated, in the highest degree, to the proposition of exterminating or clearing out all Indians. Several regiments of Texas troops attacked and destroyed Bowl's town on the Angelina River in 1839; Bowl and many others were killed, and the survivors were driven across the border into Indian Territory (where, says tradition, they were dissuaded from bootless acts of retaliation by the aging Sequoya).

In the same year Lipan Apaches very willingly sided with Texans in fighting Comanches; a few years later, however, Texas exterminators drove the Lipan people themselves into Mexico, where Mexican troops, aided by some expatriate Kickapoos, almost annihilated the remnants of the tribe. Years afterward a few Lipan survivors, a few dozen people, found homes with the Kiowa Apache or the Tonkawa or, principally, among the Mescalero people in New Mexico.

The barefoot people, the Karankawan tribes among whom Alvar Núñez Cabeza de Vaca and his companions were shipwrecked in 1528, were hunted into supposed extinction, the last being killed off some time before the Civil War.

But most of the people of the plains, Kiowas and Comanches, Arapahoes and Cheyennes and Sioux, Blackfeet and Crows, enjoyed high points of wealth and strength in these uncertain times, from the late 1750s to the early 1840s.

Situated as they were, in contact with Spanish or American settlements, some of them became practiced and prosperous middlemen. Comanche trade relations were especially complex, due to the widely separated ranges of the several important divisions. The southern division known as the Penatekas (Honey-eaters)—the name Penateka may have been at the origin of "Padouca"—and the Nokoni (Wanderer) band, did some trading with the Spanish settlements in Texas, but outlaw American traders and filibusters trickling into their country before 1812 encouraged them in quarrelsome behavior toward the settlements, an attitude of hostility that carried over into later times.

Kwahadi (Antelope) Comanches of the Staked Plains kept pretty much out of touch with whites until the closing decades of the free era, in the middle 1800s. A number of bands toward the northern frontier of Comanche country, along the Arkansas River, became first great raiders and then great traders among the Spanish settlements and Indian pueblos of New Mexico. Yamparikas (Root-eaters) made up one of the main groups in this area; the western division of the Kotsotekas (Buffalo-eaters) was another.

Ordinarily these divisions and bands did not constitute an Indian nation, with a unified council or other machinery of overall government. Some of the important divisions were so far apart—700 miles or even more—that they may hardly have been aware of each other's existence.

However, there were occasions when a man of extraordinary ability and ambition became head chief of several groups temporarily confederated. The Comanche (Padouca) head chief talking to Véniard de Bourgmont in 1724 said, "I am heard and obeyed in all the villages of our nation; I am the Emperor of all the Padoucas." He also said he could summon 2,000 warriors. Another such seems to have been the famed Cuerno Verde (Greenhorn) killed by the Spanish in 1779 near the mountain in the southern Colorado Rockies that bears his name. The leader of the 645 Spanish troops (259 of them were Indians) in this engagement (Cuerno Verde opposed them with a total of fifty warriors) was the New Mexico frontiersman Juan Bautista de Anza, who encouraged the establishment of a head-chiefship and gave Spanish support to Ecueracapa (Iron Shirt), Cuerno Verde's successor. In the usual European view only a genuinely authoritative chief, able to control all his people, could promise lasting stability.

Ecueracapa was said to represent 600 Comanche rancherias, or villages, which means either that he padded the voting lists or later estimates of Comanche population figures are much too low, since this very large figure of 600 rancherias would only have represented the western bands, exclusive of the Texas Comanches to the east and south.

Ecueracapa succeeded in overcoming the leaders of the anti-Spanish party, killing one of them with his own hands, and a Comanche-Spanish peace was made in 1786 that was fairly real in the New Mexico region for many years to come.

Not that all Comanches stopped raiding, or even that the Spanish wanted them to stop all raiding. One of the Spanish objectives in this alliance was to make use of Comanches in fighting Apaches. The Comanches obliged with an excess of zeal, continuing their traditional attacks on even the Jicarilla Apache people whom the Spaniards regarded as friendly.

It appears that a shattering Comanche raid during this period on the once-populous pueblo of Pecos may have been carried out because Pecos was harboring some fugitive Jicarillas.

Comanches had been admitted to the great Taos trading fair at least as early as 1749. Some Comanche go-getters occasionally spurred sales by early-summer raids on pueblos or settlements—not excepting Taos itself—to collect captives who were then brought in to the Taos fair to be sold, to the furious indignation of Spanish officials (but business was business).

An equally indignant Spanish cleric wrote in 1761 of some unidentified "barbarians" that when they bring Indian women to sell, "among them many maidens and young girls, before delivering them to the Christians who buy them . . . they deflower and corrupt them in the sight of innumerable assemblies of barbarians and Catholics . . . without considering anything but their unbridled lust and brutal shamelessness, and saying to those who buy them, with heathen impudence: 'Now you can take her—now she is good.'"

A report of the late 1760s speaks of Comanches and Kiowas coming to the annual Taos fair ("There they trade buckskins, buffalo hides, and slaves from various Indian nations situated to the east for clothing and horses. . . . Their arms are the bow and arrow and a few guns acquired from the French").

After the peace of 1786 these plains people were naturally more in evidence as traders. In the late years of the 1700s competition of better-made English trade goods was coming to the plains, and the Spanish needed all the trade-jobbers they could find—which was another Spanish objective in making the 1786 peace. The Taos trading fiesta, biggest doings in all the West, certainly helped to hold customers and keep them coming back.

One of the popular trade items, oddly enough, was a large size silver cross offered by the missionaries. Comanches and Kiowas generally had little interest in Christianity, but the crosses were traded for premium prices over the plains as emblems of military rank to be hung around the necks of soldier-society chiefs.

Travel and trade in the pre-wild West, before the frontier of Europeans really arrived, which is to say before the nineteenth century stamped its trademark on the American West, was as a rule open, free, and unadventurous. Fray Francisco Garcés made many of his long-distance treks alone or with only one companion, a Baja California Indian named Tarabal. The great Texas-New Mexico explorer, Pierre Vial (Pedro to the Spanish), traveled with only one companion when he "opened the road" from San Antonio in Texas to Santa Fe, in 1786, a new road to go with the Comanche peace. A serious illness en route laid him up for some weeks in a Wichita village, and he spent a couple of months in a Comanche village waiting for the good traveling weather of spring, when a half dozen Comanche families then went along to show him the best route to Santa Fe. For laying out the road to St. Louis in 1792 that became a generation later the Santa Fe Trail, Vial took along two trailhands. All three were held captive by Indians for some weeks in what is now Kansas, apparently on suspicion of illicit trading operations. In his trips Vial met many times travelers in small groups or only one or two people going about their business as matter-of-factly as so many truck drivers of today; It is the matter of factness that comes through most strongly in Vial's diaries.

Horses were, by this time, the basic goods of trade. Some, probably the best blooded, were obtained by legitimate trade or purchase from the Spanish settlements. Many more were stolen, particularly in raids on the Spanish settlements in Texas.

In those days certain western Comanche divisions and Kiowas went into winter camp on the upper Arkansas River along with Cheyennes and Arapahoes, all doing a thriving off-season business in horses and other trade articles, including captives red and white. A party of American traders camped with an enormous village—700 lodges—at a plains rendezvous of this kind in November of 1821. Crows were camped two days' journey away, on the Platte, and nearly every night brave young Crows would creep into the very center of this immense camp to steal some of the extra-fine horses that were kept there, under the most stringent security, in log corrals.

A band of western Comanches known as the Jupes even tried settling down as farmers under Spanish guidance, early in the time of Anza's great peace. Spanish authorities financed the building of a model pueblo for them in what is now southern Colorado; the town was named San Carlos de los Jupes and was the envy of mountain Utes, who began clamoring that they wanted pueblos too. But the project was a failure. Most of the hunting peoples of the plains moved their camp after the death of an important person; therefore at the first such death the Comanches packed up and moved away, leaving the neat little adobe houses of San Carlos de los Jupes to melt into ruins.

Texas Comanches asked several times for a formal peace, after Texas had won independence from Mexico, but the Comanches insisted on a definite boundary line reserving their territory from settlement, and this the office holders in the Republic of Texas refused to consider. Settlers were arriving and buying land, and Texas's official position was that any Texas citizen could be settled on any land not already occupied by a white owner. Indians must withdraw and keep away from these settlements, wherever they might appear.

One early settlement was established east of the present site of Waco by Elder John Parker and his numerous children and relatives, totaling nearly three dozen people. In the spring of 1836 Kiowas and Nokoni Comanches swept down from the north on the stockaded "Parker's Fort," killed several of its defenders, and took five captives. The tales of barbarities told by some of these captive women after their ransomed return were widely circulated and of considerable moment in making the name Comanche a byword for cruelty on the Texas frontier.

One of the captives was not recovered for many years—this was Cynthia Ann Parker, variously reported between nine and thirteen years old at the time of her capture. She eventually became a wife of Nokoni, chief of the Nokoni band, and bore him several children. Her brother visited her "in her Indian home" after some years but (rather out of keeping with the aforementioned atrocity stories) she could not be persuaded to return to civilization. Finally, in 1860, she was forcibly repatriated, together with an infant child, although both died soon afterward. A son named Quanah, about fifteen at that time, stayed with his father, who had extended his influence over other Comanche bands to become the most important of Comanche leaders. After Nokoni's death, Quanah, usually known as Quanah Parker, rose to become head chief of all the Comanche, apparently by virtue of his own outstanding ability rather than hereditary right, there being no other recorded instance of inherited chieftainship among the Comanches.

In 1839, the Texas legislature having appropriated more than $1 million for militia expenses, a number of citizen companies took the field against Comanches, sometimes traveling long distances to find and attack Comanche rancherias. In March 1840, a small band of Comanches, invited to a peace conference in the San Antonio council house, was surreptitiously surrounded by troops of this militia and captured, several dozen of the Comanches and a few of the militiamen being killed in the process. This brought an outraged reaction from Isomania, one of the best known of the Penateka Comanche leaders of the time, who a week or so afterward rode into San Antonio with a single companion, like a medieval knight with his squire, lambasted the Texans for their treachery and roared challenges to the militia to come forth and fight the army of warriors he had left parked outside of town. No fight was forthcoming, the forted-up Texas citizen-soldiers explaining that a truce was in effect, and as usual the scattered frontier settlers, sitting ducks for any handful of angry young men, suffered the most in the long run.

Later in the summer Texas troops defeated a Comanche force in a crucial battle at Plum Creek, midway between Austin and San Antonio. But Comanche fighting remained a recognized profession on the west Texas plains for a generation longer. The Comanche people remained officially at peace with the United States for much of this long time, but the peace did not include Texas, even after the admission in 1845 of Texas as a state. In this warfare, scattered travelers and scattered settlers of the Texas frontier provided, as usual, most of the suffering.

Essentially, such raiding parties were of two types: those maddened by attacks of the whites and seeking revenge, and those looking for loot. As the attrition of years of white military operation took its toll, both types naturally increased.

The ever-growing poverty of the Plains Indians has not been given its due in this connection. At each destruction of a village there went up in smoke not only the immediate food reserves of jerked meat and pemmican but also the product of years of hunting and work. Buffalo robes, beaded clothes, saddles and bridles and braided reatas, thousands of arrows, tipis and their hard-to-get poles, painted parfleches, "possible" sacks, painstakingly manufactured articles of all kinds, were burned by the museum-load.

Horses, the real treasure, were confiscated by the herd or killed on the spot, sometimes in large numbers. A U.S. Army column reportedly killed 1,400 captured horses and mules after a raid on a Kiowa camp in the Texas Panhandle in 1874.

An American general commanding a large force of troops, including the brand new (at that time) Seventh Cavalry, told several Cheyenne leaders, one of them being Roman Nose, to bring back the women and children who had just fled from their village at the approach of the troops. He wanted them all to hear his orders. But this was 1866, only two years after Sand Creek. The Cheyennes refused to place their families under the American guns. The general, Winfield Scott Hancock, affronted at this insubordination, had his men inventory the abandoned Cheyenne village—251 tipis, 962 buffalo robes, 436 saddles, plus parfleches, lariats, mats, utensils for housework and cooking too numerous to count. All this was then burned.

The general's mission had been to bring peace to the plains, still in eruption from Sand Creek.

Early reports from the plains speak of the wealth and prosperity of the Indian people; later reports indicate, decade by decade, the advancing tide of poverty. It was this long attrition that at last withered the resistance of the Plains Indians, who had no other source of supply than what they carried with them. But it was also this long attrition that drove more and more men and boys to the business of looting, especially since the business of looting became constantly easier and more tempting as the plains filled up with green pilgrims and settlers.

There was, of course, no shortage of excuses for hostility. Some footloose parties, however, were quite openly out for loot, an employment as old and honorable as humanity. One such, made up apparently of a few Comanche youths, was idling along the Cimarron cutoff of the Santa Fe Trail in the summer of 1831, and there met the Lancelot of mountain men, Jedediah Strong Smith. They told someone later, it seems, that they joked with him while they casually used the mirrors hanging in their hair to blind Jed's horse, causing him to spook, and while Jed was busy trying to manage the horse they shot him in the back and then ran him through with lances. He killed two of them, they said, before he died. His Hawken rifle and his pistols turned up for sale in Taos.

Jed Smith was far and away the greatest explorer among the mountain men, with an unequaled map of the whole wide West etched in his brain. But the days of solitary travel on the plains, the days of Francisco Garcés and Pierre Vial, were, by the 1830s, gone.

In the middle 1850s the U.S. government set up several Indian reservations in Texas, for some Comanches and Kiowas as well as other peoples of the region, including Tonkawas. The once terrible Tonkawas, much reduced by disease and evil times, had turned humble, and Tonkawa men had served the Texans faithfully as scouts in forays against Comanches and other Texas Indians. But Texas extremists reacted so violently against the reservations that the reservees, Tonkawas and all, had to be moved. The Tonkawa people were established on the Washita River in Indian Territory, where in 1862 neighboring refugees from east Texas who had suffered at the hands of the Tonkawa-guided militia massacred more than 100, leaving only 100 or so Tonkawa survivors.

The Comanche and Kiowa nations signed a treaty with the United States in 1865 reserving for them the Panhandle of Texas and sundry other lands. But Texas, which had pleaded from the outset of statehood the "perfectly irresistible" spread of settlement, insisted on the complete expulsion of all Indians. Kiowas and Comanches were persuaded to accept a revised treaty and settled in Indian Territory.

The irresistible wave of settlement for which the Indians had to give way, in the Texas Panhandle, turned out to be a team of Chicago investors, who less than twenty years later were paid some 3 million acres of Panhandle land for building a new state capitol. This acreage, with the cooperation of British financiers, was turned into the largest single cattle ranch in the history of the West, the XIT (ten counties in Texas, as they used to say) Ranch, bigger than the state of Connecticut. Eight hundred miles of barbed-wire enclosure were required to civilize this vast domain.

The irresistible pressure of settlement instanced all over the land as an inarguable reason for dispossessing Indian communities also did not seem to exist in the world inhabited by railroads, which in the ten years before 1871 were given by Congress more than 131 million acres of choice land, to which various western states added grants of 49 million more, the whole adding up to more than all the land in the country then occupied by all the remaining Indian nations.

Not all Comanches and Kiowas went to live at the Indian Agencies, and not all those who went there stayed there. A possibly apocryphal story used a Comanche for straight man in 1869. The Comanche was Tochaway (Turtle Dove) and the place was Fort Cobb, Indian Territory (where, six weeks before, Black Kettle had asked for official camping instructions before Custer's troops descended on his village). General Phil Sheridan, Custer's boss and patron, was at Fort Cobb and, so the story goes, Tochoway, to identify himself, said, "Me good Indian." General Sheridan observed that the only good Indians he'd ever seen were dead Indians. The American public took his witty remark into the language—the extermination philosophy in a high-ranked nutshell.

Quanah Parker, on his way to becoming the most influential of all Comanche leaders, refused to sign the reservation treaty of 1867 and remained on the buffalo plains, although within the area reserved for Indian use. His Nokoni band changed its name after the death of Chief Nokoni, since a man's name could not be spoken after his death; it was called the Detsanasyuka, which referred to its hasty camps made in a life of constant movement. Apparently the Kwahadi Comanches also associated themselves with young Quanah Parker's leadership.

When buffalo-hide hunters illegally invaded the Indian country by hundreds in the early 1870s, these two important Comanche bands spearheaded a desperate effort to drive them out. Hostilities began in 1874 and spread over five states, harmless settlers and travelers furnishing more victims than the guilty but tough hide-hunters. Troops immediately poured into the Indian country to put down the hostiles, and ended most of the fighting within a year or so. Quanah Parker surrendered with his band a couple of years later.

His real career, and a long and distinguished one, began at this point, as the industrious, able, and devoted savior of the remnant of his people under the galling new hardships of agency life.

The first two signers of the 1867 treaty were Setangya, known to the Americans as Satank, principal chief of the Kiowa, and Satanta, a noted orator and warrior some twenty years younger than Setangya, and regarded as the second chief of the Kiowa. However, both continued to lead raids into Texas—

one story has it that Satanta went raiding for vengeance after a practical-joking army officer gave him a swig of an emetic in place of whiskey.

Setangya's son was killed on one such raid, and the grief-stricken old man thereafter bore his son's bones along with him on a lead horse wherever he went (so they say).

Both chiefs were arrested for their part in a raid of 1871; Setangya wrenched off his manacles, taking the flesh of his hands with them, and attacked his guards until he was shot to death—he meant the act for suicide, and sang his death song first.

Satanta was given a conditional release from prison but was imprisoned again, for life, when Kiowas joined the war against the invading buffalo hunters of 1874. He too killed himself, four years later, in the Texas state prison. Their deaths may have been meant to inspire Kiowa people with an iron courage to face the iron subjugation before them; this was what many Kiowa people thought, at any rate.

The 1870s brought a number of despairing outbreaks from normally peaceful people, such as from Utes of Colorado or Bannocks of Idaho, as reservations were whittled away by "rings" of local developers, and Indian agents or other officials sprang a little too greedily at the task of "civilizing" their charges, or reservation inmates became discontented with enforced starvation—the Bannock people were being rationed at a cost of two and a half cents per day per person.

In Arizona and New Mexico the same period saw permanent peace envelop a people—the Navajo—who had been constantly warlike, by reputation at least, throughout all their known history.

Navajos had long before created a unique society, in their country of magic mesas, vermilion cliffs, and painted deserts. Captives and immigrants made them a truly composite people and triggered a vigorous growth that had increased their numbers to perhaps 10,000 by 1860, larger than the population at that time of all the other Apachean tribes put together.

The only substantial heritage they continued to share with their original Apache cousins was the Athapaskan basis of their language, but even that was much altered by accessions from new tongues. One accession the language never picked up was the letter "v"—most Navajos, in consequence, found the word "Navajo" unpronounceable. Many Navajos, in fact, scarcely knew of the word until rather modern times. Their name for themselves was and is Diné, the Folks, the People. Most of the nearly four dozen Athapaskan languages, as previously noted, use some variation of this vocable as a tribal name.

At some time after the arrival of the Spanish in the Southwest, the Navajos took to the raising of sheep and became herders and stockmen. Navajo women learned weaving and in time made the Navajo blanket world famous. The men learned silversmithing and produced work of high excellence, for which Pueblo importers came to trade, bargaining in sign language. They adopted the altars of the Pueblos, the much admired "sand paintings" that the Navajos made their own. Pueblo influences are noticeable in the sacred literature of a number of Apachean groups, but are most evident, by far, among the Navajo, even though the Navajo never adopted the formal, community-wide religious ceremonies of the Pueblos.

Religious growth from many roots became profuse in the Navajo way of life. Religious songs became so numerous, said an early investigator, that no one could ever hope to collect them all. The resulting edifice of religion has been studied as a whole and in parts perhaps more intensively than that of any other Indian group north of Mexico.

Some students have found two main strands persisting through all the alterations of Navajo history: male power, hunting and killing, and female power, fertility and life-giving. Some find the strand of order, peaceful growth, and fertility ascendant in the edifice at present (although objecting to the oversimplification of calling this theme "female"), emphasizing the current importance of the Blessingway ceremony. Some find the presence of the two strands in opposition essential to the great underlying theme of the world and life in balance.

Some find an overall theme of simply praying to live the right way, "according to the ideal," and entreating the world to do likewise.

Some prefer merely to record the songs:

In beauty
you shall be my representation
In beauty
you shall be my song
In beauty
you shall be my medicine
In beauty
my holy medicine

for an example recorded a hundred years or so ago.

Recently the linguistics people have begun to get into this act, an attractive act for such discussion, that will probably lead to a considerable literature touching on a number of differing Indian religious structures.

Navajos farmed a little, peach trees and corn patches, Hopi style, wherever a touch of moisture in the earth permitted. But they never really formed villages. Their hogans—earth lodges—were sometimes gathered in family clusters, houses of a mother and her married daughters, but otherwise were anywhere. The brush shelters of summer were as scattered as their flocks.

As with general Apachean custom, and custom frequent all over the plains, a house was usually abandoned, sometimes burnt down or otherwise destroyed, upon the death of an occupant. Ordinarily, Apachean people were very reluctant to touch a dead body, for fear of the dead and of witchcraft. Navajos, like many other Apacheans, never adopted the practice of scalping; and the Ghost Dance drew few fans within Apache and Navajo borders.

The keeping of family-owned flocks may have helped bring about a sharper distinction between rich and poor than was usual among most Indians; also, Navajos became noted for an industriousness uncommon to semi-nomadic peoples. These are highlights that blend well with the faintly Old World, almost Old Testament shadowing that falls upon the picture of the early Navajo, as the only pastoral nonvillage people in the Americas.

But there was certainly no Old Testament ring to their character—"Wit, merriment and practical jokes enliven all their gatherings," wrote one nineteenth-century observer, in an observation typical of most. And in the testimony of generations of town-dwelling neighbors, Pueblo Indians, Spanish colonials, and Mexicans alike, Navajos were raiders and warriors first and gentle shepherds a distant second, finding far more joy in coming down like wolves on a fold than in patiently tending one.

It may be significant that many Navajo war names—war names being the only formal personal names in times past—made some use of the verb "to raid." This was true for girls' names as well as boys', although a very common girl's name was simply Warrior Girl.

But it is possible that Navajos, and Apaches as well, were as much sinned against as sinning, in the matter of raids. Spanish pronunciamentos pictured New Mexico a martyr for centuries to the rapacious Navajo, the "Lords of the Soil," who reportedly boasted that they only tolerated the Spanish presence because the Spanish ranchos were so pleasant to plunder. Unquestionably Navajo raiders removed much moveable property, including children and women, from the Spanish settlers and from the Pueblos.

There must have been some plunderers from the other side, though, to capture the thousands of Navajo and Apache women and children who were commonly slaves in the New Mexico settlements. Said a New Mexico resident in the 1860s, "I think the Navahos have been the most abused people on the continent, and that in all hostilities the Mexicans have always taken the initiative with but one exception that I know of." Kit Carson spoke of the way some Mexicans were accustomed to "prey on" the Navajos, but also mentioned the "continual thieving carried on between the Navajos and the Mexicans," which may be the most accurate general summation.

Official American acquaintance with the Navajo came in the autumn of 1849, three years after the American conquest of New Mexico during the Mexican War. New Mexico was a land much troubled at this time. Early in 1847 an outbreak of Taos Indians, urged on by Mexicans who hoped to overthrow the conquest, cost the lives of a number of Americans, including the acting governor, before it was ended with a hard-fought battle at Taos and the subsequent hanging of some of the *insurrecto* leaders.

By the summer of 1849 new American arrivals, some of them on their gold-rushing way to California, were causing much concern by robbing and outraging the Indians, particularly the patient Pueblos. The Pueblos—"a more upright and useful people are nowhere to be found," said the Indian agent at Santa Fe—entreated the government for compensation and protection, but in vain, there being no way, said the American authorities, to control these lawless elements or make restitution for their misdeeds.

There were also endless complaints of Apache and Navajo raids and thefts. Between August 1846 and October 1850 some 12,000 mules, 7,000 horses, 31,000 cattle, and more than 450,000 sheep were reported as stolen by (some extremely busy) rustlers in New Mexico. It was assumed the main blame should go to Apaches and Navajos. The Indian agent at Santa Fe previously mentioned, James S. Calhoun, usually a conservative witness, remarked during the same period that it was unsafe to travel more than ten miles from Santa Fe.

To do something about this, the governor of New Mexico marched a body of troops westward from the Rio Grande to the Navajo country and made a treaty. Nothing like an authorized Navajo chief existed, each band operating with complete independence under an informally chosen head man. However, a local patriarch of repute, known as Narbona, came with several hundred of his followers to meet with the Americans. Narbona explained that lawless men were everywhere and that "their utmost vigilance had not rendered it possible for the chiefs and good men to apprehend the guilty, or to restrain the wicked."

This was rather the same situation as that just noted concerning depredations by lawless Americans, but unlike the American government Narbona offered to make every possible restitution for Navajo thefts, and as an earnest of this intention turned over 130 sheep and four or five horses and mules.

A treaty of "perpetual peace and friendship" was signed, but then a Mexican with the American command demanded still another horse, a particular horse he happened to see, the Navajos objected, the governor threatened, the Navajos wheeled their horses and "scampered off at the top of their speed," and the governor ordered his troops to fire on them.

Six or seven Navajos didn't get out of range in time and were killed, including the patriarch, Narbona. Possibly his age, about eighty, slowed him up, or possibly the business of signing the treaty of perpetual peace and friendship had left him in an unhandy getaway position.

The rest of the Navajos, "300 to 400, all mounted and armed, and their arms in their hands," fled without offering any resistance. The artillery with the troops, noted a young Army officer in his report, "also threw in among them, very handsomely—much to their terror, when they were afar off, and thought they could with safety relax their flight—a couple of round shot." He added, with a fine discernment, "These people evidently gave signs of being tricky and unreliable."

This example of statesmanship did not stop Navajo marauding, and a fort, Fort Defiance ("a wretched hole," wrote an experienced officer, "which deserves its name because its position is in defiance of nearly every principle of military science"), was established in the Navajo country in 1851. Thereafter reasonable quiet prevailed until 1858, when an altercation between a Navajo subchief and an Army officer's black slave blew up a war. It featured a massed Navajo attack on Fort Defiance, and the country was strewn anew with garlands of wild-blooming violent deaths and disasters.

Exigencies of the Civil War intervened, and it was not until the winter of 1864–1865 that Colonel Kit Carson was sent to round up the Navajos and did so. In the impregnable Navajo stronghold of the Cañon de Chelly the troops cut down 2,000 to 3,000 peach trees and found, among other plantings, one field of corn that took 300 men the better part of a day to destroy. Flocks and herds were seized or butchered.

Most of the Navajo people were starved into submission and eventually were removed to the Bosque Redondo, a (highly unsuitable) reservation established near Fort Sumner in eastern New Mexico, to be reformed from the incurable brigands everyone said they were. The idea was to turn them into peaceful small farmers.

After four years of mingled misery and unrest (and much disturbance among other Indian groups on the nearby plains) the clique of command suffered a change of policy , and the Navajo people were allowed to return to their own country, or rather to a part of it which was made the basis of a permanent reservation. The government gave them 35,000 sheep and goats to put them back in the pastoral business.

There were difficulties and hardships in getting started again, but in the main the tribe waxed greater year by year, sometimes prospered, and was at peace.

There was no peace for Apaches.

Given a large enough territory, rich enough in game and foraging, such as the great Athapaskan homeland in northwestern Canada, no outstanding war-making tradition seemed to trouble normal Apache times. But whatever circumstances set the Apache ancestors in motion southward also moved them into frequent if not incessant conflict with the peoples whose lands they traversed. Theft, raid, plunder, war became the manner of life for generation after generation.

Spanish colonial authorities, and Mexican authorities following, tried offering reservations and rationing, but policy shifted with growth of ranchos and the reservations were withdrawn, or Apaches used the safe haven of a reservation ("peace establishment," in Spanish terms) in Chihuahua as a base from which to raid Sonora—or a peace establishment in Sonora as a safe base from which to raid Chihuahua.

So at times Spanish officials, and Mexican officials after them, drew up grandiose—and far too costly—battle plans for complete extermination of Apaches, and the states of Chihuahua and Sonora offered handsome bounties for Apache scalps—200 pesos for a warrior's, 150 for the hair of a woman or child, as typical Chihuahua prices from the early 1800s. Some prices north of the border waxed even handsomer—in 1866 an Arizona county was still offering $250 for each Apache scalp. And a ready market always existed for Apache women and children as slaves.

In a bounty boom year, 1837, some American trappers obtained a great pile of scalps by inviting a band of Mimbres Apaches to a fiesta and at the height of the festivities murdering the guests. Mimbreños had been friendly toward Americans but were not very cordial thereafter, and killed quite a few trappers in their country. The fiesta took place in the neighborhood of the Santa Rita copper mine in southwestern New Mexico, which was abandoned, and the Mexican village nearby rendered uninhabitable, for several years afterward.

South of the Salt and the Gila rivers the peaceful Piman people, the O'odham (Akimel O'odham, river people, previously known as the Pimas, and the Tohono O'odham, desert people, previously known as the Papago) had, as mentioned, fought Apaches for centuries, the O'odham always winning, by the testimony of both sides—but they were, of course, fighting against hit and run raids. The Maricopa, a Yuman people from the lower Colorado River, emigrated to Piman country over a long period of time ending in the early 1800s, to escape attacks from their kinsmen the Quechan, and other Yuman groups.

It is said the O'odham made them promise to fight no wars except defensively, to which all the Maricopas agreed.

The two peoples thereupon lived together in friendship, although neither spoke the other's language, and as allies ran up occasional high scores in their defensive wars against Apaches to the east and Yuman bands to the west. Of a sizable Yuman war party that invaded Pimeria in 1857, for one example, only three (so they say) lived to get back home.

Other Yuman tribes lived above the Quechan on the Colorado: the numerous and valiant Mojave, who "talk rapidly and with great haughtiness," meanwhile giving "smart slaps with the palms on the thighs," as Fray Francisco Garcés sketched them; and smaller groups of Yuman peoples such as the Hualapai, Havasupai, and Yavapai, living from the Grand Canyon to the Gila. These made up a bloc unique in the Southwest, in that their hands were not raised against the Apache. Yavapais, in fact, mingled with Tonto Apaches to such an extent that both were called Tontos indiscriminately; Yavapais were also sometimes known as Apache Mojaves.

It may have been a gang of Yavapai hoodlums who in 1851 committed a famous massacre usually credited to Tonto Apaches, the killing of several members of the Oatman family of emigrants along the Gila, at what has been known since as Oatman Flat. Olive Oatman, twelve-year-old daughter of the family, was sold into slavery to Mojaves. She was rescued by a Quechan five years later and returned to the white world, which made a sensation of her story and the Mojave marriage marks tattooed on her chin.

More than anything else, it was probably the continuous kidnapping and enslavement of their women and children that gave Apaches their mad-dog enmity toward whites, from earliest Spanish times onward. It was officially estimated that 2,000 Indian slaves were held by the white people of New Mexico and Arizona in 1866, after twenty years of American rule—and when the Thirteenth Amendment was endeavoring to open for business over all the land. Unofficial estimates put the figure several times higher. Still more enslaved Apaches were in Sonora and Chihuahua.

"Get them back for us," Apaches begged of an Army officer in 1871, referring to twenty-nine children just stolen by citizens of Arizona; "our little boys will grow up slaves, and our girls, as soon as they are large enough, will be diseased prostitutes, to get money for whoever owns them. Our women work hard and are good women, and they and our children have no diseases."

Prostitution of captured Apache girls, of which much mention is made in the 1860s and 1870s, seemed to trouble the Apaches exceedingly. It was during this period—the 1860s—that Apaches are supposed to have overcome religious dread sufficiently to turn to the custom of mutilating enemy dead.

Enslaving captives was common practice everywhere, but the Americans seemed to make it an industry, as with scalp bounties. The universal power of money hunger among the whites may have been the keystone. One notorious American bounty hunter claimed to have collected on 478 scalps—all claimed Apache, but maybe from any chance acquaintances with long black hair. With slaving, as has been noted, bounties provided a growth industry that remained healthy for many years.

An old-timer, Pauline Weaver (honest and kind hearted, said those who knew him), guide for Colonel Philip Saint George Cooke and the Mormon Battalion in 1846, pointed out the Tonto Rim and said, "When I went over once, from the Pimos, I met some lodges and had a fuss with them." When Cooke asked what sort of fuss, Weaver replied, "Oh, we killed two or three and burnt their lodges, and took all the women and children and sold them." Cooke was shocked, but Weaver, without any sign of remorse, admitted that he had frequently sold Indian women and children in New Mexico and Sonora. "They bring a hundred dollars," he explained.

Demure overtures of friendship characterized the usual Apache approach to the first Yankees who appeared in their country. The newcomers were very different from Mexicans—a common Apache name for Americans was White-eyes—and might prove to be allies against the constant Mexican foe.

But the wonted hostile collisions were not long in arriving. Apaches looked miserably primitive, with their wild-flying hair (the custom was to shampoo it daily, which might make for cleanliness but not for neatness), their raggle-taggle bands sometimes consisting of only a few families, their dusty brush-hut rancherias in the dusty brush. They had little of the finery of the Plains Indians. And there was a great deal to create suspicion. They came and went with exceeding softness. They were often genial and talkative but without quite saying anything.

The wandering American, everybody's buddy, could usually pick up a working knowledge of a strange tribe's customs in a week, but until the 1930s Apaches remained the least known important Indian people in the United States—while, as has been noticed, "Apache" had been a familiar name worldwide for years.

In brief, Apaches were watchful. They were some of the most watchful people who ever lived, which may be one reason they had been able to go on living through centuries of playing dangerous big game for hunters with guns.

To blunt White-eyes in heavy shoes their sly, grinning watchfulness had an air of menace and guilt.

The chronology of hostile incidents that turned Apache problems in the Southwest into one of the major Indian wars in American history is of interest, and may even reveal something of the basic issues concerned.

Some American people in the region lived pretty much at peace with all the different Indian groups about them, one factor in this usually being a reasonable knowledge of the local political situation, which included knowledge of the strange ways of the different Indian groups.

One such was Pete Kitchen at his ranch south of Tucson, near the Mexican border, worked by Opata Indians hired from Sonora. True, the ranch house was fortified and always guarded, with a lookout always on the roof; in addition, Pete Kitchen was on friendly terms with the most important Chiricahua leader of the time, Cochise; there was a story that he had once saved the life of Nachez, a son of Cochise.

Another ranch in Chiricahua country, the Canoa, installed a crew of Maine lumberjacks to handle a timber operation, whence came disaster. Mexican ranchers appeared, asking for allies in ambushing Apaches who were trailing north with stolen cattle, and offering to split fifty-fifty on the take. Local residents who knew that participation in other people's wars invited retaliation were not interested, but it seemed like ready money to the Maine newcomers, who helped bring off an easy and profitable victory. But some weeks later a large Apache force swept down on the Canoa, bringing death, destruction, and the finish of the ranch.

Placer gold was found at Pinos Altos, in the middle of Mimbreños country, in 1860. A couple of dozen of the miners attacked some astonished local Apaches on suspicion of having stolen a mule—the leader of the miners said he tried to dissuade them but "the majority of the men were Texans." Several Indians were killed and, not surprisingly, the band, so their agent reported, was enraged. An important leader, a massive-headed giant, comically bow-legged, did his best to get the miners to leave, telling them he would show them more gold someplace else. The jolly miners knew a sneaky savage plotting a trap when they saw one: they tied him up and lashed his bullback to ribbons, by way of telling him to go away.

This was Mangas Coloradas (Red Sleeves, his Spanish name), a survivor of the Santa Rita scalp bounty massacre of 1837, related by marriage to leading people of the central Chiricahua bands next door west and Coyotero (White Mountain) bands next door north. He was probably close to sixty years old at the time of his flogging. By the following summer all whites had been driven out of the Mimbres valley and the Pinos Altos community had been abandoned.

A U.S. Army blunder, whether the fault of a green young officer or an Army surgeon is disputed, involved the great Cochise, an apparent violation of a truce, and matching—or overmatching—the Apaches in summarily killing captives. Whatever the course of events, they were clearly founded on ignorance and arrogance, and left Cochise an impassioned enemy of Americans.

Together, Mangas Coloradas and his lieutenants, such as Victorio, and Cochise and his lieutenants, such as Nana, laid waste white settlements and promoted hatred of Americans throughout Apacheria. As the Civil War back east got into high gear, Apaches took over virtually all of southern Arizona outside other Indian communities—only Old Tucson, in Pimeria, remained as a white settlement of any importance, its population shrunken to a beleaguered couple of hundred.

These conditions were not improved by the temporary invasion of Apache country in southern New Mexico by Confederate troops from Texas, who practiced anti-Indian measures Texas-style to an extreme degree. The Confederate commander there, Lieutenant-Colonel John R. Baylor, was named territorial governor of Confederate Arizona, with headquarters at Mesilla, New Mexico. He urged the "Arizona Guards," a vigilante group, to lure Apaches to meetings on any pretext and then kill all adults and sell the children to pay the vigilantes' expenses, claiming this was in line with a law passed by the Confederate government.

The main Confederate force was defeated by Union troops, principally from Colorado, at Glorieta (Apache Canyon) in early 1862, and when Confederate officials learned of Baylor's orders to the vigilantes he was relieved of all military duties. His mistake, understandable in view of Texas tradition in Indian matters, may have cost the Confederate cause dearly—if a way to the West Coast could have been opened and held by the Confederacy it might have been of some effect in counterbalancing the later Union blockade of Southern ports.

All these misadventures were put in the shade by the next step, the arrival of General James H. Carleton with 3,000 California volunteers to take command for the Union in New Mexico. He brought along a chronic case of California gold fever, stating plainly that his first objective was to remove Apaches so mineral prospecting could get going in New Mexico; he spoke of his troops as a regiment of "practical miners," and his military maneuvers frequently happened to maneuver into country inhabited by imaginary mines.

To get the Apache problem out of the way he set on foot a campaign of Apache extermination intended as the real thing. This began in 1863, reached all-out proportions in 1864, and continued, although declining in energy, until 1871.

In the first flush of enthusiasm the cooperation of Sonora and Chihuahua was invited; miners were encouraged to return to depopulated Arizona and were offered expenses, in the California way, for unofficial Apache-killing excursions; the Apache-fighting O'odham peoples (Pimas and Papagos, as then known) were furnished guns and American leadership; troops on hand, at a wartime high of volunteers, were employed to the full, and the California troops used California methods. This meant that any means whatever were acceptable as long as Apaches were killed. Thus there was no formal objection if Apaches were coaxed to appear for "treaty" talks and were then shot—old Mangas Coloradas was one of the first to fall for this, and was seized and killed, along with several members of his family, in 1863.

Some officers, such as Colonel Kit Carson and Colonel John C. Cremony, who had known Apaches for years, simply ignored the order to kill all men and take the women and children prisoner and, when opportunity offered, accepted Apache surrender under normal military terms.

But in general the forces combined for the great extermination program went to their work with a will, and the peak year of 1864 featured hundreds of armed encounters. However, the official score of a total of 216 Apaches killed in this big year was not terribly encouraging—and the rest of the score, 3,000 sheep captured by Indians as against 175 captured back, and 146 horses captured by Indians as against fifty-four recovered, was even less so. There was also a definite feeling in the Territories that the official white loss of sixteen was incomplete. Nevertheless, mines were reopened in Arizona, settlements were reestablished, and Apache bands were driven deep into their mountains and made destitute by ceaseless destruction of their rancherias.

But no Apache band was conquered, most of the Apache casualties were noncombatants, the life of a traveler was not secure in Apacheria, nor the lives of small groups of prospectors or settlers, and even settlements of some size lived in fear of bloodcurdling Apache raids.

In effect, the old conditions of the Spanish frontier were restored, with the difference that the methods of the war had brought bitterness and cruelty to new highs. Some of the milder frontier tales of Apache atrocities spoke of prisoners hung head downward over small fires, their uncontrollable jack-knifing affording amusement for hours while their brains slowly roasted until they died.

The tales of white atrocities that Apaches may have told each other have not been recorded. Arizona in the late 1860s and 1870s had the reputation of being the toughest territory in the West, filled with gentry who had departed other climes a quick jump ahead of the vigilantes. There is no reason to suppose they dealt gently with an Apache, when they could get hold of one.

The 1871 massacre by a Tucson mob of some eighty-five Aravaipa Apache people who had put themselves under the protection of the military at a nearby fort, Camp Grant, caused national indignation but was generally defended by the Arizona press—100 Anglo-Americans, Mexicans, and Piman Papagos were indicted and tried for these murders and declared not guilty by a jury after less than a half hour's deliberation.

A plenary representative of the president, sent to Arizona to take over Indian affairs after this incident, reported that "acts of inhuman treachery and cruelty" had made the Apaches "our implacable foes," after they had tried to be friends of the Americans in the beginning.

"How is it?" asked Cochise. "Why is it that the Apaches want to die—that they carry their lives on their finger ends?"

The Camp Grant massacre ended the war of Apache extermination—a war of almost ten years that had cost 1,000 American lives and more than $40 million and resulted in complete failure.

The special report of the president's representative concluded that the country was no quieter nor the Apaches any nearer extermination than when it all began. And so the policy of extermination was replaced by a policy of conciliation, upon which, of course, the frontier seethed with resentment.

The first moves in the new policy of conciliation did not succeed in the crucial matter of making peace with Cochise, so in 1872 a new plenipotentiary was sent to Arizona. This was General O. O. Howard, who got Tom Jeffords, the one Anglo trusted by Cochise, to take him (with no accompanying troops) to talk to Cochise and his "captains" in one of the Cochise strongholds, the "west" stronghold in the Dragoon Mountains. In this dreamland setting, surrounded by bare rock formations that at each shift of light assume new identities as figures of myth, scripture, or fantasy (depending on the viewer's cast of mind), Cochise and Howard agreed on a reservation site in the Apache Pass region of the Chiricahua Mountains—a site Cochise demanded and Howard (with some hesitation) granted. The leaders of Cochise's Chokonen band voted in favor, and the peace was made.

Unfortunately this reservation, like so many others, didn't last long, although long enough for Cochise to die there, still more or less at peace, in 1874.

At the time of this reversal of policy, in the summer of 1871, command of the military department of Arizona was given to General George Crook. General Crook was an Indian fighter of skill and wisdom, and what was still more extraordinary, of an honesty as stubborn as one of his treasured pack mules. He would no more break his word to the leader of a pack of ragged Apaches than he would break his word to a field marshal of England. Fighting was his profession but people were his business. He realized that Apaches were not the hellhounds the frontier pictured them, and they were not the saintly martyrs pictured by the sentimental friends of the Red Man back east (whose own Indian "problems" had long ago been conveniently forgotten).

Apache people were simply threatened people who were tremendously experienced at being objects of extermination, an experience of many generations that had made them the most polished masters of ruthless guerrilla fighting in the history of the United States.

Captain John G. Bourke, General Crook's adjutant for many years, became extremely well acquainted with Apaches, and wrote, "No Indian has more virtues and none has been more truly ferocious when aroused. . . . For centuries he has been preeminent over the more peaceful nations about him for courage, skill, and daring in war; cunning in deceiving and evading his enemies; ferocity in attack when skillfully-planned ambuscades have led an unwary foe into his clutches; cruelty and brutality to captives; patient endurance and fortitude under the greatest privations. . . . In peace he has commanded respect for keen-sighted intelligence, good fellowship, warmth of feeling for his friends, and impatience of wrong."

An Apache could cover forty miles in a day on foot, shambling along in his sloppy legging-like moccasins, or could reel off seventy-five miles a day on horseback, caring nothing about running his horse into the ground since his remount station was the nearest ranch. He could live off the country, "hilarious and jovial," while a town-bred pursuer was perishing of hunger, thirst, and sunstroke. He could travel as invisibly as a ghost, appear or disappear as silently as a shadow.

The soldier on his trail only knew of his presence when the lethal Apache bow or Winchester announced itself from a concealed and highly defendable position. The dusty warrior, with a dash of color at the headband or in the Pima-like turban, was seldom seen, and if seen seldom hit, and if hit seldom knocked down to stay. Apaches were terribly hard to kill—and their price in retaliation was likely to be terribly high.

But there being no solidarity among Apaches in general, Crook employed the warriors of conciliated bands to fight the bands that insisted on remaining hostile, on the premise that only an Apache could catch an Apache.

Crook's Apache scouts became famous, and by the end of summer 1874, all important hostile bands had been either conciliated or relentlessly rounded up and were settled on reservations, peaceful, industrious, and reportedly contented.

There was "almost a certainty," said the governor of Arizona Territory in 1875, "that no general Indian war will ever occur again."

This was the first phase of Crook's program. The second phase was not as easy. Its objective was to protect these peaceful Apaches from white troublemakers, well-meaning or otherwise. Said General Crook in 1879, "During the twenty-seven years of my experience with the Indian question I have never known a band of Indians to make peace with our government and then break it, or leave their reservation, without some ground of complaint; but until their complaints are examined and adjusted, they will constantly give annoyance and trouble."

The greatest cause of later trouble, among the Apaches, was the reduction or withdrawal of promised reservations or the arbitrary removal of bands from their homeland reservations to new reservations where they did not want to go. This was done by the Indian Bureau for reasons of operational efficiency, or to throw the business of an agency to some go-getting community that was pulling strings to get it, or for similar humanitarian motives. The military sometimes added complications to this by a stern desire to punish all the people of a band for the misbehavior of a few renegades.

The second greatest cause of trouble was the activity of crooked "rings" that supplied supplies Indians never received, stole reservation land by shady manipulation, or practiced other such arts and crafts. It was considered proper in many circles to settle as a squatter on reservation land, hoping for a day that your "improvements" would be bought out, thus multiplying the difficulties of the Indian people living on the land.

Captain Bourke summed up the common activity of theft from Indians by saying that the wicked Indians labored under a delusion that a ration was enough food to keep the recipient from starving to death, while the agent issued supplies by throwing them through the rungs of a ladder—the Indians getting whatever stuck to the rungs, and the agent getting what fell to the ground. (Some agents, such as Michael Steck and Tom Jeffords, emphatically excepted.)

Finally, there were the seamy whiskey wagoners and petty rustlers who were not averse to stirring up the Indians for a profit of two-bits. Alcoholism among the Indians was also a factor, according to neighboring whites, even drunks caused by the lightweight native booze, tiswin.

But General Crook again, on the subject of bad Indians: "I have never yet seen one so demoralized that he was not an example in honor and nobility compared to the wretches who plunder him of the little our government appropriates for him."

In New Mexico and Arizona these causes brought trouble from a number of Apache groups—Jicarilla people were faced intermittently with a choice of either fleeing, fighting, or starving—but the trouble that most consistently made news was from the Chiricahua, whose furious outbreaks added considerable size to the Apache legend.

Within a year and a half after the death of Cochise some of the Chiricahuas were rampaging into Sonora, killing bystanders innocent or otherwise right and left along the way, to resist removal to another reservation. ("Supt. L.E. Dudley of N. Mex. endeavored to have the Chiricahuas removed to Hot Spring, but they refused to go. Finally, in April 1876, serious trouble arose from the sale of whiskey by one Rogers at Sulphur Spring station, the drunken Ind. fighting among themselves, killing the liquor-dealer and his assistant, going on the war-path, and committing many depredations. Accordingly, by the influence of Gov. Safford and against the advice of Gen. Kautz then in command, the removal of all the Ind. was ordered.")

For a fair share of the next ten or twelve years Chiricahua groups, often including some families of the eastern or Mimbres valley division and various other in-laws, were breaking loose to storm up and down the Border country, performing ghostly raids and elusive campaigns that make the staid military reports read like fiction.

Such leaders as Victorio and Geronimo (pronounced and in his day sometimes spelled Heronimo) entered the ranks of the West's top celebrities. For some bands continuous war became the constant way of life; said in later years James Kaywaykla, who had spent his childhood in Victorio's band, "Until I was ten years old I did not know that people died except by violence." Victorio, killed in Mexico in 1880, was followed by a rheumatic old gentleman named Nana (sometimes spelled Nane), who had been present at the Cochise-Howard peace talk. For a wild, incredible couple of months in 1881 he led a handful of warriors, perhaps fifteen Chiricahuas, later joined by a couple of dozen Mescaleros, on the champion raid-and-evade campaign of them all, fighting and winning a battle a week against 1,000 U.S. troops, Texas Rangers, armies of frantic civilians, and the military and police establishments of northern Mexico.

Nana was some seventy or eighty years old at the time, and so stove up with aches and pains he had to walk with a cane. He liked to wear gold watch chains in his ears.

General Crook had been sent away to fight the Sioux in 1875, when Arizona was quiet and there was never again going to be an Indian war. He was brought back in 1882, and for four years patiently rounded up hostile Apaches and then patiently tried to pacify hostile or scheming elements on the home front, and then rounded up his Apaches again when they were prodded into another break.

Geronimo came to the fore during this period and was given enormous publicity on both sides of the border as part clown, part monster, part military genius, and has been given enormous publicity since as drunken simpleton and/or heroic freedom fighter (from all of which biographers have taken their choices).

Crook's long and laborious work was crowned with a peace he felt was fair and would survive—but which was vetoed back in Washington by General Phil Sheridan and President Cleveland, who had had enough of Crook's insistence on honorable behavior.

Crook's agreement with Geronimo's band, meeting for talk under conditions of truce, provided for the hostiles to surrender on terms of being sent east to join their families for two years, then returning to the reservation.

"The President," Sheridan informed Crook, "cannot assent to the surrender of the hostiles on the terms" presented by Crook. "He instructs you to enter again into negotiations on their unconditional surrender, sparing only their lives. Take every precaution against the escape of the hostiles." (But they were meeting for talk under conditions of truce?)

Unless these terms were accepted, Crook was to "insure against further hostilities by completing the destruction of the hostiles."

(But they were meeting for talk under conditions of truce?)

To Crook this was treachery, and he asked to be relieved of his command; however, Geronimo went on a drunk and did not "come in" as he had promised to do (some say the "Apache telegraph" had told him of the veto), so the treachery was shortstopped. This is the alleged drunken simpleton episode, since the cost to Chiricahua people of this failed "peace conference" was enormous.

Crook was replaced by General Nelson A. Miles, and when Apache scouts were able to talk Geronimo into another meeting he and his band were packed off to Florida as prisoners, and for good measure Miles sent along some of Crook's old Apache scouts as prisoners too, and just to make sure he had everyone sent along many of the other Chiricahuas he could lay hands on, including hundreds who had remained quietly on the reservation from the first.

This happened in 1886, and Crook was still waging a campaign in the halls of Congress to get his Apaches moved back west (at least as far as Oklahoma) when he died of a heart attack in 1890.

A few months before his death he visited the largest group of exiled Chiricahua people, who had been temporarily settled at Mount Vernon Barracks, near Mobile, Alabama. They crowded around him, his old scouts and his ancient enemies—and a few were both—and there was quite a reunion, and this is as good a place as any to declare a final, formal end of the Indian wars.

Old Geronimo was in the schoolroom at the time of General Crook's visit, threatening with a stick any child who misbehaved.

Through the Lookinglass IV

The New World cannot be put in one line or one page or one book. But some points can be noticed that are of importance to history—the history of the whole world, New and Old.

We have seen that the beginnings of civilization in the Americas reach back, on the coast of Peru, to an area of antiquity similar to that of such beginnings anywhere in the Old World.

We have seen, in the now widely accepted Cook and Borah pattern of estimates, that populations in the Americas at the epoch of European contact were huge, far greater than populations in Europe at the time. The population of Mexico alone was equal to or larger than the populations of Spain, France, and England combined. The Taino people of the single island of Hispaniola, an island about the size of Ireland, apparently equaled in number the total population of all Spain, or many times the combined population in 1500 of the three principal cities of England, France, and Spain.

The Tainos used raised beds (*conuco*) in farming, and grew food plants (as did many American Indians) of far greater yield per acre than any then cultivated in Europe. On Hispaniola as in Amazonian South America the chief crop was manioc, with an immense yield and remarkable storage qualities. The Tainos also raised sweet potatoes, squash, beans, maize, peppers, peanuts, and pineapples; they caught fish and turtles, so the anthropologists say, in weirs, and gathered wild fruits, nuts, and berries.

We have seen that art in the ancient societies of America was equal in both quality and quantity to art produced anywhere in the Old World. Gold and silver, used only in production of art and ornament (much of this religious), existed in amounts far more abundant than any ever known before in Europe, Asia, or Africa. Platinum was used in jewelry (in northern South

America) centuries before its use in the Old World. The first examples of etching in the world took place in the Hohokam country that is now Arizona.

And as we have seen, "business" in the Old World sense of the word did not appear to exist in the Americas. Archeologists find that markets were operated not for profit but simply for exchange. Traders did not become wealthy (although they may well have been useful at times in neighborly conquest). Private buying and selling of landed estates did not take place; land was under group control; private property as a basis for accumulated wealth was generally unknown.

Early reports from American cities remark on the complete absence of beggars.

Technologically, aside from certain work in art and abstract studies (astronomy, mathematics, calendrics), the peoples of the Americas were clearly far behind the Europeans; even such elemental mechanical devices as the wheel and the bellows were not in use; in weapons and tactics of war, particularly, the Old World was infinitely superior to the New.

Evidently these two distinctly different worlds, the Old and the New, originating in about the same era, had developed in distinctly different ways. Why?

The one basic difference in their early growth seems to have been pastoralism, the keeping and herding of livestock, at the foundation of society in the Old World, almost never followed in the New, where, except for small camelids in certain Andean areas, there was no potential livestock available.

The keeping of flocks and herds could have planted the seed of private property; in fact, with the ownership of valuable straked cattle at stake the idea of individual ownership might have been pretty hard to squelch. In any case, private property was an extremely ancient institution in the Old World, being well established, as has been mentioned, by the time of Hammurabi in the eighteenth century B.C.

Private property could have brought, down through the millennia, the organization of society around profit, wealth as the high goal of life, the organization of direct inheritance to safeguard the succession of wealth and its privileges (withering the clan, making way for the absolute succession of the absolute monarch), all serious effort focused on business and business competition.

Social structure in the Americas, in its multitudinous variety, seems to have been underlain by a quite different foundation: the group control of property, group activity and effort, group identity.

I have spoken in previous work of these basic differences as *communitas* opposed to the *dominium* of private property.

Religion, or at any rate an endless concern with teleology, may have provided, beneath its thousand faces, a principal motive for communitas achievement. In technological progress, and above all in war, it was no match for the business competition of dominium.

But communitas seemed to offer, through the thousands of years, life lived for living rather than getting, a sense of belonging rather than the acquisition of belongings, nature as a source of pleasure rather than a source of profit.

When these two worlds met, dominium of course triumphed in the centuries of real war and real subjection of peoples, matters in which it was consummately expert.

And the centuries of war and subjection were accompanied by what may have been the greatest wave of death in human history as countless multitudes of New World people died from diseases brought by the Old World invaders, diseases to which the American people had no immunity. Here again the ancient association of the Old World with pastoralism played a part, the worst of these epidemic diseases (such as smallpox) having been originally transmitted to humans from domestic animals in earlier ages, thereafter gradually building an immunity in the Old World over many generations.

The Indian world was shattered and destroyed, its cultures obliterated, as everybody knows.

But a study of history has reason to be skeptical of what everybody knows.

European historians usually date the beginning of modern European history at the discovery of America. The feudal societies, the absolute kingdoms of the Old World before that date, where are they now?

It seems apparent, from a detailed look at the two very different pre-Columbian worlds, the Old and the New, that aspects of both remain in our altered world of today. New World influences of considerable historical size appear in the evidence.

Then can it be that some of the New World ideas actually triumphed in those centuries of death and subjection?

Let's say I am suggesting they may have won some of the battles, even major battles, and may still be winning more, as the conflict, the contest of ideas, continues.

For one, let me relate again the advent of the idea of liberty, liberty for all, even for ordinary people, even for the lower classes, liberty as a way of life, plain and simple liberty.

Lord Acton, the great modern authority on liberty, could not find liberty anywhere in the Old World's past before the eighteenth century. A number of other students of the subject are pretty much in agreement: Isaiah Berlin opts for some time after the beginning of capitalism; Jean Starobinski, in *The Invention of Liberty*, also picks the eighteenth century for its arrival.

Oriental despotism, based on "natural law" as said Voltaire, ruled a great area for an incredible length of unbroken time. In Europe even the Greeks preferred upper class rule, oligarchy; Plato made a figure of fun of "one whose motto is liberty and equality." The idea of liberty for all, even for ordinary people, this idea so universally present today did not seem to exist before the discovery of America. The widest democracy of ancient times, says a nineteenth-century authority, was a narrow oligarchy in comparison to modern states.

But early accounts of the people in newly discovered America headlined reports of a popular liberty involving equality and masterlessness that, as we have just seen, really were new ideas for Europe and the Old World in general.

New World people, "gyven to Idlenes and playe," as said the New World's first historian, Peter Martyr of Anghiera, were the happiest of all men because of their long-standing liberty, free of police and deceitful judges, above all free of Mine and Thine, the seeds of all mischief.

These ideas were lead items in numerous widely circulated reports on the New World. Amerigo Vespucci's frequently reprinted and immensely popular (even though or perhaps because frequently distorted) letters spoke many times of the extraordinary New World liberty—no king or lord, no one to obey, no accumulated riches, each person as free as any other.

The narrator in Sir Thomas More's *Utopia* was started for his happy land via a voyage with Vespucci. A great variety of witnesses repeated this announcement of a new and marvelous liberty: Jean de Léry in Brazil in the 1550s, the Spanish historian José de Acosta writing in the 1580s after a number of years in Peru, and many more.

Some of these glowing New World accounts, Peter Martyr's for example, held that the lucky people there were still living in the Golden Age, an idyllic if mythic prehistory dreamland often mentioned in classic literature. Later students have sometimes wondered if Martyr, Acosta, Léry, and others might have been writing about Golden Age dreams in their own minds rather than the real world over there in the Americas. Such a tacit conspiracy lasting for generations and involving a great many witnesses with the New World real before their eyes seems rather unlikely. But even more to the point, a look at actual Golden Age descriptions finds the just rule of a good king is the typical picture. Liberty, masterlessness, kinglessness, each person as much a great lord as the other are generally quite absent. These aspects of a popular liberty being the particular high points of New World reports would seem to rule out rather decisively a Golden Age participation other than metaphorical.

Less favorable verdicts on New World people contributed to the theme of liberty by speaking of their wicked freedom that was really a captivity by Satan, or the entire liberty of brute beasts they enjoyed, or of their foolish wars that lacked any sensible motives, since they didn't have wealth or sovereignty to fight about.

But all criticisms, or sensational counter attractions such as cannibalism or nudity and red-hot sex, could not compete with liberty and equality in capturing the interest of the leading minds of Europe.

The great civilizations in the Andes and in Mesoamerica, rooted in antiquity, assumed the lead in this, and their traditions and basic social structures remained evident in the frontier nations left alive after the great civilizations had been destroyed by Europe. Pierre Ronsard, the leading poet of his age in France, and Montaigne, France's most quoted essayist, who was copied word for word by Shakespeare to describe an ideal commonwealth, both rhapsodized on the beautiful New World liberty, as did a number of anti-Spanish books and pamphlets given much attention during the religious wars of the seventeenth century, and, at the opening of the eighteenth century, the enormously influential work of the baron de Lahontan on the free life of the Indians of Canada.

Almost from the beginning France provided the main channel for these many works on the new freedoms of the New World. Why this should be so is a small but so far unsolved mystery. A similar appeal is not so evident in mainstreams of thought in either Spain or England, where New World contact was also important and of long duration.

The climax of all this, of course, is Jean-Jacques Rousseau—who "invented nothing," as said Madame de Staël, "but set everything on fire" and "produced more effect with his pen," as said Lord Acton, "than Aristotle or Cicero or Saint Augustine or Saint Thomas Aquinas or any man who ever lived."

"The first man who, having enclosed a piece of ground, thought of saying, *This is mine*, and found people simple enough to believe him, was the true founder of civil society. How many crimes, wars, murders, how many miseries and horrors, might have been spared the human race by anyone who, pulling up the boundary stakes or filling in the ditch, would have cried out to his neighbors: 'do not listen to this impostor: you are lost if you forget that the fruits of the earth belong to us all and the earth itself to nobody!'"

In sum, said Rousseau, "Man was born free, and everywhere he is in chains."

With his enormous literary ability—perhaps no other writer had ever possessed "such gifts," said Kant—Rousseau laid hold of these ideas and literally changed the world.

Wrote a modern scholar who specialized in Rousseau studies, "To debate Rousseau is really to debate the main issues in our contemporary life."

It seems fairly well established that Rousseau was quite conscious of New World associations, among others, with his thinking, that the good world of his political treatises was, in the words of a recent study, "drawn from accounts of the North American Indians, the prototype noble savages." He cites specifically the lines on the Caribs from the "good Father Du Tertre" and tells us in *Emile* that he has spent his life reading books of travel and that while he detests them as books they have taught him that the least cultivated people are the wisest. He has also learned, he says in *Emile*, that in a state of nature men are born free and in a natural brotherhood.

In *Emile* he has his student, after studying natural liberty, study the right of property—which will teach him that Nature is good and society is wicked. And since Nature has made the Savage we will make of our student a Savage, strengthen his body, develop his senses, and aid his reflection. Nature knows only God, and the dogmas of religion are the inventions of society; we will show him God without dogma. We will show him luxury and privation, riches and poverty, selfish enjoyment and slavery, and show him that all this depends on the one fact of property.

Says Gustave Lanson, the leading authority at the close of the nineteenth century on French literature, only Rousseau among eighteenth-century writers had seen and stated the question clearly—the fundamental privilege is property.

Quite a few conservative politicians in and outside of France were surprisingly tolerant of Rousseau's ideas until the French Revolution awakened their alarm. America's conservative John Adams said with satisfaction of the American Constitution he had helped construct, "It is Locke, Sidney, and Rousseau and Mably reduced to practice." But a few years later, the French Revolution in full and terrifying swing, Rousseau as quoted by the revolutionaries is to Adams a "Fool," his reasoning "Nonsense and Inconsistency," his eloquence "Wild, coarse, crude talk!" "Mad rant!" "How ignorant! How childish!"

But for the French public in general and many leading thinkers in particular, Rousseau's ideas were from the beginning, and remained, warmly acceptable. Shortly after the publication of *Emile* and Rousseau's principal political essays, a poor play, *Le Manco*, became a Paris success simply because its hero was a savage and expressed, said a critic of the time, citing the recent works of Rousseau, "all that we have been reading everywhere on Kings, on liberty, on rights of man." This was in 1763, more than a quarter of a century before the National Assembly adopted the Declaration of the Rights of Man.

It has been mentioned that Rousseau's early friend and adviser, Diderot, one of the true leaders of French thought at the time, lent his support to the

Rousseauvian objective of "a social state in which there is neither king nor magistrate nor priest nor laws nor thine nor mine nor property moveable or real."

In his later years Rousseau became increasingly unstable, alienated many friends and colleagues, including Diderot, and expressed here or there thoughts that modified or contradicted some of his revolutionary statements that had so captivated France. Later critics have made much of this but France at the time did not; France at the time remained captivated. Seven of the seventeen Articles of the Declaration of the Rights of Man were devoted to liberty; Article II ("The aim of all political association is to preserve the natural and imprescriptible rights of man") was implicitly Rousseau's social contract. The French Revolution altered Europe forever, Rousseau's revolutionary ideas remained very much alive, and the New World remained very much a part of them.

This presence of the New World in the French Revolution has been overlooked in orthodox history. But the foregoing pages do indicate that the vision of the New World established by early reports was not only a factor in the onset of the Revolution but a rather weighty one.

Rousseau was regarded from the beginning as the personification of the spirit of the Revolution—said Edmund Burke in speaking of the revolutionaries, "Rousseau is their canon of holy writ, to him they erect their first statue." Jean-Jacques was a schooldays idol for Louis-Antoine Léon de Richebourg de Saint-Just, who was to argue in the Assembly debates that there should be no rich and no poor, that the State should not permit poverty to exist. The social theories of Rousseau occupied the ardent dreams of Maximilien-Marie-Isidore de Robespierre while a student at the lycée Louis le Grand, and as a candidate for the Estates-General promising to re-establish human nature in the rights and dignity of the first ages of man. And we hear Robespierre open the debate on the Jacobin constitution of 1793 with the paraphrase from Rousseau, "Man is born for happiness and liberty, and everywhere he is a slave and unhappy."

"This sensitive and eloquent philosopher," said Robespierre, "whose writings have developed for us our principles of public morality."

It is a mistake however to see in superstar Rousseau the only spokesman for New World visions in preparing the Revolution. A modern study finds that one of the main currents of philosophical history in the eighteenth century turned to the subject of primitive society and the subsequent progress or otherwise of arts and morals, while the endless debate over natural right in history reached at that time the first of its many modern climaxes.

It is also, of course, far from correct to see Rousseau as the unanimous hero of the revolutionaries. Antoine Barnave, reputed at the time the finest orator of the Revolution, said of Jean-Jacques, "He greatly influenced the minds of the young and made madmen of people who would have been merely fools. . . . He contributed to the confusion of all accepted opinions, to the emancipation of young people from old ideas and to their adoption of bizarre and extreme ideas."

The French Revolution, upon a closer look, turns out to be a number of revolutions—as they were spoken of at the time: the Revolution of July 14, the Revolution of August 10, the Revolution of May 31, and so on to the conservative revolution of Thermidor.

The shifting tides of debate in the Assembly (under the Assembly's various names) reflect quite clearly the ebb and flow of various ideas. One of the issues thus appearing and re-appearing in various disguises was property, attacked by the left, defended by the right.

To those defending property, such as Barnave, Rousseau was no hero. Rousseau appealed, in their view, to a fanatical if immense sect but not, in their view, to reason and sanity. His name was constantly invoked in the Assembly with what conservatives called "Rousseauistic challenges from the furthest left," and he had a hundred times more readers than Voltaire among the lower classes, so his enemies admitted.

But the New World vision of propertylessness alienated even many in the left wing of the Revolution. Danton: "We must not make liberty a hateful thing by a too rigorous application of philosophical principles"—meaning by attacking property.

Liberty, equality, and property made up a continuing debate during the later years of the Revolution, and the final score seemed to agree, as Rousseau had argued, that they could not live together.

Liberty attacks royalty, said Barnave, and added, taking the thought directly from Rousseau's *Discourse on Inequality* and *Emile*, "Equality attacks property." And, said the conservative Malouet, there can be no liberty for anyone unless there is a supreme power resisting everything and anything that could threaten security and property.

Liberty and property could, however, make common cause at one point: the liberty to make as much money from property as possible, the enlistment of the idea of total liberty (freedom from any controls) to support the exploitation of property for unlimited profit, the exploitation by the propertied of the propertyless who needed to use the property.

Rousseau and New World visions may have presented to Europe the vision of liberty, but the Old World adapted it to the Old World's ruling creed of profit.

Demands, disorder, riot, and uprisings over the price of bread helped bring on the French Revolution and continued to sound, like a constant figured bass, beneath much of the revolutionary activity. To one such petition requesting price controls upon flour and bread, and protesting the freedom of commerce to profit unduly from necessary means of sustenance, the revolutionary interior minister of the moment (1792), Jean-Marie Roland de la Platière, responded that all history proves government has never meddled in any commerce, in any business enterprise, except to the disadvantage of everyone. Leave to all business, said Roland, its free and full development, for it is on this liberty that all forms of prosperity depend. The Assembly should abolish all shackles to industry, declare the most complete liberty to all commerce, and act with all force against anyone who would curtail these economic principles.

Roland's wife, Manon-Jeanne Phlipon, was thought of as one of the ablest politicians of the Revolution, and in particular as the brains of her husband. As such, she was presumably the author of this statement of laissez-faire economics that bent Rousseau's New World liberty, as it has been bent so many times since, to the service of the Old World's obsession with private gain Rousseau had so often denounced. Madame Roland was truly devoted to Rousseau, she had fallen in love with the Nouvelle Héloïse at the age of twenty-one, and visiting Geneva in later years she was scandalized to find there not a single statue of the city's most famous son, J.-J. Rousseau. (One is there now, in the Rousseau Memorial Park on Rousseau Island at the Pont Mont-Blanc, epicenter of the city.)

It was Madame Roland who made the most quoted scaffold remark of the Revolution, when taken to the guillotine: O Liberty, what crimes are committed in thy name!

Visions of New World liberty, liberty for all, even for ordinary people, liberty as "virtue" presented on the world-class stage of the French Revolution, did not go away with the demise of the revolution. (The writings of Simon Bolivar a generation later read, as says a critic, like translations of Rousseau, and they were not alone in this distinction.)

The new image of liberty, liberty for all, settled eventually into a permanent place as a vector of the world's actual living social process, in opposition to the Old World wing of authoritarian business progress.

Clearly the New World has occupied for centuries a place, beside Athens and Rome, among the most influential of our direct ancestors.

The tension, the conflict between New and Old continues. Its great tangled campaign of our time was set off by theories adapted from Rousseau and company by Pierre Joseph Proudhon and bent to the service of Old World authoritarianism by Karl Marx and Friedrich Engels.

New World images operative on the Old World soul were no doubt often a far cry from New World realities. The Old World soul thus altered often achieved an even farther cry from the expressed aim.

But the undeniable realities of the fundamental differences between New World and Old were at the origin of this process, and, for good or ill, have had their effect on the changing world of the present.

The total picture of New World life and thought is involved in the question of what those fundamental differences really are, and lends serious historical importance to that study. The question *in toto* is exceedingly complex, and cannot, as was said at the beginning of this chapter, be put in one line— such as a society without beggars versus a society with nuclear weapons, nor can it be put in one page, such as this one, or in one book, such as this one just ending.

Epilogue

In Paris the main entrance of the Bibliothèque Nationale faces a pleasant little park, the Square Louvois, decorated with a recently refurbished Visconti fountain. The Opera of Paris once stood there, where on the last Christmas Eve of the eighteenth century or the first of the nineteenth century, or 3 nivose of the year IX of the République, December 24, 1800, Haydn's oratorio "The Creation of the World" was being presented for the first time in France, and First Consul Bonaparte had announced he would attend.

Along his route, in an ancient street then called rue Saint-Nicaise, a horse and loaded wagon waited in the foggy night, the horse held by a little girl muffled in rags against the cold. At a given moment the wagon blew up with an enormous explosion, blowing horse and little girl and a number of passersby to smithereens, but missing the First Consul's vehicle—the fourth attempt on his life in three months.

The architects of, as it used to be called, the infernal machine, could have been Chouans, or maybe Jacobins, or maybe Septembrisseurs. At the time everybody just said "anarchists." Whatever they were, they would surely have said they had acted for liberty, and the little girl, whom surely they needed—what more innocent than a little girl holding a horse? One of the architects himself wouldn't have done at all—was, surely they would have maintained, a martyr for liberty.

Napoleon went on to the Opera, where he was wildly cheered when the news went round. The little girl's name—bits of blue-and-white striped skirt sticking to fragments of her legs were identified by a poor widow from the rue de Bac, a street vendor, who came to the police in search of her missing child—turned out to be, huge cloudy symbol, Marianne.

The infernal architects turned out to be Royalists with English money and Chouan pals, but this didn't turn out until Napoleon and his ministers had profited from the public indignation to carry out mass arrests of some hundreds of people, and, by means of hastily established Special Tribunals, execute or imprison or deport the more troublesome old Jacobins still left over from the Revolution, while special government agents had been assigned to visit every house in the city to "take exact information on the public opinions of each individual," and modern times, in this instance the Old World vector prevailing, had begun.

THE END

Notes

PART I

Chapter 1

3   Four to fourteen million years ago: D.R. Pilbeam, "Rethinking Human Origins," in R.L. Ciochon and J.G. Fleagle, eds., *Primate Evolution and Human Origins* (Menlo Park, California, 1985), 215. In explaining that ideas unrelated to actual fossils have dominated the way fossils are interpreted, Pilbeam adds, "I have come to believe that many of the statements we make about the hows and whys of human evolution say as much about us . . . and the larger society in which we live, as about anything that 'really' happened." (220)

- The 1994 find of a hominid molar in north-central Ethiopia, (*Australopithecus ramidus*) is believed to push back the opening of the human fossil record to 4.4 million years ago: Gen Suwa and Tim White, *Nature*, September 1994.
- "almost as many scenarios of human evolution as paleoanthropologists": D. R. Pilbeam, "Major Trends in Human Evolution," in Lars König Königsson, ed., *Current Argument on Early Man* (Oxford 1980), 270. See also Michael H. Day, *Guide to Fossil Man*, 4th ed. (Chicago 1986).

4   Theories of the past: Lee Eldridge Huddleston, *Origins of the American Indians: European Concepts, 1492–1729* (Austin 1967).

- "Even that remote date": Frank E. Poirier, *Fossil Evidence: The Human Evolutionary Journey*, 3rd ed. (St. Louis 1981), places human beings in the "western United States and northern South America by 15,000 years ago at the very latest." (369)
- Blood-group patterns: William C. Boyd, *Genetics and the Races of Man* (Boston 1950); W.S. Laughlin, ed., *The Physical Anthropology of the American Indian* (New York 1951).
- "primordial blood streams": Carl Ortwin Sauer, *Land and Life: A Selection from His Writings* John Leighly, ed., (Berkeley 1963), 239.

5   Bering Strait entry: V.L. Kontrimavichus, ed., *Beringia in the Cenozoic Era* (New Delhi 1984, trans. from Russian edition, Vladivostok 1976), *passim*. David M. Hopkins, ed., *The Bering Land Bridge* (Stanford 1967), *passim*.

6   Northeastern Siberia ice-free: C.C. Flerow, "On the Origin of the Mammalian Fauna of Canada," in Hopkins, *Bering Land Bridge*, 275.

•   Hopkins, *Bering Land Bridge*, gives a detailed timetable. (465–68)

7   The geographer is Albrecht Penck, cited in Carl Sauer, "A Geographic Sketch of Early Man in America," *Geographical Review* 14/4 (1944).

•   The paleozoologist quoted is C.C. Flerow in Hopkins, *Bering Land Bridge*, 274.

8   Paul Rivet, *Bulletin de la Société de Linguistique* 26 (Paris 1925).

•   "The story left in stone and bone": Stuart Fiedel, *Prehistory of the Americas* (Cambridge 1987), 54–60.

9   Monte Verde: Tom D. Dillehay and Michael B. Collins, " Monte Verde in Chile," *Nature* 332 (1988), 150–52.

•   Pedra Furada: M. Guidon and G. Delibras, "C-14 Dates . . . " *Nature* 321 (1986), 769–71.

•   Valsequillo: Cynthia Irwin-Williams, "Summary of Archaeological Evidence from the Valsequillo Region, Puebla, Mexico," in David L. Bowman, ed., *Cultural Continuity in Mesoamerica* (The Hague 1978). Also Virginia Steen-McIntyre, Ronald Fryxell, and Harold E. Malde, "Geologic Evidence for Age of Deposits at Hueyataco Archaeological Site, Valsequillo, Mexico," in *Quaternary Research* 16 (1981).

•   Early dates: Poirier, *Fossil Evidence*, 369–74; Alan Lyle Bryan, ed., *Early Man in America: From a Circum-Pacific Perspective* (Edmonton, Alberta, 1978), Introduction vii–viii; 1–9; 23–25; and David M. Hopkins et al., eds., *The Paleoecology of Beringia* (New York 1982), 459.

•   Old Crow earliest dates: A.V. Jopling, W.H. Irving, B.F. Beebe, "Stratigraphic, Sedimentological and Faunal Evidence for the Occurrence of pre-Sangamonian Artefacts in Northern Yukon," *Arctic* 34/1 (1981), 3–33. Several bone tools described in this study were re-dated in later laboratory tests to much more recent times, only 1,200 to 1,500 years ago; ages of 25,000 to 47,000 years for the others were confirmed—although this interpretation has been questioned. D.E. Nelson, Richard E. Morlan, J.S. Vogel, J.R. Southon, C.R. Harrington, "New Dates on Northern Yukon Artifacts: Holocene not Upper Pleistocene," *Science* 232 (May 9 1986), 749–51.

10   Piman prayer: J. William Lloyd, *Aw-aw-tam Indian Nights* (Westfield, New Jersey 1911).

11   Ales Hrdlicka, *Skeletal Remains Suggesting or Attributed to Early Man in America*, BAE Bulletin 33 (Washington 1907), 14 and 98; and *Recent Discoveries Attributed to Early Man in America*, BAE Bulletin 66 (Washington 1918).

•   Clement W. Meighan, "California," R.E. Taylor and C.W. Meighan, eds., *Chronologies in New World Archaeology* (New York 1978), gives bone collagen radiocarbon dates for the Laguna Beach bone (plus 14,000), for a Long Beach skull (plus 17,000), for a Los Angeles skull (plus 23,000), but "all these have problems of archaeological context and possible contamination. All were recovered years ago and have an uncertain history." (229)

•   "study of some thirty-odd years ago": T. Dale Stewart, "A Physical Anthropologist's View of the Peopling of the New World," in *Southwestern Journal of Anthropology* 16/3 (1960).

•   Spirit Cave Man's revised age was the subject of a story in the *New York Times*, April 27, 1996.

- Yuha Man's age of 60,000 years is suggested in George F. Carter, *Earlier Than You Think: A Personal View of Man in America* (College Station, Texas 1980), 235.
- "20,000 'possible'": Stewart, "A Physical Anthropologist's View," 260.

12 The surveying archeologist: A.D. Krieger, in Sol Tax, et al., eds., *An Appraisal of Anthropology Today* (Chicago 1953), 248.

13 C. Vance Haynes Jr., "Geofacts and Fancy," *Natural History* 97 (1988), 9, 6, and 10.

- Additional rejections of dates earlier than 12,000 years ago are from Fiedel, *Prehistory of the Americas*, 43, 52, 54–55; and from Frederick Hadleigh West, *The Archaeology of Beringia* (New York 1981), Preface, xv.
- The unlikely demography: Paul S. Martin, "The Discovery of America," *Science* 179 (1973), 969–74; the more customary explanation for the rest of the world is given by C.C. Flerow in Hopkins, *Bering Land Bridge*.
- The specialist in settlement patterns, William T. Sanders, notes for the spectacular growth of the great city, Teotihuacan, a climax population growth doubling every two centuries, a "remarkable growth rate for a pre-industrial group": William T. Sanders, "Ecological Adaptation in the Basin of Mexico," in Jeremy Sabloff, ed., with the Assistance of Patricia A. Andrews, *Supplement to the Handbook of Middle American Indians, vol. 1, Archaeology* (Austin 1981), 109 and 166, and Sanders et al., *The Basin of Mexico* (New York 1979), 107.

14 Fiedel, *Prehistory of the Americas*, 43, disqualifies finds by "non-professionals."

- Hrdlicka 1912: *Early Man in South America*, BAE Bulletin 52 (Washington 1912), 385.
- The Mexican archeologist is José Luis Lorenzo, excavator of Tlapacoya, "Early Man Research," in Bryan, *Early Man in America*, 2.
- Hrdlicka is quoted from *Melanesians and Australians and the Peopling of America*, Smithsonian Miscellaneous Collections 24/11 (Washington 1936), 34.
- "open-minded": F.H. West, "Old World Affinities of Archaeological Complexes from Tangle Lakes (Central Alaska)," in Kontrimavichus, *Beringia*, 593.
- "split into warring camps": Carter, *Personal View of Man in America*, 317.
- David Hopkins is quoted from *Paleoecology of Beringia*, 438.
- DNA research: *Science* 259 (January 15, 1993), 312–13.

15 Archeology's "masquerade as science" is questioned by the British archeologist Warwick Bray, "The Paleoindian Debate," *Nature* 332 (1988), 107. He notes, in analyzing the American debate, that "two very different questions have become confused. One is that of the oldest human presence in the New World" and the other "what the oldest American artifacts look like."

- The recent protest is from David S. Meltzer, "Why Don't We Know When the First People Came to America?" *American Antiquity* 54/3 (1989), 484.
- Monte Verde: *Arizona Daily Star* (Tucson), February 7, 1997, from *The New York Times*: "Evidence for a pre-Clovis site at Monte Verde, on the sandy banks of a creek near the Pacific 500 miles south of Santiago, Chile, has been amassed and analyzed over the last two decades by a team of American and Chilean archaeologists, led by Dr. Tom D. Dillehay of the University of Kentucky. . . . Consensus agrees that human occupation there dates back to 12,500 years ago. This represents the first major shift in more than 60 years in the confirmed archaeology . . . 'It could mean that early people first arrived in their new world at least 20,000 years before Columbus.'" See also the previously mentioned 1988 paper by Dillehay and Michael B. Collins, "Monte Verde . . . " in *Nature*.

- Wild times during deglaciation: Ronald B. Parker, *The Tenth Muse* (New York 1986), 73–81. And also see E.C. Pielou, *After the Ice Age: The Return of Life to Glaciated North America* (Chicago 1991).
- Lerma points: Fiedel, *Prehistory of the Americas*, 65.
- Plains points: Warren W. Caldwell and Dale R. Henning, "North American Plains," in Taylor and Meighan, *Chronologies in New World Archaeology*, 118–26.
- Meat-eating, bipedalism, tools, brain size: recent studies of human origins are admirably covered in Richard Leakey, *The Origin of Humankind* (New York 1994).
- "feminist critics": Pilbeam, "Major Trends in Human Evolution," in *Current Argument on Early Man*, 264. Richard B. Lee and Irven DeVore, eds., *Man the Hunter* (Chicago 1968) present detailed statistics on modern hunter-gatherers, hunting providing only 20 to 44 percent of the menu. (37–39 and 43). See also H.M. Wormington, *Ancient Man in North America*, 4th ed., (Denver 1957).

17 Some idea of samenesses and differences in legends, hero stories, creation stories, is found in the comparative notes in Stith Thompson's classic *Tales of the North American Indians* (Bloomington, Indiana 1929), 271–360.

- The interest of modern science can be illustrated by Edward O. Wilson, *The Diversity of Life* (New York 1992), "Humanity is part of nature . . . The more closely we identify ourselves with the rest of life, the more quickly . . . an enduring ethic . . . can be built. . . . Only in the last moment of human history has the delusion arisen that people can flourish apart from the rest of the living world." (348–49).

Chapter 2

19 The Boylston Street weir: J.B. Griffin, in Taylor and Meighan, *Chronologies in New World Archaeology*, 53; Thomas Harriot, *A Briefe and True Report of the New Found Land of Virginia* (1588 and the illustrated Theodor de Bry edition of 1590), 20, and 56–57, pictures the weir, with boats, and fishermen harvesting with lances. Ralph Hamor the younger, *A True discourse of the Present Estate of Virginia . . .* (London 1625) speaks of English threats "to breake downe their fishing Weares" in a dispute with the Powhatan people. (7)

- Caliban sings at the close of Act Two, *The Tempest*.
- Old Copper dates: James B. Griffin, "Eastern United States," in Taylor and Meighan, *Chronologies in New World Archaeology*, 60.

20 Lake Cochise: Fiedel, *Prehistory of the Americas*, 118.

- Desert food: E.B. Jelks, "Diablo Range," in Taylor and Meighan, *Chronologies in New World Archaeology*, 71–74.
- Peruvian coastal dates: Richard L. Burger, *Chavin and the Origins of Andean Civilization* (London 1992), 31.

21 The Koster Site: Fiedel, *Prehistory of the Americas*, 94, citing S. Struever and F.A. Holton, *Americans in Search of Their Past* (New York 1974).

- Carl O. Sauer, *Agricultural Origins and Dispersals* (New York 1952; Cambridge, Massachusetts 1969), argues that the "only explanation for the great savannas that meets all conditions is fire." (191) This has been a highly controversial point.

- The concept of "primary forest efficiency" was outlined long ago in J.B. Caldwell, *Trend and Tradition in the Prehistory of the Eastern United States* (Menasha, Wisconsin 1958).
- Lee and DeVore, *Man the Hunter*, present statistical tables on the !Kung Bushmen of Africa, who follow a hunting-gathering way of life with little stress and less work (a work week of one to three days), obtaining enough calories to support not only active adults but also large numbers of elderly and children. Their life is more secure than that of their pastoralist and farmer neighbors, who suffer hard times and even famine during droughts—which have little effect on the !Kung. (37–39)
- The introduction of agriculture as the fall from the Garden of Eden is suggested by Victoria Brandon.

22   In the concluding summation of Charles A. Reed, ed., *Origins of Agriculture* (The Hague 1977), evidence is noted of planting and tending in Mesoamerica 1,000 years earlier than 7,000 BP, but still 3,000 years before villages. (892)

- Early pottery dates derive principally from Gordon R. Willey, "A Summary Scan," in Taylor and Meighan, *Chronologies in New World Archaeology*, 513–58; tables 514–15; bibliography 558–63.
- Origins of agriculture: Reed, *Origins of Agriculture*; N.W. Simmonds, ed., *Evolution of Crop Plants* (London 1976); Charles B. Heiser, *Seed to Civilization* (San Francisco 1981). Richard I. Ford, ed., *Prehistoric Food Production in North America* (Ann Arbor 1985), emphasizes the diversity.
- Plants for fiber: Charles B. Heiser, *Of Plants and People* (Norman 1985), 218, citing Bennett Bronson, "The Earliest Farming: Demography as Cause and Consequence," in Steven Polgar, ed., *Population, Ecology and Social Evolution* (The Hague 1975).
- The *totora* fire fan: Heiser, *Of Plants and People*, 42.

23   Bitter manioc: Erland Nordenskiöld, "The Ethnography of South America Seen from Mojos in Bolivia," *Comparative Ethnographical Studies* 3 (Göteborg 1924), 36.

- Eastern United States: Heiser, *Of Plants and People*, 171, 13–14, 95, and 103–10.
- Sumpweed: Nancy and David Asch, "The Economic Potential of *Iva annua* and Its Prehistoric Importance in the Lower Illinois Valley," in Richard I. Ford, ed., *The Nature and Status of Ethnobotany* (Ann Arbor 1978), 301–43.
- *Cucurbita*: Frances B. King, "Early Cultivated Cucurbita in Eastern North America," in Richard I. Ford, ed., *The Beginning of Food Production in Prehistoric North America* (Ann Arbor 1984), 73–79. See also Thomas W. Whitaker and Hugh C. Cutler, "Prehistoric Cucurbits from the Valley of Oaxaca," *Economic Botany* 25 (1971).
- Tropical origin: Donald W. Lathrap, "Our Father the Cayman, Our Mother the Gourd . . . a Unitary Model for the Emergence of Agriculture in the New World," in Reed, *Origins of Agriculture*.

24   Sweet potato: Heiser, *Seed to Civilization*, 135 ff; 150–52.
- Agricultural frontier: Sauer, *Agricultural Origins and Dispersals*.
- Quinua: Heiser, *Of Plants and People*, 82–99; *chochos*: 120–27; meat a luxury: 123.
- Llamas: Reed, *Origins of Agriculture*, 938.
- Code of Hammurabi: Lewis Mumford, *The City in History* (New York 1961), 108.

Chapter 3

25   The "fertility goddess" identification of early figurines is questioned by Philip
     Phillips, "The Role of Trans-Pacific Contacts in the Development of New World
     Pre-Columbian Civilizations," *Handbook of Middle American Indians* 4, pointing
     out that some were made by nonagricultural people, and many offer only a crudely
     standardized female body but go to great pains with the head and hairdo.

•   Nicholas J. Saunders, *People of the Jaguar: The Living Spirit of Ancient America*
     (London 1989), calls jaguar symbolism "omnipresent." (149)

26   A sequence of different peoples through the centuries in the Olmec country is
     detailed in Wigberto Jiménez Moreno, "El Enigma de los Olmecas," *Cuadernos
     Americanos*, 1/5 (Mexico 1942).

•   The 50-ton stone is mentioned in Philip Drucker, Robert F. Heizer, and R.J. Squier,
     Excavations at La Venta, Tabasco, 1955, BAE Bulletin 170 (Washington 1959).

•   Magnetism: Vincent H. Malmstrom, "Knowledge of Magnetism in pre-Columbian
     Mesoamerica," *Nature* 259 (1976), 390–91; for the shapes of structural groups and
     "compass" orientation of towns see *The Olmec and Their Neighbors, Essays in
     Memory of Matthew W. Stirling*, M. D. Coe and David Grove, organizers, and
     Elizabeth P. Benson, ed. (Washington 1981).

•   Olmec and Chou jade are discussed in M.W. Stirling, "The Olmecs, Artists in Jade,"
     in Samuel K. Lothrop, et al., eds., *Essays in Pre-Columbian Art and Architecture*
     (Cambridge, Massachusetts 1961). See also Frederick W. Lange, ed., *Pre-Columbian
     Jade: New Geological and Cultural Interpretation* (Salt Lake City 1993), a work
     Gordon R. Willey calls "definitive." (*American Anthropologist* January 1995).

•   Trans-Pacific connections are proposed in Betty J. Meggers, "The Trans-Pacific Origin
     of Meso-American Civilisation: A Preliminary Review of the Evidence and its
     Theoretical Implications," *American Anthropologist* 77 (1975); and skeptically assessed
     in Joseph Needham and Lu Gwei-Djen, *Trans-Pacific Echoes and Resonances; Listening
     Once Again* (Singapore 1985). The question will be taken up later in this text.

27   Belize: B. L. Turner II and Peter C. Harrison, eds., *Pulltrouser Swamp: Ancient Maya
     Habitat, Agriculture, and Settlement in Northern Belize* (Austin 1984); and Mary
     De Lond Pohl, ed., *Ancient Maya Wetland Agriculture: Excavations on Albion Island,
     Northern Belize* (Boulder, Colorado, 1990).

•   Cuello dates: Norman Hammond, ed., *Cuello* (Cambridge 1990), 245–46. See also
     Norman Hammond, Duncan Pring, Rainer Berger, with V. R. Switsur and A. P. Ward
     of the Radiocarbon Dating Research Laboratory, Cambridge, "Radiocarbon chronol-
     ogy for early Maya occupation at Cuello, Belize," *Nature* 260/1976, 579–81: Occupation
     was dated at 2000 B.C. in radiocarbon years, 2600 B.C. in bristlecone pine calibration,
     thus establishing a sedentary pottery-using community in the Maya lowlands as
     early as any in Mesoamerica, 1,700 years earlier than the hitherto earliest known
     such communities on the Yucatan Peninsula or the adjacent Pacific slope. (579) .

•   Calendrics are considered in detail in Herbert J. Spinden, *The Reduction of Maya
     Dates*, Papers of the Peabody Museum of American Archaelogy and Ethnology,
     6/4 (Cambridge, Massachusetts 1924); and in J.E.S. Thompson, *Maya Chronology:
     The Correlation Question*, Contribution No. 14, Publication No. 456, Carnegie
     Institute of Washington (Washington 1935); and in Alfonso Caso, "Calendrical
     Systems of Central Mexico," *Handbook of Middle American Indians* 10, who
     remarks that the basic calendar is found at various sites dating back to 600 B.C.

and "at all these places the calendar appears as a completely established and organized system . . ." (333)

- "The sophistication of their system": John D. Barrow, *Pi in the Sky: Counting, Thinking, and Being,* (Oxford 1992, New York 1994), 87n.

28　Francisco Lopez de Gómara, *La Historia General de las Indias* (1554) quotes Friar Thomas Ortizius, before the Council of the Indies: "They sacrificed to Venus, which they considered the most excellent of stars, a royal slave on the day . . . when they perceived it in the autumn. It continued visible for 260 days. They believed that it was influential over destinies, and accordingly they practiced divination by signs, which they painted and allotted to these 260 days."

- The date 292, heralding the great 600 Classic years, might ring a bell for a Maya *halach uinic,* if one were around these days: 292 + 600 = 892 (Classic Maya collapse); 892 + 600 = 1492; 1492 + 600 = (what would the prediction be?) It should be noted that 600 years = 20 generations, perhaps a figure of interest for the vigesimal Maya.

29　One of Twain's news stories recounted a terrible massacre committed (in a locality that couldn't exist) by a man gone mad because he had bought some mining stock Goodman's *Territorial Enterprise* didn't like. Goodman left a rival editor with an honorable limp after a duel with Navy Colts; his editorials, besides once forcing "the resignation of the entire Supreme Court bench of the Territory," were believed to have been of influence in keeping Nevada in the union.

- Dr. Gustav Eisen: Joseph T. Goodman, "The Archaic Maya Inscriptions," Appendix to A.P. Maudslay, *Archaeology,* vols. 1 to 4, *Biologia Centrali-Americana; or, Contributions to the Knowledge of the Fauna and Flora of Mexico and Central America* (London 1889–1902), Preface (dated 1895, published 1897). Goodman was rather unkind to rank-happy "scientists" and their "hieratic secrecy" (which may have been one reason the professors took thirty years to swallow his findings), but with one fulsome exception for Brasseur de Bourbourg, discoverer of so many treasures of Maya information. J.E.S. Thompson, "A Correlation of the Mayan and European Calendars," *Field Museum of Natural History Publication 241* (Chicago 1927), Introductory Note: "The correlation suggested in this publication was first proposed as long ago as 1905 by J.T. Goodman . . . At that time Goodman's correlation was unanimously rejected by his fellow students of Mayology. The chronicle of Oxkutzcab was then unknown, and the astronomical information contained both in the Dresden Codex and the monuments had not been worked out." J.E.S. Thompson's obituary of Juan Martinez Hernandez (1866–1959) cites his "Parelelisme entre los calendarios maya y azteca" in *Diario de Yucatan* (Merida February 7, 1926) as having revived the Goodman correlation, a turning point in Maya research: *American Antiquity,* 25/4 (1959–1960), 392. Ignacio Bernal, *A History of Mexican Archaeology: The Vanished Civilizations of Middle America,* Ruth Malet, trans., (London 1980): Goodman invented the GMT "with a few subsequent minor modifications by Eric Thompson." (144–48).

Chapter 4

31　Little potbellied stone gentlemen: Lee A. Parsons, "Post-Olmec Stone Sculpture: The Olmec Izapan Transition on the South Pacific Coast and Highlands," in Coe, Grove, and Benson, *The Olmec.*

- Possible Zapotec origin for Maya system of writing: Coe, *The Maya,* 27 and 38.

33   Milpa remained the standard: ibid., 20.

•   Jorge E. Hardoy devotes a chapter to the question of whether or not the Maya built cities: *Pre-Columbian Cities* (Spanish 1964, English 1973), chapter 7, 241–89.

•   Habitation "virtually continuous": Coe, The Maya. A possibility of maybe 8 to 10 million people in the Lowlands in the eighth century seems not unreasonable. See also T. Patrick Culbert and Don S. Rice, eds., *Pre-Columbian Population History in the Maya Lowlands* (Albuquerque 1990).

•   Body paint symbolism: Sylvanus Griswold Morley, *The Ancient Maya*, 3rd edition revised by George W. Brainerd (Stanford 1956), 169–70 and 383.

34   Bishop Landa is quoted from *Landa's "Relacion de las cosas de Yucatan." A Translation*, Alfred M. Tozzer, ed. and trans., Papers of the Peabody Museum of American Archaeology and Ethnology, Harvard, XVIII (Cambridge, Massachusetts 1941).

•   The recent art historian: Linda Schele and Mary Ellen Miller, *The Blood of Kings: Dynasty and Ritual in Maya Art* (New York and Fort Worth 1986), 40.

•   Skilled labor: Morley, *The Ancient Maya*, 47 and 263–64. Also, Robert W. Patch, *Maya and Spaniard in Yucatan, 1648–1832* (Stanford 1993): "all peasants, men and women, carried out some form of skilled or semiskilled nonagricultural labor." (20)

•   Landa: Tozzer, *Landa's "Relacion."*

35   Thompson is quoted from J.E.S. Thompson, "A Commentary on the Dresden Codex: A Maya Hieroglyphic Book," American Philosophical Society, *Memoirs*, 93 (Philadelphia 1972), 113.

•   Maya religion, sacrifice, and penance: J.E.S. Thompson, *Maya History and Religion* (Norman 1970), 175–76.

•   Ceremonial use of decapitated skulls at Chichen Itza: ibid., 178–79.

•   Sacrificial offerings: ibid., 162–63; and J.E.S. Thompson, *The Rise and Fall of Maya Civilization* (Norman 1954), 60.

36   The Classic "palaces" not residences: ibid., 57–58.

•   "Five million" present day Maya is a guesswork figure levered rather drastically upward by a another guesswork figure in Clifford Krauss, *Inside Central America* (New York 1991), that "pure Mayan" inhabitants of Guatemala are today "about forty-five per cent of the 8.6 million population," which would give us 3,870,000 Maya people for Guatemala alone. The Maya population in Mexico could be presumed in the neighborhood of the same figure, producing a total from these two areas of some 7 million, but I have re-levered this total somewhat downward. Since a string of military dictatorships in Guatemala have bombed, burned, and shot thousands of Maya people during the last thirty-five years (120,000 Indian children as war orphans are given by Krauss from a census of 1984), perhaps the nearly 4 million guess above for Guatemala could be considered too high. Coe, *The Maya*, gives 2 million for the total present Maya population. Thompson, *Maya Civilization*, quotes Karl Sapper "nearly fifty years ago" estimating about one and a quarter million, three-fifths of them highland Maya. (29) Thompson adds that the Central Area, except for its appendage, the Chiapan uplands, is now largely uninhabited. Krauss estimates that at the turn of the present century eighty per cent of the then one and a half million Guatemalan population were "pure Mayan" (which would equal 1,200,000) (19), compared to, as stated above, 45 percent of the present 8.6 million population.

38   The present tendency is to date the opening of the Classic period a little earlier than the Stela 29 date: for example T. Patrick Culbert, ed., *Classic Maya Political History: Hieroglyphic and Archaeological Evidence* (Cambridge 1991), 7, suggests A.D. 250; and Norman Hammond suggests c. A.D. 200 (ibid., 253). And see Jeremy A. Sabloff and John S. Henderson, eds., *Lowland Maya Civilization in the Eighth Century* A.D. (Washington, Dunbarton Oaks Research Library, 1993). Thompson in the 2nd (1966) edition of *Maya Civilization*: "The division between Formative and Classic has become meaningless now that corbeled vaulting and hieroglyphic writing are known to have begun in late Formative times. As those terms are too firmly established in the literature to be dropped, we are now in the ridiculous position of having to correlate the start of the Classic period, once regarded as a great landmark, with changes in shape and color in non-utility pottery that took place around A.D. 200. There is an equally meaningless dating of the start of the Classic at Teotihuacan, falling a little earlier. One must not look on the line between these two periods as something synchronized to the year throughout middle America." (57–59).

·   Radiocarbon dates supporting the GMT correlation: Coe, *The Maya*, "Most Mayanists have given sighs of relief" (24); and Thompson himself in the *Encyclopaedia Britannica*, 15th ed., vol. 20: "carbon-14 readings overwhelmingly support the Goodman-Martinez-Thompson correlation." (652–53) The Spinden and GMT correlations are so close together, however, that either can be made to fit many of the readings, especially in view of present corrective calibration to actual age.

·   The Classic Period came to a close: according to Thompson, *Maya Civilization*, Copan ceased dedicating dated monuments A.D. 800 (GMT); Quirigua and Piedras Negras, 810; Tikal, 869; Yaxchilan-Bonampak, 870; Uaxactun, c. 889 (84).

·   Buildings left unfinished: ibid., 84.

·   Glyphs left blank: Rafael Girard, *Los Mayas* (Mexico 1966), 405 and 436; for the half-finished hieroglyphic stairs (*Dos Pilos*), foto 200 (495).

·   Postclassic resetting of stela fragments upside down: Robert Wauchope, "Late Horizons of Maya Prehistory," in Wauchope, ed., *The Indian Background of Latin American History* (New York 1970), 100.

39   Tatiana Proskouriakoff, "Historical Implications of a Pattern of Dates at Piedra Negras, Guatemala," *American Antiquity* 25/4 (1959–60).

·   Historical inscriptions: Linda Schele and Peter Matthews, "Royal Visits" in Culbert, *Classic Maya Political History*. T684 was identified by Proskouriakoff (1960) as a verb recording "inauguration." Although this glyph functions as a standard verb for accession to office, here it must refer to some other kind of ritual event, for Bird-Jaguar had acceded five years earlier on 9.16.1.0.0. (A.D. 752) according to the Yaxchilan inscriptions. It may simply refer to the presentation or offering of a "bundle" with its contents. (n5, 252)

·   Schele and Miller, *Maya Art*: "clear evidence for the Maya preoccupation with war. . . . At Piedras Negras nearly half the monuments show warriors, many of them with captives." (22)

·   The 1840 study: John L. Stephens, *Incidents of Travel in Central America, Chiapas and Yucatan*, Illustrations by Frederick Catherwood (New York 1969, 2 vols., originally 1841, 1843), 1:142. The bow had not yet reached the Maya in Classic times. Oviedo, the historian of the Indies, wrote in 1535 that the Maya of Yucatan used to fight with slings and sharp sticks. Bishop Landa, however, who describes in detail the Yucatecan weapons at the time of the Spanish conquest (bows and arrows, hatchets, *atlatl*, and a small lance with a flint point), says in the 1560s that the Maya do not have slings and have never seen one, "although they can throw a stone very hard and with accuracy by aiming at their target with the left arm and index finger." *Diego de Landa's Account of the Affairs of Yucatan: The Maya*, A.R. Pagden, ed. and trans. (Chicago 1975), 165, 84–85, and 44. Projectile points or other remains of weapons do not seem to figure prominently in archeological collections of the Classic period.

- "Emblem glyphs" as names for city-states: Heinrich Berlin, "El glifo 'emblema' en las inscriptiones Mayas," *Journal de la Société des Américanistes* 47 (1958), 111–19; and "Glifos nominales en el sarcafago de Palenque," *Humanidades* 2/10 (1959), 1–8. However, Proskouriakoff 1960 suspects these emblem glyphs might refer to dynasty or lineage rather than place. (471)
- "Bonampak," *Archaeology*, 1/1 (March 1948), 30; Giles G. Healey, "Oxlahuntun," *Archaeology*, 1/3 (September 1948), 129–34; and Healey, "The Lacanja Valley," *Archaeology*, 3/1 (March 1950), 12–15.
- The name Bonampak was suggested by S.G. Morley in a letter of July 1946 to G.G. Healey, made up from two Maya words meaning roughly "dyed wall": *Morleyana* (Santa Fe 1950).

40 "constant warfare": the enthusiast is Michael D. Coe, quoted from the preface to Schele and Miller, *Maya Art*.

- Thompson in Karl Ruppert, J.E.S. Thompson, and Tatiana Proskouriakoff, *Bonampak, Chiapas, Mexico* (Washington 1955): the "terms 'battle,' and perhaps even 'fight' are too grandiose . . . enemy are unarmed." (51) The severed head in the mural is "strongly reminiscent of the decapitated head of the maize god which rests on the earth symbol on page 34 of the Codex Dresden." (53) Bleeding hands "a baffling matter." (54)
- The "sacred text" is from the Talmud.
- Much has been published on the digging and rebuilding at Tikal. An impressive example: the multi-volume set of plans, sketches, drawings, photographs, and detailed description in William R. Coe, ed., *Excavations in the Great Plaza, North Terrace and North Acropolis of Tikal* (Philadelphia, the University Museum, University of Pennsylvania, 1990). The Guatemalan government's aggressive interest in the tourist-attraction potential of the Tikal site has given rise to some archeological murmurs, such as a letter from Heinrich Berlin in 1967, "The Destruction of Structure 5D-33 at Tikal," in *American Antiquity* 32/2 (1967), 241–42, warning against "archaeological abdication in favor of a road-builder's mentality." This was answered in the same issue by Froelich Rainey, Alfred Kidder II, Linton Satterthwaite, and William R. Coe (242–44), and in "A Third-Party Comment" by J. E. S. Thompson (244).
- Conquest and empire: Schele and Miller, *Maya Art*: "Increasingly, emerging evidence suggests that the aims of Maya conflict did include material and territorial gains, even though the outcomes of particular conflicts are unknown." (218) In contrast, see Culbert, *Classic Maya Political History*: "We are bothered by the fact that our use of the term [dynasty] does not imply an unbroken line of descent . . . It is impossible to demonstrate in the great majority of cases" that a new ruler was a direct descendant of his predecessor. (330) "I am also struck by the number of important rulers whose accessions were in some way irregularities." (332)

41   Fragmentary inscriptions: Norman Hammond, defining Maya polity in the same volume (citing W. Ashmore and R.R. Wilk, *Household and Community in the Mesoamerican Past* (Albuquerque 1988), 1–27, emphasizes "the dangers of Mesoamerican archaeologists turning to fragmentary textual evidence as inscriptions are deciphered, and investing it with overmuch significance." (263) Hammond adds, "the internal dynamics of Classic Maya polities must always be the subject of speculative reconstruction rather than observation" (283) Such reservations are nothing new in the Maya business, as witness the classic remark of George Kubler's used as a chapter heading in Francis Robicsek, *The Smoking Gods* (Norman 1978): "Mesoamerican studies often impress the reader as a Sahara of guesses where travelers crazed with a thirst for certainty suffer various mirages." The dean of American archeologists, Gordon R. Willey, *Essays in Maya Archaeology* (Albuquerque 1987): "I admit to being over-dazzled and over-optimistic. . . . Most everyone in Maya archaeology has responded positively to the recent advances on the part of the epigraphers . . . and yet we must temper our enthusiasm with caution, especially those of us who do not directly control the glyphic texts." (14) Population growth, subsistence, warfare, and trade seem to relegate ideology to a back seat. But there are indications that "idea systems" were important all through Maya development. The total ideology, rich in symbolism and ritual, "must have been crucial in maintaining the entire Maya cultural system as it was directed from its ceremonial or organizational centers" and must also have played a part "in bringing the system to decline and finish." (90) Willey continues: "A major difficulty in all of this is that we do not know—and probably will never know—the nature of the ideas involved . . . Considering this difficulty, is it worthwhile even to attempt to struggle with this dimension? . . . Should we not . . . turn our efforts to the more tangible systems that we can cope with more readily? Some archaeologists appear to think so; I do not." (90)

·   El Mirador "in sheer bulk larger than Tikal": Willey, *Maya Archaeology*, 6.

·   Nakbe, a site seven miles from El Mirado, has produced some of the earliest dates so far obtained for Maya temple construction.

·   Quoted scripture is from the *Chilam Balam of Chumayel* [the Book of the Prophet of Secrets, the Book of the Jaguar Priest], Ralph L. Roys, trans. (Washington 1933). A post-Spanish collection.

42   The remembered prayer: from the *Popul Vuh: The Sacred Book of the Ancient Quiche Maya*, translated into Spanish by Adrian Recinos and into English by S.G. Morley and Delia Goetz (Norman 1950).

·   Munro S. Edmonson, ed., *Supplement to the Handbook of Middle American Indians*, vol. 3, *Literature*, (Austin 1985), spoke of the Maya "predicting their history and then living it." (48)

Chapter 5

43   Sexy talk: see Gary H. Gossen, "Tzotzil Literature," in Edmonson, *Handbook* 3 for a ritualized example. (95)

·   Two examples of the boozy old man are pictured in Manuel Lucena Salmoral, *America 1492: Portrait of a Continent 500 Years Ago* (New York 1990), 63 and 69. Another is in Hasso von Winning, "Tlacaelel, Aztec General and Statesman," *The Masterkey* 38/2 (Southwest Museum, Los Angeles 1964).

46   The *Popol Vuh* is quoted from the edition previously cited, Recinos et al., 1950.

·   Douglas Schwartz, Arthur Lange, and Raymond de Saussure, "Split-Twig Figurines in the Grand Canyon," *American Antiquity* 23/3 (January 1958).

·   Pueblo trading area: William Brandon, *Quivira* (Athens, Ohio, 1990), 47.

47   Monte Alban: T. Patrick Culbert, "Mesoamerica," in Jesse D. Jennings, ed., *Ancient Native Americans, North America* (New York 1983), 1:60–62; Sabloff, *Handbook* 1 (Gordon R. Willey, "Introduction"; Kent V. Flannery, Joyce Marcus, Stephen A. Kowalewski, "The Preceramic and Formative of the Valley of Oaxaca"; Richard E. Blanton and S.A. Kowalewski, "Monte Alban and After"); John Paddock, ed., *Ancient Oaxaca: Discoveries in Mexican Archaeology and History* (Stanford 1966); and William T. Sanders, "The Central Mexican Symbiotic Region: A Study in Prehistoric Settlement Patterns," in Gordon R. Willey, ed., *Prehistoric Settlement Patterns in the New World* (New York 1956).

·   Teotihuacan: William T. Sanders, "Ecological Adaptation in the Basin of Mexico; 23,000 B.C. to the Present," in Sabloff, *Handbook* 1,109 and 166; William T. Sanders, Jeffrey R. Parsons, Robert S. Santley, *The Basin of Mexico: Ecological Processes in the Evolution of a Civilization* (New York 1979), 107; René Millon, "Teotihuacan: City, State, and Civilization," Sabloff, *Handbook* 1.

48   Tikal: Sanders et al., *Basin of Mexico*, speak of Teotihuacan's dominance in the fifth century (128); see also Christopher Jones, William R. Coe, and William A. Haviland, "Tikal: an Outline of its Field Study, (1956–1970), and a Project Bibliography," and Gordon R. Willey, "Introduction," 17–18, in Sabloff, *Handbook* 1.

50   A contemporary picture of central Mexican turmoil: Zelia Nuttall, ed., *Codex Nuttall, Facsimile of an Ancient Mexican Codex* (Peabody Museum of American Archaeology and Ethnology, Harvard University, Cambridge, Massachusetts 1902), half of which is the story of Eight-Deer Tiger Claw, an eleventh-century Mixtec conqueror in Oaxaca. This codex was upon its discovery in Florence in the 1860s only the tenth pre-Columbian Mexican codex to be found in the modern world.

Chapter 6

51   William T. Sanders, in Sabloff, *Handbook* 1, sees the systemic and multicausal complexities in "the rise of civilization" but is more concerned with subsistence ecology and population pressures. The normal frost season above 2,000 meters altitude is mid-October to mid-March, and can extend into September and May. (154)

·   René Millon, in Sabloff, *Handbook* 1, finds the decline due to "rival politics" or possibly urban factions, sees militarism more prominent in the last phase, "burning" only the "ritual destruction of main buildings" and such destruction limited to the center. Armed men in Teotihuacan art are found only in the phase of decline (650–750 A.D.), although Teotihuacan style military figures are found in foreign places, such as Tikal, a century or two earlier. (242, n 26) Richard Blanton, "The Rise of Cities," in Sabloff, *Handbook* 1, argues that "cultural ecology" is not sufficient as an explanation; "more powerful" causes are needed. Sherburne Friend Cook, "The Interrelation of Population, Food Supply, and Building in Pre-Conquest Central Mexico," *American Antiquity* 13 (July 1947), surveys Teotihuacan's environmental problems rather than its invaders. Sanders et al., *Basin of Mexico*, find archeological indication of residences burned, thus probably military disasters, but the "processual" cause of Teotihuacan decline is seen as the collapse of external trade networks. (137)

52   "they marched on": Fernando d'Alva Ixtlilchochitl, *Histoire des Chichimeques*, in H. Ternaux-Compans, ed., *Voyages, Relations, et Mémoires Originaux pour servir à l'Histoire de la Découverte de l'Amérique*, vols. 12–13 (Paris 1840). The *Historia Chichimeca* also appears as vol. 2 of Ixtlilchochitl's *Obras Historias* (Mexico 1891–1892).

·   Sanders et al., *Basin of Mexico*, discuss the "explosive" growth of Cholula from A.D. 750–950, and the possibility of Cholula equaling Toltec Tula in importance. (137–38)

·   Richard A. Diehl, "Tula," in Sabloff, *Handbook* 1, settles on A.D. 950–1150 for the period of Tula's florescence. (293) Archeological evidence of Tula settlement patterns is detailed in Sanders et al., *Basin of Mexico*, 143–50, 289–91, and 380–85; see also William T. Sanders, in Sabloff, *Handbook* 1, 190; Richard A. Diehl, ibid., 277, 284, 290, and 293; and Richard A. Diehl, *Tula: The Toltec Capital of Ancient Mexico* (London 1983), 13–14; 57. Angel Garcia Cook, "The Historical Importance of Tlaxcala in the Cultural Development of the Central Highlands," in Sabloff, *Handbook* 1, attacks Sanders et al., *Basin of Mexico*, for "distorting," in their Map 20, the political instability of the region. (276, n 4)

53   The "ancient prayer" is from Fray Bernardino de Sahagun, *General History of the Things of New Spain*, translation from the Nahuatl by Charles E. Dibble and Arthur J.O. Anderson (Santa Fe 1955ff), Book 2, dealing with the ceremonies.

·   Daniel G. Brinton, *Rig Veda Americana* (Philadelphia 1890), speaks of the philosophical, moralistic, and religious connotations of ballgame allusions in his notes to the very beautiful (although very garbled) "Hymn of Fasting." A less garbled (and alas less beautiful) version of this hymn is found in Sahagun (Anderson-Dibble translation), Book 2, 212. For a description of the ballgame and its paraphernalia, see Frans Blom, "The Maya Ball-Game Pok-ta-pok, called Tlachtli by the Aztec," *Tulane University, Middle American Research Series* 4, (New Orleans 1912); and Stephen F. de Borhegyi, "America's Ball Game," *Natural History*, 69/1 (January 1960).

54   Ixtlilxochitl is summarized in Frederick Peterson, *Ancient Mexico, An Introduction to the Pre-Hispanic Cultures* (New York 1959). A more detailed relation of the Topiltzin Quetzalcoatl story is in Wigberto Jiménez Moreno, "Sintesis de la Historia Pretolteca de Mesoamerica," in *Esplendor de Mexico Antiguo*, C. Cook de Leonard, Coordinator, Centro de Investigaciones Antropologicas de Mexico (Mexico 1959), 2:1019–1108.

55   Nonprofit markets: Sanders et al., *Basin of Mexico*, 298 and 404.

·   Richard A. Diehl, in Sabloff, *Handbook* 1, speaking of Tula trade items of an elite nature, finds only one elite type "for which we have archaeological evidence," this being vessels of travertine, known as *tecali*. (288)

·   Typical market of classic Greece: *Cambridge Ancient History*, 2nd edition (1982), 3:436.

·   Chaco Canyon: Fiedel, *Prehistory of the Americas*, 216. For the complexities of the Chaco Canyon settlement: Charles D. Trombold, ed., *Ancient Road Networks and Settlement Hierarchies in the New World* (Cambridge 1991), chapters 5, 6, and 10.

56   An attempt is under way to reestablish the species of parrot once present in the Chiricahua mountains in southeastern Arizona: *Arizona Daily Star* (Tucson December 17, 1992).

- Paul Radin, *The Story of the American Indian* (New York 1927, 1934, and 1944), suggested a sea route from Vera Cruz to the lower Mississippi. (155)
- Fiedel, *Prehistory of the Americas,* accepts the very early date of 1500 B.C. for the earliest "certain" (Arctic, pre-Dorset) bows in North America (146–47); and also accepts the date of A.D. 500 for a composite bow, possibly Klamath, in northeastern California. (123)
- The specialist is Dudley T. Easby, Jr., "Fine Metalwork in Pre-Conquest Mexico," in Lothrop, *Pre-Columbian Art and Architecture.* He identifies as Mixtec the treasure from Tomb 7 at Monte Alban.
- Gold and copper foil: Burger, *Chavin,* 127, 98–99.
- Chavin-era metalwork, ibid, 201.

57   Bronze in Peruvian graves: Pal Kelemen, *Art of the Americas: Ancient and Hispanic* (New York 1969), 149.

- The Old Copper Industry on Lake Superior is given a beginning dating to some 5000 years ago: James B. Griffin, "Eastern United States," in R.E. Taylor and C.W. Meighan, eds., *Chronologies of New World Archaeology* (New York 1978), 60.
- Independent centers of metalwork , such as copper and bronze near Lake Titicaca and goldwork in Colombia and Peru, and work elsewhere in other alloys and platinum, are noted in Samuel K. Lothrop, *Treasures of Ancient America* (Geneva 1964 and 1972), 147, 131, and 226. Warwick Bray, "Gold Work," in *Between Continents/Between Seas: Pre-Columbian Art of Costa Rica* (New York 1981), the catalogue of an exhibition from the Detroit Institute of Arts, describes Colombia and Central America as a single metalworking province. (153)
- Lothrop, *Treasures of Ancient America*: "use [of metals] in tools and weapons never was fully developed." (226)
- Peruvian geography, Burger, *Chavin* 12.

59   Earliest cultivated plants (Guitarrero Cave): Michael E. Moseley, *The Incas and Their Ancestors: The Archaeology of Peru* (London 1992), 96. Also see Burger, *Chavin,* 30.

- Burger, *Chavin,* young man buried with pet monkey, 73–74.
- Amazingly early dates: Burger, *Chavin,* 28–31. This work argues that various forms of society may have once existed that have no equivalent in the "historic record . . . Preceramic Peru may present one instance in which societies created truly monumental constructions without a coercive state apparatus."
- The necessity of hierarchy "upon which civilization rests" is argued by Rosa Fung Pineda, "Late Preceramic and Initial Period," Richard W. Keatinge, ed., *Peruvian Prehistory: An Overview of Pre-Inca and Inca Society* (Cambridge 1988), 80.

60   Some pots found in northern Peru were apparently formed on a potter's wheel: Terence Grieder, *Art and Archaeology of Pashash* (Austin 1979), 96ff.

- Mummification: Moseley, *The Incas,* 92–93.

61   Rafael Larco Hoyle, *Checan: Essay on Erotic Elements in Peruvian Art* (Geneva 1965), gives the god, Aia Paec, and interpretation of the name. (93) Mochica sex-centered pottery begins between 800 and 500 B.C. and reaches its highest expression in the Florescent Era (the Classic age), A.D. 1–800, "exactly when the arts and sciences do." (52) Erotic (or anti-erotic) pottery was placed in many tombs along with other funerary offerings: "The strange thing is that they are found not only in the tombs of adults but also in those of children." (44) Larco Hoyle, *Checan,*

sees the mutilation of nose and lip as "punishment," (34, 45, 80, 123, and 136) "certainly surgical, and carried out by an expert hand." (124) Elizabeth Benson, *The Mochica: A Culture of Peru* (London 1972), finds that "the deformity of faces and bodies is almost always clearly due to disease rather than to deliberate mutilation." (70) John W. Verano and Douglas H. Ubelaker, "Health and Disease in the Pre-Columbian World," in Herman J. Viola and Carolyn J. Margolis, eds., *Seeds of Change, a Quincentennial Commemoration* (Washington 1991), find that "damage to the lips and nose probably represents infection with leighmaniasis (uta) an insect-borne fungal disease endemic in parts of Peru and Brazil today." A woman sufferer is pictured in pottery. (213)

- William H. Isbell, "The Prehistoric Ground Drawings of Peru," *Scientific American* 239/4 (1978) finds that certain of the lines "mark the position of the sun at the summer and winter solstices." Evan Hadingham, *Lines to the Mountain Gods: Nazca and the Mysteries of Peru* (London 1987), finds pattern types chronological, and an Andean worldview symbolized. William J. Conklin and Michael Edward Moseley, "The Patterns of Art and Power in the Early Intermediate Period," in Keatinge, *Peruvian Prehistory*, also find the patterns chronological. Joseph A. Franch, *Pre-Colonial Art* (Paris and New York 1987) provides the apt term "geoglyphs." (206) Maria Reiche, longtime student of these desert figures, describes them in "Giant ground drawings on the Peruvian desert," in *Verhandlungen des 38 Internationalen Amerikanesten kongresses* (München 1969), 1:329–82.

62   Skull trephination in the Old World: George Grant Maccurdy, "Prehistoric Surgery—a Neolithic Survival," *American Anthropologist*, NS, 7 (1905). Neolithic skulls so operated are cited from the Seine-et-Oise northeast of Paris, and from ancient Guanche burials in the Canaries—where twenty-five of 210 skulls had been trepanned. The German pathologist Rudolf Virchow remembered the treatment in Berlin in the 1840s. (20)

- For a pair of such golden hands, see Franch, *Pre-Colonial Art*, 345.
- Larco Hoyle's article on the Mochica in Steward, *Handbook of South American Indians*, suggests similarities between the supposed Mochica lima-bean writing system and Maya ideographs.
- The "pampa-isla" ridged fields are the subject of a study by J.J. Parsons and W.M. Denevan, "Pre-Columbian Ridged Fields," *Scientific American* 217/1 (July 1967), 72.
- Chicha tasty: Harry A. Franck, *Vagabonding Down the Andes* (New York 1917), 72.
- Nordenskiöld, *Ethnography of South America*, map 19, illustrates the extensive distribution of the penis-cover in South America. A Chimu figurine of an authoritative personage wearing a gold penis-sheath is pictured in the frontispiece of Larco Hoyle, *Checan*; the same figurine, together with another personage in the identical costume, is pictured in Salmoral, *America 1492*, 103.

63   Tiahuanaco: there is a growing trend toward using non-Spanish spellings for South American pre-Columbian sites and material, thus Tiwanaku for Tiahuanaco. Unfortunately at present this leads not to simplification but to added difficulties (Qhapac for Capac, rough-breathing 'Inka for Inca), and will not be followed here.

- "A Summary View of Peruvian Prehistory," in Keatinge, *Peruvian Prehistory*, 303–16, supposes "Huari and Tiwanaku interaction" and influence over all the central Andes, but finds the Huari picture confused and "Tiwanaku understudied" relative to its magnitude and importance: "We know far more about Moche iconography and burial details than we know of the demise of Chavin and rise of Huari and Tiwanaku."

- Victor W. von Hagen, "The Pre-Columbian New World," *Encyclopaedia Britannica*, 15th ed. (1991), 26:24ff, gives A.D. 800 for the collapse of Huari and the abandonment of Tiahuanaco, this coinciding with urban development in the northern Andean region—Chan Chan, the Chimu capital, dating from A.D. 900 or 1000.
- T. Patrick Culbert, in Jennings, *Ancient Native America*, 431, says A.D. 700 to 1000 were cataclysmic evil days for all major Mesoamerican sites.
- The claim that El Niño's behavior can slow the earth's rotation: Moseley, *The Incas*, 27–28.
- The description of El Niño: Burger, *Chavin*, 13–15.

64   The evidence of El Niño's visits in the sixth and seventh centuries: Moseley, *The Incas*, 209–11.

- Victoria Brandon offers the very tentative suggestion of a parallel growth for the problems of sewage and garbage in the Classic cities of both the Andean region and Mesoamerica.
- Wendell C. Bennett and Junius G. Bird, *Andean Culture History* (New York 1949), used the City Builder designation.
- Antonio de la Calancha, *Coronica moralizada del Orden de San Augustin en el Peru* (1638), gives the Chimu double-creation story.

65   William J. Conklin and Michael Edward Moseley, in Keatinge, *Peruvian Prehistory*, find Lake Titicaca and Tiahuanaco at the focus of a great culture history which did include Inca Cuzco; Inca mythical origins were placed on islands in the lake. Tiahuanaco is seen as the major Andean population center of its time, as well as a religious center. (163)

- Hearsay dynastic history: Gary Urton, *The History of a Myth: Pacariqtambo and the Origin of the Inkas* (Austin 1990), 26, cites R. Tom Zuidema of the Collège de France, *La Civilization inca au Cuzco* (1986), since translated as *Inca Civilization in Cuzco* (Austin 1990).
- Burger, *Chavin*, suggests the telling illustration of the north-south length of the Inca empire. (1)
- von Hagen, "Pre-Columbian New World," settles on 12 million population.
- Satellite photos: Michael E. Moseley, "Central Andean Civilization," in Jennings, *Ancient Native America*, 190.

66   An Inca slinger may be seen in Arthur Baessler, *Ancient Peruvian Art, Contributions to the Archaeology of the Incas*, A.H. Keane, trans., 4 vols. (Berlin 1902–1903), Figures 73 and 76.

- Coca terracing appeared to have political significance in Inca times: Patricia J. Netherly, "From Event to Process: the Recovery of Late Andean Organizational Structure by means of Spanish Colonial Written Records," in Keatinge, *Peruvian Prehistory*, 262.

67   Juan de Sarmiento's 1550 voyage to Peru: *Relacion de la sucesion y govierno de las Yngas Señores naturales que fueron de las Provincias del Peru*, manuscript, quoted by William H. Prescott, *History of the Conquest of Peru* (1847ff, cited here from the Philadelphia 1895 edition), 1:173 and 177. The will of a conquistador (Mancio Sierra Lejesema) is also cited from Prescott, *Peru*, 1:173, and Appendix III, 2:398–99.

- Craig Morris and Donald S. Thompson, *Huánuco Pampa: An Inca City and its Hinterland* (London 1985), find a Frank Lloyd Wrightian emphasis on diversity (156) and conclude: "The Inca political and economic achievement was based in large part on principles so dynamic they almost ensured that the state itself would be ephemeral." (166)
- Theories about Andean city-building are discussed in Anthony Aveni, *Stairways to the Stars: Skywatching in Three Great Ancient Cultures* (New York 1997), 154–77.
68 Textiles: John V. Murra, *CHLA*, 1:77, and the same author's "Cloth and Its Functions in the Inca State," *American Anthropologist*, 64/1 (1962), 718, 722.
- Information differs on the matter of the four directions in Inca religion. Garcilaso Inca de la Vega, *Commentarios reales de los Incas* (1609), learned from his uncle, Cusi Hualpa, that in the beginning the deity divided the world into four parts.
- Farmers cultivating the Inca's lands were ordered to "maintain a tidy appearance, sing and dance, and at the end shout 'Hailli,' our cry of victory," according to F. Huaman Poma, sixteenth-century Indian author of the *Nueva Cronica y Buen Gobierno* (Paris 1936).
- For many years archeologists have presumed an Inca origin for Diaguita metalwork, and Tiahuanaco influences have been discerned among the Diaguita dating to long before Inca times: A.L. Kroeber, *Anthropology* (New York 1923 and 1948), 833.
69 Use of the coca and lime box is described in Baessler, *Ancient Peruvian Art*, text to Plate 39.
- A detailed description of Jibaro *tsantsa* rites is in Rafael Karsten, *Blood Revenge, War, and Victory Feasts among the Jibaro Indians of Eastern Ecuador*, BAE Bulletin 79 (Washington 1923).
- A bad *ayahuasca* trip is pictured in Dr. P. Reinburg, "Contribution à l'Etude des Boissons Toxiques des Indiens du Nord-ouest de l'Amazone, l'Ayahuasca—le Yajo—le Huanto. Etude Comparative Toxico-Physiologique d'Une Expérience Personelle," *Journal de la Société des Américanistes de Paris*, NS, 13 (Paris 1921), 25–54 and 197–216.

Chapter 7

71 Sources for prehispanic Mexico are mainly sixteenth and seventeenth century chronicles based on oral accounts and picture-writing codices. Most of these of course are by Spanish or European-educated authors and written for a European audience, and thus to some degree colored by this European translation, as was pointed out in regard to Spanish chronicles of Inca history. In addition some of these Mexican sources contain anti-Aztec (or pro-Aztec) bias clinging to the roots of original native accounts. One of the most useful such accounts (written in Nahuatl in the 1620s) is by Domingo Francisco de San Anton de Munon Chimalpahin Quauhtlehuanitzin, a native of the town of Chalco, conquered by the Aztecs in 1465. However, since one object of Chimalpahin's writing was to restore, under Spanish rule, the Chalco dynasty (of which he was a descendant), still another *ex parte* element here might reasonably be suspected. This objective figures in a number of these post-Conquest documents—designed as evidence for the ownership or overlordship of certain land or territory. Despite all such

handicaps, these "Annals" and similar chronicles are of a special value because the writers had at hand various codices that have since been lost.

- The Tula quotation is from Ixtlilchochitl, *Histoire des Chichimeques*; Tula is seen in detail in Diehl, *Tula*.

73 Karl A. Wittfogel and Feng Chia-Sheng, "History of Chinese Society Liao (907–1125)," *Transactions of the American Philosophical Society*, NS, 36 (Philadelphia 1946), give much attention to organization, supply, and tactics of Liao armies and the Mongol armies two centuries later, citing B.H. Liddell Hart, *Great Captains Unveiled* (Boston 1927), on the clock-like coordination. (533) The importance of invention (saddle with stirrups) and technology are noted. A textbook of world military history is also cited, giving Jenghiz Khan as much space as Alexander the Great and Julius Caesar: William A. Mitchell, *Outlines of the World's Military History* (Harrisburg 1940), 219–42, 38–69, and 101–25.

- The Manchu soldier's journal of 1680: *Soldier: A Journal*, Nicola di Cosmo, ed. and trans., is a recently translated diary, still in manuscript, from which Dr. di Cosmo has kindly permitted quotation.

- German organization for war: Fritz Redlich, *The German Military Enterpriser and His Work Force: A Study in European Economic and Social History*, 2 vols. (Wiesbaden 1964): "Since they did this under the spur of the profit motive, one is entitled to speak of them as military enterprisers . . . The military enterpriser . . . led the troops which he had raised for profit's sake." (Introduction, 1:3) In the early 1630s soldiers of an Imperial garrison rioted when they learned the officers had stolen their wages, and then joined the opposing army en masse. But "the practice of stealing wages was widespread." (1:371) It is not surprising some of the military entrepreneurs became "angry when a peace was concluded which deprived them of their business and magnificent sources of income." (ibid.) The disbanding of troops in winter and after a peace treaty was sensible in view of the military entrepreneurs' financial limitations, although this not only created social problems "but was also of an historical importance never yet stressed sufficiently . . . The Wars of the Roses would have been impossible without the masses of unemployed veterans returning to England after the Hundred Years' War. Nor would there have been any Peasants' War in Germany in the 1520s, had not thousands of lansquenets been discharged after the victory of Pavia in 1525 . . . the Huguenot Wars in France were possible because large numbers of unemployed mercenaries became available after the treaty of Cateau-Cambresis . . . in 1559." (1:118)

- War as the chief element: Walter Bagehot: "The beginning of civilization is a military advantage." Herbert Spencer: "The conquest of one people over another had been, in the main, the conquest of the social man over the anti-social man." Both are cited by Quincy Wright, *A Study of War* (Chicago 1942 and 1964), 41. Robert L. Carneiro, "A Theory of the Origin of the State," *Science* 169/3947, argues that victory in war is the only workable theory of the origin of states.

- E. Wyllys Andrews V, "Dzibilchaltun," in Sabloff, *Handbook* 1, finds some archeologists seeing conflict over land leading to an institutionalized elite, others see participation in regional trade bringing social change. (323)

74 Tlaxcala-Puebla "ahead" of the Valley of Mexico: Sanders et al., *Basin of Mexico*, 398; and Angel Garcia Cook, in Sabloff, *Handbook* 1, 270–75.

- Tula population pattern: William T. Sanders, in Sabloff, *Handbook* 1, 147–97; and Eduardo Matos Moctezuma, Coordinator, *Proyecto Tula*, 2 Parts (Mexico 1974 and 1976).

- Tula population: Richard A. Diehl, in Sabloff, *Handbook* 1, 277–95; and Diehl, *Tula*, 60.

75 Among the sources of Aztec history is Hernando de Alvarado Tezozomoc, a grandson of Moctezuma, who wrote in Spanish the *Cronica Mexicana* (c. 1598), Manuel Orozco y Berra, ed. (Mexico 1944); and in Nahuatl the *Cronica Mexicayotl* (1606), translated into Spanish by Adrian Leon (Mexico 1949); and with the Spanish chronicler Fray Diego Duran wrote *Historia de las Indias de Nueva España y Islas de Tierra Firma* (Mexico 1951). Hubert Howe Bancroft, *The Early American Chroniclers* (San Francisco 1883), calls Duran a "dangerously zealous priest in defending natives."

- I have made rather much in this text of the story of the old king Tezozomoc, both because it is a significant revelation of ancient Mexican political history and because it was a popular contemporary theme for poets and philosophers such as Nezahualcoyotl, one of whose purported works, as adapted from Daniel G. Brinton, *Ancient Nahuatl Poetry* (Philadelphia 1881), reads: "That great man that great conqueror Tezozomoc/ at the age of a hundred years/ his palaces and gardens surely so one thought/ would last forever . . . Sad and impressive/ indeed to reflect on that great Tezozomoc . . ."

76 The Nezahualcoyotl verses here are adapted from a translation by Fanny Calderon for William H. Prescott and printed by him in his *History of the Conquest of Mexico* (1843ff, cited here from the Philadelphia 1893 edition).

77 Alvarado Tezozomoc and Diego Duran emphasize Tlacaelel, while some other early chroniclers doubt his very existence, apparently because some sources confused him with his grandson of the same name, making it appear he had lived to the unlikely age of 120. See von Winning, "Tlacaelel." Von Winning points out that the present trend in studying ancient Mexican history concentrates on philosophical and religious thought as a key to the course of events. A.M. Garibay (1953–1954) and Miguel Léon-Portilla (1963 and 1983) are examples of such material. See also George Kubler, *Esthetic Recognition of Ancient American Art* (New Haven 1991). The quoted description of Huitzilopochtli is from Sahagun, *History of New Spain*, Book 1; his formal epithet is from a translation in Edward King, Viscount Kingsborough, *Antiquities of Mexico, etc.*, 7 vols. (London 1831), a reproduction of the Codex Mendoza, a picture-manuscript painted by Aztec artists in 1541 at the behest of Viceroy Antonio de Mendoza.

78 Tenochtitlan population estimates: Sanders et al., *Basin of Mexico*, 163. The Abbé Clavigero: Francisco Javier Clavijero, *The History of Mexico, etc.* . . . (originally published in Italian 1780; English translation London 1787) collected estimates of population for Tenochtitlan running from 60,000 to 1.5 million; cited in Alexander von Humboldt, *Political Essay on the Kingdom of New Spain, etc.*, translated from the original French by John Black, 2 vols. (New York 1811), 1–51.

- Everybody farming: ibid., quoting Fr. del Paso y Troncoso, *Epistolario de Nueva España 4* (1939), "each person should follow his trade . . . and everyone generally should plant . . . and be farmers." (169–70)

- House sizes: Richard A. Diehl, in Sabloff, *Handbook* 1, 294.

79 John H. Rowe, "Inca Culture at the Spanish Conquest," in Steward, *Handbook*, vol. 2, remains the most useful Tawantinsuyu source; this was republished separately in 1962 and also included in John H. Rowe and Dorothy Menzel, *Peruvian Archaeology: Selected Readings* (Palo Alto 1967).

- For the Tlaxcala policy attributed to Tlacaelel: von Winning, "Tlacaelel," 49. Andres de Tapia said Moctezuma gave him the same explanation: cited in A.P. Maudslay's commentary to his translation of Bernal Díaz (1908), 122.
80 Old Wolf and the following quotations are from Sahagun, *History of New Spain*, Book 2.
81 The story of Nezahualpilli's swinging "wife" and her statuesque lovers is based on Ixtlilxochitl (1568–1648) and the many annals subsequent to his work. However, Charles E. Dibble, *Codex en Cruz* (Salt Lake City 1981), 2 vols., finds no evidence that Ixtlilxochitl used this codex, which in its account of the year of (1498) Six Rabbit records the infidelity of Chalchiuhuenetzin, the daughter of Axayacatl, and her death, but with no mention of "four hundred accomplices" and various other later plot points.
82 Quotations are from Sahagun, *History of New Spain*, Book 12, and from the "Lienzo de Tlaxcala" (the "record on painted cloth from Tlaxcala") in *Antiguedades Mexicanas* (Mexico 1892), plates 66–175.

Chapter 8

83 Two of the sundry sages are the Abbé Guillaume Raynal, a voice of the Enlightenment, *Histoire Philosophique des Indes* (1770): nothing in the past equals the discovery of the New World and the route to the East Indies via Good Hope "for mankind in general and for the people of Europe in particular," and Adam Smith, *The Wealth of Nations* (1776): these two discoveries are the "two greatest and most important events recorded in the history of mankind."
- Columbus is quoted from the "Santangel letter" dated February 15, 1493, and sent from Portugal March 9, addressed to Luis de Santangel, Chancellor of the Royal Household of Aragon, as cited in John Boyd Thacher, *Christopher Columbus, His Life, His Work, His Remains*, 3 vols. (New York 1903), 2:18.
85 Kirkpatrick Sale, *The Conquest of Paradise: Christopher Columbus and the Columbian Legacy* (London 1991), lists twelve landfall candidates. (66) Samuel Eliot Morison, a knowledgeable authority on this sort of thing, says Watling's Island is the only one that fits: *Admiral of the Ocean Sea* (Boston 1942).
- The Columbus quotations on Española: December 6, 14, 23, and 16, 1492; all from Sherburne Friend Cook and Woodrow Wilson Borah, *Essays in Population History: Mexico and the Caribbean* (Berkeley 1971).
- Columbus's first remark on the Taino is from Ferdinand Columbus' biography of his father, written with the Journal before him: Morison, *Admiral of the Ocean Sea*, 1:300; the second from Las Casas' abstract of the Journal, using Columbus' own words: Bartolomé de Las Casas, *Historia de las Indias*, edicion de Agustin Millares Carlo y estudio preliminar de Lewis Hanke, 3 vols. (Mexico and Buenos Aires 1951), 1:209.
86 Sherburne Friend Cook and Woodrow Wilson Borah, authors of the most thorough and painstaking demographic studies made on the region, *Essays in Population History*, arrive at 8 million persons for pre-Columbian Hispañola. This figure was regarded as astounding at the time but is now rather generally accepted. The few thousand "Indios" shown in the censuses of 1514, 1516, and 1520 include Indians brought from other islands as servants and laborers. None at all of the

original millions of people of Hispañola (modern Dominican Republic and Haiti) may have been left by 1520, one short generation after the first appearance of the people from heaven.

- The background on Malinal is from Bishop Landa (Tozzer, *Landa's "Relacion"*).

87 E. Wyllys Andrews V, in Sabloff, *Handbook* 1, describes the clusters (327) and (citing Phillip C. Thompson's 1978 Tulane Ph.D thesis) the rotational pattern. (327–78)

- Maya "rule" as propriety: Inga Clendinnen, *Ambivalent Conquests: Maya and Spaniard in Yucatan, 1517–1570* (Cambridge 1987), says that "Priests and lords 'ruled' not through the sumptuousness of their state, nor by coercion, nor by the engrossment of material goods, but through the multitude of small gestures and formalities which suffused Maya interaction, between age and youth, male and female, and greater and lesser rank." (152)

- Ralph L. Roys, *The Political Geography of the Yucatan Maya* (Washington 1957), calls the Mayapan rule "joint government." (1)

88 Quotations describing the smallpox are from Bishop Landa (Tozzer, *Landa's "Relacion"*).

- Background on Malinal is, as above, based on what Bishop Landa heard a generation later: ibid.

89 Landa and his modern editor: ibid.

- The best population guesses: Woodrow Wilson Borah and Sherburne Friend Cook, *The Aboriginal Population of Central Mexico on the Eve of the Spanish Conquest* (Berkeley 1963), covering the area from about Nayarit to the Tehuantepec Peninsula. A.L. Kroeber, "Native American Population," *American Anthropologist* 36 (1934), provided very low population estimates many years ago. Henry F. Dobyns, "Estimating Aboriginal American Population," *Current Anthropology* 7 (1966), produced the highest guesses. A recent source is Daniel T. Neff, *Disease, Depopulation, and Culture Change in Northwestern New Spain 1518–1764* (Salt Lake City 1991). Bernard R. Ortiz de Montellano, *Aztec Medicine, Health, and Nutrition* (Rutgers 1990), supports William T. Sanders in estimating the pre-Columbian population of Mexico at only about half of the Cook and Borah figure.

90 The first Aztec treasures sent by Cortés to Europe were seen in Brussels on their arrival by Albrecht Dürer, who wrote of "the things which have been brought to the king from the new land of gold: a sun all of gold a whole fathom broad and a moon all of silver of the same size, also two rooms full of the armor of the people there, and all manner of wondrous weapons of theirs, harness and darts, wonderful shields, strange clothing, bedspreads, and all kinds of wonderful objects of various uses . . . beautiful to behold. . . . All the days of my life I have seen nothing that has gladdened my heart so much as these things, for I saw amongst them wonderful works of art." Wolfgang Stechow, *Dürer in America* (National Gallery, Washington 1971).

- Prescott, *Mexico* (1893), says Moron, whom he calls Moran, died the following day from his wounds. (1:383) Cortés, in his letters to the king (Hernando Cortés, *Five Letters*, J. Bayard Morris, trans., (London 1938); or a recent edition in Spanish, *Cartas de Relacion de la Conquista de Mejico*, Mexico 1946), acknowledges no fatalities. Bernal Díaz says that by the end of the Tlaxcalan fighting "over forty-five of our soldiers had been killed in battle, or succumbed to disease and chills." (Bernal

Díaz del Castillo, *The Discovery and Conquest of Mexico, 1517–1521*, Irving A. Leonard, ed., New York 1956, 134). Cortés says the Tlaxcalan warriors numbered 150,000; Bernal Díaz says 40,000; Francisco Lopez de Gómara, *The History and Conquest of Mexico* (1552) says 80,000—but tradition says it was due to indignation over Gómara's history, which overglorified Cortés, that Bernal Díaz wrote his account. (Irving Leonard's introduction to the 1956 edition of Bernal Díaz, xvi) The first published version of Bernal Díaz (Madrid 1632), much used by early historians, was extensively altered by its editor, Fray Alonzo Remon, who "suppressed whole pages . . . interpolated others, garbled the facts, changed the names . . . increased or lessened the numbers, modified the style . . . moved thereto either by religious fervor and false patriotism, or by personal sympathy, and vile literary taste," says Genaro Garcia in the introduction to his own correct edition of Bernal Díaz, published in English in five volumes in 1908 by the Hakluyt Society.

91   The red Flemish hat is mentioned by Bernal Díaz, *Discovery and Conquest of Mexico*, 122 and 127. The knightly scene of the mare's head presented on the point of a lance: Antonio de Solis, *Historia de la Conquista de Mexico*, 2 vols. (Madrid 1783), 1:248.

·   The Spaniards as "encantadores": Solis, *Historia*, 1:263.

·   The further quotations: Bernal Díaz, *Discovery and Conquest of Mexico*, 135.

·   Cortés gives Cholula casualty figures in his *Five Letters*. Prescott, *Mexico*, sums up reports of 6,000 or more in most other accounts. (2:39)

·   Cholula's factions: Bernal Díaz, *Discovery and Conquest of Mexico*, 179

92   The modern historian is Frans Blom.

·   Cortés is quoted from the *Five Letters*, and Juan Sedeño from Bernal Díaz, *Discovery and Conquest of Mexico*, 39.

93   Malinal's 300 Tlaxcalan handmaidens: Diego Muñoz Camargo, a native of Tlaxcala who wrote in the sixteenth century and whose manuscript *Historia de Tlaxcala* is cited here from Prescott, *Mexico*, 1:426.

·   Axayacatl's administration is usually dated from 1469 to 1481. It was during his time that the famous "Aztec Calendar Stone" was carved.

·   According to Cortés (*Five Letters*), Moctezuma explicitly abdicated: David Carrasco, *Quetzalcoatl and the Irony of Empire* (Chicago 1982), accepts the "abdication" interpretation. (202–3)

95   Moctezuma quotation: Bernal Díaz, *Discovery and Conquest of Mexico*, 309.

·   The Spanish sources generally report that Moctezuma was killed by his own people; the Indian version, as given for example in Sahagun, *History of New Spain* (Book 12), was that the Spaniards killed Moctezuma and threw his body over the walls of their quarters. Killing their hostage seems unlikely, but if Moctezuma died of wounds, however inflicted, the Spaniards in rage and frustration may well have thrown his body to the attacking Aztecs.

·   Bernal Díaz, *Discovery and Conquest of Mexico*: "and a very black affair it was for New Spain, for it was owing to him that the whole country was stricken and filled with it, from which there was great mortality." (293) Las Casas, *Historia*, described the epidemic in Hispaniola, capping a generation of death and disaster: "I do not believe that 1,000 souls can have escaped from this misery, out of the immensity of people my own eyes had seen living in this island." (3:270–71)

- Bernal Díaz, *Discovery and Conquest of Mexico*, mentions two faces flayed, the beards left on, offered on a temple altar, as well as four horse hides "with the hair on and the horse shoes." (352) The Florentine Codex pictures horses' heads included on the skull rack. (Sahagun, *History of New Spain*, Book 12)

96   The Anonymous Conqueror, *Narrative of Some Things of New Spain and the Great City of Tenochtitlan*, (New York 1917). Bancroft suggests his possible identity as Francisco de Terrazas, mayordomo for Cortés, whose account has come to us only in an Italian translation. Federico Gómez de Orozco, *Relación de Algunos Cosas* (Mexico City 1961), 23–33, guesses a probable identity as Alonso de Ulloa and finds that the compilation was prepared in Italy.

- Cortés is quoted from the third of the *Five Letters*. His figures of Aztec losses would need to be greatly reduced (especially recalling the previous losses from smallpox) to fit an estimated population much below the higher range of previous estimates. A bit of evidence that might apply to population is found in this third of the *Five Letters*, speaking of looking out over the city from the summit of the great temple of Tlatelolco, observing that the Spaniards were then in control of about seven-eighths of the city, and mentioning later that the section the enemy still held "consisted of more than a thousand houses." Arithmetic projected from this figure would produce some 8,000 houses for the entire city, with a correspondingly low figure for the total population (using the archeological estimate of ten to fifteen persons per house), of 80,000 to 120,000. The Anonymous Conqueror uses ambiguously 60,000 in speaking of the size of the city of Tenochtitlan; W. W. Borah, in William M. Denevan, ed., *The Native Population of the Americas in 1492* (Madison 1974), 25, argues that the 60,000 refers to houses, not people, but Borah in the same comment adds that "the bulk of the documentary evidence remains to be unearthed."

- The temple of Tlatelolco was reached only at the end of July (Bernal Díaz, *Discovery and Conquest of Mexico*, 447), only a couple of weeks or so before the end of the battle, and the guess by Cortés that one eighth of the city was still in enemy hands at that time might have been too large. The battle lasted ninety-three days and was really won by starvation, says Bernal Díaz. (*Discovery and Conquest of Mexico*, 424 and 444) It lasted seventy-five days, says Cortés, from May 30 to August 13: Henry Raup Wagner, *The Rise of Fernando Cortés, Documents and Narratives Concerning the Discovery and Conquest of Latin America*, New Series no. 3, the Cortés Society (Berkeley 1944), foreword, vi.

- The modern archeologist quoted: George C. Vaillant, *The Aztecs of Mexico: Origin, Rise and Fall of the Aztec Nation* (New York 1944; revised edition annotated by Suzannah B. Vaillant 1962).

97   The poem is from Antonio Peñafiel, MS Coleccion de Cantares Mexicanos, National Library of Mexico, Folio 17, reprinted here from Alfonso Caso, *The Aztecs, People of the Sun*, Lowell Dunham, trans. (Norman 1958).

- Huitzilopochtli in a cave near Tula: Diehl, *Tula*, 169, citing R.C. Padden.

- "Scarcity of water rather than the hostility of the Indians has hampered for centuries the exploration of the Chaco": Alfred Métraux, "Ethnography of the Chaco," in Steward, *Handbook* 1, 1:199.

100   Alexander von Humboldt's estimate of the ransom value, and other interesting calculations of New World wealth, are given in *Essai Politique sur la Royaume de*

la Nouvelle Espagne (Paris 1811). Prescott, *Peru*, makes the amount nearer 15 million. (1:410–11)

- Kelemen, *Art of the Americas*: "Of the tons of gold and silver objects amassed in the first decades of the Conquest, not one piece survives . . . In the inventory made in 1596 at the medieval Habsburg castle Ambras, near Innsbruck, Tyrol, a golden casque with a large eagle's beak is already missing from the often-reproduced feather headdress . . . in 1878 [in Vienna], of the more than one thousand small disks, sequins, scales, plaques, and minute decorations on the piece, not half a dozen were in place: a restoration done at that time replaced them with gilded bronze." (158)

Chapter 9

101 Burger, *Chavin*, lists a dozen sites on the Peruvian coast and eleven in the nearby highlands with radiocarbon dates such as 2772 B.C., 2903 B.C., 3001 B.C., 2483 B.C. (31) Lists of C-14 measurements are found on pages 230–33.
- Sechin Alto was "one of the largest architectural complexes in the world" c1200 B.C.: Burger, *Chavin*, 81. Some 400 stone sculptures, among the oldest stone sculptures in the New World, mainly warriors and their mutilated victims, were found at Cerro Sechin. (ibid., 78)
- Some coastal preceramic sites may be under water from sea-level changes: Michael E. Moseley, "Central Andean Civilization," in Jennings, *Ancient Native Americans*, 205–6.
- Thirty Jequetepeque sites: ibid., 97.
102 Prescott, *Peru*, 1:43.
- The Grand Khan Kublai: John Ranking, *Historical Researches on the Conquest of Peru, Mexico, Bogota, Natchez, etc., in the Thirteenth Century by the Mongols, accompanied with Elephants* (London 1827).
- The Tartar inscription: Peter Kalm, *Voyage en Amerique* (in English as *Travels into North America*, 2 vols., London 1772) states that M. de Verandier found the stone in 1746; several Jesuits assured Kalm they had held it in their hands. Cited in Edward King, Viscount Kingsborough, *Antiquities of Mexico, etc.*, 7 vols. (London 1831). In connection with the various theories of origin, see Robert Wauchope, *Lost Tribes and Sunken Continents* (Chicago 1962).
- An early work in English on the subject of Indians as lost Israelites is Thomas Thoroughgood, *Jews in America* (London 1649–1660). The Rev. John Eliot wrote the author, "By reading your book . . . I thought, I saw some ground to conceive that some of the Ten Tribes might be scattered even thus far, into these parts of America."
- The great classifier of culture-trait distribution was Erland Nordenskiöld, whose *Comparative Ethnographical Studies: Origin of Indian Civilizations in South America*, vols. 8 and 9, and "The American Indian as an Inventor," reprinted in A.L. Kroeber and T.T. Waterman, eds., *Source Books in Anthropology* (1931), relate most directly to the points here mentioned.
103 A.B. Kehoe, "A Hypothesis on the Origin of Northeastern American Pottery," *Southwestern Journal of Anthropology* 18 (1962), 20–29; and P. Ridley, "Transatlantic contacts of Primitive Man," *Pennsylvania Archaeology* 30, deal with possible pottery introduction from north Europe.
- Valdivia: Betty J. Meggers, Clifford Evans, and Emilio Estrada, *Early Formative Period of Coastal Ecuador*, Smithsonian Contributions to Anthropology, vol. 1

(Washington 1965), sum up the argument for Japanese parentage of New World civilization. Previous opposition (e.g. Julian H. Steward, *American Journal of Archaeology* 68,1964, 411) had questioned the significance of ceramic details in the structure of culture. Needham and Lu, *Trans-Pacific Echoes*, agreed with criticism of Japanologists that the techniques involved "were really too simple to allow of the certain conclusion of an influence." (50) Pre-Valdivia pottery sites (San Pedro, Loma Alta) located in the 1970s were believed by most archeologists to end support for Japanese origins, and lend support to the interior tropic lowlands as the origin point of ceramics: Robert A. Feldman and Michael E. Moseley, "The Northern Andes," in Jennings, *Ancient Native Americans*, 155.

- J.B. Hutchinson, R.A. Silow, and S.G. Stephens, *Evolution of Gossypium* (London 1947), proposed the Asiatic cotton crossing, setting off a long controversy. Needham and Lu, *Trans-Pacific Echoes*, note the negative conclusion. (62)

104 In connection with metallurgical details, Needham and Lu cite H. Lechtman, "Andean Value Systems and the Development of Prehistoric Metallurgy," *Technology and Culture* 25 (1984); and H. Lechtman, A. Erlij, and E.J. Barry, "New Perspectives on Moche Metallurgy; Techniques of Gilding Copper at Loma Negra, Northern Peru," *American Antiquity* 47/1 (1982).

- The Egyptian wall painting (in the tomb of Rekhmiré, vizier to Thothmes IV, Thebes) is pictured in Leslie Atchison, *A History of Metals*, 2 vols. (London 1960), 1:171.

- The significance of the absence of bellows in the matter of American metallurgical origins was pointed out by Victoria Brandon.

105 Description of early Sumerian gold work as amazing and breath-taking, and Egyptian work still more so: ibid., 173.

- Platinum: C.P. Bergsøe, *The Metallurgy and Technology of Gold and Platinum among the pre-Columbian Indians* (Copenhagen 1937), as cited in Donald McDonald, *A History of Platinum* (1960), 5–6. Dudley T. Easby, Jr., "Fine Metalwork in Pre-Conquest Mexico," in Lothrop, et al., *Pre-Columbian Art and Architecture*, mentions the working of platinum. (36) For a later summing up by the same author, see "Early Metallurgy in the New World," *Scientific American* (April 1966).

- Resemblances in art motifs are analyzed in Robert von Heine-Geldern and Gordon F. Ekholm, "Significant Parallels in the Symbolic Art of Southern Asia and Middle America," *Selected Papers of the 29th International Congress of Americanists*, vol. 1 (Chicago 1951).

- Robert von Heine-Geldern, "The Origin of Ancient Civilization and Toynbee's Thesis," *Diogenes* 13 (Chicago 1956), 90–99, proposes ship sailings from the Chinese coastal states of Wu and Yueh in the eighth century B.C. to plant the Chavin culture in the central Andes, and further traffic to stimulate the various other American cultures until 33 B.C., when the Dong-son folk of Vietnam took over the commerce. The Han Dynasty (202 B.C. to A.D. 220) then resumed Chinese voyages, which ended with the fall of the Han; Cambodia then took over. These theoretical voyages are not documented in the various written records of the Asian groups involved. Heine-Geldern later summed up his views in "The Problem of Transpacific Influences in Mesoamerica," in Wauchope, *Handbook* 4.

- Needham and Lu, *Trans-Pacific Echoes*, state that their position on transoceanic influence is "represented rather well" (6) by the opinion of Glyn Daniel, *The First*

Civilizations: the Archaeology of their Origins (London 1968), 189–90: "It is one thing to reject, as the archaeological and ethnological evidence tells us to reject, the idea of civilisation coming to America from outside, it is quite another thing to deny the possibility of influences coming to America from outside . . . But any contacts Trans-Atlantic or Trans-Pacific that may have occurred were slight and very infrequent, and had little effect."

106   Philip Phillips, "The Role of Trans-Pacific Contacts in the Development of New World Pre-Columbian Civilizations," in Wauchope, *Handbook* 4, a summary of the problem in its broader aspects, speaks of the nineteenth-century German theory of the universality of history and its place in the New World controversies. See also William Brandon, *New Worlds for Old* (Athens, Ohio, 1986), 164.

   ·   Steward, *Handbook* 5, in summing up New World culture development gives a total of more than 100 native American crops and the very few plants of this inventory known to the pre-Columbian Old World.

   ·   Pastoral origin of Old World epidemic diseases: William H. McNeill, *Plagues and People* (Oxford 1977). Some technicalities of man-animal disease relationships are sketched in T. Aidan Cockburn, "Infectious Diseases in Ancient Populations," *Current Anthropology* 12 (1971).

107   For a nineteenth-century listing of Asian ships driven ashore on the Northwest Coast see Charles Wolcott Brooks, "Reports of Japanese Vessels Wrecked in the North Pacific from the Earliest Records to the Present Time," *Proceedings of the California Academy of Sciences*, 6 (1875).

   ·   Pioneer Spanish transpacific seafaring is recounted in Ione Stuessy Wright, "Early Spanish Voyages from America to the Far East," in *Greater America: Essays Presented to H.E. Bolton* (Berkeley 1945).

   ·   Sauer, *Agricultural Origins and Dispersals*, mentions the Araucanian chickens with the Silkie look.

   ·   Rongo-rongo origins are discussed in Thor Heyerdahl and Edwin N. Ferdon Jr., eds., *Reports of the Norwegian Archaeological Expedition to Easter Island and the East Pacific in 1955–1956*, vol. 2 (New York 1966).

108   Some indication of flues has been reported archeologically for early New World dwellings. Small chimneys have been described for some prehistoric Hopi houses in Arizona, apparently born of the necessity for a draft to carry away the fumes of the local soft coal evidently used for heat: Paul S. Martin, George I. Quimby, and Donald Collier, *Indians Before Columbus, Twenty Thousand Years of North American History Revealed by Archeology* (Chicago 1947), 150.

   ·   There have been many summaries of the essential differences between Old World and New World societies; one that has been regarded as basic for many years is Steward, *Handbook* 5.

   ·   Lewis H. Morgan, *Systems of Consanguinity and Affinity of the Human Family*, Smithsonian Contributions to Knowledge, vol. 17 (Washington 1871); and *Ancient Society* (New York 1877), introduced "one of the most basic and significant generalizations of ethnology, namely, that primitive society is organized upon the basis of kinship relations, whereas modern society is based upon property relations." (Leslie A. White, ed., *Lewis Henry Morgan, The Indian Journals*, Ann Arbor 1956, 6). Morgan's influence on Karl Marx and Friedrich Engels will be discussed later in this text.

Chapter 10

110   The quotation from Columbus' son Ferdinand is found in Morison, *Admiral of the Ocean Sea*, 2:301–2.
  •   Columbus's letter of 1500: ibid., 2:304.
111   Spain in 1492: W. Eugene Shiels, *King and Church: The Rise and Fall of the Patronato Real* (Chicago 1961), 13.
  •   Columbus's actions as precursor to encomienda: Morison, *Admiral of the Ocean Sea*, 2:299.
112   Aztec weapons were spears and the spear-thrower, *atlatl* (sometimes double-barreled, which hurled with force javelins with fire hardened points), bows and arrows, slings, and the *macana* or *maquahuitl*, sometimes called by Bernal Díaz a broadsword, a flat blade of wood fitted along each edge with sharp bits of flint or obsidian. Thrown rocks and stones account for most of the casualties reported in the Mexican fighting and, according to Bernal Díaz, for the death of Moctezuma (Bernal Díaz, *Discovery and Conquest of Mexico*, 310)
  •   Ottoman and Spanish comparison: Leopold von Ranke, *The Ottoman and the Spanish Empires in the Sixteenth and Seventeenth Centuries* (original German edition 1827; first English edition, London 1843), a book usually regarded as the first work using modern historical techniques. Ranke was an early apostle of the German vision of universal history mentioned previously in these notes. He was also the leading political conservative in the Prussian academia of his day, and also the "Dryasdust" of Carlyle's *Frederick* (1858–1865): "The Prussian Dryasdust . . . He writes big books wanting in almost every quality."
114   The missionary quoted is Fray Toribio de Benavente, known as Motolinía, from F.B. Steck, ed., *Motolinía, Historia de los Indios de Nueva España* (Washington 1951), 91, 92, 100, and 292. The final line is corrected by comparison with editions edited by Fray Daniel Sanchez Garcia (Mexico 1914, 1941), 20, and Edmundo O'Gorman (Mexico 1971), 28.
  •   Las Casas relates the reduction of Cuba in *Historia*, 2: 505–48.
  •   Voltaire recounts the story of the Indian refusing heaven in *Essay sur les Moeurs* (1756), ch 148, 266, citing Las Casas, *Historia*, (Seville 1542); he probably saw the 1642 Lyons edition (31).
115   Las Casas is quoted from Victoria Reifler Bricker, *The Indian King, the Indian Christ* (Austin 1981), 33, citing the Cortés Society edition of Sedley J. Mackie, *An Account of the Conquest of Guatemala in 1524 by Pedro de Alvarado* (New York 1924), 126.
  •   In regard to the execution of Cuauhtemoc, a document recently found in the Archive of the Indies in Seville, seems to support Cortés' side of the story; this is a 1612 petition for a pension from the then Chontal ruler because of his grandfather's services in 1525 in refusing Cuauhtemoc's invitation to join in a conspiracy against the Spanish invaders, and, instead, informing Cortés of their plan. (Morley and Brainerd, *The Ancient Maya*, 115) However, claims brought in colonial times based on deeds or land rights of an Indian ancestor were fairly rife all over the Indies; some have suspected the presence of occasional legal shenanigans based on wishful grounds.
  •   The marriages of Marina and Tecuichpo are mentioned in Prescott, *Mexico*, 3:250, 384, and 391. Tecuichpo lived to wed two other grandees of Spain. Prescott, or at

least my 1893 edition, has a misprint (Xamarillo) for Marina's husband; I take the correct name from Wagner, *Rise of Fernando Cortés*, 443.

116   The possibility of Itza intervention to make events conform to prophecy is suggested in Bricker, *The Indian King, the Indian Christ*, 5–7, and 327–28 n3. She remarks on difficulties in correlating evidence from archeology with the 1,000 years of semi-mythic history, and matching GMT dates with dates in the prophetic Book of Chilam Balam, but finds that "the structure of Maya myth and rituals of ethnic conflict is the cumulative result of naturism, syncretism, and a cyclical notion of time." Clendinnen, *Ambivalent Conquests*, speaking not of the Itza or any particular incident but of the generalized abstract notion of cyclical time: "Thus history was simultaneously prophecy, prophecy becoming history again with the next swing of the cycle." (146)

  •   The Landa quote is from Tozzer, *Landa's "Relacion"*; the Chilam Balam quote from Maud W. Makemson, *The Book of the Jaguar Priest* (New York 1951).

  •   The most important works in pre-Columbian New World demography are still the various studies by Sherburne Friend Cook and Woodrow Wilson Borah, and the first such study by Cook and Lesley Bird Simpson. Other modern studies followed, beginning with a review of the work of Cook and Borah by Henry F. Dobyns, "Estimating Aboriginal American Population, an Appraisal of Techniques with a New Hemisphere Estimate," *Current Anthropology* (October 1966). Dobyns found a population of nearly 10 million for the area north of Mexico. His base figure, however, taken from Angel Rosenblat, *La Poblacion Indigena y Mestizaje en América*, vol. 1 (Buenos Aires 1954), is in error, as was pointed out by Harold E. Driver in the same issue of *Current Anthropology*, in adjusting Dobyns' figure downward to some 4 million for aboriginal North America north of Mexico. A later and more limited study by Dobyns, *Their Number Become Thinned: Native American Population Dynamics in Eastern North America* (Knoxville 1983), rather heartily criticized, found a pre-contact population for this limited eastern region of 750,000 to 900,000. A more recent work, Russell Thornton, *American Indian Holocaust and Survival: A Population History Since 1492* (Norman 1987), guesses the aboriginal population of the area of the United States at a minimum of 5 million.

117   With the academic boom in linguistics the literature on any and all aspects of language has become quite unwieldy. A general pre-boom view of the field can be found in C.F. and F.M. Voegelin, *Classification and Index of the World's Languages* (New York 1977); in T.A. Sebeck, *Native Languages of the Americas*, 2 vols. (New York 1976–1977); and in T.A. Sebeck, ed. *Current Trends in Linguistics*, vols. 1 to 14 (The Hague 1963–1974).

Chapter 11

118   Epidemics and population figures for the Valley of Mexico are from William T. Sanders, in Sabloff, *Handbook* 1, 194–96.

  •   The famous picture-history of the conquest, the *Lienzo de Tlaxcala*, was prepared by the Tlaxcalans to support a reward for their services.

119   The quote on the *calpulli* and description of the *calpultin* are from Sanders, et al., *The Basin of Mexico*, 160.

- The figure of sixty calpultin was used in Sanders' earlier contribution to Wauchope, *Handbook* 10:24. In this same work, Sanders describes the calpulli as a "basic pattern on which all larger social groupings were based," towns, cities, city-states, and "empires" being "growths from this pattern." As an illustration of changing interpretation with the passage of time, Adolf F.A. Bandelier, "On the Social Organization and Mode of Government of the Ancient Mexicans," *Reports of the Peabody Museum*, vol. 2 (Cambridge, Massachusetts 1880), gives the number of Tenochtitlan calpultin as twenty.
- The *tlaxilacalli*: Edward E. Calnek, "The Internal Structure of Tenochtitlan," in E.R. Wolf, ed., *The Valley of Mexico* (Albuquerque 1976),
- T.T. Waterman, *Bandelier's contribution to Study of Ancient Mexican Social Organization* (Berkeley 1916–1917), mentions the Spaniards finding the same official bearing a variety of differing titles.
- The quotations are from Sahagun, *General History of New Spain*, Book 8.
- For the *tecpan*: Edward E. Calnek, in Wolf, *Valley of Mexico*, 295.

120 Religion "intervening" in all areas of Aztec life: Caso, *The Aztecs*, 117. Caso's earlier "La Religion de los Aztecas," *Enciclopedia Ilustrada Mexicana* (Mexico 1936); and *Revista Mexicana de Estudios Antropologicos* 3/1 (Mexico 1937), expand on this point.

121 Hernando de Alvarado Tezozomoc and his collaborator Fray Diego de Duran recount Tlacaelel's role as Cihuacoatl. See also von Winning, "Tlacaelel," who remarks on the "dual principle of life and the power that governs" thus symbolized by these two representations (of the gods Quetzalcoatl and Cihuacoatl) who "functioned together as a team." (50–51)

- The idea of dualism in American Indian government has been the subject of countless studies—for example the important paper, dealing with areas far outside Mesoamerica, by William N. Fenton, "Factionalism in American Indian Society," *Actes du IVe Congrès International des Sciences Anthropologiques et Ethnologiques*, vol. 2 (Vienna 1952), which is especially instructive in its reflections on the governments "inside the wall" and "outside the wall" at Taos Pueblo, New Mexico, in recent times. As remarked by Roys, *Political Geography of the Yucatan Maya*, the "division of authority was complicated."
- The twenty maidens and the "last" Toltec: Alfonso Caso, "Land Tenure among the Ancient Mexicans," *American Anthropologist* 65 (1963), summarizes the various early sources of this story (865–67). Nobles and commoners were also of two different creations (citing a picture history to this effect), although in conclusion Caso adds that the king, "like all kings," had the power to ennoble commoners. Duran gives a similar contradiction.
- Several Aztec land claims were brought before the viceroy in colonial times based on lands (or proceeds thereof) allegedly distributed by Tlacaelel, documented by a manuscript in picture writing, the *Codex Cozcatzin*: von Winning, "Tlacaelel," 49.

122 "Such tight and enduring control": Sanders et al., *Basin of Mexico*. Adding: "however, as several writers have long argued, such 'private' estates were probably of minimal importance, and are perhaps best viewed as linked to the roles of their 'owners' in the state-level administration." (158–59)

- Roys, *Political Geography of the Yucatan Maya*, finds "some evidence" that the hereditary aristocracy among the Postclassic Maya "all considered themselves to be descended from Mexican invaders." (3) He concludes that this group "had a preferred position in regard to the apportionment of land." The tradition of the caciquedom and its perquisites remaining in a specific family line is well documented in Mexican villages remote from the seats of modern political power: for example, Sherburne Friend Cook, *Santa Maria Ixcatlan* (Berkeley 1958), with its comments on the "Cacicazgo of Ixcatlan" in Appendix 2, 73–75.

- The Tezcatlipoca sacrifice is described in Sahagun, *General History of New Spain*, Book 2.

123 "For whoever rejoices": quoted by Sahagun from Nezahualcoyatl, as adapted in William Brandon, *The Magic World* (New York 1971; Athens, Ohio 1992).

- Boethius: C.S. Lewis, *The Discarded Image* (Cambridge 1964), 83.
- The verses attributed to Virgil are from the *Copa Surisca*.

124 The Columbus quotation is from the first printed version of his Santangel letter, cited previously.

- "freedom of thought": Vaillant, *The Aztecs*, 127.

125 The English list of 200 capital crimes and 800 hangings a year is from Will and Ariel Durant, *The Age of Reason Begins* (New York 1961), 55.

- Crime statistics from Middlesex County 1609–1619: Edward Channing, *A History of the United States*, 6 vols. (New York 1905–1925), 1:183,184, 185, and n2, 184.

126 The obviously exaggerated figures of 20,000 to 80,000 sacrificed at one fell swoop are reported by Tezozomoc and Ixtlilxochitl and Duran, who all say 80,400; by Torquemada, *Monarquia Indiana*, 1:186, as 72,344; and by the *Codex Telleriano-Remensis*, Paul Radin, trans. (Berkeley 1920), as 20,000. The commemoration stone seems to indicate 20,000, a figure accepted by Manuel Orozco y Berra, "Dedication del Templo Mayor de Mexico," *Anales Museo Nacional*, 1:61. Some say two files of victims, some four files, extending miles out along the causeways. Frederick Peterson, *Ancient Mexico, An Introduction to the Pre-Hispanic Cultures* (New York 1959) settles for four files, each over three miles long, rather than a specific total. Prescott, *Mexico*, chooses an indeterminate number of files two miles long (1:97). But Prescott (alone) does give an assertion by Las Casas that figures of this range are put forward as "the estimate of brigands, who wish to find an apology for their own atrocities," and that the total number of sacrifices yearly "was not above fifty." (Quoted by Prescott from Las Casas, *Oeuvres* (Paris 1822) 1:365 and 386.) Sahagun reproduces a plan of the Tecpan, or temple enclosure, in Tenochtitlan (at the location of the Civic Center in modern Mexico City). This shows the twin temples on the great twin-topped pyramid, one temple dedicated to Tlaloc, the other to Huitzilopochtli, with twin altars, and even twin trails of blood staining the temple steps. It was at the dedication ceremonies for this great pyramid that the alleged multi-myriad sacrifices took place, and the concept of twin files of victims does seem to fit best with the picture of the twin altars at the twin temples as the focus of the action. There were, however, other temples within the Tecpan—Sahagun says a total of twenty-five—at which other sacrifices, presumably specialized (such as those at the temple of Xipe) could take place. A figure of 20,000 sacrifices for the great celebration of 1487 might be tolerable if all other temples in the city—better yet, all other temples in all the surrounding cities over the whole country—were assumed to be participating. For the ceremony as described, though, the figure is clearly out of kilter with simple arithmetic.

127   Sherburne Friend Cook, "Human Sacrifice and Warfare as Factors in the Demography of Pre-Colonial Mexico," *Human Biology* 18/2 (May 1946), makes an arithmetical calculation on the data of the great sacrifice, allowing three minutes per sacrifice. However, he opts for four lines of victims and four teams of priests, and also makes the assumption that the process was kept going day and night for four days—a total of ninety-six hours. This seems a questionable assumption, given the importance of offering the fresh-plucked hearts to the sun. Even with four lines and round-the-clock operation, Cook's calculations can only produce 11,520 total victims. Cook also offers interesting calculations based on the actual count made by two of Cortés' soldiers of the skulls in Tenochtitlan's famous skull rack: 136,000 (Andres de Tapia, *Relacion sobre la Conquista de Mexico*, J. Garcia Icazbalceta, ed. (Mexico 1866), 583), with in addition two sizable "towers" made of skulls and bones. If the skulls in the rack were all collected in the years following the dedication of the great temples in 1487, they would indicate 4,250 sacrifices per year, including the large number, whatever it was, at the dedication. (89) Or further guesses might be permissible: if kept since the last New Fire Ceremony (1507, fourteen years before) the average per year would be 9,785; if kept for the approximate 200 years of Tenochtitlan's existence, the average would be some sixty-eight per year. (ibid.)

Chapter 12

128   Garibay, Leon Portilla, Edmonson, and Bricker are examples of scholars who have studied Indian thought as a framework for Indian history; there are many more.
   • The archeologist speaking of ethnohistorians: William T. Sanders in Sanders et al., *Basin of Mexico*, 153.
   • "This is not to argue": Frank Hole, "Changing Directions in Archaeological Thought," in Jennings, *Ancient Native Americans*, 14. John W. Fox, *Maya Postclassic State Formation* (Cambridge 1987), speaks of advantageously combining ethnohistory with archeology. (285)
129   Willey, *Introduction to American Archaeology*, citing among others Wormington, *Ancient Man in North America*, expresses the usual view that the mammoth may have lingered on in southern Arizona a little longer than elsewhere, to fit the earliest radiocarbon dates of c. 7350 B.C. to 6270 B.C. (58) The calibration to real dates now in use would ease this misfit a little, by adding perhaps as much as 1,000 years or so to those radiocarbon dates.
131   Originators of some of the most drought-resistant and heat-tolerant plants in existence: *Native Seeds Search Catalogue* (Tucson 1991), 32.
   • "a very large canal": Henry Rowe Schoolcraft, *Historical and Statistical Information, Respecting the History, Condition and Prospects of the Indian Tribes of the United States*, 6 vols. (Philadelphia 1851–1857).
   • Some archeologists argue invasion and conquest from Mesoamerica, but the more generally accepted explanation settles for gradual peaceful diffusion of Mesoamerican elements. See especially H.S. Gladwin, *Excavations at Snaketown IV* (Globe, Arizona 1948); E.W. Haury et al., *The Stratigraphy and Archaeology of Ventana Cave, Arizona* (Albuquerque 1950); George J. Gumerman, ed., *Exploring the Hohokam: Prehistoric Desert Peoples of the American Southwest* (Albuquerque 1991);

Jonathan K. Ericson and Timothy G. Bough, eds., *The American Southwest and Mesoamerican Systems of Prehistoric Exchange* (New York 1993).

132 The description of a priest's house and the following quotation on authority: Frank Russell, "The Pima Indians," *26th Annual BAE Report* (Washington 1908), 353–56. Russell's work on Piman tradition is particularly noteworthy for its translations. For Tohono O'odham ethnography, see Ruth Murray Underhill, *Social Organization of the Papago Indians* (New York 1939), and *Papago Indian Religion* (New York 1946).

• "You may think this over": Russell, "Pima Indians," 362.

133 "wonderfully timorous": Morison, *Christopher Columbus Mariner*, Appendix One ("A New Translation of Columbus' Letter on His First Voyage,"), 216.

• "Although peaceful and lethargic": Steward, *Handbook* 4:552.

• The early Spanish explorer is Ruy Diaz de Guzman, *La Argentina: Historia de las Provincias del Rio de la Plata*, in vol. 9, *Anales de la Biblioteca Nacional* (Buenos Aires 1914), cited by Alfred Métraux, in Steward, *Handbook* 3:467; the unlikely association of Guarani and Chané is nevertheless here accepted by Métraux and the editors. It is also supported by a number of other sources, such as Reginalda de Lizarraga, *Descripcion . . . del Rio de la Plata*, in *Nueva Biblioteca de Autores Españoles*, vol. 15 (Madrid 1900), 552; and Ulrich Schmidel (a soldier of fortune under Pedro de Mendoza and other explorers, and the earliest source for the region), *Viaje al Rio de la Plata* (1534–1544) (Buenos Aires 1903), 252.

• The argument among present day social scientists will be discussed later.

134 Willey, *Introduction to American Archaeology*: the Mimbres painted pottery was "probably the outstanding aesthetic product of the Southwest." (1:196)

136 A couple of recent works on Southwestern petroglyphs, models of disparity: Sally J. Cole, *Legacy on Stone: Rock Art of the Colorado Plateau and Four Corners Region* (Boulder 1990); and Nancy H. Olsen, *Hovenweep Rock Art: An Anasazi Visual Communication System* (Los Angeles 1985).

• Chaco Canyon statistics in Fiedel, *Prehistory of the Americas*, are followed here: roads, rooms, great kivas with no modern counterparts. (216)

• Road networks, also questionable as to purpose, have been much studied. A recent summary is Charles D. Trombold, ed., *Ancient Road Networks and Settlement Hierarchies in the New World* (Cambridge 1991), containing four chapters dealing with road patterns in the Chaco Canyon region.

137 The Cumbemayo canal, which diverted its stream from Pacific drainage to Atlantic drainage, begins as a tiny open ditch only a couple of feet or so across, goes underground, emerges, divides, is joined together again; it "appears to have been built primarily for cult activities related to rainfall and fertility." (Burger, *Chavin*, 111)

• For a recent meticulous survey of remains of habitations dating from A.D. 500 to 1300, and flood-plain and channel deposits in a 7.5-kilometer stretch of McElmo Creek, a tributary of the San Juan River (in the heart of Mesa Verde Anasazi Region) see Eric R. Force and Wayne Howell, *Holocene Depositional History and Anasazi Occupation in McElmo Canyon, Southwestern Colorado* (Arizona State Museum Archaeological Series 188, Tucson, 1997). The study was conducted in cooperation with the Crow Canyon Archaeological Center and the U.S. Geological Survey.

• Various arrow releases are charted in Harold E. Driver and William C. Massey, *Comparative Studies of North American Indians*, Transactions of the American Philosophical Society, NS, 47, part 2 (Philadelphia 1957), 353–55, especially map

140 (354), which is based on Edward S. Morse, "Ancient and Modern Methods of Arrow-release," *Bulletin of the Essex Institute* 17 (Salem, Massachusetts 1883); and on A.L. Kroeber, "Arrow Release Distribution," *University of California Publications in American Archaeology and Ethnology* (Berkeley 1927).

138   The Puebloans resident for several generations among the Hohokam, given the name Salado by archeologists, have garnered headline comment for many years: "truly astonishing" (Martin, Quimby, and Collier, *Indians Before Columbus*, 189); "lived side by side in apparent peace for more than a century" (Willey, *Introduction to American Archaeology*, 228).

    • "of four stories": Schoolcraft, *Indian Tribes*.

139   Some traditional Pueblo recipes and foods are in Wilfred William Robbins, John Peabody Harrington, and Barbara Freire-Marreco, *Ethnobotany of the Tewa Indians*, BAE Bulletin 55 (Washington 1916).

    • E. Charles Adams, *The Origin and Development of the Pueblo Katsina Cult* (Tucson 1991), suggests that this religious structure, spelled "kachina" by the uneducated, was a key element of integration in a period of Pueblo change, 190.

    • "the corn will be glad": Robbins et al, *Ethnobotany*, 83.

141   Ritch Collection 1, "Marcos de Niza," Huntington Library, gives New Galicia as a principal source for Indians with Estevanico.

    • "with his gown gathered": Herbert E. Bolton, *Coronado, Knight of Pueblo and Plains* (New York 1949).

    • "as one dead": Vásquez de Coronado to Viceroy Mendoza, from Cibola, August 3, 1540, George P. Hammond and Agapito Rey, *Narratives of the Coronado Expedition 1540–1542* (Albuquerque 1940), 169.

142   For a close look at Zuñi-Cibola, see Frederick Webb Hodge, *History of Hawikuh, New Mexico* (Los Angeles 1937). The reported number of pueblos: ibid., 219. Hammond and Rey also give eight plazas for Pecos rather than the five archeologists accept.

    • "They do not have chiefs": Frederick Webb Hodge and Theodore H. Lewis, eds., *Spanish Explorers in the Southern United States 1528–1541* (New York 1907).

    • The best and most convenient source for tribal names and locations in North America is John R. Swanton, *The Indian Tribes of North America*, BAE Bulletin 145 (Washington 1953).

143   The routes and details of the Vásquez de Coronado expedition are closely examined in William Brandon, *Quivira* (Athens, Ohio 1991).

    • "saintly lay brother": Hammond and Rey, *Narratives of the Coronado Expedition*, 294.

    • Angelico Chavez, *Coronado's Friars* (Washington 1968), gives detailed information on the religious.

    • The beard "in braids": Bolton, *Coronado*, 359.

    • The various unofficial explorers before Oñate: George P. Hammond and Agapito Rey, eds. and trans., *The Rediscovery of New Mexico 1580–1594, the Explorations of Chamuscado, Espejo, Castaño de Sosa, Morlete, and Leyva de Bonilla and Humaña* (Albuquerque 1966).

144   Oñate: George P. Hammond and Agapito Rey, *Don Juan de Oñate, Colonizer of New Mexico 1595–1628*, 2 vols. (Albuquerque 1953).

    • The surge of conversions: France V. Scholes, "Royal Treasury Records . . ." *New Mexico Historical Review*, 50/1 (January 1975), relates that Fray Lázaro Ximénes arrived in Mexico City in December 1608 with the sensational word of thousands of conversions, and thus success of the missionary effort could be anticipated. "This optimistic report is suspect . . ." (11)

- "the reason why": Hammond and Rey, Oñate.
- France Scholes also gives pre-revolutionary details in "Civil Government and Society in New Mexico in the Seventeenth Century," *New Mexico Historical Review* 10 (April 1935).

145   The basic source on the Pueblo Revolt used here (and the source of quotations) is Charles Wilson Hackett, ed., *Revolt of the Pueblo Indians of New Mexico,* 2 vols. (Albuquerque 1942).

146   The quotations are from Diego de Vargas, *Journal of an expedition to the Moqui Provinces* (November 1692), MS RI 21 in the Ritch Collection, Henry E. Huntington Library, San Marino, California.

Chapter 13

148   Sayri Tupac's daughter, "Princess Beatriz," married Martin Garcia de Loyola, nephew of Saint Ignatius: Nathan Wachtel, *Cambridge History of Latin America* (hereafter *CHLA*) 1:225. The family was not noble, but rich: a previous Martin Garcia de Loyola, elder brother of Saint Ignatius and the head of the family a generation earlier, left in his will lands around the mansion for more than a mile, plus 21 pasture lands, plus 7 farms, plus 6 plantations: James Broderick, S.J., *Saint Ignatius Loyola* (London 1956), 20.

149   For a colorful rendition of all the adventures comic and tragic accompanying La Condamine's expedition, see Victor W. von Hagen, *South America Called Them* (London 1949), 11–105. The two young naval officers sent to Peru as members of La Condamine's scientific expedition were Jorge Juan and Antonio de Ulloa, their report, *Policias Secretas de Americas.*

- The 1960s authority: Steve J. Stern, *Peru's Indian Peoples and the Challenge of Spanish Conquest: Huamanga to 1640* (Madison 1982) states that in scarcely a century the Andean people were transformed into a proletariat perceived as racially inferior.

150   Araucanian wars are the subject of Alonso de Ercilla y Zùñiga's epic poem, *Araucana* (1569–1590), of genuine historical interest—he was there—but unfortunately, having been praised by Cervantes and Voltaire, the poem was regarded by generations of Spanish schoolteachers as of high literary value and hammered into the heads of generations of long-suffering schoolchildren, not to the benefit of Spanish literature.

- Coca "indispensable" (the coca trade in Potosí amounted to half a million pesos, or 95,000 baskets, per year): José de Acosta, *Historia natural y moral de las Indias* (Madrid 1914, originally 1590), 116, quoted in Wachtel, *CHLA*, 1:230. Indian control of the silver production lasted for over twenty-five years, until introduction of the amalgamation process in the early 1570s (ibid., 1:222, citing Carlos Sempat Assadourian, "La producciòn de la mercencia dinero . . . El caso del espacio peruano siglo XVI," in *Ensayos sobre el desarollo econòmico de Mexico y America latine*, Enrique Floressano, ed., Mexico 1979).

151   The 33,000 head of cattle are mentioned in Herbert E. Bolton and Thomas M. Marshall, *The Colonization of North America 1492–1783* (New York 1920), 58.

- "a crusade of fire. . ." : Richard J. Morrissey, "The Northward Expansion of Cattle Ranching in New Spain, 1550–1600," *Agricultural History* 25/3 (1951), 120.
152 Peru's "greatest mineral contribution" was the mercury of Huancavelica: Peter Bakewell, *CHLA*, 2:108.
- The Sierra Azul hasn't yet been found in Hopi country but appears in Carlos de Sigüenza y Góngora, *Mercurio Volante con la Noticia de la Recuperatión de las Provincias del Nuevo Mexico . . . (An Account of the First Expedition of Don Diego de Vargas into New Mexico in 1692)* first published in 1693, translated and edited with an introduction by Irving Albert Leonard (Los Angeles 1932). Also see José M. Espinosa, "Legend of Sierra Azul," *New Mexico Historical Review* 9/2 (April 1934).
153 Robert Hale Shields, "The Enchanted City of the Caesars, Eldorado of Southern South America," in *Greater America*, introduces the Land of the Caesars. The same author's collection of Cesarista material in the Bancroft Library, Berkeley, provides further information for those who may want to keep on looking.
154 Alvar Núñez Cabeza de Vaca, *La relacion que dio Alvar Núñez Cabeça de Vaca de lo acascido en las Indias en la armada donde vua por governado Pamphilo de Narvaez* (Zamora 1542), and reprinted with some alterations in the *Comentarios* (Valladolid 1555), in which Núñez also relates his later South American experiences. The 1542 edition, usually known as the *Naufragios* ("Castaways"), has endured innumerable translations, among them a translation into English by Fanny Bandelier (New York 1905). The 1555 edition was translated by T. Buckingham Smith (1851); it is reprinted in F.W. Hodge and Theodore H. Lewis, eds., *Explorers of the Southern United States 1528–1543* (New York 1907). This same volume contains the narrative of the expedition of Hernando de Soto by the Gentleman of Elvas; much understudied detail is in *Final Report of the U.S. De Soto Expedition Commission*, 76th Congress, 1st Session, House Document 71 (Washington 1939). Attention should also be called to the work of semi-fiction based on the Alvar Núñez story, *Interlinear to Cabeza de Vaca*, by the poet Haniel Long. Oviedo first recorded Alvar Núñez Cabeza de Vaca's tale of the four castaways: Gonzalo Fernandez de Oviedo Valdes, *Historia general de las Indias*, published in part in the sixteenth century, but not in a complete edition until 1851–1855, where the Núñez story is told in book XXXV, chapters 1–7. Alvar Núñez' own *Relación*, first published in Spain in 1542, contained added material evidently filched by the publisher from early reports of the Vásquez Coronado expedition, and remained a prized article of equipment for New Mexico-bound adventurers for years to come.
155 Abortion and infanticide: Fray Pedro de Cordoba (early seventeenth century), *Colección de documentos inéditos* 42 vols. (Madrid 1864–1884), 11:219, cited in Nicolas Sanchez-Albornoz, *CHLA*, 2:12.
156 Fray Bernadino de Minaya is quoted from Lewis Hanke, "Pope Paul III and the American Indian," *Harvard Theological Review* XXX (1937).
157 Motolinía (Fray Toribio de Benavente), *Memorial* to Charles V, in *Documentos inéditos*, 7:262–63.
- Spain's zenith of glory is from Americo Castro, *The Structure of Spanish History*, Edmund L. King, trans. (Princeton 1954), 190. See also Castro's *La Realidad Historica de España* (Mexico 1954), 443; and *The Spaniards: An Introduction to Their History*, Willard F. King and Selma Margaretten, trans. (Berkeley 1971), 10.

- The debate between Las Casas and Sepúlveda is the subject of Lewis Hanke, *Aristotle and the American Indians* (New York 1959, Bloomington 1970). The point of the debate is quoted from the 1970 edition, page 41.
- Las Casas: *Historia*, 112 and 113.
158 The Jesuits in Paraguay: Robert Bontine Cunninghame Graham, *A Vanished Arcadia: Being Some Account of the Jesuits in Paraguay 1607–1767* (London 1901, 1988).
- Population figures are from the report of the official "chronicler" of the Indies, appointed in 1571, Lopez de Velasco. Figures on the population decline are from Cook and Borah, *Essays in Population History: Mexico and the Caribbean*. The Cook and Borah totals, worked out from various documentary sources, reached astonishing heights, far greater than the populations of Europe, and excited much debate on their appearance in the early 1960s. Their general range is by now accepted by most authorities.
159 Andean epidemic figures: Henry F. Dobyns, "An Outline of Andean Epidemic History to 1720," *Bulletin of the History of Medicine* 37/6 (1963); the quotation is from page 514. See also Nicolás Sanchéz-Albornóz, *CHLA*, 2:5–7, citing Noble David Cook, *Demographic Collapse: Indian Peru, 1520–1620* (New York 1981).
161 Chiskiac: Clifford Merle Lewis and Albert J. Loomie, *The Spanish Mission in Virginia, 1570–1572* (Chapel Hill 1953). A similar name, Chiska, was the Muskogean name for a Yuchi band: Swanton, *Indian Tribes*, 117.
162 For priests inciting Indians against other factions: Lesley Bird Simpson, *Many Mexicos* (New York 1941 and ff.), 83–84.
- The "jockeying for power between different interest groups—between viceroys and audiencias, viceroys and bishops, secular clergy and regional clergy, and between the governors and the governed" fragmented authority and left it "filtered, mediated and dispersed." (Elliott, *CHLA*, 1:303)
- The duke of Alva's silver service, and the beggars of Madrid: Will and Ariel Durant, *The Age of Louis XIV* (New York 1963), 449–53.
- The court and grandees principal factors in Spain's downfall: J.H. Elliot, *New Cambridge Modern History* (1970), 4:444–50. "a vast court . . . ": 447.
163 The Hawkins slave run and the *Jesus: Dictionary of National Biography*, 25:213–14. Queen Elizabeth loaned the *Jesus* again as flagship for the expedition of Hawkins and Drake in 1567, but on this trip the *Jesus* was destroyed by the Spanish, in a general defeat suffered by the English privateering fleet at Vera Cruz, September 1567: *DNB*, 25:214.
- "haunted by flamingoes": R.B. Cunninghame Graham, *The Conquest of the River Plate* (London 1924), is the source of the phrase on pampas streams.
164 The missionary in Brazil, Pierre Alvarèz Cabral, in Joseph François Lafitau de la Compagnie de Jesus, *Histoire des Découvertes et Conquestes des Portugais dans le Nouveau Monde*, 3 vols, (Paris 1733 and subsequently), 2: 258.
- New World liberty is discussed in detail in William Brandon, *New Worlds for Old* (Ohio University Press, 1986).
- Religious/sexual differences in a familiar setting, based here on church records referring to Pueblo Indians: Ramon A. Guttierez, *When Jesus Came the Corn Mothers Went Away: Marriage, Sexuality and Power in New Mexico, 1500–1846* (Stanford 1991).
- The New World as a second earth: Marvin Harris, *The Rise of Anthropological Theory* (1968), 683.

PART II

Chapter 14

167   James Bryce, *The American Commonwealth*, 2 vols. (originally published 1893; revised edition New York 1924), 2:891–92.

•   Frederick Jackson Turner Papers, Huntington Library, San Marino, California (TU File Drawer no. 13). The quotation is from a handwritten draft for a summary of a half-term's work at Harvard on western history. Ray Allen Billington, Turner's biographer, through whose kindness this quotation was provided, dated the draft at about 1921.

168   DeVoto is quoted from his Introduction to Joseph Kinsey Howard, *The Strange Empire of Louis Riel* (New York 1942), vii and ix.

•   Francis Parkman examples come from *La Salle and the Discovery of the Great West*, John A. Hawgood, ed. (Boston 1869; New York 1953) 136, 175 and 177n; and from the Introduction to *The Jesuits in North America in the Seventeenth Century* (Boston 1867). But see the "heroic" Parkman persuasively presented in Wilbur R. Jacobs, *Francis Parkman, Historian as Hero: The Formative Years* (Austin, Texas 1992).

169   A.L. Kroeber, *Anthropology*, 2nd edition (New York 1948), 763–64.

•   Franz Boas, *Race, Language, and Culture* (New York 1940); and *The Mind of Primitive Man* (1938).

•   Claude Levi-Strauss, *Tristes Tropiques* (Paris 1955), 353.

•   The quotation on quinine: William Howells, *Back of History* (Garden City 1954, 1963), 286–87. William H. McNeill, *Plagues and People* (Oxford 1977): it is "practically certain that neither malaria nor yellow fever" were in America before Columbus; both were presumably brought later from Africa. (211–13)

170   The "New World's earliest historian" was Peter Martyr d'Anghiera, quoted here from the First Decade of *De Orbe Novo Decades* (1511–1525), in the words of his first (fragmentary) English translation: Richard Eden, *Peter Martyr the History of Travayle in the West and East Indies . . .* (London 1555).

•   The Caribbean quotation is from Jean-Baptiste Du Tertre, *Histoire Générale des Isles de S. Christophe, de la Guadeloupe, de la Martinique, et Autres dans l'Amérique* (Paris 1654), 2:356.

•   Joseph François Lafitau, *Moeurs des Sauvages Ameriquains*, 2 vols. (Paris 1724), 1:103–8.

•   Pierre F.X. de Charlevoix, *Letters to the Duchess of Lesdiguieres . . .* (London 1764), 28.

•   Robert Rogers, *A Concise Account of North America* (London 1765), 210.

•   Pierre de Ronsard, "Discours Contre Fortune," *Oeuvres Complètes*, 2 vols. (Paris 1950), 2:399ff.

•   Michel Eyquem de Montaigne, the Preface to *Les Essays*, Pierre Villey, ed., 3 vols. (Paris 1930).

•   Gottfried Wilhelm von Leibniz, Judgement sur les Oeuvres de M. le Comte de Shaftesbury, Publiés à Londres en 1711, Sous le Titre de Characteristiks: *Works*, 5:40.

•   Geoffroy Atkinson, *The Extraordinary Voyage in French Literature before 1700* (New York 1920), 14.

171   "full-gorged": John Florio's translation of Montaigne's *Essays* (London 1603), 106.

•   On Morgan in the Marxist canon see Leslie A. White, ed., *Lewis Henry Morgan, the Indian Journals* (Ann Arbor 1959) 11 and 202, n58.

•   Denis Diderot, "Le Temple du Bonheur" (date uncertain but probably c1770) *Ouevres Complètes*, Roger Le Winter, ed., (Paris 1971), 8:168.

•   Mark Twain, *Roughing It* (New York 1872), 154–58.

172   William Bradford, *History of Plymouth Plantation, 1620–1647*, 2 vols. (Boston 1912), 1:202–3.

•   Sir Ferdinando Gorges, *America Painted to the Life, etc . . .* (London 1659).

•   The Wappinger quotation is from "Notes by D. David Pieterez de Fries" (Hoorn 1655), in *Collections* of the New-York Historical Society, 2nd Series, vol. 3, part 1 (New York 1857).

•   Captain John Smith is quoted from *A True Relation of Virginia* (London 1608), and from a petition of 1616 to Queen Anne on behalf of the Lady Pocahontas.

173   "being of simple faith": John Boyd Thacher, *Christopher Columbus, His Life, His Work, His Remains*, 3 vols. (New York 1903), 2:xxx.

•   The Cartier incident: John Pinkerton, *A General Collection of the Best and Most Interesting Voyages and Travels in All Parts of the World*, 17 vols. (London 1808–1814), 3:650.

•   Alvar Núñez Cabeza de Vaca: F.W. Hodge and Theodore H. Lewis, eds., *Spanish Explorers in the Southern United States, 1528–1542* (New York 1907), 56 and 54.

•   All the quotes from "early explorers" are from Parkman, *La Salle*, 141, 223, 298, 194–95, and 194n, dealing with accounts of La Salle, Membré, and Hennepin.

•   Castañeda: Herbert E. Bolton, *Coronado, Knight of Pueblo and Plains* (New York 1949), 246.

•   Captain Barlow is quoted from Irwin R. Blacker, ed., *Hakluyt's Voyages* (New York 1965), 293.

174   The two failed Vial expeditions are fully treated in Noel M. Loomis and A.P. Nasatir, *Pedro Vial and the Roads to Santa Fe* (Norman 1967), 429.

175   The "untold numbers" of Indian allies are mentioned by Cortés in his third letter to Charles V (1521), quoted in Bernal Díaz del Castillo, *The Discovery and Conquest of Mexico*, Irving A. Leonard, ed. (New York 1956), 446.

176   Edmond Atkin is quoted from Wilbur R. Jacobs, ed., *Indians of the Southern Colonial Frontier*, (Columbia, South Carolina 1954), 40.

•   The Foxes "also were dismayed by the priests' reaction to several national disasters," such as, besides the epidemic of 1675–1676, late damaging frosts or fungus in stored corn. The missionary Père Allouez "said God was scourging them, but Indians wondered if the old manitous were angry." And, of course, the "Black Robes continued to befriend their enemies." R. David Edmunds and Joseph L. Peyser, *The Fox Wars* (1993), 16.

•   Apalachee "counterrevolution": John R. Swanton, *The Indian Tribes of North America*, BAE Bulletin 145 (Washington 1953), 123.

177   William Christie MacLeod, *The American Indian Frontier* (New York 1908), 423.

178   "many mistakes": ibid., 449.

•   Atkin is again quoted from Jacobs, *Indians of the Southern Colonial Frontier*, 38 and 40.

179   There is little indication: Adolph F.A. Bandelier, "On the Art of War and Mode of Warfare of the Ancient Mexicans" *Reports of the Peabody Museum* 20/2

(Cambridge, Massachusetts 1880), 99. These Bandelier reports, involved in a very public debate at the time between Lewis Henry Morgan and H.H. Bancroft, have fallen into great disfavor among anthropologists since the 1930s, but it does seem evident that no "guard" came to Moctezuma's rescue. One popular line in recent discussion of aboriginal American war follows the lead of Anthony F.W. Wallace in finding Iroquois warfare a mechanism for emotional and social "equilibrium" (*The Death and Rebirth of the Seneca*, New York 1970, 45–46).

- The Court of Claims opinion is in United States Indian Affairs, *Report of the Commissioner for 1895*, (Washington 1856), 427; see also 417–18.

183   Parkman: *Jesuits in North America*, xxvii.

- H.M. Brackenridge, *Journal of a Voyage up the River Missouri* (Baltimore 1816), reprinted as the first part of volume 6 of Reuben Gold Thwaites, *Early Western Travels* (Cleveland 1904).

- The quotes on the Opatas are from the *Rudo Ensayo*, quoted in Edward H. Spicer, *Cycles of Conquest, Indians of the Southwest 1533–1960* (Tucson 1962), 322.

184   Pablo Abeita, governor of Isleta Pueblo in New Mexico, is quoted from a 1940 speech, "About Coronado," in Jeannette Henry, ed., *The American Indian Reader*, vol. 3, *Literature* (San Francisco 1973), 115–17.

- Modern economist: Gerard Piel, *Consumers of Abundance*, (a pamphlet published by the Center for the Study of Democratic Insititutions, Santa Barbara, California 1961), 3.

- Whorf: John B. Carroll, ed., *Language, Thought, and Reality: Selected Writings of Benjamin Lee Whorf* (New York 1956).

- Teilhard de Chardin: Sol Tax, ed., *An Appraisal of Anthropology Today* (Chicago 1953), 44.

Chapter 15

185   James L. Phillips and James A. Brown, eds., *Archaic Hunters and Gatherers in the American Midwest* (New York 1983), describes life in this region 800 to 3,000 years ago.

- Dating for the red paint burials mentioned here, the Old Copper industry, and the emergence of Adena, follow James A. Tuck in *Handbook of North American Indians*, vol. 15, *Northeast*, Bruce G. Trigger, ed. (Washington 1978), 42–43.

186   Robert F. Spencer and Jesse D. Jennings, *The Native Americans*, second edition (1977) adopt 800 B.C. to A.D. 600+ for Adena-Hopewell. (25)

- Climatic changes: James E. Fitting, *Handbook* 15, 44.

187   Spencer and Jennings, *Native Americans*, find Effigy Mound dates uncertain, but risk the possibility of A.D. 300 to A.D. 1642. (32)

- Hopewell maize: Fitting, *Handbook* 15, 48. Spencer and Jennings, *Native Americans*, accept "almost no" Hopewell maize, but note squash and sunflower and evidence of Adena-Hopewell cultivation of plants now regarded as weeds, such as pigweed and lambs-quarters.

- Hopewell agriculture: Bruce D. Smith, *Rivers of Change: Essays on Early Agriculture in Eastern North America* (Washington 1992); and C. Margaret Scarny, ed., *Foraging and Farming in the Eastern Woodlands* (Gainesville 1993).

- "The sides so upright": Henry Rowe Schoolcraft, *Historical and Statistical Information, Respecting the History, Condition, and Prospects of the Indian Tribes of the United States*, 6 vols. (Philadelphia 1851–1857).
- Paul Radin, *The Story of the American Indian* (New York 1929, 1934, 1944) pictured a sea route from Vera Cruz to the lower Mississippi (155), an idea now finding a little more support than formerly. Gordon R. Willey, *An Introduction to American Archaeology*, 2 vols. (Englewood Cliffs 1966 and 1971), discusses this and other possible transmission routes. (36)

188   The Mississippian tradition: Fitting, *Handbook* 15, 52; Charles A. Bareis and James W. Porter, eds., *American Bottom Archaeology: A Summary of the FAI-270 Project Contribution to the Culture History of the Mississippi Valley* (Urbana 1984); Thomas E. Emerson and E. Barry Lewis, eds., *Cahokia of the Hinterlands: Middle Mississippian Cultures of the Midwest* (Urbana 1991).

- The erudite traveler quoting Ariosto was Louis Armand de Lom d'Arce, baron de Lahontan, *New Voyages to North America* (London 1703), 1:234.

189   John R. Swanton, *Myths and Tales of the Southeastern Indians*, BAE Bulletin 88 (Washington 1929) tells the story of the heavenly canoe.

- The great battle with Soto was in defense of a fortified village on the west bank of the Mobile River a few miles below the forks of the Tombigbee and Alabama (Swanton, *Indian Tribes*, 159). The Spaniards took the town with heavy losses on both sides, although the claim of 2,500 Indian casualties seems unlikely for the brief time involved.

192   Herbert Landar, *The Tribes and Languages of North America: A Checklist* (Center for Applied Linguistics, Washington 1972) gives "Nah-tchi" for the native pronunciation of Natchez.

193   Emerald Mound: Paul S. Martin, George I. Quimby, and Donald Collier, *Indians Before Columbus, Twenty Thousand Years of North American History Revealed by Archeology* (Chicago 1947), 411–20.

194   The five reasonably plausible contemporary accounts are assessed in detail—Le Page du Pratz taking first place—in John R. Swanton, *The Indians of the Southeastern United States*, BAE Bulletin 137 (Washington 1946).

- The quotations here, and to page 200, are all drawn from Antoine S. Le Page du Pratz, *Histoire de la Louisiane*, 3 vols. (Paris 1758; London 1763, 1774).

200   "But as the Indians": James Adair, *The History of the American Indians* (London 1775; Johnson City, Tennessee 1930).

Chapter 16

202   One recent archeological summary is Ronald J. Mason, *Great Lakes Archaeology* (New York 1981).

203   A classic study of trickster scripture, Paul Radin, *The Trickster, A Study in American Indian Mythology*, was given a new edition (New York 1972), with Commentary by Karl Kerenyi and C.G. Jung and a new Introduction by Stanley Diamond.

- "wild Irish": William Wood, *New Englands Prospect, a True, Lively, and Experimentall Description of that part of America, commonly called New England*, (London 1634).

205   Thomas Varnum Jr., *American Indian Lacrosse* (Washington 1994), emphasizes "the sacred nature of the game." (31)

- The 1586 account is Thomas Hariot, *Narrative of the First English Plantation of Virginia* (London 1588 and 1590), quoted here from Pinkerton, *Voyages and Travels*, 12:613. Hariot (a leading savant of the age) was with a supply squadron sent out by Sir Walter Raleigh to the colony of Roanoke, a colony founded the year before and fated to vanish a year or two later. Documents and drawings of these early contacts are collected in Stefan Lorant, ed., *The New World: The First Pictures of America* (New York 1946). The best known drawings were reproduced in Paul Hope Hulton and David Beers Quinn, *The American Drawings of John White, 1577–1590*, 2 vols. (London 1964), volume 1 being a study of the artist (whose granddaughter was Virginia Dare of the lost Roanoke colony).
- "running and fiercely crying": Will Wood, *New Englands Prospect*.
- "But to leave": ibid.
- Thomas Morton, *New English Canaan . . . containing an Abstract of New England* (1637, Amsterdam 1969).

206   Wallace, *Death and Rebirth of the Seneca*, mentions various traditional motives in Indian "war," such as maintaining kin-group and social equilibrium, or maintaining security and fulfillment in the family setting (44–48). George T. Hunt, *The Wars of the Iroquois, A Study in Intertribal Trade Relations* (Madison, Wisconsin 1940, 1960) makes a case for the first real war in the Northeast as an adjunct to European trade. (20–22)

207   A number of early Canadian reports listed Ottawa, Potawatomi, Missisauga, and Lake Superior as four major divisions of Ojibwa: Diamond Jenness, *The Indians of Canada*, 6th edition (Ottawa 1978), 277.

208   The great king Powhatan and his country: William Strachey, *The Historie of Travaille into Virginia Britannica* Hakluyt Society Publication, vol. 6 (London 1849).

- A map drawn by Captain John Smith in 1612 shows and names more than 160 of the nearly 200 Powhatan villages: John Smith, *Works*, Edward Arber, ed., (Birmingham, England 1884). Wilcomb E. Washburn, in *Handbook* 15, 95, gives a Virginia population roughly double Smith's figure of 8,500, from 14,000 to 22,000, citing Christian F. Feest in the Quarterly *Bulletin of the Archeological Society of Virginia* 28/2 (Richmond 1973).
- Strachey, *Historie of Travaille*.

209   Temporarily lambasted loser: Philip L. Barbour, *The Three Worlds of Captain John Smith* (Cambridge, Massachusetts, 1964), 276–80. This work contains a very full bibliography on the longlonglongstanding Smith controversy. For the legalese of Smith's deposition, see Herbert L. Osgood, *The American Colonies in the Seventeenth Century*, 3 vols. (New York 1904, 1930, Gloucester, Mass., 1957), 1:65.

210   "Why should you take by force": MacLeod, *American Indian Frontier*, 177–78.

- "it pleased God": Smith, *True Relation of Virginia*.
- "Blessed Pocahontas" is from the dedication to the *General Historie of Virginia* (1616).

211   The letter to Sir Thomas Dale is quoted in part from Charles M. Andrews, *The Colonial Period of American History*, 4 vols. (New Haven 1934–1938), 1:142 and in part from Barbour, *Three Worlds of Captain John Smith*, 329.

- The best of Pocahontas's hundred poets is Hart Crane, in whose American vision of *The Bridge* (1930) she is the chiefest heroine; the pretty cartwheeling picture from Strachey serves as her introduction in part two of this poem. The most ambitious of her hundred failed novelists is (so far) the otherwise excellent David Garnett, with *Pocahontas or the Nonpareil of Virginia* (London 1933).
- The dates and details of John Rolfe's first tobacco export and marriage are from Andrews, *Colonial Period*, 1:126, 142, 152, where n.3 mentions that "Varina" may be related to "Barinas," the name given to the finest Spanish tobacco from South America, the letters "b" and "v" being interchangeable in Spanish.
- "the permanence of English colonization": Edward Channing, *A History of the United States*, (New York 1905–1925), vol. 1:188.
- Pocahontas's brother and her several young ladies-in-waiting stayed on in England for the time, with varying adventures: Sidney Lee, *The American Indian in Elizabethan England* (1929), 287.

212   Ben Jonson is quoted from *Staple of News* (1625).

- MacLeod, *American Indian Frontier*, summarizes the background of the colonizing joint stock companies of North America (131–43).
- English companies in the Russian trade: Inna Lubimenko, "Les Marchands Anglais en Russie au XVIe Siècle," *La Revue historique*, 109 (Paris 1912).
- Peckham is quoted from William Warren Sweet, *The Story of Religion in America* (New York 1939).
- Gorges, *America Painted to the Life.*

213   The French prospectus is translated from Bibiothèque Nationale LK[12] 818-819-820, "Acte d'Association passé entre les sous-signez, et Reconnu par devant Rallu et Blanche Notaires, pour l'établissement des Colonies dans la Terre Firme de l'Amerique." Dated August 29, 1651.

- The price of tobacco: Channing, *History*, 1:188.
- "This pretious herb": Sir John Beaumont, "The Metamorphosis of Tobacco"— dedicated to Michael Drayton. Spencer went a little further still, calling it "our holy herb nicotian."
- "pleasure of drunkenness": Père du Creux, *History of Canada*, cited in Lafitau, *Moeurs des Sauvages Ameriquains*, 2:113–42.
- James II, *Counterblast to Tobacco* (1604), is quoted from Will and Ariel Durant, *The Age of Reason Begins* (New York 1961), 58, citing Kenneth Muir, ed., *Elizabethan and Jacobean Prose* (Pelican Books 1956), 89. The rest of the quotation, for the delectation of today's tobacco prohibitionists: "Is it not both great vanity and uncleanness that at the table, a place of respect, of cleanliness, of modesty, men should not be ashamed to sit tossing of Tobacco pipes, and puffing the smoke one to another, making the filthy smoke and stink thereof to exhale athwart the dishes and infect the air . . . The public use whereof, at all times and in all places, hath now so far prevailed as divers men . . . have been at least forced to take it also, without desire . . . ashamed to seem singular . . . Moreover, which is a great iniquity . . . the husband shall not be ashamed to reduce thereby his delicate, wholesome, and clean complexioned wife to that extremity, that either she must corrupt her sweet breath therewith, or else resolute to live in a perpetual stinking torment."

214   Algonquian terms for Englishmen: James Hammond Trumbull, *Natick Dictionary*, BAE Bulletin 25 (Washington 1903), 183.

215   Opechancanough as an ancestor of Jefferson Davis: Laurence M, Hauptman, *Between Two Fires; American Indians in the Civil War* (New York 1995), 12, citing *The Papers of Jefferson Davis*, James T. McIntosh, ed. (Baton Rouge 1971–1972), 1:488–89.

216   The colonial traveler: Andrew Burnaby, *Travels Through the Middle Settlements in North America* (London 1775), 31–32.

·   Early English indifference to American Indians is summed up in the quote by Wilbur R. Jacobs from "British Indian Policies to 1783," *Handbook of North American Indians, vol. 4, History of Indian-White Relations*, Wilcomb E. Washburn, ed., (Washington 1988), 5.

Chapter 17

218   The value of Indian auxiliaries: Washburn, *Handbook* 15, 99.

·   The Tuscarora expedition: J.N.B. Hewitt, in Frederick Webb Hodge, ed., *Handbook of American Indians North of Mexico*, 2 vols., BAE Bulletin 30 (Washington 1907–1910), 2:845–46.

·   Nanticoke antiquity: Maryland Archives, Proceedings of the Council, 1636–1637, 593, cited by James Mooney and Cyrus Thomas in Hodge, *Handbook*, 2:25.

219   Delaware population: Ives Goddard, *Handbook* 15, 213–39.

·   Delaware legends: E.G. Squier, "Traditions of the Algonquins," in W.W. Beach, ed., *The Indian Miscellany: Containing Papers on the History, Antiquities, Arts, Languages, Religiions, Traditions and Superstitions of the American Aborigines* (Albany 1877), speaks of finding among the papers of C.S. Rafinesque—one of the more extraordinary of early nineteenth-century characters—a manuscript entitled "the Walum Olum, (literally, painted sticks), or painted and engraved traditions of the Lenni-Lenape." Daniel G. Brinton offered a translation of the Walum Olum in volume five, *The Lenape and Their Legends*, of his *Library of Aboriginal American Literature*, 6 vols. (Philadelphia 1882–1885). A more recent edition: *Walam Olum, or Red Score, the Migration Legend of the Lenni Lenape or Delaware Indians* (Indiana Historical Society, Indianapolis 1954).

·   Archeological studies: Dean R. Snow, *Handbook* 15, "Each local (East Coast) sequence seems to reflect a long-term stability that belies the stories of recent migrations that have been popular for many years." (69)

·   Nils Gustafson is quoted from Peter Kalm, *Travels into North America* (London 1772), and this excerpt quoted in Pinkerton's *Voyages*, 13:538.

220   New Sweden colonists: Herbert E. Bolton and T.M. Marshall, *The Colonization of North America* (New York 1920), 175.

·   Manhattan: Goddard, *Handbook* 15, 236. Contemporary value of price for Manhattan: MacLeod, *American Indian Frontier*, 194. Peter Minuit's report of the Manhattan purchase is in the Holland Documents, volume one of E.B. O'Callaghan, ed., *Documents Relative to the History of the State of New York*, 15 vols. (New York 1858–1887), and in O'Callaghan, *History of New Netherlands*, 2 vols. (New York 1846–1848), 1:103.

·   Notions of land ownership among the Woodland Indians of the Northeast are analyzed in George S. Snyderman, "Concepts of Land Ownership among the

Iroquois and Their Neighbors," in William N. Fenton, ed., *Symposium on Local Diversity in Iroquois Culture*, BAE Bulletin 149 (Washington 1951).

- Brooklyn: Osgood, *American Colonies in the Seventeenth Century*, 2:49.
- The refugees were a group of Delaware "river people," the Wiechquaeskeck: Goddard, *Handbook* 15, 216.

221 Atrocities: see D. David Pieterszatz De Vries, "Notes . . ." (Hoorn 1655) in *Collections of the New-York Historical Society*, 2nd Series, vol. 3, part 1 (New York 1857); also *Broad Advice to the New Netherlands*, a calumnious pamphlet, authorship sometimes attributed to Cornelis Meyn (1649); also *Indian Tribes of Hudson's River . . .* (Albany 1872), 108; also E.M. Ruttenber, in MacLeod, *American Indian Frontier*, 224–26; also E.B. O'Callaghan, ed., *Documentary History of the State of New York*, 4 vols. (New York 1849–1851), 4:105. The word "Swannekin" is from De Vries.

- "fields lie fallow": John Romeyn Brodhead, *History of the State of New York*, 2 vols. (New York 1853, 1871), 1:398, cited in Channing, *History*, 1:458.
- Company quotes: O'Callaghan, *History of New Netherlands*, Appendix E, quoted in MacLeod, *American Indian Frontier*, 229–30.
- Repurchase of lands: Allen W. Trelease, "Dutch Treatment of the American Indian, with Particular Reference to New Netherland," in Howard Peckham and Charles Gibson, eds., *Attitudes of Colonial Powers Toward the American Indian* (Salt Lake City 1969), 55.

222 There have been a great many studies of Puritan factionalism—one of the best is Patrick McGrath, *Papists and Puritans under Elizabeth I* (London 1967). This work concludes on a note of caution "in assessing the debt to the Elizabethans of those who established Puritanism across the Atlantic" (397).

- Tamenend: John G.E. Heckewelder, *An Account of the History, Manners and Customs of the Indian Nations Who Once Inhabited Pennsylvania and the Neighboring States* (Philadelphia 1819, 1876), cited by James Mooney in Hodge, *Handbook*, 2:683. The legendary virtues are questioned in Clinton A. Weslager, *The Delaware Indians, A History* (New Brunswick, New Jersey 1972), 168–69.
- New England population density: A.L. Kroeber, Cultural and Natural Areas of Native North America, University of California Publications in American Archaeology and Ethnology, vol. 38 (Berkeley 1939, 1953), 142.

223 Tisquantum: Sir Ferdinando Gorges, *Briefe Narration . . .* (London 1658); Samuel Purchas, *Hakluytus Posthumus, or Purchas his Pilgrimes . . .* (London 1625–1626).

- Thomas Morton, *New English Canaan*, describes the plague.
- Plymouth landing: Osgood, *American Colonies in the Seventeenth Century*, 1:109; Pinkerton, *Voyages*, 12:349.

224 "scarce a bush": Will Wood, *New Englands Prospect*. Wrote Henry David Thoreau more than two centuries later: "They regularly cleared extensive tracts for cultivation, and these were always level tracts where the soil was light . . . Such was the land which they are known to have cultivated extensively in this town [Concord], as the Great Fields . . ." (Thoreau, *A Writer's Journal*, L. Stapleton, ed., (New York 1960), 14:272.

- "aloof": William Bradford, *Of Plymouth Plantation 1620–1647*, Samuel Eliot Morison, ed., (New York 1952), 83.
- Some color is lent to the Gorges claim by the fact that Squanto came back to America with a Captain Dermer, "a gentleman employed by Sir Ferdinando Gorges and others for discovery and other designs . . ." (Bradford, *Of Plymouth Plantation*, 81).

- "a speciall instrument": ibid.
- Colonies "could not survive": Alden T. Vaughan, *New England Frontier: Puritans and Indians 1620–1675* (Boston 1965),12.
- "the young men": Bradford, *Of Plymouth Plantation*, 121.

225 "the benefit of their beaver trade": Thomas Morton, *New English Canaan*. Morton also remarks that the sale of liquor brings great benefits to the planters, since for it the "Salvages . . . will pawne their wits" but that in all his commerce he has "never proffered them any such thing."

- The verse is from William Morrell, *New England, or a Briefe Narration of the Ayre, Earth, Water, Fish, and Fowles of that Country . . . in Latine and English Verse* (London 1625). This was not the first Latin poem propagandizing for the New World among the Latinist English—Stephen Parmenias, a Hungarian with Sir Humphrey Gilbert in 1583, wrote "an elegant Latin poem about Newfoundland (and died at sea, with the admiral and nearly one hundred of the crew) that same year." The poem is in volume nine of the *Collections* of the Massachusetts Historical Society: Lydia Sigourney, *Traits of the Aborigines of America* (Cambridge, Massachusetts 1822), 18–19.
- "The wonderful preparation": Captain Edward Johnson, *Wonder-Working Providence of Zion's Savior in New England* (1624; as edited by W.F. Poole, 1867).

226 Pequot antiquity: Snow, *Handbook* 15, 65.

- The Pequot argument: Bradford, *Of Plymouth Plantation*, 294.

227 The modern specialist: Vaughan, *New England Frontier*, 124.

- Cutshamekin: ibid., 129.
- Torture scenes: ibid., 133 and 141.
- The attack "before day": Bradford, *Of Plymouth Plantation*, 295.
- Several hundred dead: Bradford gives 400 (296); participants offer 400 to 600 or 700: Vaughan, *New England Frontier* (145).
- Allied Indians "mistakenly" wounded, and a half-hour duration: ibid.
- "It was a fearful sight . . . ": Bradford, *Of Plymouth Plantation*, 296.

228 An illustration of the victory: a detailed analysis is in Francis Jennings, *The Invasion of America* (Chapel Hill 1975), 224.

- The gossip of a Narraganset bribe: Bradford, *Of Plymouth Plantation*, 297.
- Washburn, *Handbook* 15, summarizes skepticism in regard to "conspiracies" (90–93).
- The death of Miantonomo, executed by order of the Commissioners of the United Colonies of New England after a "disgraceful" trial in which theological bias against Roger Williams (a friend of Miantonomo's) "played some part": Alexander F. Chamberlain in Hodge, *Handbook*, 1:855, quoting John W. De Forest, *History of the Indians of Connecticut from the Earliest Known Period to 1850* (Hartford 1851), 198.

229 "it was my chance": Thomas Morton, *New English Canaan*.

- Quotes on the murder of a Narraganset: Bradford, *Of Plymouth Plantation*, 229 and 118.
- Quotes concerning business attitudes and Protestant uneasiness: Osgood, *American Colonies in the Seventeenth Century*, 3:310, 413, and 446.

231 Today's leading expert: Washburn, *Handbook* 15, 92 and 93.

232 Another recent study finds disease the principal enemy of the Indians: Neal Salisbury, *Manitou and Providence: Indians, Europeans, and the Making of New England, 1500–1643* (New York 1983).

- The soldiers' doubts are quoted from the Ruggles Manuscript by G.E. Ellis, *King Philip's War* (1906), 152 and 155.
233 "the flower and strength: Benjamin Trumbull, *Complete History of Connecticut from 1630 to 1764*, 2 vols. (New Haven 1818).
- "My heart breaks": Nathaniel Morton, *New England's Memorial or Zion's Savior* (1669; 5th edition, John Davis, ed.,1826), 454.
234 New England Indian refugees working for La Salle: Parkman, *La Salle*, 214 and 217.
- Military expenses are as calculated by MacLeod, *American Indian Frontier*, 243.
- Edward Everett, *An Address Delivered at Bloody Brook, in South Deerfield, September 30, 1835, in Commemoration of the Fall of the "Flower of Essex" at that Spot in King Philip's War, September 18, (O.S.) 1675* (Boston 1835), 26. "It was not till the year 1759, till Quebec fell, that the settlements on Connecticut River were safe." (34)
- Douglas E. Leach, *Flintlock and Tomahawk, New England in King Philip's War* (New York 1958), states that in "proportion to population the war inflicted greater casualties upon the people than any other war in our history." Wilcomb E. Washburn, reviewing this work in *Pennsylvania Magazine of History and Biography*, 82 (1958), argues that the English were the aggressors, shed the first blood, attacked Narragansetts and Pennacooks and Connecticut Valley Indians without justification, and that the English had military successes only when they used more Indian allies than English troops.
- Philip's crippled hand (injured by the explosion of a pistol in former years) was given by Captain Thomas Church to Alerman, the Indian who shot him: Samuel Gardner Drake, *Biography and History of the Indians of North America, From Its First Discovery*, 11th ed. (Boston 1851).
- Cotton Mather, *Magnalia Christi Americana* (London 1702).
235 Theological quotations are from Nathaniel Morton, *New England's Memorial*.
- The Irish and Highland Scots sold as slaves to the West Indies by Cromwell: (MacLeod, American Indian Frontier, 170).

Chapter 18

237 Frank G. Speck, *Family Hunting Territories and Social Life of Various Algonquian Bands of the Ottawa Valley*, Memoir 70 (Ottawa 1915), and *Beothuk and Micmac*, Indian Notes and Monographs, Museum of the American Indian, Heye Foundation (New York 1922) (of which part two is devoted to Micmac hunting territories) discusses the Algonquian family hunting territory "which was first mentioned in this region by Le Clerq in 1691." (71n.) Father Chretien Leclerq, *New Relation of Gaspesia, with the Customs and Religion of the Gaspesian Indians* (Paris 1691) and in an English translation by William F. Ganong, The Champlain Society, (Toronto 1910). Speck's work on this private ownership is summarized in "The Family Hunting Band as the Basis of Algonkian Social Organization," in B. Cox, ed., *Cultural Ecology* (Toronto 1973).
- Later distinguished ethnologist: Eleanor Leacock, *The Montagnais "Hunting Territory" and the Fur Trade*, American Anthropological Association, (Washington 1954). David Riches, *Northern Nomadic Hunter-Gatherers* (London 1982), 148, calls her work "meticulous," and continues, "Leacock's achievement was to

demonstrate conclusively that the existence of the family trapping territory was in fact a post-contact phenomenon, associated with the European-introduced trading economy."

- "never had the band": Edward S. Rogers and Eleanor Leacock, "Montagnais-Naskapi," in *Handbook of North American Indians*, vol. 6, *Subarctic*, June Helm, ed., (Washington 1981), 181. See also Eleanor B. Leacock and Nan A. Rothschild, eds., *Labrador Winter: The Ethnographic Journals of William Duncan Strong, 1927–1928* (Washington 1984). Richard B. Lee, "Reflections on Primitive Communism," in Tim Ingold, David Riches, and James Woodburn, eds., *Hunters and Gatherers 1* (Oxford 1988) (a work dedicated to the memory of Glyn Isaac and Eleanor Leacock) discusses the reluctance of scholars to use the term, although it "was a perfectly acceptable concept in the nineteenth century and well into the twentieth." (252–53). "The American ethnologist Frank Speck 'discovered' the aboriginal 'family hunting territory' among the northern Algonquians (1915), a view which prevailed until Eleanor Leacock's . . . demonstration that the family hunting territory was a later arrival . . . a product of the fur trade." (260) *Hunters and Gatherers 2* (1991) includes lengthy sections on property rights, equality, and domination among hunter-gatherer societies.

238 The older traditional view of the Iroquoian people as an amalgamation of several peoples is expressed in Martin, Quimby, and Collier, *Indians Before Columbus*, 257–58. The Owasco culture, where remains offering some identity with historical Iroquoians first appear, was later dated as emerging A.D. 500–700: Willey, *Introduction to American Archaeology*, fig. 5-3, 251, and 310. Phonetic studies indicate Iroquoian people may have been in their historic homeland as long as four millennia: Floyd G. Lounsbury, *Handbook* 15, 336.

- Smith is quoted from Hodge, *Handbook* 2, 653.
- Wood, *New Englands Prospect*.
- The Cartier report is from Pinkerton's *Voyages*, 12:653. Cartier was at the time on the way to Hochelaga, later identified as an Iroquois town.
- The Five Nations farms: William N. Fenton, *Handbook* 15, 298.

239 Comments on the hardships of Indian life were by no means limited to the Iroquois. For a typical picture of the squalor, filth, and privation among the Montagnais, see *Jesuit Relations* (henceforward *JR*) 45, Document 170.

- For a story of daily cannibal dinners, and preparation for a glorious cannibal feast, see C.C. Trowbridge, *Meearmeear Traditions* (Ann Arbor 1938), 75–76: Trowbridge was secretary to the American territorial governor of Michigan in the early 1800s (Lewis Cass) and writing of the Seneca. The authoritative *Handbook* 15, however, while listing the Trowbridge material, presents only two mentions of cannibalism for the entire region, both religious and ritualistic.
- Cannibalistic Sung Dynasty restaurants are described from Jacques Gernet, *Daily Life in China on the Eve of the Mongol Invasion 1250–1276* (Paris 1959, English translation by H.M. Wright, New York 1962, quoted here from the English edition of 1971), 135, citing *Chi le pien, Shuo fu* XXVII, f. 14a-b.
- Work of 1851: Francis de Castelnau, *Expedition dans . . . l'Amérique du Sud*, 6 vols. (Paris 1850–1851), quoted in J.G. Frazer, *The Native Races of America*, Robert Angus Downie, ed. (London 1939), 300.
- Frazer is quoted from Stanley Edgar Hyman, *The Tangled Bank: Darwin, Marx, Frazer and Freud as Imaginative Writers* (New York 1962), 272.

- Recent debate on cannibalism: "Anthropologists Suggest Cannibalism Is a Myth," *Science*, vol. 232 (20 June 1986), 1497; and Bruce Bower, "The Cannibal's Signature," *Science News* 143 (January 2, 1993), 12–14.
240 "evil people": Pinkerton's *Voyages*, vol. 12.
- Wood, *New Englands Prospect*.
- The story of Aharihon: Wallace, *Death and Rebirth of the Seneca*, 31–33.
- Best early ethnography": Lafitau, *Moeurs des Sauvages Ameriquains*, 1:290.
241 Structure and operation of the Five Nations: Elisabeth Tooker, "The League of the Iroquois," in *Handbook* 15. See also James W. Bradley, *Evolution of the Onondaga Iroquois: Accommodating Change, 1500–1655* (Syracuse 1987).
243 The illustration of Patuxet, from Champlain's, *Voyages* (1613), is reproduced in Samuel Eliot Morison, *Samuel de Champlain, Father of New France* (Boston 1972), 65.
- Champlain's victory over "Mohawks": ibid., 110–14. Champlain's drawing of the engagement carries the caption, "Two chiefs killed and one wounded from one arquebus shot by the Sieur de Champlain." Jean Jacques de Waldhausen, *L'Art Militaire* (1615), gives a manual of arms for the musketeer (the musket being an improved arquebus)—in which applying the match and leveling the weapon runs to a count of fifty-seven by the time of firing. Reloading required a major delay. To go through the prolonged operation of firing three times to bring down the three chiefs might well seem to demand too much patient cooperation from the targets. Morison questions the effect of this alleged incident on future Iroquois policy (111). The description of the enemy camp—two hundred men in a stockaded campsite—also sounds a peculiar ring.
245 A different story on the derivation of "Huron" related it to "hure"—a boar's head or any striking head of hair, supposedly from the Huron (and Iroquois) occasional style of roached hair: *JR* 16:229–31.
- The number of Iroquois captives burned by the Hurons in 1639: Hunt, *Wars of the Iroquois*, 73, citing *JR* 15:185–87 and 17:63–77.
- "Did I not hope": Father Barthelemy Vimont's Relation for 1642, *JR* 22:255.
- Huron population estimates: Hunt, *Wars of the Iroquois*, 40.
- Plague losses: ibid.,188, n3.
246 "It was politic": ibid.,165, citing Governor Dubois d'Auvergne to the Minister, August 4, 1663, from *New-York Colonial Documents* 9:13.
- Guns: Hunt, *Wars of the Iroquois*, 90, discussing larger estimates in Louise Phelps Kellogg, *The French Regime in Wisconsin and the Northwest* (Madison, Wisconsin 1925), 85.
- Conrad E. Heidenreich, "Huron," in *Handbook* 15: "Prior to the late 1630s, when both the motives and methods of Iroquoian warfare changed as a result of the fur trade, warfare was largely motivated by blood revenge, the gaining of personal prestige, and to some extent religious ideals. Wars for hunting rights or territorial gains were not fought prior to the 1640s." (385) Hunt also makes a case for the first introduction of real war on the Old World model (in the Northeast at least) as an adjunct of European trade (20–22), reiterating Charles H. McIlwain in his introduction to Peter Wraxall, *An Abridgement of the Indian Affairs . . . Transacted in the Colony of New York, from the Year 1678 to the Year 1751*, C.H. McIlwain, ed. (Cambridge, Massachusetts 1915)—as have a number of other writers on the subject.

247 Population figures are based on Hunt, *Wars of the Iroquois*, 66; and J.N.B. Hewitt in Hodge, *Handbook*, 1:430–31.

248 The *Jesuit Relations* for 1656 and 1660 mention that the Five Nations people were a minority in their own towns.

• William Hand Brown, Aubrey C. Land, et al., eds., *Proceedings of the Council of Maryland, 1636–1667*, vol. 3, *Archives of Maryland* (Baltimore 1883 et seq.), 499, covers Maryland's efforts in the "matter of so great consequence"—a peace between the Susquehannas and Senecas (June 7, 1664). Maryland's deal with the Iroquois and abandonment of the Susquehanna: ibid., 2:378.

249 A single cause for these wars is no longer acceptable, but the fur trade nevertheless remains a most important and complex factor: "Too much attention in Canadian history to priests and officials, too little to traders and their employees. Traders studied Indian ways and forged alliances . . ." (Bruce G. Trigger, *Natives and Newcomers: Canada's "Heroic Age" Reconsidered* (Kingston, Ontario 1985), 341.

• "land of souls": Onaiondiont, Huron emissary to the Susquehannock in 1647, his words intended as propaganda and instead truly prophetic: *JR*, 38:67.

250 Governor Andros' remark: Osgood, *American Colonies in the Seventeenth Century*, 3:408.

• Francis Jennings, *The Ambiguous Iroquois Empire: The Covenant Chain Confederation of Indian Tribes with English Colonies* (New York 1984) has much to say of the "multiparty confederation" of the Covenant Chain, organized either in 1677 at the treaty of the Iroquois with Massachusetts and Connecticut, or in 1744 with the Onondaga "Chief" Canassatego, or possibly in 1674. Stephen Saunders Webb, *1676, The End of American Independence* (New York 1984) decides on 1675–1677 for the "forging," by Governor Andros and the Onondaga sachem Daniel Garacontie.

• The French administrator: Jean Talon in 1667, quoted in Hunt, *Wars of the Iroquois*, 138.

• Big Mouth is quoted from Louis Armand, baron de Lahontan, *New Voyages to North America*, Reuben Gold Thwaites, ed., 2 vols. (Chicago 1905), 1:82. Lahontan is also witness for the displeasure of the French governor, Lefebre La Barre.

251 The Jesuit accolade: *JR*, 44:149.

• The ennobled French frontiersman was Charles Le Moyne, called by the Iroquois The Partridge, father of the famous Iberville and Bienville.

• The councilors returned from the galleys: Pierre F. X. Charlevoix, *Historie et Description Générale de la Nouvelle France*, 3 vols. (Paris 1744) 1:509. Pierre Margry, ed., Mémoires et Documents Pour Servir à l'Histoire des Origines Françaises des Pays d'Outre-Mer—Découvertes et Etablissements des Français dans l'Ouest et dans le Sud de l'Amérique Septentrionale (1679–1754), 6 vols. (Paris 1879–1888) provides a list of twenty-one ordered released by the king. They had been held for four years, says Jacques Boulenger, in a work of 1912 published in English in 1963 as *The Seventeenth Century in France*, 342.

• "a dirty troupe": Lafitau, *Moeurs des Sauvages*, I:478–80.

• The governor of New York is quoted from MacLeod, *American Indian Frontier*, Appendix 8, 556, citing O'Callaghan, *Documentary History*, 3:595.

• The Albany commissioners: MacLeod, *American Indian Frontier*. The Pennsylvania secretary: ibid., quoted from McIlwain's Introduction to Wraxall, *Indian Affairs*, xxxvi. The French missionary recording the same thing is the Jesuit historian Charlevoix, *Letters to the Duchess of Lesdiguieres*, entry for June 1721.

- There has been some objection to the view of the Iroquois as king of the hill (Jennings, *Ambiguous Iroquois Empire*, 20), but the quarrel would seem to be with these contemporary sources. This view remains in present day studies: Elisabeth Tooker, *Handbook* 15, "As both France and England knew, their contest for control of the North American continent ultimately would be decided by the choice the Iroquois made between them." (418) The view also remains in studies focused on the continent as a whole: at the end of the seventeenth century "events in North America were dominated less by the European colonial powers, France, England, and Spain, than by the Five Nations Iroquois Confederacy." W.J. Eccles, *France in America* (New York 1972), 90.

252   The recall of nearly all French traders from the forests ruined Nicolas Perrot, a bitter experience bitterly related in his Memoir edited by Emma H. Blair in *Indian Tribes of the Upper Mississippi Valley and Region of the Great Lakes*, 2 vols. (Cleveland 1911–1912). The order, issued in Paris on May 26, 1696, reached the remote Canadian beaver country in 1698. While recognizing factors such as Iroquoian politics, the increasing number of outlaw *coureurs de bois*, the Jesuit party and the anti-Jesuit party, Fénelon's influence on Madame de Maintenon is given the chief role by Clarence W. Alvord, *The Illinois Country, 1673–1818* (Springfield, Illinois 1920), 104–9.

- "they were of us": *Documents Relative to the Colonial History . . . of New York*, Edmund B. O'Callaghan and Berthold Fernow, eds., 10 vols. (Albany 1853–1858), vol. 11, General Index, and vols. 12–15 (Albany 1881–1887); 5:376.

- "An old Mohawk sachem": Cadwallader Colden, *The History of the Five Indian Nations of Canada*, 3rd ed., 2 vols. (London 1755) 1:4.

- The Dutch pastor: "Johannes Megapolensis, Jr.," *A Short Sketch of the Mohawk Indians in New Netherland* (1644, reprinted in the Collections of the New-York Historical Society, 2nd Series, vol. 3, part 1, New York 1857). The same point is made by Colden: "Their Great Men, both Sachems and Captains, are generally poorer than the common People, for they affect to give away and distribute all the Presents or Plunder they get in their Treaties or War, so as to leave nothing for themselves. If they should once be suspected of Selfishness, they would grow mean in the Opinion of their Country-men, and would consequently lose their Authority." (New York edition of 1727, xvi)

253   Lafitau, *Moeurs des Sauvages Ameriquains*, from the dedication to the duc d'Orleans, and from 1:72. Again, Colden echoes the identical observation (Introductory Epistle to General Oglethorpe, vi).

- "You see the footprints": adapted from "At the Wood's Edge," the welcoming ceremony opening the "Ancient Rites of the Condoling Council" in Horatio Hale, *The Iroquois Book of Rites* (Philadelphia 1883).

Chapter 19

257   "with some slaughter" and "they were taken away": Osgood, *American Colonies in the Seventeenth Century*, 3:261 and 262, which adds that the Maryland commander "escaped with a light sentence."

258   Berkeley enraged: *Force Tracts* (*Tracts and Other Papers Relating to the History of America*, collected by Peter Force, Washington 1836 t.seq.), vol. 1.

- Woodrow Wilson, *History of the American People* (1902), 1:269.
- "The Indians, our neighbours": Osgood, loc.cit.
- Jefferson is quoted from his preface to *The Beginning, Progress, and Conclusion of Bacon's Rebellion in Virginia, in the Years 1675 and 1676* (Richmond, Virginia *Enquirer*, 1st, 5th, and 8th September 1804, reprinted in *Force Tracts*, vol. 1.)
- Recent scholars: Stephen Saunders Webb, *1676, The End of American Independence* (New York 1984) sees the Rebellion as very American. The *chef de file* of the opposition has been Wilcomb E. Washburn ever since *The Governor and the Rebel: A History of Bacon's Rebellion in Virginia* (Chapel Hill 1957).

260 The story of Sylvanus is from "A Narrative of the Capture of Mrs. Johnson," in John Frost, ed., *Indian Battles, Captivities, and Adventures* (New York 1856).

- Governor Keift offered scalp bounties in 1641 (MacLeod, *American Indian Frontier*, 223). Drake, *Indians of North America*, mentions that the Puritan soldiers who were in at King Philip's death were being paid (their only wages) thirty shillings for each enemy death or capture. MacLeod gives the scale of Massachusetts scalp bounties (244 n1), and those of Pennsylvania for 1756 and following years. (400–2)
- The murder of the Susquehanna people at Conestoga and its political background are the subject of a study by Wilbur R. Jacobs, *The Paxton Riots and the Frontier Theory* (Chicago 1967).
- Bounties on Beothuk heads or scalps: Jenness, *Indians of Canada*, 266; their extinction is described in Hodge, *Handbook*, 1:142.

261 "after the Indian manner": "Narrative of the Long Walk by John Watson, Father and Son, Communicated to the Historical Committee of the American Philosophical Society, Philadelphia, in 1822," reprinted from Hazard's *Register of Pennsylvania* (Philadelphia, October 9, 1830) in Beach, *Indian Miscellany*, 90–101. The account was written in 1815 by John Watson Sr., a surveyor, from the testimony and extracts found in deeds and grants used in his work, with added notes provided by the son in 1822 from oral information given him in previous years by one of the three men who undertook, for pay (never received, by the way) to perform the Long Walk.

- Various modern studies include: A.F.C. Wallace, *King of the Delawares: Teedyuscung 1700–1763* (Philadelphia 1949); pages 18–19 of this work summarize a fuller account in P.A.W. Wallace, *Conrad Weiser, 1696–1760: Friend of Colonist and Mohawk* (Philadelphia 1945), 95–99.
- Whole oceans of literature, many uncharted, pitch and toss the Walking Purchase; some accounted good are: Jennings, *Ambiguous Iroquois Empire*, appendix B and chapter 17; Jennings, "The Scandalous Indian Policy of William Penn's Sons, Deeds and Documents of the Walking Purchase," *Pennsylvania History* 37/1 (January 1970); A.F.C. Wallace, *Teedyuscung*, 25–30; Weslager, *Delaware Indians*, 173–91. Various of the accounts vary on various points.

262 Frederick B. Tolles, *James Logan and the Culture of Provincial America* (Boston 1957) mentions the need for charcoal.

- "sharp practice": ibid., 181.
- The later chronicle is the Watson Narrative cited above.
- The principal items of the three hundred pounds' worth of additional goods were 24 guns, 10 dozen knives, 25 pairs of shoes, 25 pairs of stockings, 25 hats, 50 hatchets, 50 hoes, 30 blankets, which together with the goods paid earlier necessitated

the loan of teams, wagons, and drivers to carry it all home. The gratuity was given "as a gesture of friendship, but the Indians knew what they were supposed to do in return" (Weslager, *Delaware Indians*, 190).

- "glowing with liquor": Tolles, *James Logan*, 182.
- Canassatego's speech: Carl Van Doren and Julian P. Boyd, eds., *Indian Treaties Printed by Benjamin Franklin 1736–1762; Their Literary, Historical, and Bibliographical Significance* (Philadelphia 1938). The derogatory use of "women" has enjoyed much exegesis; see for example Herbert C. Kraft, *The Lenape: Archeology, History, and Ethnography* (Newark 1986), 230; and for a recent explanation: Matthew Dennis, Cultivating a Landscape of Peace (1993), 109, n79.

263   Quotations again from the Watson Narrative.

- Drifted on westward: a hundred years later Delaware hunters were some of the most valued members of John C. Frémont's second and third western exploring expeditions.

264   MacLeod, *American Indian Frontier*, 399, lists the Braddock scalp bounties. These were widely publicized in France as a sample of enemy atrocity, a volume of current events added by a French editor, "M. de Grace," to Samuel von Pufendorf, *Introduction à l'Histoire Moderne, Générale et Politique de l'Univers* (Paris 1750), stating that the "action, as contrary to the laws of good politics as to those of justice, made so many enemies for England as there were Savages informed of a so foolhardy and cruel proclamation." (8:604)

- [Charles Thomson], *An Enquiry into the Causes of the Alienation of the Delaware and Shawanese Indians from the British Interest . . .* (London 1759), source of quotes here, is an attack on the Walking Purchase as a sample of the Indian policy of the Proprietary government of Pennsylvania, published in London through the efforts of Benjamin Franklin, who included as an Appendix "The Journal of Christian Fredrick Post, in his Journey from Philadelphia to the Ohio." The story of the embassy to the Ohio Delaware was completed by publication separately, the same year, of *The Second Journal of Christian Frederick Post, on a Message from the Governor of Pensilvania to the Indians on the Ohio* (London 1759).

265   Iroquois invitation of the English into the Ohio country brought violent French reaction and "the French and Indian War was on," argues A.F.W. Wallace, *Death and Rebirth of the Seneca* (New York 1970), 113–14. The basic cause of the war, however, is sometimes seen simply as generalized commercial rivalry: "more than half the goods exported from Cadiz to the Spanish colonies were French in origin, and in 1740 the French obtained commercial privileges in the Turkish empire. Between 1710 and 1741 French trade with her colonies rose from 25 million livres a year, and by 1741 her total overseas trade was estimated to be worth 300 million livres. In contrast, during the decade of the 1730s English overseas trade had remained almost stationary. It seemed that before too long France would overtake England as the leading commercial power, even that England might share the fate it had imposed on the Dutch and be reduced to the status of a third- or fourth-rate power, and by the same means." Eccles, *France in America*, 172–73.

- P.A.W. Wallace, *Conrad Weiser*, quotes a complacent letter from Thomas Penn to John Penn telling of the Long Walk and John's pleased reply saying "you have got the Confirmation of the Delaware Indian's at an easy rate. . . ." to which the author remarks, "The rate seemed less easy after Braddock's defeat." (99)

- Teedyuskung's acceptance of a present of £400 to drop complaints against the Walking Purchase is stated as fact by George P. Donehoo, in Hodge, *Handbook*, 2:714–17, citing *Colonial Records of Pennsylvania*, vols. 6 and 7 (Harrisburg 1851–1853), and *Pennsylvania Archives*, Samuel Hazard, ed., 2nd Series (Harrisburg 1875–1890), and also accepted by Joseph S. Walton, *Conrad Weiser and the Indian Policy of Colonial Pennsylvania* (Philadelphia, c.1900), citing *Colonial Records of Pennsylvania*, vol. 8, 708 and 749–50. A.F.C. Wallace, *Teedyuscung*, points out that matters of supposed bribes and treaties involving Teedyuscung are interwoven in the whole fabric of Pennsylvania politics of the time, Teedyuscung operating as a front man for the Quakers in the conflict between the Quaker faction and the proprietors, which is to say Colonials vs. British. (248)
- "give away their country": George Croghan to Jeffrey Amherst, April 30, 1763, in Wilbur R. Jacobs, *Dispossessing the American Indian* (New York, 1972), 79, citing Bouquet Papers, Public Archives of Canada, Ottawa.
- The exhortation of Neolin is from A.F.W. Wallace, *Death and Rebirth of the Seneca*, 118, quoting excerpts from the so-called Pontiac MS, a manuscript by an unknown author (now believed to be Robert Navarre) presumably based on information from French-Canadians who were present at Indian councils preceding the outbreak of Pontiac's war. The manuscript is the principal source on events leading up to the war. It was used by Francis Parkman, *The Conspiracy of Pontiac and the Indian War after the Conquest of Canada* (Boston 1898), and by Howard H. Peckham, *Pontiac and the Indian Uprising* (Princeton 1947). The Pontiac MS is published in French and English, M. Agnes Burton, ed., *Journal of Pontiac's Conspiracy, 1763* (Detroit 1912), and in English only, Milo M. Quaife, ed., *Journal of Pontiac's Conspiracy, 1763* (Chicago 1958).

266   Land speculators: Clarence W. Alvord, *The Mississippi Valley in British Politics: A Study of the Trade, Land speculation, and Experiments in Imperialism Culminating in the American Revolution*, 2 vols. (Cleveland 1917), 1:186.

- Amherst's suggestion of giving the Indians smallpox by means of infected blankets is mentioned in Jacobs, *Dispossessing the American Indian*, 81, and the reply to Amherst by his field commander, citing *The Papers of Col. Henry Bouquet*, Pennsylvania Historical Survey, (Harrisburg 1940–1943). A.T. Volwiler, ed., "William Trent's Journal at Fort Pitt, 1763," *Mississippi Valley Historical Review* 11/3 (December 1924), quotes the Fort Pitt commander noting that when two Indians appeared from the woods saying they were friends "we gave them two Blankets and an Handkerchief out of the Small Pox Hospital. I hope it will have the desired effect." (400) Could smallpox virus survive in infected blankets to spread the disease? Donald R. Hopkins (an authority on smallpox and former assistant director at the Centers for Disease Control in Atlanta) appears to think so, accepting an account of an outbreak from an infected flag. (Hopkins, *Princes and Peasants: Smallpox in History*, Chicago 1983, 236)
- "I traveld about 140 miles": A.T. Volwiler, *Geroge Croghan and the Westward Movement, 1741–1782* (Cleveland 1926), 164.

268   The report of 1765: Sir William Johnson to the Board of Trade, July 10, 1765: C.W. Alvord and C.E. Carter, *The Critical Period 1763–1765* (Springfield, Illinois 1915), 522–28.

269   Hendrick: Herbert L. Osgood, *The American Colonies in the Eighteenth Century*, 4 vols. (New York 1924), 4:306–7 and 316.

- Johnson's recruitment of brisk allies: William L. Stone, *Life of Joseph Brant—Thayendanegea, Including the Indian Wars of the American Revolution,* 2 vols. (New York 1838), 1:15.
- The valuable presents, actually called £1100 worth: Isabel Thompson Kelsay, *Joseph Brant (1745–1807), Man of Two Worlds* (Syracuse 1984), 60–61.
- Hendrick's supposed remark is quoted in Drake, *Indians of North America,* 536.
270   The quotation attributed to Daniel Boone is found in "The Adventures of Daniel Boone," in Gilbert Imlay, *A Topographical Description of the Western Territory of North America* (London 1797), 340.
- The price paid by Judge Henderson is from Ray A. Billington, *Westward Expansion* 2nd ed. (New York 1967), who adds, "No one paid the slightest attention to the company; the immigrants reasoned that it had obtained possession illegally and they would do the same." (169–73)
271   Reuben Gold Thwaites and Louise P. Kellog, eds, *Documentary History of Lord Dunmore's War, 1774* (Wisconsin Historical Society, Madison, Wisconsin 1905), contains in the introduction the statement, "A study of contemporary documents will convince any fair-minded student of history that Lord Dunmore acted in this episode with disinterested discretion . . ." Frederick Jackson Turner's copy of this work, now in the Huntington Library, San Marino, California, bears beside this statement a marginal note in Turner's hand: "Land spec—bndy question?"
- Quotations about Brant are from Stone, *Life of Brant:* 1:xv-xvi; 1:256 (the proclamation of Benedict Arnold); and Appendix 8.
272   Thomas Campbell is quoted from *Gertrude of Wyoming* (1807).
- Losses at Oriskany "were higher in proportion to men engaged than in any other battle of the war": Bolton and Marshall, *Colonization of North America,* 496.
- Cherry Valley and Wyoming statistics rest on the carefully researched account in A.F.W. Wallace, *Death and Rebirth of the Seneca,* 137–40. This excellent work is based on the story of the Handsome Lake Church.
273   "over the council table": ibid., 149.
- Of lasting importance was the Handsome Lake religion's revival of the Midwinter Ceremony, rites of thanks to the gods: Dean R. Snow, *The Iroquois* (Oxford 1994), 160.
- Son of Brant's: Campbell, *Gertrude of Wyoming.*
- Brant's later noble repute: Kelsay, *Joseph Brant,* 654–58.
- "Yankeys" is Joseph Brant's spelling: Wallace, *Death and Rebirth of the Seneca,* 167, quoting Stone, *Life of Brant,* 275.
274   "Now listen" is adapted from the "Ancient Rites of the Condoling Council," Hale, *Iroquois Book of Rites.*

Chapter 20

275   The numbers of treaties as indicators of the relative importance of Indian nations are especially deceptive—from 1778 to 1820 there were eight American treaties with various of the Six Nations, as against thirteen with the "Pottawatimies": *American Indian Frontier* in *Statutes at Large of the United States,* vol. 7. Dorothy V. Jones, *License for Empire: Colonialism by Treaty in Early America* (Chicago 1982): treaties set the course "for the social disaster that followed" (186).

- Washington is quoted from a message to the Senate, August 22, 1789: J.C. Fitzpatrick, ed., *The Writings of George Washington* (Washington 1939), 30:505.
- The 1790 treaty with the Creeks became the subject of comment by Thomas Jefferson, in relation to its force as law, and a subject in the classic legal analysis of the Constitution, *Story on the Constitution*. H.A. Washington, ed., *The Writings of Thomas Jefferson* (Washington 1854), 6:557–80, and 505n; and Joseph Story, *Commentaries on the Constitution of the United States*, 5th ed., Melville W. Bigelow, ed., (Boston 1905), 2:609.
- The agent (actually Deputy Agent) was Major Caleb Swan, quoted here and in the two following paragraphs from Schoolcraft, *Indian Tribes*, 5:258.

278   Yahou-Lakee is quoted from *Force Tracts*, vol. 6.
- Long King: ibid.
- "where the Savannah bends": Carolyn Thomas Foreman, *Indians Abroad* (Norman 1943), 57.

279   Florida missions: John R. Swanton, *The Early History of the Creek Indians and Their Neighbors*, BAE Bulletin 73 (Washington 1924); W. Lowery, *The Spanish Settlements Within the Present Limits of the United States*, 2 vols. (New York 1901 and 1905), vol. 2; MacLeod, *American Indian Frontier*, 104–6.
- Statistics on the 1704 raid are from Swanton, *Creek Indians*, 123. This raid was reported in England, Spain, and France, with varying statistics, and even reached the French-language republican-propaganda journal published in Holland under various titles, *L'Esprit de Cours de l'Europe, Nouvelles des Cours de l'Europe*.
- Foreign slaves freed: *Recopilacion de Leyes de los Reinos de las Indias . . .* 5th ed. (Madrid 1841), Ley 5, tit.2, lib.3 of A.D. 1550.

280   Wrongs suffered by the Tuscarora, particularly enslavement of children, are detailed in their petition to Pennsylvania in 1710, *Pennsylvania Provincial Council, Minutes*, 16 vols. (Philadelphia and Harrisburg, 1852–1853), 2:511, summarized in Hodge, *Handbook*, 2:843–84. Indian enslavement in general in the South: J. Leitch Wright Jr., *The Only Land They Knew: The Tragic Story of the American Indians in the Old South* (New York 1981).
- "We look upon them with disdain": John Lawson, *A New Voyage to Carolina* (London 1709). Also see Lawson, *History of Carolina* (London 1714; Raleigh, North Carolina 1860).

281   "great service": Swanton, *Indian Tribes*, 99 and 103. The people driven away by the Shawnee are usually called the Westo, believed by Swanton a part of the Yuchi.
- Charleston cargoes: Pinkerton, *Voyages*, 12:345. Contemporary estimates for 1734 give South Carolina 15,000 whites, 22,000 blacks, and North Carolina for 1732, 30,000 whites, 6,000 blacks: Channing, *History of the United States*, 2:366.

282   Prospectus of 1717: Sir Robert Montgomery, *A Discourse concerning the design'd Establishement of a New Colony to the South of Carolina, in the Most Delightful Country of the Universe*, in *Force Tracts*, vol. 1.
- "In America": "The Colony of Georgia under James Oglethorpe, Feb. 1, 1733," in *Force Tracts*, vol. 6.
- Jonathan Daniels, *The Devil's Backbone, The Story of the Natchez Trace* (New York 1962), 23, takes seriously the importance of the Battle of Ackia, a claim made by Adair, *History of the American Indians*.

283 "humorsome": Washington to Lieutenant-Governor Robert Dinwiddie of Virginia, September 1756, in Dinwiddie, *Official Records*, R.O. Brock, ed., (Richmond 1883–1884), 2:669–71.

• The Creek embassy: Foreman, *Indians Abroad*, 56 and 63.

284 The eighteenth-century list of goods "proper for the savages" is from Lahontan, *New Voyages to North America*.

• Benjamin Franklin, *Two Tracts: Information to Those Who Would Remove to America, and Remarks Concerning the Savages of North America*, 3rd ed. (London 1784). In this pamphlet Franklin says of the Indians, "Having few artificial wants, they have abundance of leisure for improvement by conversation. Our laborious manner of life compared with theirs, they esteem slavish and base; and the learning on which we value ourselves, they regard as frivolous and useless."

• Chickasaw and Choctaw horse talk is from Robert West Howard, *The Horse in America* (Chicago 1965), 26–27 and 184.

285 "there came a Coweta fellow": William L. McDowell Jr., ed., *Colonial Records of South Carolina* (Columbia, South Carolina 1958), "Documents relating to Indian Affairs, May 21, 1750–August 7, 1754, Report of Ludwick Grant to Governor Glen, February 8, 1755."

• "counterpoise": Richard Maxwell Brown, *The South Carolina Regulators* (Cambridge, Massachusetts 1963), 2. The South Carolina population of 1760 was 36,740 white, 94,074 black: from "Reports of Colonial Officials to Lords Commissioners of Trade and Plantation," *Historical Statistics of the United States, Colonial Times to 1957*, U.S. Bureau of the Census (Washington 1960), Z 1–19, 743 and 750.

• There were several Fort Loudouns: in Winchester, Virginia; on Conococheague Creek, Pennsylvania; and the fort here mentioned, which a force from South Carolina had built only three years earlier, in 1757.

286 Brown, *South Carolina Regulators*, 135–36: "Respectable, honest settlers dedicated to the establishment of law and order and the inviolability of property" seemed to make up the core of the regulators.

• "most of the low People": ibid., 184 n 35, citing Richard J. Hooker, ed., *The Carolina Backcountry on the Eve of the Revolution: The Journal and other Writings of Charles Woodmason, Anglican Itinerant* (Chapel Hill 1953), 10.

• The low people defined as "idle persons," etc.: Brown, *South Carolina Regulators*, 50.

• The Regulator-Rangers killed or executed many outlaws in the field; a "few more criminals were killed in skirmishes": ibid., 46. But the author had seen only one reference to undeputized "Regulator 'lynching.'" (137)

• Osgood, *American Colonies in the Eighteenth Century*, says Mary Matthews had given help to the colony of Georgia of value even beyond that "rendered by Pocahontas to the early settlers of Virginia." (3:402)

• Pushmataha is quoted (attributively, anyway) from Daniels, *The Devil's Backbone*, 188. (Pushmataha's sister married a Frenchman—their daughter, a "high-up lady," Rebecca Cravat, married Louis LeFleur; one of the eleven children born to them was Greenwood LeFleur, better known as LeFlore, very prominent in later Choctaw politics.)

• Among the important half-blood families: Colbert (Chickasaw), Folsom and LeFlore (Choctaw), McGillivray, McIntosh, Tait (Creek), Ross, Vann, Hicks, Lowry, and McCoy (Cherokee)—as listed by Robert S. Cotterill, *The Southern Indians: The Story of the Civilized Tribes Before Removal* (Norman 1954).

- "they have the French": *Colonial Records of South Carolina*, loc.cit.
- Mary A. O'Callaghan, "An Indian Removal Policy in Spanish Louisiana," in *Greater America: Essays in Honor of Herbert Eugene Bolton* (Berkeley 1945), outlines Indian movement across the Mississippi after 1763.
- Colonel Anthony Hutchins arrived at Natchez in 1772 and built his house on the White Apple Mound: Daniels, *The Devil's Backbone*, 27. The family of Joseph Williams, father of the famous mountain man Old Bill Williams, moved to the Spanish side of the river at this time, as did Daniel Boone, Moses Austin, and many other frontier Americans: Alpheus H. Favour, *Old Bill Williams, Mountain Man* (Norman 1963, originally Chapel Hill 1936), 4.

288 The bawdy song: Tom Hatley, *The Dividing Paths: Cherokees and South Carolinians Through the Era of Revolution* (Oxford 1993), 151–52.

289 Quotations referring to the Cherokee: Sigourney, *Aborigines of America*, Notes.

- McGillivray's difficulties: J. Leitch Wright, Jr., "Creek-American Treaty of 1790: Alexander McGillivray and the Diplomacy of the Old Southwest," *Georgia Historical Quarterly* 51/4 (December 1967). John Walton Caughey, *McGillivray of the Creeks* (Norman 1938), deals with Spanish efforts to turn the Creeks against the Georgians and Americans and get the 1790 treaty set aside (337–39), efforts that, says Caughey, "did not get far." (51) Mary Elizabeth Young, *Redskins, Ruffleshirts, and Rednecks, Indian Allotments in Alabama and Mississippi, 1830–1860* (Norman 1961) points out that McGillivray was the last principal half-blood Creek leader: "Where half-blood town chiefs exercised more than local influence, they wielded it through full blood chieftains." (35)
- J. Leitch Wright Jr., *William Augustus Bowles, Director General of the Creek Nation* (Athens, Georgia 1967), deals with Bowles' career and his fantasies thereof. William C. Sturtevant, "The Cherokee Frontier, The French Revolution, and William Augustus Bowles," in Duane H. King, ed., *The Cherokee Indian Nation: A Troubled History* (Knoxville 1979), gives an anthropologist's view of the Bowles story.

Chapter 21

290 McGillivray "tried during the last decade of his life to prepare the Creek Nation for its battle for survival with the United States": Michael D. Green, *The Politics of Indian Removal* (Lincoln, Nebraska 1982), 36.

- "the extraordinary step": E.J. Cashin, *Lachlan MacGillivray* . . . (Athens, Georgia 1992), 290.
- McGillivray's Creek name was said to be *Hoboi-Hili-Miko* (Good Child King): Caughey, *McGillivray*, 3. His birthdate rests on a mention in John Pope, *A Tour through the Southern and Western Territories of North America* (Richmond, Virginia 1792), 48.
- $48,000: David H. Usner Jr., "American Indians on the Cotton Frontier: Changing Economic Relations with Citizens and Slaves, in the Mississippi Territory," *Journal of American History* 72/2 (September 1985), 203.

291 "primitive honesty": Cotterill, *Southern Indians*, 159.

- Jackson is quoted from Anonymous, *Daring Deeds of American Heroes* (New York 1860), 244.

292 Charlton W. Tebeau, *A History of Florida* (Coral Gables 1971): Negro Fort was established by a British force in 1814, on the east bank of the river, at Prospect Bluff. The British stayed until the summer of 1815, and provided cannon, arms, and ammunition to the Indians and fugitive slaves who gathered there. "The banditti caused much alarm on the Georgia frontier and made travel on the river hazardous." Jackson demanded of the Spanish governor at Pensacola, April 1816, that the fort be broken up; the reply was unsatisfactory so he ordered "the fort destroyed and the Negroes returned to their owners." The explosion of the magazine killed 270 of 344 occupants. John Lee Williams, *The Territory of Florida* (New York 1837), 110: the fort was destroyed on August 27, 1816; gunboats 149 and 154 being fired on, they returned fire, and "on the fifth discharge, a hot shot from gunboat No. 154 entered the magazine, and blew up the fort. . . . The negro force had been rapidly increasing for one to two years, from runaways: their fields extended fifty miles up the river." (201–3)

293 Annie Heloise Abel, "The History of Events Resulting in Indian Consolidations West of the Mississippi," *Annual Report of the American Historical Association for the Year 1906*, vol. 1 (Washington 1908), gives a cool and careful look at Jefferson's notions in respect to Indian removal. (241–59) The idea of Indian colonies in the much-criticized Louisiana purchase is discussed in the same work. (270–75) Jefferson's opponents "denounced and ridiculed" the Louisiana Purchase "in the most unmeasured way," in the phraseology of a historian of Abel's time: James K. Hosman, *The History of the Louisiana Purchase* (New York 1902), 148–49.

- Arthur H. De Rosier, *The Removal of the Choctaw Indians* (Knoxville 1970), speaks of Jefferson's excuse of national security in Indian removal—and the fact that he did not alter his policy when the ostensible security emergency had passed—and the "even more odious aspect" of his recommended method for obtaining Indian lands. (25–28)

294 Lewis Cass is quoted from Francis Paul Prucha, *Lewis Cass and American Indian Policy* (Detroit 1967), 15.

- "we may secure a part": De Rosier, *Removal of the Choctaw Indians*, 60, citing a letter to John C. Calhoun, then secretary of war, while preparing for the huge Choctaw cession of 1820.

- "private" group: Francis Paul Prucha, "Thomas L. McKenney and the New York Indian Board," *Mississippi Valley Historical Review* 47 (March 1962), 637. Prucha, in "Thomas L. McKenney," accepts the pro forma excuse of Jackson and his advisers as the true motive for removal; most specialists in the subject reach opposite conclusions. Wilcomb E. Washburn, "The Writing of American Indian History: A Status Report," *Pacific Historical Review* 40/3 (August 1971), greets Father Prucha's thesis with "incredulity."

- Richard M. Johnson built a Choctaw Academy on his own plantation at Blue Springs, Kentucky: Samuel J. Wells, "Federal Indian Policy: From Accommodation to Removal," in Carolyn Keller Reeves, ed., *The Choctaw Before Removal* (Jackson, Mississippi 1985), 205.

- Jedidiah Morse, *Report to the Secretary of War* (New Haven 1822), 10–14 and 93–95.

295   Three missions turning into twenty-five: Cotterill, *Southern Indians*, 227.

- Choctaw black and white census figures: De Rosier, *Removal of the Choctaw Indians*, 126.

- In the early eighteenth century the Mohawk people had refused to surrender an indentured servant who had escaped to their country, although they were willing to pay his "Value . . . to his Master." Colden, *History of the Five Indian Nations*, 1:13.

- "convert their country": De Rosier, *Removal of the Choctaw Indians*, 91.

296   "galled and butchered": Avery O. Craven, *Soil Exhaustion as a Factor in the Agricultural History of Virginia and Maryland, 1606–1860* (Urbana, Illinois 1926), 90–91. Craven continues: "exhausted and abandoned lands behind the advancing frontier were but a counterpoint to the mineral waste and charred stumps in the train of the exploiter of mineral wealth or of virgin forest." (22)

- Frank L. Owsley, "The Pattern of Migration and Settlement on the Southern Frontier," *Journal of Southern History* 11 (May 1945), finds that until the annexation of Oregon the open land area in the South was twice as great as that of the North, while the white population was less than half. (148–49)

- "encourage immigration": De Rosier, *Removal of the Choctaw Indians*, 107.

- Paul Wallace Gates, *The Farmer's Age: Agriculture 1815–1860* (New York 1960), writes that pioneering in the new cotton areas of the Old Southeast ("rich planters with their scores of slaves clearing the forests,") differed from the typical "frontier" image. (140) He adds, "the great profits in agriculture came not from tillage but from buying virgin land cheaply, improving and selling it while its fertility was still rich." (143)

- Cass is quoted in Prucha, *Lewis Cass*, 13.

297   Policy of the new United States toward the Scioto Land Company is weighed and found wanting in Abel, "Indian Consolidations West of the Mississippi," 265–67.

- John C. Calhoun remarked that almost every man in the country who had any cash or credit was engaged in land speculation: James Parton, *Life of Andrew Jackson* (1859–1860), 3:453.

- John Spencer Bassett, ed., *Correspondence of Andrew Jackson* (Washington 1928–1929), sums up Jackson's character in his preface to volume 3: "He was nearly incapable of seeing any side of a question but that on which he had ranged himself." (3:xv) Jackson's mid-nineteenth-century biographer, James Parton, assessing Jackson's weaknesses: "No man in this country has ever been subjected to such a torrent of applause, and few men have been less prepared to withstand it." (Parton, *Jackson*, 3:639)

- Jackson as a treaty commissioner: Cotterill, *Southern Indians*, 204, 202, 165, and 206. See also De Rosier, *Removal of the Choctaw Indians*, 63 and 69. The Benjamin Hawkins letters denouncing Jackson as a treaty commissioner are all missing from the files of the secretary of war's office, although they are listed, with brief summaries, in the register of letters received. "That these letters were deliberately removed is certain." (Frank Lawrence Owsley Jr., *Struggle for the Gulf Borderlands: The Creek War and the Battle of New Orleans 1812–1815*, Gainesville, Florida 1981, 90n.)

- Jackson is quoted from Bassett, *Correspondence*, 3:88.

- The Mississippi thanks and gifts to the Choctaw are detailed in *Chronicles of Oklahoma* 6/4 (1928), 481–82. The 1816 promise of everlasting friendship: De Rosier, *Removal of the Choctaw Indians*, 17.

298 "prime cotton land": Florette Henri, *The Southern Indians and Benjamin Hawkins, 1797–1816* (Norman 1986), 302. See also Joel W. Martin, *Sacred Revolt: The Muskogee Struggle for a New World* (Boston 1991).

· Choctaw details: De Rosier, *Removal of the Choctaw Indians*, 36; Cotterill, *Southern Indians*, 183–84 and 190; Bassett, *Correspondence*, 2:73–74.

299 *Speeches on the Passage of the bill for the Removal of the Indians, Delivered in the Congress of the United States, April and May, 1830* (Boston 1830), viii. Thomas Hart Benton, *Abridgement of the Debates of Congress from 1789 to 1836*, 16 vols. (New York 1860) gives, in volume 10, speeches on both sides of the Removal bill. Speakers are typically aligned by party rather than by North and South; for example, Woods of Ohio and Smith of Indiana, one against and one for the "emigration" of the Indians, speaking successively, February 18 and 19, 1828.

· Famous anti-Removal speech: *Abridgement of Debates*, 10:526. William Lloyd Garrison, editor of the Baltimore paper *The Genius of Universal Emancipation*, had been fined $50 and costs for libel, having published an attack on a slave-ship owner from Newburyport, Massachusetts (Garrison's home town). Garrison, of course, chose to go to jail rather than pay the fine, and entered Baltimore City Jail on April 7, 1830—the day Senator Frelinghuysen began his speech. (Russell B. Nye, *William Lloyd Garrison and the Humanitarian Reformers*, Boston 1955, 28–29.)

· Pro-Removal Congressional maneuvering: Wells, "Federal Indian Policy," 203.

· McKenney's Indian Board "was soon joined by other proremoval forces consisting mainly of southern congressmen." (ibid., 202)

301 Evasion by "obvious" and "overwhelming" fraud of an article permitting individual Choctaws to enroll as allottees and remain in their homeland is detailed in De Rosier, *Removal of the Choctaw Indians*, 136–37.

· The story of Emubby's murder is one of many related in Grant Foreman, *Indian Removal: The Emigration of the Five Civilized Tribes* (Norman 1932, 1953).

· Appeal after appeal: Thomas L. McKenney, *Memoirs Official and Personal; with Sketches of Travels among the Northern and Southern Indians*, 2 vols. in one (New York 1846), 1:254.

302 Quotations on Southern dissent and ethnocentricity: De Rosier, *Removal of the Choctaw Indians*, 105–6 and 108.

· Bribes to Greenwood LeFlore and other chiefs: ibid., 114 and 125.

· The "hot-gospel" motto: Young, *Redskins, Ruffleshirts, and Rednecks*, 28–29.

303 "In the woods, saloons and gambling tables were set up inside tents, and plenty of *Okahomi*, an alcoholic drink, was available." But "there could be no missionaries on the treaty grounds" (Robert B. Ferguson, "Treaties between the United States and the Choctaw Nation," in Reeves, *The Choctaw Before Removal*, 221). See also De Rosier, *Removal of the Choctaw Indians*, 120–21.

· "literally in mourning": Muriel H. Wright, "The Removal of the Choctaws to Indian Territory," *Chronicles of Oklahoma*, 6/2 (1928).

305 Washington Irving is quoted from his note "for the Conspiracy of Neamathla," 1833, MS, Huntington Library. His published sketch is found in *Wolfert's Roost and Other Papers* (New York 1863).

· "The Chickasaws have": Foreman, *Indian Removal*, quoting from Irving, *Wolfert's Roost*.

306 "Among the Creeks": D.W. Eakins, quoted in Schoolcraft, *Indian Tribes*, 1:277.

307 Creek quotes: Foreman, *Indian Removal*, 113 and 108, n 7.

- The U.S. marshal: ibid., 154.
- Wording of the Georgia Compact: S.G. McLendon, *History of the Public Domain of Georgia* (Atlanta 1924), 112.

308 Article Two of the Creek treaty of 1790 stipulated that the "Creek nation will not hold any treaty with an individual State" (Charles L. Kappler, *Indian Affairs: Laws and Treaties*, 3 vols. (Washington 1904), 2:25), thus specifically prohibiting state jurisdiction for the Creek nation.

- Foreman, *Indian Removal*, 251, citing the Memorial and Protest of the Cherokee Nation to Congress, June 21, 1836: "Joseph Vann was a prosperous Cherokee" with a large plantation—800 acres under cultivation and a costly brick mansion. "On the pretence that he had violated a law of Georgia by employing a white man to oversee his farm while he was absent from home, his property was seized in December, 1833."
- The story of Corn Tassel: Marquis James, *The Life of Andrew Jackson* (Indianapolis 1938), 580–82 and 603. Georgia versus the Supreme Court: Carl Brent Fisher, *American Constitutional Development* (Boston 1943), 87.

309 *Worcester v. Georgia* decision (1832): Henry Steele Commager, ed., *Documents of American History* (New York 1949), 259.

310 Jackson is quoted from McKenney, *Memoirs*, 1:258–59; Parton, *Jackson*, 3:283, quoting a toast delivered by President Jackson at the Jefferson Day Dinner of 1830; and Bassett, *Correspondence*, 4:504 (an extract from a letter to Martin Van Buren of December 23, 1832), and 4:498.

- Frances Trollope is quoted from *The Domestic Manners of the Americans* (1832).
- Hardeman Owen: Foreman, *Indian Removal*, 251–52 (the name spelled Hardiman).

311 Frauds and floats: Green, *Politics of Indian Removal*, 184.

- Creek "War" of 1836, and General Jesup's orders: ibid., 184–85, quoting the *Montgomery Advertiser's* contemporary suspicion of "a humbug," from Foreman, *Indian Removal*, 147. Green cites the "best analysis of the 1836 'War'" as Kenneth L. Valliere, *Chronicles of Oklahoma*, 57 (1979–1980).
- Eneah Emathla: Foreman, *Indian Removal*, 153.

312 The major cause of suffering seemed to come from a murderous shortage of supplies—blankets, clothing, transport, food—as the Indian people, under control of the military, were herded away westward. Stories of huge frauds in connection with these shortages were common—McKenney, *Memoirs*, tells of Sam Houston offering him a $50,000 bribe to throw a provisioning contract to a group Houston represented. The consequences of such shortages may be seen in detail in the account of a group of Creeks given as good care as their honest and humane conductor, Captain John Page, could manage, numbering 630 on departure in December 1834, and suffering so many deaths en route that only 469 arrived at Fort Gibson at the end of March 1835. (Foreman, *Indian Removal*, 121–25)

- "I am not much": ibid., quoting from Irving, *Wolfert's Roost*.
- The John Howard Payne arrest: ibid., 268n; Payne's own account of this was published in the Knoxville Tennessee *Register* of December 2, 1835, and in the Augusta *Georgia Constitutionalist* of December 24, 1835. "The people of Tennessee generally were incensed at the outrage and at least one Georgia newspaper, the *Georgia Journal* of Milledgeville, deplored the lawless proceeding."
- Jackson's message to Congress 1835: Commager *Documents*, 260.

313   The Jackson administration's capital-letter assurance: McKenney, *Memoirs*, 1:249. George Washington: ibid., 1:130–31.

•   Henry Clay: Thurman Wilkins, *Cherokee Tragedy: The Story of the Ridge Family and the Decimation of a People* (New York 1970), 256–57.

•   John Ross quotation: ibid., 257.

•   National Archives, *List of Documents Concerning . . . Indian Treaties*, provides a summary of treaties between the United States and the Cherokee Nation from 1785 to 1835, a great deal of correspondence from the treaty commissioners, William Carroll and the Reverend John F. Schermerhorn, various drafts, instructions, and proclamations concerned with the treaty, and supplemental articles signed in March 1836. The Reverend Schermerhorn (McKenney in his *Memoirs* sarcastically underlines his title) was much in demand at the time as a treaty commissioner, having produced treaties in 1833 with the Western Cherokee and in 1832, 1834, and 1835 with the Potawatomi. See also Morris L. Wardell, *A Political History of the Cherokee Nation 1838–1907* (Norman 1938); Grace Steele Woodward, *The Cherokees* (Norman 1953); John Philip Reid, *A Law of Blood: The Primitive Law of the Cherokee Nation* (New York 1970); Brad Agnew, *Fort Gibson: Terminal on the Trail of Tears* (Norman 1980), especially chapter 13.

•   Military quotations: Francis Paul Prucha, *The Sword of the Republic: The United States Army on the Frontier 1783–1846* (New York 1969), 263–64.

314   Russell Thornton, *The Cherokees: A Population History* (Lincoln 1990), gives the "most complete and reliable measurement of Cherokee population ever available": William G. McLoughlin, *Pacific Historical Review*, November 1992.

•   Jackson is quoted from Wilkins, *Cherokee Tragedy*, 254.

•   McKenney, *Memoirs*, 1:272; 2:126. Herman J. Viola, *Thomas L. McKenney, Architect of America's Early Indian Policy, 1816–1830* (Chicago 1974), quotes McKenney in a letter to his friend John McLean: "I *knew* all was wrong—*deeply* so." (235)

•   Costs of the Seminole War: Prucha, *Sword of the Republic*, 301.

315   "I do hereby": *U.S. House Document 285*, 25th Congress, 2nd Session.

•   Captives taken under flag of truce: Foreman, *Indian Removal*, citing *Army and Navy Chronicle*, vol. 5; *American State Papers*, "Military Affairs," vol. 7, 690; *New York Observer*, December 16, 1837, et seq.

•   Jesup quote: E.C. McReynolds, *The Seminoles* (Norman 1953), 181.

•   "Five years ago": Foreman, *Indian Removal*, 378n.

•   Hitchcock in Oklahoma: Grant Foreman, ed., *A Traveller in Indian Territory, The Journal of Ethan Allen Hitchcock, late Major General in the United States Army* (Cedar Rapids 1930). John R. Swanton's Foreword says of Colonel Hitchcock's missing report, "its mysterious disappearance from all official files proves at one and the same time the honesty of the report and the dishonesty of the national administration of the period." (8)

316   Official quotes: Prucha, *Sword of the Republic*, 294 and 300.

•   Creek "volunteers" : General Jesup forced the Creeks to provide six hundred to one thousand men to fight the Seminoles, before he would recommend that money be released from their own annuity to pay debts alleged against them. This money made it possible for the departing Creeks to save some of their personal belongings from claims of creditors: "by which the Indians were enabled to ransom themselves from the whites." (Foreman, *Indian Removal*, 161)

317   Menewa is quoted from Thomas L. McKenney and James Hall, *History of the Indian Tribes of North America*, 3 vols., (Philadelphia 1838–1844, and various subsequent editions).

·   A removal population of 80,000 was an official estimate of the Indian Office: McKenney, *Memoirs*, 229–31.

Chapter 22

318   Early mention of Sequoya (the *Cherokee Phoenix*, 1828) gave him a white paternal grandfather; later he was endowed with a white father, sometimes vaguely described as a German trader named Gyst or Guess. Later still this parentage was transferred to Nathaniel Gist, a frontier personage of some note in pre-Revolutionary days, thus relating Sequoya to various later American families of distinction, including the Blairs of the famous Blair House in Washington. Since even the decade of Sequoya's birth is uncertain (1760? 1770?), and even his mother's identity (other than her clan) is uncertain, all this must be considered speculation. John B. Davis, "The Life and Work of Sequoyah," *Chronicles of Oklahoma*, 8 (1929), gives a bibliography of printed sources, including Emmet Starr, the Reverend Samuel Worcester, James Mooney, Charles C. Royce, Albert V. Goodpasture, George E. Foster, John R. Swanton, and other well-known writers on early Cherokee history. Grant Foreman, *Sequoyah* (Norman 1932, 2nd edition 1959, 6th printing 1980) is by far the best-known biography. This work accepts a Gist as the father, a more likely candidate, says the (otherwise usually astute) author, than some "clod" of a German trader—unfortunately typical of much thinking on the parentage of genius.

322   The missionary linguist: Edmund Schwarze, *Moravian Missions among the Southern Indian Tribes* (Bethlehem, Pennsylvania 1923), 123.

·   Samuel A. Worcester, "The Cherokee Language," in Schoolcraft, *Indian Tribes*, vol. 2.

323   The emininent ethnologist: James Mooney, *Sacred Formulas of the Cherokees*, BAE 7th Annual Report (Washington 1891).

·   A recent picture of the Cherokees in the period following Removal is William G. McLoughlin, *After the Trail of Tears: The Cherokees' Struggle for Sovereignty, 1839–1850* (Chapel Hill 1993). The same author's *Champions of the Cherokees: Evan and John B. Jones* (Princeton 1990), gives a detailed account of the troubles of the summer and fall of 1839. (199)

324   "The Story of Sequoyah's Last Days," *Cherokee Advocate*, June 26, 1845.

Chapter 23

331   Paul W. Gates, *History of Public Land Law Development* (Washington 1968), 174: 25 million-plus acres, citing Young, *Redskins, Ruffleshirts, and Rednecks*, 164–67. Gates lists lands proclaimed and sold by states, citing General Land Office Annual Reports. (165–66) The American Land Company is discussed as an example of large scale land speculation. (171–74) In documenting the general attitude toward land speculations, Andrew Jackson's public remarks inveighing against the "frauds,

speculations, and monopolies, in the purchase of the public lands," is quoted in Gates, *Public Land Law*, 175–76, with the comment that "there is little in his past to indicate that he disapproved of large scale purchases of public land solely for speculation." (174)

- The "principal authority" quoted is Abel, "Indian Consolidations West of the Mississippi."
- The total of traders' claims: James L. Clayton, "The Impact of Traders' Claims on the American Fur Trade," in David M. Ellis, ed., *The Frontier in American Development, Essays in Honor of Paul Wallace Gates* (Ithaca 1966).
- Cass: Prucha, *Lewis Cass*, 18.

332 "valuable lands": from the foreword by Frederick Merk to Ellis, *Frontier in American Development*.

- Tipton: Paul Wallace Gates, introduction to *The John Tipton Papers*, Nellie Armstrong Robertson and Dorothy Riker, eds., 3 vols. (Indianapolis 1942), 49.
- "On the mid-continent frontier": Leslie E. Decker, "The Great Speculation: An Interpretation of Mid-Continent Pioneering," in Ellis, *Frontier in American Development*, 379.
- Treaty of Greenville: Abel, "Indian Consolidations West of the Mississippi," 266.

334 The Cherokee after Removal made an effort to follow Tecumseh's example by trying to forge an agreement in 1843 among sixteen Indian nations not to sell or cede any part of their territory without the consent of all: McKenney, *Memoirs*, 2:128. Cherokee political activity during this period: Gary E. Moulton, *The Papers of Chief John Ross* (Norman 1985), vol. 2.

- The purported Tecumseh quote: Anonymous, *Daring Deeds of American Heroes*, 108–9.

335 Quotations referring to the Potawatomi: Gates, Introduction to *Tipton Papers*, 45. See Irving McKee, ed., *The Trail of Death, Letters of Benjamin Marie Petit*, Indiana Historical Society Publication 14/1 (Indianapolis 1941) for the letters of a priest who accompanied the Indiana Potawatomi on their forced march into exile. Lewis Cass, secretary of war in 1834, is quoted as objecting to any Potawatomis remaining in their homeland: "they ought all speedily to go." (19) However, Commissary General Gibson, "upon whose department lay the responsibility of conducting an emigration," said the intention of the government was not to remove all the Potawatomi to the west "but rather to extinguish their nationality." Petit concludes that Gibson's statement reveals "either a lack of unity or a duplicity in the policy of the War Department." (21) To a Potawatomi protest (1838) showing that the "treaty" was a fraud, a letter from Petit to his bishop quotes the secretary of war as replying, "I do not need to be shown, and we did not need your signatures; the great chiefs of the nation were entitled to sell your reserve."

- Richardville: ibid., 49. The name may derive from Claude Drouet de Richardville, who was active in this region from 1736 to 1759 (Paris, Archives Nationales C 13 C4, page 202).
- "all rules": ibid., 44.
- Horace Greeley, *New York Tribune*, June 2 and 9, quoted in Paul Wallace Gates, *Fifty Million Acres: Conflicts over Kansas Land Policies, 1854–1890* (Ithaca 1954, New York 1966), 102.

338 The record number of memorials to Sacagawea is mentioned in W.J. Ghent's biographical sketch in the *Dictionary of American Biography*.

Chapter 24

339 Politian (1454–1494) is quoted from Lewis Mumford, *Technics and Human Development*, vol. 1 of *The Myth of the Machine* (New York 1966–67), 283.

- Columbian material: John Boyd Thacher, *Christopher Columbus, His Life, His Work, His Remains*, 3 vols. (New York 1903), and Samuel Eliot Morison, *Admiral of the Ocean Sea* (Boston 1942).

- Latin quotation: *Mémoires de la Société d'Ethnographie*, 2ième Série, Tome Premier (Paris 1879).

340 The theory quoted here on the origin of syphilis: E.H. Hudson, "Treponematosis and Man's Social Evolution," *American Anthropologist* 67/4 (1965). Later discussion: Alfred W. Crosby Jr., *The Columbian Exchange; Biological and Cultural Consequences of 1492* (Westport, Connecticut 1977, originally published 1972), 147.

341 "they are agitated": Maud W. Makemson, *The Book of the Jaguar Priest; a Translation of the Book of Chilam Balam of Tizimin, with Commentary* (New York 1931).

- "I wolde think": Eden, *Peter Martyr.*

- Vespucci: Clements Markham, ed., *The Letters of Amerigo Vespucci, and Other Documents Illustrative of His Career* (London 1894), 46 and 6–7.

- Léry: *Histoire d'un Voyage Faict en la Terre du Brésil, autrement dite Amerique . . .* (La Rochelle 1578), 303.

- Acosta: *Historia Natural y Moral de las Indias* (Seville 1590), translated into Latin, French, Dutch, German, Italian, and English within the next fifteen years; the quotations here are from the first French edition (Paris 1598), 1:274; and the second French edition (Paris 1600),1:288.

342 Vespucci: *Lettres* (Jean Temporal edition, 1556).

- Ronsard: "Discours contre Fortune," *Oeuvres Complètes*, 2 vols. (Paris 1950), 2:399–409.

- Montaigne: *Les Essays*, Pierre Villey, ed., 3 vols. (Paris 1930).

- The first English translation: *The Essayes of Michael Lord of Montaigne*, translated by John Florio (London 1603), quoted here from the 3rd edition (1632)

343 *André Thevet, Les Singularités de la France Antarctique* (1557), chapter 39.

- Francisco López de Gómara, *Histoire Générale*, (French edition, 1568, originally published in Spain 1552), book 5, chapter 217, 251.

344 Montaigne: the essay "Des Coches."

- Du Tertre: *Histoire Générale . . .* (Paris 1654), 396–97.

- Benzoni/Chauveton: Hierosme Benzoni (Urbain Chauveton, trans.), *Histoire Nouvelle du Nouveau Monde* (Geneva 1579), 326.

- Lahontan: *Nouveaux Voyages de Mr. le Baron de Lahontan, dans l'Amerique Septentrionale . . .* (La Haye 1703); and Tome 2, *Memoires de l'Amerique Septentrionale, ou la Suite des Voyages de Mr. le Baron de Lahontan . . .* (La Haye 1703); and *Supplement aux Voyages du Baron de Lahontan où l'on trouve des Dialogues curieux entre l'Auteur et un Sauvage de bon sens qui a voyagé. . .* (La Haye 1703).

345 Lahontan's "modern editor": Gilbert Chinard, ed., *Dialogues Curieux* (Baltimore 1931).

- Gottfried Wilhelm von Leibniz, *Jugement sur les Oeuvres de M. le Comte de Shaftesbury, Works*, 5:40. Chinard discusses Leibniz' references to Lahontan, *Dialogues Curieux*, 52–56.

- Louis François Delisle de la Drevetière, *Arlequin Sauvage, Comedie en Trois Actes* (Paris 1756).
- For Morgan to Engels to Marx, see White, *Lewis Henry Morgan, the Indian Journals.*

346   Max Weber's fragmentary *The Protestant Ethic and the Spirit of Capitalism*, first published in German in1904–5; later, much revised, in 1920, the year of Weber's death, was translated by Talcott Parsons (Oxford 1930) and is quoted here from the paperback edition (New York 1958), 53.

- Cotton Mather: *Magnalia Christi Americana*, Book 7.
- "For the honour of humanity": Clark Wissler, *Indians of the United States* (New York 1940), 254, quoting from *Historical Account of Bouquet's Expedition against the Ohio Indians, in 1764* (Cincinnati 1808), 80–91.

347   Anonymous, *Indian Anecdotes and Barbarities . . .* (Barre, Massachusetts 1837), 32 pages.

348   "It was a horrid sight . . .": Allan Nevins and Henry Steele Commager, *A Short History of the United States* (New York 1966).

- The epic poem: Elbert M. Smith, *Ma-Ka-Tai-Me-She-Kia-Kiak; or, Black Hawk, and Scenes in the West, a National Poem in Six Cantos* (New York 1849).

349   Francis Parkman is quoted from his prefatory note to *The Oregon Trail* (Boston 1849).

- The story of Petalesharo: McKenney, *Memoirs*, 2:94–96.
- Eleazar Williams: biographical sketch by J.N.B. Hewitt, in Hodge, *Handbook*, 2:955.

350   The Jesuit priest (Le Jeune) and the (probably) Algonkin priests are paraphrased from the *Jesuit Relations* as quoted in D'Arcy McNickle, *They Came Here First: The Epic of the American Indian* (Philadelphia 1949).

- The Dutch pastor, "Johannes Megapolensis, Jr.," *Mohawk Indians*, chapter 17; the Seneca sachem is Red Jacket, quoted in McKenney and Hall, *Indian Tribes.*
- The Mohawk duke of Northumberland is quoted from W.L. Stone, *Life of Joseph Brant* (1838).

352   Government pets: Robert M. Utley, *The Last Days of the Sioux Nation* (New Haven 1963), 264. The rancher (an ex-convict) and his two brothers killed one person in this 1891 incident.

353   "The Blue Juniata," by Marian Dix Sullivan, is a fair example of false-flying folklore, antelopes not through forests going and wild-roving Indian girls' tresses surely not wavy-flowing, leastways not without the help of curling-irons. The Indian created in the white man's image: a very nineteenth-century practice.

Chapter 25

354   Exploited "European traders and their promoters, many of whom found Indian price manipulation ruinous": Robin Fisher, *Contact and Conflict: Indian-European Relations in British Columbia, 1774–1800* (Vancouver 1977), 9, cited by Douglas Cole and David Darling, "History of the Early Period," in *Handbook of North American Indians*, vol.7, *Northwest Coast*, Wayne Suttles, ed. (Washington 1990), 125.

- Eskimos in Tudor England: *Handbook of North American Indians*, vol. 5, *Arctic*, David Damas, ed. (Washington 1984), reproduces drawings of a 1576 Eskimo captive, and a 1577 Eskimo family.

355   "about five" centuries: Ólafur Halldórsson on Greenland in Phillip Pulsiano, ed., *Medieval Scandinavia: An Encyclopedia* (New York 1993), 240–41.

357   Siberian-American Paleo-Arctic tradition: Don E. Dumond, "Prehistory: Summary," *Handbook* 5, 73, citing Dumond, *The Eskimos and Aleuts* (London 1977), and Frederick Hadleigh West, *The Archaeology of Beringia* (New York 1981).

•   Anangula: Allen P. McCartney, "Prehistory of the Aleutian Region," *Handbook* 5, 122, citing among others William S. Laughlin and Gordon H. Marsh, "The Lamellar Flake Manufacturing Site on Anangula Island in the Aleutians," *American Antiquity* 20/1 (1954).

•   Aleuts, 6000 B.C.: Dumond, *Handbook* 5, 73, citing Robert F. Black, "Geology and Ancient Aleuts, Amchitka and Umnak Islands, Aleutians," *Arctic Anthropology* 11/2 (1974).

•   *Excomminquois*: Hodge, *Handbook*, 1:434, citing Pierre Biard, "Excomminquois," 1611, 1616, *JR*, 2:66 and 3:68. Father Biard's *Relation* from Acadia in 1614 was far earlier than the continuous series forming the *Jesuit Relations*, which began with Paul Le Jeune's *Brieve Relation* (Paris 1632).

•   "less controversial": Anthony Woodbury, "Eskimo and Aleut Languages," 62.

358   The Danish scholar: H.P. Steensby, "An Anthropographical Study of the Origin of the Eskimo Culture," *Meddelser om Grønland*, 53 (Copenhagen 1917).

359   *Igdlo*: Kaj Birket-Smith, *The Eskimos* (London 1936, 1959), 120n.

360   Mummies: Jens Peder Hart Hanson, Jørgen Meldgaard, Jørgen Nordquist, eds., *The Greenland Mummies* (The British Museum 1991, originally published in Danish and Greenlandic 1985), 3.

•   Eskimo lamps: Elisha Kent Kane, *Arctic Explorations: The Second Grinnell Expedition—in Search of Sir John Franklin, 1853, '54, '55*, 2 vols. (Philadelphia 1856), 2:9–10. Kane writes, "our faces [were] begrimed with fatty carbon like the Esquimaux of South Greenland." Could special lamp problems have existed in Greenland?

362   The poems are from Knud Rasmussen, *The Intellectual Culture of the Iglulik Eskimos, Report of the Fifth Thule Expedition, 1921–24* (Copenhagen 1929).

•   Hospitality: Peter Freuchen, *Book of the Eskimos* (Cleveland 1961): "The Eskimos' extraordinary delight at visiting and eating together must be seen against the background of their basic loneliness and isolation." (151)

363   Aggressive Inuit of northwestern Alaska: John Bookstoce, ed., *The Journal of Rochfort Maguire 1852–1854*, 2 vols. (London, Hakluyt Society, 1988), 159ff. The editor of this work cites, apparently as expressing an opposite view of the people of northwestern Alaska, Ernest S. Burch Jr., "Traditional Eskimo Societies in Northwestern Alaska," in V. Kotani and W.B. Workman, eds., *Alaskan Native Culture and History* (Osaka 1980); and Dorothy Jean Ray, "Ethnology in the Arctic: the Bering Strait Eskimos," *Handbook* 5.

•   Trade: John Simpson report, Appendix 7 in Bookstoce, *Journal of Rochfort Maguire*, (2:505 and 539–40)

•   Various names for "She Down There": Birket-Smith, *The Eskimos*, 165.

364   The "methods of travel and transportation evolved long before by the Indian . . . the snow shoe and the toboggan, in summer the birchbark-canoe": Diamond Jenness, *The Indians of Canada* (Ottawa 1932, 1960), 250.

365   Cree women "had a widespread reputation for beauty": ibid., 284, citing Alexander MacKenzie, *Voyages from Montreal, on the River St. Lawrence, through the Continent*

of North America, to the Frozen Pacific Oceans; in the years 1789 and 1793 (London 1801, Philadelphia 1802).

- Henry Wadsworth Longfellow published *Hiawatha* (1855) after reading Schoolcraft's *Indian Tribes*, in which the name of Hiawatha, legendary Iroquois hero, mistakenly appears as a legendary Ojibwa hero. Jeremiah Curtin, in the notes to *Creation Myths of Primitive America* (London 1899): "Schoolcraft, with his amazing propensity to make mistakes, with his remarkable genius for missing the truth and confusing everything with which he came in contact, gave the name Hiawatha to his patchwork." (498–99)
- Scattered bands: Jenness, *Indians of Canada*, 123.
- MacKenzie, *Voyages* (London 1801); Albert Gallatin, *A Synopsis of the Indian Tribes in North America* (Worcester, Massachusetts, 1836).

366   John Wesley Powell, *Indian Linguistic Families of America North of Mexico*, 7th Annual BAE Report (Washington 1881). The name Athapaska not from the Athapaskan language: Swanton, *Indian Tribes*, 552. For a recent study of MacKenzie River Athapaskan people, see Kerry Abel, *Drum Songs: Glimpses of Diné History* (Buffalo 1993).

- Slavey eccentricities: Jenness, *Indians of Canada*, 391.

368   Sir Edward Belcher, *Narrative of a Voyage Round the World,* 2 vols. (London 1843). On the Arctic map: Belcher Island in Hudson Bay; Belcher Channel in the Arctic Ocean.

- The American captive is quoted from John R. Jewitt, *A Narrative of the Adventures and Sufferings of John R. Jewitt, Only Survivor of the Ship Boston, During a Captivity of Nearly Three Years Among the Savages of Nootka Sound* (Middletown, Connecticut 1815).

369   The spirit story: Ruth Benedict, *Patterns of Culture* (New York 1934).

- Wayne Suttles' Introduction to *Handbook 7* cites Boas of sixty years ago warning against regarding "marginal" cultures as inferior. (12)
- One of the first great men in linguistics: Edward Sapir, *Language* (New York 1921), 214.

370   The potlatch description is from Benedict, *Patterns of Culture.*

- The Kwakiutl system is detailed by Helen Codere in *Handbook 7*. Franz Boas, *The Ethnology of the Kwakiutl, Based on Data Collected by George Hunt*, 35th Annual BAE Report (Washington 1921) describes a young man beginning his business career among the Kwakiutl.
- Claude Lévi-Strauss, *The Way of the Masks* (Seattle 1982), 163–87, compares the *numaym* to a noble house of medieval Japan.

372   The Bear Dancing and Cannibal Dancing scenes are drawn from Benedict, *Patterns of Culture*, who bases the passage on Boas, *Ethnology of the Kwakiutl.*

373   Oscar O. Winther, *The Great Northwest* (New York 1947), states in his chronology, under the date of 1796, that "no less than 195,000 gallons of liquor were expended by the rivals" in the split of the North-West Company.

- David Thompson, *Narrative of His Explorations*, J.B. Tyrrell, ed., (Toronto 1916), 321.
- The medical historian: J.J. Heagarty, *Four Centuries of Medical History in Canada* (Toronto 1928), 1:56, cited in Jenness, *Indians of Canada*, 252.
- MacKenzie, *Voyages* (London 1801).
- "High wine": David Lavender, *Westward Vision* (New York 1963), 121.

374   The Aleuts: Martin Sauer, *Account of a Geographical and Astronomical Expedition to the Northern Parts of Russia* (London 1802).

·   Tlingit and Sitka: Wayne Suttles, "History of Research: Early Sources," *Handbook* 7, 70–71; and Cole and Darling, *Handbook* 7.

376   The young army officer's journal was that of Charles Erskine Scott Wood, in manuscript in the Huntington Library, San Marino, California.

·   The standard history of Alaska: Hubert Howe Bancroft, *Alaska* (San Francisco 1886).

·   Sixteen stockholders: Samuel P. Johnston, ed., *Alaska Commercial Company, 1868–1940* (San Francisco 1940).

·   1876 investigation: *House Committee Reports*, 44th Congress, 1st Session, 623 ff.

·   In 1888 the revenue cutter reported some 300 Eskimo people dead on St. Lawrence Island in Bering Strait as the result of a great summer binge: J. Arthur Lazell, *Alaskan Apostle, The Life Story of Sheldon Jackson* (New York 1960).

377   Wendell H. Oswalt, *Bashful No Longer: An Alaskan Eskimo Ethnohistory, 1778–1988* (Norman 1990), makes an effort to "examine changes from an Eskimo perspective" (Introduction, xvi). Norman A. Chance, *The Iñupiat and Arctic Alaska: An Ethnography of Development* (Fort Worth 1990), is an updated edition of a 1966 work analyzing social change.

·   Michael Healy, captain of the revenue cutter *Bear*, suggested the reindeer idea to Jackson in 1890 and for several years took an active interest in the project; the notion first came, he said, from the naturalist Charles H. Townsend during an Alaska cruise in 1885: Dorothy Jean Ray, *The Eskimos of Bering Strait, 1650–1898* (Seattle, University of Washington Press, 1992; first edition 1975), 227.

·   Victor William Henningsen III, *Reading, Writing and Reindeer*, a 1987 thesis in the Graduate School of Education at Harvard, mentions that some scholars estimate a population loss of as much as 50 percent among the Eskimos of northwestern Alaska between1850 and 1880. (167) The same work speaks of a 1902 Russian ban on the export of reindeer. (173) Frank Darnell, an authority on Alaskan education past and present, very kindly provided the above thesis for me, as well as *A Schoolteacher in Old Alaska; The Story of Hannah Breece* (New York 1995). Breece was a great-aunt of Jane Jacobs, who edited her memoir and added commentary on Sheldon Jackson's role among other matters.

Chapter 26

378   *The Voyage of Sebastian Vizcaino to the Coast of California* (San Francisco 1933) is the first English edition of Miguel de Venegas, *Noticia de la California* (Madrid 1759), pieced together from excerpts previously published (Seville 1615 onward) of Father Antonio de la Ascensión's records of the voyage. For earlier voyages to the Pacific Coast see Henry Raup Wagner, *Spanish Voyages to the Northwest Coast of America in the Sixteenth Century* (San Francisco 1929).

·   Vizcaino is quoted from George Butler Griffin, ed., "Documents of the Sutro Collection," *Publications of the Historical Society of Southern California*, Part 1 (Los Angeles 1891).

379   Earliest days: Jon M. Erlandson, *Early Hunter-Gatherers of the California Coast* (New York 1994).

381   Jimson weed, *Datura meteloïdes*, was used also as an element in the Chingichnich cult, described in the notes kept during mission times by Father Geronomo Boscana—translated in J.P. Harrington, *A New Original Version of Boscana's Historical Account of the San Juan Capistrano Indians of Southern California*, Smithsonian Miscellaneous Collections, 92/4 (Washington 1934).

382   The Owens valley pre-agricultural irrigation was described in the Los Angeles *Star*, August 17, 1859. The account is reprinted in J.M. Guinn, ed., "Some Early History of Owens River Valley," *Annual Publications of the Historical Society of Southern California*, 10/3 (Los Angeles 1917), 41–47. Julian H. Steward, "Ethnography of the Owens Valley Paiute," *University of California Publications in American Archaeology and Ethnology*, 13/3 (Berkeley 1933) gives a reconstruction of this pre-agricultural irrigation. Martha C. Knack and Omer C. Stewart, *As Long as the River Shall Run: An Ethnography of Pyramid Lake Indian Reservation* (Berkeley 1984) is of (much) related interest.

·   Salvador Palma (Olleyquotequiche) is quoted from a letter to Viceroy Antonio Bucareli, November 11, 1776 (the letter was written by Juan Bautista de Anza at the Indian captain's dictation), printed in J.N. Bowman and R.F. Heizer, *Anza and the North West Frontier of New Spain*, Southwest Museum Papers, 20 (Los Angeles 1967), 154.

·   The explorer was Anza, quoted in Robert Glass Cleland, *Wilderness to Empire* (New York 1944).

·   Charles L. McNichols, *Crazy Weather*, a novel set among Colorado River people (New York 1944 and 1967) is "an extraordinary perception of the psychology of a native culture . . . wholly accurate." (A.L. Kroeber, *American Anthropologist* 46, 1944, 394).

383   Kuksu distribution among the Maidu: Francis A. Riddell, *Handbook of North American Indians*, vol. 8, *California*, Robert F. Heizer, ed. (Washington 1978). Riddell lists the entire cycle of dances from late September-October to May. (384)

385   The ironic commander was Gaspar de Portola, quoted from Charles Edward Chapman, *A History of California: The Spanish Period* (New York 1921), 227.

386   Campbell Grant in *Handbook* 8 , 506, estimates the pre-Columbian Chumash population at18,000 to 22,000, and calls their work the "finest example of prehistoric rock art in the United States." (534) See also Grant's *Rock Paintings of the Chumash* (Berkeley 1965).

·   Quotations on the Chumash "gentle" life: Father Juan Caballeria y Collel, *History of the City of Santa Barbara California from its Discovery to our Own Day*, Edmund Burke, trans. (Santa Barbara 1902), 17–18.

·   Mission Indian birth rate: Warren A. Beck and David A. Williams, *California, a History of the Golden State* (New York 1972), 76. Maynard Geiger, O.F.M., *Mission Santa Barbara 1782–1965* (Santa Barbara 1965), gives the total number of local baptisms from 1786 to 1804 as 3000, while for "the next fifty-five years only 1,771 baptisms were administered," one factor being the "preponderance of deaths over births after about 1812." (31)

·   Altered descriptions: James J. Rawls, *Indians of California: The Changing Image* (Norman 1984); see also William Brandon, "The California Indian World," *The Indian Historian*, (San Francisco, Summer 1969).

387   "lazy, stupid": Louis Choris, *Voyage Pittoresque Autour du Monde*, Part 3, "Port San-Francisco et ses habitants," (Paris 1822), 5.

388   The Spanish quotation: A. R. Rojas, *The Vaquero* (1964).

- "a young centaur": George Frederick Augustus Ruxton, *Life in the Far West*, Leroy R. Hafen, ed., (London 1848, Norman 1951).
- The Indian population of California was (wild-guess) estimated at 20,000 after 1848, 30,000 before that date: J.P. Dunn, *Massacres of the Mountains: A History of the Indian Wars of the Far West* (New York 1886, London 1963), 117. More accurate figures for California Indian populations are from the generally accepted authority in this field, Sherburne Friend Cook, *The Aboriginal Population of Upper California*, Actas y Memorias del XXXV Congreso Internacional de Americanistas (Mexico 1962), with estimates in the range from 250,000 to 300,000. Later, however, Cook studied new data dealing with the populations of the Sacramento valley and Mission areas, and gave 325,000 as his reconsidered estimate (personal communication, May 1973). See also Cook's *The Population of California Indians, 1769–1970* (Berkeley 1976). The 1848 figure is from Sherburne Friend Cook, "The Destruction of the California Indian," *California Monthly*, 76/3, 16.

389   Hubert Howe Bancroft, *History of California* (San Francisco 1886–1890), 7:477: "the California valley cannot grace her annals with a single Indian war bordering on respectability" but it could boast a hundred or more instances of "brutal butchering." Detail regarding attacks in this era on the Hupa people and their neighbors is found in Jack Norton, *Genocide in Northwestern California: When Our Worlds Cried* (San Francisco 1979).

- Some Chivalry politicos had a dream of two Californias—one slave and one free: Beck and Williams, *California*, 164.

390   The Clear Lake massacre: Robert F. Heizer, ed., *Collected Documents on the Causes and Events in the Bloody Island Massacre of 1850* (Berkeley 1971). "Bloody Island" is now a hill well inland on the lake shore, marked by a monument near the town of Upper Lake. See also Edward D. Castillo, *Handbook 8*, 107–8.

- The Pomo interpreter, Ralganal, also known as William Benson, wrote out his account c1931. (Heizer, *Collected Documents*, 54)
- Bill's obituary: Red Bluff *Beacon*, January 7, 1858, quoted in Cook, "Destruction of the California Indian."
- The dog murder: Marysville *Democrat*, May 1859, quoted in Robert F. Heizer, ed., *They Were Only Diggers: A Collection of Articles from California Newspapers 1851–1866* (Ramona, California 1974), 300. This episode was brought to my attention by Tom Nixon, chief ranger at Anderson Marsh State Park, Lower Lake, which may have been the locality of the attack.

391   The Wappo: Jess O. Sawyer, *Handbook 8*, 262.

- Pomo government: Sally McLendon and Michael J. Lowy, *Handbook 8*, 318.
- Wintu tales: Cora A. Du Bois and Dorothy Demetracopoulou, *Wintu Myths*, University of California Publications in American Archaeology and Ethnology, 28/5 (Berkeley 1931), 279–403. The authors speak of a still earlier collection, Jeremiah Curtin, *Creation Myths of Primitive America* (Boston 1898), which relied on a single informant, Norlputus, a man of unusual intelligence and "philosophic inclination," for all of its material. Du Bois and Demetracopoulou use however "a cross-section of the population." The choice of one method over the other raises quite a serious question.
- The Wintu poem is slightly altered from the version in William Brandon, *The Magic World* (New York 1971, Athens, Ohio, 1992), 132. It is found in its original

form in Curtin, *Creation Myths*, as one of the contributions of the informant Norlputus. (516)

392   The massacre of the Yana is also drawn from Curtin, but from the London edition of 1899, Notes, 517–20. "That year the Yanas had worked a good deal, and it was not uncommon for single persons to have from $40 to $60. One informant told me that a man showed a friend of his $400 which he had taken from murdered Indians." (520) The Yahi, southernmost cousins of the Yana, contained two bands in the 1860s, the Mill Creek and Deer Creek bands; the Mill Creek band had acquired a bad reputation among neighboring Indians, as mentioned in the reminiscences of a Maidu woman born in 1895, whose grandmother had been, briefly, a Mill Creek captive in 1863: Marie Potts, *The Northern Maidu* (Happy Camp, California, 1977), 40–42. T.T. Waterman, *The Yana Indians*, University of California Publications in American Archaeology and Ethnology, 8/2 (Berkeley 1918), finds the mid-1860s date of the massacre uncertain, but "the undoubted fact remains that after this period only remnants of the Yana people survived." (50–51) Nine Yanan persons appeared in the census of 1930: John R. Swanton, *The Indian Tribes of North America* (Washington 1953), 523.

·   The "modern specialist": Jerald Jay Johnson, *Handbook* 8, 362–63.

·   Stolen Indian children: Cook, "Destruction of the California Indian," 16; the same source provides the news item from the Sacramento *Union*, July 19, 1862.

·   1850 report: William H. Ellison, "Indian Policy in California 1846–60," *Mississippi Valley Historical Review* 9/1 (1922).

·   Don Benito Wilson is quoted from John W. Caughey, ed., *The Indians of Southern California in 1852, the B.D. Wilson Report and a Selection of Contemporary Comment* (San Marino, California 1952)

393   Los Angeles quotations: Horace Bell, *Reminiscences of a Ranger* (Santa Barbara 1927).

·   The government inspector: J. Ross Browne, quoted in Caughey, *Indians of Southern California*, xxxiii.

·   The cave murders: Waterman, *Yana Indians*; the Yahi Yana children killed in the cave were members of the band that included Ishi, himself then a child of eight or nine. Theodora Kroeber, *Ishi in Two Worlds* (Berkeley 1961), tells in detail the story of attempted Yahi extermination. (56–90)

394   R.F. Heizer and A.B. Elsasser, *Original Accounts of the Lone Woman of San Nicolas Island*, University of California Archaeological Survey No. 55 (Berkeley 1961). For a first-hand account of the lost woman of San Nicolas see George Nidever, *The Life and Adventures of a Pioneer in California since 1834*, W.H. Ellison, ed., (Berkeley 1937).

Chapter 27

395   Shoshonean languages of the Uto-Aztecan language family: Wick R. Miller, *Handbook of North American Indians*, vol. 11, *The Great Basin*, Warren L. D'Azevedo, ed. (Washington 1986), 98.

396   Reuben Gold Thwaites, ed., *Original Journals of the Lewis and Clark Expedition* (Cleveland 1904).

397   Plains horse societies: Demitri B. Shimkin, *Handbook* 11, 517.

400   In connection with the Whitman massacre, see Senate Executive Document No. 37, 41st Congress (Washington 1903).

401   Leschi on the land of darkness: Dunn, *Massacres of the Mountains*, 197.

•   Figures on the Rogue River "war" are from Hubert Howe Bancroft, *History of Oregon*, 2 vols. (San Francisco 1886–1888). For the squad records see also Dunn, *Massacres of the Mountains*. The Rogue River "War" is examined in detail as a focus for the general malaise of the Indian service in the 1830s in Stephen D. Peckham, *Requiem for a People: The Rogue Indians and the Frontiersman* (Norman 1971).

402   "Apart from sickly sentimentalism": Frank Soulé, John H. Gihon, and James Nisbet, *The Annals of San Francisco* (San Francisco, 1855 and 1938; Palo Alto, 1966). The "ruthless philosophy" of the book in regard to Indians and Catholics, as quoted in the introduction by R.H. Dillon: "the sooner the aborigines of California are altogether weeded away quietly, the better for humanity. Yet the Fathers would retain them; then sweep away the Fathers, too." (xi–xii)

•   Motto: Bancroft, *History of Oregon*, 2:311, n 2

405   The heads of Captain Jack, John Schonchin, Boston Charly, and Black Jim found their final resting place in the Smithsonian: Richard H. Dillon, *The Burnt-Out Fires: California's Modoc Indian War* (Englewood Cliffs, New Jersey 1973), 335–36. The hangman's knots from the necks of Kintpuash and Schonchin John were obtained by the Indian Museum at Fort Sutter, California. (333)

•   The rest of Captain Jack's band at the finish: Ralph K. Andrist, *The Long Death: The Last Days of the Plains Indians* (New York 1964), 237.

•   Young Joseph, "An Indian's View of Indian Affairs," *North American Review*, 128 (New York 1879), says that his father, Old Joseph, refused to sign the June 1855 treaty (417), although Joseph's attested mark appears on the treaty, third among the Nez Perce signers, after Lawyer and Looking Glass (Kappler, *Indian Affairs*, 2:705). The wording of Young Joseph's account would seem to apply better to a later treaty conference, since in 1855 Joseph was not being asked to surrender his home country of Wallowa. Old Joseph's name is conspicuously absent from later agreements. He also refused any annuity goods, even from the 1855 treaty, saying, "If we take the pay, the white man will say he has bought the land also."

406   "As to the merderer": Dunn, *Massacres of the Mountains*, 639.

•   An amendment to the 1863 treaty, signed August 13, 1868, by Lawyer, Timothy, and Jason for the Nez Perce (not signed by Joseph), provided for those outside the reservation to remain "on lands now occupied and improved by them and provided, that the land so occupied does not exceed 20 acres for each and every male person 21 years of age or head of a family" with military protection (Kappler, *Indian Treaties*, 2:1024–25). These restrictions, plus Young Joseph's observation ("An Indian's View of Indian Affairs," 422) that there was no good land left unoccupied on the reservation, accounted for the Indians' supposition that if they should go to "Lapwai reservation or one similar, they will be obliged to give up their horses, which constitute their main wealth, and that as a community they will cease to exist." (Dunn, *Massacres of the Mountains*, 637)

•   "Christianizing influence": Father Wilbur as quoted in ibid., 640

407   Dunn puts the blame for the war squarely on the Commission of 1876, and points out that in Howard's later public writing (his 1879 article in the *North American Review*, and his 1881 book *Nez Perce Joseph*, he does not mention his part in the Commission.

- "rather than have war": Young Joseph, "An Indian's View of Indian Affairs," 423.
- The C.E.S. Wood quotations are from his manuscript journal of 1877 in the Huntington Library.
- Joseph as commanding general of the Nez Perce has been questioned by, among others, Edward S. Curtis, *The American Indian*, 15 vols. (New York 1907–1930), 8:163–69; Lucullus Virgil McWhorter, *Yellow Wolf: His Own Story* (Caldwell, Idaho 1940), 501–7; Merrill D. Beal, *"I Will Fight No More Forever," Chief Joseph and the Nez Perce War* (Seattle 1963); Alvin M. Josephy Jr., *The Nez Perce Indians and the Opening of the North West* (New Haven 1965); and Mark H. Brown, *The Flight of the Nez Perce* (New York 1967). Contemporary accounts, including reports by the principal U.S. Army officers involved, generally accepted the notion of Joseph's leadership. The issue seems to lie in the difficulty, often mentioned in these pages, of discussing New World organization in Old World terms.

408   James Reuben is quoted from the abridgment in Brandon, *Magic World*, 133–34. The original text was deposited in the cornerstone of the Nez Perce and Ponca school on October 20, 1880, recovered when the schoolhouse was torn down, and first printed in the *Chronicles of Oklahoma* 12 (September 1934).

409   "No, a war": *San Francisco Chronicle*, October 10, 1877, quoted in Brown, *Flight of the Nez Perce*, 415.
- "They rode at full gallop": Dunn, *Massacres of the Mountains*, 660.
- Sherman: ibid.
- General Nelson A. Miles: "The Indian Problem," *North American Review*, 128 (1879), says of "Our relations with the Indians . . . by treaties and trade" that "we find the record of broken promises all the way from the Atlantic to the Pacific, while many of the fortunes of New York, Chicago, Saint Louis, and San Francisco can be traced directly to Indian tradership." (306)

410   Joseph was only released because an American lieutenant had been seized by the Indians as a hostage to guarantee his safety. Joseph's own account of this incident has been substantiated by testimony gathered by McWhorter (*Yellow Wolf*, 489), from Wood, and from the hostage lieutenant. Brown, *Flight of the Nez Perce*. Brown concludes that the Nez Perce surrender three days later was delayed by the air of treachery proceeding from this little *pas de deux*.
- C.E.S. Wood is quoted from a letter published in the *Oregon Inn-Side News* (Portland, November-December 1947). Wood told the story of Chief Joseph many times in his long life, with occasional disparity in the details bringing woe to researchers, as Brown, *Flight of the Nez Perce*, bears witness.
- Joseph's lost daughter was not sent to Indian Territory but instead to the Lapwai Reservation, where eventually she married and had a family.

411   The famous surrender speech is most often quoted from U.S. Secretary of War, *Report*, (1877), 630–31.

Chapter 28

412   Buffalo Bill Show and London quote: Ray Allen Billington, *Land of Savagery, Land of Promise* (New York 1981), 49.

413   Peter Masten Dunne, "Pioneer Jesuit Missionaries on the Central Plateau of New Spain," in *Greater America*, mentions the mounted Lagunero chieftain in 1594. (164)

414   Padouca-Comanche: William Brandon, *Quivira* (Athens, Ohio 1990), 306n, citing *Archives Nationales*, Paris, Col. C13 C4.

·   Bourgmont: Brandon, *Quivira*, 193–97.

·   La Salle and Caddoan horses: ibid., 107.

·   Pawnee horse traders: ibid., 113.

·   Route of plains trade: ibid., 124.

·   Plains Apache traders: ibid., 143, citing the Vargas journal, RI 26, in the Ritch Collection, Huntington Library.

·   Apaches still on the horse/dog fence: ibid, 124, citing La Harpe in BN F.F. 8989.

416   The recollection of the first horse seen by Blackfoot people was recorded by David Thompson in 1782: J.B. Tyrrell, ed., *David Thompson's Narrative* (Toronto 1916), 330 and 334.

·   Lavish beadwork is another inseparable element of the Plains Indian image, though one by no means limited to the plains or to post-European times: William Orchard, *Beads and Beadwork of the American Indians*, Museum of the American Indian, Heye Foundation (New York 1929), estimates more than 16,500 beads in a dentalium-shell string 41.5 feet long, from the Chumash of California.

417   Waldo R. Wedel, "Changing Perspectives in Plains Archaeology," *Plains Anthropologist* 28/100 (1983): "we see now a depth of at least ten millenia of human habitation, and . . . many among us . . . will argue vigorously and with some justification for twice that much time, or more."

·   Inexhaustible buffalo: "There is a narrow ravine in Sarsi Territory near Calgary, Canada, at the bottom of which have been found the bones of buffalo in such numbers that modern Sarsi Indians (1920) made a business of collecting and selling them for fertilizer." Harold E. Driver and William C. Massey, *Comparative Studies of North American Indians*, Transactions of the American Philosophical Society, N.S., 47/2 (Philadelphia 1957), 191.

419   William Wildschut, *Crow Indian Medicine Bundles*, John C. Ewers, ed., Museum of the American Indian, Heye Foundation (New York 1960), cites George Catlin, writing in the 1830s, and Edwin Thompson Denig writing in 1854 after twenty-one years in the country, as believing that the Crows, so badly outnumbered by the Blackfeet moving into their country from the north and the Dakota invading from the east, were facing extermination.

421   La Harpe: Brandon, *Quivira*, 190, citing extracts from the La Harpe manuscript, F.F. 8989, in Pierre Margry, ed., *Découvertes et Etablissements des Français dans l'Ouest et dans le Sud de l'Amérique Septentrionale (1679–1754)*, 6 vols. (Paris 1879–1888), 6:293. Hereafter cited as Margry.

422   "fruitful commerce": Brandon, *Quivira*, 194.

·   "oppose a peace?": ibid.

·   Alligator perfume: ibid., 195–96, citing the *Mercure*, vol. 1, December 1725.

·   The neglected Bourgmont report: ibid., 220.

·   Bourgmont's patent of nobility: ibid., 196.

424   George Catlin, *Letters and Notes on the Manners, Customs, and Conditions of North American Indians*, 2 vols. (1844, New York 1973), 2:66.

425   The *coureur de bois* killed in eastern Colorado in 1706: Brandon, *Quivira*, 149–52, citing Alfred Barnaby Thomas, *After Coronado* (Norman 1935, 1966), 65–74.

·   Canada's leading businessman in the 1690s: Charles Aubert de La Chesnaye, quoted from Margry, 6:3.

- Ann Woodbury Hafen, "Son of Bird Woman," *Denver Post*, July 21, 1946, tells the story of Baptiste Charbonneau.

426 Old Fraeb: LeRoy R. Hafen, "Fraeb's Last Fight," *Colorado Magazine* 7 (1930).

427 "would pay": ibid.

428 Blackfoot tourists: John C. Ewers, *The Blackfeet: Raiders on the Northwestern Plains* (Norman 1958, 1961), 198–99.

429 Mari Sandoz, *Hostiles and Friendlies* (Lincoln 1959), writes that the site of Conquering Bear's burial scaffold "later became part of our orchard on the Niobrara. In my childhood an occasional old Sioux used to come to dance a few solemn steps there, and then smoke a pipe in the evening sun."

431 "Greed and avarice": F.C. Lockwood, *The Apache Indians* (New York 1938).

- "Nothing can be done": Dunn, *Massacres of the Mountains*, 524.

432 It was a Sioux spokesman at a council in 1876 who suggested putting the Indians on wheels: Dee Brown, *Bury My Heart at Wounded Knee* (New York 1971), 285.

434 "You must begin anew": Ruth Murray Underhill, *Red Man's America* (Chicago 1953), 172.

- Cherokee Trail: George R. Stewart, "Travelers by Overland," *The American West* 5/4 (July 1968), 12.

435 George Bird Grinnell, *The Fighting Cheyennes* (New York 1915, Norman 1956), quotes Kit Carson before the Joint Special Committee of Congress speaking of herders frequently blaming Indians for losses caused by their own negligence.

436 The government report: *Condition of the Indian Tribes: Report of the Joint Special Committee Under Joint Resolution of March 3, 1865* (Washington 1867), containing material also gathered in *Senate Report, No. 142, 38th Congress*, and *Senate Report No. 156, 39th Congress, Senate Executive Document, No. 26*.

- The warbonnet of Roman Nose: George E. Hyde, *The Life of George Bent, Written from His Letters*, Savoie Lottinville, ed. (Norman 1968), 307.

437 "All those people": Grinnell, *Fighting Cheyennes*, 286.

438 Sheridan: Dunn, *Massacres of the Mountains*, 534.

439 Custer psychobizarrerie: Charles K. Holling, "George Armstrong Custer: a Psychoanalytic Approach," *Montana the Magazine of Western History* 31 (April 1971).

440 "sheer starvation" : James Mooney, in Hodge, *Handbook*, 2:571.

- Clown: Utley, *Last Days of the Sioux Nation*, 261–64.

441 Ankle: Grinnell, *Fighting Cheyenne*, 391–93.

- Lame Deer: ibid.

- The *Herald*: Oliver Knight, *Following the Indian Wars* (Norman 1960), 289.

- The remaining land base was taken mainly by the Allotment Act: Janet A. McDonald, *The Dispossession of the American Indians, 1887–1934* (Bloomington 1991).

- Annie Oakley's comment: Stanley Vestal, *Sitting Bull, Champion of the Sioux, A Biography* (Boston 1932, Norman 1956), 250–51.

442 Indian Police were given strict orders to bring in Sitting Bull dead or alive: ibid., 306. Agent James McLaughlin to Bull Head, leader of Indian Police: "if he does not listen to you do as you see fit, use your own discretion in the matter, and it will be all right." Utley, *Last Days of the Sioux Nation*, 153, citing Stanley Vestal, *New Sources on Indian History, 1850–1891* (Norman 1934), 12. The New York *Herald*, December 17, 1890, reported that to kill Sitting Bull was the tacit under-

standing given the Indian Police. (Utley, 310) One of the first dispatches to the press from Standing Rock, December 16, 1890: "That the Government authorities . . . preferred the death of the famous savage to capture whole-skinned, few persons here, Indian or white, have any doubt." (ibid.)

443   Miles to General John R. Brooke, "Big Foot is cunning and his Indians are very bad and I hope you will round up the whole body of them, disarm, and keep under close guard." (ibid., 192) General Brooke's orders to Colonel James W. Forsyth were "to disarm Big Foot's band, take every precaution to prevent the escape of any; if they fought, to destroy them." (ibid., 197) Brooke's previous orders to Forsyth: "Capture him. If he fights, destroy him." (ibid., 192)

   •   James Mooney, *The Ghost-Dance Religion and the Sioux Outbreak of 1890*, 14th BAE Report, Part 2 (Washington 1896): "In obedience to instructions the Indians had pitched their tipis on the open plain a short distance west of the creek and surrounded on all sides by the soldiers. In the center of the camp the Indians had hoisted a white flag as a sign of peace and a guarantee of safety." (115) Mooney continues, "a young Indian, said to have been Black Fox from Cheyenne river, drew a rifle from under his blanket and fired at the soldiers, who instantly replied with a volley directly into the crowd of warriors. . . . At the first volley the Hotchkiss guns trained on the camp opened fire and sent a storm of shells and bullets among the women and children . . . The guns poured in 2 pound explosive shells at the rate of nearly fifty per minute, mowing down everything alive . . . In a few minutes 200 Indian men, women, and children, with 60 soldiers, were lying dead and wounded on the ground, the tipis had been torn down by the shells and some of them were burning above the helpless wounded, and the surviving handful of Indians were flying in wild panic to the shelter of the ravine, pursued by hundreds of maddened soldiers and followed up by a raking fire from the Hotchkiss guns, which had been moved into position to sweep the ravine. . . . There can be no question that the pursuit was simply a massacre where fleeing women, with infants in their arms, were shot down after resistance had ceased and when almost every warrior was stretched dead or dying on the ground." (118)

444   Miles to General John M. Schofield, January 2, 1891, on the defective disposition of the troops: Utley, *Last Days of the Sioux Nation*, 244.

445   John Shangreau quotation: ibid., 192.

   •   The relation of Dewey Beard, formerly known as Dewey Horn Cloud: ibid., citing the Eli J. Ricker Collection in the Nebraska State Historical Society. Various persons at Pine Ridge, speaking of the last words of Dewey Horn Cloud's dying mother, give them a slightly different phrasing from the quotation in the Ricker Collection.

Chapter 29

446   Mescalero song: Brandon, *Magic World*, 58, adapted from P.E. Goddard, "Gotal: a Mescalero Apache Ceremony," in *Putnam Anniversary Volume* (1909). For a description of the Mescalero ceremony as still performed, see Claire R. Farner, *Thunder Rides A Black Horse: Mescalero Apaches and the Mythic Present* (Prospect Heights, Illinois 1994).

447   Morris E. Opler, *Handbook of North American Indians*, vol. 10, *Southwest*, Alfonso Ortiz, ed. (Washington 1983), argues that the Apaches originally came south via the Great Basin.

·   Spanish missionary: F.W. Hodge and C.F. Lummis, eds., *The Memorial of Fray Alonso de Benavides 1630* (Chicago 1916), 39–40.

448   "Little is known of events in the Hopi towns in 1680. The date was sometime between August 10 and 13. All the priests were killed, two at Oraibi, two at Shongopavi, and one at Awatovi": J. O. Brew, "Hopi Prehistory and History to 1850," *Handbook of North American Indians*, vol. 9, *Southwest*, Alfonso Ortiz, ed. (Washington 1979), 521.

·   Fray Francisco: Herbert E. Bolton, *Guide to Materials for the History of the United States in the Principal Archives of Mexico* (Washington 1913), and from Bolton, *Anza's California Expedition* (Berkeley 1930), IV, 121.

·   Note to Escalante: Thomas M. Griffiths. *San Juan Country* (Boulder, Colorado, 1984), 83, drawing on Herbert E. Bolton, "Pageant in the Wilderness, the Story of the Escalante Expedition to the Interior Basin, 1776," *Utah Historical Quarterly* 18 (1950). Escalante had himself attempted a visit to the Hopis in the summer of 1775.

449   Granville Goodwin, in *American Anthropologist* 37 (1935), 55–64, reckoned domesticated plants as furnishing 20 to 25 percent of the diet for Western Apaches.

·   Arthur L. Campa, "Piñon as an Economic and Social Factor," *New Mexico Business Review* 3 (1932), describes the use of a wild food, piñon nuts, still very popular in the Southwest.

·   Present cultivation of amaranth: E. Barrie Kavasch, *Enduring Harvests* (Old Saybrook, Connecticut, 1995), 277.

450   Llanero, Ollero, Hoyeros: Veronica E. Tiller, *Handbook* 10, 441 and 460.

451   The "far superior" Comanches: Fray Juan Agustin Morfi, *History of Texas 1673–1779*, translated and edited, with an introduction, by Carlos Eduardo Castañeda, 2 parts (Albuquerque 1935), 1:88–89.

452   John P. Harrington, "Kiowa Memories of the Northland," in Donald D. Brand, ed., *So Live the Works of Men* (Albuquerque 1939), examines in detail place-name evidence of Kiowa residence in the north.

·   Donald D. Brand speaks of the Kiowa-Taos relationship in *American Anthropologist* 12 (1910), 119–23. Some further discussion of Kiowa-Taos possibilities: Kroeber, *Cultural and Natural Areas*, 46 and 80; Robert H. Lowie, *The Indians of the Plains* (New York 1954), 1–4; Waldo R. Wedel, *An Introduction to Kansas Archeology*, BAE Bulletin 174 (Washington 1959), 78–79.

·   The difficult Kiowa language: Old Bill Williams is quoted in Brandon, *Men and the Mountain*, 111, citing Albert Pike, *Prose Sketches and Poems* (Boston 1834).

453   Plains sign language: W.P. Clark, *The Indian Sign Language* (Philadelphia 1883).

454   Karankawa extinction: W.W. Newcomb Jr., *Handbook* 10, 362.

455   "I am heard": Brandon, *Quivira*, 306.

456   The indignant cleric was the Reverend Father Provincial, Fray Pedro Serrano, to the Most Excellent Señor Viceroy, the Marquis of Cruillas, in regard to the Custodia of New Mexico in the year 1761, published in C.W. Hackett, ed., *Historical Documents Relative to New Mexico, etc.* collected by A.F. and Fanny Bandelier (Washington 1937), 479–501. The report adds (487) that Indian slaves of both sexes, small and large, constitute "the richest treasure for the governors, who gorge themselves . . . while the rest eat the crumbs." Hubert Howe Bancroft, *History of*

Arizona and New Mexico 1530–1888 (San Francisco, 1889) points out that this report is part of a lengthy and bitter quarrel between the friars and the governors, with flaming charges and counter-charges from both sides. "The partisan bitterness and prejudice of the writers . . . indicate clearly enough that the accusations are too sweeping, and often grossly over-colored, yet enough of candor and honest evidence remains to justify the conclusion that New Mexican affairs were in a sad plight, and that the pueblo Indians were little better than slaves." (272–73)

- Report of the late 1760s: Lawrence Kinnaird, ed., *The Frontiers of New Spain: Nicolas de Lafora's Description 1766–1768*, vol. 13 of the Quivira Society Publications (Berkeley 1958), 94. Lafora's report states that sometimes the French come to the Comanche rancherias "and live there for years."
- Vial: Noel M. Loomis and A.P. Nasatir, *Pedro Vial and the Roads to Santa Fe* (Norman 1967).

457 The 1821 party of traders was the Jacob Fowler-Hugh Glenn trading expedition: see George E. Hyde, *Indians of the High Plains from the Prehistoric Period to the Coming of the Europeans* (Norman 1959), 208–9.

- San Carlos de los Jupes: Alfred Barnaby Thomas, "San Carlos: A Comanche Pueblo on the Arkansas River, 1787," *Colorado Magazine* 6/3 (1929).

458 Grace Jackson, *Cynthia Ann Parker* (San Antonio 1959), says of Texas's most famous captive, after her "liberation": "She would take a knife and hack her breast until it would bleed, then put the blood on some tobacco and burn it, and cry for her lost boys." (98)

- Comanche fighting: Rupert N. Richardson, *The Comanche Barrier to South Plains Settlement* (Glendale 1933).

459 The destruction, by a U.S. Army force under Colonel Ranald Mackenzie, of a reported 1,400 Kiowa horses and mules took place in Palo Duro Cañon on September 26, 1874.

- Abandoned Cheyenne village: Dee Brown, *Wounded Knee*, 157.

460 Dale L. Morgan, *Jedediah Smith and the Opening of the West* (Indianapolis 1953), brings together the various accounts of Smith's death. (329–30 and 435–36)

- "perfectly irresistible": a 1847 pronunciamento by Texas politician David G. Burnet, in Schoolcraft, *Indian Tribes*, 1:240.

461 Railroad land-grant totals: Billington, *Westward Expansion*, 701. Allan Nevins and Henry Steele Commager, *Short History of the United States* (New York 1966), quote Robert Louis Stevenson on the transcontinental railroad: "When I think how the railroad has been pushed through this unwatered wilderness and haunt of savage tribes . . . how at each stage of the construction, roaring, impromptu cities, full of gold and lust and death, sprang up and then died away again . . . and then when I go on to remember that all this epical turmoil was conducted by gentlemen in frock coats and with a view to nothing more extraordinary than a fortune and a subsequent visit to Paris, it seems to me as if this railway were the one typical achievement of the age in which we live." (342)

- General Sheridan's much-quoted remark rests entirely on the journalistic source in Edward S. Ellis, *Ellis's History of the United States, from the Discovery of America to the Present Time*, 6 vols. (St. Paul 1899), 4:1483. It seems reasonably possible that the phrase was simply attached to a celebrity's name, in the traditional way of the media in such things, and it certainly seems reasonably possible that the story as Ellis has it is apocryphal. De Bonneville Randolph Keim went with Sheridan through the whole winter campaign of 1868–1869 as a correspondent for the *New York Herald* and doesn't seem to have mentioned this celebrated *bon mot* (see Knight, *Following the Indian Wars*, and Philip T. Sheridan, *Personal Memoirs*, 2 vols. (New York 1888), 2:346). Carl Coke Rister, *Border Command, General Phil Sheridan in the West* (Norman 1944), while full of comments that could qualify, in spirit, does not repeat this particular remark; nor does Captain H.C. Greiner, *General Phil Sheridan as I Knew Him, Playmate—Comrade—Friend* (Chicago 1908), even though this volume makes a considerable effort to show us Sheridan's "Irish wit."

- Glenn Danford Bradley, *The Story of the Santa Fe* (Boston 1920), 156, describes buffalo bones "stacked up way above the tops of the box cars, and often there were not sufficient cars to move them. Dodge excelled in bones, like she did in buffalo hides, for there were ten times the number of carloads shipped out of Dodge than out of any other town in the state, and that is saying a great deal for there was a vast amount shipped from every little town in western Kansas."
- White encroachment on Comanche and Kiowa reservations is detailed in William T. Hagan, "Kiowas, Comanches, and Cattlemen, 1867–1906, A Case Study of the Failure of U.S. Reservation Policy," *Pacific Historical Review* 40 (1971).
- Forrest D. Monahan Jr., "Kiowa-Federal Relations in Kansas, 1865–1868," *Chronicles of Oklahoma* 49 (Winter 1971–1972), gives archival evidence on Kiowa efforts to maintain peace with the United States.

462   The tale of the army officer's bad practical joke is told in Paul I. Wellman, *The Indian Wars of the West* (New York 1954).

463   Two main strands: Guy H. Cooper, *Development Stress in Navajo Religion* (Stockholm 1984), 113. The theme of two opposites as part of a necessary balance is treated in many works. See Clyde Kluckhohn and Dorothea Leighton, *The Navaho* (New York 1962), and Berard Haile, *Women versus Men, a Conflict of Navajo Emergence* (Lincoln 1981). For the two Navajo worlds expressing universals in opposites, see John R. Farella, *The Main Stalk: a Synthesis of Navajo Philosophy* (Tucson 1984); also, by the same author, *The Wind in a Jar* (Albuquerque 1993).

- Leland C. Wyman, *Blessingway* (Tucson 1970).
- "According to the ideal": Gladys Reichard, *Navajo Religion: A Study of Symbolism* (Princeton 1970), 47.
- The lines quoted from Brandon, *Magic World*, 62, are adapted from Washington Matthews, *The Night Chant, a Navaho Ceremony*, Memoirs of the American Museum of Natural History, vol. 6 (New York 1902). (For a recent account of this ceremony see James C. Faris, *The Nightway: A History and a History of Documentation of a Navajo Ceremonial*, Albuquerque 1990.) Some of the early and still some of the finest translations from Navajo religious literature were made by Washington Matthews, as in *Navaho Myths, Prayers and Songs, with Texts and Translations*, University of California Publications in American Archaeology and Ethnology, 5/2 (Berkeley 1907). The Song of Talking God as translated in Robert W. Young, ed., *The Navajo Yearbook* (Window Rock, Arizona 1961), 523, is of particular interest.
- One example of a linguistic approach to Indian religion is William K. Powers, *Sacred Language: The Nature of Supernatural Discourse in Lakota* (Norman 1986).

464   Wit and merriment: J.H. Beadle, *The Undeveloped West; or, Five Years in the Territories* (Philadelphia c1873), quoted in Young, *Navajo Yearbook*, 546. Similar sentiment is recorded a century later by a longtime Navajo-country resident, Bernice Eastman Johnston, in *Two Ways . . . in the Desert: A Study of Modern Navajo-Anglo Relations* (Pasadena 1972).

- "I think the Navahos": Dr. Louis Kennon, quoted in Young, *Navajo Yearbook*, 542. The same witness, writing in 1865, estimated the number of Navajo slaves in the Territory as "five to six thousand." (ibid., 543)

465 Kit Carson: ibid., 544.

- "a more upright and useful": James S. Calhoun, *Official Correspondence while Indian Agent at Santa Fe and Superintendent of Indian Affairs in New Mexico*, Annie Heloise Abel, ed. (Washington 1915).
- Busy rustlers' loot: Donald E. Worcester, *The Apaches, Eagles of the Southwest* (Norman 1979), 44.
- Narbona is quoted from Calhoun, *Official Correspondence*.
- Narbona's death: ibid.
- The young Army officer: J.H. Simpson, *Journal of a Military Reconnaissance from Santa Fe, New Mexico, to the Navajo Country, etc.* (Philadelphia 1852), entry for August 31, 1849.
- "a wretched hole": John G. Bourke, "Bourke on the Southwest," *New Mexico Historical Review* 11/1 (1936), 81.
- Lawrence C. Kelly, *Navajo Roundup: Select Correspndence of Kit Carson's Expedition against the Navajo, 1863–1865* (Boulder, Colorado 1971), presents Carson as a humanitarian, who forced the Navajo to surrender by destroying crops rather than people.

467 Scalp bounties: Worcester, *Apaches*, 25, 28, and 46. Typical Chihuahua bounties of the early nineteenth century were 150 pesos for a scalp of a woman or child, 200 for a mature male, and 250 for a live warrior (but live "warriors were much more dangerous to transport than bales of scalps").

468 Dunn, *Massacres of the Mountains*, quotes the official estimate of 2,000 Indian slaves in New Mexico. Benjamin M. Read, *Illustrated History of New Mexico* (Santa Fe 1895, 1912), 60: "Indian captives were bought and sold, one or more serving in each family of the wealthier class. This slavery existed by mere popular sufferance and not by law."

- "Get them back": Dunn, *Massacres of the Mountains*, 723.

469 The notorious American scalp hunter was James Kirker (Worcester, *Apaches*, 46).

- Weaver quotation: ibid., citing Philip St. George Cooke, *The Conflict of New Mexico and California: An Historical and Personal Narrative* (New York 1878, Glorieta, New Mexico 1964). Pauline (or Powell) Weaver, in the mountains from 1830, was described in a letter of 1850 from American emigrants as "an honest, kindhearted man, of strong intellect." (Hafen and Hafen, *The Far West and the Rockies*, 15:56)

470 The Canoa story: Worcester, *Apaches*, 74.

- Pinos Altos and Mangas: Dan L. Thrapp, *Victorio and the Mimbres Apaches* (Norman 1979), 67, 71, and 74, citing John C. Cremony, *Life among the Apaches* (Santa Fe 1868; Tucson 1954), 172–73. Thrapp's version of the Army blunder alienating Cochise differs from those in Edwin R. Sweeney, *Cochise, Chiricahua Apache Chief* (Norman 1991), and in Worcester, *Apaches*.

471 Baylor: Worcester, *Apaches*, 81–82.

- General Carleton: Opler, *Handbook* 10: "many of his forays were thinly veiled explorations to find mines . . . He wrote more than once that he considered his main mission to 'brush' Apaches aside so mineral exploration could proceed unhindered." (404) Nine thousand Navajo and Apache prisoners at Fort Sumner went hungry as a result of one of General Carleton's many official feuds, as detailed in Edward J. Danziger Jr., "The Steck-Carleton Controversy in Civil War New Mexico," *Southwestern Historical Quarterly* 74 (1970).

473   "How is it?": Dunn, *Massacres of the Mountains*.

•   Dr. Eric R. Force of the United States Geological Survey showed me the Cochise "west" stronghold in November 1993.

474   Bourke: *An Apache Campaign in the Sierra Madre*, a new edition with an introduction by J. Frank Dobie (New York 1958), 18.

475   Crook is quoted from Dunn, *Massacres of the Mountains*.

•   Bourke: *An Apache Campaign*, 20.

•   In defense of Indian agents: William E. Unrau, "The Civilian as Indian Agent: Villain or Victim," *Western History Quarterly* 3 (October 1972).

•   "I have never yet seen": from a contemporary account of the short life (four years) of the Chiricahua reservation promised to Cochise: Bancroft, *Arizona and New Mexico*, 566 n18. The continuation of the same note on the next page gives details on the shrinkage of the San Carlos Reservation.

476   Kaywaykla is quoted from Angie Debo, *Geronimo, The Man, His Time, His Place* (Norman 1976), 5, citing Eve Ball, *In the Days of Victorio: Recollections of a Warm Springs Apache* (Tucson 1970). Victorio's band called itself the Chihenne, and was the specific Red Paint band, because of a line of red across the face (Debo, *Geronimo*, 12). Geronimo's band was known among Apaches as the Bedonkoke, referring to its home at Geronimo's birthplace on the upper Gila river, on the present Arizona-New Mexico line near present Clifton, Arizona. When Geronimo chanced to pass by there he was, naturally, rolled in the four directions.

477   General Sheridan to General Crook: Worcester, *Apaches*, 297–99.

Chapter 30

478   The high population range of Cook and Borah (and earlier Cook and Simpson) brought a "lively debate among demographic historians" (Leslie Bethell, ed., *The Cambridge History of Latin America*, vol. 1, 1984, 145). William T. Sanders, specialist in settlement patterns in precolumbian Latin America, was inclined to reduce Cook and Borah's 23 million for central Mexico by about half, in William M. Denevan, ed., *The Native Population of the Americas in 1492* (Madison 1974), a work containing several other contributors eager to cut Cook and Borah's estimates. Many historians, however, noting Cook and Borah's meticulous scrutiny of sources, were favorably impressed. The Cook and Borah technique was used for additional areas (Noble David Cook, *Demographic Collapse: Indian Peru, 1520–1620*, Cambridge 1981, gives a nine million total for that region), or as a basis for further calculation (Henry F. Dobyns, *Their Number Become Thinned: Native American Population Dynamics in Eastern North America*, Knoxville 1983, which uses social organization, technology, and food resources as factors in estimating population). W. George Lovell's entry on Hispaniola in vol. 3 of *The Encyclopedia of Latin American History and Culture*, (New York 1996), asserts that "Controversy . . . still abounds" but without citing historians in opposition. *The New Cambridge Modern History* gives population figures on London in 1500 as "not more than 60,000," and on Paris as "approaching 200,000"; Madrid was "a small agricultural town at that time and only became the capital of a united Spain in 1560." "Seville the Great," as a slogan of the epoch had it, was given a population of 25,000 in 1518. (1:42–43)

- Taino agriculture is described in Sherburne Friend Cook and Woodrow Wilson Borah, *Essays in Population History: Mexico and the Caribbean* (Berkeley 1971), 1:408; and in Irving Rouse, *The Tainos: Rise and Decline of the People Who Greeted Columbus* (New Haven 1992), 12–13. Rouse prefers a pre-Columbian population of 500,000 for Hispaniola, citing Karen Anderson-Córdova, *Hispaniola and Puerto Rico: Indian Acculturation and Heterogeneity, 1492–1500* (Ann Arbor 1990). See also Samuel M. Wilson, *Hispaniola: Caribbean Chiefdoms in the Age of Columbus* (Tuscaloosa 1990).

479 For a detailed treatment of private property in the Code of Hammurabi, see Lewis Mumford, *The City in History* (New York 1961), 108.

- *Dominium* and *Communitas* are discussed more fully in William Brandon, *New Worlds for Old* (Athens, Ohio 1986), 124.
- On the primacy of religion to American Indians: "Most—if not all—Native American history basically is sacred history. For, in Indian thought, there is no separation between the sacred and the secular." From Father Peter J. Powell, Journey to the sacred mountain: personal reflections upon a priest's role in recording Cheyenne Indian history, a talk delivered at the Newberry Library, October 2, 1974.

480 Acton Papers, Cambridge University Library, Add. 4870.

481 Voltaire, *The Age of Louis XIV* (1751), translated by Martyn F. Pollack (London 1961), 453: "The laws and internal tranquillity of this vast empire [China] are based on the most natural and sacred law of nature, the respect of children for their parents."

- Plato is quoted from *The Republic*, Francis Cornford ed. (Oxford 1941), 286.
- "a nineteenth century authority": Acton Papers, Add. 4938, citing William Mitchell Ramsay, *The Church in the [Roman] Empire* (London 1895), 175.
- Peter Martyr is quoted, as before, from Eden, *Peter Martyr*.
- The Classic Golden Age in the New World is discussed more fully in Brandon, *New Worlds for Old*, 148–54.
- France provided the main channel: French writers on this theme began with Pierre de Ronsard and Michel Eyquem de Montaigne and include Jean de Léry, Antoine S. Le Page du Pratz, Chretien Leclerq, André Thévet, Gabriel Bonnot de Mably, Joseph François Lafitau, Jean-Baptiste du Tertre, Louis François Delisle de la Drevetière, Louis Armand de Lom d'Arce baron de Lahontan, Jean Macer, Pierre Margry, Pierre F. X. de Charlevoix, and eventually not only Rousseau but Voltaire (in his *Alzire* and in *L'Ingénu*). Many authors of geographies and travel books picked up the theme as did French translations of works in Spanish and Italiam, such as early French editions of Peter Martyr d'Anghiera and the Jean Temporal edition of Amerigo Vespucci, Urbain Chauveton's translation of Hierosme Benzoni, and many others.

482 Acton is quoted from Irving Babbitt, *Spanish Character and other Essays* (Boston 1940), 225.

- "The first man who": J.-J. Rousseau, *Discours sur l'Origine et les Fondements de l'Inégalité parmi les Hommes* (1755). Notes to this discourse are included in vol. 2 of *Oeuvres* (Amsterdam 1769).
- "Man was born free": "Réponse à Borde," *Correspondance Complète de Jean Jacques Rousseau* (Geneva 1966), vol. 3.
- Kant on Rousseau: Jean Ferrari, *Les Sources Françaises de la Philosophie de Kant* (Paris 1980), 174.
- Irving Babbitt is the modern scholar quoted on Rousseau's ideas.

483   "drawn from accounts": Geoffrey Symcox, "The Wild Man's Return: The Enclosed
       Vision of Rousseau's Discourses," in Edward Dudley and Maximilian E. Novak,
       eds., *The Wild Man Within, An Image in Western Thought from Renaissance to
       Romanticism* (Pittsburgh 1972).
 •   Gustave Lanson, *Histoire de la Littérature Française* (Paris 1912), 795.
 •   John Adams on Rousseau is reported in *More Books: Bulletin of the Boston Public
       Library,* March 1926, which prints marginal comments written by President Adams
       in 1794 in his copy of a work of Rousseau's, including the *Essay on Inequality.*
 •   The comment on "Le Manco": *Mémoires Secrets Pour Servir à l'Histoire de la
       République des Lettres en France,* Tome Premier (London 1784), entry for June 13, 1763.
484   "a social state": Diderot is quoted from "Le Temple du Bonheur," date uncertain
       but probably c.1770, in *Oeuvres Complètes,* ed. Roger Lewinter (Paris 1971). 8:168.
 •   Burke, "Letter to a Member of the National Assembly," in *Reflections on the French
       Revolution* (London 1790).
 •   Saint-Just and Robespierre: *Biographie Universelle*; and from Paul H, Beik, ed., *The
       French Revolution,* a volume in *The Documentary History of Western Civilization*
       (New York 1970), 143–55.
 •   The modern study: Emmanuel Chill, "Introduction to the French Revolution," in
       Power, Property, and History (New York 1971).
485   Barnave: ibid., 93.
 •   Danton: *Biographie Universelle.*
 •   Malouet is quoted from Beik, *French Revolution,* 212.
486   Roland on business liberty: ibid., in a ministerial letter answering the price-con-
       trol petition of November 19, 1792.
 •   Madame Roland was guillotined, in the aftermath to the fall of the Girondins, on
       November 8, 1793. Roland, in hiding, committed suicide a few days later.
 •   The deeper meaning of the liberty proposed by the Revolution's Declaration of
       the Rights of Man and Citizen as "'virtue' in the language of Montesquieu,
       Rousseau and Robespierre" is the subject of the concluding paragraph in the clas-
       sic study, Georges Lefebvre, *Quatre-vingt-neuf* (Paris 1939); in English, *The Coming
       of the French Revolution* (Princeton 1947).
 •   *The Area Handbook for Colombia* (Washington 1970, a State Department publi-
       cation for the use of diplomatic employees), speaks of the resemblance between
       the writings of Bolivar and Rousseau. See also the discussion in R. D. Hussey,
       "Traces of French Enlightenment in Colonial Hispanic America" in *Latin America
       and the Enlightenment,* 2d ed. (Ithaca, 1961).
 •   The origin of modern liberty is studied in detail in Brandon, *New Worlds for Old.*

Epilogue

489   See "Les Derniers Terroristes" in *Revue des Deux Mondes,* V, LX, 15 (November 1930);
 •   F.-A. Aulard, *Paris Sous le Consulat,* T. II, du 1er frimaire an IX au 30 germinal an
       X (Paris 1904), 84; Jean Loredan, *La Machine Infernale de la rue Nicaise* (Paris
       1924), 65; and Archives de France, F^7 3702, *Minutes des Bulletins de Police, An IX*
       and sd.

Index